Applications of Formal Methods

C.A.R. Hoare, Series Editor

BACKHOUSE, R.C., *Program Construction and Verification*
BACKHOUSE, R.C., *Syntax of Programming Languages*
DE BAKKER, J.W., *Mathematical Theory of Program Correctness*
BARR, M. and WELLS, C., *Category Theory for Computing Science*
BEN-ARI, M., *Principles of Concurrent and Distributed Programming*
BEN-ARI, M., *Mathematical Logic for Computer Science*
BIRD, R. and WADLER, P., *Introduction to Functional Programming*
BORNAT, R., *Programming from First Principles*
BOVET, D.P. and CRESCENZI, P., *Introduction to the Theory of Complexity*
DE BROCK, B., *Foundations of Semantic Databases*
BUSTARD, D., ELDER, J. and WELSH, J., *Concurrent Program Structures*
CLARK, K. and McCABE, F.G., *Micro-Prolog: Programming in Logic*
DAHL, O.-J., *Verifiable Programming*
DROMEY, R.G., *How to Solve It by Computer*
DUNCAN, E., *Microprocessor Programming and Software Development*
ELDER, J., *Construction of Data Processing Software*
ELDER, J., *Compiler Construction*
ELLIOTT, R.J. and HOARE, C.A.R. (eds), *Scientific Applications of Multiprocessors*
FREEMAN, T.L. and PHILLIPS, R.C., *Parallel Numerical Algorithms*
GOLDSCHLAGER, L. and LISTER, A., *Computer Science: A modern introduction (2nd edn)*
GORDON, M.J.C., *Programming Language Theory and Its Implementation*
GRAY, P.M.D., KULKARNI, K.G. and PATON, N.W., *Object-oriented Databases*
HAYES, I. (ed.), *Specification Case Studies (2nd edn)*
HEHNER, E.C.R., *The Logic of Programming*
HENDERSON, P., *Functional Programming: Application and implementation*
HOARE, C.A.R., *Communicating Sequential Processes*
HOARE, C.A.R. and GORDON, M.J.C. (eds), *Mechanized Reasoning and Hardware Design*
HOARE, C.A.R. and JONES, C.B. (eds), *Essays in Computing Science*
HOARE, C.A.R. and SHEPHERDSON, J.C. (eds), *Mechanical Logic and Programming
    Languages*
HUGHES, J.G., *Database Technology: A software engineering approach*
HUGHES, J.G., *Object-oriented Databases*
INMOS LTD, *Occam 2 Reference Manual*
JACKSON, M.A., *System Development*
JOHNSTON, H., *Learning to Program*
JONES, C.B., *Systematic Software Development Using VDM (2nd edn)*
JONES, C.B. and SHAW, R.C.F. (eds), *Case Studies in Systematic Software Development*
JONES, G., *Programming in Occam*
JONES, G. and GOLDSMITH, M., *Programming in Occam 2*
JONES, N.D., GOMARD, C.K. and SESTOFT, P., *Partial Evaluation and Automatic Program
    Generation*
JOSEPH, M., PRASAD, V.R. and NATARAJAN, N., *A Multiprocessor Operating System*
KALDEWAIJ, A., *Programming: The derivation of algorithms*
KING, P.J.B., *Computer and Communications Systems Performance Modelling*
LALEMENT, R., *Computation as Logic*
LEW, A., *Computer Science: A mathematical introduction*
McCABE, F.G., *Logic and Objects*
McCABE, F.G., *High-level Programmer's Guide to the 68000*
MEYER, B., *Introduction to the Theory of Programming Languages*
MEYER, B., *Object-oriented Software Construction*
MILNER, R., *Communication and Concurrency*
MITCHELL, R., *Abstract Data Types and Modula 2*
MORGAN, C., *Programming from Specifications*
PEYTON JONES, S.L., *The Implementation of Functional Programming Languages*
PEYTON JONES, S. and LESTER, D., *Implementing Functional Languages*

Series listing continued at back of book

Applications of Formal Methods

edited by

Michael G. Hinchey
and
Jonathan P. Bowen

PRENTICE HALL
London   New York   Toronto   Sydney   Tokyo   Singapore
Madrid   Mexico City   Munich

First published 1995 by
Prentice Hall International (UK) Limited
Campus 400, Maylands Avenue
Hemel Hempstead
Hertfordshire, HP2 7EZ
A division of
Simon & Schuster International Group

Printed and bound in Great Britain by
Hartnolls Ltd., Bodmin, Cornwall

Library of Congress Cataloging-in-Publication Data

Applications of formal methods / edited by Michael G. Hinchey and
    Jonathan Bowen.
            p.   cm. – (Prentice–Hall international series in computer
    science)
      Includes bibliographical references (p.   ).
      ISBN 0-13-366949-1 (alk. paper)
      1. System design.   2. Computer software–Development.
    I. Hinchey, Michael G. (Michael Gerard), 1969-   .   II. Bowen, J. P.
    (Jonathan Peter),   1956-   .   III. Series.
    QA76. 9 . S88A68   1996
    620' . 0042' 015113–dc20

                                                                    95-11111
                                                                    CIP

British Library Cataloguing in Publication Data

A catalogue record for this book is available
from the British Library

ISBN 0-13-366949-1

1 2 3 4 5 99 98 97 96 95

Why does this magnificent applied science which saves work and makes life easier bring us so little happiness? The simple answer runs: because we have not yet learned to make sensible use of it.

Albert Einstein

Contents

Foreword

The best way to learn the practice of large-scale engineering is to engage in real projects of industrial and commercial interest. The best way to learn the relevant theory is by education, which includes the reading of books, case studies, and conduct of practical exercises on the smallest possible scale. However, the primary goal of the theory is to inspire invention and to underpin confidence in practical applications on any scale from the smallest to the largest.

This book is published in a series which has been devoted to broadening the link between theory and practice in the engineering of computer systems. We have established a record for publication of theoretical results and case studies to support education of the highest quality. The contribution of this book is exceptionally welcome, since it reports on a range of independent experiments in the application of theories on an industrial scale. In spite of diversity in the areas of application and in the formalisms selected, there is an encouraging uniformity in the overall conclusion: if appropriate attention is also paid to commercial, managerial and educational implications, there is a positive benefit to be achieved by increasing the level of formalism at the earliest possible stages of specification and design; and this benefit can be felt, if not measured, on the occasion of first use. There are grounds for optimism that second use may be even more beneficial.

That is why I regard the publication of this book as a milestone in the development of the series. It is a confirmation of the soundness of the goals that we have pursued in the past, and a promise of further achievement in the future.

C.A.R. Hoare

Preface

Formal methods continue to grow in popularity; growing numbers of delegates at conferences such as the Formal Methods Europe (FME) symposia and the International Conferences of Z Users (ZUM) are indicative of this. Perhaps more interesting in this respect is the increasing number of papers devoted to formal methods and more formal approaches that surface at conferences with which one would not normally associate formal methods.

Unfortunately, as interest in formal methods increases, the number of misconceptions regarding formal methods continues to grow in tandem. While formal methods have been employed, to some extent, for over a quarter of a century, there are still very few people who understand exactly what formal methods are, and how they are applied in practice. Many people completely misunderstand what constitutes a formal method, and how formal methods have been successfully employed in the development of complex systems. Of great concern is the fact that we must place many professional system developers and project managers into that latter category.

The question arises as to how the technology transfer process from formal methods research to practice can be facilitated. More real links between industry and academia are required, and well publicized demonstrations of successful uses of formal methods are needed to disseminate the benefits of their use.

This collection aims to play its part in this by providing a collection of descriptions of the use of formal methods at an industrially useful scale written by the experts involved.

Choosing a suitable order for such a collection of papers proved to be problematic, due to the inherent subjectivity of any particular ordering. Whatever order we chose, another equally (or sometimes, more) logical ordering presented itself. Perhaps what we really needed was an electronic "book" with many different indices for the reader to traverse.

In the absence of such developments, we have settled on the current ordering, and hope that the reader finds it logical. In essence, there is no prefered order of reading, although Chapter 1 does provide an overview of the book, and attempts to guide the reader to the chapters that may be of most interest to his or her situation. We hope that the papers will provide the reader with a better understanding of what formal methods are and how they should be applied, and will provide interesting reading and examples of some of the highly successful applications of formal methods.

Following the overview in Chapter 1, the next three chapters, although addressing specific examples of the application of formal methods, provide excellent overviews of formal methods and their application.

In Chapter 2, David Parnas argues in favour of the use of mathematical descriptions in the certification of safety-critical systems, based on his experiences with the Darlington Nuclear Facility in Ontario.

In Chapter 3, Bruns and Anderson provide an account of how formal methods can greatly increase confidence levels and help us to gain assurance in the "correctness" and appropriateness of complex systems using concise and pertinent certification data based on a requirements-based approach. They relate this back to their experiences with the analysis of a protocol employed in the Sizewell B nuclear reactor.

Garlan and Delisle, in Chapter 4, describe how formal methods (specifically Z) were effectively scaled in the development of a range of oscilloscopes at Tektronix Corporation. The approach employed focused at an architectural level, concentrating on compositional techniques for a family of designs.

An unusual application of formal methods is the use of VDM in the specification of the single-transferable voting algorithm used by the Church of England, as described by Mukherjee and Wichmann in Chapter 5. The formal specification served to highlight a number of ambiguities in the natural language description of the algorithm.

In Chapter 6, Jonathan Hoare discusses IBM's experiences in the formal development of a new component of their CICS system using the B-Method. Part of the system had previously been restructured using Z in the specification stages, and most new components of the system are now formally specified.

Chapter 7, by Srivas, Miller and Rushby, details the formal verification of Rockwell's AAMP5 microprocessor using SRI's Prototype Verification System, PVS. This represents one of the most impressive formal developments of hardware yet undertaken in industry.

The railway industry has provided a very suitable "test-bed" for formal specification languages, and verification techniques. William Young describes the real-time gate controller and its modeling and verification using Nqthm in Chapter 8. The example acts as a useful "yard-stick" for comparing various methods.

Indeed, the railway industry is not forgotten, with two examples of the use of formal methods: Dürr, Plat and de Boer describe the development of a rail traffic tracking and tracing system with VDM^{++} in Chapter 9, while in Chapter 10 Dehbonei and Mejia describe the GEC Alsthom experiences in the development of safety-critical signalling systems using B, most notably for the Paris rapid transit system.

In Chapter 11, Hamer and Peleska describe the application of Z to the cabin communication system of the European Airbus A330/340 aircraft.

Chapter 12 concerns the development of the kernel for the THETA Distributed Operating System. The system development, as described by Guaspari, Seagar and Stillerman, was undertaken in both Ada and C, using Larch and ORA's Penelope system.

Barroca et al. describe experiences in the formal specification of the attitude monitor for an aircraft in Chapter 13, demonstrating the need for multiple formal and informal notations in the development process.

Fitzgerald *et al.* report on the parallel development of a security-critical system using both formal and conventional methods in Chapter 14, as part of an investigative study for British Aerospace.

In Chapter 15, Vivien Hamilton gives practical advice on the construction of a formal specification and on the successful use of a formal method, based on the Rolls-Royce & Associates experiences in using both formal and structured methods.

Chapter 16 provides an excellent discussion of how various formal and informal notations may be integrated to exploit the benefits of each paradigm in the system development process. Mataga and Zave relate this to the multiparadigm specification of an AT&T switching system.

Finally, in Chapter 17, Craigen, Gerhart and Ralston provide an overview of a now well-known survey of the industrial use of formal methods, focusing on how technology transfer was impeded, and how such impediments have been successfully overcome.

We should like to express our grateful appreciation to Professor C.A.R. Hoare, who first suggested the project to us, for his encouragement and support in the prepartion of this collection.

Our sincerest thanks also to the following for their help in securing excellent contributions for this book: Professor Robert S. Boyer, Professor David Garlan, Dr. Jim Horning, Dr. Leslie Lamport, Professor Robin Milner, Dr. Yuan Yu, and Professor Jeannette Wing. Thanks also to Dr. Neville Dean and Dr. Peter Scharbach for their useful comments on earlier drafts, to Steven Scott, who guided us through the production stages, and, lastly but by no means least, to Jackie Harbor at Prentice Hall, for her support, encouragement ...but most of all, her patience.

M.G.H.
Cambridge

J.P.B.
Oxford

Trademarks

Ada® is a Registered Trademark of the US Department of Defense.

DEC® and VAX/VMS® are Registered Trademarks of Digital Equipment Corporation.

Framemaker® is a trademark of Frame Technology Corporation.

Hypercard® is a Registered Trademark of Apple Computer Inc.

IBM®, CICS®, CICS/ESA®, System/360®, DB/2® are trademarks or service marks of International Business Machines Corporation in the United States and other countries.

Intel® and Pentium® are trademarks or service marks of Intel Corporation.

Occam® is a Trademark of Inmos Limited.

RTM® is a Registered Trademark of GEC Marconi.

Teamwork® is a Registered Trademark of Cadre Technology Inc.

UNIX® is a Registered Trademark in the United States and other countries, licensed exclusively through X/Open Company Ltd.

List of Contributors

Stuart Anderson, University of Edinburgh, Department of Computer Science, The King's Buildings, Edinburgh EH9 3JZ, UK.

Leonor Barroca, The Open University, Walton Hall, Milton Keynes MK7 6AA, UK.

Jonathan Bowen, Oxford University Computing Laboratory, Programming Research Group, Wolfson Building, Parks Road, Oxford OX1 3QD, UK.

Glenn Bruns, University of Edinburgh, Department of Computer Science, The King's Buildings, Edinburgh EH9 3JZ, UK.

Michiel de Boer, Cap Volmac, P.O. Box 2575, 3500 GN Utrecht, The Netherlands.

Tom Brookes, British Aerospace (Systems and Equipment) Ltd., Clittaford Road, Plymouth, Devon PL6 6DE, UK.

Andy Coombes, University of York, Department of Computer Science, Dependable Computing Systems Centre, Heslington, York YO1 5DD, UK.

Dan Craigen, ORA Canada, 100–267 Richmond Road, Ottawa, Ontario K1Z 6X3, Canada.

Babak Dehbonei, GEC Alsthom, FTC Department, PO Box 165, 33 Rue des Bateliers, 93404 Saint-Ouen Cédex, France.

Norman Delisle, Raytheon Company, 528 Boston Post Road, Sudbury, MA 01776, USA.

Eugène Dürr, Cap Volmac, P.O. Box 2575, 3500 GN Utrecht, The Netherlands.

John Fitzgerald, University of Newcastle upon Tyne, Centre for Software Reliability, Bedson Building, Newcastle NE1 7RU, UK.

David Garlan, Carnegie Mellon University, School of Computer Science, 5000 Forbes Avenue, Pittsburgh, PA 15213-3890, USA.

Susan Gerhart, University of Houston at Clear Lake, Research Institute for Computing and Information Systems, Houston, TX 77058-1098, USA.

Peter Gorm Larsen, Institute for Applied Computer Science, Forskerparken 10, DK-5230 Odense M, Denmark.

Michael Green, British Aerospace (Systems & Equipment) Ltd., Clittaford Road, Plymouth, Devon PL6 6DE, UK.

David Guaspari, Odyssey Research Associates, 301 Dates Drive, Ithaca, NY 14850, USA.

Ute Hamer, DST Deutsche System-Technik, Edisonstraße 3, 24145 Kiel, Germany.

Vivien Hamilton, Rolls-Royce & Associates Ltd., Industrial Power Group, Eastgate House, PO Box 31, Derby DE24 8BJ, UK.

Mike Hinchey, New Jersey Institute of Technology, Department of Computer and Information Science, University Heights, Newark, NJ 07102, USA.

C.A.R. Hoare, Oxford University Computing Laboratory, Programming Research Group, Wolfson Building, Parks Road, Oxford OX1 3QD, UK.

Jonathan Hoare, IBM United Kingdom Laboratories Ltd., Hursley Park, Winchester, Hampshire SO21 2JN, UK.

Peter Mataga, AT&T Bell Laboratories, 1000 East Warrenville Road, Naperville, IL 60566, USA.

John McDermid, University of York, Department of Computer Science, High Integrity Systems Engineering Group, Heslington, York YO1 5DD, UK.

Fernando Mejia, GEC Alsthom, FTC Department, PO Box 165, 33 Rue des Bateliers, 93404 Saint-Ouen Cédex, France.

Steve Miller, Rockwell International, Advanced Technology and Engineering, Collins Commercial Avionics, 400 Collins Road NE, Cedar Rapids, IA 52398, USA.

Paul Mukherjee, Royal Holloway, University of London, Department of Computer Science, Egham Hill, Egham, Surrey TW20 0EX, UK.

David Lorge Parnas, McMaster University, Department of Electrical and Computer Engineering, Communications Research Laboratory, Hamilton, Ontario L8S 4K1, Canada.

Jan Peleska, JP Software-Consulting, Goethestraße 26, D-24116 Kiel, Germany.

Nico Plat, Cap Volmac, P.O. Box 2575, 3500 GN Utrecht, The Netherlands.

Ted Ralston, Odyssey Research Associates, 301A Dates Drive, Ithaca, NY 14850, USA.

Amer Saeed, University of Newcastle upon Tyne, Dependable Computing Systems Centre, 20 Windsor Terrace, Newcastle NE1 7RU, UK.

Mike Seagar, Odyssey Research Associates, 301 Dates Drive, Ithaca, NY 14850, USA.

Lynn Spencer, BAe Defence Ltd., Systems Computing Department, Military Aircraft Division, Warton Aerodrome, Preston, Lancashire PR4 1AX, UK.

Mandayam Srivas, SRI International, 333 Ravenswood Avenue, Menlo Park, CA 94025, USA.

Matt Stillerman, Odyssey Research Associates, 301 Dates Drive, Ithaca, NY 14850, USA.

Brian Wichmann, National Physical Laboratory, Teddington, Middlesex TW11 0LW, UK.

William D. Young, Computational Logic Inc., 1717 West Sixth Street, Suite 290, Austin, TX 78703, USA.

Pamela Zave, AT&T Bell Laboratories, Murray Hill, NJ 07974, USA.

Chapter 1

Applications of Formal Methods FAQ*

Michael G. Hinchey and Jonathan P. Bowen

> Right now it's only a notion but I think I can get money to make it into a
> concept and then later change it into an idea.
>
> *– Woody Allen (Annie Hall, 1977)*

1.1 Introduction

We pose a number of questions concerning the application of formal methods, and attempt to answer them with practical information and guidance. It is intended that the information provided should be of use for both potential and existing practitioners of formal methods, and also for technically aware managers of formal methods. In addition, the material may be of interest to academics and advanced students with an interest in the practical application of formal methods. Where appropriate, reference is made to other chapters in the book, which provide more detailed expositions of some of the concerns that are covered in outline here.

1.2 The nature of formal methods

Q. What are formal methods?

A. Formal methods are different things to different people. The term itself is a misleading one, originating in formal logic, but now used in computing to refer to a wide range of mathematically based activities (Dean and Hinchey, 1995).

For the purposes of this book, a formal method is a set of tools and notations (with a formal semantics) used to specify unambiguously the requirements of a computer system that supports the proof of properties of that specification and proofs of correctness of an eventual implementation with respect to that specification.

Following this definition, formal methods are not so much "methods" as formal systems. While they provide support for a formal notation, or formal specification language, and some form of deductive apparatus, or proof system, they fail to support many of the methodological aspects of the more traditional structured development methods.

---

* Frequently Asked Questions

1

In the context of an engineering discipline, a **method** describes the way in which a process is to be conducted. In the context of system engineering, a method is defined to consist of (1) an underlying model of development, (2) a language, or languages, (3) defined, ordered steps, and (4) guidance for applying these in a coherent manner.[1]

Most so-called formal methods do not address all of these issues. While they support some of the design principles of more traditional methods, such as top-down design and stepwise refinement, there is very little emphasis on an underlying model that encompasses each of the stages of the system development lifecycle or any guidance as to how development should proceed. Indeed, the formal methods community have been slow to address such methodological aspects.

A number of the applications reported in this book do, however, address such issues. Chapter 14, for example, reports on the parallel development of a security-critical system. This work was undertaken for British Aerospace to confirm the appropriateness of formal techniques in the development of such a system, with the formal development being subjected to the same quality standards. While the parallel development was completely separated, such a development facilitated insights into the formal development process.

The use of both structured and formal methods at Rolls-Royce & Associates, as described in Chapter 15, gave interesting insights into the effectiveness of modern software engineering techniques, and of how formal methods could be successfully integrated with other techniques in the system development lifecycle.

Q. Do I need formal methods?

A. There is no definitive answer to this question; rather it depends on your circumstances — the organization in question, the system to be developed, the expertise available, etc.

Formal methods should not be employed merely to satisfy company whim, or as a result of peer pressure. Just as the advent of "object orientation" saw many firms incur needless expense as they unnecessarily converted their systems to object-oriented implementations, there is a danger that many could unnecessarily adopt formal methods. Realistically, the first thing that must be determined is that you really do need to use formal methods — whether it is for increased confidence in the system, to satisfy a particular standard required by procurers, or to aid in conquering complexity, etc.

Even the most fervent supporters of formal methods must admit that there are areas where formal methods are just not as good as more conventional methods. In user interface (UI) design, for example, although there have been a number of somewhat successful applications using formal specification techniques (Dix, 1991), it is generally accepted that UI design falls within the domain of informal reasoning in the main.

Applying formal methods to all aspects of a system would be both unnecessary and costly. Even in the development of the CICS system (futher developments of which are reported on in Chapter 6), which resulted in Oxford University Computing Laboratory and IBM being jointly awarded a UK Queen's Award for Technological Achievement,

---

[1]This definition is modified from Kronlöf (1993).

only about one-tenth of the system was subjected to formal development. This still resulted in 100 000s of lines of code and thousands of pages of specifications. Having saved 9% over costs using conventional methods (confirmed by independent audit) it is often cited as a major successful application of formal methods (Phillips, 1990).

However, there are many situations where the use of formal methods is very desirable. In fact, the use of formal methods is recommended in any system where the issue of correctness is of concern.

This clearly applies to safety-critical and security-critical systems, but equally to systems which are not classified in these terms, but where one needs, or wishes, to ensure that the system operates correctly owing to the potentially catastrophic consequences of a system failure. Consider, for example, the formal specification of the algorithm used by the Church of England in its single transferable voting system, as described in Chapter 5, and the ambiguities that were uncovered in its natural language description.

There are also occasions where formal methods are not only desirable, but positively required. A number of standards bodies not only have used formal specification languages in making their own standards unambiguous, but have strongly recommended and in the future may mandate the use of formal methods in certain classes of applications (Bowen and Hinchey, 1994a; Bowen and Stavridou, 1993b).

The International Electrotechnical Commission specifically mentions a number of formal methods (CCS, CSP, HOL, LOTOS, OBJ, VDM, Z) and temporal logic in the development of safety-critical systems. The European Space Agency suggests that VDM or Z, augmented with natural language descriptions, should be used for specifying the requirements of safety-critical systems. It also advocates proof of correctness, a review process, and the use of formal proof in advance of testing (European Space Agency, 1991).

The UK Ministry of Defence (MoD) draft Interim Defence Standards 00-55 and 00-56 mandate the extensive use of formal methods (Ministry of Defence, 1991a,b). 00-55 sets forth guidelines and requirements; the requirements include the use of a formal notation in the specification of safety-critical components, and an analysis of such components for consistency and completeness. All safety-critical software must also be validated and verified; this includes formal proof and rigorous (but informal) correctness proofs, as well as more conventional static and dynamic analysis. 00-56 deals with the classification and hazard analysis of the software and electronic components of defence equipment, and also mandates the use of formal methods. Indeed, the work reported in Chapter 15 attempts to apply these standards, and has served to identify omissions from the standards themselves.

The Atomic Energy Control Board (AECB) in Canada has commissioned a report on software for computers in the safety systems of nuclear power stations in conjunction with David Parnas at McMaster University. Ontario-Hydro has developed a number of standards and procedures within the framework set by AECB and further procedures are under development. Some procedures developed by Canadian licensees mandate the use of formal methods (Atomic Energy Control Board, 1991), and together with 00-55 are still some of the few to go so far at the moment.

Whether or not one believes that formal methods are necessary in system development, one cannot deny that they are indeed strongly advisable in certain classes of applications, and are likely to be required in an increasing number of cases in the future (Bowen and Hinchey, 1994b).

Q. Which formal method should I use?

A. As already highlighted above, formal methods are distinguished by their specification languages, which should have a well-defined formal semantics.

Choosing the most appropriate notation is not as trivial as one might think. There are now a myriad of specification languages available, each making its own claims to superiority. Many of these claims are quite valid — different specification languages do indeed excel when used with particular classes of system.

In Chapter 12, Odyssey Research Associates' difficulties in finding an appropriate "readymade" formal method for development of a secure system implemented in Ada are discussed. In the end, a combination of LSL (the Larch Shared Language) and Larch/Ada was chosen, but required modifications to handle concurrency aspects.

In the development of an avionics subsystem, as described in Chapter 13, multiple formal and graphical notations were used in an attempt to derive a more "complete" method of development.

In fact, the development of many complex systems is likely to require the use of multiple formal and informal notations at various stages in the development, or to address various aspects of the development (Hoare, 1987). In Chapter 16, the integration of various notations is addressed in the specification of an AT&T switching system, using a first-order logic semantics as a means of unifying the diverse notations.

There is always, necessarily, a certain degree of trade-off between the expressiveness of a specification language and the levels of abstraction that it supports (Wing, 1990). Certain languages may indeed have wider "vocabularies" and constructs to support the particular situations with which we wish to deal. However, they will also force us towards particular implementations, and while they will shorten the specification, they generally make it less abstract.

Languages with small "vocabularies" on the other hand, while generally resulting in longer specifications, offer high levels of abstraction and little implementation bias. Consider CSP, Hoare's language of communicating sequential processes (Hoare, 1985; Hinchey and Jarvis, 1995), for example. The only first-class entities are processes (or pipes and buffers, which are merely particular types of processes). CSP specifications can become quite lengthy as a result, but the fact that there are so few constructs with which to become familiar makes them readily understandable. Likewise, there is minimal bias towards the implementation of communication primitives, and CSP channels may be implemented as physical wires, buses, mailboxes, or even just shared variables.

The vocabulary is not the only issue to consider, however. Some specification languages are just not as good as others when used with particular classes of system. Trying to specify a concurrent system in a model-based specification language such as Z (Spivey, 1992) or VDM (Jones, 1990), for example, is rather like using a hammer to insert a screw ... it can be done, but it is certainly not the best way to go about things (although various variants and extensions of Z and VDM have been used successfully).

A process algebra such as CSP or CCS (Milner, 1989) is generally far more appropriate, but these suffer from the drawback of paying very little attention to state-based aspects of the system. This has resulted in much research aimed at integrating process algebras with model-based specification languages, such as the RAISE development method (RAISE Language Group, 1992), and extending model-based specification languages to handle concurrency and temporal aspects.

The real-time community has proposed a number of "test-bed" case studies to enable the comparision of "real-time" specification languages. The example that is currently enjoying most popularity — the railway crossing and gate example (Heitmeyer *et al.*, 1993b) — is described in Chapter 8, along with its specification in Nqthm, and an evaluation of the approach.

It is important to choose a well-established notation with a good user base to ensure successful application in an industrial setting. Typically the development of a formal notation for industrial use takes at least a decade from conception to real application. It takes this long for the notation to be developed by researchers, taught to students, promulgated via academic-industrial liaison, for textbooks to be written, industrial courses to be developed, support tools to be marketed, a user community to be established, and so on. The technology transfer of formal notations, as with many new developments, is fraught with hurdles any one of which could cause its downfall. Chapter 17 discusses a number of inhibitors to the transfer of formal methods technology to industry, and discusses potentially successful innovations in this area.

An important part of the general acceptance of a notation is the production of an international standard. This is of course a chicken-and-egg situation, since developers desire its existence and influence on its contents, but would rather not be involved in the expensive and time-consuming process of its production. However, it is essential to have some sort of standard, be it *de facto* or official, to ensure a reasonably uniform and compatible set of tools to support the notation. It may be noted that conformance to a standard for a specification notation is somewhat more problematic compared with a programming language since it is inherently non-executable in the general case (otherwise it would be a programming language). There is some dispute about the benefit of so-called "executable specification languages" and we refer the reader elsewhere for a discussion on this topic (Hayes and Jones, 1989; Fuchs, 1992).

1.3   Costs and benefits

Q. Are formal methods expensive?

A. Formal methods are expensive when applied extensively or for the first time. There is quite a learning curve in becoming *au fait* with their effective use, and their initial introduction into a development environment is likely to require significant amounts of training, contract consultancy, and investment in support tools. Set-up costs aside, there is considerable evidence that formal methods projects can be run as cheaply (and possibly more cheaply overall) than projects developed using conventional methods.

For example, evidence of this has been provided by the award of the Queen's Award for Technological Achievement to two formal methods projects in the UK in 1990 and 1992. Auditors checked for the financial benefits gained as part of the award process. In the first, an estimated 12 months reduction in testing time was gained in the development of the Inmos floating-point unit for the T800 Transputer by formally developing the microcode using machine-supported algebraic techniques (May *et al.*, 1992). In the second case an estimated 9% was saved in the development costs for part of the very large IBM CICS transaction processing system by using the Z notation to respecify the software, resulting in a reduction of errors and an increase in quality of the code produced (further work on this, using Abrial's B-Method, is described in Chapter 6).

Chapter 4 also details how the use of formal methods to describe the architecture of a range of oscilliscopes at Tektronix Corporation resulted in significant cost reductions, and how the cost of formal specification could be spread over a number of product developments. Similiar results are reported in Chapter 11, where a less complex software architecture reduced implementation and integration costs for the Airbus A330/340 cabin illumination system.

A number of formal methods projects have run notoriously over schedule and over budget. The assumption that this is inherent in the nature of formal methods is a rather irrational deduction. Certainly these projects were delayed not because of the lack of ability of the formal methods specialists, but rather a lack of experience in determining how long development should take. That is to say, the projects were not necessarily delayed, but development time was severely underestimated. (This is not an uncommon occurrence in the computer software industry, whatever the method used.)

For example, the application of SCR to the Darlington Nuclear Facility, as detailed by David Parnas in Chapter 2, was notoriously expensive, but is still widely regarded as a success story for formal methods. The levels of assurance that were achieved as a result are deemed to have warranted such a major investment.

Project cost estimation is a major headache for any development team. If one follows the old adage, "estimate the cost and then double it", one is still likely to underestimate. Determining project development time is equally difficult (in fact, the two are inevitably intertwined).

A number of models have been developed to cover cost and development time estimation. Perhaps the most famous is Boehm's COCOMO model (Boehm, 1981), which weights various factors according to the historical results of system development within the organization.

Here we have the crux of the problem. Any successful model of cost and development-time estimation must be based on historical information and details such as levels of experience, familiarity with the problem, etc. Even with traditional development methods, such information might not be available. Using formal development techniques historical information is likely to be even more scarce, as we have not yet applied formal methods to a sufficient number of projects on which to base trends and observations.

Moreover, many of the factors that Boehm uses to weight his model would naturally be expected to have a significant effect on the cost of developing systems using formal methods. The fact that formal methods are employed in systems where the highest integrity, or reliability, is required, and are likely to be very complex systems, or complex components of larger systems, means that the weightings for *RELY* (required software reliability) and *CPLX* (product complexity) are likely to be very high. As formal methods are employed increasingly in real-time systems, *TIME* (execution time constraints) is also likely to have a significant influence on costs. The remainder of Boehm's "computer attributes" are unlikely to have a significant influence, nor are many of his "personnel attributes". In fact, the latter are likely to need to be augmented with new attributes, such as *SEXP* (specification language experience), *MCAP* (mathematical Capability), *FMEX* (formal methods experience) and *DEXP* (domain experience).

While his "project attributes" are all likely to remain valid, *MODP* (modern programming practices) is likely to be constant, while the development of more useful tools and IFDSEs (integrated formal development support environments) (Bowen and Hinchey, 1995b) should greatly increase the impact of the *TOOL* (software tools) attribute. Again, new attributes are likely to be required, such as *DFOR* (the percentage of the system that has been subjected to formal specification techniques and formal analysis) and *PROF* (the degree of rigorous and formal proof required).

One would expect that the use of formal methods would greatly increase the weightings of many of these attributes. It is our contention, however, that this does not mean that formal methods themselves are expensive, but rather is symptomatic of the fact that they are used in high-integrity systems, and it is the systems themselves that are expensive, especially if we require high levels of confidence in their "correct" operation.

In Chapter 17, Craigen, Gerhart and Ralston point out that the absense of appropriate cost models prohibits accurate evaluation of projects employing formal methods. Discussions of formal development (such as the chapters in this book), surveys of industrial usage (Bowen and Stavridou, 1993a; Craigen *et al.*, 1993), and a highlighting of successes, failures, hindrances, etc., will eventually provide us with the levels of information we require to cost formal methods adequately. Perhaps entirely new cost models are required, but for the time-being extending existing models is a useful starting point, provided that we allow for significant margins of error.

Q. What do I do about the development techniques I've used in the past?
A. There is considerable investment in existing software development techniques and it would be foolhardy to replace these *en masse* with formal methods. Instead it is desirable to integrate formal methods into the design process in a cost-effective manner. One way to do this is to investigate how an existing formal method can be combined effectively with an existing structured method already in use within industry. One attempt to do this is the "SAZ" method, a combination of SSADM and Z (Mander and Polack, 1995). Of course structured methods and formal methods each have their strengths and weaknesses and ideally the combination of the two should make the most of the benefits of both. For example, formal methods allow increased precision in a specification, whereas a structured method may be more presentable to a non-expert.

In Chapter 14, structured and formal methods are used side by side, and the formal specification is used to highlight errors in the conventional development, while the conventional development highlights means by which the formal development process can be improved. Chapter 15 takes a different view, in that both structured and formal methods are successfully used at different stages in the system lifecycle.

The Cleanroom approach is a technique that could easily incorporate the use of existing formal notations to produce highly reliable software by means of non-execution-based program development (Dyer, 1992). This technique has been applied very successfully using rigorous software development techniques with a proven track record of reducing errors by a significant factor, in both safety-critical and non-critical applications. The programs are developed separately using informal (often just mental) proofs before they are certified (rather than tested). If too many errors are found, the process rather than the program must be changed. The pragmatic view is that real programs are too large to be formally proven correct, so they must be written correctly in the first place. The possibility of combining Cleanroom techniques and formal methods has been investigated (Normington, 1993), but applying even semiformal development is difficult at an industrial scale without appropriate machine assistance.

Sometimes it is possible to combine different formal methods together usefully and effectively. For example, HOL (Gordon and Melham, 1993) has been used to provide tool support for Z (Bowen and Gordon, 1994). This allows the more readable Z notation to have the benefit of mechanical proof checking by HOL, thus increasing confidence in the development.

The management of a project using formal methods must be more technically aware than is perhaps normally the case. The use of a formal approach means that code is produced much later on in the design cycle. Far more effort than normal is expended at the specification stage. Many more errors are removed at this point, but early progress might not be as obvious as in a more typical project. One way to provide feedback, particularly for a customer, might be to produce a rapid prototype from the specification (Breuer and Bowen, 1994). The advantages of such an approach in the development of a pan-European rail-tracking network are discussed in Chapter 9.

Q. Can I use formal methods in my hardware development?

A. Formal methods can equally well be applied to hardware design as to software development. Indeed, this is one of the motivations of the HOL theorem prover which was used to verify parts of the Viper microprocessor (Cohn, 1988).

Other theorem proving systems which have been applied to the verification of hardware include the Boyer–Moore, Esterel, HOL, Nuprl, 2OBJ, Occam transformation system and Veritas proof tools. Model checking is also important in the checking of hardware designs if the state space is sufficiently small to make this feasible. However, techniques such as binary decision diagrams (BDDs) (Bryant, 1986) allow impressively large numbers of states to be handled.

One of the most convincing and complete hardware verification exercises is the FM9001 microprocessor (Hunt and Brock, 1992) produced by Computational Logic Inc. in the US, and which has been verified down to a gate level netlist representation using the Boyer–Moore theorem prover (Boyer and Moore, 1979, 1988). Two examples of real industrial use are provided by Inmos. The T800 Transputer floating-point unit has been verified by starting with a formalized Z specification of the IEEE floating-point standard, and using the Occam Transformation System to transform a high level program to the low level microcode by means of proven algebraic laws (May, 1990). More recently, parts of the new T9000 Transputer pipeline architecture have been formalized using CSP (Hoare, 1985) and checked for correctness (May *et al.*, 1992). A collection of invited papers written by experts in the field covers the applications outlined above, and others, in more detail (Hoare and Gordon, 1992).

Chapter 7 of this book reports on one of the most substantial uses of formal methods in hardware development yet undertaken — the verification of Rockwell's AAMP5 microprocessor using SRI's Prototype Verification System (PVS).

A more recent approach to the development of hardware is hardware compilation (Bowen *et al.*, 1994). This allows a high-level program to be compiled directly into a netlist, a list of simple components such as gates and latches together with there interconnections. The technology of field programmable gate arrays (FPGAs) allows this process to be undertaken entirely as a software process if required (which is particularly useful for rapid prototyping) since these devices allow the circuit to be configured according to the contents of a static RAM within the chip. It is possible to prove the compilation process itself correct (He *et al.*,1993). In this case the hardware compiled each time need not be separately proven correct, thus reducing the proof burden considerably. For instance, a microprocessor could be compiled into hardware by describing the microprocessor as a interpreter written in a high-level language. Additions and changes to the instruction set could easily be made by editing the interpreter and recompiling the hardware with no additional proof of correctness required.

In the future, such an approach could allow the possibility of provably correct combined hardware–software co-design (Hoare and Page, 1994). A unified proof framework would facilitate the exploration of design trade-offs and interactions between hardware and software in a formal manner.

1.4 Quality

Q. Can formal methods guarantee correctness?

A. Formal methods are not a panacea; they are just one of a number of techniques that when applied correctly have been demonstrated to result in systems of the highest integrity, and one should not dismiss other methods entirely. Formal methods are no guarantee of correctness; they are applied by humans, who are obviously prone to error. Various support tools such as specification editors, type checkers, consistency checkers and proof checkers should indeed reduce the likelihood of human error ... but not eliminate it. System development is a human activity, and always will be. Software engineering will always be subject to human whim, indecision, the ambiguity of natural language, and simple carelessness.

One can never have absolute correctness, and to suggest that one can is ludicrous. Ongoing debates in *Communications of the ACM* (Fetzer, 1988) and other fora, have been criticized on the grounds that there is a mismatch between the mathematical model and reality (Barwise, 1989). This is no great deduction — no proponent of formal methods would ever make a claim of definitive correctness. In fact, one should never speak arbitrarily of correctness, but rather of correctness with respect to the specification. As such, an implementation — or rather a mathematical model of it — may be proven to be correct with respect to the specification derived at the outset, but if the specification was not what the procurers really intended, then their (albeit subjective) view will be that the system is incorrect.

One must be conscious of the need to communicate with procurers and the systems users, and one should not be afraid to admit that the specification was not what was intended, and to go back and rework portions of it. System development is by no means a straightforward one-pass process. Royce's model of system development (Royce, 1970), now generally known as the "waterfall" model, was abandoned because of the simplistic view it held of system development. Every developer has experienced the need to revisit requirements and to rework the specification at various stages in the development. Ideally all inconsistencies will be discovered during implementation, or at least during post-implementation testing. However, in the worst case, errors in the system specification may be uncovered during post-implementation execution.

System development is not so simple as the model proposed by Royce (Gladden, 1982; McCracken and Jackson, 1982), but rather an iterative and non-linear process as exemplified by Boehm's "spiral" model (Boehm, 1988). As such, the developer should not make claims to having determined all of the requirements just because a certain stage in the development process has been reached; indeed such claims should be considered dubious even post-implementation. The developer must always be ready to make changes to the specification to meet the procurer's requirements, which are likely to change continually over time anyway; after all, in the best traditions of R.H. Macy, "the customer is always right"[2]. Even if the requirements have been fully satisfied, there are still plenty of opportunities for error.

One must always be conscious of the level of abstraction. If one is too abstract, then it is difficult to determine omissions and to determine what the system really is intended to do (one well-known formalist once joked that "everything is a set"). If one is not sufficiently abstract, however, there is a tendency, or bias, towards particular implementations. Couching the specification at the appropriate level of abstraction is a matter of experience — experience with both the specification language and the application domain. One should never be afraid to admit that the level of abstraction is not the most appropriate and to rework the specification accordingly.

Similarly, no proof should be taken as definitive. Hand proofs are notorious not only in admitting errors as one moves from one line to the next, but also at making gigantic leaps which are unfounded. From experience of machine checking proofs, most theorems are correct, but most hand proofs are wrong (Rushby, 1993). Even the use of a proof checker does not guarantee the correctness of a proof, but it does aid in highlighting unsubstantiated jumps, and avoidable errors.

---

[2]Of course, in the best traditions of P.T. Barnum, "there's a sucker born every minute".

Having said that, using formal methods to examine existing systems has proven to be very beneficial in highlighting errors and inconsistencies that were admitted by more conventional development methods.

The application of SCR to the certification of a safety-critical component of the system software at the Darlington Nuclear Facility, as described in Chapter 2, highlighted a number of errors in the code and eventually resulted in an implementation of much higher quality. A similiar application, described in Chapter 3, involved the use of CCS to highlight inconsistencies in the MSMIE protocol used between dedicated processors and the control and protection systems of the Sizewell B nuclear power plant in the UK.

In a non-safety-critical domain, another interesting example is the use of formal methods to highlight inconsistencies in the description of an algorithm used in voting by the Church of England; this is discussed in Chapter 5.

Q. Do I still need to test my system?

A. Definitely. Dijkstra (1981) has pointed out a major limitation of testing — while it can demonstrate the presence of "bugs", it cannot demonstrate their absence. Just because a system has passed unit and system testing, it does not follow that the system will necessarily be bug free.

That is where formal methods offer considerable advantages over more traditional structured methods when developing systems where the highest integrity is required. Formal methods allow us to propose properties of the system and to demonstrate that they hold. They make it possible for us to examine system behaviour and to convince ourselves that all possibilities have been anticipated. Finally, they enable us to prove the conformance of an implementation with its specification.

In this way, one would hope to eliminate the ubiquitous bug. Unfortunately, contrary to the hyperbolic claims made by many so-called "experts", formal methods are no guarantee of correctness. Certainly the use of formal methods can give increased confidence in the integrity of the system, and more confidence that the system will indeed perform as expected, but errors still exist and bugs are still found post-implementation.

Even where full formal development is employed (i.e. the specification is refined to executable code) there must be a certain degree of human input. It is debatable as to whether automatic refinement can ever realistically be achieved in a beneficial manner, and indeed whether it ever should be achieved.

A formal specification is an abstract representation of reality. It has an infinite (up to renaming) number of potential implementations. However, when we turn from the abstract world of sets, sequences and formal logic to considering an implementation in a conventional programming language, we find that very few programming languages support the required structures explicitly (and certainly not in an efficient manner). We must then determine the most appropriate data structures to implement the higher-level entities (data refinement) and translate the operations already defined to operate on pointers, arrays, records, etc. If a computer program is allowed to choose the eventual implementation structures (assuming that it could be relied upon to choose these appropriately), it will cause a bias towards particular implementations ... one of the things that should be avoided if possible to give the implementor the greatest possible freedom of choice in the design. As such, refinement will always require a certain degree of human input, admitting possibilities of human error.

Even when formal methods are used in the design process, testing, at both the unit and system level, should never be completely abandoned. On the contrary, a comprehensive testing policy should be employed to trap those errors that have been admitted during refinement and/or cases that have not been considered earlier. Although such testing would not need to be as exhaustive as in the case where formal methods had not been employed, a substantial degree of testing is still required.

In the case of the formally developed Inmos floating-point unit for the T800 Transputer, one error was found by testing. This was as a result of an "obviously correct" change to the microcode being made after the formal development had been undertaken. We should never underestimate human fallibility, and testing will always be a useful check that a formally produced system does work in the real world.

Testing may be performed in a traditional fashion, using techniques such as McCabe's complexity measure to determine the required amount of testing. Alternatively it may employ some form of simulation, using executable specification languages, or some form of specification animation (such as that described in Chapters 5 and 6 of this book).

Formal methods offer yet another alternative when it comes to testing, namely specification-based testing. The formal specification may be used as a guide for determining functional tests for the system and automating test coverage evaluation. The tester may exploit the abstraction made in the specification to concentrate on the key aspects of the functionality. The approach offers a structured means of testing, which simplifies regression testing (Carrington and Stocks, 1994) and helps to pin-point errors.

The specification itself can be used to derive expected results of test data, and to aid in determining tests in parallel with the design and implementation, hence enabling unit testing at an earlier stage in the development, as described in Chapter 11.

1.5   Support for formal methods

Q. Are there any tools available?

A. Yes. Just as in the late 1970s and early 1980s, when CASE (computer-aided software engineering) and CASP (computer-aided structured programming) tools were seen as a means of increasing programmer productivity and reducing programming "bugs", tool support is now seen as a means of increasing productivity and accuracy in formal development.

Craigen, Gerhart and Ralston conclude this in Chapter 17, as an analysis of various formal methods projects as part of their international survey (Craigen *et al.*, 1993) highlights the trend towards, and need for, further tool support. This is a trend that seems set to continue, and we expect that in the future more emphasis will be placed on IFDSEs (integrated formal development support environments) to support formal specification, just as CASE workbenches support system development using more traditional structured methods.

Indeed most of the projects discussed in this book placed great emphasis on tool support. Chapter 12 describes ORA's experiences in the development of a secure kernel for a distributed operating system using their own tool, Penelope, and highlights how this and other tool support was essential to a large-scale development.

In Chapter 9, the development of a rail traffic tracking and tracing system by CAP Volmac involves the use of their own VDM^{++} tool. Various tools were also used extensively in the BAe experiment reported in Chapter 13, in particular the Teamwork CASE tool and IFAD's VDM-SL Toolbox.

Less integrated tools were used at DST in their work on the Airbus CIDS system (Chapter 11), and editing and type-setting tools for formal methods were commonly used. Indeed, in Chapter 15, Hamilton concludes that although CADiZ proved to be extremely useful, a more integrated tool would have been a distinct advantage.

Conversely, from their work at Tektronix Corporation (described in Chapter 4), Garlan and Delisle conclude that they did not require sophisticated tool support in their formal development, although much use was made of basic tools such as type checkers.

A number of formal methods incorporate tool support as part of the method itself. PVS, as used in the development of the AAMP5 microprocessor in Chapter 7, for example places great emphasis on the use of an integral theorem prover, as does Nqthm, described in Chapter 8.

Abrial's B-Method (Abrial, 1995), as used in Chapter 6 in the further development of IBM's CICS system, was supported by the B-Toolkit, an integrated set of tools from B-Core (UK) Ltd. These augment Abrial's method for formal software development by addressing industrial needs in the development process. At GEC Alsthom Transport, development in B (discussed in Chapter 10) necessitated a not insubstantial investment in the development of a suite of tools to support the development process.

Many believe B and the B-Method to be representative of the next generation of formal methods; if this is true, then the B-Toolkit, and other similar such toolkits, will certainly form the basis of future IFDSEs.

Q. Where can I learn more?

A. There are now a number of outlets for practitioners to discuss formal methods, notations and tools, and to seek advice and solutions to problems and difficulties from other practitioners.

Chief among these outlets are various (especially electronic) distribution lists, such as the Z FORUM (contact zforum-request@comlab.ox.ac.uk) and the more recently established VDM FORUM (vdm-forum-request@mailbase.ac.uk). A larch-interest group (larch-interest-request@src.dec.com) and an OBJ FORUM (contact objforum-request@comlab.ox.ac.uk) are also in operation.

Z FORUM has spawned comp.specification.z, a gatewayed electronic newsgroup which is read regularly by around 40 000 people worldwide. A newsgroup devoted to specification in general, comp.specification, regularly generates discussions on formal methods, as well as the more traditional structured methods, object-oriented design, etc., as does the comp.software-eng newsgroup.

A recently established mailing list at University of Idaho (contact `formal-meth-ods-request@cs.uidaho.edu`) addresses formal methods in general, rather than any specific notation, and a new mailing list run by the Z User Group addressing educational issues (to subscribe, contact `zugeis-request@comlab.ox.ac.uk`) has also been established. In addition, the newsletter of the IEEE Technical Segment Committee on the Engineering of Complex Computer Systems (contact `ieee-tsc-eccs--request@cl.cam.ac.uk`) addresses issues related to formal methods and formal methods education.

Electronically accessible on-line archives for Z (including an on-line and regularly revised comprehensive bibliography) and other formal methods exist on the global Internet computer network. The global World Wide Web (WWW) electronic hypertext system provides significant support for formal methods. A useful starting point is the following WWW page which provides pointers to other electronic archives concerned with formal methods throughout the world, including substantial publicly accessible tools such as HOL, Nqthm and PVS for downloading on the Internet:

`http://www.comlab.ox.ac.uk/archive/formal-methods.html`

It should be noted, however, that most existing formal methods tools have grown out of research work in the area. It is questionable whether the formal methods market is sufficiently large to support more commercial development of tools. This has, until now, limited the production of industrially robust tools with appropriate maintenance support.

A plethora of formal methods books are now available, and most reputable computer science publishers carry a title on the Z notation, or on discrete mathematics looking suspiciously like Z. The proceedings of various symposia and workshops offer invaluable reading on up-to-date developments in formal methods. The proceedings of the Formal Methods Europe symposia (and their predecessors, the VDM symposia) are available in the Springer *Lecture Notes in Computer Science* (LNCS) series, while the proceedings of the Refinement Workshops and five Z User Meetings have been published in the Springer *Workshops in Computing* (WiCS) series. The proceedings of the most recent International Conference of Z Users (Bowen and Hinchey, 1995c) are published in LNCS. Both LNCS and WiCS contain the proceedings of many other interesting colloquia, workshops and conferences on formal methods.

Formal methods are not quite so popular in North America as in Europe, although they are gaining momentum. While papers on formal methods are becoming well established at a number of US conferences, there is as yet no regular conference in the US devoted to formal methods. Perhaps the Workshop on Industrial-strength Formal Specification Techniques (WIFT) represents a step in that direction.

Again the main journals and publications devoted to formal methods are based in Europe, and the UK specifically. These include *Formal Methods in System Design*, *Formal Aspects of Computing* and the *FACS Europe* newsletter run jointly by Formal Methods Europe and the British Computer Society Special Interest Group on Formal Aspects of Computing Science, among others. *The Computer Journal*, *Software Engineering Journal* and *Information and Software Technology* regularly publish articles on, or related to, formal methods, and have run or plan a number of special issues on the subject.

In the US, there are no journals devoted specifically to formal methods, although some of the highly respected journals, such as *IEEE Transactions on Software Engineering* (TSE) and the *Journal of the ACM*, and the popular periodicals such as *IEEE Computer*, *IEEE Software* and the *Communications of the ACM* regularly publish relevant articles. IEEE TSE, *Computer* and *Software* ran very successful coordinated special issues on formal methods in September 1990. More recently, in January 1994 an *IEEE Software* special issue on safety-critical systems also devoted a not inconsiderable amount of attention to formal methods, as has a journal in this area entitled *High Integrity Systems*, launched in 1994.

Formal methods (in particular Z, VDM, CSP and CCS) are taught in most UK undergraduate computer science courses. Although still quite uncommon in the US, a recent NSF-sponsored workshop aims to establish a curriculum for teaching formal methods in US undergraduate programmes. One would hope that this will become a regular event, and will help to establish formal methods as a regular component of US university curricula.

A number of industrially based courses are also available, and in general can be tailored to the client organization's needs. Popular Z courses are run by Logica Cambridge Ltd., Praxis, Formal Systems (Europe) Ltd., as well as by the Oxford University Computing Laboratory. In fact, the majority of all industrially based formal methods courses focus on the Z notation. Formal Systems (Europe) Ltd. also run a CSP course and a CSP with Z course, both of which have been given in the US as well as the UK. IFAD in Denmark run an industrially-based formal methods course using VDM and the object-oriented variant VDM^{++}.

1.6 Conclusions

We have given some brief practical hints on how to apply formal methods. The remainder of this book consists, in the main, of a presentation of examples of industrial usage of formal methods, the accounts written by the actual practitioners involved. We hope that these will inspire and help to guide others who may wish to apply formal methods (to whatever extent) in their own domain.

Acknowledgements

Parts of this chapter are based on Bowen and Hinchey (1995a,b).

Chapter 2

Using Mathematical Models in the Inspection of Critical Software

David Lorge Parnas

2.1 Introduction

Professional engineers are required to accept responsibility for the reliability and trust-worthiness of their products. A major part of their education is devoted to mathematics; they learn to use mathematics to specify, describe, and analyse their products. No professional engineer would claim that intuition alone is sufficient, or that mathematics is too difficult for an engineer. The major exception to this pattern is the activity that we euphemistically call software engineering. Software design methods have been developed outside the traditional engineering establishment and many program developers do not have much professional training. As a result, mathematics is rarely used in industrial practice. In fact, it is frequently argued that the use of mathematics is not practical in this area of engineering. Programs are often considered to be self-documenting, and testing, sometimes called animation of models, is substituted for mathematical analysis.

For more than three decades, computer scientists have sought a mathematical basis for programming and developed "formal methods" for verifying the correctness of software. The first breakthrough came in 1968 when Robert Floyd introduced a means of using mathematical pre-conditions and post-conditions to describe what a program accomplishes (Floyd, 1967). After Floyd, many other researchers proposed variations on that approach. The method described in this work derives from the work of Mills (1975). Mills, like several others, showed how to use the classical mathematical concept of function rather than the pre- and post-conditions approach introduced by Floyd. Unfortunately, in spite of many years of effort, and hundreds of papers, industrial applications of formal (mathematical) methods remain rather rare. One notices that the same examples of applications are cited repeatedly. These cases serve as "existence proofs", proofs that the methods can work, but, if one visits typical programming shops, one rarely finds anyone who has used these methods. Existence proofs are not proofs of practicality.

When new methods do not catch on, there are two obvious possible explanations. Either the methods are not yet good enough, or practitioners are too conservative, unwilling to learn, and resistant to change. In most cases, there is truth in both explanations. The best known formal methods clearly work, but it is equally clear that they require a lot of tedious writing of expressions that are difficult to read. In fact, some of the methods are

17

so tedious that people take short-cuts and make mistakes. It is also true that the people who should be using these methods entered the computer field because they enjoy the immediate feedback that they get from writing and running programs; they are often reluctant to do the tedious analysis that is required if we are to be certain that a complex product is correct.

This chapter explains a relatively unknown approach that was applied as part of the licensing process for the Darlington Nuclear Power Generating Station in Canada. The application was reported to the nuclear industry in Parnas *et al.* (1991). The work is characterized by several factors.

1. The use of mathematical methods was required by a governmental agency.
2. The work was not motivated as research in formal methods; instead, it was motivated by safety-requirements and executed by programmers and engineers who had no previous contact with any of the "formal methods" developed by computer scientists.
3. The method was applied to previously written software, including assembler programs; no program was modified in order to ease the use of mathematical methods.
4. Although the work used mathematical methods, we thought of it as a disciplined and formal inspection, not as a mathematical proof.
5. We took a "divide and conquer" approach, breaking the inspection task down into many small and simple tasks. We will argue that the last point may be the most important characteristic of the approach.

2.2   Safety-critical software in the Darlington Nuclear Power Generating Station

Canadian nuclear stations are required to have three control systems, each one capable of shutting down the station if a serious problem is detected.

- The reactivity control system is a real-time control system that is responsible for power adjustments under normal operating conditions; it is also required to initiate a shutdown of the reactor whenever key measurements deviate from specified safe ranges. Reactivity control systems have long been computerized. However, because of their complexity, and a history of some failures, the AECB[1] does not assume that the reactivity control system will work correctly when they perform their safety analysis. They assume that these systems will fail and look for assurance that the plant will be safe even if the reactivity control system fails to shut down the plant.
- In addition to the reactivity control system, there are two systems whose only job is to shut the reactor down in the event of an accident. The two systems are completely separate (from each other and from the reactivity control system) and play

---

[1]The AECB (Atomic Energy Control Board) is the Canadian governmental agency charged with certifying that nuclear plants are safe to operate.

no rôle in normal plant operations. Known as the safety systems or shutdown systems, they have no task other than their shutdown rôle; consequently, they are much simpler than the reactivity control system. Canadian regulations forbid assigning any functions that are not essential for the shutdown task to a shutdown system.

Any of the three systems can bring about a reactor shutdown even if the other two systems are not calling for such action. Each of the systems has its own sensors and control mechanisms.

The Nuclear Power Generating Station in Darlington, Ontario, was one of the first nuclear plants constructed with shutdown systems that are entirely computer controlled. In Canadian nuclear plants built before Darlington, each safety system was constructed as a network of analog components and relays. At Darlington, the safety systems are computerized. The two shutdown systems used different types of computers, were programmed in different languages, and were created by different teams of programmers. This was intended to assure design diversity and thereby to reduce the likelihood that both systems would fail simultaneously.

The AECB customarily inspects both the design and the construction of nuclear power stations very carefully; it is quite normal for them to require changes. When they tried to inspect the software in the safety systems, they became concerned. Although the two programs were relatively simple (approximately 10 000 lines in a mixture of a compiler language and assembly code), the inspectors found them much more complex than the hardware systems that they were replacing. Although the two systems had been implemented by different teams, a design error common to both of them had been found in an informal analysis. Although the code had been tested extensively for several years, that shared design error had not been uncovered by the (carefully planned) tests. The AECB could not state, with confidence, that there were no errors in the code. They were unwilling to grant a licence without further inspection.

A team comprising about 60 people conducted an inspection of the code over a period of nearly one year. During that inspection, a number of unsuspected discrepancies between the code and the requirements were discovered. Those that were found to be safety relevant were corrected and the plant is now operating.

The inspection was based on the preparation of precise mathematical documentation for the code. Sections 2.4 to 2.9 will describe the method that was used.

The inspection process at Darlington has been discussed by several other authors in Archinoff *et al.* (1990) and Bowman *et al.* (1991).

2.3 Why is software inspection difficult?

Regulatory authorities routinely inspect safety-critical installations, both while they are being designed and during construction. The AECB employs very experienced and competent engineers; they are usually confident of their ability to detect safety-relevant flaws. When software is involved, that confidence evaporates. When inspecting all but the smallest programs, the complexity overwhelms the inspectors. They are faced with a lot of detailed information without the clear structure usually present in physical mechanisms. They are aware that any small detail in any part of the program could cause a serious failure. In commonly used programming languages, the interactions between code sections are almost unrestricted and, most often, undocumented. There are many situations that must be considered and it is hard to be confident that one has not overlooked something important.

Years of practical experience have shown that people cannot easily understand long programs. When asked to study such programs, we tend to focus on little details while making use of vague and inaccurate descriptions of the overall structure. The combination of a large amount of detail with inaccurate or vague descriptions of the structure makes it quite common for serious errors to escape our attention.

When studying a long program, we must decompose it into small parts and then, provisionally, associate a function with each one. We must then convince ourselves that

1. if each part implements its assigned function, the whole program will be correct, and
2. each part implements its assigned function.

Frequently, we find that our provisional assumptions were not exactly what the programmer had in mind and are not accurate descriptions of the program. After revising our initial division and function descriptions, we try again. In principle, this iterative process converges and we learn whether or not the program is correct. In practice, we usually give up before we have a complete and precise understanding of the program. The process terminates when we run out of time or patience, not because we are sure that the program is correct.

In inspecting a safety-critical program, one cannot rely upon *ad hoc* inspections in which people stare at code until they run out of energy. One needs a systematic process in which it is possible to be sure that one has covered all possible situations. Such a procedure, must have a sound basis, i.e. a mathematical foundation.

2.4   Functional documentation

As with any engineering product, one cannot certify that software meets its requirements unless one has a clear and precise statement of those requirements. That statement must be written in a way that allows those who really know the requirements to read it; those experts may not be computer specialists. Because of the complexity of software products, inspection also requires clear and precise statements of what the components of the system are supposed to do; we cannot examine the whole system at once, and we can only examine the components in isolation if the interfaces are properly described. In other words, documentation plays an essential rôle in inspecting software.

In recent years, a small group of collaborators has developed a general approach to software documentation, which we call "functional documentation" (Parnas *et al.*, 1991). We define the required content of documents in terms of mathematical relations. Each of the documents is associated with certain relations; the document must contain a representation of those relations. A document that does not fully describe the associated relations is incomplete; one containing additional information is also considered to be faulty. By defining documents in these abstract terms, we have succeeded in being precise about their contents without specifying the notation or "language" to be used.

The documents described in Parnas *et al.* (1991) include: the system requirements document, the system design document, the software requirements document, an optional software behaviour specification, the module interface specifications, and module internal design documents. Hardware descriptions and communication protocol descriptions are also discussed.

Elsewhere (Parnas, 1992; Janicki, 1993; Zucker, 1993, 1994), we have discussed notations for representing relations in any of these documents. If our method of software documentation is to be practical, we need a representation of relations that is easily read. In practice, the use of conventional notation results in very complex, deeply nested, expressions that are difficult for anyone to use. Practitioners are quickly turned off by notations that require them to parse long expressions in order to learn simple facts. We have discovered that a multidimensional notation, tables whose entries can be mathematical expressions (including other such tables), results in a precise notation that can be used by engineers in industry. In spite of the fact that there is no increase in theoretical expressive power over conventional notations, the tabular format has several practical advantages.

One of the goals of our research is to be able to use the same tabular notations in all of our documents. All of the documents describe mathematical relations, but the ranges and domains of those relations vary from document to document.

The Darlington inspection process used two of the documents mentioned above. The first was a system design document written and reviewed by nuclear engineers, not software specialists. Like most such systems, the shutdown systems were written as a periodic loop. The requirements document could be interpreted as a description of the actions that must be taken on any pass through that loop.

The second document was a set of program-function (see Section 2.7) descriptions derived from the code by software experts. These tables described the effects of the execution of the body of the outermost loop. The ultimate goal was to have both documents describe the same functions and to be confident that those functions were the "right" functions.

2.5 Specifications vs descriptions or models

Engineers make a useful distinction between specifications, descriptions, and models of products. This distinction seems to be forgotten in the computer science literature.

- A **description** is a statement of some of the actual attributes of a product, or a set of products.
- A **specification** is a statement of properties required of a product, or a set of products.

- A **model** is a product, neither a description nor a specification. Often it is a product that has some, but not all, of the properties of some "real product".

A description may include attributes that are not required, i.e. incidental properties. For example, a description of a program may include the number of ones in its binary representation; usually there is no requirement to have any particular ratio of zeros to ones. A specification may include attributes that a (faulty) product does not possess. The statement that a product satisfies a given specification constitutes a description of the product. Perhaps it is this fact that has led some to confuse descriptions and specifications.

Any list of attributes may be interpreted as either a description or a specification. "A volume of more than 1 cubic metre" may be either an observation about a specific box that has been measured, or a requirement for a box that is about to be purchased. If one is given a list of attributes, one must be told whether it is to be interpreted as a description or as a specification. Sometimes one may use one's knowledge of the world to guess whether a statement is a description or a specification; for example, when discussing milk, the attribute "spoiled" is unlikely to be a specification. Moreover, while a specification may allow a choice of attributes, a description must describe the actual attributes.

We often try to use models as descriptions or specifications by accompanying a model with a statement such as, "It looks like this but is 100 times larger" or "Make it look like this". Before the work of Floyd (1967) several authors proposed using one program to specify another and thus to accomplish proofs of correctness by proving equivalence. In discussions of communications protocols, researchers and developers often present finite state machines that conform to a protocol as if it was a specification of the protocols. In fact, these are models, products that purportedly satisfy unstated requirements. I see the same tendency to use models as if they were specifications in most current work on "formal methods".

Descriptions and specifications are both predicates on observable attributes of a product. Models will include information that is not observable. Models generally have attributes that are neither requirements nor properties of the "real product".

When talking about aircraft, we do not have trouble distinguishing between "model", "prototype", "specification", and "description". A model 747 may fit on my desk and be unable to fly. A prototype 747 would have been one of the first built, would have held 350 people and have been able to carry them a long distance. A specification of the 747 would tell us, among other thing, that it must be able to carry 350 persons a certain distance. The statement "has a funny looking bump on top at the front" could be part of a description, but I doubt that it was part of a specification. We should learn to make the same distinctions in software engineering but because specifications, descriptions, models, and prototypes and the final product are all abstract mathematical in nature, and consist of text, we seem to find this difficult.

2.6   The mathematical content of requirements documents

A critical step in documenting the requirements of a computer system is the identification of the environmental quantities to be measured or controlled and the representation of those quantities by mathematical variables. The environmental quantities include physical properties (such as temperatures and pressures), the readings on user-visible displays, administrative information (such as the number of people assigned to a given task), and even the wishes of a human user. These quantities must be denoted by mathematical variables and, as is usual in engineering, that association must be carefully defined; coordinate systems, signs, etc. must be unambiguously stated. Often diagrams are essential to clarify the correspondence between physical quantities and mathematical variables.

It is useful to characterize each environmental quantity as either monitored, controlled, or both. **Monitored** quantities are those that the user wants the system to measure. **Controlled** quantities are those whose values the system is intended to regulate[2]. For real-time systems, time can be treated as a monitored quantity. In the following, we will use $m_1, m_2, \ldots, m_p$ to denote the monitored quantities, and $c_1, c_2, \ldots, c_q$ to denote the controlled ones. If the same quantity is to be both monitored and controlled, the corresponding values must be specified to be equal (by relation *NAT*, cf. Section 2.6.1 below). Note too that some systems are expected to monitor the status of their own (internal) hardware components. Since these are often determined later in the design process, we may add to the set of monitored variables long after design has begun.

Each of these environmental quantities has a value that can be recorded as a function of time. When we denote a given environmental quantity by v, we will denote the time function describing its value by v^t. Note that v^t is a mathematical function whose domain consists of real numbers; its value at time t is denoted by $v^t(t)$.

The vector of time-function $(m_1^t, m_2^t, \ldots, m_p^t)$ containing one element for each of the monitored quantities, will be denoted by $\underline{m}^t$. Similarly, $(c_1^t, c_2^t, \ldots, c_q^t)$ will be denoted by $\underline{c}^t$.

2.6.1   The relation *NAT*

The environment, i.e. nature and previously installed systems, places constraints on the values of environmental quantities. These restrictions must be documented in the requirements document and may be described by means of a relation, which we call *NAT* (for nature), defined as follows:

- *domain(NAT)* is a set of vectors of time functions containing exactly the instances of $\underline{m}^t$ allowed by the environmental constraints;
- *range(NAT)* is a set of vectors of time functions containing exactly the instances of $\underline{c}^t$ allowed by the environmental constraints;
- $(\underline{m}^t, \underline{c}^t) \in NAT$ if and only if the environmental constraints allow the controlled quantities to take on the values described by $\underline{c}^t$, if the values of the monitored quantities are described by $\underline{m}^t$.

---

[2]Frequently, it is not possible to monitor or control exactly the variables of interest to the user. Instead one must monitor or control other variables whose values are related to the variables of real interest. Usually, one obtains the clearest and simplest documents by writing them in terms of the variables of interest to the user in spite of the fact that the system will monitor other variables in order to determine the value of those mentioned in the document.

NAT is not usually a function; if *NAT* were a function the computer system would not be able to vary the values of the controlled quantities without effecting changes in the monitored quantities. Note that if any values of m^t are not included in the domain of *NAT*, the system designers may assume that these values will never occur.

2.6.2   The relation *REQ*

The computer system is expected to impose further constraints on the environmental quantities. The permitted behaviour may be documented by describing a relation, which we call *REQ*. *REQ* is defined as follows:

- *domain*(*REQ*) is a set of vectors of time functions containing those instances of m^t allowed by environmental constraints;
- *range*(*REQ*) is a set of vectors of time functions containing only those instances of c^t considered permissible, i.e. values that would be allowed by a correctly functioning system;
- $(m^t, c^t) \in REQ$ if and only if the computer system should permit the controlled quantities to take on the values described by c^t when the values of the monitored quantities are described by m^t.

REQ is usually not a function because one can tolerate "small" errors in the values of controlled quantities.

2.6.3   Requirements feasibility

Because the requirements should specify behaviour for all cases that can arise, it should be true that

- $domain(REQ) \supseteq domain(NAT)$, and
- $domain(REQ \cap NAT) = (domain(REQ) \cap domain(NAT))$.

That is, the relation *REQ* can be considered feasible with respect to *NAT* if the first condition above holds.

Feasibility, in the above sense, means that nature (as described by *NAT*) will allow the required behaviour (as described by *REQ*); it does not mean that the functions involved are computable nor that an implementation is practical.

Note that the above implies that

- $domain(REQ \cap NAT) = domain(NAT)$.

Discussions of the use of this model in practice can be found in Archinoff *et al.* (1990), Hester *et al.* (1981), Heninger *et al.* (1978), Heninger (1980) and Parnas *et al.* (1990, 1991). Further examples and discussion can be found in van Schouwen (1990) and van

Schouwen *et al.* (1993). In all of these papers the reader will find that the functions and relations are described using tabular expressions as in Parnas (1992) and Janicki (1993). We return to this aspect of the work in Section 2.8.

2.7   Program descriptions

A digital computer can usefully be viewed as a finite state machine and a program as a description of a behaviour pattern for that machine. The following terminology is useful in talking about programs and their behaviour

- An **execution** is a sequence (either finite or infinite) of states. A **program** is an initial state of a machine that determines a set of executions, sometimes called the executions of that program. We denote the set of all executions by $Exec(P,S)$.
- The subset of $Exec(P,S)$ that begins with the state x, $x \in S$, is denoted by $e_P(x)$, and x is called the **starting state** of those executions.
- If there exists an execution in $e_P(x)$ that is finite and its last state is z, then we may write $\langle x, \ldots, z \rangle \in e_P(x)$, and say that this **execution terminates (in z)**, and call z the **final state (of this execution)**. We may also say that the **program P may start in x and terminate in** z.
- An infinite sequence in $e_P(x)$ (i.e. of the form $\langle x, \ldots \rangle$) is called a **non-terminating execution**.
- If there exists a state x, $x \in S$, such that $e_P(x)$ contains two or more distinct executions, then P is called a **non-deterministic program**.
- If for a given state x, $x \in S$, every member of $e_P(x)$ is finite, x is called a **safe state** of P. The set of safe states of P is denoted S_P.

We have found it useful to extend the notion of relations a little in order to have convenient mathematical descriptions of programs

- A binary relation R on a given set U is a set of ordered pairs with both elements from U, i.e. $R \subseteq U \times U$. The set U is called the **Universe of R**. The set of pairs R can be described by its characteristic predicate, $R(p,q)$, i.e. $R = \{(p,q) : U \times U \mid R(p,q) = \textbf{\textit{true}}\}$. The domain of R, denoted $Dom(R)$, is $\{p \mid \exists q \, [R(p,q)]\}$. The range of R, denoted $Range(R)$, is $\{q \mid \exists p \, [R(p,q)]\}$. Below, "relation" means "binary relation".
- A **limited-domain relation** (LD-relation) on a set, U, is a pair, $L = (R_L, C_L)$, where R_L, the relational component of L, is a relation on U, i.e. $R_L \subseteq U \times U$, and C_L, the competence set of L, is a subset of the domain of R_L.

A more complete discussion of these issues can be found in Parnas (1994).

$(\exists i, B[i] = x)$	$(\forall i, ((1 \leq i \leq N) \Rightarrow B[i] \neq x))$

$j'\ \mid$	$B[j'] = x$	*true*	
$present' =$	true	false	$\wedge\ NC(x, B)$

Figure 2.1 Specification of a search program.

2.8 Program-function tables

The previous section describes an abstraction. It does not tell how to represent the LD-relations. Although LD-relations can be described by Boolean expressions that describe the characteristic predicate of the sets involved, we have not found this to be satisfactory in practice. The programs that we encounter alter many variables and distinguish many different cases. The Boolean expressions become long, deeply nested, and visually unapproachable. An early version of the tabular notations subsequently described in Parnas (1992), the program-function table[3] was used in the inspection at Darlington. This section gives an informal introduction to program-function tables based on the example in Figure 2.1.

The table in Figure 2.1 describes a program that must find an element of an array, B, whose value is that of the variable x. The program is to determine the value of two program variables called j and *present*. The variable j (presumed to be of type integer) is to record the index of one element of B whose value is the value of the variable x (if one exists). The variable called *present*, presumed to be Boolean, is to indicate whether or not the desired value could be found in B. If B does not contain the value sought, the value of j is allowed to be any integer value.

The header at the top of the table in Figure 2.1 shows that two situations must be distinguished. The first column of the main grid (under the first element of the top header) describes the case where the value sought can be found in the array. The second column describes what the program must do if the value is not present.

Each row in the main grid of a program-function table corresponds to a program variable and describes the value that this variable must have upon termination. The header to the left of the table identifies the variable whose value is described in each row and also indicates how that variable will be described. A "$\mid$" in the vertical header indicates that the variable's final value must satisfy a predicate given in the main grid. When "$=$" appears instead of "$\mid$", the final value of the variable can be obtained by evaluating the expressions in that row of the main grid. The symbols "*true*" and "*false*" represent values of predicates, while the symbols "**true**" and "**false**" represent the possible values of Boolean variables.

The table describes a predicate on a set of pairs (a relation) representing the values of the variables before and after execution. The value of a variable named v on termination

---

[3]Program-function tables are essentially mixed-vector tables.

$$(((\exists i, B[i] = x) \land (B[j'] = x) \land (present' = \textbf{true})) \lor$$
$$((\forall i, ((1 \leq i \leq N) \Rightarrow B[i] \neq x)) \land (present' = \textbf{false}))) \land ('x = x' \land 'B = B')$$

Figure 2.2 Conventional expression equivalent to Figure 2.1.

is denoted by v'. Its initial value is denoted $'v$. The program must terminate in a state in which the predicate represented by the variable evaluates to ***true***. The Boolean expression $NC(x, B)$ represents a predicate whose value is ***true*** if x and B are not changed by the program; in other words, it is a shorthand notation for "$'x = x' \land 'B = B'$". Because the table represents a predicate, it can be part of a conjunction with another such table or any Boolean expression. The table in Figure 2.1 is equivalent to the Boolean expression in Figure 2.2.

In practice, program-function tables have many more rows and columns. Although the tables can be understood intuitively, we have described their meaning formally as well. More extensive discussions of these, and other types of tables can be found in Janicki (1993), Parnas (1992) and Zucker (1993, 1994).

There is nothing that can be said with such a table that cannot be said using equivalent conventional Boolean expressions. Figure 2.2 shows a Boolean expression that is equivalent to Figure 2.1. However, the table parses the expression for the reader and presents the reader with a set of simple Boolean expressions instead of a single complex expression. Using the table, one can select the row and column of interest and one need not understand the whole expression in order to find out what must happen to a particular variable in a specific case. The number of characters that appear in the tabular expression is usually smaller than the number of characters in the equivalent conventional expression because in the conventional expression some of the expressions that appear once in one of the headers would have to be repeated several times[4]. In spite of the fact that the tabular representation takes up more space on paper, we all found the tables far easier to work with than the equivalent Boolean expressions. In larger tables, involving many cases, many variables, and longer identifiers, the advantages of the table format are more dramatic. In the Darlington inspection, programs that altered a dozen or more variables and for which 6–10 different cases had to be distinguished were common. In such circumstances, the tables are far easier to read than the equivalent Boolean expressions.

2.9 The inspection process

The AECB designed an inspection process that recognized the following pragmatic limitations on the task of inspecting large programs.

---

[4]Note how "*present'* =" appears only once in the table, but twice in the conventional expression. The repetition becomes more serious when there are more rows. More advanced forms of these tables reduce the repetition of subexpressions even more (Parnas, 1992; Iglewski *et al.*, 1993).

- Inspectors looking for errors in a program need "quiet time" to think.
- The results of their contemplation must be scrutinized in an open discussion.
- Inspections must be interrupted by breaks, evenings and weekends, which means that the inspection must compose of a sequence of small, almost independent examinations.
- Inspection must focus on small amounts of the program at any one time, because if we examine large portions at once, the inspectors may miss important problems.
- It is essential that all cases be considered and all parts of the program be inspected.

The combination of tabular representation of the requirements functions and the program-function tables were well suited for this task. Tabular expressions were used to represent the results of the private analysis of inspectors and were well suited for scrutiny by others. The tabular format allows inspectors to focus on simple cases, while supporting a systematic procedure (proceeding column by column, and then row by row) for covering all cases.

The AECB inspection process called for an inspection by four teams:

- a requirements team, which produced tabular representation of the requirements;
- a code inspection team, which derived program-function tables from the code;
- a comparison team, which attempted to establish equivalence between requirements tables and program-function tables by showing step-by-step transformations from one to the other;
- an audit team, which checked the work of the other teams on a "random sample" basis.

The requirements tables were based on Heninger *et al.* (1978); more up-to-date descriptions of this method are to be found in van Schouwen (1990) and van Schouwen *et al.* (1993). Their output was a set of tables like those in Heninger *et al.* (1978). We found that, although these tables use mathematical notation, they can be read by engineers with no training in either computer science or abstract mathematics. For example Heninger *et al.* (1978), the A-7 Aircraft Software Requirements Document, could be read by the pilots available to advise our software team. In fact, pilots found several hundred detailed errors in the early drafts. The team that produced the requirements document for the Darlington shutdown system comprised people considered experts in nuclear safety, not programming. Most of the members of this team were employed by AECL, who manufacture the equipment.

The second team consisted mostly of software consultants who were not active in the nuclear power industry. They were chosen for their expertise in the programming language and had little knowledge of the requirements. They were hired as consultants by the owner of the plant, Ontario Hydro. They were not given a description of the requirements to work with.

The third team was trained to understand program-function tables. They did not look at the code; instead they worked from the program-function tables and the requirements tables. They had to show step-by-step transformations of the tables that would cause both tables to look alike. Unfortunately for this team, in most cases the tables were not equivalent and no such sequence of transformations could be found. The team would then report the discrepancies that kept them from doing their job.

The fourth team was hired by AECB, and worked in Ottawa while the other teams were based in the Toronto area. They were primarily software experts and their task was to be sure that the other teams did their work in a disciplined and rigorous way.

Whenever a discrepancy was first reported, the team that produced the program-function tables was asked to check its work. They were not told what the problem was, just asked to check their work again. If there was still a discrepancy it would be reported to a set of safety experts for evaluation. Evaluation usually revealed one of the following situations.

- The requirements tables were wrong; they were corrected and the process repeated.
- The programmers had added "something extra", thinking that they were improving things. In many cases, the "extra" was a positive change and accepted.
- There was a coding error, but it would not adversely affect safety. It was allowed to remain.
- There was a coding error that did affect safety. It was corrected and the review was repeated.

The fourth team sampled the work of the first three, after those teams were satisfied that their work was correct. In the early phases, they found numerous problems. As skills developed, the process became fairly routine and the audit found fewer problems.

Perhaps because the code had tested for many years before the inspection[5], the number of changes required was relatively small, but each change made was deemed important. Nonetheless, the main product of the inspection was confidence. The plant was allowed to go into service and all involved felt confident about the thoroughness of the inspection.

2.10   Hazard analysis using functional documentation

Ontario Hydro brought in its own consultant[6] before the inspection described in this paper was undertaken. She concluded that, in addition to the inspection discussed here, a form of hazard analysis was needed. The inspection described here showed that the requirements document and the code were consistent, but it did not show that there were no hazards. A particular form of hazard analysis, involving inspection of the code, was carried out and reported in Bowman *et al.* (1991).

It is the opinion of this author that, although a hazard analysis was necessary, it should not have been performed on the code. When applied to code, "fault-tree" analysis looks

---

[5]Although the software was behind schedule, the physical plant was much further behind its schedule. This software should have been inspected much earlier.

[6]Professor Nancy Leveson, now at the University of Washington.

suspiciously like weakest-precondition analysis and duplicates the analysis that is required to derive the program-function tables. It is possible to perform a fault-tree analysis using the functional requirements document instead of the code. In fact, the method described in Section 2.6 treats the computer system in exactly the same way that engineers treat other components. That description should allow fault-tree analysis to be carried out without giving the software any special consideration. By using an abstraction of the code instead of the code itself, one saves a great deal of effort and can put more time and energy into defining hazards and investigating the ways that they might occur. Just as the program-function tables provided an abstraction of the code that was easier to work with than the code itself, the requirements tables provide an abstraction of the system that summarizes everything one needs to know for any analysis of the effects of the system on its environmental variables. In electronics, for example, one always uses abstractions of components rather than returning to the basic physics for each new analysis. Software should be handled in the same way.

2.11   Conclusions

One important test of the value of any technology that has been transferred from the research laboratory or university to industry is whether the practitioners continue to use the technology when the researcher is no longer involved. Often an idea is used by newly graduated Ph.D.s on their first job, but their employer does not follow up and continue to use or develop the ideas. The experience with program-function tables has been quite different. None of the practitioners in the four teams mentioned had any previous contact with the technology. Ontario Hydro and AECL were initially strongly opposed to using what they viewed as a completely new method. All three organizations involved (AECB, Ontario Hydro, AECL) called in other experts looking for an alternative that was more mature and supported by tools. They reluctantly concluded that the approach described was the best one and completed the inspection described above. After the process was completed, the author was asked to give two one-week courses on software engineering to others in the Canadian nuclear industry. The organizations involved have since published widely (within their industry) on their experience with the method and have offered their expertise to others. Ontario Hydro has developed the methods further and incorporated them in a software development standard which has now been approved for trial use by the AECB. They now organize their own courses on the documentation methods. New software is being developed using program-function table methods. AECL has used the ideas on software being developed for nuclear power plants being built in South Korea. The AECB, apparently convinced that this approach is essential to the use of software in safety-critical applications, continues to study similar approaches in its own research program. The author, who introduced the ideas to those involved, has not been involved with the nuclear industry in the past few years, but the work goes on. This is the best evidence of success.

Acknowledgements

I am indebted to Harlan D. Mills and N.G. de Bruijn who first introduced me to the concept of program functions–relations. A.J. van Schouwen contributed a great deal to the early work on these methods and Jan Madey has helped to formalize the model behind them. Some of the formulations here are modified versions of explanations used by the author and Jan Madey in technical reports.

Chapter 3

Gaining Assurance with Formal Methods

Glenn Bruns and Stuart Anderson

3.1 Introduction

We would like to be as confident in the safety of complex systems as we are in simple
systems. Typically, the safety of simple systems is certified by exhaustive testing. For
complex systems exhaustive testing is impossible, and random testing precludes strong
claims of safety (Littlewood and Strigini, 1993). Standards for complex systems therefore attempt to ensure safety by regulating the production process (RTCA, 1992; Ministry
of Defence, 1991a). This approach has the adverse economic consequence of making the
production process more rigid. More importantly, it does not directly justify the safety of
the final system. Empirical arguments founder for lack of evidence; arguments in principle founder on the difficulty of establishing a clear connection between the process and
the final product.

A product-oriented certification regime may yet be feasible despite the limitations of
testing. Some advocates of formal methods argue that these methods can provide objective evidence of the adequacy of a system's requirements, and of the satisfaction of
the requirements by the actual system. This claim suggests that future standards should
ask for such evidence rather than mandate aspects of the production process. Here we illustrate the use of formal methods in providing evidence that requirements are correctly
formulated and are satisfied by a system.

The Sizewell B nuclear power plant (now under construction) is the first such plant in
the UK to have software components which contribute to its primary safety system. The
software system implementing both plant control and primary safety has been developed
over more than a decade and has about 100 000 lines of code written in three different
programming languages. The software is developed to conform with IEC 880 (International Electrotechnical Commission, 1986), the international standard for nuclear power
systems. However, because this is the first such plant to be installed in Britain the UK
regulatory body, the Nuclear Installations Inspectorate, has required a detailed assessment of the code to convince them that the implemented system achieves a suitable level
of safety assurance.

The assessment programme for the code was carried out by Nuclear Electric, the British
utility company responsible for the operation of Sizewell B. The programme activities
ranged from conventional dynamic testing and review to a formal methods analysis of
the code.

The formal methods activity was the verification (Ward, 1993) of the code modules making up the system with the MALPAS (Ward, 1989) code analyzer. The verification was a bottom-up process, moving up the call tree of the system from modules which make no calls to the top-level modules. Verification of a module is achieved by automatically translating the code to the intermediate language used by MALPAS and by expressing the specification of the module in pre-condition-post-condition form. Then verification conditions are generated using the code analyzer and one attempts to discharge these conditions (using a rewriting system). This process is known as compliance analysis. It requires considerable skill because an analyst must annotate the code with logical assertions before the verification conditions can be generated. The consultancy firm involved in the analysis employed up to 80 people full time on the Sizewell assessment.

It is not surprising that problems in the Sizewell B code were identified by such intensive study. However, because the verification is code driven it generates a low-level analysis that is hard to relate to requirements. Because it is process oriented, being applied uniformly to all modules, it generates a large volume of certification data.

By contrast, our approach is requirements driven. We aim to show that requirements are adequate and are met by the system. We do this by verifying that properties hold of system models. This raises issues in the validation of system models, the adequacy of formalizations of requirements and how failure to meet a requirement should influence the system model. Rushby (1993), Leveson (1986) and others have identified omitted and misinterpreted requirements as a major source of potentially critical software failures.

We are especially interested in system components that involve the interaction of some independent components. Littlewood and Strigini (1993) mention that faults which resist discovery by testing are typically the result of unforeseen interaction between components. Our experience suggests that modelling and property-based specification help in focusing on deviant behaviour arising from complex interaction of system components.

In the spring of 1990 we met with members of the Nuclear Electric validation and verification team engaged in assessing the code for the Sizewell B system. At the meeting we attempted to identify components of the Sizewell B protection system whose analysis might prove challenging. Our preference was for a component which would permit some analysis of the requirement and whose structure involved concurrent interaction of system components. We were given a public-domain document (Santoline *et al.*, 1989) describing the Multiprocessor Shared Memory Information Exchange (MSMIE) protocol used for communication from dedicated processors to the control and protection systems. This document provides both a statement of the requirements and a detailed description of the protocol.

We present some of the modelling and analysis work carried out on the MSMIE protocol. We begin by constructing a formal model of the MSMIE protocol in CCS (Milner, 1989). We provide two different kinds of models. The first is a natural one in which hardware components are modeled as CCS agents. The similarity of the model to the description of the protocol helps raise our confidence that the formal model is valid. The second model is more abstract, focusing on the transitions that are possible between states of shared memory. This model allows us to identify important features of MSMIE which are hard to describe in the first model. An important question is whether the two models are interchangeable. Part of our analysis is a comparison of the models, using notions of behavioural equivalence from CCS.

Next, we take the main requirements given in the protocol description and formalize them in a temporal logic. We use the Concurrency Workbench (Cleaveland *et al.*, 1993) to check that these properties hold of our model. In formalizing the requirements we identify unstated assumptions without which MSMIE fails to meet the requirements. We also identify a failing in the basic protocol. Fortunately, the actual protocol uses timing constraints to prevent this problem from occurring. Elsewhere (Bruns and Anderson, 1994) we present a modified version of the protocol that satisfies the property without using timing constraints.

Finally we describe the contribution this form of analysis can make to providing evidence for the certification of safety systems. We also contrast the evidence provided by our approach to that provided by the MALPAS analysis of the Sizewell B code. The Sizewell verification places formal methods in a restricted context. Though the data provided by the MALPAS analysis is useful, the analysis of the system we present here shows that formal methods can play a broader role in the development of safety systems.

3.2   Modelling MSMIE

In this section we describe the protocol informally and show how it can be formalized as a CCS agent.

3.2.1   The MSMIE protocol

The Multiprocessor Shared-Memory Information Exchange (MSMIE) is a protocol for communication between processors in a real-time control system. The processors are classified as either **masters**, which perform application-related tasks, or **slaves**, which provide dedicated functions. For example, a monitoring system might contain slave processors that sense various temperatures, and a master processor that ensures the temperatures are within prescribed bounds.

Communication between slave and master processors is made via shared memory, as shown in Figure 3.1. A shared-memory cell can be used for either slave-to-master communication, or for master-to-slave communication, but not both. The details of slave-to-master and master-to-slave differ; we look only at the slave-to-master part of the protocol. Here, a cell can be written by a single slave, but read by many masters. Reading and writing are performed asynchronously. For example, a slave processor might sense temperatures and write them to shared memory at one rate, while a master processor reads the values and checks them at a different rate.

The requirements that guided the design of MSMIE are described informally (Santoline *et al.*, 1989). Some of these provide for fault tolerance and standardized design.

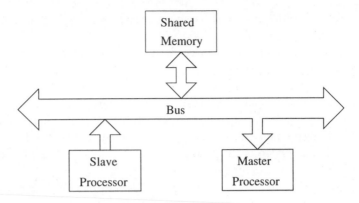

Figure 3.1 System architecture for the MSMIE protocol.

Others concern the behaviour of the protocol. Of these, the primary requirement is

1. "prevent simultaneous access to a given memory resource"

Adherence to this requirement avoids **data tearing**, in which one processor reads an item of data while another processor is in the middle of writing it. Data tearing is possible when a data item is too large to be stored in a single memory cell, and must be stored in a buffer built from two or more cells.

A naïve solution to this requirement is to protect a single shared-memory buffer with a semaphore, so that only one processor at a time can access it. This approach leads to delays. For example, if the slave processor is writing to a buffer, a master processor must wait before it can begin to read. The second requirement states that delays are unacceptable:

2. "a buffer is guaranteed to be available to each processor at the time it requests access to a buffer"

Implicit in this requirement is the understanding that delays can be avoided only if multiple buffers are used for each data item to be communicated. For example, if two buffers are used, the slave buffer can write a new value to one buffer while a master processor reads the previous value from the other buffer.

A third requirement in (Santoline *et al.*, 1989) also concerns delays:

3. "information exchanges between the processors [must occur] within a minimal and deterministic time frame"

Requirement 3 implies that delays must be avoided; requirement 2 explicitly prohibits them. However, requirement 3 also demands that the passing of data from slave to masters be timely.

The MSMIE protocol is a three-buffer protocol. To motivate the need for three buffers, we will sketch a two-buffer protocol and show that delays are inevitable with it. We attach to each buffer a status value to coordinate the slave and master processors. Status

data$_1$	status$_1$	semaphore
data$_2$	status$_2$	

Figure 3.2 A two-buffer memory image.

value **slave** indicates that a slave can write to the buffer, value **newest** indicates that writing by a slave is complete, value **master** indicates that a master process can read from the buffer, and value **idle** indicates that the buffer is unused. The buffer values are manipulated by the slave and master processors. For example, when a slave finishes writing to a **slave** buffer, it changes the status of the buffer to **newest**. Access to the status values is controlled by a semaphore so that only one processor can change them at a time. However, a slave may write data to a **slave** buffer, and a master may read data from a **master** buffer, without acquiring the semaphore. We refer to a set of buffers and a semaphore as a **memory image** (see Figure 3.2). No two buffer protocol can avoid all delays. For example, suppose one buffer has status **newest**, another has status **master**, and that the slave processor is ready to write. Now the slave must either delay or overwrite the newest data, causing the next read by a master to be out of date.

The MSMIE protocol is like the protocol just sketched, but uses three buffers. Also, each memory image now contains a count of the number of currently reading processors. Initially one buffer has status **slave** and the others have status **idle**. The number-of-readers count is initially zero.

The operations of the MSMIE protocol are as follows. As already mentioned, the master-to-slave part of the protocol is ignored. We also ignore an "access mode" feature of MSMIE.

Slave write
1. Acquire semaphore
2. If there is a **newest** buffer, change its status to **idle**
3. If there is a **slave** buffer, change its status to **newest**, else an error has occurred
4. If there is an **idle** buffer, change its status to **slave**, else an error has occurred
5. Release semaphore

Master acquire
1. Acquire semaphore
2. If there is a **newest** buffer, but not a **master** buffer, then
   change status of **newest** buffer to **master**
3. If there is a **master** buffer, then increment number-of-readers count
4. Release semaphore

Master release
1. Acquire semaphore

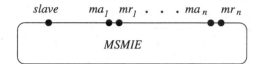

Figure 3.3 Interface to a shared-memory service for *n* masters.

2. Decrement number-of-readers count
3. If number-of-readers = 0, then
      if there is a **newest** buffer, then
           change status of **master** buffer to **idle**
      else change status of **master** buffer to **newest**
4. Release semaphore

When a slave processor is ready to write, it can immediately begin writing its data item to a buffer having status **slave**. After the data item has been completely written, the slave performs the **Slave write** operation, causing the buffer to become a **newest** buffer. At the same time, another buffer acquires status **slave**, so that a buffer is available when the slave processor is ready to write again.

A master processor performs the **Master acquire** operation when it is ready to read. If a buffer with status **master** is available after the operation is performed, then the master reads from that buffer. If not, then the slave has never written a data item, so the master must try again later. After the master has completed reading the buffer, it performs operation **Master release**, which, if no other masters are reading, will cause the buffer status to become **newest** or **idle**.

Notice that buffer data values are not mentioned in the operations of the protocol. Data values are read and written between these operations.

3.2.2   Formalizing the protocol

Our aim is to discover whether MSMIE satisfies the requirements listed in the previous section. To be able to check the requirements, and even to state them precisely, we need a more precise description of MSMIE. Here we develop a formal model of the protocol in CCS. To avoid breaking up the presentation of the model we confine information about CCS to Appendix A. For a complete account of CCS see Milner (1989).

Our first modelling step is to consider which of the MSMIE requirements we hope to check. We will concentrate first on requirements 1 and 2, since requirement 3 is less clear.

Next we must choose the interface to the protocol. The informal description of the protocol does not specify an interface; it is implementation oriented rather than service oriented. We will define a precise interface to the shared-memory communications service provided by the protocol to slave and master processors. The actions provided by this service are *slave*, ma_k, and mr_k, where k ranges over the master processor indices. Figure 3.3 shows the interface to a shared-memory service for *n* masters.

This simple interface is intended to capture only the observable behaviour of the protocol that we need to express requirements 1 and 2. For example, we cannot ask, using the actions of the interface, whether a value written by a slave is correctly read by a master. In contrast, in a bottom-up verification a complete specification of the code is carried along throughout the analysis. The choice of this interface shows that we are choosing to focus on synchronization issues rather than on correctness of data transmission. The ability to narrow the range of the assessment allows us to make the analysis more tractable and comprehensible.

Now we are ready to start defining parts of our CCS model. We begin by modelling a shared-memory image, consisting of three buffers, a counter, and a semaphore. A single buffer stores a status value, and allows the value to be read and written. It can be described in CCS as a kind of shared-memory cell:

$$Cell(v) \overset{def}{=} \overline{read}(v).Cell(v) + write(v').Cell(v')$$

The agent C can perform the output action $\overline{read}(v)$ to supply the stored value and evolve to a cell storing the same value, or it may perform the input action $write(v')$ to accept new value v' and evolve to a cell storing this value.

A single buffer with address i is obtained from agent $Cell$ by relabelling the read and write actions:

$$Buf_i(v) \overset{def}{=} Cell[read_i/read, write_i/write]$$

For example, the read and write actions of Buf_1 are $read_1$ and $write_1$.

A set of three buffers can be built by putting single buffers in parallel. Writing buffer status values with the single letters **i,s,n**, and **m**,

$$Buffers \overset{def}{=} Buf_1(\mathbf{s}) \mid Buf_2(\mathbf{i}) \mid Buf_3(\mathbf{i})$$

A shared-memory image also contains a counter of the number of readers. This is just another case of the memory cell *Cell*. We obtain the counter by relabelling the read and write actions:

$$Counter(n) \overset{def}{=} Cell[cr/read, cw/write]$$

The read and write actions of $Counter(n)$ are cr and cw.

Finally, we need a semaphore to provide for exclusive access to the image:

$$Semaphore \overset{def}{=} take.give.Semaphore$$

A memory image can now be described:

$$MemImage \overset{def}{=} Buffers \mid Counter(0) \mid Semaphore$$

The next step in modelling the protocol is to formalize the **Slave write** operation, which is performed by a slave processor when it has finished writing its data to the buffer with status value **s**.

$$
\begin{aligned}
Slave \quad &\overset{def}{=} \quad slave.Sl_1 \\
Sl_1 \quad &\overset{def}{=} \quad \overline{take}.read_1(v_1).read_2(v_2).read_3(v_3).Sl_2((v_1, v_2, v_3)) \\
Sl_2(B) \quad &\overset{def}{=} \quad \sum_{i=1}^{3} \text{if } B_i = \mathbf{n} \text{ then } Sl_3(B[i \rightarrow \mathbf{i}]) \\
&\qquad + \text{if } \mathbf{n} \notin \{B_1, B_2, B_3\} \text{ then } Sl_3(B) \\
Sl_3(B) \quad &\overset{def}{=} \quad \sum_{i=1}^{3} \text{if } B_i = \mathbf{s} \text{ then } Sl_4(B[i \rightarrow \mathbf{n}]) \\
Sl_4(B) \quad &\overset{def}{=} \quad \sum_{i=1}^{3} \text{if } B_i = \mathbf{i} \text{ then } Sl_5(B[i \rightarrow \mathbf{s}]) \\
Sl_5(B) \quad &\overset{def}{=} \quad \overline{write_1}(B_1).\overline{write_2}(B_2).\overline{write_3}(B_3).\overline{give}.Slave
\end{aligned}
$$

The structure of this agent mirrors the steps listed in the informal description of the protocol in Section 3.2.1. Tuples of buffer status values are used as parameters. We write $(v_1, \ldots, v_n)$ for the tuple containing values $v_1, \ldots, v_n$; T_i for the ith element of tuple T; and $T[i \rightarrow v]$ for the tuple that agrees with tuple T except that the ith value is v.

The errors mentioned in the informal description of the protocol are not modelled explicitly in agent *Slave*. For example, in state $Sl_3(B)$, no error action occurs if no buffer has status **s**. Instead, such a condition will result in deadlock. Later in the paper, the model will be checked for deadlocks.

We have finally to formalize the **Master acquire** and **Master release** operations of the protocol. As we have mentioned when discussing the interface of the protocol, this part of the protocol will provide, for the *i*th master processor, the actions ma_i and mr_i. A important issue faced in formalizing MSMIE, and not raised in the informal description of the protocol, is how to handle an acquire request from a master if no slave has yet written to the memory image. If we model the master acquire action as the single, instantaneous CCS action *ma*, then the only solution is to allow these actions to occur only when data is available for reading. However, to determine whether data is available for reading it is necessary to read the memory image. The memory acquire part of the protocol therefore autonomously checks the memory image. If data is available for reading, the protocol allows the master to perform an acquire action. If not, the protocol checks the memory image again.

A related issue arises in handling master release actions. For every master, a release action should only be possible after an acquire action. This could be modelled in two ways. The first is to model acquire and release actions as two, concurrent CCS processes, and to store in shared memory the identification of masters that have acquired, but not yet released, a buffer. The second way, which we will adopt, is to model acquire and release actions as a single CCS process that alternately accepts acquire and release actions.

The CCS agent *Master* models the master acquire and release operations. In the following agent definition, *MA* and *MR* refer to the **Master acquire** and **Master release** operations:

$$
\begin{aligned}
Master &\stackrel{def}{=} MA_1 \\
MA_1 &\stackrel{def}{=} \overline{take}.read_1(v_1).read_2(v_2).read_3(v_3).MA_2((v_1, v_2, v_3)) \\
MA_2(B) &\stackrel{def}{=} \text{if } \mathbf{n} \in \{B_1, B_2, B_3\} \wedge \mathbf{m} \notin \{B_1, B_2, B_3\} \\
&\quad \text{then } \sum_{i=1}^{3} (\text{if } B_i = \mathbf{n} \text{ then } MA_3(B[i \rightarrow \mathbf{m}])) \\
&\quad \text{else } MA_3(B) \\
MA_3(B) &\stackrel{def}{=} (\text{if } \mathbf{m} \in \{B_1, B_2, B_3\} \text{ then } ma.cr(x).\overline{cw}(x+1).MA_4(B)) \\
&\quad + \overline{give}.Master \\
MA_4(B) &\stackrel{def}{=} \overline{write_1}(B_1).\overline{write_2}(B_2).\overline{write_3}(B_3).\overline{give}.MR_1
\end{aligned}
$$

It may seem strange that, in MA_3, the protocol may choose to give up the semaphore and check the memory image again even if the master wants to acquire the buffer. This alternative is necessary because the protocol cannot wait, holding the semaphore, for the master to acquire a memory buffer. Unfortunately, this means our model has the possibility of forever re-checking the buffer even if the master is waiting to perform an acquire action.

$$MR_1 \stackrel{def}{=} mr.\overline{take}.read_1(v_1).read_2(v_2).read_3(v_3).MR_2((v_1, v_2, v_3))$$

$$MR_2(B) \stackrel{def}{=} cr(x).\overline{cw}(x-1).MR_3(B)$$

$$MR_3(B) \stackrel{def}{=} cr(x).\text{if } x = 0$$
$$\text{then } \sum_{i=1}^{3} (\text{if } B_i = \mathbf{m}$$
$$\text{then } (\text{if } \mathbf{n} \in \{B_1, B_2, B_3\} \text{ then } MR_4(B[i \rightarrow \mathbf{i}])$$
$$\text{else } MR_4(B[i \rightarrow \mathbf{n}])))$$
$$\text{else } MR_4(B)$$

$$MR_4(B) \stackrel{def}{=} \overline{write}_1(B_1).\overline{write}_2(B_2).\overline{write}_3(B_3).\overline{give}.Master$$

As with the shared memory buffers, we can model the part of the protocol that handles the ith master by relabelling the agent *Master*.

$$Master_i \stackrel{def}{=} Master[ma_i/ma, mr_i/mr]$$

All parts of the MSMIE protocol have now been described as agents, and we are ready to assemble them using the CCS composition and restriction operators. For simplicity, our model contains just one slave processor, two master processors, and one memory image:

$$Msmie \stackrel{def}{=} (MemImage \mid Slave \mid Master_1 \mid Master_2) \backslash L$$

where L is the set of all actions found in the CCS definitions for the MSMIE protocol except the *slave*, *ma*, and *mr* actions.

A flow diagram for our CCS model showing the top-level components is the given in Figure 3.4.

The dotted lines between the components are intended to show that the master and slave agents synchronize with the shared-memory agent, but do not synchronize between themselves.

We claim that the final model for MSMIE is faithful to the synchronization aspects of the informal presentation of the protocol. Validation of the model can be done in a sys-

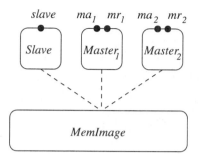

Figure 3.4 Flow diagram of CCS model.

tematic way because CCS supports agents built of subagents. First, we check that the component structure of the model reflects the component structure of the informal description. Secondly, we check that each component agent is faithful to the corresponding process in the informal description.

The process of formalization forces us to face issues which are not considered in the informal description. Most important is the treatment of initial conditions, which are a rich source of potential error. In the CCS model we must decide on the action taken when a master reads before the slave has written; this case is ignored in the informal description.

3.2.3   Simplifying the model

The model given above is a natural description of the MSMIE protocol in the sense that the components of the model correspond to hardware or software components of the system. Further, the slave and master agents were written to reflect the details of the informal description of the protocol. Such a description is essential for validation. However, our analysis concerns only the protocol's behaviour. An abstract model of the protocol can be made by considering only shared-memory buffer states and the observable actions that are possible between them. The new model is a sequential agent with a parameter that represents the state of shared memory. As we will see, CCS provides a framework that shows when these two models can be interchanged.

The MSMIE protocol is now described as the agent $M(B, r)$. The parameter B represents the state of the shared memory buffers. It is a set of three pairs (a, l), where a is the buffer status, drawn from $\{\mathbf{i}, \mathbf{s}, \mathbf{n}, \mathbf{m}\}$, and l is the buffer identification, drawn from $\{1, 2, 3\}$. The buffers are given as a set rather than a tuple to enable pattern-matching rules to be used in the description of the protocol. Thus the set $\{(\mathbf{s}, 1), (\mathbf{i}, 2), (\mathbf{i}, 3)\}$ is used rather than $(\mathbf{s}, \mathbf{i}, \mathbf{i})$. The parameter r is the set of master processors reading from the master buffer, drawn from subsets of the set $\{1, 2\}$ of master processor identifiers.

Instead of describing M as a CCS agent, we present the transitions of M's behaviour graph directly:

Slave actions

$$M(\{(\mathbf{s},l),(\mathbf{n},l'),(\mathbf{i},l'')\},r) \overset{slave}{\to} M(\{(\mathbf{n},l),(\mathbf{s},l'),(\mathbf{i},l'')\},r) \tag{1}$$

$$M(\{(\mathbf{s},l),(\mathbf{n},l'),(\mathbf{i},l'')\},r) \overset{slave}{\to} M(\{(\mathbf{n},l),(\mathbf{i},l'),(\mathbf{s},l'')\},r) \tag{2}$$

$$M(\{(\mathbf{s},l),(\mathbf{i},l')\}\cup B',r) \overset{slave}{\to} M(\{(\mathbf{n},l),(\mathbf{s},l')\}\cup B',r) \quad \forall l.(\mathbf{n},l)\notin B' \tag{3}$$

$$M(\{(\mathbf{s},l),(\mathbf{n},l')\}\cup B',r) \overset{slave}{\to} M(\{(\mathbf{n},l),(\mathbf{s},l')\}\cup B',r) \quad \forall l.(\mathbf{i},l)\notin B' \tag{4}$$

Master acquire actions

For $k \in MI$:

$$M(\{(\mathbf{m},l)\}\cup B',r) \overset{ma_k}{\to} M(\{(\mathbf{m},l)\}\cup B',r\cup\{k\}) \quad k\notin r \tag{5}$$

$$M(\{(\mathbf{n},l)\}\cup B',\emptyset) \overset{ma_k}{\to} M(\{(\mathbf{m},l)\}\cup B',\{k\}) \quad \forall l.(\mathbf{m},l)\notin B' \tag{6}$$

Master release actions

$$M(\{(\mathbf{m},l)\}\cup B',r\cup\{k\}) \overset{mr_k}{\to} M(\{(\mathbf{m},l)\}\cup B',r) \quad r\neq\emptyset,k\notin r \tag{7}$$

$$M(\{(\mathbf{m},l),(\mathbf{n},l')\}\cup B',\{k\}) \overset{mr_k}{\to} M(\{(\mathbf{i},l),(\mathbf{n},l')\}\cup B',\emptyset) \tag{8}$$

$$M(\{(\mathbf{m},l)\}\cup B',\{k\}) \overset{mr_k}{\to} M(\{(\mathbf{n},l)\}\cup B',\emptyset) \quad \forall l.(\mathbf{n},l)\notin B' \tag{9}$$

The initial state of the protocol is:

$$M_0 \overset{def}{=} M(\{(\mathbf{s},1),(\mathbf{i},2),(\mathbf{i},3)\},\emptyset)$$

Each clause of the definition shows how a slave or master processor action can change the buffer contents. For example, clause 1 shows that if the memory buffers contain status values $\mathbf{s}$, $\mathbf{n}$, and $\mathbf{i}$, then a slave action can change the $\mathbf{s}$ buffer to a $\mathbf{n}$ buffer and the $\mathbf{n}$ buffer to a $\mathbf{s}$ buffer. Notice that the variables in the definition of M allow a clause to be applied in more than one way to a particular state. For example, by clause 3 both of the following transitions are possible for $M(\{(\mathbf{s},1),(\mathbf{i},2),(\mathbf{i},3)\},\emptyset)$:

$$M(\{(\mathbf{s},1),(\mathbf{i},2),(\mathbf{i},3)\},\emptyset) \overset{slave}{\to} M(\{(\mathbf{n},1),(\mathbf{s},2),(\mathbf{i},3)\},\emptyset)$$

$$M(\{(\mathbf{s},1),(\mathbf{i},2),(\mathbf{i},3)\},\emptyset) \overset{slave}{\to} M(\{(\mathbf{n},1),(\mathbf{i},2),(\mathbf{s},3)\},\emptyset)$$

We could have defined M as the CCS agent $M(B, r) \stackrel{def}{=} C_1 + \cdots + C_9$, where the agent C_i captures the ith clause above. For example, C_3 could be defined as

$$\sum_{(l, l', B') \in S} slave.M(\{(\mathbf{n}, l), (\mathbf{s}, l'), (\mathbf{i}, l'')\}, r)$$

where set S is all tuples (l, l', B') such that $B = \{(\mathbf{s}, l), (\mathbf{i}, l')\} \cup B'$ and B' contains no buffer with status $\mathbf{n}$. We find our definition easier to read.

We now have two models of the protocol. Our first, natural model, has several concurrent components. Externally observable actions have internal synchronization actions interspersed between them. For example, the buffer status changes via internal synchronizations. Our new model has no internal actions. It describes just the possible externally observable behaviour. Each action of the new model causes the buffer parameters to change. The new model highlights the role of the buffer status as our principal abstraction in describing the behaviour of the protocol. However, does it provide an adequate description of the externally observable behaviour?

To answer this question we must consider the theory provided by CCS. Central to CCS are a variety of notions of process equivalence. The central one is observation equivalence, which attempts to formalize the idea that two processes are equivalent when they cannot be distinguished by an external observer. Our two models of the system are observation equivalent. For finite-state systems the observation equivalence is decidable and can be checked automatically. The Concurrency Workbench (Cleaveland *et al.*, 1993) is a tool which (amongst other things) checks for observation equivalence of agents. This provides a high level of assurance that our models really are interchangeable.

Even though our models are observation equivalent there are significant differences between the models. The natural model, but not the abstract one, can **diverge**; that is, it may perform internal τ actions forever, not responding at all to the environment. This fact may seem surprising in light of the tight relationship defined by observation equivalence. However, most other common notions of behavioural equivalence allow even greater differences between equivalent processes. For example, if two processes can perform the same sequences of actions, then one may be able to deadlock while the other cannot.

This section has shown two advantages of using an expressive formal method as a modelling tool. First, it eases the task of validation. Because the operators of CCS provide a flexible structure for modelling processes we can model the system in a way that accurately reflects the informal specification. Secondly, it contributes to intellectual tractability. The notion of observation equivalence allows us to build models which highlight the abstractions we want to work with but which can be shown to be equivalent.

3.3   Reasoning about MSMIE

Having a precise model of the behaviour of the MSMIE protocol allows us to verify aspects of that behaviour. Modern safety-critical standards (Ministry of Defence, 1991a,b; RTCA, 1992) stress that the verification process should be driven by system requirements not by the structure of the system design. Thus the verification process will involve three stages: identifying a requirement, formalizing the requirement, and checking whether the formal requirement holds of of the system model. Since requirements often change as a system is required to function in new circumstances, a flexible means of formalizing requirements is needed.

Our approach is to formalize requirements as a collection of properties expressed in a temporal logic, the modal mu-calculus (Kozen, 1983; Stirling, 1989, 1991). We view the formalized requirements as an open-ended collection of formulae in this logic, which we may add to as analysis proceeds or as further requirements are identified. If a CCS agent has finitely many states, then we can automatically check whether a modal mu-calculus formula is satisfied by a CCS agent using the Concurrency Workbench.

We will now attempt to formalize the three main requirements of MSMIE.

The first requirement, that simultaneous access to shared-memory cells is prevented, is guaranteed by the presence of buffer status values, provided that the processors observe the rules of the protocol. Since we have not modelled slave and master processors, we cannot determine this.

The second requirement is that buffer contention is prevented: buffer access should always be possible without delay. For a slave processor, this means that a *slave* action should always be possible. This requirement is formalized as the formula *Slave always possible*:

$$Always(\phi) \stackrel{def}{=} \nu Z.\phi \wedge [-]Z$$

$$Slave\ always\ possible \stackrel{def}{=} Always(\langle slave \rangle \mathtt{tt})$$

MSMIE has the *Slave always possible* property. This critical property ensures that a slave processor will never be delayed from writing a buffer by the protocol. Notice that this property implies that the protocol is deadlock free. As mentioned in Section 3.2.2, this means that the errors in the informal description of the protocol cannot occur.

For a master processor, the requirement means that, after an initial write by the slave, each master should always be able to perform either a master acquire or master release action. This idea can be expressed as the formula *Master always possible*:

$$Master\ always\ possible \stackrel{def}{=} [slave]Always(\langle ma_1, mr_1 \rangle \mathtt{tt} \wedge \langle ma_2, mr_2 \rangle \mathtt{tt})$$

MSMIE also has the *Master always possible* property.

The third requirement, that information exchange occur within a minimal and deterministic time frame, is difficult to make precise. During our analysis it became clear that one facet of this requirement is that master processors must eventually read data written by the slave. More precisely, if fresh data is continually written by the slave, then it should be continually read by the masters, provided they are continually reading data. This property cannot be expressed using the actions of our current CCS model. To express it, it is necessary to define "freshness" and to add a new action to the model.

We call a buffer **fresh** if its status is **n** and its previous status was **s**. Not every buffer with status **n** is fresh; such a buffer may have previously had status **m**. We will insert a new "probe" action *update* into the abstract model of the protocol to indicate that on the next ma_k action a fresh buffer will be acquired by the kth master. This will be the case when either

- a *slave* action occurs and there is no buffer with status **m** or,
- an mr_k action occurs, there is a buffer with status **n**, and k is the only master currently reading a buffer.

In the abstract model it is straightforward to identify those transitions in which a master processor acquires a fresh buffer.

Adding *update* actions to clauses 1–4 of agent M of the previous section gives the following:

$$M(\{(\mathbf{s},l),(\mathbf{n},l'),(\mathbf{i},l'')\},r) \stackrel{slave}{\rightarrow} \stackrel{update}{\rightarrow} M(\{(\mathbf{n},l),(\mathbf{s},l'),(\mathbf{i},l'')\},r)$$

$$M(\{(\mathbf{s},l),(\mathbf{n},l'),(\mathbf{i},l'')\},r) \stackrel{slave}{\rightarrow} \stackrel{update}{\rightarrow} M(\{(\mathbf{n},l),(\mathbf{i},l'),(\mathbf{s},l'')\},r)$$

$$M(\{(\mathbf{s},l),(\mathbf{i},l'),(\mathbf{m},l'')\},r) \stackrel{slave}{\rightarrow} M(\{(\mathbf{n},l),(\mathbf{s},l'),(\mathbf{m},l'')\},r)$$

$$M(\{(\mathbf{s},l),(\mathbf{i},l')\}\cup B',r) \stackrel{slave}{\rightarrow} \stackrel{update}{\rightarrow} M(\{(\mathbf{n},l),(\mathbf{s},l')\}\cup B',r) \quad \forall l.(\mathbf{n},l),(\mathbf{m},l)\notin B'$$

$$M(\{(\mathbf{s},l),(\mathbf{n},l'),(\mathbf{m},l'')\},r) \stackrel{slave}{\rightarrow} M(\{(\mathbf{n},l),(\mathbf{s},l'),(\mathbf{m},l'')\},r)$$

$$M(\{(\mathbf{s},l),(\mathbf{n},l')\}\cup B',r) \stackrel{slave}{\rightarrow} \stackrel{update}{\rightarrow} M(\{(\mathbf{n},l),(\mathbf{s},l')\}\cup B',r) \quad \forall l.(\mathbf{i},l),(\mathbf{m},l)\notin B'$$

Adding an *update* action to clause 8 gives:

$$M(\{(\mathbf{m},l),(\mathbf{n},l')\}\cup B',\{k\}) \stackrel{mr_k}{\rightarrow} \stackrel{update}{\rightarrow} M(\{(\mathbf{i},l),(\mathbf{n},l')\}\cup B',\emptyset)$$

The sole reason for the introduction of *update* actions is to aid in the analysis of the protocol. The requirements we have identified force us to introduce observable *update* actions so we can express the informal requirement in formal terms. These considerations should also affect more conventional verification activities. If the requirements demand some notion of *update* be observable then it should be observable during testing. This suggests that the implemented code should detect *update*, at least for test purposes, though this may be disabled when the code is in operation.

Since *update* roughly reflects the availability of fresh data to the master processors, we formalize our property by the formula *Update always*, which states that updates happen infinitely often.

$$\text{Update eventually} \stackrel{def}{=} \mu Z.\langle-\rangle\mathsf{tt}\wedge[-update]Z$$

$$\text{Update always} \stackrel{def}{=} \text{Always}(\text{Update eventually})$$

The MSMIE protocol fails to have this property. One reason for the failure is that the slave and master processes of the model need not make progress, even if they are able to. For example, the slave process can cease to supply fresh information, and therefore after the last value supplied by the slave has been read by the master processors no further *update* action can occur.

This failure of the *Update always* property identifies the progress assumptions we have brought to formalizing the protocol. In the informal requirement there is an unspoken assumption that all processors make progress and so this source of failure can never occur. The formalization forces us to make the assumption explicit and to evaluate the validity of the assumption. Since master processors are introduced to provide resilience to failure it may not be reasonable to assume no master will fail.

Our solution is to refine further the property to incorporate the idea that the slave and the two master processors always makes progress. To capture the idea that each processor makes progress requires consideration of infinitely long behaviours of the system. A processor makes progress within an infinite behaviour if it contributes infinitely many actions to the behaviour. The formula *Update often* formalizes the property that infinitely many *update* actions occur if the master and slave processors always make progress.

$$\text{Update often} \ \overset{def}{=} \ \text{Always}(B)$$

$$[L^*]\phi \ \overset{def}{=} \ \nu Z.\phi \wedge [L]Z$$

$$B \ \overset{def}{=} \ \mu X.[slave][-update^*][ma_1][-update^*][ma_2][-update^*]X$$

Update often can be paraphrased in English as "it is always the case that no sequence of non-update actions containing infinitely many occurrences of each of *slave*, ma_1, and ma_2 can occur". The order of the actions *slave*, ma_1, and ma_2 in the formula is not important; to say that they occur infinitely many times in a particular order is logically equivalent to saying that they occur infinitely many times.

Does *Update often* hold of our model of MSMIE? No, because a buffer can remain in the master state indefinitely, as shown by the following possible behaviour of our model.

$$\ldots M(\{(\mathbf{s},1),(\mathbf{n},2),(\mathbf{m},3)\},\{1\}) \overset{slave}{\rightarrow} M(\{(\mathbf{n},1),(\mathbf{s},2),(\mathbf{m},3)\},\{1\}) \overset{ma_2}{\rightarrow}$$

$$M(\{(\mathbf{n},1),(\mathbf{s},2),(\mathbf{m},3)\},\{1,2\}) \overset{mr_1}{\rightarrow} M(\{(\mathbf{n},1),(\mathbf{s},2),(\mathbf{m},3)\},\{2\}) \overset{slave}{\rightarrow}$$

$$M(\{(\mathbf{s},1),(\mathbf{n},2),(\mathbf{m},3)\},\{2\}) \overset{ma_1}{\rightarrow} M(\{(\mathbf{s},1),(\mathbf{n},2),(\mathbf{m},3)\},\{1,2\}) \overset{mr_2}{\rightarrow}$$

$$M(\{(\mathbf{s},1),(\mathbf{n},2),(\mathbf{m},3)\},\{1\}) \ldots$$

In the first state shown, only master processor 1 has a buffer acquired for reading. The same is true in the last state shown. However, according to clause 5 above, a master will always acquire the current master buffer if one is present. Therefore it is possible for the master processors to acquire and release a buffer in such a way that the master processors make progress but one buffer has master status continuously. In other words, our model violates the *Update often* property, since masters can continually read old data forever even in the presence of newer data.

Property *Update often* is a reasonable one to require of the protocol. In Bruns and Anderson (1994) we present a modified version of the protocol for which the property holds.

We believe we can develop variants of the protocol which tolerate master processor failures and still retain the property.

The failure of MSMIE to satisfy *Update often* is recognized in Santoline *et al.* (1989). The solution there is to impose, for systems with multiple masters, a limit on the amount of time a master may assign a buffer to itself. This strategy guarantees the requirement captured in the *Update often* property.

3.4   Formal methods and certification

Many modern standards, for example MoD DIS 00-55 (Ministry of Defence, 1991a) and the FAA DO-178B (RTCA, 1992) take a process-oriented view. These standards, which require certification data on planning, standards, process and product for each major stage in the development process, generate large amounts of certification data. For example, DO-178B lists 20 different sets of certification data. Although the generation of certification data may benefit the developer by helping to regulate system development, the benefit to the certifier is less clear. Certification data is often closely connected to the construction of the system and tends to be detailed, obscuring the overall case for the safety of the system.

The standards recognize this problem. For example, DO-178B states that data should be unambiguous, complete, verifiable, consistent, modifiable and traceable. It is difficult to structure large amounts of data into a safety case while maintaining these properties. The standards give little guidance on maintaining the coherence of all the process data generated for certification.

The Nuclear Installations Inspectorate required that the Sizewell B safety case be constructed in a process-oriented manner. Thus the MALPAS verification was carried out under a process-oriented regime. We argue that this has had a strong influence on the kind of data generated by the formal code analysis. MALPAS was mandated as the only formal methods tool to be used and the verification process was applied uniformly to each module. There appears to have been little attempt to select particularly critical modules for intensive analysis. Because the Sizewell B system is large, verification took about 200 person-years of effort and generated a huge volume of data.

The formal verification identified many problems in the specification and code but did not identify any safety-critical faults. In part this was probably due to the maturity of the code but one could argue that a uniform approach to the verification of all modules regardless of their function results in a shallow analysis of the system. A uniform approach also tends to discourage the investigation of features which are hard to formalize. This is reinforced by the selection of a single tool, which limits analysis to what is easily expressible within the tool. For example, it appears that some aspects (particularly those involving timing) of communication protocols in Sizewell B remain unanalyzed by MALPAS (Ward, 1993). This suggests that protocols cannot be treated by MALPAS, or at least that there is no mature process for dealing with them in MALPAS. The need to fit into a process-oriented regime diminishes the advantages of the formal methods approach.

Other problems in the formal analysis of Sizewell B are related specifically to MAL-PAS. First, there is the issue of controlling detail. Experience with static analysers has been mostly in the analysis of small-scale embedded systems. Because the bottom-up analysis approach remains close to the code this means that the requirements must be close to the code. In small systems this may be acceptable but in large systems requirements must often state high-level, behavioural properties of the system. Secondly, there is the issue of validation. In analyzing Sizewell B the code of the system was automatically translated into MALPAS intermediate language. No fully rigorous verification of the translation was given. In addition, certain features were hand translated since the translator could not handle them. Thus the MALPAS verification has been carried out on a model of the system, albeit a low-level model.

By contrast, our work with the MSMIE protocol demonstrates an approach which is oriented more towards a "goal-setting" certification regime, and in which the quality, relevance, and comprehensibility of evidence are paramount. Underlying our work is the belief that quality evidence must be diverse and at the right level of detail.

Diversity of evidence depends on a corresponding diversity of methods, especially for a system of the size and complexity of Sizewell B. This is because the clarity of evidence provided by a method will vary according to the particular requirement and design of interest. Providing clear evidence for all requirements will therefore often require several methods. Our example shows the lucidity of our choice of method for the requirements of MSMIE we have chosen. We believe that a MALPAS analysis of MSMIE would result in evidence that is less clear.

Getting evidence at the right level of detail requires abstraction. The models we use here are abstract in that they capture only the design level of interest and have interfaces that capture only the parameters of interest. Our MSMIE model focused on the interface between MSMIE and the slave and master processors, and did not capture the items of data to be communicated. Furthermore, our models abstract away from implementation details in the sense that the logic we use to formalize requirements is only able to express behaviour. Our first MSMIE model, even though it explores properties of a low-level component, was replaced by an abstract model with little connection to the implementation. Using abstract models driven by formalized requirements allows one to concentrate on particularly critical properties of the system while ignoring others.

Our approach has been subjected to certain criticisms. First, the use of abstract models poses a serious validation problem. The models of the MSMIE protocol illustrate one approach to this problem. By using a flexible modelling language with a non-trivial equivalence we can develop models whose structure is close to the real system yet analyze equivalent models which highlight important features. The problem of validation also arises in deciding whether a set of properties adequately formalize the informal requirements. We do not believe the validation problem is more serious with formal methods than with any other approach. Secondly, we have the problem of relating different formal methods used in analyzing a system. Such questions can be difficult to answer but at least they can be clearly stated. Answering such questions would address problems of consistency and completeness of the evidence provided for certification.

As work on incorporating formal methods into system development continues we believe we will see increasing demand for requirements-driven approaches to standards. Such a change in focus will result in better-structured cases for certification.

3.5   Conclusions

Certification data is supposed to help certifiers assess whether a system meets its safety requirements. Traditional standards for safety software require the generation of large amounts of process-oriented certification data. The value of such data to certifiers is questionable. A requirements-driven approach can increase the quality of certification data and decrease its volume.

Our approach is a formal one in which a system (or subsystem) is formalized as a CCS model, requirements are formalized as a collection of modal mu-calculus formulae, and the meeting of requirements by the system is formalized as the satisfaction of the formulae by the CCS model. Formalization generally tends to help expose problems of incompleteness and ambiguity. For example, modelling MSMIE led us to discover that the informal description does not state the intended result of performing a master acquire action in the absence of a **newest** or **master** buffer. In formalizing the *Update often* property, it was realized that needed progress assumptions were being implicitly assumed. Another benefit of formalization is that automated analysis with the Concurrency Workbench is possible, providing evidence with a high probability of correctness. The Concurrency Workbench is useful both in answering validation questions by showing models are equivalent, and in performing requirements-driven analysis by showing that properties hold of models.

A particular benefit of CCS is that it addresses the issue of validity of formal models. The concurrent composition operator of CCS allows the structure of the formal model to reflect the structure of the system. Our formal model of MSMIE has components that represent shared memory, slave processors, and master processors. The notion of equivalence in CCS allows these easy-to-validate models to be replaced by other formal models with equivalent behaviour but with different structure. Our second MSMIE model, which focuses on buffer states, has no concurrency at all.

A formal approach to requirements-driven certification must also address the issue of expressiveness. The modal mu-calculus is an expressive logic, allowing complex liveness properties such as *Update often* to be expressed. The expressiveness of the modal mu-calculus is closely tied to CCS: any behavioural difference between two CCS agents can be detected with a modal mu-calculus formula. On the other hand, there are ways in which expressiveness should be limited. For example, it is often desirable to give safety-critical requirements in terms of behaviour only, not implementation. The requirement that data tearing be prevented in MSMIE violates this principle, because data tearing is not directly observable. The explicit interface of CCS models makes it easy to see when a property describes more than behaviour. In fact, it is not possible to express in the modal mu-calculus anything more than behaviour that can observed through a model's interface. In formalizing the liveness properties we identified a new action, *update*, which is essential to the observation of our liveness properties. This required us to change the interface to reflect a new observation.

These features of our formal approach contribute to deriving evidence about systems which is concise, directly related to the system and expressed at an appropriate level of detail.

Our approach contrasts with the MALPAS verification of the full Sizewell B system. We chose to model a small critical component and to work directly from formalized requirements while the MALPAS verification worked directly with the code and the design specification documents. The MALPAS work was undertaken within a process-oriented certification regime which emphasized uniformity of approach to the running code rather than being driven from system requirements. The results of the two approaches contrast sharply. The MALPAS verification identified many deviations from detailed design-level specifications but did not identify any safety-critical errors. Significantly, some areas remain unanalyzed by MALPAS. By contrast our approach concentrates on requirements and on complex aspects of the interaction between concurrent components. Our analysis of MSMIE identified a difficulty relating to a requirement which was clarified by the formal modelling process. Both our work and the MALPAS verification used formal methods; the crucial difference is the regime under which the work took place. We believe that the benefits of formal methods can be better realized in a requirements-driven certification regime than in a process-oriented one.

Appendix A

CCS

Systems are modelled in CCS as algebraic expressions called **agents**. The events that a system can perform are modelled as actions of the agent. **Actions** can be **names** $a, b, c, \ldots$ or **co-names** $\overline{a}, \overline{b}, \overline{c}, \ldots$. The interface between a system and its environment is modelled as the **sort** of an agent, which is the set of actions that the agent can perform.

Agent 0 is the **inactive** agent, which can perform no actions. Other agents are built up from 0 using operators. We now informally describe the CCS operators by stating the conditions under which an agent can perform an action. The operator . is called **prefixing**. Agent $a.P$ can perform action a and thereby become agent P.

The operator $+$ is called **summation**. If an agent P can perform a and become P', then so can $P + Q$, and symmetrically so can $Q + P$.

The operator $|$ is called **composition**. If P can perform a and become P', then $P \mid Q$ can perform a and become $P' \mid Q$, and symmetrically $Q \mid P$ can perform a and become $Q \mid P'$. If, additionally, Q can perform $\overline{a}$ and become Q', then $P \mid Q$ can perform the special action τ and become $P' \mid Q'$. Thus parallel composition in CCS allows both independent action by one component, and synchronized action. The special action τ is neither a name nor a co-name; it is an anonymous action regarded as invisible to observers of an agent.

The operator $[f]$ is called **relabeling**. Function f, called a **relabeling function**, is a function from names to names. It is extended to co-names by $f(\overline{a}) \stackrel{def}{=} \overline{f(a)}$, and is extended to τ by $f(\tau) \stackrel{def}{=} \tau$. If P can perform a and become P', then $P[f]$ can perform $f(a)$ and become $P'[f]$. When f is an identity on all but finitely many names it is usual to write it as $a_1/b_1, \ldots, a_n/b_n$, which denotes the function that maps b_i to a_i and is otherwise the identity.

The operator $\backslash$ is called **restriction**. If P can perform a and become P', and a and $\overline{a}$ are not in the action set L, then $P\backslash L$ can perform a and become $P'\backslash L$. The most common use for restriction is in enforcing synchronization between agents. For example, in agent *Msmie*, a $\overline{take}$ action of *Slave* can occur only through synchronization with *MemImage*.

It is also possible to define agent constants. If **agent constant** A is defined by $A \stackrel{def}{=} P$, and P can perform a and become P', then so can A.

In value-passing CCS, actions and agents can be parameterized with values. Parameterized actions are either **input** or **output** actions. If expression e has value v, then $\overline{a}(e).P$ can perform output action $\overline{a}(v)$ and become P. If v is a value, then $a(x).P$ can perform input action $a(v)$ and become P with free occurrences of x in P bound to v. As for parameterized agents, if A is defined by $A(x) \stackrel{def}{=} P$, and the value of e is v, and P with free occurrences of x bound to v can perform a and become P', then so can $A(e)$.

Value-passing CCS also allows **conditional expressions**. If P can perform a and become P' and if value expression c is true, then *if c then* P can also perform a and become P'.

Appendix B

The modal mu-calculus

The modal mu-calculus is a modal logic having propositional operators $\neg$ and $\wedge$, modal operator $[\ ]$, and fixed-point operator ν. Additionally, the logic contains the atomic formula tt and fixed-point variables. The fixed-point operator ν is useful because system properties can often be naturally expressed recursively. For example, a property always holds if it holds now, and after any action occurs, the property always holds. The definition of *Always*(ϕ) in Section 3.3 reflects this idea.

The meaning of modal mu-calculus formulae is briefly as follows. All agents satisfy tt. An agent satisfies formula $\neg\phi$ if it does not satisfy ϕ; it satisfies $\phi_1 \wedge \phi_2$ if is satisfies both ϕ_1 and ϕ_2; it satisfies $[L]\phi$ if every agent reached by an action in the set L satisfies ϕ; it satisfies $\nu Z.\phi$ if it satisfies the greatest solution to the recursive equation $Z = \phi$.

The modal mu-calculus is a small but powerful logic. Some abbreviations are often used to make it more convenient. First, there are abbreviations for within modal operators.

$$[a_1, \ldots, a_n]\phi \stackrel{def}{=} [\{a_1, \ldots, a_n\}]\phi$$

$$[-]\phi \overset{def}{=} [Act]\phi$$

$$[-L]\phi \overset{def}{=} [Act-L]\phi$$

The modal operator $\langle \rangle$ and the least fixed-point operator μ are defined as duals of $[\,]$ and ν.

$$\langle L \rangle \phi \overset{def}{=} \neg[L]\neg\phi$$

$$\mu Z.\phi \overset{def}{=} \neg\nu Z.\neg\phi\{\neg Z/Z\}$$

Here $\phi\{\neg Z/Z\}$ is the formula obtained by replacing free occurrences of Z in ϕ by $\neg Z$. An agent satisfies $\langle L \rangle \phi$ if some agent reached by an action in L satisfies ϕ. An agent satisfies $\mu Z.\phi$ if it satisfies the least solution to the recursive equation $Z = \phi$.

Finally, the modal operator $[L^*]$ is also an abbreviation.

$$[L^*]\phi \overset{def}{=} \nu Z.\phi \wedge [L]Z$$

Formula $[L^*]\phi$ is similar to $Always(\phi)$, but says that ϕ continues to hold only along paths built of actions from the set L.

Chapter 4

Formal Specification of an Architecture for a Family of Instrumentation Systems

David Garlan and Norman Delisle

4.1 Introduction

An important challenge for formal methods is to develop techniques of system specification that scale in a cost-effective way to large, commercial systems. For such systems key issues include reducing the engineering effort and time in bringing a new product to market, guaranteeing "non-functional" system properties, such as latency, throughput, and interoperability with external systems, and supporting developmental concerns, such as maintainability and low-risk incorporation of new methods into existing practice.

To date formal methods have not been successful in addressing these concerns. Indeed, current approaches to formal methods may very well exacerbate the problems. Costs of development (although, many would argue, not overall lifecycle costs) may be increased because of the extra overhead of formal specification and the need to train engineers to use formalisms. Non-functional system properties are typically ignored by most formal methods, in favour of attention to functional correctness and completeness. Finally, little attention has been paid to making formal artifacts maintainable, or finding ways to ensure that their development fits smoothly with other more established software engineering procedures.

In this chapter we describe an approach to the application of formal methods to industrial software development that seems to have a better chance of finding a cost-effective place in large-scale software development. Rather than specify a specific system, we use formal methods to describe an architecture for a family of systems. Such a specification focuses on the broader systemic properties of a class of hardware-software system by providing a formal compositional model in which many different products can be assembled from reusable parts.

An architectural approach to formal specification addresses many of the defects of current techniques. First, since a single architectural specification can serve a number of distinct — although probably related — products, the cost of developing that specification can be amortized over those products. Second, the development of different products from the same specification can lead to a desirable uniformity across those products. Third, in many cases reusability in a specification translates to correspondingly reusable software components. For example, it may be possible to implement the basic abstractions of an architectural framework as "abstract classes" in an object-oriented language.

Fourth, the requirement of producing an architectural specification for several products forces the developers of that specification to strive for particularly elegant abstractions. This in turn can lead to much cleaner definitions of the fundamental concepts behind an application. Fifth, since reusing an existing framework is considerably easier than specifying it in the first place, in many cases the job of defining the framework can be allotted to a small team of highly skilled engineers. This addresses the very real problem in industry — that currently all too few software engineers are capable of producing good specifications. Sixth, by exposing the architectural structure of a system, it may be possible to reason about high-level properties of that system, such as potential for deadlock, locations of possible performance bottlenecks, and assumptions about the environment in which the system is to operate. Finally, since existing software engineering practices usually have very little to say about techniques for carrying out architectural design, a formal approach to architectural design can be integrated smoothly into current practice.

In the remainder of this chapter we describe our experience in formally specifying the architecture of a family of instrumentation systems. This work was done during the period 1987–1990 at Tektronix, Inc. in Beaverton, Oregon, and contributed to the development of an oscilloscope family that was brought to market in 1991. We begin by outlining the problem domain and key challenges that we faced. Then we present the formal specification, and describe its distinctive properties. Finally we reflect on the advantages and disadvantages of this approach with respect to the broader context of industrial software development and related work in formal methods.

4.2   The problem and its context

Instrumentation systems are hardware-software systems that sample external electrical phenomena and present various kinds of information about those phenomena to users. An important class of instrumentation systems are oscilloscopes, which display pictorial representations of time-varying electrical signals. As Figure 4.1 illustrates, electrical signals enter an oscilloscope through one or more channels and are converted into waveforms. After some internal processing, the waveforms are displayed as pictures called traces.

While at first glance the function of such an instrumentation system may seem simple, several factors complicate the situation. First, an oscilloscope user is typically interested in only certain aspects of a signal, such as its periodic nature, its form over some small time interval, or its deviation from some other signal. So the user must have some way to acquire the portions of the signal of interest. Typically, this is done with a trigger, which determines when waveform acquisition should occur. The trigger could be obtained from one of the signal channels or from an external signal source.

A second complication is that oscilloscopes are limited in their ability to acquire and display a signal faithfully. To get the best performance from an oscilloscope, the user may have to adjust several parameters so, for example, the signal falls within the appropriate dynamic range of acquisition hardware and so the waveform fits on the small display.

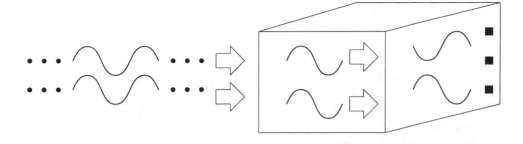

Figure 4.1 A simple view of an oscilloscope.

This means that oscilloscopes must also allow user-level reconfiguration inputs as well as signals.

A third complication is that an oscilloscope usually can do many things besides displaying waveforms: it can measure the waveform (for example, calculate rise time), store and retrieve waveforms, perform arithmetic operations on waveforms (such as, add two waveforms or produce the Fourier transform of a waveform), display simultaneous views of one or more waveforms, and interact with external devices (such as workstations). Indeed, there may be more than 300 user-level commands for configuring and operating an oscilloscope.

This complexity is reflected in the relative complexity of the software used to implement current oscilloscopes. Early electronic instruments consisted almost entirely of analog hardware controlled by hard-wired knobs and switches. However, in the last decade software has come to dominate the implementation of electronic instruments. For example, a modern oscilloscope's software component may consist of more than a megabyte of code providing features such as complex measurements, waveform storage, and control via a local-area network. Its internal architecture typically includes multiple microprocessors running real-time operating systems, special-purpose coprocessors for digital signal processing, and user interfaces that support windows, pop-up menus, and soft knobs and switches.

The incorporation of software technology into electronic instruments has happened so rapidly that software engineers in this area have not had a rich history of theory and practice to draw on. Of course, electronic instrument developers are not alone — this problem faces developers of many contemporary embedded systems. In contrast, a software engineer developing a routine application, such as a compiler, can base his designs on a well-accepted high-level architecture and considerable supporting detail in areas such as algorithms and data structures for parsing and semantic analysis.

The lack of good abstract models for such systems often becomes apparent in a practical way as companies look for improved productivity in their product development. In particular, it is frequently the case that several product divisions within a company all find themselves building different versions of the same kind of product. In the case of oscilloscopes, for example, one division might be building small, inexpensive, portable systems for one market segment, while another division builds large, high-end versions for a different market segment. Unfortunately, however, because there are no shared models each product development effort tends to operate independently from the others, resulting in costly duplication of design and implementation efforts.

So it was with oscilloscopes at Tektronix. In an effort to improve the situation a group of researchers and developers met over a period of three years to develop a software architecture for oscilloscopes. The result was a shared architectural design that formed the foundation for an emerging line of oscilloscope products. Part of this effort involved formalizing various architectural models. In this chapter we describe one of those models.

4.3   Overview

At an abstract level an electronic instrument can be viewed formally as a mathematical function that transforms electrical signals into viewable representations. Thus in its simplest form an oscilloscope might be thought of as a function:

Oscilloscope : *Signal* → *Trace*

where *Signal* and *Trace* are suitably defined data types.

However, two things cause this simple view to be unrealistic. First, even if we could write down a single *Oscilloscope* function it would not be intellectually (or practically) manageable. Second, the user can dynamically modify the function performed by the oscilloscope. This occurs when the user manipulates the knobs and buttons on the instrument front panel. Thus a single function will not suffice.

Summarized briefly, our plan of attack for dealing with the first problem will be to handle the intrinsic complexity of the "oscilloscope function" by treating it as a composition of simpler functions, each of which describes part of the oscilloscope's processing.

To account for a user's ability to configure an oscilloscope — the second problem — we treat the oscilloscope building blocks as higher-order functions. Thus, given a set of user-provided parameters, an oscilloscope component produces a new function that performs some transformation on its input data. Higher-order functions nicely model both the user's intuition of configuring an oscilloscope and the actual operating behaviour of oscilloscopes. Typically, the user sets values for operating parameters and then the oscilloscope repeatedly applies the resulting functions in real time to produce a series of traces that are overlaid on a display screen.

This formulation of the architecture of an oscilloscope as a composition of higher-order, functional building blocks has a natural analog at an implementation level. Each of the functional building blocks can (in principle) be implemented in software or hardware as a data transformation module. These modules are then composed as a data flow system by connecting the outputs of one transformer to the inputs of another.

Let us now see how we apply these ideas to characterize a simple two-channel oscilloscope. We begin by defining the basic types of entities used by the system. Next we describe how signals are converted into waveforms and traces. Then we show how the

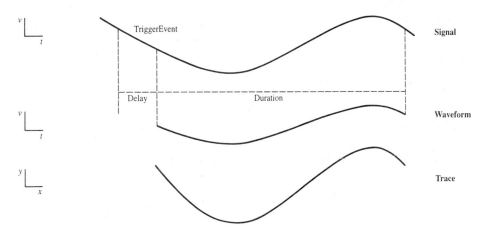

Figure 4.2 Signals, waveforms, and traces.

scope determines which parts of the signal should be extracted for display. Finally, we combine the pieces to arrive at the overall oscilloscope specification.

4.4 Data Types

Two kinds of time occur when characterizing oscilloscopes: **absolute time** refers to clock time; **relative time** refers to the passage of time between two absolute time values. Using the Z specification language (Spivey, 1992), we model both kinds of time as natural numbers ($\mathbb{N}$), and voltage and screen coordinates in terms of integers ($\mathbb{Z}$).

$AbsTime == \mathbb{N}$
$RelTime == \mathbb{N}$
$Volts == \mathbb{N}$
$Horiz == \mathbb{Z}$
$Vert == \mathbb{Z}$

We choose to base the time domain on natural numbers instead of real numbers because an oscilloscope has a finite bandwidth, and so it has finite time resolution. One can think of *AbsTime* as the number of time ticks since some absolute reference time (say, nanoseconds since the invention of the oscilloscope). Similarly, one can think of *RelTime* as the number of ticks since a relative reference time (say, nanoseconds since a particular trigger event). We use a discrete definition of volts for a similar reason — an oscilloscope has a finite voltage resolution owing to the thermal noise of its electrical components.

To account for the time-varying behaviour of the signal data that is being processed by an oscilloscope, we can model signals, waveforms, and traces as functions over the primitive domains of time, volts, and coordinates.

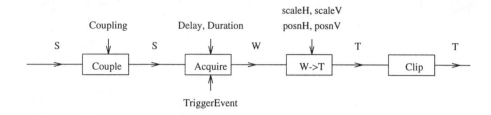

Figure 4.3 An acquisition channel.

$Signal == AbsTime \rightarrow Volts$
$Waveform == AbsTime \nrightarrow Volts$
$Trace == Horiz \nrightarrow Vert$

A *Signal* is defined as a total function from time to voltage values. (In doing this, we take the abstract view that a signal's voltage values are available at all times.) A *Waveform* is an "acquired" signal, and (as we will see presently) represents the sampling of the signal over some time interval: it is defined as a partial function from time to volts. Finally, a *Trace* is defined as a mapping between horizontal and vertical coordinates. Figure 4.2 illustrates the relationship between signals, waveforms, and traces.

4.5   The channel subsystem

A channel represents the path along which a signal is converted to a trace; it is modelled as a function from signals to traces. As indicated earlier, we define a channel's behaviour as a composition of higher-order functional components. Figure 4.3 shows a road map for this part of the specification, which is decomposed into components that handle coupling, acquisition, scaling, and clipping.

In most oscilloscopes an incoming signal undergoes certain conditioning before waveforms are extracted from it. As an example of this kind of processing we define a function, *Couple*, that is used to subtract a DC offset from a signal. A user's inputs to this function determine exactly how it behaves. In this specification the user has three choices: DC, AC, and ground. A choice of "DC" leaves the signal unchanged; a choice of "AC" subtracts the appropriate DC offset[1]; a choice of "GND" produces a signal whose value is zero volts at all times.

$Coupling ::= DC \mid AC \mid GND$

$Couple : Coupling \rightarrow Signal \rightarrow Signal$

$Couple\ DC\ s = s$
$Couple\ AC\ s = (\lambda t : AbsTime \bullet s(t) - dc(s))$
$Couple\ GND\ s = (\lambda t : AbsTime \bullet 0)$

---

[1]We assume, but do not show here, a function *dc* that computes the DC component of a signal.

A *Waveform* is obtained from a *Signal* by extracting a time slice. The waveform is identical to the signal, except that it is defined only over a bounded interval. That interval is determined by three things: a reference time, called a trigger event, and two other relative time values, called delay and duration.[2]

$TriggerEvent == RelTime$

$Acquire : RelTime \times RelTime \rightarrow TriggerEvent \rightarrow Signal \rightarrow Waveform$
___
$Acquire\ (delay, dur)\ trig\ s =$
$\quad \{\ t : AbsTime \mid trig + delay \leq t \leq trig + delay + dur\ \} \lhd s$

A *Trace* is obtained from a *Waveform* in two steps. The first step converts time volt pairs into appropriate coordinates. The second step clips the trace so it will fit on the display screen. The dimensions of the screen are given by two global constants, *maxH* and *maxV*. For simplicity we have elided the definition of *WaveformToTrace*. (For details see Delisle and Garlan (1990).)

$WaveformToTrace : RelTime \times Volts \times Horiz \times Vert \rightarrow Waveform \rightarrow Trace$
___
$\cdots$

$maxH : Horiz$
$maxV : Vert$
$Clip : Trace \rightarrow Trace$
___
$\forall tr : Trace \bullet Clip\ tr = (0 .. maxH) \lhd tr \rhd (0 .. maxV)$

We would now like to assemble these functional components into a definition of the channel subsystem. To do this we will make the channel configuration state explicit as a collection of (user-supplied) parameters. This can be done by defining a Z schema that encapsulates those parameters. To obtain a channel subsystem we then apply the previously defined components to those parameters and compose the resulting functions.

___*ChannelParameters*_____
$c : Coupling$
$delay, dur : RelTime$
$scaleH : RelTime$
$scaleV : Volts$
$posnV : Vert$
$posnH : Horiz$
_____

---

[2]As illustrated in Figure 4.2, duration determines the length of the interval, while delay determines when the interval is sampled relative to the trigger event.

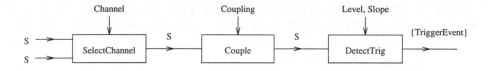

Figure 4.4 Trigger selection.

ChannelConfiguration : *ChannelParameters* → *TriggerEvent* → *Signal* → *Trace*

ChannelConfiguration p = (λ *trig* : *TriggerEvent* •
$\qquad$ *Clip* ∘ *WaveformToTrace*(*p.scaleH*, *p.scaleV*, *p.posnH*, *p.posnV*)
$\qquad$ ∘*Acquire*(*p.delay*, *p.dur*) *trig* ∘ *Couple p.c*)

Note how *ChannelConfiguration* defines yet another higher-order function which neatly combines and encapsulates the components of the channel subsystem. This new transformation maps the entire channel configuration state into the desired function from *Signal* to *Trace*.

4.6   The trigger subsystem

As noted earlier, a waveform is acquired relative to a reference time, called a trigger event. In this section we show how these events are obtained. Figure 4.4 provides an overview of this part of the specification.

Loosely speaking, a trigger event is a time value that represents the occurrence of an interesting signal feature. The meaning of "interesting" is defined by several user-settable parameters. First, however, the user must pick one of the channels on which trigger events are observed. *SelectChannel* does this.

Channel ::= *CH*1 | *CH*2

SelectChannel : *Channel* → *Signal* × *Signal* → *Signal*

*SelectChannel CH*1 (s_1, s_2) = s_1
*SelectChannel CH*2 (s_1, s_2) = s_2

After picking a signal source for the trigger, the user sets the coupling, which acts as described earlier. We therefore use the same coupling function (*Couple*) defined above. However, in this case a trigger coupling value of *GND* is not allowed because a constant 0-valued function would be useless as a trigger. We will see later how this restriction is imposed.

Having selected a signal source and conditioned that signal, we are ready to look for trigger events. In this simplified description an interesting event will be defined as one for which the signal crosses a given voltage level along a given slope orientation. From these parameters the function *DetectTrig* produces a set of time values representing the observed trigger events.[3]

Slope ::= *POS* | *NEG*
Level == *Volts*

$DetectTrig : Level \times Slope \rightarrow Signal \rightarrow \mathbb{P}\, TriggerEvent$

$\forall l : Level;\ sl : Slope;\ s : Signal;\ t : RelTime \mid t \in DetectTrig\ (l, sl)\ s\ \bullet$
$\quad (sl = POS) \Rightarrow s(t-1) \leq l \leq s(t)\ \wedge$
$\quad (sl = NEG) \Rightarrow s(t) \leq l \leq s(t-1)$

As with *ChannelConfiguration*, we now bundle up our trigger components to produce an overall description of the trigger subsystem. In doing this we reuse *Couple*, but constrain the values of its input parameter in the predicate of the *TriggerParameters* schema.

__*TriggerParameters*__

$l : Level$
$sl : Slope$
$ts : Channel$
$tc : Coupling$

$tc \in \{AC, DC\}$

$TriggerConfiguration : TriggerParameters \rightarrow Signal \times Signal \rightarrow \mathbb{P}\, TriggerEvent$

$TriggerConfiguration\ p =$
$\quad DetectTrig\ (p.l, p.sl) \circ Couple\ p.tc \circ SelectChannel\ p.ts$

4.7   The overall oscilloscope

We can now assemble the pieces. Figure 4.5 illustrates the final result: two channels, each with its own set of parameters, produce traces as defined by trigger events selected from one of those signals. The overall oscilloscope is defined succinctly as follows:

---

[3]It is interesting to note that according to this definition *DetectTrig* need not produce a set containing every point on signal with the given slope and level. It does, however, say that that every point selected has those properties.

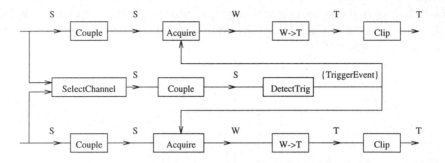

Figure 4.5 The whole oscilloscope.

___Oscilloscope_____
$s1, s2 : Signal$
$cp1, cp2 : ChannelParameters$
$tp : TriggerParameters$
$ts1, ts2 : \text{seq } Trace$
———
$\forall t : \text{ran } ts1 \bullet$
        $\exists trig : TriggerConfiguration\ tp\ (s1, s2) \bullet$
                $t = ChannelConfiguration\ cp1\ trig\ s1$

$\forall t : \text{ran } ts2 \bullet$
        $\exists trig : TriggerConfiguration\ tp\ (s1, s2) \bullet$
                $t = ChannelConfiguration\ cp2\ trig\ s2$
_____

Note that this specification relates each trace in the displayed sequence to the *Trigger-Event* used to acquire it. It does not, however, require that every trigger produce a trace, only that every trace must have been produced by a trigger.

4.8 Properties of the specification

The oscilloscope that we have specified is a particularly simple one. However, the value of this specification is not so much the specific system it defines, but the architectural framework that it embodies. As we have seen, this framework defines an oscilloscope as a composition of functional building blocks. Each building block encapsulates a part of the overall system function that can be combined with other building blocks to produce complex applications.

This kind of specification has a number of distinctive properties. One important property is its support for reusability. For example, even in this limited example we were able to reuse *Couple* in both the definitions of *ChannelConfiguration* and *TriggerConfigur-*

ation. We were also able to reuse *ChannelConfiguration* for both of the channels in the definition of *Oscilloscope*. This form of reuse is made possible by the simple compositional framework and the ability to build new encapsulated components out of existing ones. (A more detailed account of the properties of reusability appears in Garlan and Delisle (1990).)

A second, closely related property is extensibility: the architectural framework provides an extensible model for describing new designs. For example, to scale this specification to a more realistic system, we could provide more accurate definitions of the transformations. These might account for details of electrical behaviour such as time skew and jitter, bounded frequency response, and both voltage and time calibration inaccuracies. (Ian Hayes (Hayes, 1990) has done just that by extending our work in a similar formal model of an oscilloscope.) This would complicate the definitions of the specific atomic functions, but otherwise would not affect the overall system structure.

Other forms of extensibility are made possible by extending the types of data processed by the system. For example, a more realistic specification would require the specification of new types for the results of measurements, as well as special waveform types that require more than one voltage value for each time-domain element.

Yet other forms of extensibility come about by modifying the structure of the transformation graph. For instance, consider the problem of augmenting the oscilloscope channel definition so that signal voltages above a certain maximum value are clipped after the couple function is performed. To accomplish this extension we can simply define a new building block, *ClipVoltage*, and then compose that function with the others, as before.

$$MaxVolts : Volts$$
$$ClipVolts : Signal \rightarrow Signal$$

$$MaxVolts > 0$$
$$ClipVolts\ s = (s \oplus \{\ t : \text{dom}\,s \mid s(t) > MaxVolts \bullet t \mapsto MaxVolts\ \})$$
$$\oplus \{\ t : \text{dom}\,s \mid s(t) < MaxVolts \bullet t \mapsto -MaxVolts\ \}$$

$$ChannelConfiguration : ChannelParameters \rightarrow TriggerEvent \rightarrow Signal \rightarrow Trace$$

$$ChannelConfiguration\ p = (\lambda\,trig : TriggerEvent \bullet$$
$$Clip \circ WaveformToTrace(p.scaleH, p.scaleV, p.posnH, p.posnV)$$
$$\circ Acquire(p.delay, p.dur)\ trig \circ ClipVolts \circ Couple\ p.c)$$

A third important property of this architectural specification is that it provides a domain specific computational model that matches the intuitions of product engineers. In this case the model was that of data flow. The components of that computation fit well with an engineer's view of the hardware and software transformations that take place in an actual oscilloscope. This is in contrast to more traditional views of a system specification that would typically reduce the design to a system of data types that interact through procedure calls.

A fourth property is that it exposes important structural properties of the system design. For example, it immediately raises the question as to whether cycles should be allowed in the graph. It also serves as a starting point for analyses of non-functional system properties, such as throughput, latency, and schedulability. (Although we did not carry out such analyses ourselves, for an example of what is possible see the work by Jeffay (1993) on analysis of dataflow systems.)

A fifth property is that the specification picks a high level of abstraction to characterize the system. This allows us to articulate an architectural structure, and to provide a simple user-level model of the functions of an oscilloscope. The primary conceptual abstraction that made this possible was an idealization of the passage of time. In this case, the specification gives the illusion that when a user modifies a parameter the oscilloscope can reacquire a waveform whose acquisition window has already passed. Abstracting away from time turns out to be a useful approach because there is much to gain from a steady-state description of oscilloscope behaviour. An alternative, more detailed formal model could be developed to explore some of the dynamic issues, but would be considerably more complex and would perhaps obscure some of the architectural issues.

4.9   Putting our experience into perspective

To put this experience into perspective let us now address a number of broader questions: what were the main benefits and non-benefits of carrying out this kind of formal exercise? How were the formal development methods integrated into software development practices of the company? How does our approach relate to other efforts to apply formal methods to industrial problems?

4.9.1   Gaining insight

The primary benefit of our use of formalization was to gain insight into the system architecture for this family of applications. Confronted with a large space of existing and potential designs (with an equal number of zealots arguing for their adoption), it is a considerable intellectual challenge to find abstractions that provide a common, unifying view.

To illustrate how a formal model led to this kind of insight, consider arithmetic operations on waveforms. For example, most oscilloscopes provide an operation to subtract one signal from another to examine their differences. As it turns out, there are three types of formal entities in our oscilloscope model on which you might define subtraction: it could operate on two signals, two waveforms, or two traces.

$SubtractS : Signal \times Signal \rightarrow Signal$
$SubtractW : Waveform \times Waveform \rightarrow Waveform$
$SubtractT : Trace \times Trace \rightarrow Trace$

$SubtractS(s1, s2) = \lambda t : \mathrm{dom}(s1) \mid \mathrm{dom}(s1) = \mathrm{dom}(s2) \bullet s1(t) - s2(t)$
$SubtractW(w1, w2) = \lambda t : \mathrm{dom}(w1) \mid \mathrm{dom}(w1) = \mathrm{dom}(w2) \bullet w1(t) - w2(t)$
$SubtractT(t1, t2) = \lambda x : \mathrm{dom}(t1) \mid \mathrm{dom}(t1) = \mathrm{dom}(t2) \bullet t1(x) - t2(x)$

Subtracting signals and waveforms yields similar results: at each time in either domain the result is the voltage difference between the two operands. Trace subtraction, however, is performed on graphical objects, so the result depends on current graphical scaling and positioning of the operands.

All three subtraction types could be useful; indeed, different oscilloscopes have defined subtraction differently. Our formal oscilloscope model exposes these distinctions to help the developer define a product that meets user requirements.

Another example that illustrates use of formalism to gain insight into architectural abstractions concerns the definition of a waveform. Establishing a common vocabulary of such types was one of our first challenges in developing an oscilloscope model. We first asked software engineers who had built oscilloscopes to define the term "waveform". Invariably, their answers reflected an implementation-level view, such as

A waveform is a 1-Kbyte array of eight-bit samples.

After some discussion it became clear that waveforms store time voltage values, so we volunteered a second definition:

A waveform is a function from time to volts.

Although this was a pleasing mathematical abstraction, we quickly discovered a technical flaw: formally, this definition requires a voltage value for every time value. However, when oscilloscope designers refer to a waveform, they are referring to acquired data, which represents voltage values only over some time interval. This observation led to an improved definition:

A waveform is a partial function from time to volts.

This is much better (and is the definition we used in our simple model above), but on closer inspection it is apparent that it cannot handle all waveforms that an oscilloscope can manipulate. In particular, some digital acquisitions store several values for each time value, such as the maximum and minimum value over some small interval centered on that time value. Since the previous definition associates a unique voltage with each time value, a fourth, more general definition is more appropriate:

A waveform is a relation between time and volts.

A relation is a collection of time–voltage pairs, so this definition encompasses the waveforms presented so far. However, further discussion with the software engineers revealed that there are still other waveforms. In certain acquisition modes, waveforms are built out of repeated samplings. Many of these samples will be duplicates. For these waveforms, it is important to know how many repetitions there are of each time–voltage pair. As a set of pairs, our definition above precludes this. Thus we arrived at our final definition:

A waveform is a bag of time voltage pairs.

This example illustrates several things. First, it underscores the discrepancy between common practice in building software systems — in which designers view notions such as waveforms at a detailed, implementation level — and the practice of modelling such entities in an abstract mathematical form. Second, it shows how precise mathematical notation helps analyze the adequacy of a proposed definition. Third, it illustrates that developing a good formal model is an iterative process that requires not only mathematical expertise, but also considerable domain-specific knowledge.

Fourth, it shows how the resulting abstraction both unifies and simplifies the ideas lurking behind a complex implementation. This in turn can lead to much cleaner implementations. For example, in the past, oscilloscope builders have had some difficulty managing the many varieties of waveforms that exist in an oscilloscope. In previous implementations, this was reflected in complex, special-purpose code for handling special waveform cases. The formal definition exposes what is common to all of these and leads to a much cleaner, and more general implementation.

4.9.2   Formal reasoning

Our use of formal methods to gain insight into system architecture raises questions about the role of formal proof. In most applications of formal methods, proofs are used to verify an implementation's correctness: given a specification and a proposed implementation, a proof formally demonstrates that the implementation actually does what the specification says it should.

While the goal of producing provably correct software is a laudable one, our use of formal reasoning had very different goals. Instead of establishing a formal relationship between specifications and their implementations, we used mathematical reasoning to explore the properties of those specifications.

In this oscilloscope work our arguments were almost always informal, as the waveform example illustrates. Of course, if necessary, we could turn these informal arguments into formal theorems and proofs. Further, we have found that if it is difficult to reason about some expected property of a specification, it is usually a sign that the specification is poorly structured, if not wrong.

In the oscilloscope model, for example, we might want to argue that traces portray input signals accurately. This is relatively easy to show for our oscilloscope specification. However, had we tried to demonstrate that all trigger values result in the acquisition of some waveform, a formal argument would quickly reveal that our oscilloscope model is deficient. (This follows from our use of a model that allows an oscilloscope to ignore certain triggers if it is not yet ready to process the associated waveforms.)

4.9.3   The rôle of formalism in software development

The project was initiated when a small group of system architects came together with a small group of researchers to explore the possibilities of developing a common architecture for instrumentation systems. Over the course of three years a number of architectural models were developed, one of which is described formally above. During this period, as the architectural models became clearer — in part as a result of our formalization of them — the design group began to work with product developers to apply the ideas to the actual design of the next generation of products. This led to a number of revisions and refinements of the models. Eventually the product development and architectural design converged and the ideas were transitioned into product development.

Focusing on the role of formalism in this process a number of salient characteristics stand out.

- Formalization clarified architectural frameworks, not a specific product. As we have noted above, the essential technical core of our formal models was the architectural frameworks that they embodied. When reduced to practice, these frameworks determine two things. First, they identify a set of shared resources for composing new products out of smaller pieces. In the case of the model outlined in this paper, that infrastructure would handle the data flow communication between transformation steps. Second, they identify a way of conceptualizing new systems. In the case of the model above, this required engineers to think of their applications as a graph of transformations. Over time such conceptualizations, if effective, become part of the design culture of an organization, independent of the formalism that initially characterized them.

- Formalization was accompanied by prototyping. As the architectural models began to emerge during discussions, two kinds of clarifying activities were performed. The researchers attempted to formalize the ideas, and the product engineers began to prototype run-time mechanisms to support the architectural model. These two efforts complemented each other nicely. The formalism clarified the basic concepts and kept the design clean, while the prototyping served as a reality check, and often generated new kinds of problems not exposed by the formalism.

- More than one formal model was needed. The first model that we developed was the one described in this paper. However, we soon discovered that it alone was not sufficient. First, while it defines an abstract interface through which a user can change oscilloscope operating parameters it says nothing about how the user interface is structured to accomplish this. For example, how are menu selections and changes in knob settings resolved into modifications to specific parameters? Second, the data flow model characterized by this formal model cannot run directly on existing hardware platforms. For example, there need to be buffering mechanisms to hold data communicated between the transformations. To clarify these concrete details we developed a refinement of the initial signal processing model. This helped bridge the gap between the conceptual structures and the concrete implementation mechanisms.[4]

- Formalization did not require sophisticated tools. Beyond a document processor and a type checker for Z, we did not find the need to exploit any automated tools

---

[4] These more detailed architectural specifications are proprietary — this is probably the strongest possible endorsement that formal specifications can play a valuable role in industry.

for formal development. In part this was a consequence of the way in which we used proofs. However, it also reflected the fact that our specifications tended to be fairly small. Unlike some industrial projects in which formal specifications run to hundreds or even thousands of pages (Nix and Collins, 1988; Hall, 1994), each of our specifications was under 50 pages in length. On the other hand, we found that it was helpful to have tools for engineers when actually using the models to construct systems. For example the architectural style for composing an application naturally lends itself to a graphical tool for system construction. Such a tool was developed by the product engineers.

- Formalization played several distinct roles. As detailed above, the primary rôle was gaining insight into system architecture. However, a secondary rôle was documentation of our designs. The formal models were used to communicate our ideas to other engineers during presentations, as well as to augment the formal system design documentation. This had several implications. First, there were only a small number of writers of specifications — two or three at any given time — but a larger number of readers. Second, the formalism supplemented existing forms of documentation: the main ideas were conveyed through prose and informal diagrams, while the formal models augmented that description, conveying some aspects of those ideas to some of the engineers. This is unlike many other efforts in which a formal specification provides a more central function in determining what is to be built (for example, in Hall (1994)).

4.9.4   Relationship to other industrial uses of formal methods

Many other projects have attempted to specify real systems in an industrial context. This book includes accounts of several. Others are described in detail elsewhere (such as Craigen *et al.* (1993)).

Our work shares with many of these projects the conviction that if formal methods are to have a long-term future in industrial software development, they must establish an appropriate place within the context of existing development practices.

However, we differ in several ways from most applications of formal methods to industrial problems. The most salient difference is our focus on families of systems. Most industrial projects are concerned with a specific system. In contrast, we were concerned with providing an architectural framework for a collection of related applications — viz. electronic instrumentation systems.

This focus on architecture had three important ramifications. First, as we have noted, our specifications tended to be relatively small. Second, the specifications were constructed by a small, highly skilled group. Rather than attempting to propagate skills for formal specification across the company or engineering division, a small group of about five specialists in architecture and formalism were involved in the construction of the formal models. A much larger group of engineers, however, were exposed to the models through documentation, briefings, and short courses in how to read Z specifications.

Third, our criteria for what constituted a "good" specification were somewhat unusual.

Typically, a good specification is one that provides a complete and consistent definition of some desired system behaviour. The specification is then used as a "contract" against which implementors can evaluate their implementations. The trick is finding an appropriate level of abstraction that completely captures the users' requirements without overly constraining implementations. In our case, however, a good specification was one that captured a set of common abstractions that could serve as a shared architectural model for the application family. The trick was finding an appropriate level of abstraction that was abstract enough to satisfy a range of product instances, but concrete enough to provide a substantive basis for product design.

4.9.5   Relationship to other work on architecture

Research on applying formal methods to the development of architectural frameworks falls into several categories.

The first category is formal specifications with an architectural flavor. A good example is Flinn and Sorensen's (1992) CAVIAR case study. This specification provides a set of conceptual building blocks for producing different kinds of reservation systems. The main formal device used in the specification is instantiation of generic Z schemas. Schema inclusion is used as the main kind of architectural "glue".

A second category uses formal specification to clarify specific architectural styles. Within this category specifications can vary from highly domain specific (such as the one presented in this chapter), to very generic. Examples of generic specifications include a formalization of a "pipe–filter" style (Allen and Garlan, 1992) and a formalization of an "implicit invocation" style (Garlan and Notkin, 1991). In both of these cases the goal was to make precise a commonly used mechanism for structuring systems, and to clarify the design space of variations.

A third category is concerned with developing new formal models for the description of software architectures. Recently there has been considerable interest in software architecture as an emerging field within software engineering (Shaw and Garlan, 1995; Garlan and Shaw, 1993; Perry and Wolf, 1992). Several researchers are now developing formal models to put architectural engineering on a more scientific foundation. Different approaches have adopted different formal models: Rapide (Luckham *et al.*, 1995) is based on POSETs; Wright (Allen and Garlan, 1994a) is based on CSP; Inverardi and Wolf's work (1995) is based on the Chemical Abstract Machine; others have used Z (Abowd *et al.*, 1993). These efforts differ from the one described in this chapter, in that they focus on the more general questions of what is software architecture, and how notations can be tailored to the task of specifying architectural design.

4.10   Conclusions

In this chapter we have presented a formal model of oscilloscopes and discussed some of the ways in which our use of formal methods differs from more traditional approaches. The main novelty of this work is its focus on clarifying system architecture for a family of products. This contrasts with more typical approaches in which formal methods have been used to specify individual systems. As we have tried to show, this shift in focus has a significant effect on the way in which formal models are developed, the nature of the formal artifacts themselves, the use of formal analysis and proof, and the broader relationship between formal specification and industrial practice.

In retrospect it would appear that our goals were both more and less ambitious than traditional approaches. They were less ambitious in that they did not attempt to provide a complete definition of any specific product, to infuse formal methods into the product divisions, or to produce provably correct implementations. On the other hand, they were more ambitious in that they attempted to derive a set of abstractions that would serve a wide range of products, to improve overall software productivity and quality through a shared architectural design, and to fit smoothly within existing development practices in the company. Although it would be unwise to generalize too much from a single experience such as ours, we believe that this approach has much to recommend itself as a technique for system specification that can scale in a cost-effective way to large, commercial systems.

Acknowledgements

The work described in this paper was the result of a collaborative effort between members of what was then referred to as the Computer Research Labs and the Test and Measurement Division at Tektronix. We would like to thank our past colleagues from both organizations. In particular, we thank Don Birkley, Steve Lyford, David Olson, Jim Stanley, and John Wiegand for their partnership in this effort. We would also like to thank Ian Hayes, Ralph London, Kathleen Milstead, and Mayer Schwartz for their insightful comments on the specification described in this paper.

This paper extends results published earlier as Delisle and Garlan (1990). It also includes some material from Garlan and Delisle (1990).

Chapter 5

Formal Specification of the STV Algorithm

Paul Mukherjee and Brian A. Wichmann

5.1 Introduction

Most published examples of the application of formal methods have been in the areas of security- or safety-critical systems. The property that such systems share is the value that society at large places on the safe and correct service that they provide. However, this property is not unique to such systems. In this chapter we describe the use of formal methods in a system with no safety or security requirements, but which society nonetheless requires to have the highest level of integrity, namely a computerized voting system.

In July 1991, the Church of England changed the regulations used to specify the method of electing representatives to its main bodies. The key change was that, for the first time, a computer could be used to determine the result of the election which is conducted according to the single transferable vote (STV) method. These elections are controlled by statute since the Church of England is the established church. Hence, legally, the use of STV is similar to that of the Northern Ireland European Parliament public elections, except that the Northern Ireland elections do not allow the use of a computer.

It is clear, therefore, that the electorate must have absolute confidence in the use of the computer in a similar manner to that of a safety-critical application (such as railway signalling, for instance). Hence we believe that the application of formal methods to this example is appropriate.

5.1.1 1991 Synod elections

The actual regulations allowed a program to be used for Church elections provided that the Electoral Reform Society (ERS) certified that the computer program does implement the specific rules that the Church uses. These rules are based upon hand counting, so, in essence, the computer program must simulate the actions that would otherwise be undertaken manually.

Since the Synod elections were due in October 1991 and the regulations were published in July 1991, only a short time was available for the certification by ERS. In fact, only about 36 person-hours could be devoted to the certification process. This was undertaken without the use of formal methods, but is reported here so that the development process can be properly understood.

The program which was eventually certified was written by I.D. Hill and consisted of about 1000 lines of Pascal. In fact, the complete system was rather more since it included a data preparation program and other utilities to enable a complete election to be handled.

The certification was undertaken by one of the authors for the ERS and consisted of the following process.

Checking the program was based upon the analysis of statement execution applied to the main 1000 line program. The reason for analyzing just the main program was that errors elsewhere are likely to be immediately apparent, while the work needed to check the main logic is quite significant.

The main program was transferred from an IBM PC to an Archimedes. This transfer was done for practical reasons but acted as a cross-check on the code. The program was then instrumented by hand (by using a different compiler) to discover the statements executed. Special test data was constructed to execute all the statements. All statements proved executable except two which would not be executable on either the Archimedes or IBM PC. In fact, a program was already available to generate random test cases, so there was a potentially large source of data.

The specification of the computer program was to follow the same logic as the hand counting rules. Thus, in principle, it was easy to check the output from any specific test. However, for the larger tests, the amount of hand checking was significant, so it was important to minimize the checking required. This was done by computing the minimum number of test cases which would ensure all the (feasible) statements were executed. This left 13 test cases which were hand checked by the ERS expert — the ideal 'oracle' in this case.

The result of this exercise was that one significant bug was found and about six minor ones. No fault has been found subsequently in the program (although a minor fault has been found in another program concerned with the data preparation). An amusing example of a minor bug was in the handling of an elections in which no votes were cast — a random choice was made (correct), but one too many people selected (wrong!).

The ability to use a computer was exercised by two dioceses in the elections to the General Synod — in fact, the elections to the Synod which made the historic decision to allow women priests.

5.1.2   Methods and tools used

The previous section indicates the position prior to the start of the application of formal methods to this example, namely an existing program and a set of test cases thought to ensure the correctness of at least one algorithm. In this study we have specified the STV algorithm using the specification language VDM-SL (Dawes, 1991), and performed analysis on this specification, using the set of test cases.

We chose VDM-SL as our specification language for a variety of reasons. VDM-SL is a relatively mature formal specification language, and has a large body of associated literature. It is also currently being standardized, so a specification written in VDM-SL gives an unambiguous description of how a system is to behave.

Another consequence of the use of VDM-SL is the availability of tools with which specifications may be analyzed mechanically. In this study we used two such tools: we used the tool SpecBox (Froome, 1990) initially, to perform syntax analysis on the specification. At a later stage we used the IFAD VDM-SL Toolbox (IFAD, 1994) to perform type analysis of the specification, and also to execute the specification against the test set.

In fact, as we shall see, we executed the specification twice: the first time by animating the specification in the programming language SML (MacQueen *et al.*, 1986), and the second time using the IFAD Toolbox. SML was chosen to animate the specification as it provides many data structures that are natural analogs of VDM-SL's data structures.

5.1.3   Overview

Having described what languages and tools were used in this study, we now describe how they were used. The process which was followed in this study was as listed below:

1. the formulation of the Church of England STV rules in VDM-SL, see Section 5.2;
2. mechanical checking of the VDM-SL using the tool SpecBox;
3. review of the rules by hand by several people;
4. animation of the VDM-SL using SML, see Section 5.3;
5. execution of the 13 test cases (devised for the certification, see above) with the SML version;
6. revision of the VDM-SL in the light of bugs discovered during the animation;
7. mechanical validation of the VDM-SL using the IFAD VDM-SL Toolbox;
8. further revision of the VDM-SL.

This method is very similar to that advocated in the UK Interim Defence Standards (Ministry of Defence, 1991a,b). The main difference is that there was no iteration on the specification (the ambiguities were merely noted), and that the production algorithm was produced without the aid of formal methods.

Section 5.4 draws some conclusions from this study, particularly on the relevance to the production of safety-critical software to Defence Standard 00-55.

5.2   Specification

Below is a brief overview of the algorithm. In this section we describe the data types used in the specification and by way of example present a particular branch of the specification. We do not present formal definitions for all the auxiliary functions used here; those functions whose intended meaning is not obvious from their context will be defined informally and their formal definitions may be found in Mukherjee and Wichmann (1993).

```
Start;
Count_First_Preferences;
while Vacancies_Left loop
   if Number_Continuing_Candidates =Number_Unfilled_Vacancies
      then Elect_All_Continuing_Candidates;
      exit;
   end if;
   if Number_Continuing_Candidates_Satisfying_Quota <=
                              Number_Unfilled_Vacancies then
      Elect_All_Such_Candidates;
      exit;
   end if;
   if One_Vacancy and Large_Lead then
      Elect_Leading_Candidate;
   else
      if Exists_NonDeferable_Surplus then
         Transfer_Surplus;
      else
         Exclude_Candidate;
      end if;
   end if;
end loop;
```

Figure 5.1 Ada code illustrating the basic algorithm.

The basic algorithm is illustrated by the fragment of Ada code in Figure 5.1. The algorithm hinges on the concept of the quota. The **quota** is a value dependent upon the total number of valid voting papers cast and the number of vacancies to be filled. Roughly speaking, the three main ideas in the algorithm are as follows. Candidates whose total vote is greater than or equal to the quota are deemed to be elected. If, after a candidate (or candidates) has been deemed to be elected, there are still unfilled vacancies, then the candidate with the greatest vote (whether continuing or deemed to be elected), will have his or her surplus transferred (the "surplus" being the difference between the candidate's total score and the quota). If, after a candidate (or candidates) has been deemed to be elected, there are still unfilled vacancies and no candidate has a surplus, then the candidate possessing the fewest votes will be excluded and have his or her votes transferred.

In this chapter we describe the specification of the operations involved in excluding a candidate. The complete specification appears in Mukherjee and Wichmann (1993). Note that for the remainder of this chapter we will use the word "elected" interchangeably with the phrase "deemed to be elected".

5.2.1   Definitions

The 3 parameters of the algorithm are the number of candidates seeking election (*Number-of-candidates*), the number of vacancies to be filled (*Number-of-vacancies*) and the collection of candidate names (*Candidate-names*). The former two will not be given values in the current study. Elements of the type *Candidate-names* will be used purely to tag various different objects, so the only operation that will be performed on them is testing for equality. Hence we define the type to be the type of tokens, token. In a particular election, the names of the candidates standing is given by *Cand-names*: *Candidate-names*-set.

Below are some basic definitions; they are reproduced verbatim and are followed by some examples.

1. Definitions:
In these Regulations:

(3) The expression 'continuing candidate' means any candidate neither deemed elected nor excluded from the poll at any given time.

(4) The expression 'first preference' means the figure '1' standing alone opposite the name of a candidate; 'second' preference means the figure '2' standing alone opposite the name of a candidate in succession to the figure '1'; 'third preference' means the figure '3' standing alone opposite the name of a candidate in succession to the figure '1', '2', and so on.

(5) The expression 'next available preference' means a second or subsequent preference recorded in consecutive numerical order for a continuing candidate, the preferences next in order on the voting paper for candidates already elected or excluded from the poll being ignored.

(8) The expression 'original vote' in regard to any candidate means a vote derived from a voting paper on which a first preference is recorded for that candidate.

(9) The expression 'transferred vote' in regard to any candidate means a vote derived from a voting paper on which a second or subsequent preference is recorded for that candidate.

(10) The expression 'surplus' means the number of votes by which the total number of the votes, original and transferred, credited to any candidate exceed the quota.

(11) The expression 'stage' means -

(a) all the operations involved in the counting of the first preferences recorded for candidates; or

(b) all the operations involved in the transfer of the surplus of an elected candidate; or

(c) all the operations involved in the transfer of the votes of an excluded candidate.

Consider the voting paper shown below. For candidate Hoare, this paper would be an original vote. On the other hand, if Hoare had been elected, the remaining candidates were continuing and we wished to transfer this paper from Hoare, then the next available preference would be Dijkstra and this paper would become one of Dijkstra's transferred votes. If Hoare had been elected, Dijkstra excluded and we wished to transfer this paper from Hoare, then the next available preference would be Wirth.

Dijkstra	2
Hoare	1
Knuth	
Lamport	4
Wirth	3

Voting papers

Next, we specify precisely what a voting paper shall be. From the regulations, we find the following requirements:

3. Voting papers:

   (1) In an election to be conducted by post, the voting paper shall consist of a paper containing a list of the candidates, described as their respective nomination papers.

   (2) In an election to be conducted at a meeting, or partly at a meeting and partly by postal voting, the voting paper shall consist of a paper containing a list of candidates, described in a such a way as to ensure that the identity of each candidate is known to each voter and to the presiding officer.

6. Invalid voting papers:

A voting paper shall be invalid if:

   (a) it is not signed by a voter on its reverse; or
   (b) the figure 1 standing alone indicating a first preference is not placed against any candidate; or
   (c) the figure 1 standing alone indicating a first preference is placed opposite the name of more than one candidate; or
   (d) the figure 1 indicating a first preference and some other figure are placed opposite the name of the same candidate; or
   (e) it cannot be determined for which candidate the first preference of the voter is recorded.

Below are some examples of invalid voting papers. In voting paper (i), no first preference is specified (satisfying clause 6(b)). In voting paper (ii), more than one first preference is specified (satisfying clause 6(c)).

Dijkstra	2
Hoare	
Knuth	5
Lamport	4
Wirth	3

(i)

Dijkstra	2
Hoare	4
Knuth	1
Lamport	1
Wirth	3

(ii)

We define a voting paper to be a map from the set of candidate names to the non-zero natural numbers, each candidate name being associated with a preference.

types

$$Voting\text{-}paper = Candidate\text{-}names \xrightarrow{m} \mathbb{N}_1$$

$$\text{inv } v \triangleq \exists! name : Candidate\text{-}names \cdot v(name) = 1$$

Thus the voting paper

Dijkstra	2
Hoare	4
Knuth	1
Lamport	5
Wirth	3

would be represented by

$$\{Dijkstra \mapsto 2, Hoare \mapsto 4, Knuth \mapsto 1, Lamport \mapsto 5, Wirth \mapsto 3\}$$

Note that on a physical voting paper, a name might occur with no preference next to it. In our representation of voting papers, the only names which occur are ones which have a preference next to them on the corresponding physical paper. So the following voting paper

Dijkstra	2
Hoare	4
Knuth	3
Lamport	1
Wirth	

corresponds to the map

$$\{Dijkstra \mapsto 2, Hoare \mapsto 4, Knuth \mapsto 3, Lamport \mapsto 1\}$$

We assume that all invalid voting papers are removed before transcription of papers occurs. This assumption is made explicit by the invariant that we place on voting papers. However, we clearly cannot specify clauses (a), (d) and (e).

Using this representation, it is easy to extract those names which occur on (i.e. with a preference) a voting paper by looking at the domain of the map. We can also represent voting papers in which two names might have the same preference next to them (provided that it is not the first preference, which would invalidate the paper).

Transferable and non-transferable papers

Voting papers cast may be divided into two categories: transferable and non-transferable papers.

> (6) The expression 'transferable paper' means a voting paper on which, following a first preference, a second or subsequent preference is recorded in consecutive numerical order for a continuing candidate.

> (7) The expression 'non-transferable paper' means a voting paper on which no second or subsequent preference is recorded for a continuing candidate; provided that a paper shall be deemed to have become a non-transferable paper whenever

> > (a) the names of two or more candidates (whether continuing or not) are marked with the same number, and are next in order of preference; or

> > (b) the name of the candidate next in order of preference (whether continuing or not) is marked -

> > > (i) by a number not following consecutively after some other number on the voting paper; or

> > > (ii) by two or more numbers; or

> > (c) for any other reason it cannot be determined for which of the continuing candidates the next available preference of the voter is recorded.

We make an assumption here: because we have chosen to model voting papers using maps, it is not possible for us to have a voting paper where the name of a candidate is marked by two or more numbers since this would violate the well-definedness of maps. Therefore, we assume that any such papers are transcribed so that if a candidate's name is marked with two or more numbers, then that candidate and any subsequent preferences are treated as if no preference were made against them. This conforms to the regulations but places additional responsibility on the transcription process.

So for instance, the voting paper

Dijkstra	2 3
Hoare	4
Knuth	1
Lamport	5
Wirth	3

would be represented by

$$\{Hoare \mapsto 4, Knuth \mapsto 1, Lamport \mapsto 5, Wirth \mapsto 3\}$$

Note that even though there is no preference number 2, we include preferences 3,4 and 5; however, if the paper were to be transferred from Knuth then it would become non-transferable because there is no second preference.

With this proviso, most of the conditions of (7) can be translated into predicates. If *paper* represents a voting paper and *continuing-names* represents the names of the continuing candidates, then we have the following.

(7) The second and subsequent preferences on *paper* are given by $paper \triangleright \{1\}$. So the names of those candidates with a second or subsequent preference against them are given by $\text{dom}(paper \triangleright \{1\})$. Hence the first condition translates to

$$\text{dom}(paper \triangleright \{1\}) \cap continuing\text{-}names = \{\}$$

(a) If *discontinuing* is the name of the candidate currently credited with this paper (i.e. the current preference), subsequent preferences are given by

$$paper \triangleright \{1, \ldots, paper(discontinuing)\}$$

Assuming this map is non-empty, if m is the minimum of the range of this map, then the name corresponding to m must be the next preference. So the requirement is

$$\text{card dom } paper \triangleright m > 1$$

(b)(i) Using m as defined above, this translates to:

$$m - 1 \notin \text{rng } paper$$

(b)(ii) With the above proviso, this case will not occur.

(c) Obviously, we cannot specify a "catch-all" clause such as this.

Combining the above predicates, we can formally characterize a paper which is non-transferable:

> *non-transferable-paper*:
>   *Voting-paper* × *Candidate-names* × *Candidate-names*-set → $\mathbb{B}$
>
> *non-transferable-paper*(*paper*, *discontinuing*, *continuing-names*) $\triangleq$
> $\text{dom}(paper \triangleright \{1\}) \cap continuing\text{-}names = \{\}$ ∨
>   let $s = (\text{rng}(paper \triangleright \{1, \ldots, (paper(discontinuing))\}))$ in
>   if $s = \{\}$ then true else let $m = min(s)$ in
> $(\text{card dom}(paper \triangleright \{m\}) > 1$ ∨
> $m - 1 \notin \text{rng } paper)$

This function is used when voting papers are transferred be it due to transfer of surplus or exclusion of a candidate.

Scores and stages

In the process of conducting an election, we will wish to know the total number of votes currently credited to each candidate. To do this, we define the composite type *Score*, which associates with each candidate their current total value of votes credited. (Where the total value of votes is the sum over all voting papers credited to the candidate, of the value at which each paper was transferred to the candidate.)

$$Score :: name : Candidate\text{-}names$$
$$count : \mathbb{R}$$

Note that the count is a real number rather than a natural number because when voting papers are transferred, the value at which they are transferred need not be integral.

The total value credited to each continuing or elected candidate will need to be known at the end of each stage. Therefore, we define a *Stage* to be an ordered sequence of scores of continuing and elected candidates, the ordering being on the value of votes credited to each candidate.

$$Stage = Score^*$$

$$\text{inv } s \triangleq \forall i,j \in \text{inds } s \cdot$$
$$((i < j) \implies (s(i).count \geq s(j).count)) \land$$
$$i \neq j \implies s(i).name \neq s(j).name$$

Parcels, subparcels and bundles

A collection of voting papers is referred to as a *Parcel*. We define a parcel to be a map from the type *Voting-paper* to the non-zero natural numbers, where the number associated with each paper indicates the number of occurrences of that paper.

$$Parcel = Voting\text{-}paper \xrightarrow{m} \mathbb{N}_1$$

If the papers in a parcel belonging to a particular candidate are transferred then the parcel is divided into a collection of *sub-parcels*, the papers in each subparcel sharing the same next available preference. Similarly a subparcel itself, when transferred, gives rise to a collection of subparcels. However, when a parcel or subparcel is transferred, the voting papers contained therein need not necessarily be transferred at the same value that they held originally. Therefore, each subparcel needs to carry the value at which the papers contained therein were transferred. If the type *Value* denotes the positive real numbers, then we obtain the following definition:

$$Sub\text{-}parcel :: votes : Parcel$$
$$value : Value$$

When a parcel or subparcel is transferred, the papers contained in it are divided up as follows: all those papers which show a next available preference are divided up according to the name of the next available preference and those papers without a next available preference are held separately and the total value of such papers is recorded. Thus we obtain: a collection of subparcels, where in any one subparcel, each paper has the same next available preference, a subparcel containing all the non-transferable papers and the loss of value due to the non-transferable papers. Modelling this in VDM-SL, the last two are obviously represented using a *Sub-parcel* and a real number respectively. We model the first using a map from *Candidate-name* to *Sub-parcel*. Combining the three we obtain the type *Sub-parcel-bundle*.

$$Sub\text{-}parcel\text{-}bundle::sub\text{-}parcels: Candidate\text{-}names \overset{m}{\longrightarrow} Sub\text{-}parcel$$
$$non\text{-}transferable: Sub\text{-}parcel$$
$$loss\text{-}of\text{-}value: \mathbb{R}$$

Candidates

During the process of electing candidates, each candidate will have a certain number of parcels and subparcels containing votes with preferences for him or her. We tag these parcels and subparcels with the candidate's name so that we will be able to keep track of where all the parcels and subparcels are.

The votes credited to a candidate fall into two natural categories: original votes and transferred votes. For each original vote, *ov*, credited to a candidate, we require the candidate is the first preference on *ov* and no other candidate is the first preference on *ov*. (In fact, assuming *ov* is a valid voting paper, the former implies the latter since valid voting papers have unique first preferences. However, we retain both for clarity.) For each transferred vote *tv*, we require the candidate's name has a preference next to it.

Again, these requirements are simple to formulate in VDM-SL. Assuming the candidate's name is *name*, the first requirement translates to the following predicate:

$$ov \triangleright \{1\} = \{name \mapsto 1\}$$

The second requirement translates to

$$\{name\} \triangleleft ov = \{name \mapsto 1\}$$

and the last requirement translates to

$$name \in \text{dom } tv$$

We therefore define a *Candidate* to be the composite type consisting of the candidate's name, the parcel of original votes and the (sequence of) sub-parcels of transferred votes.

$$Candidate::name: Candidate\text{-}names$$
$$original\text{-}votes: Parcel$$
$$transferred\text{-}votes: Sub\text{-}parcel^*$$

inv *candidate* $\triangle$
   $(\forall ov \in \text{dom } candidate.original\text{-}votes \cdot$
      $(ov \triangleright \{1\} = \{candidate.name \mapsto 1\} \land$
      $\{candidate.name\} \triangleleft ov = \{candidate.name \mapsto 1\})) \land$
   $(\forall sub\text{-}parcel \in \text{elems } candidate.transferred\text{-}votes \cdot$
      $\forall tv \in \text{dom } sub\text{-}parcel.votes \cdot candidate.name \in \text{dom } tv)$

We are required to use a sequence for the collection of subparcels because of the following regulation:

12. <u>Papers transferred to be placed on top of parcel</u>
Whenever any transfer is made under any of the preceding Regulations each
sub-parcel of papers transferred shall be placed on top of the parcel or subparcel, if any, of papers of the candidates to whom the transfer is made, and
that candidate shall be credited with a value ascertained in pursuance of these
Regulations.

State
At the end of any stage in the electoral process, to be able to conduct the next stage,
we will require the sets of continuing, excluded and elected candidates, the sequence of
stages that have already occurred (in chronological order) and the quota.

Note that the sets of continuing, excluded and elected candidates must be disjoint and
the names of the candidates therein must span the type *Candidate-names*. Also, we require that a candidate is uniquely defined by name.

We encapsulate the above information in the state of the specification and specify the
above requirements in the invariant on the state:

> state *St* of
>   *elected* : *Candidate*-set
>   *excluded* : *Candidate*-set
>   *continuing* : *Candidate*-set
>   *stages* : *Stage**
>   *quota* : $\mathbb{R}$
>
>   inv *mk-St*$(el, ex, co, s, q) \triangleq$
> $(\{cand.name \mid cand \in el \cup ex \cup co\} = Cand\text{-}names) \wedge$
> $disjoint(\{el, ex, co\}) \wedge$
> $(\forall cand_1, cand_2 \in el \cup ex \cup co \cdot$
> $cand_1 = cand_2 \Leftrightarrow cand_1.name = cand_2.name)$
> end

5.2.2   Beginning an election

Once all voting papers have been cast, there are three main operations involved in performing the first stage of the election: arrange voting papers into parcels according to
first preference then credit each candidate with the number of first preferences counted;
on the basis of the number of voting papers cast and the number of candidates, calculate
the quota; and elect any candidates whose value is greater or equal to the quota, provided
that the number of such candidates does not exceed the number of vacancies.

We now describe these operations in turn.

Sorting and counting papers
From the regulations, we find the following information:

7. Sorting and counting papers:

> (1) The presiding officer, after rejecting any voting papers that are invalid, shall cause the valid voting papers to be arranged in parcels according to the first preferences recorded thereon for each candidate.

> (2) The presiding officer shall count the number of papers in each parcel, and credit each candidate with a number of votes equal to the number of valid papers on which a first preference has been recorded for such candidate.

As explained in Section 5.2.1, a vote v is a first preference for candidate *name* if $\operatorname{dom} v \triangleright \{1\} = \{name\}$. Hence, given a parcel of votes *votes*, the collection of first preferences for *name*, will be the submap of *votes* whose domain satisfies the above condition, namely

$$\{v \mid v \in \operatorname{dom} votes \cdot \operatorname{dom} v \triangleright \{1\} = \{name\}\} \triangleleft votes$$

Clearly, in the first instance no candidate will have any transferred votes. Thus we obtain the VDM-SL function *sort-papers* which distributes voting papers according to first preference.

$$sort\text{-}papers : Parcel \times Candidate\text{-}names\text{-set} \to Candset$$

$$sort\text{-}papers\,(votes, names) \;\triangleq$$
$$\{\text{mk-}Candidate\,(name, \{v \mid v \in \operatorname{dom} votes \cdot$$
$$(v \triangleright \{1\}) = (\{name \mapsto 1\})\} \triangleleft votes, [\,]) \mid$$
$$name \in names\}$$

To satisfy requirement (2) we need to count the number of votes each candidate has received. We do this using the function *size*, defined in Mukherjee and Wichmann (1993), which counts the number of voting papers in a parcel, and then we build a stage. Using the invariant of the type *Stage*, we only need to describe the elements of the stage; the remaining structure is implied by the type invariant. Thus we obtain the function *build-first-stage*.

$$build\text{-}first\text{-}stage\,(candidates : Candidate\text{-set})\; stage : Stage$$

$$\text{post elems}\, stage =$$
$$\{\text{mk-}Score(candidate.name, size(candidate.original\text{-}votes)) \mid$$
$$candidate \in candidates\} \land$$
$$\text{len}\, stage = \text{card elems}\, stage$$

Calculating the quota

The quota is the value of voting papers which any candidate must satisfy to be elected. The formula for calculating the quota is given by the following regulation:

8. Quota:

The presiding officer shall add together the number of votes credited to all the candidates and then divide the sum by a number exceeding by one the number of vacancies to be filled, the division being continued to two decimal places. If the result is not exact the remainder after two decimal places shall be disregarded, and the result increased by 0.01. This number, being sufficient to ensure the election of a candidate, is herein called the 'quota'.

That is, the quota is given by:

$$quota = \frac{total\ number\ of\ valid\ papers\ cast}{1 + number\ of\ vacancies\ to\ be\ filled}$$

with the value being rounded up after two decimal places if it is not exact to two decimal places. We say that a candidate "satisfies" the quota if the value of votes credited to that candidate is no less than the quota.

Elected candidates

We now define precisely what it means for a candidate to be deemed elected. If after the initial count or after a surplus is transferred, one or more continuing candidates satisfy the quota, then those candidates are elected, subject to the following two regulations:

9. Candidate with quota deemed to be elected:

If the value credited to a candidate is equal to or greater than the quota, that candidate shall be deemed to be elected, provided that the number of candidates deemed to be elected does not exceed the number of vacancies to be filled.

10. Surplus to be transferred:

(8) Candidate deemed to be elected after transfer of a surplus:

If, after the transfer of a surplus, the value credited to a continuing candidate is now equal to or greater than the quota, that candidate shall be deemed to be elected, provided that the number of candidates deemed to be elected does not exceed the number of vacancies to be filled.

Assuming the auxiliary functions *num-candidates-satisfying-quota* and *number-of-remaining-vacancies* which respectively return the number of candidates with a total value of votes exceeding the quota and the number of vacancies still to be filled, this leads directly to the following operation:

CHANGE-STATUS-OF-ELECTED-CANDS ()
  ext rd *stages* : *Stage**
    rd *quota* : $\mathbb{R}$
    wr *continuing*, *elected* : *Candidate*-set

pre *num-candidates-satisfying-quota(continuing, stages, quota)*
$\leq$ *number-of-remaining-vacancies(elected)*

post let *candidates-satisfying-quota* =
$$\{candidate \mid candidate \in \overline{continuing} \cdot$$
$$\exists count : \mathbb{R} \cdot$$
$$(mk\text{-}Score(candidate.name, count) \in \text{elems hd } stages)$$
$$\land (count \geq quota)\} \text{ in}$$
$$(elected = candidates\text{-}satisfying\text{-}quota \cup \overline{elected}) \land$$
$$(continuing = \overline{continuing} \setminus candidates\text{-}satisfying\text{-}quota)$$

Note that candidates who satisfy the quota after having received the votes of an excluded candidate are elected separately.

Initialization

Here we describe the operation which initializes the state. We begin by counting voting papers and sorting them according to candidates, to get the local value, *cur-cont*. Candidates cannot be excluded by this operation so we initialize the excluded set to be empty. If any candidate satisfies the quota, provided that the total number of such candidates does not exceed the number of candidates to be elected, such a candidate will be deemed to be elected, using the predicate *post-CHANGE-STATUS-OF-ELECTED-CANDS* and the set of continuing candidates will be all other candidates. Otherwise, we set *elected* to be empty and *continuing* to be *cur-cont*. The quota will be as described in Section 5.2.2 and the stage will be constructed using the function *build-first-stage*. So we obtain:

PREPARE-ELECTION (votes : Parcel)
ext wr *excluded, elected, continuing : Candidate*-set
  wr *stages : Stage**
  wr *quota : $\mathbb{R}$*
post $(excluded = \{\}) \land$
  let *cur-cont* = *sort-papers(votes, Cand-names)* in
  $(quota = two\text{-}dec\text{-}places(size(votes)/(Number\text{-}of\text{-}vacancies + 1))) \land$
  $(stages = build\text{-}first\text{-}stage(cur\text{-}cont)) \land$
  if $0 <$ *num-candidates-satisfying-quota(cur-cont, stages, quota)*
    $\land$ *num-candidates-satisfying-quota(cur-cont, stages, quota)*
        $\leq$ *Number-of-vacancies*
  then *post-CHANGE-STATUS-OF-ELECTED-CANDS(*
        mk-St(\{ \}, \{ \}, cur-cont, stages, quota),
          mk-St(elected, \{ \}, continuing, stages, quota))
  else $(elected = \{ \} \land continuing = cur\text{-}cont)$

where *two-dec-places* is the auxiliary function which rounds a real number to two decimal places.

5.2.3   Excluding a candidate

In order to illustrate how the algorithm operates, we now consider the circumstances in which a candidate might be excluded from the election. We have the following regulation:

11. Exclusion of a candidate:

   (1) Candidate with lowest value excluded:

   If at the end of any stage of the count no candidate has a surplus other than a surplus whose transfer is deferred, and one or more vacancies remain unfilled, the presiding officer shall exclude the candidate credited with the lowest value.

To illustrate this idea we give another example. Suppose we wish to elect two candidates from six and 120 valid voting papers are cast as follows:

Name	Value
Dijkstra	35
Hoare	30
Wirth	24
Knuth	20
Milner	6
Lamport	5

The quota is $120/3 = 40$. Thus no candidate has a surplus. Therefore we exclude the lowest placed candidate – in this case Lamport. On transferring his papers, we arrive at the following situation:

Name	Value
Dijkstra	35
Hoare	30
Knuth	25
Wirth	24
Milner	6

Once more, no candidate has a surplus so we exclude the lowest placed candidate – in this case Milner:

Name	Value
Dijkstra	35
Hoare	35
Wirth	25
Knuth	25

Again, no candidate has a surplus, so we exclude the lowest placed candidate. However, in this situation there are two candidates credited with the lowest value. The regulation for dealing with such situations is given below.

(2) Selection of candidate for exclusion:

If when a candidate is to be excluded, two or more candidates are each credited with the same lowest value, the presiding officer shall exclude the candidate (of those two or more) who was credited with the lowest value at the earliest stage at which they were credited with unequal values.

If the relevant candidates were each credited with the same value at all stages of the count, the presiding officer shall determine by lot which of these candidates to exclude.

Thus, because Wirth was credited with a greater value than Knuth at the first stage, Knuth is the candidate who is excluded.

We now translate these ideas into VDM-SL. We begin by defining the predicate *sole-trailer* which takes a stage (*stage*), a candidate's name (*name*) and a set of candidate's names (*lowest*) and is true exactly when *name* has a value of votes credited which is strictly less than that of any member of *lowest* at this particular stage.

$$sole\text{-}trailer : Stage \times Candidate\text{-}names \times Candidate\text{-}names\text{-set} \to \mathbb{B}$$

$$sole\text{-}trailer(stage, name, lowest) \triangleq$$
$$\text{let } cand = \iota c \in \text{elems } stage \cdot c.name = name \text{ in}$$
$$\text{let } lowest\text{-}scores = \{sc \mid sc \in \text{elems } stage \cdot sc.name \in lowest\} \setminus cand\text{-set in}$$
$$\forall sc \in lowest\text{-}scores \cdot cand.count < sc.count$$

Using *sole-trailer*, we can define the predicate *trailing-candidate*. This takes a candidate's name (*name*) and all the stages that have occurred so far (*all-stages*) and is true precisely when there exists a stage at which *name* satisfies *sole-trailer* and no other candidate with a score currently equal to *name*'s score satisfies *sole-trailer* at any earlier stage.

$$trailing\text{-}candidate : Candidate\text{-}names \times Stage^+ \to \mathbb{B}$$

$$trailing\text{-}candidate(name, all\text{-}stages) \triangleq$$
$$\text{let } lowest = \{score.name \mid score \in \text{elems hd } all\text{-}stages \cdot$$
$$score.count = bk(\text{hd } all\text{-}stages).count\} \text{ in}$$
$$\exists i \in \text{inds } all\text{-}stages \cdot$$
$$sole\text{-}trailer(all\text{-}stages(i), name, lowest) \land$$
$$(\forall j \in \{i+1, \ldots, \text{len } all\text{-}stages\}, other \in lowest \cdot$$
$$\neg(sole\text{-}trailer(all\text{-}stages(j), other, lowest)))$$

where *bk* returns the last element in a sequence. Now, choosing which candidate to exclude is trivial. We do this as follows.

1. Extract the names of those candidates whose count equals the current minimum count. Call this set *lowest*.

2. If *lowest* is singleton, then no more work need be done.

3. If *lowest* contains more than one element, we obtain

   Either (a) At some earlier stage, a member of *lowest* had a vote strictly less than all the other members of *lowest* – in which case *trailing-candidate* is satisfiable.

   Or (b) The members of *lowest* had the same score as each other at every previous stage, in which case we return a random element of *lowest*.

This can be expressed concisely in VDM-SL:

$$CHOOSE\text{-}CANDIDATE\text{-}TO\text{-}EXCLUDE\,()\ name : Candidate\text{-}names$$

ext rd   *stages* : *Stage**

pre   *stages* ≠ []

post let *lowest* = {*score.name* | *score* ∈ elems hd *stages* ·
$$\qquad\qquad\qquad\qquad score.count = bk(\text{hd}\,stages).count\}\ \text{in}$$
$$(name \in lowest)\,\wedge$$
$$((\text{card}\,lowest > 1)\ \Rightarrow$$
$$\qquad (\text{if } \exists n \in lowest \cdot trailing\text{-}candidate(n, stages)$$
$$\qquad \text{then } trailing\text{-}candidate(name, stages)$$
$$\qquad \text{else } post\text{-}RANDOM\text{-}ELEMENT(lowest,$$
$$\qquad\qquad mk\text{-}St(\{\,\},\{\,\},\{\,\},[],0,[]),$$
$$\qquad\qquad\qquad mk\text{-}St(\{\,\},\{\,\},\{\,\},[],0,[]), name)))$$

5.3   Animation

5.3.1   The principles

Given a specification of reasonable complexity, it is clear that it is very hard to be totally confident of its correctness. The last section indicates that in this case, the complexity of the STV algorithm is quite high, in spite of an English description of modest length.

The method chosen here to validate the VDM-SL specification is one of **animation**. By this, we mean converting the VDM-SL into a form which can be directly executed, and using the execution as a means of checking the correct operation of the specification. The conversion of an arbitrary VDM-SL specification into an executable form is not, in general, feasible, since VDM-SL allows the use of implicit specifications. Hence if an algorithm is specified by a post-condition, then there may be no way of providing an implementation, and indeed, the post-condition could prove impossible to satisfy. However, one objective of the animation exercise would be to highlight such unsatisfiable post-conditions.

In the current study, the VDM-SL specification is algorithmic and therefore the problem with implicit specifications does not arise. However, the conversion must follow the VDM-SL precisely, otherwise the validation process will be flawed. In consequence, the automatic conversion of the VDM-SL specification would be advantageous, or failing that, the conversion to a language which has similar constructs to those used in VDM-SL so that the conversion process itself can be easily checked.

Given an executable version of the specification, it is essential to execute it in as searching a manner as possible if confidence is to be gained in the specification. In this case, we have an almost ideal situation of 13 carefully constructed test cases which are thought to be adequate to validate (another version) of the algorithm.

5.3.2 SML

SML originally arose as a tactics language for use in theorem proving in LCF logic (MacQueen *et al.*, 1986). However, it has developed into a respectable programming language in its own right. SML has functional programming features such as lists, recursive data types and curried functions as well as imperative features such as assignment, sequential composition and loops. This latter feature is based on the presence of "reference variables".

The presence of both of these facilities makes SML an attractive choice to animate VDM-SL specifications. This is for the following four reasons.

- The presence of lists in SML (which are dynamic structures) provides a natural way to interpret sets, sequences and maps. In other languages we might have to build separate abstract data type modules for these to cope with their changing size during computation.
- Functions in VDM-SL can be interpreted directly as functions in SML.
- Operations in VDM-SL can be implemented as SML functions over reference variables.
- Operation pre-conditions can be checked in SML using SML's exception handling mechanism.

Few languages other than SML satisfy the four requirements listed above, so SML was an obvious choice.

5.3.3 Example

To illustrate how animation was performed, we describe the SML version of the function *sole-trailer* (the VDM-SL definition of which is given in Section 5.2.3). Since all sets in VDM-SL are finite, they were implemented using SML's lists, and therefore set comprehensions were translated into list expressions using the functions map and filter. Also, universal quantification was implemented using distributed conjunction over a list (denoted by the SML operator `conjl`). Records in VDM-SL were implemented using SML's records, the difference being in the syntax of selection, e.g. if *c* is a candidate then in VDM-SL the name of *c* would be given by *c.name* whereas in SML the name of c would be given by #name(c). Thus the SML version of *sole-trailer* was

```
fun sole_trailer (stage:Stage, name:Candidate_names,
                  lowest:Candidate_names set) =
    let val name_sc = hd (filter (eq name o (#name)) stage)
        val lowest_scores =
                filter ((mem (set_seq lowest)) o #name) stage
        fun lt (sc1:Score) (sc2:Score) = sc1 = sc2 orelse
                                  (#count(sc1)) < (#count(sc2))
    in
      conjl (map (lt name_sc) lowest_scores)
    end;
```

5.3.4   Errors discovered by the animation process

Testing of the SML program was performed against a suite of test data first used for testing the original Pascal program for performing STV elections. 13 test cases were used for the original program but we only used 10 of these tests here because our program did not implement options such as withdrawal of a candidate following casting of votes. We do not describe the data sets — details of these may be found in Mukherjee and Wichmann (1993).

Before animation the specification was analyzed using SpecBox (Froome, 1990). The SpecBox tool checks VDM-SL specifications for conformance with BSI-VDM syntax and performs weak type analysis. The type analysis it performs is based on arity checking: function and operation calls are checked to make sure that the number of arguments provided conforms to the number of parameters in the corresponding definitions. In fact, SpecBox was used throughout the construction of the specification and uncovered many syntax and type errors. However, as described below, a few type errors remained.

Animation of the specification revealed the following errors: two type errors in the specification (i.e. type errors missed by SpecBox); three errors due to correct interpretation but incorrect specification of requirements; two errors due to misinterpretation of English requirements; one error introduced during translation of VDM-SL into SML. A more detailed discussion of the errors uncovered by animation may be found in Mukherjee and Wichmann (1993).

5.3.5   Execution using the IFAD Toolbox

Having animated the specification in SML, the corrected specification ws executed using the IFAD VDM-SL Toolbox. This execution was intended to measure the efficacy of animation in SML, as in theory the animation should have removed all the errors in the specification.

In practice, execution uncovered some errors in the specification. These errors may be divided into two categories:

- errors found and corrected in the SML program, but not corrected in the VDM-SL specification;
- errors present in the VDM-SL specification but absent in the SML program due to incorrect translation of VDM-SL's data structures into SML's data structures.

The first category is essentially a problem of maintaining consistency between the VDM-SL specification and the SML program. This could be avoided by (for instance) automating the translation process and then only allowing the specification to be altered. This forces errors found in the SML program to be corrected by correcting the corresponding errors in the specification.

The second category relates to the informal nature of the translation. This suggests that even if no formal link between the two languages is given, it might be useful to state abstraction functions and representation invariants in order to avoid incorrect translation of data structures.

The issues arising from animation in SML compared to execution using the IFAD Toolbox are discussed at length in Mukherjee (1995). Here, we simply observe that because of its informal nature, animation in SML only gives us evidence that the number of errors in the specification has been reduced.

5.4   Discussion

5.4.1   Was VDM-SL suitable?

One can argue that VDM-SL is being used as a programming language in this case study, and therefore perhaps a different choice should have been made. Using a conventional programming language instead would have avoided the conversion process for animation, so the balance would seem to be against VDM-SL. However, a conventional programming language, even Pascal, has quite complex semantics which could make the code difficult to understand. In fact, some of the limitations of Pascal, particularly that functions cannot return composite values, mean that a version of the STV algorithm in Pascal would be very different from the VDM-SL specification.

In fact, the Pascal program which was certified contains a significant fraction of the code for the input and output which is not formally defined in Section 2. This is an inherent danger in the use of a conventional language in that implementation considerations tend to predominate so that the simple expression of the semantics is lost amongst other verbiage.

In this case, we feel that the use of VDM-SL has proved its worth. The semantics of the algorithm has been captured at the suitable level of abstraction. The complexity of the VDM-SL specification reflects that of the STV algorithm. Part of the difficulty in reading the algorithm is that the notation of sets and maps is less familiar than, say, differential calculus (even though the underlying mathematics is simpler).

5.4.2   The value of animation

The use of animation in this case was highly effective, owing to the simple conversion process and the existence of good test data. Note that we cannot claim that the VDM-SL specification is necessarily correct because it has passed the validation process. Indeed, the twice-through process revealed ten errors overall, so that one could argue that at least one further error might be found via extensive back-to-back testing of the SML and Pascal versions. Also, use of the IFAD Toolbox suggests that a great deal of care must be taken when performing the translation from VDM-SL to SML.

The most worrying aspect of the process is that the number of bugs per source line of VDM-SL is rather similar to that noted from conventional programs. This implies that reliance upon a formal specification without any animation (or other validation procedure of similar strength) seems unwise.

5.4.3   The 00-55 development model

Two parts of the Interim Defence standard (Ministry of Defence, 1991a) are particularly relevant to this study and therefore we repeat them in full.

> "29.3.1 The Design Team shall validate the Software Specification against the Software Requirements Specification by animation of the Formal Specification. Animation shall be carried out by both of the following:
>
> - By the construction of Formal Arguments in accordance with 32.1 showing that the Formal Specification embodies all the safety features described in the Software Requirements Specification.
>
> - By the production of an Executable Prototype derived from the Formal Specification. The minimum number of changes shall be made to the Formal Specification in the construction of the Executable Prototype; Formal Arguments shall be constructed in accordance with 32.1 to show the link between the two.
>
> 29.3.2 The Executable Prototype shall be tested by the Design Team. The aim of each test and the expected results shall be determined before the test is executed. As a minimum, the tests shall exercise all the safety functions of the SCS. The results shall be recorded in the Software Specification.
> 33.3 The integrated SCS shall be tested in a test harness that enables the results to be compared with the Executable Prototype. During these tests, the SCS shall be run on the target hardware or an an emulator that has been shown by Formal Arguments to be equivalent to the target hardware."

In this study, we do not have safety features, and hence the first itemized paragraph cannot be undertaken as it stands. However, the general requirement that if there are n

places, then exactly *n* people must be elected should be capable of formal verification. Indeed we prove this in Mukherjee and Wichmann (1993).

We believe that we have followed the spirit of the second itemized paragraph. The executable prototype followed the specification very closely with the exception of the additional input–output which is obviously necessary. Prototyping tools should perhaps provide a simple means of undertaking input/output to simplify the process. The link between the SML code and the VDM-SL has not been subject to "Formal Arguments" in the sense of the standard. However, in the light of the errors discovered using the IFAD Toolbox, it might be prudent to sketch out the formal links.

Concerning section 29.3.2, we believe the testing is adequate. The fact that the results were checked by the ERS expert, and that the algorithm docs mimic the manual method, gives us a high degree of confidence in the validation of the SML code.

On the question of section 33.3, the position is not quite so strong. No attempt has been made to use the "target hardware" (the Church program uses an IBM PC). Indeed, configuration problems can arise, such as lack of disc space and conflicts in file names, etc., unless elaborate checks are undertaken. It would be possible to undertake back-to-back testing of the Pascal program with the SML version. However, there are some practical problems with this. Firstly, the output would have to be identical if automatic comparison of the output was to be used. Secondly, in the case of ties, the computer programs can legally make different choices, and hence some means must be devised of avoiding this if completely automatic comparisons were to be undertaken. These problems are akin to the consistent comparison problem in N-version software (Brilliant *et al.*, 1989). Of course, it would be feasible to undertake further test cases with manual checks on the output, but at this stage any remaining errors are very unlikely, and hence this option is not attractive.

5.4.4 Conclusions

We believe that this case study supports the use of formal methods. Ambiguities were located in the English text, although the experts (in ERS) have an agreed interpretation of these points. The problems of specifying an algorithm in English are well known (Hill, 1972). Mistakes do occur in public elections and one of the attractions of using computers would be to reduce the frequency of such errors. However, errors could not be eliminated completely by such means, even if the program were error free, since the input of the data is likely to be a significant source of errors.

The results obtained here strongly support the need for validation of a formal specification, and that providing an executable prototype would appear to be a good method for this, provided that the execution tests are thorough enough.

We have not undertaken back-to-back execution of the executable prototype and the production program. This would appear to be a strong method of testing, provided that the comparison process can be automated. It would be easy to envisage situations in which such an automatic comparison would be difficult. For instance, if the specification involves real arithmetic, there may be different rounding between the two systems, given differences which are nevertheless within the specification. In general, implicit specification methods can easily yield different but valid implementations. Such a situation could make back-to-back testing uneconomic owing to the need to undertake large numbers of hand comparisons or write elaborate software for an automatic process.

It must be admitted that the use of a formal notation for the expression of the STV algorithm is much less attractive than that produced for the formulation of the regulations for the storage of explosives (Mukherjee and Stavridou, 1993). In general, one must expect the formal specification to reflect the closeness of the subject matter to classical mathematics. The regulations for the storage of explosives can be represented as a set of pure functions, and hence the main complexity is in the classification of the explosives themselves and in the buildings (which is easier to understand). It is difficult to obtain the same level of understanding of the STV algorithm without conducting some elections by hand.

It did not prove possible to validate the explosives example by animation, since searching test cases were not available. This study therefore provides better insight into animation. This indicates that one should expect faults in specifications to appear at a comparable frequency to that of programs, say one fault every 70 lines of VDM-SL, which was the rate observed here.

Acknowledgements

We would like to thank I.D. Hill for pointing out some errors in an early version of the specification. The first author was supported by a CASE award jointly funded by the National Physical Laboratory and the Science and Engineering Research Council.

Chapter 6

Application of the B-Method to CICS

Jonathan P. Hoare

6.1 Introduction

This chapter describes the experiences gained on a project involving the application of the B-Method to the development of part of a new component in a future release of the CICS/ESA transaction processing product.

6.1.1 CICS

CICS (Customer Information Control System) is an IBM family of software products which is used by businesses worldwide to manage and process their business information. At its heart CICS comprises a monitor system providing generic facilities for online transaction processing, which can be tailored to meet customers' exact business requirements, by means of an application programming interface (API), used to invoke CICS services from within the customer's own business applications.

Designed for continuous operation without the need for periodic interruptions in availability, CICS offers services such as data access and communications for multiple users in a parallel processing environment. In addition, CICS has built-in facilities for ensuring data integrity, for failure recovery and transaction backout, and for providing transactional characteristics to database management systems, e.g. DB/2.

The first version of CICS developed for System/360 mainframes became generally available in the USA over 25 years ago, and since then it has grown into one of IBM's most widely used and commercially successful software products. The Hursley Laboratory took over responsibility for CICS development in 1975, and new versions of CICS have been developed subsequently for most IBM operating systems and recently for some non-IBM systems. Members of the CICS family now exist for a variety of different hardware platforms and operating systems, any of which may be required to work together in a distributed environment.

Used by banks, insurance companies and finance houses, CICS is also found in manufacturing industry, airlines and many other areas of business that depend upon high integrity services to manage their day-to-day business transactions. There are currently in excess of 35 000 licensees worldwide for CICS on mainframe operating systems, including most of the world's top businesses. Typical applications for CICS include the cashpoint services operated by banks and building societies, stock control in manufacturing industry and payroll administration.

6.1.2   Formal methods

The application of mathematical methods to the development of CICS began in 1982 with a collaboration between Hursley and the Programming Research Group at Oxford University on the use of the Z notation for specification. Initially Z was used in the CICS code restructuring initiative for version 3.1.1 and since then it has been used for the specification of most new components of CICS as well as parts of the API. In recognition of this work, the Queen's Award for Technological Achievement was conferred jointly upon IBM Hursley and the Oxford University Computing Laboratory in 1992.

The CICS restructuring initiative was aimed at providing future CICS implementations with a framework for modular design. Within this new structure, code modules are grouped according to the data upon which the code operates. Such a group of code modules was given the name **domain**.

Z is well suited to the specification of CICS domains, and consequently a considerable degree of success has been achieved with its use for specification by CICS designers. The use of Z resulted in a tangible increase in the quality of the CICS product while maintaining the overall programmer productivity (Collins *et al.*, 1989). Although extra work was involved in writing the formal specifications and holding inspections, this additional effort was offset by a reduction in the amount of rework required during the subsequent design and coding stages. The majority of the actual savings which have been realized so far through the use of formal methods have resulted from a reduction in service costs after the product's release.

In the Z-based development method, whilst the specification stage was formal, the rest of the process did not change. The aim of IBM's use of the B-Method is to reduce the effort in design and coding by extending the use of mathematical techniques and associated tools to cover these later stages, consequently allowing developers to concentrate on the creative aspects of software design.

6.1.3   The B-Method and B-Toolkit

The B-Method (Neilson and Sorensen, 1994) is a rigorous approach to software design drawing together the principles of structured programming, formal specification and object orientation, supported by a uniform notation, the abstract machine notation (AMN). The method covers the complete software development life cycle from initial specification to final code.

The B-Toolkit (B-Core (UK) Ltd., 1993) is a suite of tools supporting all stages of the B-Method in a unified development environment.

The mathematical basis of AMN is similar to that of Z, in that state models are given in terms of set theory and predicate calculus. It differs from Z, however, in that operations are specified in terms of a generalized substitution language (GSL) instead of post-conditions.

The basis of the method was proposed by J.-R. Abrial and others while working on a three-year research project at the Programming Research Group, Oxford University, sponsored by British Petroleum Research. The method and associated tools were further developed over a seven year period by a team at BP working in consultation with J.-R. Abrial. The B-Method and an early version of the B-Toolkit were in use within BP from 1990 to develop operational software for the BP group of companies. During 1991 and 1992 the B-Toolkit underwent alpha-testing in a number of other organizations ranging from transport companies to telecommunications businesses. B-Core (UK) Ltd. purchased the B technologies from BP International in 1993, and have subsequently commercialized and continued the development of the B-Toolkit.

In late 1992, the CICS development organization entered the alpha-test programme. A copy of the B-Toolkit was installed at Hursley and initially one programmer began a series of small pilot developments aimed at investigating the capabilities of the B-Toolkit and its suitability for more widespread use. Following a favourable report from this study it was decided to extend the trial by using the B-Method and the B-Toolkit within a real development project.

The current project began in March 1993, when a site licence for the B-Toolkit was obtained for Hursley, and a collaborative contract was set up with B-Core (UK) Ltd. The contract covered consultancy on the B-Method and the tailoring of the toolkit for CICS. With regard to education and training, it was decided that the team members would be capable of acquiring the necessary skills through intrateam communication and consultancy contacts while the project was underway.

6.2   The development process

The process adopted for the development of the new CICS component followed the standard CICS guidelines, adapted for the B-Method and the use of the B-Toolkit. B prescribes a design strategy not fully covered by the CICS development guidelines. In particular, B encourages an iterative design approach for the stepwise refinement of specifications into code. The stages of the process are illustrated in Figure 6.1, and are discussed below.

6.2.1   Initial requirements

The development began with what has become standard practice in the CICS organization: the production of an initial requirements document called the Product Level Design (PLD). This laid out the requirements which were to be addressed by the proposed component and included an abstract Z specification of the new functions which were to be provided. Details of non-functional characteristics which needed agreement prior to the

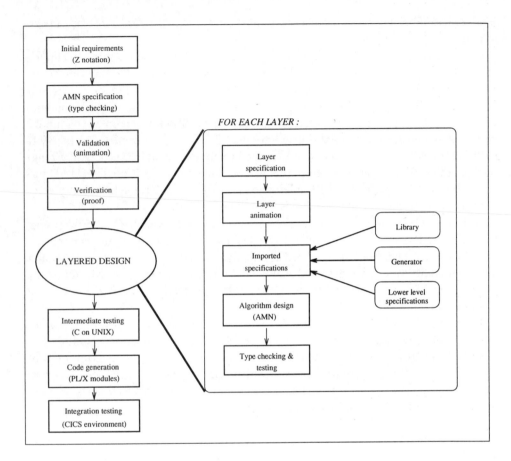

Figure 6.1 The CICS development process using the B-Method.

design phase were also included. After the Z specification had been type checked, the complete PLD was subjected to the IBM inspection process (which includes a thorough peer review and revision by the author as necessary).

6.2.2 AMN specification

Whilst the PLD was written according to standard procedure and inspected as usual, at this point the process adopted in the project departed from the usual course. The Z specification from the PLD was manually translated into AMN and entered into the B-Toolkit. The static analysis tools were then used to parse and type check the AMN.

This manual translation was performed from the Z specification alone without any prior knowledge of the component or its intended usage. That this was possible clearly demonstrates the value of an initial formal definition of the requirements.

6.2.3   Validation

The AMN specification of the system made it possible, with the use of the B-Toolkit, to carry out a form of validation not possible using traditional means. This extra level of checking involved the use of the standard B-Toolkit animation tool to "execute" the specification interactively and thereby to gain confidence in the behaviour of the proposed component.

During animation, the AMN specification was subjected to a number of typical usage scenarios such as might be expected to occur after delivery of the component. By this approach, it was possible to validate, in a considerably more convincing way than usual, the specification against requirements not formalised in the PLD.

Validation by animation is a form of early testing and consequently can only demonstrate the absence (or presence) of undesirable behaviour within the scenarios used for animation. It is possible therefore that some unchecked, but valid, implementation will not necessarily exhibit the desired behaviour.

Even though this form of validation is limited, it nevertheless provided a useful check on the specification and increased the level of confidence that the software, when implemented, would satisfy its behavioural requirements.

Three categories of error were detected during animation of the AMN.

1. *Errors introduced in the translation process.* These were mainly due to the difficulty of identifying the set of constraints affecting operations composed from Z schemas using the schema calculus.
2. *Errors in the Z.* These resulted in the initial formal specification not reflecting the intentions of the author.
3. *Errors in the author's conception of the system.* These were typically reflected in omissions and inconsistences in the Z.

The findings of the animation resulted in revisions to the Z specification as well as to the AMN and each time, the revised AMN specification was subjected to reanimation covering the same usage scenarios. These were again employed when testing the prototype implementations.

6.2.4   Verification

In addition to validation by animation, the existence of the AMN specification made it possible to attempt a formal verification of its internal consistency using the proof facilities provided in the B-Toolkit. In the B-Method this consists of proving that, when an operation of the specification is invoked within its precondition, it preserves the invariant of the system state. This proof work was carried out by Chris Pratten, a postgraduate student from Southampton University, working at IBM.

Several errors in the AMN specification were found during the verification stage. The main difficulties arose because the stated preconditions of the operations were insufficiently strong to guarantee that the invariant conditions were maintained. This in turn arose from the difficulty of identifying the complete set of predicates constraining the system state during the translation from Z to AMN.

When the operation pre-conditions were strengthened appropriately, and additional logic rules particular to the problem in hand were supplied, all the proofs became feasible and many were discharged automatically by the B-Toolkit proof tool. The revised AMN specification was then subjected to re-animation, to ensure that the strengthened preconditions were still acceptable.

Whereas animation was used to validate the specification against the informal behavioural requirements of the software, proof work enabled the mathematical consistency of the AMN to be verified. The two techniques address different aspects of correctness, and one cannot act as a substitute for the other. Both are valuable and were used in conjunction.

6.2.5   Layered design

The design phase in the B-Method involves the refinement of high-level specifications into successively more detailed layers, until library functions can be used for implementation at the lowest level. The design process will be treated in detail in Section 6.3.

6.2.6   Intermediate testing

When the overall structure of the layered design had been finalized and the implementation of all intermediate layers had been finished, a complete interactive version of the design was created using the AMN to C translation and interface generation facilities of the B-Toolkit. The purpose of this was to build an executable prototype to test in the UNIX environment before generation of PL/X code modules for migration to CICS. This prototype was subjected to the same test scenarios which had been used for the animation of the original AMN specification. These scenarios were also used for regression testing.

6.2.7   Code generation

After the complete design had been checked by the methods described earlier, as well as by a manual inspection of the algorithms in the various layers, the toolkit was used to build the final code modules which were to be compiled and linked into CICS. Versions of all required library modules, hand coded into the target language, PL/X, were therefore added to the B-Toolkit library. This code consists mainly of the interfaces to existing CICS functions, though with some minor adaptations.

6.2.8   Integration testing

With the PL/X code now generated, the final modules were transferred to the mainframe system for compilation and integration with the rest of CICS. The standard testing procedures of the CICS development process were then resumed.

6.3   The design process

The principal elements of sound software engineering practice encouraged by the B-Method are formal specification, object orientation, stepwise refinement, reuse and configuration control. Together, these permit the construction of a layered design and provide the ability to split the development into smaller parts, each of which may be considered in isolation.

6.3.1   Layered design

The design of a single software layer using the B-Method begins with a specification of the required functionality as an abstract machine expressed in AMN, and ends with an implementation of that machine which refers only to the operations of machines in lower levels. The specification encapsulates a set-theoretic model of the state and the definitions of operations which may be performed upon that state, in an object-oriented style. An implementation is an algorithm that refers only to the operations of subsidiary machines which are imported from lower layers.

Given the specification of a particular layer, design proceeds by imagining a new lower layer of abstract machines in terms of which the current layer can be implemented. First the lower level is specified, animated and reworked until the designer is satisfied that it provides a set of operations sufficient for the implementation of the layer above. Then the implementation of the upper layer is written and analyzed, and proofs carried out where desirable.

To produce a complete design for a large-scale piece of software using this method, it may be necessary to repeat the above process many times to build successive layers of software, each more concrete than the next. The design iteration ends when the final layer is implemented purely in terms of library machines.

This approach combines top-down and bottom-up styles. The creation of the specification of the next layer down is an opportunity to consider the target facilities, and to converge on them in a bottom-up fashion. At the same time, the consideration that each layer has to implement the layer above focuses the designer's mind on the top-down aspect of the design process. Although responsibility for ensuring the convergence of these opposing directions remains with the software engineer, the animation facility of the B-Toolkit can be used to assist in this task by ensuring that the function of an intended intermediate layer will be appropriate for use by higher layers. This approach also encourages reuse of the library modules supplied with the B-Toolkit.

When the implementation of all underlying layers has been completed, it is possible, by using the B-Toolkit automatic interface generator, to test a particular layer interactively against a possible usage scenario, without the overhead of writing test programs.

6.3.2　Relationships between layers

Between an abstract machine and its implementation, there may be a number of optional intermediate steps, termed **refinements**, in which the abstract state can be refined. Although helpful if a fully formal mathematical development is to be attempted, refinements are not mandatory. The layered software structure enforced by the B-Method, and the benefits of type checking at each level, can represent a degree of rigour sufficient for many developments.

To allow the separate provability and implementability of subsystems, the B-Method provides various different forms of information hiding, or data encapsulation. For instance, the implementation of one design layer imports a specification from the next level down, and here full information hiding is enforced: the state of the imported machine can only be accessed through its visible operations. This allows the imported machines to be implemented entirely independently. It is this feature that gives the B-Method characteristics of an object-oriented approach.

Other relationships between machines allow the sharing of their associated mathematics in such a way that their proof concerns can still be separated. For example, specifications may include or "see" others, which allows read-only access to those machines: modifying their state is not allowed since it might invalidate the invariants of their encapsulated data. Such forms of partial access are said to enforce semihiding.

6.3.3　Design structure

Figure 6.2 illustrates the tree-like structure of the hierarchical design of the component developed in the course of this project. The pairing is shown between specifications and their corresponding implementations. Arrows indicate the importation of low-level specifications into higher-level implementations.

There is a considerable amount of flexibility in the method, allowing designers to select the level of formality most appropriate to their particular situation. The minimum is to write specifications for the intermediate layers which simply list the operations available, together with the names and types of their input and output parameters. This serves purely to define the operation signatures of the machines. The other extreme is to write fully formal abstract specifications for each layer with a complete state model and GSL definitions of the operations. The various possible levels of formality can be freely mixed within a single development, permitting, where appropriate, some short cuts to be taken while maintaining the option for more formal verification elsewhere.

In the current project this flexible approach was indeed adopted and full AMN specifications were used only for

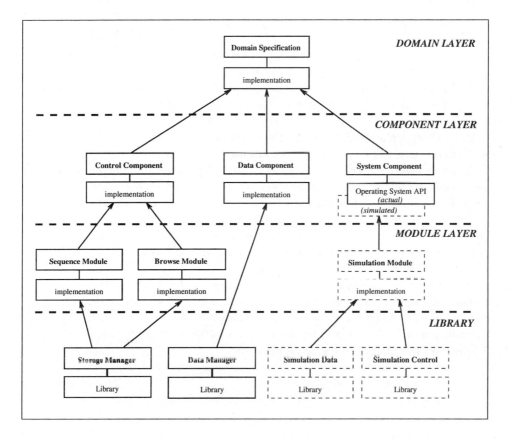

Figure 6.2 Layered design structure (simplified).

- the highest level specification, produced by translation from the existing Z specification,
- the operating system facility upon which the development was to be based,
- pre-existing library functions of the B-Toolkit, and
- some intermediate layers, where a simple abstract view of the functions could be given, yet the implementation would be relatively complex.

For all other layers, skeleton specifications were written defining only the type signatures for all the operations which were to be implemented. Informal annotations were used to keep track of the effect of these operations on the encapsulated abstract state, yet the benefits of structured design and type checking were still present. No intermediate refinements were used between specifications and implementations.

6.3.4   Target platforms

The design phase is complete when all the lowest-level machines are implemented solely in terms of library modules. The B-Toolkit library contains specifications and C code for a number of reusable modules which form a target platform adequate for most developments. If another target language or special-purpose functions are needed, then these must be supplied and added to the library.

Various target platforms were used successively during the CICS project. The first AMN implementation of the system component of the design was based on the B-Toolkit C library modules. Later, PL/X versions of the library modules were added, allowing the same AMN implementation to be ported, without modification, to the CICS environment. Eventually the interface to the actual operating system code was encapsulated as a library module, and the entire AMN implementation collapsed into a single layer, while preserving the original specification. This is illustrated in Figure 6.2 where the simulated implementation of the system component, ultimately based on the library, has been replaced by an interface to the operating system API.

This incremental approach was adopted to allow the development to progress in the absence of both the PL/X library code and the new operating system feature. Thus it was possible to perform intermediate testing of a prototype in C before porting to the CICS environment, followed by early testing in CICS by other users months in advance of the delivery of the first operating system code.

6.4   Example

In this section we present a small example of a development using the B-Method, starting with an AMN specification and giving an implementation based on the library provided with the B-Toolkit.

The purpose of this is to give the reader who is unfamiliar with the B-Method and AMN a flavour of the style and syntax used in the method, and an idea of the level of formality which was employed in the current project.

The example chosen is a simplified version of a component which forms part of the overall development described in Section 6.3. It is a module which encapsulates a sequence of items. There are three operations:

- append an item to the sequence;
- delete a previously added item;
- return the oldest surviving item.

Such a module might have uses in a variety of situations, such as the following.

- In a database of all the people in the country, it might be desired to know who is the oldest person.

- In a class manager's assistant, it might be desirable to know which student has been enrolled on the course for the longest period without graduating.
- In the CICS development, it is necessary to keep track of the oldest block of data which needs to be kept when backing out from a transaction.

The specification was written with both its intended use and a possible implementation in mind. This ensured that the module would be useful and would admit an efficient implementation.

A typical scenario for the use of this module would be in the first case above: a database pertaining to each individual in the country. When a person is born, their personal data is recorded and a new "token", or identity number, such as a social security number, is assigned to them. This identity number is then used to represent the person instead of any part of his or her personal information, which may not be unique.

The nature of the personal data stored is left completely undetermined in this module. It may be a simple name, or perhaps another token referring to some complex data structure stored elsewhere.

When a person dies, the token for that person's entry in the machine is supplied, and is used to delete the entry. When it is required to know who is the oldest person, we simply invoke the operation on our module to return the earliest surviving entry.

Figure 6.3 gives an overview of the structure of the example development.

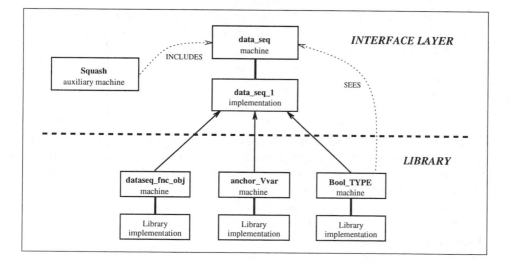

Figure 6.3 Structure of the example development.

6.4.1   Specification

MACHINE   *data_seq (DATA , any_data)*

CONSTRAINTS   *any_data* ∈ *DATA*

This machine is parameterized by *DATA* and *any_data*, which allows the machine to be instantiated for use with different kinds of data. *DATA* is assumed to be a set, and *any_data* a particular element of that set to be used as the default value in the implementation.

SEES   *Bool_TYPE*

The SEES clause makes the mathematics of the stateless machine *Bool_TYPE* visible within this specification, so that Boolean types and their associated operations can be used.

INCLUDES   *Squash (TOKEN)*

The specification includes another stateless machine called *Squash* which simply defines an auxiliary mathematical function *squash* used in the specification of the *DeleteItem* operation below.

SETS   *TOKEN*

TOKEN is the type of the tokens which are returned when a new item is added, and which can be used to delete the associated item later. This type is not given as a parameter of the machine, because this machine "owns" and controls the tokens: it allocates them and issues them.

VARIABLES   *token_seq* , *token_map*

INVARIANT

$token\_seq \in$ iseq $(TOKEN) \land$
$token\_map \in TOKEN \nrightarrow DATA \land$
dom $(token\_map) =$ ran $(token\_seq)$

The VARIABLES clause introduces two state components: *token_seq*, which will hold a sequence of tokens in order of creation, and *token_map*, which maps each known token to its associated data.

The INVARIANT gives the types of these variables: *token_seq* is an injective[1] sequence of tokens, and *token_map* is a partial[2] mapping from tokens to data. The invariant additionally states that the tokens known to *token_map* are exactly those that appear in *token_seq*.

INITIALISATION   *token_seq* , *token_map* := [ ] , $\varnothing$

Initially both the sequence and mapping are empty.

Although the := operator looks like an assignment statement here, it is properly interpreted as a substitution, with semantics based on set theoretic notions. The initialization is a simultaneous substitution of the empty sequence for *token_seq* and the empty set for *token_map*.

DEFINITIONS   *known* $\hat{=}$ dom (*token_map*)

known is the set of all tokens currently in use. It is shorthand for the domain of *token_map*.

OPERATIONS

success , *token* $\longleftarrow$ *AddItem*(*data*) $\hat{=}$
    PRE   *data* $\in$ *DATA*   **THEN**
        CHOICE
            ANY   *new_token*
            WHERE   *new_token* $\in$ *TOKEN* $-$ *known*
            THEN
                token_seq := *token_seq* $\leftarrow$ *new_token* $\|$
                token_map (*new_token*) := *data* $\|$
                success , *token* := *TRUE* , *new_token*
            END
        OR

---

[1]In an **injective** sequence, elements only ever occur once. In this instance, the same token cannot be repeated in *token_seq*.

[2]A **partial** function need not have every possible token in its domain. In this case, not every possible token appears in the domain of *token_map*: only those that also occur in *token_seq*.

$$success := FALSE \;\|$$
$$token :\in TOKEN$$

END

END ;

AddItem takes a single argument *data*, the value of some new data, and returns two values: *success* indicating the success or failure of the operation, and *token*, the token assigned to the new data. The latter is also appended to the end of the sequence *token_seq*.

The $\|$ operator is a means of composing substitutions in parallel, which avoids the implementation concept of sequences of assignments. It is like saying that we do not care in which order these substitutions are carried out.

This operation is deliberately non-deterministic, at two levels. Firstly, it contains the CHOICE clause, offering alternative substitutions. This is to allow for failure of the operation under certain circumstances only relevant to the implementation (such as lack of memory). So either the operation is successful, the state of the machine is changed, and the return value of *success* is *TRUE*, or the operation fails, the state of the machine is unchanged, and the return value of *success* is *FALSE*.

Secondly, the successful branch is non-deterministic in its choice of the new token. The ANY clause allows the implementation to be completely free in the way it selects *new_token* from the set *TOKEN – known* (which is the set of all tokens not currently in use).

There is a similar level of non-determinism in the unsuccessful case, in that the substitution *token* $:\in TOKEN$ allows *token* to take any value from the set *TOKEN*.

DeleteItem(token) $\widehat{=}$

    PRE   *token* $\in known$ **THEN**

        $token\_seq := squash \,(\, token\_seq \rhd \{\, token \,\}\,) \;\|$

        $token\_map := \{\, token \,\} \lhd token\_map$

    END ;

DeleteItem takes a token, which must be valid, and deletes it and its corresponding data. The operation is not expected to fail.

The auxiliary function *squash*[3] is used to simplify the deletion of items from sequences.

---

[3]The definition of *squash* is deliberately hidden in another machine in this example, since its definition is not simple, and it would distract from the current purpose. It is imported from the included machine *Squash* — see the INCLUDES clause above. For a definition of the *squash* function, see Wordsworth (1992).

A sequence of length N is a total function from the set of natural numbers from 1 to N inclusive, to a set of values. Deleting an element from a sequence may leave a "hole" in its domain. To prevent this, *squash* takes a "sequence with holes" (a partial function from natural numbers to values), and turns it into a proper sequence by "shuffling" the domain down.

$success$, $data \longleftarrow OldestItem \quad \widehat{=}$

    IF $known = \varnothing$

    THEN $success := FALSE \parallel data :\in DATA$

    ELSE $success$, $data := TRUE$, $token\_map$ (first ($token\_seq$))

    END

OldestItem takes no arguments, and delivers two values: *success*, a Boolean value indicating the success or failure of the operation; and *data*, the value of the data associated with the oldest token stored (the first in the sequence).

If no items are stored, then *success* is *FALSE*, and an arbitrary data value is returned.

END

6.4.2   Implementation

The purpose of the implementation is to represent the abstract state in terms of the concrete state of some imported machines, and subsequently to propose an algorithm for each operation. Figure 6.4 illustrates the abstract state and the concrete state which we have chosen. The abstract state is a sequence of tokens mapped onto a set of data values. In the concrete state, we use a doubly linked list of elements to store the sequence of values. Elements consist of a forward link, backward link, and the data value stored. Tokens are the addresses of elements.

IMPLEMENTATION   *data_seq_1*

This is an efficient implementation of *data_seq* based around the use of a doubly linked list of values. An anchor element contains base pointers to the beginning and end of the list.

New values are linked into the list next to the anchor point, but may be deleted at random. The earliest written value (if there is one) is held in the element previous to the anchor.

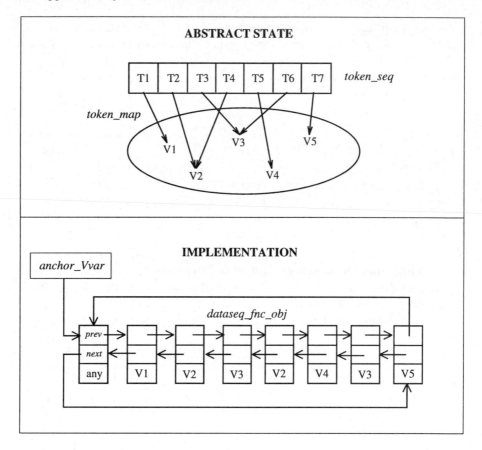

Figure 6.4 Comparison of the abstract and concrete state representations.

REFINES   *data_seq*

The REFINES clause provides the link back to the specification which this construct is intended to implement. This information is required by the analysis tools to ensure signature and type compatibility between the specification and implementation.

IMPORTS

dataseq_fnc_obj (*dataseq_FNCOBJ* ∪ *DATA* , 3 , 1001) ,
anchor_Vvar (*dataseq_FNCOBJ*) ,
Bool_TYPE

The concrete state is constructed using an instantiation of the function-object library machine, which provides storage management for fixed size units of storage, in this case the list elements. These can contain values of two types:

dataseq_FNCOBJ — tokens refering to neighbouring elements;

DATA — stored values associated with each element.

Each list element has three slots, one each for the forward and backward chaining tokens, and one for the stored data value. There are to be at most 1001 storage units: one for the anchor element, and 1000 for the list elements.

We also require a simple variable to hold the token referring to the anchor element of the doubly linked list. This is supplied by importing another machine, *anchor_Vvar*, instantiated to hold values of the correct type, *dataseq_FNCOBJ*.

CONSTANTS   *prev_index , next_index , data_index*

PROPERTIES

$TOKEN = dataseq\_FNCOBJ \wedge$

Here we make explicit the relationship between the type of the internal tokens of the specification, and the token type used by the function-object library machine. They are the same.

$prev\_index = 1 \wedge$
$next\_index = 2 \wedge$
$data\_index = 3$

We also declare constants to refer to the available slots within each list element. One each for the forward and backward chaining tokens, and one for the stored *DATA*.

INITIALISATION

VAR   *ok , anchor*   **IN**

   ok , anchor ⟵ *dataseq_CRE_FNC_OBJ* **;**

   dataseq_STO_FNC_OBJ (anchor , prev_index , anchor) **;**

   dataseq_STO_FNC_OBJ (anchor , next_index , anchor) **;**

   dataseq_STO_FNC_OBJ (anchor , data_index , any_data) **;**

   anchor_STO_VAR (anchor)

END

To initialize the machine, the anchor element is allocated, its forward and backward chaining tokens are set to point to itself, and the *any_data* value is stored in it. The anchor's token is stored in the anchor variable.

In an implementation, we use the semicolon operator to compose substitutions. This looks like sequencing of program statements, but has a well-founded semantics in set theory.

The specification of the function-object machine guarantees that this first element allocation will succeed, so in this case there is no need to test for the success of *dataseq_CRE_FNC_OBJ*.

OPERATIONS

success , *token* ⟵ *AddItem*(*data*)   ≙
    VAR   *created_ok* , *new_token* , *anchor* , *next_token*   **IN**
        created_ok , *new_token* ⟵ *dataseq_CRE_FNC_OBJ* ;
        IF   *created_ok* = *TRUE*   **THEN**
            anchor ⟵ *anchor_VAL_VAR* ;
            next_token ⟵ *dataseq_VAL_FNC_OBJ* (*anchor* , *next_index*) ;
            dataseq_STO_FNC_OBJ (*anchor* , *next_index* , *new_token*) ;
            dataseq_STO_FNC_OBJ (*new_token* , *prev_index* , *anchor*) ;
            dataseq_STO_FNC_OBJ (*new_token* , *next_index* , *next_token*) ;
            dataseq_STO_FNC_OBJ (*next_token* , *prev_index* , *new_token*) ;
            dataseq_STO_FNC_OBJ (*new_token* , *data_index* , *data*)
        END ;
        success := *created_ok* ;
        token := *new_token*
    END ;

AddItem: a new list element is allocated, and if this is successful, it is inserted into the doubly linked list next to the anchor element and the input data is stored in its value slot. The element's token is returned to the caller.

The first four calls to *dataseq_STO_FNC_OBJ* update the pointers in the new element and two existing elements. The last call stores the data value in the new element.

Here we see how the non-determinism inherent in the specification is resolved. The CHOICE depends on the success or otherwise of the new element allocation, and if successful, the ANY choice is resolved within the library machine.

DeleteItem(*token*) $\;\widehat{=}$

    VAR   *prev_token* , *next_token*   **IN**

        prev_token ⟵ *dataseq_VAL_FNC_OBJ* (*token* , *prev_index*) **;**

        next_token ⟵ *dataseq_VAL_FNC_OBJ* (*token* , *next_index*) **;**

        dataseq_STO_FNC_OBJ (*prev_token* , *next_index* , *next_token*) **;**

        dataseq_STO_FNC_OBJ (*next_token* , *prev_index* , *prev_token*) **;**

        dataseq_KIL_FNC_OBJ (*token*)

    END ;

DeleteItem: the doubly linked list implementation permits an efficient delete operation. The precondition of the abstract operation means that we can safely assume that the input refers to a valid list element, so we need not perform any checking.

The next and previous list elements are updated to chain directly to each other, and the referenced element is freed.

---

success , *data* ⟵ *OldestItem* $\widehat{=}$

    VAR   *anchor* , *first_token*   **IN**

        anchor ⟵ *anchor_VAL_VAR* **;**

        first_token ⟵ *dataseq_VAL_FNC_OBJ* (*anchor* , *prev_index*) **;**

        data ⟵ *dataseq_VAL_FNC_OBJ* (*first_token* , *data_index*) **;**

        IF   *first_token* = *anchor*

        THEN   *success* := *FALSE*

        ELSE   *success* := *TRUE*

        END

    END

OldestItem: again, the use of a doubly linked list leads to a fast retrieve of the oldest surviving list value.

If the list is non-empty, then the element previous to the anchor will be distinct from it, and will contain the required value.

If no items are stored, the anchor element points to itself. In this case, *success* takes the value *FALSE*, and the data returned is the *any_data* value stored in the anchor element.

END

Once the specification has been written, potential users of the module can use it in their programs, basing their use of it entirely on the specification. The implementor, correspondingly, can work from the specification alone, except with regard to the performance of critical operations.

Reuse of software modules is encouraged in the B-Method by the existence of documentation in the form of AMN specifications. The suitability of a module for a particular application can be checked in a number of ways: type compatibility through static analysis of the AMN, behavioural validation through animation, and formal verification through use of the proof tools.

This example has illustrated the level of formality employed in the CICS project.

Proofs of implementations were not attempted, and some of the mathematical annotations required for proof, such as refinement invariants, were not specified.

6.5   Tools support

An essential feature of this project has been the availability of a comprehensive suite of tools to support each stage of the development process. The tools used fall into two categories:

- those which constitute the base B-Toolkit, i.e.

    - analyzer/type checker,

    - animator,

    - proof tools,

    - AMN to C translator,

    - configuration manager;

- those which were developed specifically to support this project, i.e.

    - AMN to PL/X translator,

    - generator tools for CICS,

    - CICS module construction facilities,

    - a tool for the IBM mark-up language, GML.

The underlying dependency and configuration manager of the B-Toolkit is used to integrate these into a unified environment.

Tool development has proceeded in parallel with the CICS design work and there has been a significant amount of feedback from the project in this area, influencing not only the evolution of the CICS specific tools, but also parts of the base toolkit.

6.5.1   Base B tools

Here we describe very briefly the major components of the base B-Toolkit (B-Core (UK) Ltd., 1993) — those which are supplied with the commercially available version of the toolkit.

- *Analyzer/type checker.* As each new or modified AMN construct is brought into the toolkit it must be passed through the analyzer and type checker before it can be accessed by any other tool. This checks the syntax of the construct and verifies its type correctness, including consistency with any other referenced constructs.
- *Animator.* This tool allows the software designer to "execute" an AMN specification interactively to check that its behaviour matches their informal understanding of its intended function. Because of the nature of abstract specification as used in the B-Method, the designer is obliged to resolve any non-determinism as the animation session proceeds.
- *Proof obligation generator and proof tools.* Each AMN construct in a development will typically give rise to a number of proof obligations which must be discharged in order to guarantee its mathematical consistency (for a specification) or correctness (for a design). The proof obligation generator produces the proof obligations for any given construct, and then the proof tools can be invoked to attempt to discharge these obligations either automatically or interactively.
- *AMN to C translator.* When the algorithm design for the implementation of an AMN specification has been completed, the resulting AMN design can be automatically translated into C code and compiled. Eventually, when an implementation exists for each machine in the development (except library machines), the corresponding object files can be linked to produce a complete executable program.
- *Interface generator.* An AMN specification typically represents a component of a larger piece of software rather than a complete program in its own right. The interface generator will automatically generate all the code which is needed to interface to an AMN specification, allowing the designer to execute the design interactively at any level for validation purposes.
- *Reusable component library.* The B-Toolkit includes a library of general-purpose, reusable software modules comprising a set of AMN specifications, together with their implementations in C. These may be imported into the implementation of a higher-level machine, completing the refinement of that specification.

6.5.2   CICS tools

This section describes those elements of the toolkit which have been developed primarily to support the current project, under the tools development component of the contract with B-Core (UK) Ltd.

- *AMN to PL/X translator.* The base toolkit provides the ability to translate an AMN implementation into C code only. The language used for CICS development is the

IBM internal PL/X language and so an appropriate translator for AMN implementations was incorporated into the toolkit.

- *PL/X library coding tool.* In addition to the PL/X translator it was necessary to provide suitable versions of the B-Toolkit library modules. These were written by a member of the IBM team, and the integration mechanism was added to the toolkit by B-Core. Additional library machines were written to interface to other CICS components and to the MVS operating system. These PL/X implementations include not only the code to implement the operations of the specification, but also a number of associated files with additional definitions which are needed to ensure the correct integration of the code into the CICS environment.

- *Control block generator.* The base B-Toolkit includes a utility called the base generator to produce a complex specification and its AMN implementation from a high-level description of the encapsulated state, written in a special definition language. A similar facility has been provided for CICS whereby the software developer can give an abstract description of the control blocks needed in his or her design. The control block generator takes this description, and produces a specification which encapsulates access to the control block, together with a corresponding PL/X implementation.

- *CDURUN generator.* The internal interfaces between CICS components (domains) are defined using a special language called CDURUN. In order for other parts of CICS to be able to use a new component it is necessary to produce a CDURUN definition for the domain level interface. To meet this requirement a generator tool has been written which produces a CDURUN definition and an AMN specification from a high level description of the interface. An output from this tool is also used to determine the action of the final CICS module construction tool.

- *Module construction.* The physical organization of code into modules in the CICS environment typically does not correspond to the layered logical structure of a B development. Instead, a vertical partitioning is used, in which all the PL/X code needed to implement a group of top-level operations is collected into a single compilable file or module. The CICS module construction tool performs this vertical partitioning for a B development.

- *Trace formatting.* While CICS is running, execution trace entries may be appended to a log file. An offline utility program is used to interpret the trace entries, allowing CICS's internal processing to be reconstructed. A facility has been added to the B-Toolkit to add trace entries semiautomatically into the PL/X generated from AMN implementations, and to produce the corresponding trace interpretation code.

- *Dump formatting.* If an error occurs during CICS execution, or if explicitly requested, a storage dump is written to disk. A utility program is used to reconstruct the state of each CICS component at the time that the dump was taken. A facility has been added to the B-Toolkit to generate code automatically for this utility.

- *Code annotation.* CICS maintenance requires code to be well annotated. The B-Toolkit translation process has been extended by adding facilities that produce automatic annotation, hence increasing the traceability of program fragments back to AMN designs.

- *The GML mark-up tool.* The base B-Toolkit produces formatted output documents in the form of LATEX source; however, IBM uses its own proprietary mark-up language, GML, for its documentation. It has therefore been necessary to add an option to the toolkit to produce GML output instead of LATEX.

It is important to note that whilst the above tools have been described as though they are all distinct components operating independently, they do, in fact, form an integral package with significant interdependencies. For example, the translators and code generators produce output conforming to the CICS library format, the CDURUN tool produces a definition file which is subsequently used by the module construction tool when building the final outputs, and the trace and dump formatting facilities span the libraries, code generation and module construction tools.

The CICS specific tools have all been incorporated into the same dependency and configuration management environment as the base tools in the B-Toolkit.

Figure 6.5 shows how the various tools specific to the IBM project interact and the entities that they exchange. Processes appear as diamond shapes; objects acted upon by those processes as rectangles. The rounded box marked "Layered Design Process" embodies all the other work carried out within the base tools of the B-Toolkit.

6.6   Project evaluation

In this section we summarize the results of the project to date, and evaluate the success of the approach adopted for the development of CICS. At the time of writing, the project is still underway, and it is therefore not possible to give a definitive evaluation of its commercial success at this stage. We can, however, describe the current state of the project, and its achievements, and review those aspects of the work which have been particularly challenging.

In spite of the incremental approach adopted in the project in which tool development proceeded in parallel with software design, the achievements of the project can best be described in two parts: the enhancements to the B-Toolkit, and the design of the new CICS component.

The toolkit has been extended with the following facilities:

- an AMN to PL/X translator;
- a coding tool for PL/X library functions;
- a control block generator, with tracing and dump formatting support;
- a CICS module construction tool;
- a CDURUN generator, integrated with the module construction tool;
- a GML mark-up tool for the production of documents.

The state of the project at the time of writing is that an almost complete system is running in the CICS environment. There have been a number of major stages in the development process.

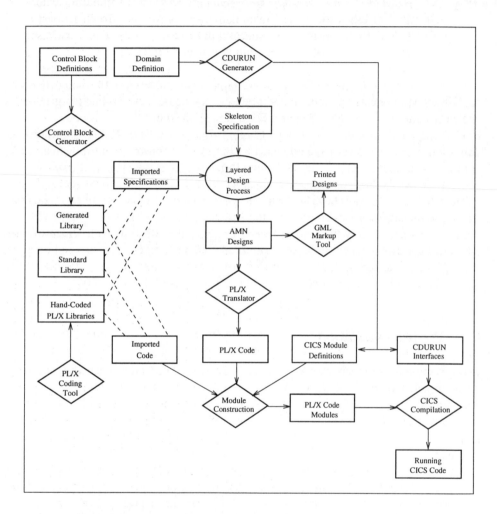

Figure 6.5 Work flow between the project-specific tools.

1. A simulation of the new operating system feature which would form the basis for the final system was specified and implemented in AMN. This enabled the first designs to be completed and tested prior to the delivery of the actual operating system code.

2. A prototype design for the new component was developed, based on the simulation described above and other B-Toolkit library functions. By using the standard B-Toolkit facilities for C code generation, this allowed the design to be tested in the UNIX environment before porting to CICS.

3. The simulated platform and prototype design were ported, without modification, into PL/X by supplying appropriate implementations for the B-Toolkit library modules. This ported prototype was successfully integrated into CICS and used by other teams for their early testing.
4. The actual operating system code was delivered, and it was encapsulated in the form of a library module, to replace the temporary simulated platform and its AMN implementation. This change required no modification to the design of the new component.
5. The prototype design was reworked to cater for concurrency, and other differences between CICS functions and those of the B-Toolkit library, such as the use of the CICS storage manager in place of the B-Toolkit function object machine.
6. Additional functions were implemented which were absent from the original specification and early prototype.

The remaining work consists primarily of incorporating into the development various housekeeping and diagnostic functions required in all CICS domains.

6.6.1 Technical issues

An undertaking to provide a new tool-supported software development process could not realistically have proceeded without challenges during its course. The most significant of these arose from four main factors.

1. *The need for modifications to the B-Toolkit to cater for CICS.* The CICS-specific elements of the toolkit were developed at the same time as the design of the software itself, and so requirements for enhancement of the toolkit arose during the course of design work, and the toolkit had to be modified accordingly. Because of this, modifications to the PL/X library code also had to be made to keep it in step with the latest tools development. These additional factors created much unplanned work in the face of stringent deadlines. In retrospect it would have been preferable if the early stages of the project had concentrated on building the CICS extensions to the toolkit, perhaps basing requirements around the development of a small, well-understood example design, before beginning the main design phase.
2. *Inconsistencies between the functionality of the PL/X and C libraries.* Early in the project it was noticed that the functionality provided by the B-Toolkit library modules was very close to that which could be readily provided by encapsulated software modules in the CICS environment. The early design work was therefore based on the toolkit library, allowing the prototypes to be completed comparatively quickly and tested in the UNIX environment. Later, it transpired that there were subtle differences between the B library functions and those which were available within the CICS programming environment, some relating to concurrency. This meant that in the production of the final designs intended for use in CICS the prototype had to be substantially reworked. A preferable approach would have been

to specify and implement in AMN the precise functionality which could be made available in the target environment, allowing testing under UNIX and direct portability to CICS.

3. *The concurrent processing inherent in CICS*. The B-Method is not designed to deal formally with the complexities of programming for a concurrent environment. Initially, some attempts were made to find a simple way of treating concurrency issues in the design, but no satisfactory approach was found which could be used as a basis for extending the B-Toolkit. A pragmatic approach was adopted eventually whereby the synchronization primitives available in the CICS environment were encapsulated within library modules with skeleton specifications, thus making them available from AMN implementations.

4. *The requirement for code level maintainability*. One of the main intentions of the B-Method is that, through the use of translators for the generation of code, maintenance of the resulting software can be carried out at the design level: designs are modified, and the code is regenerated. The nature of CICS, however, means that it is not practical to consider maintaining parts of the overall system in such a radically different manner. It was necessary, therefore, to make a considerable investment in annotation tools so that the generated code could be maintained using the standard CICS service procedures.

6.6.2   Research issues

The use of the B-Method on the current project has highlighted a number of areas where further research is required to increase the applicability of formal methods, and these are described below.

Concurrency. The integration of state-based modelling techniques with process algebras is a theoretically difficult area currently under study by a number of research groups (Hoare, 1985; Jones, 1990; Morgan, 1994). Until a standard method has emerged from these efforts, tool support for a proper treatment of concurrency will not be possible.

Data sharing. Conventional programming techniques sometimes result in a violation of the strict encapsulation rules which are inherent in rigorous object-oriented approaches such as the B-Method. These techniques amount to the exploitation of side effects for efficiency reasons. Research is required to study this problem, and to find means of accommodating such techniques in the method.

Multiple refinement. This refers to the implementation of more than one abstract component by a single implementation. More work is needed to confirm that a corresponding change to the method presents no fundamental difficulty.

Type confusion. Because the B-Method supports design right down to the code level, a system is required whereby the rich type environment of an abstract specification can be mapped into the primitive types available at the machine level.

An example of type confusion can be found in the example implementation given in Section 6.4.2 where, in the IMPORTS clause, the *dataseq_fnc_obj* machine is instantiated with the union of two incompatible types.

Although a mechanism supporting this technique is built into the B-Toolkit, its mathematical basis is not well understood, and research is needed to establish a sound theoretical foundation for its use.

6.7   Conclusions

Formal methods will undoubtedly continue to play an important role in the software development process at Hursley. During the last ten years a considerable body of experience in formal methods has been built up, and in more recent times new education initiatives have begun to implant an extended awareness of the benefits of formal techniques amongst the programming community at Hursley.

The B-Method was not introduced in the absence of any prior formal methods experience: the Z notation was already in use for specification within CICS/ESA. However, as applied in the current project, the B-Method has extended the use of formal methods much further into the design process. Whilst the pseudoprogramming syntax used in AMN makes it more suitable than Z for the design of actual software modules, the primary benefit of the B-Method and B-Toolkit is that they have been designed specifically to support the complete software development process, from specification to code.

The use of advanced tools to assist in the process of software development is essential if improved productivity is to be achieved in the production of high quality large-scale systems. Such tools can be applied to good effect even where formal verification is not part of the development process, or where only certain critical components of a system are subjected to rigorous analysis: the benefits derived from the application of the B-Method and B-Toolkit in this project have not been due to the pursuit of formal proof, but to the availability of automated support.

The extended application of formal methods to the CICS project has certainly presented considerable challenges, and a major contributory factor in overcoming them has been the close and productive collaboration between IBM and B-Core (UK) Ltd. Taken together, the experiences on this project so far have demonstrated that some formal methods have reached a level of maturity where they can be realistically applied to industrial-scale software development.

Chapter 7

Formal Verification of the AAMP5 Microprocessor

Mandayam K. Srivas and Steven P. Miller

7.1 Introduction

Software and digital hardware are increasingly being used in situations where failure could be life threatening, such as in aircraft, nuclear power plants, weapon systems, and medical instrumentation. Several authors have demonstrated the infeasibility of showing that such systems meet ultrahigh reliability requirements through testing alone (Butler and Finelli, 1993; Littlewood and Strigini, 1993). Formal methods are a promising approach for increasing our confidence in digital systems, but many questions remain as to how they can be used effectively in an industrial setting.

This chapter describes a project, specifically the formal verification of the microcode in the AAMP5 microprocessor, conducted to explore how formal techniques for specification and verification could be introduced into an industrial process. Sponsored by the Systems Validation Branch of NASA Langley and Collins Commercial Avionics, a division of Rockwell International, it was conducted by Collins and the Computer Science Laboratory at SRI International. The project consisted of specifying a portion of a Rockwell proprietary microprocessor, the AAMP5, at both the instruction set and the register-transfer levels, in the PVS language developed by SRI (Owre et al., 1993), and using the PVS theorem prover (Owre *et al.*, 1992; Shankar *et al.*, 1993) to show that the microcode correctly implemented the specified behaviour for a representative subset of instructions.

The central result of this project was to demonstrate the feasibility of formally specifying a commercial microprocessor and the use of mechanical proofs of correctness to verify microcode. This result is particularly significant since the AAMP5 was not designed for formal verification, but rather to provide a more than threefold performance improvement while retaining object-code compatibility with the earlier AAMP2. As a consequence, the AAMP5 is one of the most complex microprocessors to which formal methods have yet been applied.

Besides demonstrating the verification of a subset of AAMP5 microcode, an equally important accomplishment of the project was the development of a methodology that can be used by practicing engineers to apply formal verification technology to a complex microprocessor design. This includes techniques for decomposing the microprocessor veri-

125

fication problem into a set of verification conditions that the engineers can formulate and strategies to automate the proof of the verification conditions.

This methodology was used to verify formally a core set of eleven AAMP5 instructions representative of several instruction classes. Although the number of instructions verified is small, the methodology and the formal machinery developed are adequate to cover most of the remaining AAMP5 microcode. The success of this project has lead to a sequel in which the same methodology is being reused to verify another member of the AAMP family.

Another key result was the discovery of both actual and seeded errors. Two actual microcode errors were discovered during development of the formal specification, illustrating the value of simply creating a precise specification. Two additional errors seeded by Collins in the microcode were systematically uncovered by SRI while performing correctness proofs. One of these was an actual error that had been discovered by Collins after first fabrication but left in the microcode provided to SRI. The other error was designed to be unlikely to be detected by walk-throughs, testing, or simulation.

Several other results emerged during the project, including the ease with which practicing engineers became comfortable with PVS, the need for libraries of general-purpose theories, the usefulness of formal specification in revealing errors, the natural fit between formal specification and inspections, the difficulty of selecting the best style of specification for a new problem domain, the high level of assurance provided by proofs of correctness, and the need to engineer proof strategies for reuse.

7.2 Background

NASA Langley's research programme in formal methods (Butler, 1991) was established to bring formal methods technology to a sufficiently mature level for use by the United States aerospace industry. Besides the in-house development of a formally verified reliable computing platform, RCP (Di Vito *et al.*, 1990), NASA has sponsored a variety of demonstration projects to apply formal methods to critical subsystems of real aerospace computer systems.

The Computer Science Laboratory of SRI International has been involved in the development and application of formal methods for more than 20 years. The formal verification systems EHDM and the more advanced PVS were both developed at SRI. Both EHDM and PVS have been used to perform several verifications of significant difficulty, most notably in the field of fault-tolerant architectures and hardware designs. Recently, SRI has been actively involved in investigating ways to transfer formal verification technology to industry.

Collins Commercial Avionics is a division of Rockwell International and one of the largest suppliers of communications and avionics systems for commercial transport and general aviation aircraft. Collins' interest in formal methods dates from 1991 when it participated in the MCC Formal Methods Transition Study (Gerhart *et al.*, 1991). As a result of this study, Collins initiated several small pilot projects to explore the use of formal methods, with verification of the AAMP5 microcode being the latest and most ambitious in the series.

7.2.1   AAMP family of microprocessors

The Advanced Architecture Microprocessor (AAMP) consists of a Rockwell proprietary family of microprocessors based on the Collins Adaptive Processor System (CAPS) originally developed in 1972 (Best *et al.*, 1982; Rockwell International, 1990). The AAMP architecture is specifically designed for use with block-structured, high-level languages, such as Ada, in real-time embedded applications. It is based on a stack architecture and provides hardware support for many features normally provided by the compiler run-time environment, such as procedure state saving, parameter passage, return linkage, and re-entrancy. The AAMP also simplifies the real-time executive by implementing in hardware such functions as interrupt handling, task state saving, and context switching. Use of internal registers holding the top few elements of the stack provides the AAMP family with performance that rivals or exceeds that of most commercially available 16-bit microprocessors.

The original CAPS architecture, a multiboard minicomputer, was developed in 1972 and was quickly followed by the CAPS-2 through CAPS-10. In 1981, the original AAMP consolidated all CAPS functions except memory on a single integrated circuit. It was followed by the AAMP2, AAMP3, and AAMP5. Members of the CAPS–AAMP family have been used in an impressive variety of Collins products and other avionics applications, including the Boeing 737, 747, 757, and 767.

The AAMP5 was designed as an object-code compatible replacement for the earlier AAMP2 (Rockwell International, 1990), with advanced implementation techniques such as pipelining providing a more than threefold performance improvement. The AAMP5 is designed for use in critical applications such as avionics displays, but is not intended for use in ultracritical systems such as autoland or fly-by-wire.

7.2.2   PVS

PVS (Prototype Verification System) (Shankar *et al.*, 1993) is an environment for specification and verification that has been developed at SRI International's Computer Science Laboratory. In comparison with other widely used verification systems, such as HOL (Gordon and Melham, 1993) and the Boyer–Moore prover (Boyer and Moore, 1979), the distinguishing characteristic of PVS is that it supports both a highly expressive specification language and a very effective interactive theorem prover in which most of the low-level proof steps are automated. The system consists of a specification language, a parser, a typechecker, and an interactive proof checker. The PVS specification language is based on higher-order logic with a richly expressive type system so that a number of semantic errors in specifications can be caught by the typechecker. The PVS prover consists of a powerful collection of inference steps that can be used to reduce a proof goal to simpler subgoals that can be discharged automatically by the primitive proof steps of the prover. The primitive proof steps involve, among other things, the use of arithmetic and equality decision procedures, automatic rewriting, and BDD-based Boolean simplification.

7.2.3   Historical perspective and the scale of the challenge

Microprogram verification has much in common with processor verification, in that both relate the programmer's view of a processor to its hardware implementation. A number of microprocessor designs have been formally verified (Beatty and Bryant, 1994; Carter *et al.*, 1978; Cook, 1986; Hunt, 1994; Saxe *et al.*, 1994; Srivas and Bickford, 1990; Windley, 1990). However, the AAMP5 is significantly more complex, at both the macro- and microarchitecture levels, than any other processor for which formal verification has yet been attempted; it has a large, complex instruction set, multiple data types and addressing modes, and a microcoded, pipelined implementation. Of these, the pipeline and autonomous instruction and data fetching present special challenges. One measure of the complexity of a processor is the size of its implementation. In the case of the AAMP5, this is some 500 000 transistors, compared with some tens of thousands in previous formally verified designs and 3.1 million in an Intel Pentium (Intel Corporation, 1993).

Microcode verification is not new: it was pioneered by Bill Carter at IBM in the 1970s and applied to elements of NASA's Standard Spaceborne Computer (Leeman *et al.*, 1974); in the 1980s a group at the Aerospace Corporation verified microcode for an implementation of the C/30 switching computer using a verification system called SDVS (Cook, 1986); and a group at Inmos in the UK established correctness across two levels of description (in Occam) of the microcode for the T800 floating-point unit using mechanized transformations. Similarly, several groups have performed automated verification of non-microcoded processors, of which Warren Hunt's FM8501 (Hunt, 1994) and subsequent FM9000 (Hunt and Brock, 1992) are among the most substantial. The problems of pipeline correctness were also studied previously by Srivas and Bickford (1990), Saxe *et al.* (1994), Burch and Dill (1994), and Windley and Coe (1994). A very simple microcoded processor design developed by Mike Gordon called "Tamarack" serves as something of a benchmark for microprogram verification and was considered quite a challenge not so long ago (Joyce, 1988). PVS is able to verify the microcode of Tamarack and Saxe's pipelined processor completely automatically in about five minutes (Cyrluk *et al.*, 1994).

7.3   Project goals and organization

Formal verification of the AAMP5 microcode was selected for this project for a number of reasons. Both Collins and SRI wanted to explore the usefulness of formal verification on an example that was large enough to provide realistic insight, yet small enough to be completed at reasonable cost. Verification of the AAMP5 microcode fitted these crite-ria well. While the AAMP5 was one of the most complex microprocessors Collins had built, its requirements were well understood since it was to be object-code compatible with the earlier AAMP2. This allowed the formal methods team to concentrate on for-mal specification and verification rather than on designing a new product. Also, much of the complexity of an AAMP microprocessor resides in the microcode, and past expe-rience has shown that this is one of the most difficult parts of the microprocessor to get right. Success with formal verification in other significant projects suggested that this technology might be ready for application to an industrial microprocessor.

7.3.1 Project organization

Because of the importance of the AAMP5 to Collins' product line, the formal specifi-cation and verification of the AAMP5 were performed as a shadow project and did not replace any of the normal design and verification activities performed on a new micro-processor. This parallel approach also allowed us to relax some of the steps that would be required on a production project and focus instead on the application of formal methods. To fit the scope of the project to the time available, a core set of 13 instructions, each rep-resentative of a class of AAMP instructions, was identified to be specified and verified by SRI. An additional set of 11 instructions was identified to be specified and verified by Collins as time permitted. Even so, it was necessary to specify the entire AAMP5 archi-tecture and to develop the infrastructure needed to verify the entire instruction set since the core set contained at least one member from each of the major instruction classes.

A summary of the level of effort is presented in Table 7.1. As can be seen, relatively little time was spent on training the Collins' engineers in PVS. The small amount of struc-tured training needed was one of the surprises of the project. Early on, SRI conducted a one-week course on the use of PVS and formal specifications at the Collins Cedar Rapids facility for the five engineers who would be involved with the project. The course con-sisted of five half-day lectures with related laboratory exercises in the afternoon. No ad-ditional formal training seemed necessary. When new team members joined the project, they were provided access to the PVS documentation and trained by inclusion in review of the PVS specifications. The most effective form of education seemed to be hands-on development with frequent peer review.

Apart from overall management and education, the project split naturally into three phases: specification of the macroarchitecture (Section 7.4), specification of the microar-chitecture (Section 7.5), and proofs of correctness of the microcode (Section 7.6). The basic process followed in the first two phases was that Collins would provide design spec-ifications to SRI, SRI would provide first drafts of PVS specifications to Collins, and Collins would informally review these specifications and return comments to SRI for re-vision. At some point, the Collins team would take the specifications, prepare them for formal inspections (Fagan, 1986), conduct the inspections, correct the defects found, and send the revised specifications back to SRI. This approach was chosen both to validate the correctness of the specifications and to ensure that Collins personnel became actively

Table 7.1 Level of effort

Task	Performed	Start	Stop	Hours
Project management				
Planning and monitoring	Collins	Jan 93	Aug 94	123
Education				
PVS Course	Collins	Feb 93	Feb 93	125
	SRI	Feb 93	Feb 93	68
Specification of the macroarchitecture (2550 lines of PVS)				
Initial development	Collins	Mar 93	May 93	172
	SRI	Mar 93	May 93	360
Revision and extension	Collins	May 93	Sept 93	289
	SRI	May 93	Sept 93	120
Inspection	Collins	Sept 93	Feb 94	96
Resolve inspection issues	Collins	Feb 94	May 94	64
Revision to support proofs	Collins	Mar 94	Aug 94	54
Specification of the microarchitecture (2679 lines of PVS)				
Initial development	Collins	May 93	Feb 94	137
	SRI	May 93	Feb 94	520
Revision	Collins	Feb 94	Aug 94	160
	SRI	Feb 94	Aug 94	120
Inspection	Collins	Mar 94	Aug 94	83
Resolve inspection issues	Collins	Mar 94	Aug 94	66
Translate microcode to PVS	Collins	Jun 94	Aug 94	21
Revision to support proofs	Collins	Jun 94	Aug 94	12
Proofs of correctness				
Development of correctness criteria	SRI	Mar 94	Jun 94	320
Developing proof infrastructure	SRI	May 94	Aug 94	240
Verification of core instructions	SRI	Jun 94	Aug 94	240

involved in developing the PVS specifications. A similar process was followed for performing proofs of correctness of the microcode, with SRI providing the first examples and strategies that Collins would use on similar instructions.

To reduce the potential for missing errors in the microcode due to errors in the PVS specifications, independent teams were assigned to different portions of the project. While all early drafts of the specifications were produced by SRI, different individuals at Collins were assigned to review and revise the macroarchitecture and microarchitecture specifications. Different teams were also used to inspect the macroarchitecture and the microarchitecture. The microcode itself was produced by a member of the original AAMP5 team without any knowledge of the formal specifications and translated into PVS by yet another individual. As a result, the process of proving the microcode correct often revealed errors in the specifications, but once a proof was completed, confidence in the correctness of the associated microcode was high.

7.4   The macroarchitecture: programmer's view of the AAMP5

In this section, we first give an informal description of the AAMP5 macroinstruction architecture and then present its formal specification. Important features of the AAMP macroarchitecture include its organization of memory, process stack, internal registers that affect its observable behaviour, instruction set, and support for multitasking and error handling. These are discussed in the following sections. A more detailed discussion can be found in Best *et al.* (1982).

7.4.1   The AAMP5 macroarchitecture: informal view

The AAMP provides separate address spaces for code memory and data memory. While not required by the AAMP architecture, code memory is typically implemented in ROM. Both code and data memory are segmented, with code memory organized into 512 code environments, each containing 64K 8-bit bytes of code. Data memory is organized into 256 data environments, each containing 64K 16-bit words of data. Actual memory addresses are formed by concatenating a 9-bit code environment pointer (CENV) with a 16-bit program counter for instruction addresses, or an 8-bit data environment pointer (DENV) with a 16-bit offset for data addresses. The processor also provides data-transfer status lines which can be used by an external memory management unit for protection against improper accesses to memory, allowing code fetches to be distinguished from data accesses and executive task accesses to be distinguished from user task accesses.

Process stack
The process stack is central to the AAMP macroarchitecture, implementing in hardware many of the features needed to support high-level block-structured languages and multitasking. Each task maintains a single process stack in the task's data environment. Many of the internal registers maintained by the AAMP are used to define the process stack. The DENV (data environment) register contains the pointer to the data environment of the current active task. The TOS (top of stack) register points to the topmost word in the process stack and the SKLM (stack limit) register points to the lower limit beyond which the stack is not allowed to grow (the stack grows downward in memory). The LENV (local environment) register points to the local environment of the current procedure and is used in addressing local variables. The CENV (code environment) and PC (program counter) registers point to the code environment and address of the next instruction to be executed.

Internal registers
Many of the internal registers maintained by the AAMP are used to define the process stack. The DENV (data environment) register contains the pointer to the data environment of the current active task. The TOS (top of stack) register points to the topmost word in the process stack and the SKLM (stack limit) register points to the lower limit beyond

which the stack is not allowed to grow. The LENV (local environment) register points to the local environment of the current procedure and is used in addressing local variables. The CENV (code environment) and PC (program counter) registers point to the code environment and address of the next instruction to be executed. Finally, the AAMP maintains two Boolean flags, a USER flag to indicate whether the processor is in user or executive mode, and the INTE flag indicating whether or not the maskable interrupt is enabled (see below).

The AAMP instruction set is large and CISC like. It closely resembles the intermediate-level output of many compilers, directly supporting high-level language constructs such as procedure calls and returns. The instructions vary in length from 8 to 56 bits, although most are only 8 bits long, yielding improved throughput and code density.

The instruction set supports a variety of data types, including 16- and 32-bit integer, 16- and 32-bit fractional, 32- and 48-bit floating-point, and 16-bit logical variables. The floating-point formats have an 8-bit, excess-128 exponent and, respectively, 24 and 40 bits of fractional mantissa. Addition, subtraction, multiplication, division, and type conversions are provided for all of the arithmetic types. Computational exceptions, such as arithmetic overflow and divide-by-zero, are detected and handled automatically.

The original AAMP had 153 instructions. The AAMP5 has 209, which can be divided into several classes. Of these, 72 are Reference or Assign instructions that move data between the top of the process stack and data memory. The logical, arithmetic, relational, type conversion, shift, rotate, and field classes account for another 81 instructions, each of which performs a prescribed operation on the top few elements of the process stack and pushes the result back onto the stack. An additional 20 instructions deal with program control, such as branch, loop, call, and return instructions. The remaining 31 instructions are used for block data memory transfers, pushing literals on the stack, locating operands in the stack, and miscellaneous functions.

Multitasking and error handling

The AAMP stack architecture is designed for real-time multitasking applications, wherein the processor is time shared among two or more concurrent tasks. Each task maintains its own process stack in its assigned data environment. Most multitasking operations, including context switching, are performed automatically by the AAMP. Since many errors generate a context switch to executive mode, the multitasking and error-handling features of the AAMP are closely intertwined.

Scheduling of user tasks is performed by an executive task assigned to code environment 0 and data environment 0. During execution, the executive selects one of several user tasks to be activated or resumed, then executes a RETURN instruction from its outer procedure. This causes the AAMP to transfer control to the selected user task. Normal execution of a user task can be suspended by an exception, an external interrupt, a trap, or an outer procedure return.

Exceptions are erroneous events, such as arithmetic overflow, that are primarily relevant to the user task currently executing. These are handled by the AAMP within the context of the user task, i.e. a context switch to the executive is not initiated. When an exception is detected, the exception error code is placed on the task's process stack and the AAMP calls the appropriate exception handler.

External hardware interrupts and traps differ from exceptions in that they are handled in executive mode and initiate a transfer of control to the executive, which schedules the appropriate interrupt or trap handler. External interrupts may arrive at any time during an instruction execution, and are recognized on master clock boundaries. Four interrupts are supported. Reset (RST) and memory transfer errors (XER) are processed immediately. The maskable interrupt (IRQ) and the non-maskable interrupt (NMI) are held pending completion of the current instruction.

Traps are handled in a manner very similar to interrupts, initiating a context switch to the executive, which schedules the appropriate trap handler. Traps come in two varieties. A "hardware" trap is generated when the AAMP detects an error that must be processed in executive mode, such as stack overflow. "Software" traps are generated when the user process executes a TRAP instruction to request an executive service such as masking interrupts or transfering control to another user task. A user task may also suspend its execution by executing an outer procedure return. An outer procedure return from a user task is handled in the same way as a trap.

Finally, normal execution of the executive can be suspended by detection of an unrecoverable error, such as overflow of the executive stack, while in executive mode. Such errors initiate a context switch to the executive error handler. If the executive error handler is undefined or an unrecoverable error is detected while in the executive error handler, the AAMP is forced into an idle loop pending a reset.

7.4.2   The macroarchitecture formal specification

The macroarchitecture specification formalizes an assembly-level programmer's view of the AAMP and its instruction set, hiding most of the internal state and pipelining of the processor. The PVS specification of the AAMP models the processor as a state machine: the state of the macromachine includes external memory and the internal state that affects its observable behaviour, such as the internal registers defining the process stack; the next state function specifies the effect of executing the "current" instruction pointed to by the program counter.

An overview of the import chain for the macroarchitecture specification is shown in Figure 7.1. In PVS, a theory gains access to another theory's definitions and axioms by importing that theory. Each box in the figure represents a theory in the specification. Importation of a theory is depicted by an arrow from the importing theory to the imported theory.

At the topmost level is the `normal_macro_machine` theory that defines the behaviour of the AAMP in the absence of interrupts and unrecoverable errors such as stack overflow. The `next_macro_state` function for each instruction class is specified in an `update` theory for that class. Some instructions, such as the `branch` instructions, are simple enough that they can be defined directly in terms of changes to the macromachine

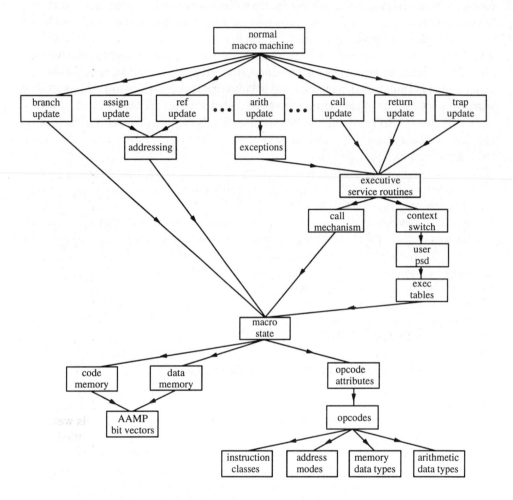

Figure 7.1 Macroarchitecture specification hierarchy.

state defined in the `macro_state` theory. More complex instructions require additional definitions provided in supporting theories. For example, the `assign` (assignment) and `ref` (reference) instructions import the `addressing` theory that determines the source or target data memory address based on the addressing mode of the current instruction. Instructions that can raise exceptions require the definitions found in the `exceptions` theory. CALL, RETURN, and instructions that require executive services cause the most complex changes to the macrostate and import a family of theories defining the executive services provided by the AAMP.

The `macro_state` theory defines the state of the macromachine and functions useful in manipulating that state. This includes the internal registers that affect the observable behavior of the AAMP and instantiations of memory defined in the `code_memory` and data_memory theories. The AAMP_bit_vectors theory imports the bit_vectors library, adding to it the specific bit vectors found in the AAMP such as words and bytes. To simplify the import chain, the macro_state theory also imports the enumeration of the instructions, or opcodes, of the AAMP and their attributes. Representative samples of this hierarchy are discussed in the following sections, beginning with the theories lowest in the hierarchy. It should be noted that the PVS theories shown in this report have been edited to remove material not relevant to the text.

Data and code memory

The PVS specification of data memory is shown in Figure 7.2. AAMP data memory is organized into 256 possible data environments, each containing 64K 16-bit words of data. Data memory itself is defined as a function from 8-bit data environment pointers to data environments, where each data environment is another function from 16-bit data environment addresses to 16-bit words of memory. Standard bit vectors used in the AAMP, such as 16-bit words, are defined in the imported AAMP_bit_vectors theory, which also defines operations over bit vectors such as concatenation and extraction of bits. The specification of data memory also introduces unspecified constants of type data environment pointer and data environment address used in later theories.

The specification of code memory is similar except that code memory is organized into 512 possible code environments, each containing 64K 8-bit bytes.

Macroarchitecture state

The macrostate defines the minimal view of the AAMP's state an application programmer must understand to write assembly code. Choosing the best representation is important since its form heavily influences the rest of the specification. Several models were considered, each with its own advantages and disadvantages. In the end, we settled on the simple structure shown in Figure 7.3, largely because this seemed to reflect best the view of the AAMP designers.

The macrostate is defined as a record type with several fields. Code memory and data memory are defined separately, since this is the conceptual model presented to a programmer. While it is possible for an external memory unit to implement code and data memory in the same address space, and even to overlap code and data memory, code memory is normally implemented in ROM and is physically distinct from data memory.

The remaining items in the macrostate define the CENV, PC, DENV, SKLM, LENV registers and the USER and INTE flags discussed in Section 7.4.1. The macrostate theory also defines a number of auxiliary functions that manipulate the macrostate to make later theories more readable. For example, push pushes a word on the current process stack.

The next state function

The next state function (next_macro_state) takes an arbitrary macrostate and returns the macrostate that would result after the current instruction is executed. The next state function is defined for each instruction class in an update theory for that class. For

```
% The data_memory theory defines the AAMP's view of data memory.
% Data memory is organized into 256 possible data environments,
% each addressed by an 8-bit data environment pointer.
% Each data environment contains 64K words of data,
% each addressed by a 16-bit data environment relative address.

data_memory: THEORY
BEGIN

  IMPORTING AAMP_bit_vectors

  % A data environment address is a 16-bit word.
  data_env_addr: TYPE = word

  % An unspecified constant data environment address
  unspecified_data_env_addr: data_env_addr

  % A data environment is a function from data environment
  % addresses to words of memory.
  data_env: TYPE = [data_env_addr -> word]

  % A data environment pointer is a bit vector of size 8.
  data_env_ptr: TYPE = bvec[8]

  % An unspecified constant data environment pointer.
  unspecified_data_env_ptr: data_env_ptr

  % Data memory is defined as a function from data environment
  % pointers to data environments.
  data_memory: TYPE = [data_env_ptr -> data_env]

  % Converts a word to a data environment pointer.
  word2denv(wd: word): data_env_ptr = wd^(7,0)

  denv2word(denv: data_env_ptr): word = zero_extend[8](16)(denv)

END data_memory
```

Figure 7.2 PVS specification of AAMP data memory.

example, the next state function for reference instructions is defined in the `ref_update` theory and for arithmetic instructions in the `arith_update` theory.

The text of the `arith_update` theory that helps specify the `next_macro_state` function for the arithmetic instructions is shown in Figure 7.4. Arithmetic instructions perform a specific operation, such as addition or subtraction, on the top few elements of the accumulator stack and push the results onto the stack after consuming the operands. Two functions are used in the definition of the `next_macro_state` function for the arithmetic operations. The `exception_number` function determines whether the instruction will result in an exception given the current macrostate. The `normal_result`

```
% The macro state theory defines the state of internal registers
% in the AAMP, code memory, and data memory. Basic operations
% based on the combined state of these registers and memory are
% also defined here.

macro_state: THEORY

BEGIN
  IMPORTING opcodes_attributes, code_memory, data_memory

  % The macro state of the AAMP consists of code memory, data
  % memory, the user/executive mode indicator, the interrupt
  % enabled indicator, the cenv, pc, denv, sklm, lenv,
  % and tos registers.

  macro_state: TYPE = [# cmem  : code_memory,
                         dmem  : data_memory,
                         user  : bool,
                         inte  : bool,
                         cenv  : word,
                         pc    : word,
                         denv  : word,
                         sklm  : word,
                         lenv  : word,
                         tos   : word #]

  % Pushes a word on the process stack. If the stack is full,
  % tos is decremented but the word is not written.
  push(wd:word, st:macro_state):macro_state =
    IF tos(st) > sklm(st)    THEN
        st WITH [(dmem)(word2denv(denv(st)))(tos(st)-1) := wd,
                 (tos)  := tos(st) - 1 ]
      ELSE
        st WITH [(tos)  := tos(st) - 1 ]
      ENDIF
                          ...
END macro_state
```

Figure 7.3 The AAMP5 macrostate.

function defines the change in state returned by the `next_macro_state` function when an exception does not occur. If an exception does occur, this state and the exception number are given as parameters to the `exception_macro_state` function, defined in the `exceptions` theory, that pushes the exception number on top of the (erroneous) result and invokes the exception handler. The auxiliary functions of `push`, `multipop`, and `data_memory_ref` (defined in the imported `macro_state` theory) are used to define the change to the macrostate.

Note that the argument to the `next_macro_state` function is of type `arith_state`. This subtype is defined immediately following the `IMPORTING` clause. Its use causes PVS to generate a type correctness condition, or TCC, requiring

```
% The arith_update theory defines the change on the macro state
% caused by arithmetic instructions in the absence of stack overflow.
% The instruction result is computed and pushed on the stack.
% If the instruction results in an exception, the state defined by
% the exceptions theory is returned.
 arith_update: THEORY

BEGIN

  IMPORTING exceptions

  % Subtype of macro state in which current instruction is an
  % arithmetic instruction.
  arith_state: TYPE =
   {st: macro_state|
            instruction_class_of(current_opcode(st)) = arithmetic}

  % Returns the exception number associated with an instruction.
  % Zero is used to indicate the absence of an exception.
  exception_number(st:arith_state): below[29] =
    LET nstkwds = number_of_stack_words(current_opcode(st)),
        args    = top_elements(st,nstkwds)
     IN IF current_opcode(st) = ADD THEN
            IF overflow(args(0), args(1)) THEN 7 ELSE 0 ENDIF
        ELSIF current_opcode(st) = ADDD THEN
            IF overflow(args(1) o args(0), args(3) o args(2))
                     THEN 8 ELSE 0 ENDIF
        ELSE 0 ENDIF

  % Returns normal result obtained in the absence of an exception.
  % Arguments to the instruction are popped from the stack, results
  % are pushed on the and the PC advanced to the next instruction.
  normal_result(st: arith_state): macro_state =
    LET nstkwds = number_of_stack_words(current_opcode(st)),
        args    = top_elements(st, nstkwds),
        popped  = multipop(st, nstkwds)
     IN IF current_opcode(st) = ADD THEN
            push(args(0) + args(1), popped)
        ELSIF current_opcode(st) = ADDD THEN
            LET result = (args(1) o args(0)) + (args(3) o args(2))
            IN push(result^(31, 16), push(result^(15, 0), popped))
        ELSE st  ENDIF WITH [(pc) := next_pc(st)]

  % Returns the next macro state for an arithmetic instruction.
  next_macro_state(st: arith_state): macro_state =
    IF exception_number(st) = 0 THEN normal_result(st) ELSE
        exception_macro_state(normal_result(st),exception_number(st))
    ENDIF

END arith_update
```

Figure 7.4 PVS specification of arithmetic instructions.

that the instruction be a reference instruction. This TCC can be discharged with the PVS theorem prover as an additional check on the consistency of the specification.

Similar update theories are defined for each instruction class. All the update theories are imported into the `normal_macro_machine` theory which defines the overall behavior of the AAMP in the absence of interrupts and unrecoverable user errors. The `normal_macro_machine` theory is shown in Figure 7.5.

```
% The normal macro machine theory defines the behavior of the AAMP
% in the absence of interupts and unrecoverable user errors.
% It computes the next macro state of the microprocessor
% based on its current state.

normal_macro_machine: THEORY
BEGIN

   IMPORTING arith_update,       assign_update,       block_update,
             branch_update,      call_update,         halt_update,
             return_update,      trap_update,         literal_update,
             misc_update,        mutex_update,        ref_update,
             relational_update,  shift_update

   next_macro_state(st: macro_state): macro_state =
     CASES instruction_class_of(current_opcode(st)) OF
       arithmetic : arith_update.next_macro_state(st),
       assign     : assign_update.next_macro_state(st),
       block      : block_update.next_macro_state(st),
       control    : CASES control_class_of(current_opcode(st)) OF
                       branch  : branch_update.next_macro_state(st),
                       call    : call_update.next_macro_state(st),
                       halt    : halt_update.next_macro_state(st),
                       return  : return_update.next_macro_state(st),
                       trap    : trap_update.next_macro_state(st)
                    ENDCASES,
       literal    : literal_update.next_macro_state(st),
       misc       : misc_update.next_macro_state(st),
       mutex      : mutex_update.next_macro_state(st),
       reference  : ref_update.next_macro_state(st),
       relational : relational_update.next_macro_state(st),
       shift      : shift_update.next_macro_state(st)
     ENDCASES

END normal_macro_machine
```

Figure 7.5 Top-level specification of the next macrostate function.

Constructive vs descriptive specifications

One of the early choices facing us in specifying the macroarchitecture was whether to specify the `next_macro_state` function **constructively**, i.e. by explicitly defining how the result of the function is to be constructed, or **descriptively**, i.e. by stating a set of properties (axioms) that the function is to satisfy. The main advantage of a constructive style of specification is that the PVS language mechanisms will ensure that the function is not only well defined but total. A disadvantage is that it is difficult to leave parts of the specification deliberately underspecified. A descriptive style is naturally suited for underspecification, but makes it possible to introduce inconsistent axioms. In addition, descriptive specifications are often more difficult to understand than constructive specifications for an uninitiated reader. Most earlier processor verification efforts have used a constructive style of specification.

We initially chose the constructive style since (besides the reasons given above) many of the AAMP instructions are similar enough (for example, a REFS and a REFSL differ only in the addressing mode) that they could be compactly specified using a constructive style. Also, much of the most complex behaviour of the AAMP instructions was already specified at Collins using a procedural style (in the form of pseudocode) that could be easily translated into a constructive specification. One result of this choice was to make the effort required to specify a single instruction quite high since most of the infrastructure for an entire class of instructions was required to complete the first instruction in that class. A benevolent side effect was that this made it easy to specify far more instructions (108) than the 13 instructions originally planned.

However, while doing the correctness proofs it became clear that a more descriptive style of specification in which the change in state was defined more directly would be helpful as an intermediate step in the proof. Fortunately, these could be stated as lemmas that could be proven from the original specification, preserving our investment in the original specification. As these lemmas were created, it became evident that they were in many ways a preferable style of specification. They were more readable, simpler to validate, and closer to what a user wanted to know in the first place. They also made it possible to specify a small portion of the next_macro_state function, i.e. to specify one instruction or part of an instruction at a time. An example of the descriptive style of specification is presented below for the ADD instruction for the case when addition doe not overflow. The other cases is characterized similarly by other lemmas. In the constructive style all the cases were embedded inside a function definition in an algorithmic style.

```
%------------------------------------------------------------
% ADD - Two's Complement Add, Single Word (no exception).
%        The two words on the top of the stack are added.
%        The resulting sum replaces the two original values
%        on top of the stack.
%------------------------------------------------------------
ADD_lemma_1: LEMMA
  LET X = current_data_env(st)(tos(st)+1),
      Y = current_data_env(st)(tos(st))
  IN current_opcode(st) = ADD
        & arith_update.exception_number(st)=0  =>
     normal_macro_machine.next_macro_state(st) =
       st WITH [(dmem)(word2denv(denv(st)))(tos(st)+1) := X + Y,
                (pc)  := pc(st)  + 1,
                (tos) := tos(st) + 1]
```

The stack cache abstraction

One of the most interesting issues pertaining to the use of abstraction in specification arose in modelling the process stack. Conceptually, it is desirable to hide the presence of the stack cache so that an application programmer does not have to be concerned with it. In actuality, effect of the stack cache is visible at the macro level in two ways.

For performance reasons, the AAMP does not check memory accesses to determine whether the word being referenced lies in the vicinity of the stack cache. As a result, REF and ASSIGN instructions that access the region of memory between the physical TOS and the logical TOS may obtain values different from those held in the stack cache. In practice this does not pose a problem since well-behaved applications do not directly access the process stack. Since applications seldom write assembly code for the AAMP (recall that it is designed for use with high-level, block-structured languages such as Ada), this is primarily a concern for the compiler writers. The second manifestation of the stack cache arises because the AAMP signals an overflow when the physical TOS exceeds the stack limit, rather than when the logical TOS exceeds the stack limit. In effect, the existence of the stack cache allows a few more words to be written to the process stack than should strictly be allowed. While benign, these two manifestations of the stack cache made it difficult to write a precise definition of the AAMP5's behaviour without bringing the details of the stack cache into the macro level specification. To avoid this, two adjustments were made to the specification of the macroarchitecture. To reflect the constraint that memory accesses should not be made to the vicinity of the stack cache, we left the effect of such accesses unspecified as shown below.

```
not_stack_cache_address(st:macro_state, base:data_env_ptr)
                    (offset:data_env_addr): bool

data_memory_assign(st      : macro_state,
                   base    : data_env_ptr,
                   offset : (not_stack_cache_address(st, base)),
                   wd      : word): macro_state =
                           st WITH [(dmem)(base)(offset) := wd]

data_memory_ref(st      : macro_state,
                base    : data_env_ptr,
                offset : (not_stack_cache_address(st, base)))):
                        word = dmem(st)(base)(offset)
```

The functions `data_memory_ref` and `data_memory_assign` are used exclusively for direct data memory accesses at a given base (data environment pointer) and offset. These functions are constrained by defining them on an appropriate subtype of the type of all possible address offsets. The predicate `not_stack_cache_address` is used to define a subtype dependent [1] on `st` and `base` to restrict the offset to locations that are not overlaid by the stack cache. (In PVS a subtype is declared by enclosing the predicate defining the subtype in parentheses.) The exact definition of the `not_stack_cache_address` predicate is left unspecified in the macroarchitecture

---

[1]Dependent subtypes are an important PVS feature allowing a type component to depend on earlier components.

since it varies with the specific AAMP microprocessor. One approach would be to be overly conservative and define it at the maximum number of words the stack cache can hold (nine for the AAMP5) above the logical TOS. Another approach is to define it as an abstraction of the micromachine state that contains information about the stack cache as shown below. Such a specification was used in the proofs of correctness relating the micro and macro levels.

```
not_stack_cache_address(ABS(micro_state), base)(offset) =
   (base /= denv(ABS(micro_state)))   OR   offset >= TOS(micro_state) OR
   (offset < TOS(macro_state) - (SV(macro_state) + TV(macro_state)))
```

Using the physical TOS rather than the logical TOS to detect stack overflow was a more difficult problem to resolve. This is dealt with in the proofs (1) by showing the correspondence between the two levels only as long as there is no stack overflow and (2) by proving a correctness statement about the behaviour of the stack overflow condition as a separate property of the micromachine. In the AAMP5 a stack overflow can occur only during a procedure call or at the beginning of an instruction during the execution of a special-purpose micro subroutine that performs stack adjustment. The stack overflow correctness is proved as a property of the stack-adjustment micro routine independent of the instruction being verified.

The issues raised by the stack cache are an excellent illustration of the need for formal, or at least precise, specifications. While the need for speed makes it unlikely that the AAMP will be changed to prevent direct memory accesses in the region of the stack cache, explicitly capturing this constraint provides important documentation for the users of the AAMP, particularly the compiler writers. Using the logical TOS rather than the physical TOS to signal stack overflow is a relatively minor change that may well be incorporated into future AAMPs — this issue had simply never arose since it has such a benign effect. Both issues were brought forward by the requirement to create an abstract, yet precise, specification of the AAMP macroarchitecture.

7.4.3   Development of the macroarchitecture specification

The macroarchitecture specification of the AAMP was developed through gradual refinement by SRI and Collins and resulted in several iterations, each incorporating increasing amounts of detail. Since the AAMP5 was to be object-code compatible with the earlier AAMP2, this work was based on the AAMP2 Reference Manual (Rockwell International, 1990). Each iteration was reviewed via informal walk-throughs by Collins and the comments returned to SRI. This phase lasted approximately three months, took 532 person hours to complete, and resulted in a first draft of the specification consisting of 1595 lines of PVS organized into 25 theories. Several issues emerged during this period.

As the specification grew in size, an ever-increasing portion of it was devoted to defining the properties of bit vectors, i.e. sequences of bits such as words of memory and internal registers. Ultimately, these theories evolved into a reusable library of 2030 lines of PVS organized into 31 theories. The bit vector library was developed at NASA Langley

Research Center by Rick Butler and Paul Miner. Availability of this library at the start of the project would have greatly shortened this phase.

Large parts of the specification were simply tables of attributes of the various AAMP instructions. While the PVS representation of this information was readable, a PVS construct explicitly designed to support the expression of tabular data would have improved their clarity. Such a construct has been added to the latest version of PVS.

Revision and extension

Once SRI and Collins were satisfied with the overall structure of the specification, its completion was taken over by Collins. This was done for several reasons, the most pragmatic being to allow SRI to move on to the specification of the microarchitecture. Ownership by Collins also encouraged transfer of the formal methods technology. There was also growing concern whether the AAMP domain experts, who were not skilled in PVS, would be able and willing to read the PVS specification. It was felt the Collins team was best situated to facilitate this.

Over the next five months, the roles of SRI and Collins on the macroarchitecture were reversed, with Collins revising and extending the specifications and SRI providing informal review. More of the executive service functions were specified and the number of instructions specified was increased to 108 of the AAMP's 209 instructions. NASA Langley also took over completion and validation of the bit vector theories. To make the specifications more accessible to the AAMP domain experts, considerable effort was invested in improving their readability by choosing more meaningful names, adding general comments, adding comments tracing the specifications back to the AAMP2 Reference Manual, and ensuring that all functions were written as clearly as possible. Approximately 409 person hours were invested in this effort. At its conclusion, the macroarchitecture specification consisted of 2550 lines of PVS organized into 48 theories, not including the bit vectors library discussed earlier.

Inspection

Formal inspection (Fagan, 1986) of the macroarchitecture was felt to be essential, both to validate the correctness of the specification and to familiarize more engineers at Collins with PVS. In preparation for these inspections, an overview of the specifications was presented in four reviews of two hours each. At the end of these sessions, the engineers were divided into two teams, one that would review the macro-level specifications and one that would review the micro-level specifications. Checklists were drawn up for use in the inspections based on earlier checklists used in inspecting VDM specifications (Jones, 1990), the RAISE Method Manual (Brock and George, 1990), and checklists used for code inspections at Collins.

Eleven inspections were held of the macro-level specification covering 31 of the most important theories. Inspectors were required to review the designated theories ahead of time, using the checklists as guides, and to record all potential defects encountered. Defects were classified as trivial, minor, and major. Trivial defects were defined as those that did not affect correctness and for which an obvious solution existed, such as spelling errors. Minor defects included those that might affect clarity or maintenance but did not affect correctness. As a rule of thumb, a defect was classified as minor if two reasonable people could disagree on whether it was a defect. Major defects were defined as those that affected correctness and obviously should be corrected. Despite their name, most of the major defects were very limited in scope and could be corrected in a few minutes. Some of the errors were misunderstandings by SRI, some were errors in the original AAMP documentation, and some had been inserted by Collins during the revisions. During the inspections, each inspector presented the minor and major defects they had found. While consensus of the team was required for a defect to be officially recorded, the majority of issues raised were recorded as defects. Later, each defect recorded was corrected. Total time spent in preparation by all participants, time spent in inspection, and number of defects found are shown in Table 7.2.

During the first inspection, team members were still uncomfortable with PVS, as indicated by the number of hours spent in preparation. This apprehension dissipated quickly and the inspectors settled down to a rate of approximately 150 lines of PVS and comments per hour of preparation time (the inspection rate increased during inspections nine through eleven since these were of simple tables). This rate is probably somewhat high since the inspectors were well aware that this was a shadow project. On an actual project, more preparation time would have been required. Even so, 53 minor (style) defects and 28 major (substantive) defects were discovered in specifications that had been carefully prepared prior to inspection. As shown in Table 7.1, approximately 96 hours were spent conducting the inspections and 64 hours were spent correcting the defects found.

The ease with which the inspectors became comfortable with PVS was one of the main surprises of the project. A similar result was observed with a different team on the inspections of the microarchitecture. Much of this was due to the time that was spent preparing the theories for inspection. While the purpose of the inspections was to validate the accuracy of the formal specifications, issues of style and clarity could dominate an inspection if a theory was not well organized. On the few occasions that unprepared theories were submitted to inspection, the result was quick rejection by the inspection team. Clear organization, standard naming conventions, and meaningful comments were essential.

Also surprising was the extent to which formal specifications and inspections complemented each other. The inspections were improved by the use of a formal notation, greatly reducing the amount of debate over whether an issue really was a defect or a personal preference. In turn, the inspections served as a useful vehicle for education and arriving at consensus on the most effective styles of specification. This was reflected by the lower number of defects recorded in the later inspections.

7.5   The microarchitecture: the pipelined view of the AAMP5

The internal microarchitecture of the AAMP5 employs four major, semiautonomous, functional units as shown in the block diagram of Figure 7.6.

The data processing unit (DPU) provides the data manipulation and processing func-

Table 7.2 Macroarchitecture inspection results

Inspection	No. of PVS theories	Lines of PVS	Inspectors	Prep. (hours)	Inspect. (hours)	Minor defects	Major defects
1	3	203	3	12.0	0.8	6	1
2	3	281	3	3.0	0.8	6	6
3	4	216	3	4.0	0.8	12	3
4	2	116	3	4.3	1.0	3	5
5	2	195	3	3.5	1.0	5	6
6	3	149	3	3.0	0.5	3	2
7	4	147	3	2.7	0.4	6	2
8	3	135	3	3.5	0.6	4	3
9	3	332	3	1.5	0.5	5	0
10	2	204	3	1.2	0.4	1	0
11	2	79	3	0.9	0.3	2	0
Total	**31**	**2057**		**39.6**	**6.3**	**53**	**28**

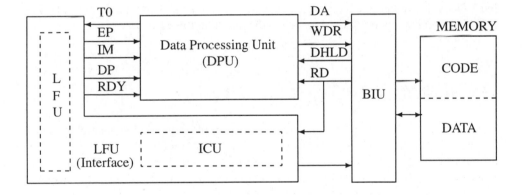

Figure 7.6 AAMP5 block diagram.

tions to execute the AAMP5 instruction set. Instructions are executed in a series of smaller operations in a pipeline, so that portions of multiple instructions can execute simultaneously. Included in the DPU are an ALU, combinational multiplication facilities, barrel shifter, multiport register file, and address computation hardware, all under microprogram control.

Instruction fetching is performed by the lookahead fetch unit (LFU) by maintaining a 4-byte-long instruction queue that it endeavours to keep full. In addition to prefetching into the instruction queue, the LFU parses the instruction stream, assembles immediate operands (IM), and provides the DPU with a microprogram entry point (EP) translated from the instruction opcode. The LFU also passes the program counter (DP) associated with the parsed instruction.

The AAMP5 includes 1024 bytes of direct-mapped instruction cache. Each cache "hit" provides two bytes of code to the LFU in a single clock cycle. During a "miss," two bytes are fetched from external memory and provided simultaneously to the instruction cache unit (ICU) storage and to the LFU for queuing. Because the operational details of ICU are hidden from the DPU, the LFU and the ICU are shown in Figure 7.6 enclosed inside a shell with which the DPU interacts directly. We have highlighted only those signals that are significant for our specification.

The bus interface unit (BIU) performs external fetches for the LFU, as well as data reads and writes initiated by the DPU. It supports 24 bits of word address, a 16-bit data bus, and several control and status signals.

7.5.1   The data processing unit

The DPU provides the data manipulation and processing functions required to execute the AAMP5 instruction set. A block diagram of the DPU that includes most of the details of the DPU is shown in Figure 7.7, which also includes some of the details of the LFU. The DPU has two main parts: the datapath and the microcontroller.

7.5.2   The datapath

The datapath consists of the components that perform the required data manipulation for instruction execution. It includes a 10-word multiport register file, a 48-bit ALU, shifters, multiplication support, and several registers. Some of the registers (R and W) are used to hold the operands of the ALU and some are used to hold the results (T, Q, and M triplets) after ALU and shift operations.

The ALU and the Reg File (register file) are two of the most complex units in the DPU. The ALU supports a large number of logical and 2's complement and 1's complement arithmetic operations on 48-bit bit vectors. Besides the two bit vector operands, the ALU accepts a carry-in input and produces a carry-out. The ALU can, if necessary, bypass the operand registers (R and W) and get its operands directly from the result registers (T, Q, and M).

The Reg File is a complex multiport register file that can be read (and written) simultaneously from (into) up to three registers relative to a read (write) index controlled by the microcode. It contains bypass logic to use the write value instead of the contents of a register during a read if there is a read–write clash. Six designated registers (STK0 through STK5) in the register file (along with the T registers) are used to implement the stack cache as described in Section 7.5.4. The remaining registers in the register file are used as pointers to the code and data memory such as the top-of-stack and data environment pointer (DENV).

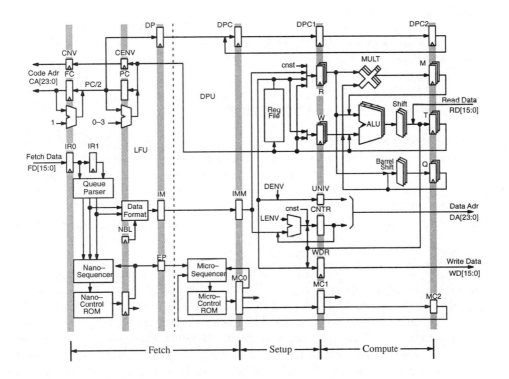

Figure 7.7 The LFU and DPU datapath.

7.5.3 The microcontroller

The microcontroller generates the signals that control the movement of data within the datapath as well as the next microinstruction to be read from the ROM. It contains the microprogram store, the microsequencer, which computes the next microaddress, and the microinstruction control registers (MC0, MC1, and MC2).

Once an instruction moves into MC0, it is interpreted in a two-stage pipeline. The signals for controlling the operations in the first stage are generated from MC0. The operations performed in the first (setup) data-path stage typically include setting up the operands for the ALU operation as well as determining the next microaddress. A subset of the fields of the microinstruction in MC0 is passed onto MC1, which controls operations in the second data-path stage. The second (compute) stage typically involves ALU computation, register write-back and memory operations. Finally, the jump-address field of MC1 is passed onto MC2 as the target microaddress of a potential delayed jump, typically used to implement exceptions such as arithmetic overflow. If a delayed jump is detected (as a function of the ALU outputs) in the second stage, then both MC0 and MC1 are cleared to abort the operations normally performed by the MC0 and MC1 microinstructions and then the microinstruction at the jump address is fetched and loaded into MC0. The program counter DP is also pipelined using a sequence of registers so that DPC, DPC1, and DPC2 contain the program counters corresponding to the instructions in MC0, MC1, and MC2, respectively.

7.5.4   The stack cache and stack adjustment

As mentioned in Section 7.4.2, the DPU holds up to nine words of the top of the process stack in its internal registers. The T register triplet always holds the latest data item, which can be one, two, or three words long, pushed on to the top of the stack. In other words, if the latest data item pushed is a triple-word item, then it is held in T0, T1, and T2, with T0 holding the least significant part. If the data item occupies two words, then they are held in T0 and T1, with T2 being "empty." The rest of the stack cache elements are stored in the register file with the stack growing from STK0 up to STK5, i.e. STK0 is at the bottom.

The occupancy state of the stack cache that would result if an instruction were completed is maintained in a pair of registers for each of the AAMP5 instructions being executed in MC0 (SV and TV) and MC1 (SV1 and TV1). The circuit that maintains the SV–TV registers is shown in Figure 7.8. TV contains the number of words that would be occupied in the T register triplet and SV contains the number of registers in the register file that are used for the stack cache. When an instruction to be executed requires more operands than are available in the cache, the processor automatically reads additional locations from memory to the stack cache. Similarly, when an instruction will place more operands on to the stack than there are empty spaces in the stack cache, the processor automatically writes the cache register contents to memory.

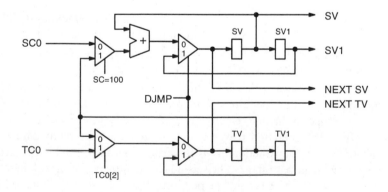

Figure 7.8 SV and TV logic.

The process of maintaining the proper number of operands in the stack cache is called a **stack adjustment**. Prior to loading into MC0 the first microinstruction of an instruction, the DPU compares the stack cache occupancy state corresponding to MC0 against the **entry condition code** of the instruction. This code, which is stored for every instruction in a read-only memory, gives the stack cache requirements for the instruction. If the stack cache occupancy is not acceptable, the DPU automatically executes microcoded push or pop stack adjustments, causing a minimum number of 16-bit words to be written to or read from the active process stack area in memory to satisfy the entry condition of the instruction.

7.5.5   Formal specification of the microarchitecture

Since our goal was to verify the microcode residing in the DPU, the formal specification of the microarchitecture abstracts the internal details of all of the blocks of the AAMP5 except the DPU. The DPU is specified at the same level of detail given in the informal microarchitecture document. The rest of the AAMP5 is specified by formalizing the behavior of the other blocks expected by the DPU. The DPU directly interacts only with the LFU and the BIU. The ICU is maintained and managed entirely by the LFU and its effect on the DPU is observed only via the LFU interface. Hence, the DPU interface specification is divided into two parts: the DPU–LFU part and the DPU–BIU part.

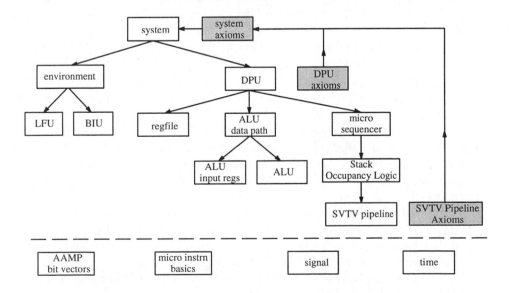

Figure 7.9 Microarchitecture specification hierarchy.

An overview of the theory hierarchy comprising the microarchitecture specification is shown in Figure 7.9. Again, an arrow drawn from theory A to B indicates that A imports B. The hierarchy closely parallels the structural decomposition of the DPU into smaller circuit blocks in the AAMP5 microarchitecture document (Rockwell International, 1990). Note that the ALU and the regfile are treated as black boxes in our specification. Every node in the graph shown in Figure 7.9 contains the PVS theories associated with a block of the circuit of the DPU. As described in the next section, each circuit block is specified by a pair of theories: one that declares the signals generated in the circuit block and one containing the axioms that constrain the signals (shown in Figure 7.9 as shaded boxes for some of the circuit blocks).

The theory pair at the root, system and system_axioms, denotes the specification for the entire system. system is constructed from environment, which combines the DPU–BIU and DPU–LFU interface specifications, and DPU. The set of basic theories imported by all the theories in the hierarchy are shown below the dashed line in Figure 7.9. Note that system is imported by all the theories thereby permitting signals generated in one circuit block at an arbitrary level to be easily used in another block. Separating the signal declarations from the axioms constraining their values made it possible to use signals globally without complicating the name structure of the signals. In the following sections, we describe the formal specifications of the DPU and its environment in more detail.

DPU specification

The DPU is constructed by combining the specifications of the datapath, namely regfile, ALU_data_path, and the microcontroller. The micropipeline part, i.e. MC0, MC1, and MC2 registers along with the abort logic, of the microcontroller is specified in the DPU theory. The parts of the microcontroller determining the next microaddress and the stack occupancy logic are specified in microsequencer, StackOccupancyLogic and SVTVpipeline. The ALU_data_path is decomposed into specifications of the input registers (ALU_input_regs) of the ALU and the ALU itself (ALU).

In most applications of formal logic for the verification of register-transfer-level hardware, the design is modelled as a finite state machine with an implicit clock. The state of the machine consists of the states of the sequential components, such as registers, in the design. The next state function defines the new state value at the next cycle of the implicit clock. The exact style used to specify the state machine implemented by the design can vary. For the AAMP5, we used a **functional** style of specification.

In this style, the inputs and outputs of every component are modelled as signals, where a **signal** is a function that maps time, i.e. number of cycles of the implicit clock, to a value of the appropriate type. Every signal that is an output of a component is specified as a function of the signals appearing at the inputs to the component. The signal definitions implicitly specify the connectivity between the components.

This style should be contrasted with the predicative style (Gordon, 1985) that is commonly used in most HOL (Gordon and Melham, 1993) applications. In the **predicative** style, every hardware component is specified as a predicate relating the input and output signals of the component and a design is specified as a conjunction of the component predicates, with signals on the internal wires used to connect the components hidden by existential quantification. We decided to use a functional style because proofs based on functional specifications tend to be more automatic than those involving predicative specifications. A proof of correctness for a predicative style of specification usually involves executing a few additional steps at the start of the proof to transform the predicative specification into an equivalent functional style. For a more detailed look at the two styles and their impact on proofs see Srivas *et al.* (1995).

```
SVTVpipeline: THEORY

  BEGIN
  IMPORTING micro_instrn_basics, AAMP_bit_vectors, signal

  % Extract the required control fields from MC0
  SC0: signal[SC_field]
  TC0: signal[TC_field]

  SV, SV1, TV, TV1: signal[bvec[3]]

  NEXT_SV: signal[bvec[3]]
  NEXT_TV: signal[bvec[3]]

  END SVTVpipeline
```

Figure 7.10 Signals for the SV–TV pipeline.

As an illustration, a complete specification in PVS of the circuit block (shown in Figure 7.8) that updates the pipelined stack pointer registers SV, TV, SV1, and TV1 is given in Figures 7.10 and 7.11. The specification of a circuit block is divided into two theories: a signals theory and an axioms theory. The **signals** theory (Figure 7.10) declares all the signals used to represent the state of the circuit. For the SV–TV circuit, these consist of the inputs (the control signals SC0 and TC0 originating from the microinstruction register MC0) and the outputs at the various registers used in the circuit. We also include NEXT_SV and NEXT_TV as signals since they are also used as outputs of the circuit.

The types of all the signals in the design, except the one used for microinstructions, are bit vectors of the actual size used in the design. An AAMP5 microinstruction is 88 bits wide organized into 27 different fields. In our specification, a microinstruction is represented symbolically as a record type with enumerated types for the microinstruction fields. The enumerated type associated with a microinstruction field contains a distinct literal for every bit pattern value possible for the field. The microinstruction record type, the default values for the fields, and related functions are specified in the theory micro_instrn_basics, which is one of the basic theories imported by the SV_TV_pipeline theory.

The **axioms theory** (Figure 7.11) for the circuit defines the values of the declared sig-

```
SVTVpipeline_axioms: THEORY

 BEGIN
 IMPORTING system
 IMPORTING micro_instrn_basics, signal, AAMP_bit_vectors

 t: VAR time

 % Extract the required control fields from MC0
 SC0ax: AXIOM SC0(t) = SC(MC0(t))
 TC0ax: AXIOM TC0(t) = TC(MC0(t))

 NEXT_SVax: AXIOM NEXT_SV(t) =
   (IF DJMP(t) THEN SV1(t)
      ELSE CASES SC(MC0(t)) OF
         NO_SV : SV(t),
         SPUSH1: SV(t) + 1,
         SPUSH2: SV(t) + 2,
         SPUSH3: SV(t) + 3,
         SPOP1 : SV(t) - 1,
         SPOP2 : SV(t) - 2,
         SPOP3 : SV(t) - 3,
         SPUSHT: SV(t) + bv2nat(TV(t))
      ENDCASES
    ENDIF)

 SVax: AXIOM SV(t+1) = IF DHLD(t) THEN SV(t) ELSE NEXT_SV(t) ENDIF

 SV1ax: AXIOM SV1(t+1) = IF DHLD(t) THEN SV1(t) ELSE SV(t) ENDIF

 NEXT_TVax: AXIOM NEXT_TV(t) =
    IF DJMP(t) THEN TV1(t)
    ELSIF TV_TO_0?(TC(MC0(t))) THEN nat2bv[3](0)
    ELSIF TV_TO_1?(TC(MC0(t))) THEN nat2bv[3](1)
    ELSIF TV_TO_2?(TC(MC0(t))) THEN nat2bv[3](2)
    ELSIF TV_TO_3?(TC(MC0(t))) THEN nat2bv[3](3)
    ELSE TV(t) ENDIF

 TVax: AXIOM TV(t+1) = IF DHLD(t) THEN TV(t) ELSE NEXT_TV(t) ENDIF

 TV1ax: AXIOM TV1(t+1) = IF DHLD(t) THEN TV1(t) ELSE TV(t) ENDIF

 END SVTVpipeline_axioms
```

Figure 7.11 Specification of the SV–TV pipeline.

nals. Every signal is specified by means of an axiom that constrains the way the values of the signals change over time. For example, the axiom TVax specifies the value of the signal TV to be equal to that of NEXT_TV delayed by one cycle unless the updating of the signal is disabled when data hold (DHLD) is asserted to be high.

The axioms and the signals theories import a number of other theories besides `micro_instrn_basics` described above. `AAMP_bit_vectors` defines the different kinds of bit vectors used in the specification. `system` is the top-level theory that imports all the signals declared in different parts of the circuit so that a signal generated in one circuit block can easily be used as an input in another block. For example, the signals DJMP and MC0 used here are generated in another part of the circuit defined by the DPU theory. For the sake of brevity, certain parts of a circuit, usually those denoting a combinational block, are abstracted in a single signal specification. For example, the axiom NEXT_SVax combines the entire combinational logic in the circuit shown in Figure 7.8 that generates the NEXT_SV signal.

The DPU interface specification

In this section, we describe the specification of the interaction between the DPU and its environment. We specifically illustrate the interaction between the DPU and the LFU. The DPU–BIU interface is specified similarly.

The DPU and the LFU undertake a "hand-shake" protocol to accomplish the proper transfer of information between them. The LFU independently prefetches instructions into a queue, decodes the instruction in the front of the queue, and presents the decoded information to the DPU via the signals EP, DP, and IM described below. The LFU signals the availability of a new instruction on its output lines by making RDY true. Whenever RDY is true, the LFU ensures that the following conditions hold.

1. EP has the entry-point (starting microaddress) of the microcode of the instruction associated with the value of DP.
2. IM has the first unit of immediate data, if any, of the instruction associated with the value of DP.

DP is an offset (actually one greater than the real offset since it is "delayed" by a byte for technical reasons) into the code environment from which the instruction is fetched. The real address of the instruction is formed as a concatenation of the code environment pointer in CENV, which resides in the LFU (but can be read as a register in the register file), and DP.

Once RDY becomes true, the LFU idles, i.e. does not change its outputs, although it may be filling up the instruction queue. The idling state continues until the DPU expresses its intent to consume, or sends a request to the LFU to discard the current instruction and start fetching from a different target address. The DPU controls the operation of the LFU by means of the NC field of the microinstruction in MC0. A value of CLR_RDY for NC means the DPU is ready to consume a new instruction and will cause the LFU to assemble information about the instruction following DP and to present it the next time RDY becomes true. However, if the DPU instructs the LFU to retarget its fetching (NC is NANO_SKIP, for instance) then the new target address (presented by the DPU in T0) is transferred into the LFU. After that, the LFU presents the instruction at the new target address the next time RDY becomes true. For the protocol to work correctly, the microcode in the DPU must obey the following conditions.

1. The DPU must consume a new piece of information from the LFU only when RDY is true. That is, if the DPU is ready to issue a CLR_RDY signal to the LFU when the LFU is not ready with the required information, the DPU must wait until RDY is true.

2. Every issue of a request to change the normal sequence of instruction fetching, such as NANO_SKIP, NANO_CALL, etc., must be followed by a CLR_RDY. For example, if a NANO_SKIP is issued before the results of a previous request are consumed, the second request may override the first one.

Our LFU–DPU interface specification states only those assumptions we made about the behaviour of the LFU in our proofs. It is not a complete specification of the LFU interface. Section 7.6.9 discusses a possible approach for validating these assumptions. Figure 7.12 shows part of the LFU interface specification.

CODE_MEMORY, declared in the theory MEMORY, denotes the portion of the external memory where the code is stored. Although the AAMP5 microarchitecture does not require external memory to be separated into mutually exclusive code and data areas, our specification uses two distinct memory objects, CODE_MEMORY and DATA_MEMORY. Both of these memories map 24-bit addresses to 16-bit words. All instructions are assumed to be fetched from CODE_MEMORY and all data reads or writes are assumed to only affect DATA_MEMORY. That is, we assume that the CODE_MEMORY state remains constant. This simplification restricts the validity of our proofs of correctness of microcode to programs that are not self-modifying.

The first axiom (RDYinv) states a condition on the LFU outputs that the DPU can rely on whenever LFU is ready with a decoded instruction. It states that whenever RDY is true, EP and IM have the appropriate information pertaining to the instruction associated with the program counter DP.

The remaining axioms specify the expected responses to some of the different instruction-fetching requests originating from the DPU. The axioms beginning with the prefix CLR_RDY specify the possible LFU behaviours in response to a request (CLR_RDY) by the DPU to consume an instruction from the LFU. If the LFU is ready with an instruction when the DPU issues a CLR_RDY, which is the case covered by the first axiom, the LFU goes into a state normal_fetching where it presents instructions sequentially. Note that the DP is updated only if the next instruction can be presented in the following cycle (otherwise, the invariant RDYinv will not be preserved). If the LFU is not ready with an instruction when NC is CLR_RDY, the case covered by the second axiom in the set, we assume that the LFU will eventually present the DPU with a new instruction, provided DPU holds the NC0 line stable with CLR_RDY.

The behaviour specified by the second axiom applies only when the LFU is in a normal_fetching state. We do not need an analogous axiom for the case when LFU is not in a normal_fetching state because the LFU can get into such a state

```
LFU: THEORY
  BEGIN
  IMPORTING micro_instrn_basics, AAMP_bit_vectors, signal
  IMPORTING opcodes, temporalops, MEMORY, system, EPROM_basics

  t, t1, t2: VAR time

  NC0(t): NC_field = NC(MC0(t))
  normal_fetching: signal[bool]

  % Invariant constraints on the outputs when LFU is RDY
  RDYinv: AXIOM
    RDY(t) =>
      LET opcode = opcode_at(CENV(t), DP(t), CODE_MEMORY(t))
        IN EP(t) = EP_ROM(opcode) &
           (has_imm_data(opcode) => IM(t) = first_unit_of_imm_data(t))

  % CLR_RDY behavior specification
  CLR_RDY_no_wait: AXIOM
     RDY(t) & CLR_RDY?(NC0(t)) =>
      normal_fetching(t+1) &
      DP(t+1) = IF RDY(t+1) THEN DP(t)+length_of_instruction(opcode)
                 ELSE DP(t) ENDIF

  CLR_RDY_wait: AXIOM
     NOT RDY(t) & normal_fetching(t) & CLR_RDY?(NC0(t)) =>
       (EXISTS (t1 | t1 > t):
           stays_same(NC0(t))(t, t1)  =>
             stays_same(RDY)(t, t1-1) & RDY(t1) &
               normal_fetching(t1) &
                 DP(t1) = DP(t)+length_of_instruction(opcode) )

  % SKIP behavior specification
  no_change_in_flow(t): bool = ((NC0(t) = CLR_RDY) OR
                                (NC0(t) = NO_NANO))

  NANO_SKIPax: AXIOM
    NANO_SKIP?(NC0(t1)) =>
      NOT RDY(t1+1) & NOT(normal_fetching(t1+1)) &
       (EXISTS (t2 | t2 > t1+1):
           stays_high(no_change_in_flow)(t1+1, t2-1)) =>
             stays_same(RDY)(t1+1, t2-1) & RDY(t2) &
               stays_same(normal_fetching)(t1+1, t2) &
                 DP(t2) = T0(t1) )
```

Figure 7.12 DPU–LFU interface specification.

only after a DPU request, such as NANO_SKIP, that causes a change in the flow of instruction fetching. The requirement that RDY must eventually become true in such a state is covered by the axioms constructed for those other DPU requests, as we have shown for NANO_SKIP in Figure 7.12. In addition to ensuring that RDY eventually becomes true, the NANO_SKIP axiom updates DP to the target address (T0) and makes the normal_fetching signal false. It guarantees the outcome only if the DPU does not issue another request for a change of instruction flow. That is, the DPU must keep the NC signal input to the LFU either NO_NANO or CLR_RDY until RDY becomes true for proper action.

The axiom NO_NANOax states that the LFU idles, i.e., the values of EP, IM, DP and CENV stay the same, once RDY becomes true as long as NC0 stays NO_NANO.

7.5.6   Development of the microarchitecture specification

This section describes how the microarchitecture specification was developed and the techniques used for its validation. Development of the microarchitecture specification mirrored that of the macroarchitecture. As indicated in Table 7.1, initial development of the microarchitecture specification by SRI took approximately 657 person hours over 10 months. The specification closely followed the block structure of the microarchitecture, usually with one theory per component. Surprisingly, the specification of the microarchitecture without the PVS version of the microcode was only slightly larger than the specification of the macroarchitecture, an indication how much of the complexity of the AAMP5 is contained within the microcode. Once decisions about the data types to be used to model signals and states are made, it should be possible to derive automatically a PVS specification of a hardware design from its description in a more traditional hardware description language.

Completion of the microarchitecture specification took longer than the specification of the macroarchitecture for a number of reasons. The AAMP5 microarchitecture document, unlike the AAMP2 Reference Manual, is targeted for an audience that is familiar with the basic architecture of the AAMP processor family. As a result, SRI had to spend considerable time becoming familiar with the design. In particular, the interactions between the DPU and its environment were difficult to specify. Although the design of the LFU and the BIU were well documented, the interface conditions that the DPU has to obey to ensure proper LFU and BIU services were not explicitly stated. This information had to be extracted through reverse engineering of the detailed designs and extensive discussions with the Collins staff. The time spent on both these efforts could have been substantially reduced if formal specification activity were integrated earlier and more closely into the conventional design cycle.

Revision

To make the specifications acceptable to the AAMP5 designers for inspection, the initial microarchitecture specifications developed by SRI were informally reviewed by three

Collins engineers familiar with both PVS and the AAMP5 and revised as was done for the macroarchitecture. Since the initial specifications covered the entire microarchitecture, there was no need for Collins to extend the specification. Most of the changes consisted of modifying names to reflect local conventions, adding comments tracing back to the design documents, and improving the clarity of the specifications. Even so, this was a sizeable effort, requiring 280 hours spread over seven months. When completed, the microarchitecture specification consisted of 2679 lines of PVS and comments organized into 20 theories.

Revisions were also made later to the microarchitecture specifications to facilitate proofs, but these were more technical in nature and not as significant as the ones made to the macroarchitecture specification. Most involved trading the use of an advanced and expressive construct of the specification language for a more basic construct to improve the efficiency of proofs.

Inspection

Formal inspections of the microarchitecture were conducted just as for the macroarchitecture. To maximize the independence between the macro and micro specifications, only one participant from the macroarchitecture inspections was included in the microarchitecture inspection team. Ten inspections were held, including two reinspections, covering 15 of the most important theories.

Again, the inspectors quickly adapted to PVS, reaching an average inspection rate of approximately 290 lines of PVS and comments per hour. Interestingly enough, the designers of the AAMP5, who were the least familiar with the PVS language, found the specifications the simplest to read, consistently turning in the most major defects and the lowest preparation times. This was a direct result of their detailed knowledge of the AAMP5 and the close correspondence between the AAMP5 design and the specifications. As with the macroarchitecture specification, more preparation time would have been required on an actual project. 64 minor (style) defects and 19 major (substantive) defects were discovered.

7.6 Formal verification of AAMP5

7.6.1 General microprocessor correctness

In most mechanical verifications of microprocessors, the general correctness criterion used is based on establishing a correspondence, as shown in Figure 7.13, between the execution traces of two state machines that the specifications at the macro and micro levels denote. In the figure, E denotes the micromachine state transition function. The objective of the correctness criterion is to ensure that the micromachine does not introduce any behaviors not allowed by the macromachine. The macromachine uses two kinds of abstraction to hide details of the micromachine.

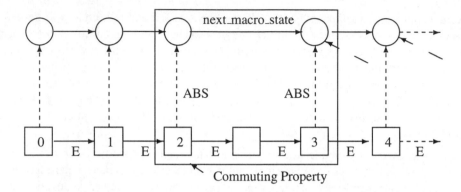

Figure 7.13 General microprocessor correctness.

- *Representation abstraction.* Not every component of the micromachine state is visible at the macro level. Even the visible part of the micromachine state can take on quite a different form at the macro level. For example, the process stack, which is viewed as residing entirely in the data memory in the macromachine, is actually split between the memory and internal registers in the micromachine.
- *Temporal abstraction.* The macro- and the micromachines do not run at the same speed. For example, while every instruction in the macromachine is viewed as being executed atomically in one unit of time, the same instruction may take a number of clock cycles to complete in the micromachine. The difference in speed means that the micromachine trace may have "intermediate" states for which there are no corresponding macromachine states.

To deal with representation abstraction it is necessary to define an **abstraction** function (ABS) that returns the macrostate corresponding to the state of the micromachine at any given time. This function must be surjective to ensure that if the macromachine starts at some initial state, the micromachine is able to start at a corresponding state. One way to deal with the consequences of temporal abstraction is to characterize the set of microstates that have corresponding macrostates as **visible** states. For example, a possible definition of a visible state is one in which an instruction is completed and a new instruction begins. In Figure 7.13, a visible state in the trace is shown with the number of the instruction that begins executing in that state.

Given the notions of ABS and visible state, the correctness criterion described by Figure 7.13 can be stated as follows[2]: "Every micromachine trace starting with an initial state (S0) that abstracts to a macrostate (s0) must be abstractable to the macromachine trace starting with the initial state s0." To prove such a correspondence between two infinite traces, it is sufficient to prove the commuting property formally stated below and depicted by the boxed region in Figure 7.13. The commuting property captures the cor-

---

[2]We also need to ensure that processor resetting will always lead to an initial state in which the correspondence required by ABS holds.

respondence between the traces for one step of the macromachine, i.e. between two successive visible states. The formalization of the commuting diagram has two additional preconditions to handle the consequences, described in Section 7.4.2, of the hiding of the stack cache from the macro level. `proper_instrns_in_pipe(t)` ensures that the memory address operands (if any) of every macroinstruction in the pipeline are not within the area overlaid by the stack cache. `no_logical_stack_overflow(t)` ensures that the logical process stack would not overflow as a result of executing the current instruction.

```
visible_state(t) &
  proper_instrns_in_pipe(t) &
    no_logical_stack_overflow(t) => EXISTS (tp: time | tp > t):
      stays_low(t+1, tp-1)(visible_state) &
        visible_state(tp) & ABS(tp) = next_macro_state(ABS(t))
```

David Cyrluk has developed a general framework for proving correspondence between state machines in PVS and has shown its application for pipelined microprocessors. The characterization of microprocessor correctness described here is similar to the visible state approach given there (Cyrluk, 1993). Windley (1990) also develops a general framework for microprocessor correctness, although it is not applicable to pipelined processors.

7.6.2 Impact of pipelining and asynchronous memory interface

The basic idea behind pipelining is to increase the instruction execution rate of a processor by executing different stages of more than one instruction within the same clock cycle. Thus, although execution of an instruction is still spread over multiple clock cycles, it is possible to complete up to one instruction every cycle.

The general correctness criterion shown in Figure 7.13 is still applicable for pipelined processors with some adjustment as long as instructions are completed in the same order as they enter the pipeline. An adjustment is needed to handle the fact that when a new instruction enters the pipeline, the results of the previous uncompleted instructions may not yet be at their destinations. The definition of the abstraction function ABS may have to peek to a future microstate, possibly non-visible, following the current visible state (as shown in Figure 7.14) to obtain correct values for some of the macrostate components. Typically, the values for all but the program counter must be obtained from the future state. We refer to the distance into the future from the current visible state where the information is to be obtained as the **latency** for the abstraction function.

In principle, it should be possible to define the abstraction function as a function of the current visible state alone because the information necessary to compute the result of the to-be-completed instructions is stored in various hidden registers in the micromachine. In the MiniCayuga verification (Srivas and Bickford, 1990), which is one of the earliest efforts in the mechanical verification of a pipelined processor, the abstraction function was defined in this fashion. However, it is easier and conceptually clearer to define the abstraction in a "distributed fashion" using the future visible or non-visible states,

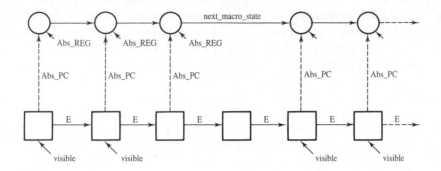

Figure 7.14 Impact of pipelining on abstraction.

which is the approach taken for the AAMP5. The pipelined verifications described in Cyrluk (1993), Saxe *et al.* (1994), Tahar and Kumar (1993), and most recently Windley and Coe (1994), also define the abstraction function in a distributed fashion. Burch and Dill (1994) use a slightly different approach to handle the time skew between the two levels. They "run" the micromachine longer by an appropriate number of cycles by streaming in NOP instructions before relating the states of the macro- and micromachines.

In Figure 7.14, the distance between two consecutive visible states can vary for a number of different reasons, although a pipelined design strives to keep the distance to one cycle as often as possible. For example, an instruction requiring a memory access may take longer than a register-to-register instruction, or an instruction that signals an exception may take a few extra cycles for completion. The distance can usually be expressed as a function of the class of the new instruction entering the pipeline in the visible state. For the AAMP5, however, the distance can be arbitrary in some situations because the DPU relies on two semiautonomous units (the LFU and the BIU) for instruction and data fetches. While we do rely on having the LFU and the BIU guarantee correct services, we cannot make any assumptions about the time taken for those services (other than that they are finite) for two reasons. First, the internal details of the LFU and BIU have been abstracted in the micromachine specification. Second, the time of service is determined by factors that are not completely under the control of the DPU.

7.6.3 The AAMP5 Pipeline

The reader is advised to refer to Figure 7.7 in Section 7.5.1 while reading this section. The AAMP5 executes its instructions in a three-stage pipeline where we identify the stages with the names fetch, setup, and compute. The fetch stage consists of the DPU activities that occur prior to the entry of the first microinstruction of an AAMP5 instruction into MC0. The setup stage consists of the activities controlled while the microinstruction is in MC0. The compute stage consists of the activities determined by the part of the microinstruction that moves from MC0 to MC1. Note that the register MC2 is only used for delayed jump execution and does not add a stage under normal instruction execution.

The different components of an AAMP5 instruction enter the DPU through the following input signals: DP, which is the program counter value associated with the instruction entering the DPU; EP, which gives the entry point, i.e. the beginning microaddress, of the microcode of the instruction; IM, which is the first unit of immediate data, if any, of the instruction. A summary of the activities that take place in each of the three pipeline stages is given below.

Fetch stage

- Read the microinstruction at EP from ROM.
- Read the entry condition code for the instruction from SROM (not shown in Figure 7.7).
- Perform any stack adjustments required.

Setup stage

- Compute the stack cache occupancy state (NEXT_SV and NEXT_TV) that would result if the instruction were performed.
- Read the register file to determine the sources for the ALU input registers R and W.
- Compute memory sources and destination addresses (needed only for memory access instructions).

Compute stage

- Compute the results of the ALU.
- Check whether there is going to be a delayed jump, i.e. an exception, such as an arithmetic overflow, that arises as an outcome of the ALU computation.
- Initiate writing into the stack cache.
- Initiate memory read/write (needed only for memory access instructions).

7.6.4 Normal pipeline operation

The DPU logic is designed so that the DPC0 register always contains the program counter value associated with the macroinstruction that is being interpreted in MC0. A similar correspondence holds between DPC1 and MC1 as well as DPC2 and MC2. We use the macroinstruction associated with DPC0 as the reference point and refer to it as the **current** instruction. Under **normal** pipeline operation, i.e. when AAMP5 instructions are being completed at the rate of one per cycle, the DPU performs the setup stage of the current instruction along with the compute stage of the previous instruction and the fetch stage of the next instruction.

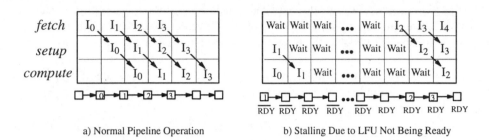

Figure 7.15 Pipeline execution traces.

The normal pipeline operation along with the execution trace of the micromachine is shown in Figure 7.15(a). A state (square) in the execution trace (shown at the bottom of Figure 7.15(a)) with a number n in it denotes the visible state where instruction n is the current instruction. The column above a state transition arrow shows the instructions in the pipeline and the stages that are being performed in a given cycle.

We define a visible state as one in which the first microinstruction of a new AAMP5 instruction is in MC0 and is guaranteed to advance to MC1 in the next cycle. That is, the left-over effects of the previous instruction are guaranteed to be completed in the next cycle. Under this characterization of the visible state, the latency for the ABS function is exactly one cycle. During normal pipeline operation, the distance between consecutive visible states is exactly one cycle. A formal characterization of a visible state is given below. `visible_state_with(op)(t)` defines the condition that must be satisfied for a micromachine state to be visible with the opcode of the current instruction being op. The first condition in the conjunction ensures that MC0 contains the first microinstruction of the microcode corresponding to op. The remaining conditions ensure that the previous instruction will complete in the next cycle: DHLD being false ensures that the previous instruction will not be held due to data memory transfer; `nextDJMP(t)` (which is the value of the DJMP register one cycle later) being false ensures that the previous instruction will not cause a delayed jump; `entry_cond_met` ensures that the entry conditions of the instruction in MC0 are met by the stack occupancy state determined by the SV1 and TV1 registers.

```
visible_state_with(op: opcodes)(t): bool =
  MC0(t) = ROM(zero_extend[8](11)(EP_ROM(op)(t))) &
    & NOT(DHLD(t)) & NOT(nextDJMP(t)) & entry_cond_met(op)(t)

visible_state(t): bool =
    EXISTS (op: opcodes): visible_state_with(op)(t)
```

7.6.4.1   Pipeline stalling and delayed jumps
One of the challenges posed by the AAPM5 from the point of view of verification is that there are a number of conditions under which the normal operation of the pipeline can be interrupted. Verification under these conditions has to be handled in special ways.

When the AAMP5 pipeline is at a visible state, the pipeline operates normally (i.e. the distance to the next visible state is one cycle) only if the following conditions hold. (1) The current instruction, i.e. the one in the setup stage in the pipeline, is implemented by a single microinstruction. (2) The previous instruction, i.e. the one in the compute stage, (a) does not cause a delayed jump (nextDJMP, the value assigned to DJMP in the next cycle, is false), and (b) will not not cause a data hold (DHLD is false). (3) The LFU is ready with the next instruction (RDY is true). (4) The next instruction will not need a stack adjustment (SADJcondn is false).

If any of the conditions listed does not hold, the distance to the next visible state will be more than one cycle and its value will depend on which of the conditions in the list are violated. We classify these situations in which the next visible state is more than one cycle away from the present one as follows. The behaviour resulting from violations of conditions 2(b), 3, or 4 is referred to as pipeline **stalling**; in these situations, the micromachine performs a computation that has no visible effect on the macro state. Violations of the other two cases (1, 2(a)) are referred to as pipeline **extension**. In a pipeline extension, the micromachine components that affect the macro state are updated incrementally in two or more cycles. In all these situations, the compute stage of the previous incomplete instruction is always completed in the following cycle.

For example, Figure 7.15(b) shows the trace when the LFU is not ready with the next instruction. In this case, a jump is made to a special microroutine (MAP_WAIT) that implements a busy wait loop which is exited only when RDY becomes true again. The distance to the next visible state can be arbitrarily large depending on when RDY becomes true.

7.6.5   Our approach to verification

To prove the general correctness criterion for the AAMP5, shown in Figure 7.13, we have first to define the abstraction function. The components of the micromachine state that are relevant in determining the corresponding macro state are the following.

1. The registers DENV, CENV, and SKLM map to their corresponding counterparts in the macro state.
2. The registers TOS, TV1 and SV1 define the value of TOS in the macro state.
3. DATA_MEMORY and CODE_MEMORY
4. The DPC register is mapped to the macro state program counter.
5. The registers T0, T1, T2, and the STKi registers in the register file, where i ranges from 0 through SV1, determine the contents of the macro state data memory that are overlaid by the stack cache.

A formal definition of the abstraction function for AAMP5 is shown below. The abstraction is divided into a separate function for each of the components in the macro state. Given a time t, an abstraction function returns a component of the macro state corresponding to the micro state at t. Every abstraction function except the one associated with the program counter actually constructs the macro state component from the micro-machine state one cycle later to account for the pipeline latency. The definition given below is applicable to only those situations where the process stack at the macro level does not cause an overflow. As was explained in Section 7.4.2, the correctness of the microcode in the presence of stack overflow is shown as a separate property.

```
ABSpc(t): word = DPC(t)

stack_cache_size(t): nat = bv2nat(SV1(t)) + bv2nat(TV1(t))

ABStos(t): word = TOS(t+1) - stack_cache_size(t+1)

ABSsklm(t): word = SKLM(t+1)

ABSdenv(t): word = DENV(t+1)

ABSlenv(t): word = LENV(t+1)

ABScenv(t): word = CENV(t+1)

i: VAR nat
ith_top_of_scache: [time -> [nat -> word]]
ith_top_of_scache: AXIOM i < stack_cache_size(t)   =>
 ith_top_of_scache(t)(i) =
   IF i < bv2nat(TV1(t)) THEN IF i = 0    THEN T0(t)
                              ELSIF i = 1 THEN T1(t)
                              ELSE T2(t) ENDIF
   ELSE REG(t)(stack_cache_size(t)-i-1) ENDIF

ABSdmem(t)(dptr: data_env_ptr)(daddr: word): word =
   IF bv2nat(daddr) < bv2nat(TOS(t+1)) &
       bv2nat(daddr) >= bv2nat(TOS(t+1)) - stack_cache_size(t+1)
      THEN LET offset =  stack_cache_size(t+1) - (bv2nat(TOS(t+1))
                           - bv2nat(daddr))
         IN ith_top_of_scache(t+1)(offset)
      ELSE DATA_MEMORY(t+1)(dptr o daddr) ENDIF
```

Every macro state component, except TOS and dmem, has a direct correspondence with a micromachine component. Since the elements of the stack cache are viewed as being in the data memory at the macro level, the macro TOS is smaller than the micro TOS by the size of the stack cache, i.e. (SV1 + TV1). The locations of dmem correspond to the locations in DATA_MEMORY except for those that range from the micromachine (TOS - 1) to (TOS - (SV1+TV1)).

7.6.6   The verification conditions

A common strategy used to prove the commuting property of Figure 7.13 is to start from an arbitrary visible state at the lower left-hand corner of the diamond, to traverse the two possible paths to the top right-hand corner of the diamond, and then to check whether the two states resulting from the traversals are equivalent. Traversing the top path, which entails applying the abstraction function followed by "running" the macromachine one step, results in the **expected** state. Traversing the bottom path, which consists of running the micromachine a multiple number of cycles followed by an application of the abstraction function, gives the **actual** state.

In a proof, running the micro- and the macromachines can be accomplished by **rewriting**, which consists of unfolding every occurrence of a defined function with its definition until all the functions have been simplified to primitive expressions. Checking whether the expected and actual states are equivalent is essentially a problem of checking the equivalence of Boolean or bit vector expressions since the state of most of the machine components is modelled as either Boolean or bit vector types.

As discussed in Section 7.6.3, the number of cycles that the micromachine needs to be run depends on the type of current instruction and whether one or more of the stalling conditions apply. Hence, a proof typically consists of a case analysis on these conditions.

We used a bottom-up incremental approach to mechanizing the verification of the correctness criterion. In this approach, we formulate a set of properties, called **verification conditions**, about the execution traces of the micromachine that can originate from a visible state under restricted scenarios.

The verification conditions are formulated so that the commuting property can be proved by combining the verification conditions using higher-level proof techniques, such as induction and case-splitting, without having to reason with the AAMP5 microcode. The formulation of the verification conditions reflects the initial case analysis that must be performed in constructing a proof of the commuting property to determine the number of cycles the micromachine must be run in the proof.

The main reason for taking the bottom-up approach was that the macro specification, which was primarily written at Rockwell, was still evolving when the verification task was begun at SRI. Also the amount of rewriting that would have to be done in a top-down undecomposed approach would strain the capacity of the PVS rewriter. This increased demand on the rewriter arises in part from the constructive style of specification that the macro specification was initially written in, as described earlier. The constructive style increased the depth of the hierarchy in the definition of the next state function of the macromachine.

The decision to take a bottom-up approach, while chosen for technical reasons, had several beneficial consequences. The proofs of the verification conditions can be constructed almost completely automatically because the crucial case splitting that determines the number of cycles on the micromachine has already been done. The Rockwell engineers related much more readily to the verification conditions than to the general correctness criterion.

However, most important, the approach provided a convenient method for partial verification of a complex and big design, such as the AAMP5. It was the quickest and, perhaps, the only way we could have obtained useful feedback from the verification exercise within the time allotted for the project.

Instruction-specific verification conditions

The verification conditions are organized into a number of sets, with a separate set for each specific instruction and a general set of that consists of properties common to all instructions. In this section, we discuss the instruction-specific verification conditions using the ADD instruction for illustration. The set of general verification conditions in discussed below.

The verification conditions[3] for the ADD instruction, assuming there will be no exception, are shown in Figure 7.6.6. The exception case has a separate set of verification conditions. A number of observations are in order regarding the verification conditions.

```
% Verification conditions for ADD in the absence of exception
ADD_correctness: THEORY

  BEGIN

  IMPORTING global_assumptions, invariants, reg_file_theorems,
            next_instrn_correctness_general, ADD_correctness_setup,
            bv_rules, more_bv_rules

 t, t1, t2: VAR time

SVTV_correctness: LEMMA
   visible_state_with(ADD)(t) & SysInv(t) =>
     bv2nat(SV1(t+2)) = bv2nat(SV1(t+1))-1 &
           bv2nat(TV1(t+2)) = bv2nat(TV1(t+1))

T0_correctness: LEMMA
   visible_state_with(ADD)(t) & SysInv(t) =>
      T0(t+2) = (sign_extend[16](48)(ith_top_of_scache(t+1)(1))
                  + sign_extend[16](48)
                         (ith_top_of_scache(t+1)(0)))^(15,0)

i: VAR below[10]
REG_correctness: LEMMA
   visible_state_with(ADD)(t) & SysInv(t) =>
                 REG(t + 2)(i) = REG(t + 1)(i)

DATA_MEMORY_correctness: LEMMA
   visible_state_with(ADD)(t) & SysInv(t) =>
     DATA_MEMORY(t+2) = DATA_MEMORY(t+1)

next_macro_instrn_entry: LEMMA
  visible_state_with(ADD)(t) & SysInv(t) & NOT Soverflow(t + 1) =>
    (EXISTS (tp: time | tp > t):
```

Figure 7.16 Verification conditions for ADD.

The verification conditions state the effect on the state of each of the micromachine

[3]The PVS text of the verification conditions and other formalizations shown in this report is a slightly edited version of the PVS theories actually used in the proofs.

components relevant to the macro state by the execution of an instruction, in this case ADD. In Figure 7.6.6, the predicate `visible_state_with(ADD)(t)` (defined in Section 7.6.4) is included as a precondition to the verification conditions because we are interested in analyzing properties of execution traces that start from a visible state where the instruction of interest is the current instruction. It is important to note that the expected value for the state of a component is expressed only in terms of the initial values of the states of the macro-level-relevant components. Thus, although the verification conditions do not relate the micro state to the macro state, they are, in effect, making assertions about the intended changes to the macro state.

The other precondition, `SysInv`, in the verification conditions consists of a set of conditions that are expected to hold in every visible state of the micromachine. `SysInv`, whose definition is shown below, is also included as a post-condition in the `next_macro_instrn_entry` verification condition to ensure that it is preserved at the next visible state.

```
% DJMP and SADJ flip-flops can't be high at instruction entry point
% for, if they were, then MC0 would be null_MC0, which is not the
% case at an instruction entry point.
  DJMPinv_ep(t): bool = NOT DJMP(t)
  SADJinv_ep(t): bool = NOT SADJ(t)

  % Constraints on stack occupancy registers SV and TV
  SVinv(t): bool = bv2nat[3](SV(t)) <= 6
  TVinv(t): bool = bv2nat[3](TV(t)) <= 3

  SysInv(t): bool =
    SADJinv_ep(t)& DJMPinv_ep(t) & SVinv(t) & TVinv(t)
```

`SVTV_correctness` states that SV1 should be decreased by one and TV1 should remain unchanged, which reflects the fact that ADD, by popping two elements and pushing one element, decreases the net size of the process stack by one. Since the number of microinstructions executed for ADD is one, in the absence of exception, all the results (except for the next instruction moving in) would be at their destinations two cycles from the initial visible state. Thus, every verification condition, except `next_macro_instrn_entry`, relates the state of a component at `t+2` with those at `t+1`. The reason for using `t+1` instead of `t` is to adjust for the one cycle latency for the abstraction function.

`T0_correctness` states that the T0 register, which holds the top of stack, must contain the result of adding the top two elements of the current process stack. The function `ith_top_of_scache(t)(i)`, which returns the element at a given distance `i` from the top of the stack cache state at time `t`, is used to fetch the process stack elements. The required arguments for ADD are guaranteed to be resident in the stack cache because the entry condition for the instruction is satisfied in a visible state.

`REG_correctness` states that the register file must remain unchanged as a result of ADD. This condition ensures two requirements on the normal execution of ADD. (1) The contents of none of the special registers (SKLM, TOS, DENV, CENV) ought to change, and (2) the contents of the stack cache registers unused by the ADD instruction remains unchanged. DATA_MEMORY_correctness requires that the contents of the physical memory remain unchanged. The only time a stack instruction, such as ADD, can affect physical memory is as a result of a stack adjustment performed prior to the entry of the instruction. In our approach, the correctness of stack adjustment, which is described below, is proved separately.

The next_macro_instrn_entry verification condition ensures that the next instruction, i.e. the first microinstruction of the next macroinstruction, moves into MC0 and the processor enters a visible state. Since the distance to the next visible state is indefinite depending on whether and how long the pipeline will be stalled, this verification condition, unlike the rest of the verification conditions for ADD, has to be expressed as an eventuality property using an existential quantifier. To prove this verification condition, it is necessary to reason about the stalling behaviour of the pipeline. Since the behaviour of the pipeline during stalling is uniform over all instructions, we separated their formalization into the general verification conditions discussed in the next section. The general verification conditions are used as lemmas in proving next_macro_instrn_entry.

General verification conditions

The general (i.e. instruction-independent verification) verification conditions characterize the behaviour of the micromachine when the AAMP5 pipeline stalls. The general verification conditions that characterize three possible ways in which the pipeline can stall are shown in Figure 7.17.

The DPU_freeze_lemma asserts that the state of every micromachine register, including those in the register file, remain unchanged as long as DHLD is true. The LFU_induced_stalling lemma states a property about the MAP_WAIT loop microcode that the DPU executes while the LFU is not ready with the next instruction. It asserts that if (1) MC0 has the last microinstruction of an arbitrary macroinstruction (MAP?(MC0(t))) and (2) the LFU is not RDY, then the next time when RDY becomes true, the relevant information about the next macroinstruction will move into MC0 and DPC. It also asserts that during the time the DPU is waiting for RDY to become true, the state of every component (except DPC) relevant to the macrostate remains unchanged. This lemma also includes several ancillary conditions that were brought out during the proof process. For example, NOT nextDJMP(t) and NOT nextDJMP(t+1) are imposed as pre-conditions to the lemmas because the MAP_WAIT loop will be entered only when a delayed jump does not occur. NOT SADJcondn(t+i+1) is a pre-condition to the lemma since the next macroinstruction will move into MC0 when the MAP_WAIT loop is exited, i.e. at t+i+2, only if the next macroinstruction does not require a stack adjustment. The lemma also ensures that the invariants will be true at t+i+2.

The stack_adjust_lemma states a property about the behaviour of the execution of the stack adjustment microcode. It asserts that if (1) MC0 has the last microinstruction of a macroinstruction (MAP?(MC0(t))) and (2) the LFU is RDY with the next instruction, and (3) that instruction needs a stack adjustment (SADJcondn(t)), then the micromachine will eventually reach the state in which the following conditions hold.

1. CENV and DPC point to the next instruction.

```
all_but_DPC_and_dmem_stays_same(t1, t2): bool =
  SV1(t1) = SV1(t2) & TV1(t1) = TV1(t2) &
    SKLM(t1) = SKLM(t2) & TOS(t1) = TOS(t2) & LENV(t1) = LENV(t2) &
      DENV(t1) = DENV(t2) & CENV(t1) = CENV(t2)

all_but_data_mem_stays_same(t1, t2): bool =
  DPC(t1) = DPC(t2) & all_but_DPC_and_dmem_stays_same(t1, t2)

% Stalling due to DHLD
DPU_freeze_lemma: LEMMA
  stays_high(DHLD)(t1, t2) =>
    all_but_data_mem_stays_same(t1, t2+1)

% Stalling due to LFU not being ready
LFU_induced_stalling: LEMMA
 MAP?(MC0(t)) & NOT RDY(t) & stays_low(RDY)(t, t+i) & RDY(t+i+1)
  & NOT nextDJMP(t) & SysInv(t) & NOT nextDJMP(t+1) &
      NOT SADJcondn(t+i+1)=>
        MC0(t+i+2) = ROM(zero_extend[8](11)(EP(t+i+1))) &
          DPC(t+i+2) = DP(t+i+1) &
            all_but_DPC_and_dmem_stays_same(t+1, t+i+2) &
              NOT nextDJMP(t+i+1) & NOT nextDJMP(t+i+2) &
                SysInv(t+i+2)

% Stalling due to stack adjustment
stack_adjust_lemma: LEMMA
  MAP?(MC0(t)) & RDY(t) & SADJcondn(t) & NOT nextDJMP(t) &
    NOT stack_overflow_condn(t)
      => EXISTS (tp: time | tp > t):
            CENV(tp) = CENV(t) &
            DPC(tp) = DP(t) &
            MC0(tp) = ROM(zero_extend[8](11)(EP(t))) &
            entry_cond(next_opcode_at_DPC(t))(tp) &
            ABSdmem(tp) = ABSdmem(t) &
            NOT nextDJMP(tp) & SysInv(tp)

% A general lemma about fetching next instruction
guaranteed_fetch_of_next_instrn: LEMMA
  NOT nextDJMP(t) & NOT nextDJMP(t+1) & SysInv(t) &
      MAP?(MC0(t)) & NOT stack_overflow_condn(t)
  => (EXISTS (tp: time | tp > t):
      DPC(tp) = DPC(t) + length_of_instruction(opcode_at_DPC(t)) &
      MC0(tp) = ROM(zero_extend[8](11)
                          (EP_ROM(next_opcode_at_DPC(t)))) &
      entry_cond(next_opcode_at_DPC(t))(tp) &
      SysInv(tp) & NOT nextDJMP(tp) )
```

Figure 7.17 General verification conditions.

2. The first microinstruction of the next macroinstruction is back in MC0.
3. The entry condition (entry_cond) for the opcode associated with the macroinstruction is met.
4. The data memory as viewed by the macromachine (ABSdmem) is unchanged.

As before, this lemma also includes several preconditions that define the context in which the stack adjustment microroutine is entered. We have proved this lemma only in the absence of a stack overflow. (Section 7.6.9 discusses the scope of the verification work completed so far.) These lemmas can be combined to prove a general lemma guaranteed_fetch_of_next_instrn that guarantees the entrance of the first microinstruction of the next macroinstruction, whenever the DPU is at the end of the microcode of an arbitrary macroinstruction.

7.6.7   Bridging the micro–macro gap

The following proof tasks have to be performed to establish the relationship characterized by the commuting diagram shown in Figure 7.13.

1. *Micro-leap.* Prove the existence of a common time, the next visible state point, at which all of the verification conditions associated with a particular instruction will hold simultaneously.
2. *Macro-elevate.* Use the abstraction function to prove that the expected values, guaranteed by the verification conditions, for the macro-relevant micromachine components indeed correspond to the macro state conjectured by the next_macro_state function.

It is important to observe that neither of the above tasks requires any reasoning about the AAMP5 microcode. The need for a micro-leap proof arises primarily to relax the assumption that the DPU is never stalled for data memory accesses. A micro-leap proof involves performing a case analysis on the number of times the DPU would have to be stalled before the next visible point is reached. Each of these cases can be discharged using the general verification condition for the appropriate stalling condition.

Macro-elevate involves applying the abstraction function to elevate the microstate to the macrostate as well as unwinding the next_macro_state function. The proof effort (rewriting) involved in applying the abstraction function is not particularly complex because the abstraction function definition, except for data memory, is straightforward for AAMP5. The effort required to rewrite the definition of next_macro_state, however, is quite complex. This complexity is partly due to the constructive style chosen for the macro specification, which introduced a significant number of intermediate definitional layers, and partly because the specification was not written in a fashion amenable to efficient rewriting.

As a result, we decided to decompose the macro-elevate step by first formulating a set of macro lemmas that characterized the value returned by next_macro_state for each of the restricted scenarios for which a separate set of verification conditions was set up. The macro lemma for the ADD instruction for the case where the instruction does not yield an exception is shown in Section 7.4.2.

7.6.8   Mechanization of proofs of verification conditions

In an interactive theorem prover, such as PVS, proof of a goal (i.e. a formula) is constructed by interactively (or automatically) invoking inference steps to simplify the given goal into simpler subgoals until all the subgoals are trivially true. At the highest level, the user directs the verification process by elaborating and modifying the specification, providing relevant lemmas, and backtracking on the fruitless paths in a proof attempt. Given our style of hardware specification, proof of a formula relating two states of a state machine that are a fixed distance apart usually follows a standard pattern consisting of a sequence of proof tasks shown below. Note that every verification condition in Figure 7.6.6 except the last one is a formula of this form.

- *Quantifier elimination.* Eliminate (skolemize) the universally quantified variable (t) by skolemization and simplify the pre-conditions. **Skolemization** consists of replacing the universally quantified variable by a new constant symbol denoting an arbitrary value for that variable. This technique is a simple and general way to prove a property for all values in a set that a variable ranges over.
- *Unfolding definitions.* Simplify selected expressions and defined function symbols in the goal by rewriting using definitions, axioms or previously established lemmas in the micromachine specification.
- *Case analysis.* At the end of the unfolding step, the original goal will have been simplified to an equation on two nested IF-THEN-ELSE expressions, not necessarily identical, involving user-defined as well as primitive function symbols. The IF-THEN-ELSEs are introduced by the unfolding of the defined function symbols. To prove such an equation, it may be necessary to split the proof, based on selected Boolean expressions in the current goal, and to further simplify the resulting goals.

The complexity and the degree of automation of the proof required to perform the above tasks depend on the level and efficiency of the primitive proof steps supported by a theorem prover. If the primitive inference steps are powerful and efficient, then one can use more brute-force and automatic strategies to perform the unfolding and case-analysis steps. If not, it is necessary to exercise more intelligent manual control in the proof to keep the size and number of cases small. The primitive inference steps of PVS are implemented using powerful and efficient decision procedures for linear arithmetic, equality on uninterpreted function expressions, and Boolean tautology checking. The primitive steps also use an efficient conditional rewriter that interacts with the decision procedures to simplify conditions. The following short PVS proof strategy, called the **core** strategy, can accomplish the above proof tasks:

```
1: ( then*
2:         (skosimp*)
3:         (auto-rewrite-micro-theories)
4:         (repeat (assert))
5:         (apply (then* (repeat (lift-if))
6:                       (bddsimp)
7:                       (assert)))))
```

*then** on line 1 is a strategy constructor that composes a sequence of commands. The proof command on line 2 performs the skolemization task. The command on line 3 makes rewrite rules out of all the definitions and axioms in our specification, after which, the command on line 4 rewrites all the expressions in the goal until no further simplification is possible. `assert` is the PVS primitive command that performs rewriting as well as simplifications using arithmetic and equality decision procedures. In the case of our verification conditions, this rewriting step has the effect of reducing all expressions into ones that involve only values of signals in the initial state. The compound proof step on lines 5 through 7 performs the case-analysis and further simplification task. The case analysis is performed by lifting all the `IF-THEN-ELSE` structures to the top and then simplifying the resulting expression propositionally (`bddsimp`). (*apply* applies a compound proof step as an atomic step.)

We have used the core strategy (or slight variants of it) to prove completely automatically the correctness of several microprocessor designs that have served as informal hardware verification benchmarks for theorem provers. See Cyrluk *et al.* (1994) for more details about application of this strategy for hardware verification. The core strategy was, however, not adequate to automate proofs of the AAMP5 verification conditions. The core strategy is usually successful in constructing a proof if the rewriting step simplifies the original goal into a relation on expressions involving either operations on primitive PVS types that the decision procedures are capable of handling or user-defined functions that can be left uninterpreted.

The AAMP5 specification, at both the micro and macro levels, uses a number of complex bit vector operations, such as concatenation (o), subsetting (^), shifting, etc. All bit vector operations are specified as parameterized functions that are defined recursively in the bit vector library. The core strategy, when unsuccessful in proving a verification condition, simplifies the original goal into equations on bit vector expressions. These expressions can be shown to be equivalent only by using properties about the bit vector operations as lemmas. To automate the bit vector equivalence checking step of the proof, we formulated a number of bit vector lemmas in the form of rewrite rules. Most of these lemmas have been proved as theorems by Rick Butler using the bit vector library. A subset of these rules can be used to first attempt to simplify the bit vector expressions into a common normal form. If the rules are unsuccessful in normalizing the expressions into a common form, then another set of rules can be used to convert the bit vector equivalence into an equivalence on natural numbers that can most likely be handled by the decision procedures.

A significant portion of our verification effort was devoted to formulating the bit vector simplification rules. The rules formulated are parameterized with respect to the size of the bit vectors involved, but are not complete enough to decide equivalence for all possible bit vector expressions. They were able to decide successfully equivalence of expressions in most of our proofs. Even when they were unsuccessful, we had to perform only a few standard case splits manually to complete the proof.

The core strategy can automate the proofs of only those verification conditions relating micromachine states that are a fixed distance apart. The general verification conditions do not fall into the above category. The general verification conditions are proved using induction on the length of the execution trace that the verification conditions constrain. For example, the `stack_adjust_lemma` has to be proved by induction on the number of stack cache elements that have to be moved to satisfy the entry condition. Once the proper induction scheme is set up, the core strategy can be used to complete the proofs of the different cases.

7.6.9   Scope of the verification performed

The goal of this project was multifold. Besides demonstrating the verification of a portion of AAMP5 microcode, we were interested in investigating how formal verification technology can be packaged so that practicing engineers could use it productively, with some expert help, for verifying a complex microprocessor design. Hence the contributions of this project extend beyond what was mechanically verified. In the following, we discuss the scope and some of the limitations of our verification effort.

1. We developed a methodology for incremental verification of a complex microprogrammed and pipelined microprocessor design. The methodology includes the following three components:

   - a style of specification that strikes a good compromise between the competing demands of efficient verifiability vs readability by practicing engineers;

   - an approach to systematically decomposing the problem of verifying the general correctness criterion for a processor specified at two levels to a set of smaller more automatically provable verification conditions;

   - a proof strategy that can be used to verify the verification conditions completely automatically or that can be used within a higher-level proof technique, such as induction, to construct a proof of the verification conditions.

2. We formalized the verification conditions of a total of eleven instructions and verified them completely using the core strategy. Seven of these verified instructions are from the core set and are representative of several of the main classes—literal data, assign data, reference data, and branch—of AAMP5 instructions. The rest of the verified instructions are from a supplementary set that has instructions drawn from the same class as the core set. One of the instructions from the supplementary set (AND) was partly verified by one of the Rockwell staff members (Al Mass) working on the project.

3. We have developed the basic formal machinery required to specify the entire macroinstruction set architecture of AAMP5 and used it to specify over 100 of its instructions.

4. We have derived a set of macro lemmas from the macro specification that specify the instructions in the core set in a declarative style.

Of the accomplishments listed above, the one whose impact is, perhaps, the most enduring is the development of the methodology. Not only can a significant part of the methodology be reused in the verification of another member of the AAMP5 family of processors, but many of the general ideas are useful in verifying any complex microprocessor design.

Some of the limitations of the project are the following.

1. The verification conditions that were mechanically verified prove the correctness of instructions only in the absence of any external interrupts. The framework and the methodology developed here are capable of formalizing and verifying correctness of instructions in the presence of interrupts. We have formalized the correctness of the `reset` interrupt although it was not included in the report.

2. Not every AAMP5 instruction class had a representative among the instructions that were verified. For example, instructions, such as CALL, RETURN, belonging to procedure call class were not verified. One of the reasons the verification did not address stack overflow was because a stack overflow condition, in general, involves procedure calling. Arithmetic instructions implementing floating point calculations were not addressed by the verification.

3. The correspondence between the verification conditions and the macro lemmas was verified only for the ADD instruction. The strategies used to perform this proof task for ADD should be applicable for other instructions.

4. The proof of correctness is only valid for programs that are not self-modifying.

5. The correctness of our verification is predicated on the correctness of the interface specification, which has been inspected by Collins but has not been verified with respect to the LFU and BIU. Verification of the interface specification, which is expressed as properties of the protocol used by the DPU to interact with its environment, is best done using state enumeration verification tools, such as CTL model checkers (Gupta, 1992) on an abstract global state machine of the DPU–BIU–LFU system. We have verified some the properties in the interface specification for a simplified model of the DPU–BIU–LFU interface using *Murφ* (Melton and Dill, 1993) and the recently implemented connection between PVS and a model checker.

7.6.10   Errors discovered by the verification effort

Analysis of a system by means of formal methods can reveal errors in two ways. First, the act of formalizing the system specification by itself forces a closer scrutiny of the design than would be performed using traditional methods. Second, mechanizing the proof of correctness has the effect of "testing" the design for all possible inputs. In the AAMP5 verification exercise, both the specification and the proof phases revealed errors in the microcode.

Two errors in the microcode were found while constructing the macroarchitecture specification. Both errors were found while trying to specify formally the behaviour of the AAMP under unusual circumstances that were not clearly specified in the AAMP2 Reference Manual, prompting a team member to examine the microcode in the AAMP5. The first was a logic error that allowed the top-of-stack register (TOS) to wrap around a data environment instead of raising a stack overflow. To result in a failure, this error required the very unlikely combination of an unusual system configuration, an improperly sized stack, and a specific sequence of instructions. The second error was made precisely because the reference manual was unclear on how the AAMP should update the local environment register (LENV) when a procedure call caused a stack overflow. This was implemented by setting the LENV to its "overflow" value, while the correct behaviour was to leave the LENV unchanged. While this error would have been discovered during Ada validation testing, the validation suite would not have been executed until after the first AAMP5 chips were in hand. Both errors were unique to the AAMP5 and corrected before first fabrication.

Errors were also found in the formal specifications through inspections as discussed in Sections 7.4.3 and 7.5.6. These revealed 28 correctness errors in the macro specification and 19 correctness errors in the micro specification. Even so, constructing proofs of correctness found several additional errors in our specifications. In the initial stages, most of the errors found were mistakes in our micromachine specification. Some of these were due to ambiguities or mistakes in the microarchitecture document and the rest were errors in our transcription of the design document into a formal specification.

One technique used to find errors in our specifications was to assign independent teams to different portions of the project. For example, different individuals at Collins were assigned to review and revise the macro and micro specifications. While this independence undoubtedly introduced some errors of communication, it also reduced the likelihood of coincident errors in the macro and micro specifications, greatly increasing our confidence in the specifications once the proof was actually completed.

More significant were errors discovered in the microcode itself by the proof process. Since only a small set of instructions were to be formally verified and because these instructions had already been verified by traditional methods, it was unlikely that any errors would be found through the correctness proofs. Two address this, two memory calculation errors were deliberately inserted in the microcode without the knowledge of SRI. The motivation behind this was not only to check whether the proof process would reveal the errors but also to see whether it would provide enough information to show how the errors could be corrected.

One of the microcode errors was in the ASNDXI instruction, which moves data in the process stack to a location in memory. The other was in the REFBXU instruction, which loads data from memory to the top of process stack. The ASNDXI error was deliberately planted by Collins. The REFBXU error was an actual error that had not been detected by traditional verification methods such as walk-throughs and testing, but was found by

Collins while running samples of application code on early prototypes of the AAMP5 chip. This error was left in the microcode delivered to SRI to determine whether the proof process would find an error that was discovered late in the traditional verification process.

The two errors were similar in that they occurred in the calculation of the memory address and were hard to spot during microcode walk-throughs owing to the pipelining of microinstructions. The address of an AAMP5 memory location is constructed as a concatenation of a pointer to a data environment and an offset into the data environment. The REFBXU instruction, for example, uses the top three elements—A, B, and I—of the process stack to determine the source data address. The least significant byte of B is used as the data environment pointer part of the address while A+I/2 forms the offset. The error in the microcode had the effect of I being used for the data environment instead of B.

This error was not detected during simulation owing to a limitation in the simulator's memory model. The memory model has since been enhanced, but, even with this change, errors such as these could still be missed since a simulation run can only exercise a small fraction of the input space. One of the advantages of formal verification is that it has the effect of exhaustive testing since the proof performs symbolic reasoning for all possible inputs.

An error in the microcode manifests itself during a proof in the form of a verification condition reducing to a goal that is unprovable. The error in the REFBXU instruction, for instance, was detected during the proof of the verification condition that characterized the correctness of the T0 register. The unprovable proof goal that was produced at the end of the application of the proof strategy described in Section 7.6.8 is shown below.

```
[-1]    nmod(bv2nat[3](SV(t0)) + bv2nat(TV(t0)) + 5, 6) >= 0
[-2]    nmod(bv2nat[3](SV(t0)) + bv2nat(TV(t0)) + 5, 6) < 6
        . . . .
[-7]    (bv2nat(TV(t0)) = 2)
[-8]    islow(REG(t0 + 1)(bv2nat(SV(t0)) + bv2nat(TV(t0)) - 3) ^ 0)
      |-------
[1]     nextDJMP(t0)
[2]     SADJ(t0)
[3]     DJMP(t0)
{4}     fill[8](0)
          ((DATA_MEMORY(t0 + 1)(REG(t0 + 1)
              (bv2nat[3](SV(t0)) - 1))^ (7, 0) o (T0(t0 + 1) ^ (15, 0)
              + (fill[1](0) o REG(t0 + 1)
                    (bv2nat[3](SV(t0)) - 1) ^ (15, 1))))^(7,0))
          = fill[8](0) o ((DATA_MEMORY(t0 + 1)(T1(t0 + 1) ^ (7, 0) o
                    (T0(t0 + 1) ^ (15, 0) +
              (fill[1](0) o REG(t0 + 1)
                    (bv2nat(SV(t0)) - 1) ^ (15, 1)))))^ (7, 0))
```

A careful reading of the succedent labelled 4, which is the reduced form of the equation that compares the actual (on the left hand side) and the expected values (on the right hand side) for the T0 register, in the sequent shows that the equation is false. The two sides are identical except for the term appearing in the data environment part of the memory address.

While the expected result is supposed to get this from the T1 register (T1(t0 + 1)^(7, 0)), the microcode actually uses the REG register instead, which contains the third element from the top of stack.

7.7 Conclusions and lessons learned

7.7.1 Feasibility of formal verification

The central result of this project was to demonstrate the technical feasibility of formally specifying the AAMP5 and the use of mechanical proofs of correctness to verify its microcode and microarchitecture. A much larger fraction of the AAMP instruction set was specified than originally planned, with 108 of the AAMP's 209 instructions completed. The portion completed is actually greater than this, since many of the instructions specified are representative of an entire family of instructions. This is notable since the AAMP has a large and complex instruction set, providing in hardware many of the features normally provided by the compiler's run-time environment and the real-time executive.

All of the microarchitecture needed for formal verification of the microcode was formally specified. Because of the style of specification chosen, translation of the microcode into PVS was a simple exercise that should be easy to automate.

At this time, eleven instructions have been proven correct in the absence of interrupts. Since these are representative of several major instruction classes, most of the low level proof strategies could be reused in verification of the remaining instructions. The existence of these strategies will also make it simpler to transfer this technology to Collins. We do not see any technical obstacles to extending either the specification of the macroarchitecture or the correctness proofs.

7.7.2 Benefits of formal verification

Many benefits were obtained on this project through the use of formal specifications alone. Our experiences suggest that one of the most important benefits of formal specification is to define precisely the interface between users and developers, encouraging the development of a clean interface. For example, the difficulty of formally specifying when stack overflow is detected pointed out the need to hide the stack cache better from an application programmer. The process of completing a formal specification encourages the specifier to "look in the corners" and to consider unusual cases and boundary conditions that are often sources of errors. To our surprise, this process alone uncovered two errors in the microcode that had not yet been discovered by traditional methods. Formal specification also pointed out several situations that the AAMP2 Reference Manual (Rockwell International, 1990) and the AAMP5 design documents left unspecified or stated unclearly. This seems to be a general deficiency of any English specification and not of the AAMP documentation.

The process of performing mechanical proofs has detected several errors in the formal macro and micro specifications. More importantly, the correctness proofs systematically found two errors seeded in the microcode. Our belief is that construction of a proof does force a much more detailed review of the microcode than is achieved through traditional methods such as walk-throughs.

7.7.3   Cost of formal verification

The cost of developing and validating the macro- and microarchitecture specifications and developing the proofs of correctness were significant, but many of these expenses have to be attributed to the exploratory nature of the project. Reuse of specifications, proof strategies, and expertise should greatly reduce these costs in the future. Some portions of the specification, such as the bit vector theories, can be reused across a wide range of hardware applications. For microprocessors in the AAMP family, virtually the entire macroarchitecture specification can be reused. Even for new development, the examples created in this project are rich enough to allow the designers to write similar specifications, eliminating the time spent by SRI in studying the AAMP5 and by Collins in reviewing and revising the formal specifications.

A large portion of the time spent on the correctness proofs was invested in the development of reusable proof strategies rather than just proving the correctness of the core set of instructions. Also, much of the overhead of completing the proofs was due to inefficiencies in the implementation of PVS then available. Improvements to PVS incorporated as a direct result of this project rectify most of these problems. Even so, formal verification is likely to remain more expensive than traditional methods. This should not be surprising. Traditional methods rely on reviews, partial analyses, and testing a portion of the input space. Proofs of correctness are a rigorous form of analysis that verifies the design for all possible inputs. To provide the same level of assurance, traditional methods would be just as expensive as formal methods, if not more so.

7.7.4   Transferring formal methods to industry

It is very difficult to inject new methodologies into an industrial setting since one of the ways industry remains competitive is to use tried and tested approaches within a well-understood problem domain. Despite their name, formal methods provide remarkably little methodology to guide their use in a new setting. The difficulties in specifying and verifying a real-time executive are likely to be very different from those of verifying microcode. Given this, it seems prudent to plan for costs to be high the first time around and to expect most of the benefits to appear on subsequent projects of a similar nature. It is our belief that the groundwork performed on this project will greatly lower the cost of specifying and verifying another member of the AAMP family, a hypothesis we plan to demonstrate in the upcoming year.

We did not feel that it was particularly difficult for the engineers at Collins to learn to use either the PVS language or the theorem prover. In fact, it was much easier for them to apply formal methods than it was for the formal methods experts to become knowledgeable about the AAMP5. The real problem was not how to use PVS, but how to build a precise mathematical model of our own microprocessor. Even so, widespread acceptance of a general-purpose specification language such as PVS or Z by practicing engineers is likely to be an uphill battle (Burns *et al.*, 1992). A more productive approach may be to develop specialized notations or models that fit a specific problem domain and that can automatically be translated into an underlying formalism such as PVS. This would allow the domain experts to work in a familiar and natural notation while a small group of formal methods experts (and tools) check their work for consistency and completeness.

In the near term, an important goal on future projects will be to have formal specification integrated into the early design effort. This will eliminate many of the costs of developing and validating the specifications, particularly if they can be used as the primary specification, not just as an add-on. Enhancements to PVS could facilitate this. In particular, integrating PVS with the standard document preparation system used at Collins would allow us to intersperse the formal specification with the text and diagram style used currently, i.e. the "specification as a document" concept promoted in Z and CaDiZ (Burns *et al.*, 1992).

Validation of formal specifications is essential to have confidence in the correctness proofs. We found inspections worked well with formal specifications, were quite inexpensive, and provided a natural vehicle for training. Maximizing the independence of the teams producing the specifications greatly increased our confidence in both the proofs and the specifications. When combined with proofs of correctness, this is a very powerful validation technique that should not be overlooked. Other forms of validation that could have been used more extensively in this project include early proof of the type correctness conditions generated by PVS and proving expected properties, or putative theorems, of the specification. Even our limited experience with proving putative theorems suggests that this is a useful validation technique.

Full proofs of microcode correctness are a very rigorous form of analysis, enabling one person to achieve a much higher level of confidence than can now be achieved by a team. Even so, there is very little in existing verification practices that would be eliminated by formal proofs. It may be possible to decrease the time spent on inspections, but some level of peer review will still be necessary to ensure good style and maintainability, and to check for issues not modelled in the specifications. It may be possible to replace some testing with proofs, but testing would not be eliminated since it provides an important check on the fidelity of the specifications and low-level properties not modelled in the specification. In the specific case of the AAMP family, large libraries of simulations and diagnostics have been built up over the years. These cost very little to modify and execute, so it is unlikely that any testing would be eliminated on future AAMP projects.

Formal methods provide the means to improve, not replace, existing practices. Formal specification can play an important role by improving the precision and clarity of communication, particularly when the specification language closely matches the problem domain. Formal verification of selected properties can provide validation of the specifications that would be particularly valuable during early lifecycle activities such as requirements capture. Finally, formal proofs of correctness provide a rigorous analysis of the consistency between a specification and its design appropriate when extremely high levels of assurance are essential or when the complexity of interacting components is so great that analysis is the only adequate means of verification.

Acknowledgements

The authors thank Rick Butler of NASA Langley for his support and refinement of the bit vectors library, Sam Owre and Natarajan Shankar of SRI International for the development and maintenance of PVS, and Al Mass and Dave Greve of Rockwell International for their many hours on this project. We also thank John Rushby of SRI and John Gee, Dave Hardin, Doug Hiratzka, Ray Kamin, Charlie Kress, Norb Hemesath, Steve Maher, Jeff Russell, and Roger Shultz of Rockwell for their support and assistance.

Chapter 8

Modelling and Verification of a Simple Real-time Railroad Gate Controller

William D. Young

8.1 Introduction

Safety-critical systems with real-time aspects often involve complex and time-sensitive interactions between the environment and the system. Consequently, informal reasoning may be inadequate for providing assurance of the correct functioning of such systems (see for example Lincoln and Rushby (1993)). The use of mechanically supported formal reasoning can often provide a much higher level of assurance than informal reasoning alone.

Given the diversity of automated reasoning systems, it is reasonable to ask which is the "right" system for a given problem. Often it is infeasible to experiment with multiple automated reasoning systems in the context of a realistic real-time application owing to the considerable effort required to model a complex system in even one formal framework. There are seldom sufficient resources to model and compare the performances of several competing formalisms. An alternative approach is to compare the performance of various formal reasoning systems on benchmark problems of manageable complexity. Ideally, the benchmark problem should be solved by expert users of the various tools to give the clearest indications of the strengths and weaknesses of the tools. Then, an independent evaluation of the tools can be made based on the results. Hopefully, the lessons of such comparisons can be extrapolated to gain insights into the applicability of these systems on problems of interest.

A potential benchmark in the area of safety-critical systems is a simple problem suggested by Leveson and Stolzy (1987) involving modelling of a controller for a gate at a railroad crossing. This problem has been proposed (Heitmeyer *et al.*, 1993b) as a benchmark for investigating the expressiveness and proof power of various formal systems. Specifications of the gate controller have been performed in the EVES prover of Odyssey Research (ORA, 1992), with SRI's PVS prover (Shankar, 1992), and with the Modechart graphical language (Jahanian and Stuart, 1988). Heitmeyer *et al.* (1993a) describe a solution using CSP and the FDR tool (Formal Systems (Europe) Ltd., 1992). A related problem has been specified by Wood (1992) using the Z specification language (Spivey, 1992) and in Nqthm (Smith, 1993).

We accepted the challenge of formalizing the Leveson-Stolzy benchmark with the Boyer–Moore logic Nqthm (Boyer *et al.*, 1991; Boyer and Moore, 1988; Kaufmann, 1992) and proving the relevant safety and utility properties with the Nqthm theorem prover. Because of limited time, the problem we solved is slightly more restricted than that proposed as a general benchmark by Heitmeyer *et al.* (1993b). In particular, we do not consider multiple trains. However, we believe that our solution could be readily extended to handle this case and we hope to do so in the future. Our goal was to provide the most natural solution to the problem with an eye to using Nqthm to best advantage. We have not attempted to compare our formulation with that in other systems. Several such comparisons are available (Heitmeyer and Lynch, 1994a,b; Heitmeyer and Jeffords, 1995).

In the following sections, we briefly describe the Nqthm logic and prover, outline the railroad gate problem, and present our solution to it. In the final section, we discuss the performance of Nqthm on this problem and draw some conclusions from this research. The appendix contains the complete text of the railroad gate specification in an infix form derived from our Nqthm script.

8.2   Nqthm

The logic in which we performed our modelling work is the Nqthm computational logic of Boyer and Moore (1988). Nqthm is well known for the extensive body of verification work done with it. We briefly review the logic, its mechanization, and the body of work performed with the system.

The Nqthm logic is a first-order, quantifier-free[1] logic resembling pure Lisp. The rules of inference are propositional calculus with equality, together with instantiation and mathematical induction up to ε_0. Two extension principles—recursive definition and conservative axiomatization of functions—are also provided. These permit extending the logic with new functions symbols in a conservative and sound manner.

The mechanization of the logic is a system of Common Lisp programs allowing the user to define functions in the logic, to execute them on concrete data, and to state and prove theorems about such functions. The Nqthm theorem prover is a collection of hundreds of heuristics to orchestrate the application of rewrite rules, decision procedures, mathematical induction, and other proof techniques. An interactive proof checker for Nqthm, called "Pc-Nqthm", has also been developed (Kaufmann, 1991, 1992).

Important to Nqthm's success has been the fact that when a new user-supplied theorem is proved, rules are derived from it and stored in its data base; these rules change the way the system behaves. By formulating an appropriate library of lemmas the user can effectively program Nqthm to prove theorems in a given domain. A well-chosen sequence of lemmas can lead Nqthm to the proofs of very deep theorems. Target theorems can often be changed and "re-proved" automatically because proof scripts tend to describe powerful and general-purpose rules for manipulating the concepts rather than particular proofs. That is, the user programs Nqthm to deal with the concepts and expects Nqthm to fill in the gaps between system-specific lemmas describing the proof at a high level. This makes it easy to "maintain" an evolving system of definitions and theorems if the system

---

[1] A treatment of quantified formulas has been added by Kaufmann (1992), and used in our work.

was initially verified with Nqthm. That, in turn, has allowed Nqthm to accumulate a vast quantity of benchmark theorems.

For example, some theorems from traditional mathematics that have been mechanically checked using the system include Gauss' law of quadratic reciprocity, the Church–Rosser theorem for lambda calculus, the infinite Ramsey theorem for the exponent 2 case, and Gödel's incompleteness theorem. Outside the range of traditional mathematics, the theorem prover has been used to check the recursive unsolvability of the halting problem for pure Lisp, the proof of invertibility of the RSA public key encryption algorithm, the correctness of numerous metatheoretic simplifiers for the logic, the correctness of several control algorithms, and the correctness of an implementation of an algorithm for achieving agreement among concurrently executing processes in the presence of faults. In the area of "systems verification" the prover has been used in the verification of the "CLI short stack" comprising a chain of abstract machines starting with a microprocessor (the FM8502) described at the gate level and ending with an operational semantics for a simple high-level programming language (Micro-Gypsy). Numerous other proofs have been done in the area of hardware and software verification; many of these are described in Boyer and Moore (1988).

Boyer, Kaufmann, and Moore are currently developing ACL2, an extended, reimplemented version of Nqthm that supports the applicative subset of Common Lisp as its logic. By formalizing a logic around applicative Common Lisp they take advantage of the exceptionally good optimizing compilers for Common Lisp to obtain, in many cases, execution speeds comparable with those of C. Two guiding tenets of the ACL2 project are to conform to all compliant Common Lisp implementations and to add nothing to the logic that violates the understanding that the user's input can be submitted directly to a Common Lisp compiler and then executed in an environment where suitable ACL2-specific macros and functions are defined. We expect to redo our railroad gate problem and many of the other Nqthm benchmarks in ACL2.

Though our specification and proof work was done entirely in Nqthm, in this paper we have chosen not to use the Lisp-like Nqthm syntax, but an infix transliteration. For example, to define a function to sum a list of numbers, the Nqthm user might type

```
(defn add-list (l)
  (if (nlistp l)
      0
      (plus (car l) (add-list (cdr l))))).
```

We will use the following alternative syntax.

Definition 1 (Add-list) The function *add-list*: $\mathcal{N}^* \to \mathcal{N}$ is defined as follows:

$$add\text{-}list\,(lst) \;\equiv\;$$

$$\begin{cases} 0 & if\ train\text{-}tr = \langle\,\rangle; \\ x + add\text{-}list\,(lst') & if\ lst = x \circ lst'. \end{cases}$$

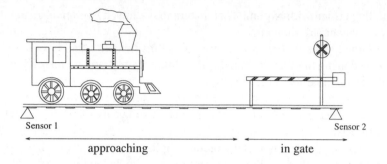

Figure 8.1 Train and gate system.

The primitive types appearing in function signatures are $\mathcal{L}$ for literal atoms, $\mathcal{N}$ for naturals, and $\mathcal{B}$ for Booleans. We use $\mathcal{S}^*$ to denote the type of finite lists of elements of set $\mathcal{S}$. Since Nqthm is an untyped logic, function "signatures" should be read as merely suggestive. All Nqthm-defined functions are total but may operate "strangely" on objects outside their intended domain. Guards on the various cases in function definitions usually will be disjoint, but should be considered as evaluated in order until some guard is true. Finally, we use the syntax $x \circ y$ for the Nqthm (cons x y), i.e., adding element x to the front of list y.

8.3 The Railroad gate problem

The problem we set out to solve with Nqthm may be stated very simply — design and verify a system to operate a gate at a railroad crossing safely. The system should have the properties that

- the gate is down whenever the train is in the crossing, and
- the gate is up as often as possible.

These are called, respectively, the **safety property** and **utility property** (Heitmeyer *et al.*, 1993b). Whether this is genuinely a "real-time" problem is a matter of debate; trains and crossing gates have very coarse timing requirements compared with the microsecond response time requirements of some application areas. In particular, we imagine that the computation time is not a significant fraction of the response time of the system. Nevertheless, we believe that our approach, if not our exact solution, is adaptable to other domains.

Figure 8.1 illustrates the system and its environment. Our task in modelling this system is to devise a control algorithm for the gate that preserves the safety and utility properties. To do so we make certain assumptions about the responses of the gate to the controller and about the general behaviour of trains on this line. We assume that

- trains on this line have a known maximum speed,
- the gate has known response parameters, including maximum and minimum times for opening and closing,
- sensors are available that can reliably determine when a train is within a given region of track,
- arrivals of trains at the gate are spaced sufficiently widely that we need only consider one train at a time.

The first assumption is required for any safe gate; an arbitrarily fast train could always race into the crossing before the gate could close. Placement of sensors to signal an approaching train assumes that we know the response parameters of the gate; a very sluggish gate will require placing Sensor$_1$ at a greater distance than a quick gate. The requirement that we treat only one train at a time is a significant simplification, but one that we believe would not be difficult to relax.

Given these assumptions, we have devised a simple gate control system and proved that the resulting system satisfies the safety and utility requirements.

8.4   Our formalization

Our model of system behaviour is essentially a discrete-time simulation of the system. At each "tick" of the global clock, the controller determines the position of the train with respect to the gate and generates a control pulse for the actuator that raises and lowers the gate. The granularity of time is not specified, but can be as fine or as coarse as desired. The behaviours of the controller, gate, and train are each specified independently; the system is specified in terms of their interactions. Finally, the system behaviour is related to the behaviour of the various subsystems by the correctness theorems.

8.4.1   The sensors and controller

Conceptually, the train can be in any of three "regions": approaching the gate, in the gate, or somewhere else. With reference to Figure 8.1, **approaching** means that the train has triggered Sensor$_1$; **other** means that the train has not yet triggered Sensor$_1$ or has already passed Sensor$_2$ indicating that the train has left the crossing. Being **in the gate** is a specification construct and is not really relevant to the controller behaviour; hence no sensor is needed directly in front of the crossing.

According to its current reading of the train's position, the controller generates a control pulse, which affects the position of the gate at the next clock tick. The control algorithm is trivial: if the train is in the other region, generate command open; otherwise, generate command close.

8.4.2   The gate

As we noted in Section 8.3, we require that the gate have known operational parameters. In particular, we assume that the gate responds reliably to open and close commands from the controller, and that there are known minimum and maximum times required for the gate to open fully or to close fully[2]. We record the state of the gate at any time in a "ghost" record with components ⟨*position, duration*⟩, recording the current position— open, closed, going-up, or going-down—and a duration indicating how long the gate will remain in its current position. Duration is meaningful only when the gate position is going-up or going-down.

   The state of the gate is re-computed at each tick based on the command received from the controller (in response to the sensed position of the train in the previous tick). When the gate receives a command, the new position is computed as a function of the previous position and the command. For example, given a command to close and a current gate state ⟨*pos, dur*⟩, the new gate position is computed as follows:

$$\begin{cases} \langle \texttt{going-down}, k-1 \rangle & \textit{if pos} = \texttt{open}; \\ \langle \texttt{closed}, \textit{dur} \rangle & \textit{if pos} = \texttt{closed}; \\ \langle \texttt{going-down}, k-1 \rangle & \textit{if pos} = \texttt{going-up}; \\ \langle \texttt{closed}, 0 \rangle & \textit{if pos} = \texttt{going-down} \wedge \textit{dur} = 0; \\ \langle \texttt{going-down}, \textit{dur}-1 \rangle & \textit{if pos} = \texttt{going-down} \wedge \textit{dur} \neq 0. \end{cases}$$

Here k is some unspecified natural number in the range [*gate-closing-min-time* ... *gate-closing-max-time*]. For any particular gate, we would compute k from the response parameters of the gate and its current position; we do not specify this computation. A similar specification applies to the next state of the gate when commanded to open.

8.4.3   The train

The train is that component of the system that is not under our control. However, to reason about the properties of the complete system, we must make certain reasonable assumptions about the behaviour of the train and model its behaviour under those assumptions.

   We model the behaviour of the train with a trace of the "position" of the train at each tick of the simulation clock. Here "position" refers to our very coarse notion of whether the train is approaching, in the gate, or elsewhere. Therefore, a legal trace of the train behaviour over time is a sequence of positions — in-gate, approaching, and other — subject to the following two constraints.

- The train may remain in a position for arbitrarily many ticks, but may only advance from other to approaching, from approaching to in-gate, and from in-gate to other.

---

[2]For technical reasons, we insist that the gate closing and gate opening maximum times be non-zero.

- Moreover, there is a system-dependent parameter *approaching-min-time* that specifies the minimum number of ticks the train must remain approaching before entering the gate.

For example, if *approaching-min-time* were 2, the following would be a legal partial train trace:

⟨other, approaching, approaching, in-gate, other⟩.

This would not

⟨other, approaching, in-gate, approaching⟩,

both because the approach is too short and because the train illegally jumps directly from in-gate to approaching.

These constraints on train traces are reasonable consequences of the assumptions we have made about our system. The progression from other to approaching to in--gate to other is merely the natural semantics of train behaviour in our system, given our assumptions that we are considering only one train at a time and that the sensors reliably detect the progression of the train. The constraint that the approach be of a given minimum duration follows from our requirement that there is a known maximum speed of trains on the line. We always can adjust the placement of Sensor₁ to ensure that we have enough advance warning of the imminent arrival of the train to enforce this constraint. As faster trains appear on the line, we may need to move Sensor₁ farther from the gate. Without some such assumption, we could never be assured of having enough time to lower the gate in time to satisfy our safety requirement.

Given that we can specify a minimum approaching interval and can adjust the placement of Sensor₁ to implement it, we enforce the following requirement:

$$approaching\text{-}min\text{-}time > gate\text{-}closing\text{-}max\text{-}time.$$

That is, we position Sensor₁ in such a way that it will signal the imminent arrival of the train in time always to allow us to lower the gate.

Notice that the farther from the gate we place Sensor₁, the "safer" the system but at a cost to "utility." Placing Sensor₁ at exactly the distance the fastest train could cover in *gate-closing-max-time* + 1 time units is adequate to ensure safety in our system and also to guarantee that the gate is open "as much as possible", as required by the utility property. It would be easy to show that any shorter distance would not satisfy the safety property for the fastest train. However, we do not require this in our proof. Instead, we only consider utility after the train has left the gate.

8.5 Specifying system behaviour

Given any legal trace of the train's position over time and an initial gate position, we can deterministically simulate the behaviour of the system. This simulation involves computing successive gate states in response to the advancing train position and the resulting control action. The output of this simulation is a trace of the gate behaviour, where each successive gate state $\langle$*position, duration*$\rangle$ in the trace is a function of its current state and the controller's current command (based upon the train position at the previous tick). Reasoning about this simulation is what allows us to prove that the system satisfies the desired safety and utility properties.

Our safety property is simple: the gate is down whenever the train is in the crossing. The formal statement is merely a relationship between any legal train trace and the corresponding trace of the gate. The desired relationship is captured in the following Boolean-valued recursive function[3]:

Definition 21 (Safety) The function *safety* : $L^* \times \langle L, \mathcal{N} \rangle^* \to \mathcal{B}$ is defined as follows:
$$safety\,(train\text{-}tr,\,gate\text{-}tr) \;\equiv$$

$$
\begin{cases}
true & \text{if } train\text{-}tr = \langle\rangle; \\[4pt]
\begin{array}{l} g = \texttt{closed} \\ \wedge\, safety\,(train\text{-}tr',\,gate\text{-}tr') \end{array} & \begin{array}{l} \text{if } train\text{-}tr = \texttt{in-gate} \circ train\text{-}tr' \\ \wedge\, gate\text{-}tr = g \circ gate\text{-}tr'; \end{array} \\[8pt]
safety\,(train\text{-}tr',\,gate\text{-}tr') & \text{otherwise.}
\end{cases}
$$

Since safety can be violated by beginning the simulation in a perverse state (as with the train `in-gate` and the gate `open`), we must specify a safe initial state. We choose to consider that the train is initially `other` and the gate is `open`. The safety theorem demonstrates that for a legal train trace (as described in Section 8.4.3) starting in this initial state the gate will always be `closed` whenever the train is *in-gate*[4]. This appropriate theorem is shown below:

Theorem 27 (Controller Safety)
   For all $train\text{-}tr' \in L^*,\, x, g \in L,\, a \in \mathcal{N}$,

$$initial\text{-}statep\,(x, g) \wedge legal\text{-}train\text{-}trace\,(train\text{-}tr, a)$$
$$\to \quad safety(train\text{-}tr,\, gate\text{-}behavior\,(train\text{-}tr, g, n)),$$

where $train\text{-}tr = x \circ train\text{-}tr'$.

The variable a in this theorem records how long the train has been in the approaching region before the beginning of the trace. This is useful is specifying recursively when a final segment of a trace is legal.

The utility property is somewhat more difficult to state. Recall that utility means that the gate is open as much as possible. This is interpreted by Heitmeyer *et al.* (1993b) to mean that there are some δ_1 and δ_2 such that the gate is open whenever the train is more than δ_1 before the crossing or more than δ_2 after the crossing. Our gate controller begins lowering the gate as soon as a train approaches. Therefore, δ_1 is essentially the interval between Sensor$_1$ and the gate. As we noted in Section 8.4.3 above, this can be as short as *gate-closing-max-time* $+ 1$.

---

[3]Definitions and theorems are numbered as in the appendix.

[4]Actually our inductive proof deals with traces beginning in any safe state. This theorem is a trivial consequence.

The gate is raised as soon as the train leaves the crossing and may take as much as *gate-opening-max-time* to open fully. Our version of utility asserts that the gate is open whenever the train is `other` and has been `other` for at least *gate-opening-max-time* units. The amount of time that the train has been `other` is recorded in the variable *m*. Again, the property is expressed recursively as a relation between the train and gate traces.

Definition 23 (Utility) The function *utility* : $\mathcal{L}^* \times \langle \mathcal{L}, \mathcal{N} \rangle^* \times \mathcal{N} \to \mathcal{B}$ is defined as follows:

$$utility\,(\text{\textit{train-tr}, \text{\textit{gate-tr}, m}}) \quad \equiv$$

$$\begin{cases} true & \text{if \textit{train-tr}} = \langle \rangle; \\[2mm] (\quad \text{\textit{gate-opening-max-time}} < m & \text{if \textit{train-tr}} = \texttt{other} \circ \textit{train-tr}' \\ \quad \to g = \texttt{open}) & \wedge \textit{gate-tr} = g \circ \textit{gate-tr}'; \\ \wedge\, utility\,(\textit{train-tr}', \textit{gate-tr}', m+1) & \\[2mm] utility\,(\textit{train-tr}', \textit{gate-tr}', 0) & \textit{otherwise}. \end{cases}$$

The theorem that establishes that our system satisfies this version of utility is given below:

Theorem 28 (Controller Utility)
For all *train-tr'* $\in \mathcal{L}^*$, $x, g \in \mathcal{L}$, $a, m, n \in \mathcal{N}$,

$$\begin{aligned} & \textit{initial-statep}\,(x, g) \wedge \textit{legal-train-trace}\,(\textit{train-tr}, a) \\ \to \quad & utility(\textit{train-tr}, \textit{gate-behavior}\,(\textit{train-tr}, g, n), m), \end{aligned}$$

where *train-tr* $= x \circ$ *train-tr'*.

This theorem says that the utility relation holds between any legal train trace and the trace of the gate behaviour as a response to the train's movement.

Notice that more utility could be gained at the cost of complicating the control mechanism. We have taken a conservative approach by starting the gate closing whenever a train reaches Sensor$_1$. This means that very slow trains may cause the gate to remain down for long periods before they reach the gate. However, modifying the controller to take advantage of the varying speeds of trains would require a much more complicated control algorithm and would also assume that trains never accelerate during the approach to the gate.

8.6   An alternative version

We have specified our system model and safety and utility properties using recursive function definitions in a style natural to Nqthm. It is frequently remarked that using recursive functions as we have makes Nqthm specifications somehow less intuitive or less readable than versions in some other specification languages, e.g. those making more extensive use of quantification. We would argue that this is simply false. Recursive functions are no less natural or intuitive than other formalisms and have a completely rigorous semantics. However, it is worth noting that we can give quantified versions of our safety and utility properties in Nqthm, using the first-order quantifiers implemented by Kaufmann (1991).

For example, our definition of safety can be rephrased as follows:

Definition 29 (Safety2) The function *safety2* : $L^* \times \langle L, \mathcal{N} \rangle^* \rightarrow B$ is defined as follows:

$$safety2\,(train\text{-}tr, gate\text{-}tr) \;\equiv$$

$$\forall i \in \mathcal{N}, (i \leq len\,(train\text{-}tr) \land train\text{-}tr[i] = \texttt{in-gate}) \rightarrow gate\text{-}tr[i] = \texttt{closed}.$$

We have proved, using the Nqthm prover, that this version of safety is implied by our earlier version. Thus, our train controller satisfies this "more intuitive" characterization. However, no additional assurance of correctness is gained by the exercise.

Similar remarks apply to our specification of the utility property. Definitions and lemmas involving these alternative versions are given in the appendix.

8.7   Proofs of the properties

It is quite easy to see why safety and utility hold for our simple control system. The controller prompts the gate to begin lowering when it senses a train entering the approaching region at Sensor$_1$. Since the approach is guaranteed to be longer than the maximum time for the gate to close, the gate always will have closed fully by the time the train reaches the crossing. Similarly, the controller raises the gate when it senses that the train has left the crossing. The gate will therefore be open no later than the maximum opening interval[5] after that point.

However, as is often the case for system invariants, neither of the theorems given in the previous section is provable directly. Proving each of them requires showing that a more complex invariant is maintained during the system simulation. This invariant (given in the following definition) establishes the necessary relationship among the current train position (p), current gate state ($\langle g, n \rangle$), distance (d) from the present position to the gate, time (e) already spent in the `other` state, and the opening and closing parameters of the gate. We prove that if this `good-statep` property is true initially, it will be maintained by the system.

Definition 19 (Good-statep) The function *good-statep* : $L \times L \times \mathcal{N} \times \mathcal{N} \times \mathcal{N} \rightarrow B$ is defined as follows:

$$good\text{-}statep\,(p, g, n, d, e) \;\equiv$$

---

[5]Actually, it may require one more tick to open fully since the control action trails the train position by one tick.

$$g = \texttt{going-down} \rightarrow n < \textit{gate-closing-max-time}$$
$$\wedge \quad g = \texttt{going-up} \rightarrow n < \textit{gate-opening-max-time}$$
$$\wedge \quad p = \texttt{in-gate} \rightarrow g = \texttt{closed}$$
$$\wedge \quad p = \texttt{approaching} \rightarrow$$
$$(g = \texttt{closed}) \vee (g = \texttt{going-down} \wedge n < d)$$
$$\vee \ (\textit{gate-closing-max-time} < d)$$
$$\wedge \quad p = \texttt{other} \rightarrow$$
$$(\ \textit{gate-opening-max-time} < e \rightarrow g = \texttt{open})$$
$$\wedge \ [\ (g = \texttt{closed} \wedge e = 0) \vee (g = \texttt{open})$$
$$\vee \ (g = \texttt{going-up} \wedge n \leq \textit{gate-opening-max-time} - e)\ ]$$

Proving that this property is maintained throughout the simulation is the key inductive component of the proof. We prove that this in turn implies both the safety and utility properties. The requisite lemmas are given in the appendix.

8.8   Conclusions

We have given a specification of a simple real-time railroad gate controller and its environment. We have stated and proved safety and utility theorems for this simple system. All proofs have been stated in the Nqthm logic, as enhanced by Kaufmann, and mechanically checked with the Nqthm prover of Boyer and Moore.

Nqthm proved to be an excellent tool for modelling and reasoning about this problem. Our specification took a very "operational" form, a style quite familiar to seasoned Nqthm users (see for example Bevier *et al.* (1989)) and well supported by the Nqthm prover. We would argue that an operational specification style such as we used is very natural for a control system such as this one where the behaviour of the system is determined by a series of sensor "readings" taken at discrete time intervals and resulting in a series of actuator commands. We have previously used such an operational model to reason about some simple fuzzy controllers (Carranza and Young, 1992) and about a Byzantine-resilient control system (Bevier and Young, 1992).

The major proof effort involved identifying an appropriate system property and proving that our control algorithm maintained it invariantly. This is an inductive proof over the structure of legal train traces. Nqthm excels at just such tasks. Moreover, because of the number of possible combinations of train positions, gate states, and relations of the various parameters, a fairly large number of tedious subcases must be considered. Nqthm handles these expeditiously and entirely automatically[6]. We can easily imagine that this conceptually simple proof would be daunting for a more interactive proof system. However, it is likely that a simple finite state system such as our train–gate system would be amenable to more fully automated analysis, perhaps using model checking techniques (McMillan, 1993).

---

[6]Some 740 cases were generated for the large inductive theorem; all were handled automatically in around 250 seconds on a Sun Sparc2 workstation.

It is worth noting that we chose quite deliberately to implement an operational solution that we believe is in keeping with the "standard" uses of Nqthm. This contrasts with some published solutions to this problem such as the PVS solution (Shankar, 1992) which involves embedding temporal operators in the PVS logic[7]. Nqthm is certainly powerful enough to embed a rich specification language and this has been done several times, e.g. Brock *et al.* (1992) and Goldschlag (1991). However, we feel that while such an approach may be a specification and proof *tour de force* it does not necessarily reflect well the strengths and weaknesses of the underlying logic and theorem prover. We believe that our solution reflects a natural style of using Nqthm and is, therefore, more in keeping with the spirit of a benchmark problem. Still, faced with the prospect of attacking a large class of similar problems, we might feel the need to embed more specialized capabilities within the logic. One of the strengths of Nqthm is its proven versatility in the face of a wide variety of specification and proof challenges.

Acknowledgements

We wish to acknowledge the assistance of our colleagues at Computational Logic, Inc., particularly Bob Boyer, Matt Kaufmann, J. Moore, and Matt Wilding. We would also like to acknowledge the helpful suggestions of an anonymous reviewer. This research was supported in part by ONR Contract N00014-91-C-0130 and by the Defense Advanced Research Projects Agency, ARPA Order 7406. The views and conclusions contained in this document are those of the author and should not be interpreted as representing the official policies, either expressed or implied, of Computational Logic, Inc., the Office of Naval Research, the Defense Advanced Research Projects Agency, or the US Government.

Appendix

Train gate system specification

This appendix contains the complete specification and major lemmas relating to the train crossing gate problem. We use an infix notation derived (by hand) from the Nqthm script. Seasoned Nqthm users will note that we have taken some liberties. In particular, we have suggested the intended "signatures" of functions despite the fact that Nqthm is an untyped logic. In doing so we use the types L for literal atoms, $\mathcal{N}$ for naturals, and $\mathcal{B}$ for Booleans. We use $x \circ y$ for the Nqthm (cons x y), i.e. adding element x to the front of list y. The "official" and replayable Nqthm event list is available by request from the author.

---

[7]See Heitmeyer and Jeffords (1995) for a more extensive comparison of several automated reasoning systems and their performance on this problem.

The latest version of Nqthm was released in 1994 along with a companion version of Pc-Nqthm. Nqthm is documented in two books (Boyer and Moore, 1979, 1988). The release includes 1.3 megabytes of updated documentation consisting of new versions of the five most important chapters in Boyer and Moore (1988). In addition, the release includes more than 15 megabytes of example input for Nqthm and Pc-Nqthm, including many of the important benchmarks listed in Section 8.2. The system is available free of charge by anonymous ftp.

A conservative axiom (Nqthm `constrain` event) is a means of introducing new function symbols into the logic in a sound manner. The axiomatization is supplied with a previously defined "witness function" for each of the new function symbols to ensure satisfiability. The following conservative axiom introduces a new function that selects an arbitrary member of the designated range.

Conservative axiom 1 (choose time introduction)
We introduce a new function symbol *choose-time* : $\mathcal{N} \times \mathcal{N} \to \mathcal{N}$ via the following conservative axiom:

$$mn \le mx \to mn \le \textit{choose-time}\,(mn, mx) \le mx.$$

The gate

The gate is our controlled system; we assume that it responds reliably to a series of commands that are generated by the control algorithm. These commands are either `open` or `close`. The simulation of the gate tells us its state at each moment of time. The following gives the response parameters of the gate.

Conservative axiom 2 (gate parameters introduction)
We introduce the new constant function symbols *gate-closing-min-time* $\in \mathcal{N}$, *gate-closing-max-time* $\in \mathcal{N}$, *gate-opening-min-time* $\in \mathcal{N}$, and *gate-opening-max-time* $\in \mathcal{N}$ via the following conservative axiom:

$$
\begin{aligned}
& 0 < \textit{gate-closing-max-time} \\
\wedge\ & \textit{gate-closing-min-time} \le \textit{gate-closing-max-time} \\
\wedge\ & 0 < \textit{gate-opening-max-time} \\
\wedge\ & \textit{gate-opening-min-time} \le \textit{gate-opening-max-time}
\end{aligned}
$$

The gate state is a pair $\langle l, n \rangle$, where l is one of `open`, `closed`, `going-up`, or `going-down`. n is the time that the gate can be expected to remain in that state. This is only meaningful when the gate is `going-up` or `going-down`.

Definition 3 (gate-positionp) The function *gate-positionp* : $L \rightarrow \mathcal{B}$ is defined as follows:

$$gate\text{-}positionp(x) \equiv (\quad x = \texttt{open} \lor x = \texttt{closed}$$
$$\lor x = \texttt{going-up} \lor x = \texttt{going-down}).$$

Definition 4 (gate-current-state) The function *gate-current-state* : $\langle L, \mathcal{N} \rangle \rightarrow L$ is defined as follows:

$$gate\text{-}current\text{-}state(\langle s, n \rangle) \equiv s.$$

Definition 5 (gate-duration) The function *gate-duration* : $\langle L, \mathcal{N} \rangle \rightarrow \mathcal{N}$ is defined as follows:

$$gate\text{-}duration(\langle s, n \rangle) \equiv n.$$

Definition 6 (compute-going-down-state) *compute-going-down-state*: $\langle L, \mathcal{N} \rangle \rightarrow \langle L, \mathcal{N} \rangle$ is defined as follows:

$$compute\text{-}going\text{-}down\text{-}state(\langle l, n \rangle) \equiv \langle l', n' \rangle \text{ where}$$

$$\begin{cases} l' = \texttt{closed} \land n' = 0 & \text{if } n = 0; \\ l' = \texttt{going-down} \land n' = n - 1 & \text{otherwise.} \end{cases}$$

Definition 7 (compute-going-up-state) *compute-going-up-state*: $\langle L, \mathcal{N} \rangle \rightarrow \langle L, \mathcal{N} \rangle$ is defined as follows:

$$compute\text{-}going\text{-}up\text{-}state(\langle l, n \rangle) \equiv \langle l', n' \rangle \text{ where}$$

$$\begin{cases} l' = \texttt{open} \land n' = 0 & \text{if } n = 0; \\ l' = \texttt{going-up} \land n' = n - 1 & \text{otherwise.} \end{cases}$$

The following function gives the next state for any potential current state of the gate.

Definition 8 (gate-next-state) *gate-next-state* : $L \times \langle L, \mathcal{N} \rangle \rightarrow \langle L, \mathcal{N} \rangle$ is defined as follows:

$$gate\text{-}next\text{-}state(c, \langle l, n \rangle) = \langle l', n' \rangle \text{ where}$$

if $c = \texttt{close}$,

$$\begin{cases} l' = \texttt{going-down} \land n' = k - 1 & \textit{if } l = \texttt{open}; \\ l' = l \land n' = n & \textit{if } l = \texttt{closed}; \\ l' = \texttt{going-down} \land n' = k - 1 & \textit{if } l = \texttt{going-up}; \\ \langle l', n' \rangle = compute\text{-}going\text{-}down\text{-}state(\langle l, n \rangle) & \textit{if } l = \texttt{going-down}; \end{cases}$$

if $c = \texttt{open}$,

$$\begin{cases} l' = l \land n' = n & \textit{if } l = \texttt{open}; \\ l' = going\text{-}up \land n' = k - 1 & \textit{if } l = \texttt{closed}; \\ \langle l', n' \rangle = compute\text{-}going\text{-}up\text{-}state(\langle l, n \rangle) & \textit{if } l = \texttt{going-up}; \\ l' = \texttt{going-up} \land n' = k - 1 & \textit{if } l = \texttt{going-down}; \end{cases}$$

where $k = choose\text{-}time(gate\text{-}closing\text{-}min\text{-}time, gate\text{-}closing\text{-}max\text{-}time)$.

Modelling the train

The train provides the input to our control system; the gate must act in response to the train. It can do so only if the behaviour of the train meets certain reasonable criteria. Therefore, the specification of the train consists of a set of constraints on the possible traces of the train behaviour, as sensed by input sensors along the track. The train can be in one of three possible states: approaching the gate, in the crossing, or elsewhere.

Definition 9 (train-positionp) The function *train-positionp* : $L \to \mathcal{B}$ is defined as follows:

$$train\text{-}positionp\,(x) \quad \equiv \quad (\quad x = \texttt{approaching} \lor x = \texttt{in-gate}$$
$$\lor x = \texttt{other})$$

A train can only make certain legal transitions from one position to another. For example, the train must pass through the approaching region before entering the gate.

Definition 10 (legal-transitionp) The function *legal-transitionp* : $L \times L \to \mathcal{B}$ is defined as follows:

$$legal\text{-}transitionp\,(x, y) \quad \equiv$$
$$\begin{cases} y = \texttt{other} \lor y = \texttt{approaching} & \textit{if } x = \texttt{other}; \\ y = \texttt{approaching} \lor y = \texttt{in-gate} & \textit{if } x = \texttt{approaching}; \\ y = \texttt{in-gate} \lor y = \texttt{other} & \textit{if } x = \texttt{in-gate}. \end{cases}$$

The following function partially defines what it means for a train trace to be legal. Notice that this definition ensures that we cannot skip a region and go directly, say, from other to in-gate.

Definition 11 (train-tracep) The function *train-tracep* : $L^* \to \mathcal{B}$ is defined as follows:

$$train\text{-}tracep\,(tr) \quad \equiv$$
$$\begin{cases} true & \textit{if } tr = \langle \rangle; \\ train\text{-}positionp\,(x) & \textit{if } tr = \langle x \rangle; \\ \\ \begin{aligned} & train\text{-}positionp\,(x) \\ & \land\, train\text{-}positionp\,(y) \\ & \land\, legal\text{-}transitionp\,(x, y) \\ & \land\, train\text{-}tracep\,(y \circ tr') \end{aligned} & \textit{if } tr = x \circ y \circ tr'. \end{cases}$$

We introduce a new constant that characterizes the amount of time the train must spend in the approaching region before it can enter the gate. We enforce this by placing $Sensor_1$ far enough in front of the gate to allow time for the gate to close.

Conservative axiom 12 (train constraint introduction)
We introduce the new constant function symbol *approaching-min-time* $\in \mathcal{N}$ via the following conservative axiom:

$$gate\text{-}closing\text{-}max\text{-}time < approaching\text{-}min\text{-}time.$$

Definition 13 (seq-long-enough) The function *seq-long-enough* : $\mathcal{L} \times \mathcal{L}^* \times \mathcal{N} \times \mathcal{N} \to \mathcal{B}$ is defined as follows:

$$seq\text{-}long\text{-}enough\,(l, tr, n, mn) \;\equiv$$

$$
\begin{cases}
true & \text{if } n = 0 \wedge tr = \langle\rangle; \\
seq\text{-}long\text{-}enough\,(x, rst, 1, mn) & \text{if } n = 0 \wedge tr = x \circ rst; \\
seq\text{-}long\text{-}enough\,(x, rst, 0, mn) & \text{if } n = 0 \wedge tr = y \circ rst \\
& \qquad \wedge x \neq y; \\[1em]
mn \leq n & \text{if } n \neq 0 \wedge tr = \langle\rangle; \\
seq\text{-}long\text{-}enough\,(x, rst, n+1, mn) & \text{if } n \neq 0 \wedge tr = x \circ rst; \\[1em]
\quad mn \leq n & \text{otherwise.} \\
\wedge \; seq\text{-}long\text{-}enough\,(x, rst, 0, mn)
\end{cases}
$$

The following predicate checks a train trace to see that each time period spent in the `approaching` region is at least *approaching-min-time* units in length, where we assume we have already spent n units approaching at the start of the trace.

Definition 14 (approaches-long-enough) The function *approaches-long-enough*:
$\mathcal{L}^* \times \mathcal{N} \to \mathcal{B}$ is defined as follows:

$$approaches\text{-}long\text{-}enough\,(tr, n) \;\equiv$$
$$seq\text{-}long\text{-}enough\,(\texttt{approaching}, tr, n, approaching\text{-}min\text{-}time)$$

This function computes the distance from the beginning of a train trace until the train enters the gate. If the trace is empty, it assumes a minimal safe distance.

Definition 15 (distance-to-gate) The function *distance-to-gate* : $\mathcal{L}^* \to \mathcal{N}$ is defined as follows:

$$distance\text{-}to\text{-}gate\,(tr) \;\equiv$$

$$
\begin{cases}
approaching\text{-}min\text{-}time + 2 & \text{if } tr = \langle\rangle; \\
0 & \text{if } tr = x \circ tr' \wedge x = \texttt{in-gate}; \\
distance\text{-}to\text{-}gate\,(tr' + 1 & \text{otherwise.}
\end{cases}
$$

Definition 16 (legal-train-trace) The function *legal-train-trace* : $\mathcal{L}^* \times \mathcal{N} \to \mathcal{B}$ is defined as follows:

$$legal\text{-}train\text{-}trace\,(tr, n) \;\equiv$$
$$train\text{-}tracep\,(tr) \wedge approaches\text{-}long\text{-}enough\,(tr, n)$$

The controller

The control algorithm is very simple: generate a control pulse of open or close depending on the current position of the train.

Definition 17 (control-output) The function *control-output* : $L \to L$ is defined as follows:

$$control\text{-}output\,(i) \quad \equiv$$
$$\begin{cases} \text{open} & \textit{if } i = \text{other;} \\ \text{close} & \textit{otherwise.} \end{cases}$$

Modelling the system

Given specifications of the train, gate, and controller, we can now combine them to analyze the behaviour of the system. The following function returns a trace of successive states of the gate, given a trace of the train and an initial gate state.

Definition 18 (gate-behavior) The function *gate-behavior*: $L^* \times \langle L, \mathcal{N} \rangle \to \langle L, \mathcal{N} \rangle^*$ is defined as follows:

$$gate\text{-}behavior\,(tr, \langle l, n \rangle) \quad \equiv$$
$$\begin{cases} \langle \rangle & \textit{if } tr = \langle \rangle; \\ \langle l', n' \rangle \circ gate\text{-}behavior\,(tr', \langle l', n' \rangle) & \textit{if } tr = x \circ tr', \end{cases}$$

where $\langle l', n' \rangle = gate\text{-}next\text{-}state\,(control\text{-}output\,(x, l, tr), \langle l, n \rangle, x)$.

This function defines the key system property in terms of the relation between the train's current position and the state of the gate at that step. It assures that the gate has time to close before the train reaches it, and that the gate starts up as soon as possible after the train has left the gate.

Definition 19 (good-statep) The function *good-statep* : $L \times L \times \mathcal{N} \times \mathcal{N} \times \mathcal{N} \to \mathcal{B}$ is defined as follows:

$$good\text{-}statep\,(p, g, n, d, e) \quad \equiv$$
$$\begin{array}{ll} & g = \text{going-down} \to n < gate\text{-}closing\text{-}max\text{-}time \\ \wedge & g = \text{going-up} \to n < gate\text{-}opening\text{-}max\text{-}time \\ \wedge & p = \text{in-gate} \to g = \text{closed} \\ \wedge & p = \text{approaching} \to \\ & \quad (g = \text{closed}) \vee (g = \text{going-down} \wedge n < d) \\ & \quad \vee (gate\text{-}closing\text{-}max\text{-}time < d) \\ \wedge & p = \text{other} \to \\ & \quad (gate\text{-}opening\text{-}max\text{-}time < e \to g = \text{open}) \\ & \quad \wedge [\ (g = \text{closed} \wedge e = 0) \vee (g = \text{open}) \\ & \quad \quad \vee (g = \text{going-up} \wedge n \le gate\text{-}opening\text{-}max\text{-}time - e)\,] \end{array}$$

su-invariant checks that *good-statep* is maintained invariantly over a train trace and corresponding gate trace.

Definition 20 (su-invariant) The function *su-invariant* : $L^* \times \langle L, \mathcal{N} \rangle^* \times \mathcal{N} \to \mathcal{B}$ is defined as follows:

$$
su\text{-}invariant\,(tr, gate\text{-}tr, n) \quad \equiv
$$

$$
\begin{cases}
true & \text{if } tr = \langle \rangle; \\
false & \text{if } gate\text{-}tr = \langle \rangle; \\
\begin{aligned}
&good\text{-}statep\,(\texttt{other}, z, d, n) \\
&\land su\text{-}invariant\,(y, w, 0)
\end{aligned} & \begin{aligned}&\text{if } tr = \texttt{other} \circ y \\ &\land gate\text{-}tr = z \circ w;\end{aligned} \\
\begin{aligned}
&good\text{-}statep\,(x, z, d, n) \\
&\land su\text{-}invariant\,(y, w, n+1)
\end{aligned} & \text{if } tr = x \circ y \land gate\text{-}tr = z \circ w;
\end{cases}
$$

Now we define the desired safety and utility properties and prove that they follow from the *su-invariant* property.

Definition 21 (safety) The function *safety* : $L^* \times \langle L, \mathcal{N} \rangle^* \to \mathcal{B}$ is defined as follows:

$$
safety\,(train\text{-}tr, gate\text{-}tr) \quad \equiv
$$

$$
\begin{cases}
true & \text{if } train\text{-}tr = \langle \rangle; \\
\begin{aligned}
&g = \texttt{closed} \\
&\land safety\,(train\text{-}tr', gate\text{-}tr')
\end{aligned} & \begin{aligned}&\text{if } train\text{-}tr = \texttt{in-gate} \circ train\text{-}tr' \\ &\land gate\text{-}tr = g \circ gate\text{-}tr';\end{aligned} \\
safety\,(train\text{-}tr', gate\text{-}tr') & \text{otherwise.}
\end{cases}
$$

Theorem 22 (su-invariant implies safety)
For all *train-tr* $\in L^*$, *gate-tr* $\in \langle L, \mathcal{N} \rangle^*$, $n \in \mathcal{N}$,

$$
su\text{-}invariant\,(train\text{-}tr, gate\text{-}tr, n) \to safety\,(train\text{-}tr, gate\text{-}tr).
$$

Definition 23 (utility) The function *utility* : $L^* \times \langle L, \mathcal{N} \rangle^* \times \mathcal{N} \to \mathcal{B}$ is defined as follows:

$$
utility\,(train\text{-}tr, gate\text{-}tr, m) \quad \equiv
$$

$$
\begin{cases}
true & \text{if } train\text{-}tr = \langle \rangle; \\
\begin{aligned}
&(gate\text{-}opening\text{-}max\text{-}time < m \\
&\quad \to g = \texttt{open}) \\
&\land utility\,(train\text{-}tr', gate\text{-}tr', m+1)
\end{aligned} & \begin{aligned}&\text{if } train\text{-}tr = \texttt{other} \circ train\text{-}tr' \\ &\land gate\text{-}tr = g \circ gate\text{-}tr';\end{aligned} \\
utility\,(train\text{-}tr', gate\text{-}tr', 0) & \text{otherwise.}
\end{cases}
$$

Theorem 24 (su-invariant implies utility)

For all *train-tr* $\in L^*$, *gate-tr* $\in \langle L, \mathcal{N} \rangle^*$, $n \in \mathcal{N}$,

$$su\text{-}invariant\,(train\text{-}tr,\, gate\text{-}tr,\, n) \rightarrow utility\,(train\text{-}tr,\, gate\text{-}tr,\, n).$$

Theorem 25 (controller maintains safety and utility)

For all *train-tr* $\in L^*$, $x, g \in L, n, e, a \in \mathcal{N}$,

$$
\begin{aligned}
&\quad legal\text{-}train\text{-}trace\,(train\text{-}tr,\, a) \\
\land\ &\ good\text{-}statep\,(x,\, g,\, n,\, distance\text{-}to\text{-}gate\,(train\text{-}tr),\, e) \\
\rightarrow\ & \\
&\quad safety(train\text{-}tr,\, gate\text{-}behavior\,(train\text{-}tr,\, g,\, n)) \\
\land\ &\ utility(train\text{-}tr,\, gate\text{-}behavior\,(train\text{-}tr,\, g,\, n),\, e)
\end{aligned}
$$

where *train-tr* $= x \circ train\text{-}tr'$.

We now characterize an initial state and show that our invariant is true in that initial state.

Definition 26 (initial-statep) The function *initial-statep* : $L \times L \rightarrow \mathcal{B}$ is defined as follows:

$$initial\text{-}statep\,(train,\, gate) \ \equiv \ train = \text{other} \land gate = \text{open}.$$

The following two theorems establish that our system maintains the safety and utility properties if started in a safe initial state.

Theorem 27 (controller safety)

For all *train-tr* $\in L^*$, $x, g \in L, a \in \mathcal{N}$,

$$
\begin{aligned}
&\quad initial\text{-}statep\,(x,\, g) \land legal\text{-}train\text{-}trace\,(train\text{-}tr,\, a) \\
\rightarrow\ &\ safety\,(train\text{-}tr,\, gate\text{-}behavior\,(train\text{-}tr,\, g,\, n)),
\end{aligned}
$$

where *train-tr* $= x \circ train\text{-}tr'$.

Theorem 28 (controller utility)

For all *train-tr* $\in L^*$, $x, g \in L\ a, m, n \in \mathcal{N}$,

$$
\begin{aligned}
&\quad initial\text{-}statep\,(x,\, g) \land legal\text{-}train\text{-}trace\,(train\text{-}tr,\, a) \\
\rightarrow\ &\ utility\,(train\text{-}tr,\, gate\text{-}behavior\,(train\text{-}tr,\, g,\, n),\, m),
\end{aligned}
$$

where *train-tr* $= x \circ train\text{-}tr'$.

An alternative version

Here we present alternative versions of the safety and utility properties using quantifiers, and prove that they are consequences of our earlier versions.

Definition 29 (safety2) The function *safety2* : $L^* \times \langle L, \mathcal{N} \rangle^* \to \mathcal{B}$ is defined as follows:

$$safety2\,(train\text{-}tr, gate\text{-}tr) \quad \equiv$$

$$\forall i \in \mathcal{N}, (i < len\,(train\text{-}tr) \land train\text{-}tr[i] = \texttt{in-gate}) \to gate\text{-}tr[i] = \texttt{closed}.$$

Theorem 30 (safety implies safety2)
　　For all *train-tr* $\in L^*$ and *gate-tr* $\in \langle L, \mathcal{N} \rangle^*$,

$$safety\,(train\text{-}tr, gate\text{-}tr) \to safety2\,(train\text{-}tr, gate\text{-}tr).$$

Theorem 31 (controller safety2)
　　For all *train-tr'* $\in L^*, x, g \in L\, a \in \mathcal{N}$,

$$initial\text{-}statep\,(x, g) \land legal\text{-}train\text{-}trace\,(train\text{-}tr, a)$$
$$\to \quad safety2(train\text{-}tr, gate\text{-}behavior\,(train\text{-}tr, g, n)),$$

where *train-tr* $= x \circ train\text{-}tr'$.

Like *distance-to-gate* this is purely a specification function. It computes the time we have been in the `other` region at location i in the trace. It assumes that we have already been in the `other` region for n time units at the beginning of the trace.

Definition 32 (time-other) The function *time-other* : $\mathcal{N} \times \mathcal{N} \times L^* \to \mathcal{N}$ is defined as follows:

$$time\text{-}other\,(i, n, train\text{-}tr) \quad \equiv$$

$$\begin{cases} n & \textit{if } i = 0; \\ time\text{-}other\,(i-1, n+1, train\text{-}tr') & train\text{-}tr = \texttt{other} \circ train\text{-}tr'; \\ time\text{-}other\,(i-1, 0, train\text{-}tr') & train\text{-}tr = y \circ train\text{-}tr', \end{cases}$$

where $y \neq \texttt{other}$.

Definition 33 (utility2) The function *utility2* : $L^* \times \langle L, \mathcal{N} \rangle^* \times \mathcal{N} \to \mathcal{B}$ is defined as follows:

$$utility2\,(train\text{-}tr, gate\text{-}tr, n) \quad \equiv$$

$$\forall i \in \mathcal{N},$$

$$\begin{aligned} & \quad i \leq len\,(train\text{-}tr) \\ \land \quad & train\text{-}tr[i] = \texttt{other} \\ \land \quad & gate\text{-}opening\text{-}max\text{-}time < time\text{-}other\,(i, n, train\text{-}tr) \\ \to \quad & gate\text{-}tr[i] = \texttt{open}. \end{aligned}$$

Theorem 34 (utility implies utility2)
   For all *train-tr* $\in L^*$, *gate-tr* $\in \langle L, \mathcal{N} \rangle^*$, and $n \in \mathcal{N}$,

$$utility\,(train\text{-}tr,\, gate\text{-}tr,\, n) \rightarrow utility2\,(train\text{-}tr,\, gate\text{-}tr,\, n).$$

Theorem 35 (controller utility2)
   For all *train-tr′* $\in L^*$, $x, g \in L, n, a, e \in \mathcal{N}$,

$$initial\text{-}statep\,(x,\, g)$$
$$\wedge \quad legal\text{-}train\text{-}trace\,(train\text{-}tr,\, a)$$
$$\rightarrow$$
$$utility2\,(train\text{-}tr,\, gate\text{-}behavior\,(train\text{-}tr,\, g,\, n),\, e),$$

where *train-tr* $= x \circ train\text{-}tr'$.

Chapter 9

CombiCom: Tracking and Tracing Rail Traffic using VDM^{++}

Eugène H. Dürr, Nico Plat and Michiel de Boer

9.1 Introduction

In this chapter the CombiCom (Combined Transport Communication System) information architecture is described. CombiCom is a distributed system capable of tracking and tracing rail traffic across Europe. The Dutch company Cap Volmac was the coordinator of the project, in which seven companies (mainly from the transportation industry) participated, and was responsible for the hardware and software implementation of the system. The system was designed during 1992, implemented in 1993 and has been operational since the end of 1994.

9.2 Background

The use of railways for long-distance ($\geq$ 200 km) freight transport in Europe has a number of advantages over the alternative of road traffic. Especially in environmentally sensitive areas, such as the Alps, rail is the preferred mode of traffic; moreover, in view of increasing traffic demands within the growing European market, rail transport offers a very viable alternative to other means of transportation. The combination of a long-distance rail corridor and local road transport between terminals at both ends of the corridor (thus a combined-traffic mode), provides attractive transportation possibilities. There is, however, a serious problem: because the load itself is not accompanied by a driver, there is a "black hole" of information during the rail part of the journey. Nowadays, one waits at a receiving terminal for the arrival of a train without any early warnings about possible delays. Statistics show that approximately 20% of freight trains suffer a delay of more than 15 minutes.

This lack of scheduling information as compared with road transport, where a driver can give the client a telephone call immediately when a delay occurs, makes the use of combined-traffic alternatives unattractive for just-in-time logistic applications, for example the transport of fruits or hazardous goods, or for use in tightly coupled production schemes. The introduction of a real-time information system with automatic identification monitoring the movements of load units (containers, swap-bodies, semitrailers, etc.) can provide detection of deviations from a schedule and inform traffic agents and their clients at an early point. The aim of the CombiCom project was the introduction of such an information system in the Rotterdam (The Netherlands) ↔ Cologne (Germany) ↔ Verona (Italy) corridor.

Because the world of combined-traffic agents consists of separate railway-affiliated companies in different countries, no central authority exists; political reasons prevent a centralized solution all over Europe. We therefore decided to design a distributed system in which each terminal would have a workstation, providing access to the shared data. The workstations are linked to each other by means of a network. Entry and exit of a workstation in the system had to be realized without interruption of the functions of the other nodes. A number of so-called automatic identification equipment units (AIEs) are coupled to each terminal.

Identification of transport units is done by sending a high frequency beam (2–5 GHz) from an antenna to a "tag" — an electronic transponder which is attached to the load unit and the wagon. The reflected beam is modulated by the contents of the tag. A concentrator takes care of the translation into an ASCII pattern. There are 128 bytes available in the programmable tag for a (unique) identification number and for some additional information such as owner, size, maximum payload, etc. The reading equipment along the railway track is able to provide this information with train speeds of up to 280 km h^{-1} with a fault rate of less then one per million readings.

An agent at a terminal is (through a graphical user interface) given the opportunity to enter a so-called transport transaction (TT) into the system before a load unit enters the corridor. A transport transaction also contains (apart from an identification) a planned time table (PTT), which is a combination of locations, times, and allowed time windows. This information is distributed to all locations en route.

When the train is on its way, the sensor installations provide the system with the real-time observations on the movements of the load units. Deviations from the planned schedule cause an alarm (an internal event in the system at the node) to be raised. An alarm message is transferred to the terminal agent responsible for the transport transaction.

A query mechanism is available to obtain information about which transport transactions are planned from other terminals in the near future and to enquire about the exact position of given load units. The system also provides clients of terminal agents with the opportunity to make bookings and request status reports through EDI messages. Ultimately, the system is capable of relaying an internal alarm message as an EDI message directly to the client. The processes involved in the system and their communication links are shown in Figure 9.1.

9.3   The use of formal methods in CombiCom

9.3.1   Motivation

At an early stage, we realized that this system, operating at several cooperating combined-traffic agent sites in Europe simultaneously, had a distributed real-time characteristic and

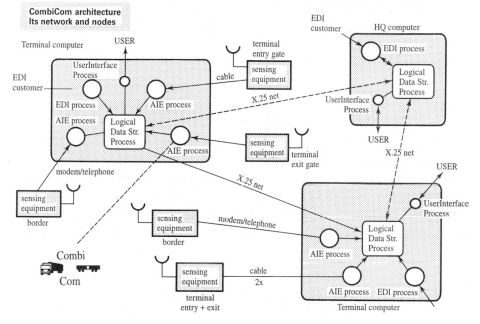

Figure 9.1 Architectural components of CombiCom.

that the consequences of a failure in its architecture would be considerable (economic) damage. These "observations" led to the decision to use formal specifications for the design, and Ada for the implementation. The choice of the latter was also motivated by the fact that a wide range of different UNIX workstations would be used.

The real-time requirements were focused on

- the incoming stream of data from the readers at arbitrary moments, and
- the generation of alarms at each relevant node, which the system had to be able to do within one minute after the detection of the event that caused it.

However, other than these, at the start of the project our transport partners had no clear idea of the consequences of introducing such a system and were unable to describe their requirements more precisely. We therefore decided to start with a functional specification of a non-distributed version of the system in VDM (Jones, 1990; International Standards Organization, 1993). Our insight into the logic of the system increased and therefore we were able to direct the questioning of our transportation partners in a better way. This analysis activity could be described as an effective way of requirements elicitation and formalization.

The next step was to transform this functional specification into an object-oriented specification using VDM[++] (see Section 9.3.2). With this step the (formal) description of message passing through the network and the additional data structures needed to describe the system's fault-tolerant behaviour (i.e., the concurrency protocols) also came in. We divided the introduction of the system into three phases (subsystems):

- phase 1, wagon monitoring;
- phase 2, monitoring of load units, and
- phase 3, the EDI interface.

The phased introduction enabled the transport partners to become gradually accustomed to the complete system and provided us with early reactions to the behaviour of the system. Each of the phases again consisted of three steps:

1. the description of a protocol defining the functions that had to be implemented during this phase;
2. the collection of reactions to this protocol and the derivation of the formal specification of the subsystem;
3. the implementation of the subsystem and its user interface.

Because all subsystems were derived from one global functional formal specification, all future interactions were already included.

9.3.2   The object-oriented specification language VDM^{++}

The formal specification language we chose to use for this project was VDM^{++}. Although a complete description of VDM^{++} lies far beyond the scope of this chapter (and of this book), we will present a few characteristics of VDM^{++} in this section. VDM^{++} (Dürr 1992, 1994; Dürr and Plat, 1995) is a formal specification language that extends VDM-SL, the formal specification language used in VDM (Jones, 1990; International Standards Organization, 1993), with constructs to support object orientation and concurrency, primarily. The object-oriented extensions are based on the language SmallTalk (Goldberg, 1984). The notation provides a wide range of constructs: as well as VDM-SL constructs, and extensions that allow the definition, creation, and manipulation of objects, the notation contains constructs for specifying concurrent and real-time systems.

A VDM^{++} specification consists of (a number of) class descriptions. Each of these may contain the following.

- A class header, with an optional subclass clause, specifies the superclass(es) of the class.
- A state internal to the object is built up from a collection of instance variables. For these instance variables, invariant expressions and initialization expressions can be formulated in a manner similar to the corresponding VDM-SL mechanisms.
- Methods, i.e. operations which can be used to update the instance variables of the objects are defined via imperative statements. Operational abstraction, as, for example, embodied by VDM-SL's pre- and post-condition mechanism, is available in VDM^{++} in the form of a so-called specification statement. Provision is also made for deferring the specification, in a manner similar to Eiffel's "deferred" methods, and "virtual" functions in C^{++}.
- A behaviour inheritance declaration, declares which methods are inherited from which superclasses.

- There is a specification of the synchronization constraints on the use of an object's methods, either in a declarative manner or by using traces (van de Snepscheut, 1983). If no synchronization constraints are specified then execution of methods is assumed to be mutually exclusive.

- There is a specification of the internal process of the object (relevant for active objects only), by using so-called threads. Threads can be specified in a declarative manner (by specifying intervals during which methods must be periodically invoked) or in a procedural (operational) manner.

- A place holder specifies predicates about the properties of a class; in VDM^{++} terminology this part is called auxiliary reasoning.

Furthermore, VDM^{++} offers facilities for specifying real-time properties; see Dürr (1994) and Mahony and Hayes (1991) for background material. A complete VDM^{++} specification consists of a set of class specifications together with a so-called workspace specification. The **workspace** — the term has been inherited from SmallTalk — contains declarations, object instantiations and some mechanisms needed for the specification of links between objects and other forms of initialization.

VDM^{++} specifications are usually presented at different levels of abstraction (called *Models* in the VDM^{++} terminology), where lower levels are more concrete (i.e. constructs are refined, conforming to the approach as presented by Jones (1990) and others) and contain more "details" which are not essential, at a higher level of abstraction, in order to understand the functionality of the system. In this chapter we will focus on the first two layers (Figure 9.2).

1. This is a rather abstract level at which only the essential features of CombiCom are specified, in order that the overall functionality of the system may be understood. The VDM^{++} specification at this level is referred to as the *Model$_0$* specification, and presents a "client view" of the system.

2. In a more concrete level several design details (which are not present in the *Model$_0$* specification) are introduced, and constructs are refined. The VDM^{++} specification at this level is referred to as the *Model$_1$* specification and presents a more "technical view" of the system.

Both levels are directly based on the user requirements. It should be noted, however, that the choice of exactly what to present at which level, and even at which level to start or stop, are not endorsed by the VDM^{++} methodology (although, of course, a number of guidelines exist; see for example Dürr (1994)); such decisions usually depend on the complexity of the specific application at hand, on the intended audience and also on the purposes for which the specification will be used (e.g. for communication purposes between various partners, as in the case of CombiCom, for prototyping, or for proving characteristics of the system).

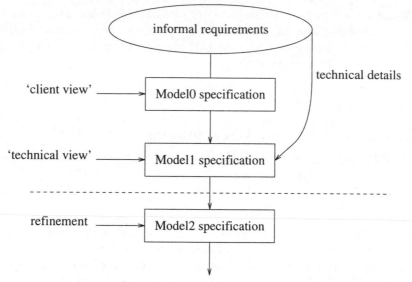

Figure 9.2 The VDM^{++} development cycle for CombiCom

9.4 Technical description of the CombiCom system

9.4.1 The CombiCom *Model*$_0$ description

The *Model*$_0$ specification represents the conceptual view offered to an operator while working with the system. The central task of the system is to monitor the movements of the wagons and UTIs[1] in real time. The movements are represented by sequences of place–time combinations. The comparison of planned and real place–time combinations can cause alarms to be raised, signalling transport irregularities. This observation leads to the conclusion that a so-called "place–time field" (PTF) is a primitive unit of information. The SOLL situation — the list with places and times at which the unit is expected on its journey — is called the planned time table (PTT). The list with places and actual passing times — the IST situation — coming from the readers on the route is stored in a real time table (RTT). For signalling alarms, a time-window concept is used to specify the allowed tolerance in time before an alarm is raised. In order to accommodate the use of different tolerances at different locations a delta time table (DTT) is used. Four different types of alarms can be distinguished:

---

[1]A UTI (Unité de Transport Intermodale) covers containers, swap-bodies and semi-trailers.

Alarm	Condition
TOOLATE	real time ≥ planned time + delta time
UNEXPECTED	real time ≤ planned time − delta time
NOSHOW	no real time exists at planned time + delta time
UNKNOWN	for this unit no planning data is available

Alarms are events generated by the system intended to inform the operator of transport deviations in real time. They have the form of messages which are sent to an alarm store, and their arrival at the store is signalled through icons on the operator's screen. Each timetable entry (except for the entries in the DTT) has a flag which registers an alarm event, mainly to enable statistical analysis at a later stage.

The formal specification of CombiCom's $Model_0$ specification begins with the definition of some types basic to the system, bundled in the class *CombiTypes*[2]:

class *CombiTypes*

    types
        PTF :: *place* : *Location*
                time : *Time*
                flag : *Alarm*;
        Location = *IsoLocationCode*;
        Time   = token;
        Alarm = TOOLATE | NOSHOW | UNEXPECTED |
                UNKNOWN | OK | NIL;
        PTT   = $\mathbb{N}_1 \xrightarrow{m} PTF$
          inv *ptt* $\triangle$ ∀ *mk-PTF* (-,-,*flag*) ∈ rng *ptt* ·
                  flag ∈ {NOSHOW, OK, NIL};
        RTT   = $\mathbb{N}_1 \xrightarrow{m} PTF$
          inv *rtt* $\triangle$ ∀ *mk-PTF* (-,-,*flag*) ∈ rng *rtt* ·
                  flag ∈ {TOOLATE, UNEXPECTED, OK, NIL};
        DTT   = $\mathbb{N}_1 \xrightarrow{m} PTF$
          inv *dtt* $\triangle$ ∀ *mk-PTF* (-,-,*flag*) ∈ rng *dtt* · *flag* ∈ {NIL};
        ...   = ...

    end *CombiTypes*

The system signals the alarm events directly and stores the fact that an alarm has been raised in the flag fields of the tables. A number of relations hold between the flags in the various tables, expressed using invariants. In the DTT, the flag is not used; this is indicated by an invariant expressing that *flag* permanently has the value NIL.

---

[2]Specifications in this chapter have been produced and checked (including the generation of their LaTeX representations) with the VPP toolset. More information on the toolset can be found in *The Formal Methods Tools Database*, available by anonymous ftp from chopwell.ncl.ac.uk in directory /pub/fm_tools, or on World-Wide Web at URL ftp://chopwell.ncl.ac.uk/pub/fm_tools/fm_tools_db.

The system maintains data about wagons and UTIs. The lifetimes of both entities are different. When a wagon has entered the system it is generally not removed for a long time. A transport transaction (TT) on the other hand, which is the carrier of all UTI information before, during, and after the actual transportation, has a limited lifetime and disappears from the system after regular completion of the transport.

The data structure for wagons and their movements is modelled as follows:

class *WData*

    instance variables
        wagon_id   : *WagonId*;
        description   : char*;
        tag   : *TagId*;
        tag_description : char*;
        load_units   : *TTId*-set;
        departure   : *PTF*;
        arrival   : *PTF*;
        ptt   : *PTT*;
        rtt   : *RTT*;
        dtt   : *DTT*;
        inv *ptt*, *rtt*, *dtt* $\triangle$
            dom *ptt* = dom *rtt* $\wedge$ dom *rtt* = dom *dtt* $\wedge$
            $\forall i \in$ dom *ptt* ·
                ptt(*i*).*place* = *rtt*(*i*).*place* $\wedge$ *rtt*(*i*).*place* = *dtt*(*i*).*place* $\wedge$
                (*ptt*(*i*).*flag* = NOSHOW $\Rightarrow$
                  (*rtt*(*i*).*flag* = NIL $\vee$ *rtt*(*i*).*flag* = TOOLATE)) $\wedge$
                (*rtt*(*i*).*flag* = TOOLATE $\Rightarrow$
                  (*ppt*(*i*).*flag* = NOSHOW $\wedge$
                  rtt(*i*).*time* > *ptt*(*i*).*time* + *dtt*(*i*).*time*));
      inv *departure*, *arrival* $\triangle$
        let *mk-PTF*(-, *departure_time*, -) = *departure*,
          mk-PTF(-, *arrival_time*, -) = *arrival* in
        Earlier(*departure_time*, *arrival_time*)

    methods
       ...

    end *WData*

For TTs, a similar class definition is used, with some slight differences in the instance variables used. The wagons and UTIs all have their own (unique) number and description fields. The associated tag must contain that same number eventually. When the pilot implementation of the system was tested, operators used removable tags for UTIs, and as a consequence the equipment number and the tag number were no longer the same, as was foreseen and taken into account during the specification stage. The wagon identifier

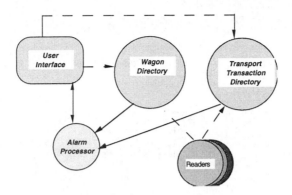

Figure 9.3 Objects in *Model*$_0$.

(of type *WagonId*) is a unique number assigned by the Union Internationale de Chemin de Fer (UIC).

A TT is identified by its place and time of creation and by the name of the agent who created it, specified as a record:

TTId :: *place* : *Location*
        time   : *Time*
        agent : char*

Because an agent can only create one transaction at one place at a time, this identifier is unique over the lifetime of the system for all locations and times. The main objects in the *Model*$_0$ specification are given in Figure 9.3.

For the activities of the operators, we developed a wagon monitoring protocol (WMP) with the following phases (and associated methods in the VDM^{++} specification):

Phase	*Server method*
create	*Create*
plan trip	*Update*
new trip	*Update*
destroy	*Destroy*
query	*Read*
alarms	*alarm_processor!Read*

An extra operation is added to isolate the input from the readers, which must be fed directly into the RTT. In principle this can be done using the *Update* method, but to control the autonomous behaviour a separate *Log* method is used instead:

Phase	*Server method*
reader	*Log* (special version of *Update*)

The class hierarchy for wagon parts is given in Figure 9.4.

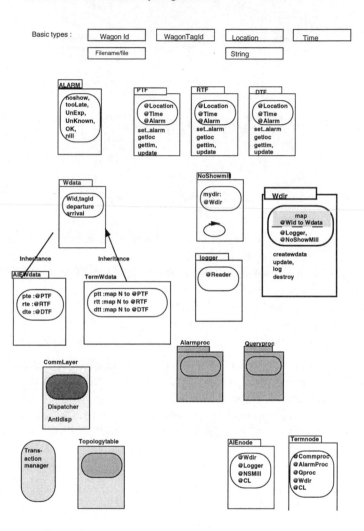

CombiCom Class Hierarchy Wagon Part

Figure 9.4 Class hierarchy for wagon parts.

The resulting VDM[++] specification of class *WDir* is

class *WDir*

values
  MaxEntriesInWDir : $\mathbb{N}$ = undefined

instance variables
  wdir   : *WagonId* $\xrightarrow{m}$ @*WData*;

alarm_processor : @*AlarmProcessor*;
init *wdir* $\triangleq$ *wdir* = {$\mapsto$};
inv objectstate $\triangleq$
    card dom *wdir* $\leq$ *MaxEntriesInWDir* $\wedge$
    $\forall$ *wagon_id* $\in$ dom *wdir* ·
        wagon_id = *wdir*(*wagon_id*).*wagon_id* $\wedge$
        tdir(*wagon_id*) = *wdir*(*wagon_id*).*tag_id*

methods
  IsEmptyWDir() value $\mathbb{B}$ $\triangleq$
  return (*wdir* = {$\mapsto$}) ;

  IsFullWDir() value *full* : $\mathbb{B}$ $\triangleq$
  return (card dom *wdir* = *MaxEntriesInWDir*) ;

  Create(*wid* : *WagonId*, *tid* : *TagId*, *dep* : *TP*, *arr* : *TP*,
      pt : *PTF*, *dt* : *PTF*) $\triangleq$
  pre *wid* $\notin$ dom *wdir*
  (dcl *wdata* : @*AIEWData* := *AIEWData*!new;
     wdata!*SetWData*(*wid*, *tid*, *dep*, *arr*, *pt*, nil, *dt*);
     wdir := *wdir* † {*wid* $\mapsto$ *wdata*}
  );

  Update(*wid* : *WagonId*, *dep* : *TP*, *arr* : *TP*, *pt* : *PTF*, *dt* : *DTF*) $\triangleq$
  pre *wid* $\in$ dom *wdir*
  let *wdata* = *wdir*(*wid*) in
  wdata!*SetWData*(*wid*, nil, *dep*, *arr*, *pt*, nil, *dt*);

  Read(*wid* : [*WagonId*], *tid* : [*TagId*], *dep* : [*TP*], *arr* : [*TP*],
      pt_loc : [*Location*], *pt_begin* : [*Time*], *pt_end* : [*Time*],
      rt_loc : [*Location*], *rt_begin* : [*Time*], *rt_end* : [*Time*], *dt* : [*DTF*])
  value *wdatas* : @*WData** $\triangleq$
  (dcl *wdatas* : @*AIEWData** := [];
     for all *wdata* $\in$ rng *wdir*
     do def *selection* = *wdata*!*WRead*(*wid*, *tid*, *dep*, *arr*, *pt_loc*, *pt_begin*,
                    pt_end, *rt_loc*, *rt_begin*, *rt_end*, *dt*) in
        wdatas := *wdatas* $\frown$ *selection*;
     return *wdatas*
  );

  Destroy(*wid* : *WagonId*) $\triangleq$
  pre *wid* $\in$ dom *wdir*
  wdir := {*wid*} $\lhd$ *wdir*;

$Log\,(tid:TagId, now:Time)$ value $\mathbb{B}$　$\triangleq$
(　dcl $lresult:\mathbb{B}:=$ true;
　　def $loc:Location=$ self!$GetLocation\,()$ in
　　if $tid\notin$ rng $tdir$
　　then $lresult:=$ false
　　else let $wid\in$ dom $wdir$ be st $tdir\,(wid)=tid$ in
　　　　def $wdata:@WData=wdir\,(wid)$;
　　　　　　$mk\text{-}\,(\text{-},\text{-},\text{-},\text{-},\text{-},ptt,\text{-},dtt)=wdata!GetWData\,()$ in
　　　　let $i:\mathbb{N}_1$ be st $ptt\,(i).loc=loc$ in
　　　　if $Earlier\,(TimePlusDelta\,(ptt\,(i).time, dtt\,(i).time), now)$
　　　　then (　$wdata!SetWData\,(\text{nil},\text{nil},\text{nil},\text{nil},\text{nil},$
　　　　　　　　　　　　　$mk\text{-}TF\,(loc, now, \text{TOOLATE}), \text{nil})$;
　　　　　　　　$alarm\_processor!Create$
　　　　　　　　　　$(mk\text{-}AlarmMessage\,(\text{TOOLATE}, tid, loc, now))$
　　　　　)
　　　　elseif $Earlier\,(TimeMinusDelta\,(ptt\,(i).time, dtt\,(i).time), now)$
　　　　then (　$wdata!SetWData\,(\text{nil},\text{nil},\text{nil},\text{nil},\text{nil},$
　　　　　　　　　　　　　$mk\text{-}TF\,(loc, now, \text{UNEXPECTED}), \text{nil})$;
　　　　　　　　$alarm\_processor!Create$
　　　　　　　　　　$(mk\text{-}AlarmMessage\,(\text{UNEXPECTED}, tid, loc, now))$
　　　　　)
　　　　else $wdata!SetWData\,(\text{nil},\text{nil},\text{nil},\text{nil},\text{nil},$
　　　　　　　　　　　$mk\text{-}TF\,(loc, now, \text{OK}), \text{nil})$;
　　return $lresult$
)

end *WDir*

The corresponding Ada code for the body of method *Create* is shown in Figure 9.5. Apart from the implementation of the data structure for *wdir* and the auxiliary code needed to check boundary cases, the close correspondence between the specification and the implementation is clear.

The alarm store is represented by an object from class *AlarmProcessor*, in which incoming alarm messages are stored.

For a TT, a similar approach is followed. The transport transaction monitoring protocol (TTMP) has the following phases:

Phase	Server method
preliminary booking	*Create*
final booking	*Update*
assign time planning	*Update*
destroy	*Destroy*
query *TTDir* or *WDir*	*Read*
alarms	*alarm_processor!Read*

begin

```
if not combi_types.equal_wagonId (wagonId, combi_types.nilWagonid) and
    not tag_types.equal_wagonTagId (tagId, tag_types.nilWagonTagId) then
    MyDir_WdataArray(free) :=
        (N => thisNode, wagonId => wagonId, tagId => tagId,
        TTIdArr => TTIdArr, departure => departure,
        arrival => arrival, pt => pt, rt => rtf.nilRealTimeField,
        dt => dt);
    wagonTagId_idxs.insert_sortArr (tagId, free, insErrorWagonTagId,
                                    myDir_wagonTagId_idx);
    if not insErrorWagonTagId then
        wagonId_idxs.insert_sortArr (wagonId, free, insErrorWagonId,
                                     myDir_wagonId_idx);
        if insErrorWagonId then
            wagonTagId_idxs.delete_sortArr (tagId, myDir_wagonTagId_idx);
        end if;
    end if;
    if not (insErrorWagonTagId or insErrorWagonId) then
        free:= free + 1;
    end if;
end if;
```

end WcreateP;

Figure 9.5 Ada code corresponding to *Create*.

Here also, an extra operation is added to isolate the input from the readers, which must be fed directly into a TT's RTT:

Phase	Server method
reader	*Log* (special version of *Update*)

In the protocol overview sketched above, the symmetry with the wagon registration is clearly visible. Another recognizable aspect here is that, apart from the *Destroy* and *Log* methods, all basic functions represent an activity that can also be invoked through an EDI message. Therefore, for each function a corresponding EDIFACT definition is available which enables agents to electronically exchange information with their clients. At the functional level of this model, however, there is no difference between access via the operator's user interface and the client's EDI message. In the next stages of refinement several kinds of protections are introduced to limit these basically equal rights.

A reader is — at this level — quite a simple piece of equipment, modelled by a separate active object which is activated by an event outside the system, namely the passing of a train. For reasons of simplicity a periodic obligation is used to invoke the *Decode* method; a complete specification of the (time-wise) randomly distributed events is also possible, but this does not add to the fundamental concepts of a reader.

class *Reader*

    instance variables
      wdir : @*WDir*;
      ttdir : @*TTDir*;
      tag : *WagonTag* | *UTITag*;
      time : *Time*

    methods
      Decode () $\triangle$
      if *is-WagonTag* (*tag*)
      then *wdir*!*Log* (*tag*, *time*)
      else *ttdir*!*Log* (*tag*, *time*)

    thread
      periodic (*t*)(*Decode*)

end *Reader*

Finally, the entire system specification with the creation and connection of the objects, as depicted in Figure 9.3, is formally specified by the *Model*$_0$ workspace.

class *WorkSpace*

    instance variables
      wdir   : @*WDir*;
      ttdir   : @*TTDir*;
      alarm_processor : @*AlarmProcessor*;
      reader   : @*Reader*

    methods
      Init () $\triangle$
    (*wdir* := *WDir*!new;
        ttdir := *TTDir*!new;
        alarm_processor := *AlarmProcessor*!new;
        reader := *Reader*!new;
        topology [ext wr *wdir*, *ttdir*, *reader*
                 rd *alarm_processor*
             post *wdir.alarm_processor* = *alarm_processor* $\wedge$
                   ttdir.alarm_processor = *alarm_processor* $\wedge$
                   reader.wdir = *wdir* $\wedge$ *reader.ttdir* = *ttdir*];
        startlist ({*wdir*, *ttdir*, *reader*})
)

end *WorkSpace*

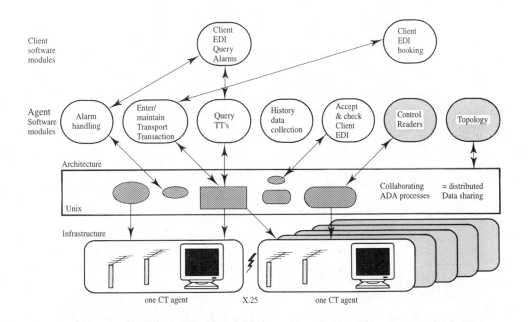

Figure 9.6 System layers.

9.4.2   The distributed character: *Model₁*

The most important addition to the formal specification in its transition from *Model₀* to *Model₁* is the introduction of the distributed characteristics of the system. The most important reasons for using the concept of loosely coupled parallel processes as the basis for the design were as follows.

- *Extendability.* The system must operate reliably under dynamic changes of its topology: new readers may be added, new terminal nodes may come in, new routes may be added. Processes can cope with this role.
- *Fault tolerance.* The effect of a failing system component should be encapsulated as much as possible, limiting the reduction of the functionality still available at other places (graceful degradation).
- *No centralized solution.* The organizational structure of cooperating independent companies on a pan-European scale prohibits the introduction of any centralized role in the architecture.

To achieve this the system was designed with three layers of parallelism (Figure 9.6):

- level 1 (computer level), distributed system with terminal computer vs terminal computer;

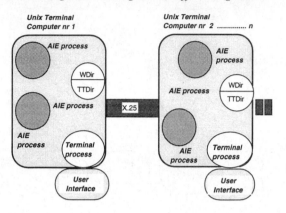

Figure 9.7 System units.

- level 2 (UNIX level), independent reader and terminal processes, and
- level 3 (Ada level), where each process is built up from several Ada tasks in client server mode.

This principle required special design measures to find a balance between minimal communication costs on the one hand and real-time sharing of data and alarm events on a geographically wide scale on the other.

9.4.3 Distributing the data

In line with the principle that at each location only a small part of the global data is needed to perform the comparison between the SOLL and IST values of the time–place combinations, we now consider the *WData* and *TTData* composed types as the logically global data sets. With respect to the distributed nature of the system a distinction is made between the terminal processes and the set of AIE processes. The main rôle of a terminal process is to play the counterpart of the user interface. An AIE process controls the data stream of one reader.

Taking the global *TTData* set as an example, a complete "frame" for this data is copied to the receiving and sending terminal processes and, if needed, to a number of intermediate transit agent nodes, i.e. the processes communicating directly with the operator's user interface. These initially empty frames are "loaded" with the static description data of *TTData*; they play the rôle of a cache copy during the life time of the TT. Thus, before a timetable is initially assigned to this TT, it resides only in the departure and arrival terminal processes. The set of AIE processes plays this rôle by virtue of their distributed nature, and collectively hold the real up-to-date values of all PTT and RTT data, i.e. the real most recently planned times and measured times.

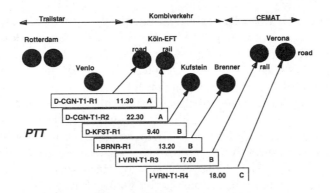

Figure 9.8 Globally distributed data.

After the assignment of a PTT to a TT, the tables are distributed by loading the relevant part of the planned timetable into each location (see Figure 9.8). First the table is split into its entries: the *ptf*, *rtf* and *dtf* fields. Then a small identifying header and the *ptf*, *rtf* and *dtf* fields (for that location) are loaded into the *TTDir* of the corresponding AIE process. In other words, only one line of the tables is available at each node; the collection of these lines together (logically) forms the complete set of tables.

Because an AIE node is directly connected to a reader (through the *Log* methods), the local value of the AIE directory entry is maintained in real time, without any network delay, because no copying to other nodes is required.

The object-oriented solution chosen here becomes visible through the subclass relations of the *TTData* set, in which the data frames *TermTTData* and the real fields *AIETT-Data* are distinguished.

The distribution operation is specified in principle as follows:

$DistributeTTData\,(ttdata:@TermTTData)\;\triangleq$
def $mk\text{-}\,(ttid,\text{-},\text{-},\text{-},\text{-},\text{-},\text{-},\text{-},\text{-},\text{-},\text{-},\text{-},\text{-},ptt,\text{-},\text{-}) = ttdata!GetTTData\,()$ in
for all $i \in$ dom ptt
do let $aienode = ptt\,(i).place$ in
$aienode!Create\,(ttid,ptt\,(i))$

Notice that the *GetTTData* method returns a compound value with 16 different components; because we only need to know the *ttid* and *ptt* components of that value, so-called "don't care" patterns are used to discard the need to introduce new identifiers not used in that part of the specification.

The result of the chosen distribution scheme is that

- the set of *AIETTData* objects represent at all times the real-time values, as soon as they are available from the readers, and
- the two *TermTTData* objects play the role of caches, which hold some older value of the passing times.

The AIE processes can be characterized as completely event driven, and by their nature they realize the real-time property of the distributed system; their local job is done within one millisecond. The AIE processes can start their job of checking whether an unusual situation has occurred, by comparing local *ptf* and *rtf* fields with one another, in principle for each TT. This is done each time a log operation is called by a reader or by maintaining a candidate queue with the expiration times of each time window for the NOSHOW alarms. The result can be either an OK situation or one of the alarms, and is initially stored in the *flag* field of the local PTF. In the case of an alarm, an alarm message is sent to the departure and arrival terminal process where appropriate action is taken by the local alarm processor. The *TTData* server at a terminal node is connected to this alarm processor. Besides signalling the operator that an alarm has occurred, a log operation on the *TTDir* is performed as a side effect. The resulting effects of this approach are given in the following table:

Alarm occurred yes/no	Condition	Effect
yes	RTT is up-to-date	$rtf = aie(i).rtf$
no	RTT is empty	$rtf = $ NIL
no	with a remote read	real-time is updated once

Thus, the principle that when there are no actual times at a terminal process the train was still on schedule, otherwise there would have been alarms and flags set, could be used for query operations. This, of course, is under the assumption that all readers function properly and that the network connections are intact. The principle was particularly useful for handling queries where all TT identifiers had to be checked to find out whether they belong to the answer set or not. Doing this by interrogation over the network of all nodes would become overly expensive and impossible to realize within response times that were acceptable to the operators. The result was that 90% of the queries could be mapped to the local read operations.

Only one distributed read operation was necessary for the situation in which an operator or an EDI client wants to know the last time a UTI was signalled, even when the train was on schedule. In this case the TT identifier is known and therefore also its PTT. Only those nodes which have a planned time before the current time have to be interrogated by a remote read. The next node is also included to ensure that a very early appearance is also covered; however, after two NIL values it can be safely assumed that the train is not yet there and thus could not have been signalled by any reader further on the route. Again, the design trade-off was in favour of minimizing communication costs.

Thus, for the planned times

$$pt_{departure} \cdots \rightarrow \cdots pt_i(now) \cdots \rightarrow \cdots pt_{arrival}$$

all AIE processes are sequentially interrogated from the start until pt_i. The interrogation is abandoned when two empty real times are encountered. This *GetRealTimes* operation can be specified as

GetRealTimes $(tid: TagId, ptt: PTT)$ value *result*: $\mathbb{N}_1 \overset{m}{\to} PTF$ $\triangleq$
(dcl $loc: Location$,
        $counter: \mathbb{N}_1 := 1$,
        $try: \mathbb{B} :=$ true;
    while *try*
    do (def $ptf = ptt(counter)$ in
            $loc := ptf\,!GetLocation\,()$;
            $rtf(counter) := loc\,!Read\,(tagid, rtf.time)$;
            $result(counter) := rtf$;
            $try := (rtf.time = $ nil$)$;
            $counter := counter + 1$
        );
    return *result*
)

9.4.4   Handling concurrency conflicts

The distribution philosophy described in the previous section is called **partial replication**, with the property that transactions with a rather long execution time have to be taken into account. This means that the following distribution and concurrency conflicts must be considered for the updates:

- updates of the PTT for the global *WData* and *TTData* data sets by two operators at the same time;
- changes in the topology, i.e. adding and removing AIE nodes.

For the read-only operations it is acceptable that the local data sets at the terminal nodes are considered to be sufficiently up to date to serve the information needs, but it cannot be guaranteed that these local data sets always represent the latest real-time information. At the level of an AIE node all servers are Ada tasks, locally protected against simultaneous update calls by the Ada rendezvous mechanism.

The second kind of conflict stems from the distribution and unpredictable message-handling times. Each update is performed as a global transaction consisting of a set of local operations. Two simultaneous update transactions on the global system level may result in several local updates, executed in a different time order, invalidating the expected final result. A time stamp ordering protocol is used to achieve a protection scheme which enforces the same sequence of updates at each node by locally aborting update transactions that appear to be out of sequence. The transaction number is derived from the place–time combination of the initiating node. A two-phase-commit protocol ensures that after an update transaction, all AIE nodes again have the same *TTData* (or *WData*). This mainly concerns the creation and deletion of the entries in the directory (Cellary *et al.*, 1988).

The architectural choices made it simple to deal with the following operations from *Model*$_1$:

- log operations, where only local AIE nodes are affected;
- for all reads, the fact is accepted that during a global transaction the "old" values will be returned and only after the second commit phase is the new value written into the directories.

9.4.5   The topology of the system

The topology table *TopTab*, which is a fully replicated table at each node, holds the entries *location_name*, *host_computer_name*, *headquarters*, *status*, *access_mode*, and *addresses*, where *status* can be one of the following: ACTIVE, SLEEPING or DEAD. The states SLEEPING and DEAD are used to distinguish between the state that the process itself is running and the sensor is working or not. Even if the sensor is (temporarily) inactive, the AIE process can remain active to maintain consistency of data with the other nodes, by participating in the global creation and deletion of *TTData*s and *WData*s from the directories. Of course no real time readings appear in this state.

A node is connected to the distributed system by adding its entry through a global *AddNode* operation into each topology table and by starting its UNIX process. The node itself takes a copy of a recent *TopTab* as one of its input parameters at start up. Redirection of the communication towards a node, or even towards an entire computer by redirecting all of its local nodes, is achieved by a global change of the addresses.

9.4.6   Communication

The communication was designed at the level of the Ada servers. The other two (higher) levels of parallelism, the computer-to-computer and the UNIX-to-UNIX process communication are handled by the communication layer in terms of Ada tasks which run on each AIE and terminal process. The communication layer uses the entries of *TopTab* to select the appropriate *MediumLayer* for the location name. Currently the system contains a *MediumLayer* for UNIX-to-UNIX process communication on one computer using writing and reading of plain UNIX files. For computer-to-computer communication, the UUCP protocol is used to write the message file into the (remote) receiver's directory. An X.25 version of this layer, using FTAM, is foreseen.

Physically, communication is based on the use of secondary storage. The use of existing interprocess communication facilities based on volatile storage was deliberately avoided because the existence of a file as a communication mechanism made it possible to build a restart capability that can cope with temporarily defective communication lines in the communication layer, in this way realizing fault-tolerant behaviour.

The communication layer attempts to reach the other system to deliver the message for a node on that system. An acknowledgement protocol was not used because the network protocols used by the *MediumLayer*, such as X.25 and UUCP, already have their own error recovery mechanisms, signalling the failure of communication after an (adjustable) number of re-attempts. If such a communication error occurs the *TopTab* entry is informed that this node is no longer reachable and the operator is informed. All currently active global transactions involving the faulty process are automatically blocked because the two-phase-commit protocol can no longer be completed. Ultimately, they abort. If the operator then performs a retry of the operation, the faulty node is excluded, but all the other reachable nodes are kept up to date. If a node comes into existence (again) after a communication failure, it uses its own stored copies of the *TTDir* and *WDir* directories and processes all remaining messages in the stored queue. From then on it joins in again with all global changes of the directories.

9.4.7 *Model₂* and further refinements

The select-statement in the code represents the server's methods available to the outside world. For one operation, *Create*, the complete code is presented. The *WData* records are stored in the first three positions of one large array `MyDir_WDataArray` in such a way that storage fragmentation is prevented.

Two sorted index arrays `myDir_wagonTag_idx` and `myDir_wagonId_idx` are maintained which preserve the relations *WId* $\xrightarrow{m}$ *Position* and *TId* $\xrightarrow{m}$ *Position*. A binary search algorithm is used to find the position in the data array. The implementation has an access time of $O(log^2(n)+1)$ for both wagon identifiers and tag identifiers.

The total current size of the software can be given, as is usual, in terms of the number of lines of source code. However, the use of functional symmetry (between *TTData* and *WData*) and the object-oriented multiple instantiation of the parallel tasks enabled us to realize the system with much fewer lines of code. Secondly, it is well known that the semantic content of one line of Ada code is approximately 10 times that of a line of, for example, C code. In this sense, we consider the small size of the system to be an asset, which will provide flexibility and ease of maintenance.

Performed function	#packages	average size	total kilo lines	size per unit
base types	4	....	21	
reader drivers	3	....	4.2	
semaphores	3	....	1.3	
testdrivers	10	...	3	
ASCII UI	...	C++	30	
graphical UI	...	HyperCard	10	
AIE node	6	....	8	8+21+4.2+3=36
terminal node	3	....	22	22+21=45+UI
total system			270	5*AIE-node+ 2*terminal node

9.5 Technology transfer

9.5.1 Rôle of the formal specification for the project partners

From the start of the project, it was clear that our transport partners were not able to read a formal specification and did not want to learn to read it. We therefore invested extra energy in making readable representations of the specifications for them, in the form of the following:

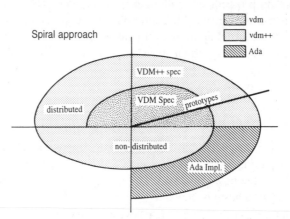

Figure 9.9 Spiral approach using formal specifications.

- pictorial representations of the system components;
- descriptions in internal documents of how the system would behave at the user interface level;
- a set of protocol descriptions in which we indicated the input actions the system would expect and which reactions it would issue;
- a fairly complete demonstration, based on the first prototype with which they could "play" just five months after the project started;
- two informal architecture descriptions in the form of reports.

From the reactions it became clear that they appreciated these representations very much. One of the partners even indicated that he liked these things much more than other representations such as data flow diagrams, E–R diagrams and structure charts. The fact that there was a formal specification was considered to be very reassuring by the other partners. It was accepted that all questions were answered by our team on the basis of these documents. It gave us the opportunity of reacting to all issues raised long before there was one line of software really running.

In the end an analogous situation to that in construction engineering was established, using a "spiral" model as illustrated in Figure 9.9. There was a maquette-like representation for the users and the construction drawings were only used by the specialists. The formal specification functioned as our internal "construction drawing" and the users accepted that we needed it for our work. The division of these two target groups for the communication only had advantages: it forced us to make our ideas clear to the transport partners, and avoided the need to use all kind of specialists terms and concepts in the presentation.

9.5.2 Rôle of the prototypes

Especially in this project it was important to provide early results, to ensure real involvement of the other partners and to get concrete reactions as soon as possible. We therefore constructed a prototype with a rather complete user interface and a functionally complete logical structure. We derived this first prototype from the VDM specification and implemented it in Ada. A graphical user interface was added — realized with HyperCard — and the communication with the Ada kernel was implemented.

This complete demonstration gave rise to a large number of reactions and enabled our partners to start thinking about the consequences of such a system in their daily work. The first versions of the EDI messages were agreed upon and internally these messages were parsed by software generated using Aflex and Ayacc, the Ada counterparts of Lex and Yacc. All the comments and changes were recorded as changes in the formal specification. The formal specification was also the basis for answers to questions such as "what if ... ?". The formal specification can function as a description of the logical behaviour of the system in the future. These changes could much more easily be carried out at the smaller specification level than would ever have been possible at the program level. The prototype implementation made use of the file-sharing capability of our local network, thus creating the illusion of a distributed system. The prototype itself was a collection of Ada tasks running on one machine. Together, however, they realized the entire functionality of the VDM^{++} $Model_0$ specification. However, there was no notion of distribution in this software prototype.

Acknowledgement

The work reported in this chapter was partially funded by the EU as part of the Drive-II programme for Advanced Transport Telematics (project number V2003).

Chapter 10

Formal Development of Safety-critical Software Systems in Railway Signalling

Babak Dehbonei and Fernando Mejia

10.1 Introduction

Jointly owned by The General Electric Company, plc. and Alcatel Alsthom, GEC Alsthom is a world leader in energy and rail transport. The company is well established internationally with around 77 000 employees in 22 countries, and 8 billion ECU of total sales. The company operates through seven divisions: Electromechanical, Gas Turbines and Diesels, Boilers and Environmental Systems, Power Transmission and Distribution, Transport, Industrial Equipment and Marine Equipment. The Transport division provides a full design, supply, commissioning and after-sales support service for a complete range of railway equipment. Its Rolling Stock group employs 13 000 people and develops and manufactures main line and urban trains, tramcars, etc. Its Signaling group employs 1800 people and develops and manufactures trackside equipment, automatic train control and supervision systems, passenger information systems, etc.

From the early days of railways, signalling has played a major rôle in assuring the safety of passengers. Since 1898, the date of introduction of the first signal box at the Gare de Lyon in Paris, GEC Alsthom has installed a large number of safety transport systems in France and throughout the world. The design and manufacture of the earliest railway safety equipment was based on mechanical and electromechanical principles and technology. Thus, safety shunts and relays, counterbalances, etc., are still used today within level crossing barriers, semaphores, track circuits (which detect trains in track sections) and points (US switches) interlocking systems. The introduction of electronic devices and microprocessors during the last 15 years gave rise to a new generation of railway safety systems. Automatic train protection (ATP) systems, computerized interlocking (CI) systems, and computerized data transmission (CDT) systems were designed using hybrid safety circuits, redundant hardware, formally validated and developed software, and sophisticated program encoding techniques (Chapront, 1992).

An ATP system supervises the adequacy of the current dynamics of the train (speed, position, etc.) with respect to the curent signalling and, whenever it detects a potentially unsafe behaviour, it activates the emergency brake of the train. For instance, a yellow signal means that the next signal is red and thus the train driver must reduce the train speed. In case of omission, the emergency brake is activated by the ATP. A CI system controls and commands points in order to set up safe, protected routes for trains. A CDT system is a high-integrity device that encodes the data exchanged between trains and trackside equipment or between trains and centralized systems.

This equipment is composed of predominantly electronic circuitry controlled by one or several computers. Standard microprocessors are used on the CPU boards and software plays a major rôle. An obvious advantage of computerized systems is that they can be easily adapted to the requirements of customers and to specific railway networks. In such safety systems, the safe state is to stop all trains. In case of failure of the equipment, the emergency brake must be triggered in order to stop all trains as soon as possible.

As mentioned above, safety has been a major concern of the signalling industry. Systematic and rigorous safety procedures must be respected in the design, development and manufacture of safety equipment. For decades, the safety procedures related to electromechanical and electronic devices have been well understood and fully established. For computer-based systems, the safety procedures are not so well established. While intensive work has been done in the field of dependable computer systems, software safety remains an unresolved issue. It has been proven (Bicarregui and Ritchie, 1993) that the quantification of safety software reliability is infeasible using classical statistical methods. These approaches lead to an exorbitant amount of testing when applied to safety software. Formal development is an alternative to these approaches. The proof procedure associated with formal methods is intended to lead to full confidence in the development process.

This chapter presents our experience of using the B formal method in the development of computer-based railway signalling systems. One of these systems is briefly described and its formal specification and implementation are investigated.

10.2   Background

The first French railway signalling project where software was intensively involved was the Système d'Aide à la Conduite et à la Maintenance (SACEM). SACEM is an ATP system ordered by the Paris Transport Authority (RATP) and has been in operation since 1988 on the Paris fast subway RER line A. The basic purpose of the system was to permit the safe reduction of the headway between two consecutive trains from $2\frac{1}{2}$ minutes to 2 minutes. Note that this leads to the situation where, during the rush hour, the first of two consecutive trains leaves the station while the second train enters the same station.

In order to increase confidence in the software, a range of techniques were applied for the validation of SACEM. Besides the standard testing phase (unit tests, integration tests and functional tests), an extra formal verification has been performed. Firstly, from an informal design document a validation team drew pre- and post-conditions for each safety procedure of SACEM and, using Hoare logic (Hoare, 1969), showed that the corresponding Modula-2 implementation satisfied them. Secondly, from the same design document a different validation team wrote a formal specification using the earliest version of Abrial's abstract machine notation (AMN) and drew from it a second version of the pre- and post-conditions. The two versions were compared and the differences were analyzed and explained.

This first satisfactory use of formal methods encouraged the management to make use of B as a complete development method and not only of AMN for validation purposes. The choice of B was motivated by the following.

1. Our concern was not only to specify the system formally but also to check the compliance of the code with respect to its specification and the consistency of the refinement process. B provides a framework for proving these properties.

2. An embryonic set of tools were available to assist the developers. It was inconceivable to start a real-life project without any tool support.

3. A certain familiarity with the B notation had been gained during the SACEM validation phase.

4. Living in Paris, J.-R. Abrial was available for consultancy and advice on request.

Thus, in order to introduce the B-Method in an industrial setting, a technology transfer programme was established. It started in 1988 and covered three topics: training of project teams, definition of guidelines based on the development of a real-life project, and the development of a computer-supported environment. The first phase of the programme has been financially supported by RATP and the French National Railway Network (SNCF). The whole technology transfer programme took approximately 10 person years.

10.2.1 Training

Approximately twenty engineers have been trained. The trained population is composed of ten development engineers, two project leaders, one validation engineer, one quality engineer and six engineers from the customer's side. Almost all the trained people have an engineering degree. Two courses of one week each are provided. The first week is devoted to specification; it concentrates on logic, set theory, basic generalized substitutions and abstract machines. The second week is dedicated to design; it introduces refinement theory and programming substitutions with emphasis on data and algorithmic refinement, proof obligations and loop invariants. We noticed that, in general, the most difficult part from the attendee's viewpoint was abstraction and mathematical proof. Despite their mathematical background, people with substantial programming experience seem to have lost the ability for mathematical proof. Obviously, the programming notations are easily understood by this audience. Despite these intensive courses, following our experience, three to six more months are necessary for a developer to be familiarized with all facets of formal development.

10.2.2   Development guideline

Prior to our applications, there were no significant applications developed in B and therefore no development guidelines were available. Such guidelines cannot be produced without experience of a real-life project. It was then decided to start the development of an upgraded version of an ATP system already in use. This was the ideal opportunity to introduce formal methods because the basic features of the system were quite well established in the previous version. The new system integrated new functionalities. We ended up with a relatively large safety program (19 000 lines of Ada code). The proof obligations generation and their associated proofs were laborious with the earliest versions of the tools. We learnt by experience, resulting in some B development guidelines. We discovered some wrong ways of specifying or implementing B modules. We investigated solutions that gave satisfactory results on one project but then failed on another. As the result of this study, some guidelines have been written out and are being used on a recently started application.

10.2.3   Support environment

We were aware that no industrial applications could be developed without appropriate tools. We started a collaboration with J.-R. Abrial, as a consultant, and BP Innovation Center, as a partner, in order to provide a complete set of tools supporting the B-Method.

10.2.4   Further B developments

The B-Method has been used for the development of six other projects: three ATP systems for urban lines; a component of a CI system that commands and supervises points; a track allocator component of the same CI system; a CDT system. The development of all but the track allocator and the CDT systems is finished. The programs obtained are relatively small (1500 to 3200 lines of Modula-2 or Ada) and their development generated 600 to 1200 proof obligations. In this chapter we shall present the first levels of the specification and design of the track allocator system.

10.3   The B-Method

Devised by Abrial (1995), like Z (Spivey, 1992) and VDM (Jones, 1990), B is a model-oriented method based on set theory and refinement theory. B has been designed to cover all the development phases of the software lifecycle, from specification to implementation, with special emphasis placed on modularity and data encapsulation. The formal specification, as well as the design and the implementation, are expressed in the abstract machine notation.

An **abstract machine** specifies a program by a state, an initialization of the state and a collection of operations. The **state** specifies the static properties of the program; it is defined by means of a collection of variables characterized by an **invariant**, which is a conjunction of first-order predicates of a typed set theory. AMN offers a large variety of data structures: Booleans, integers, Cartesian products, sets, power sets, relations, functions, sequences and trees. It thus possible to use very abstract data structures for specification. The initialization defines the initial values of the state variables and the operations specify the procedures offered by the program. The initialization and the operations are expressed in terms of generalized substitutions, an extension of Dijkstra's guarded commands (Dijkstra, 1976), that describe state transformations. Quite abstract substitutions are available for specification: pre-conditions, multiple assignment, bounded and unbounded non-determinism, etc. An abstract machine has to be proved consistent, i.e. the initial values of the variables must satisfy the invariant and the operations must preserve the invariant. These are the **proof obligations** associated with abstract machines.

In general, an abstract machine is a non-executable mathematical model of a program. It has to be progressively implemented with actual programming data structures and statements. A **refinement** is an intermediate implementation of an abstract machine. As well as an abstract machine, a refinement is defined by a state, an initialization of the state and a collection of operations. Its variables implement the abstract variables; its invariant characterizes the concrete variables and expresses the implementation relation that links these variables to the abstract variables; its initialization and operations correspond to the abstract initialization and operations expressed in terms of concrete variables and more detailed algorithms. The designer must prove that the refinement implements the behavior of its abstraction and that it preserves its properties. These are the refinement proof obligations.

The last refinement of an abstract machine, the one that will be translated into an executable programming language module, is called an **implementation**. It may import abstract machines whose variables are used as concrete variables in the implementation and whose operations may be called from the implementation operations. Because it will be translated into a programming language module, several restrictions are placed on an implementation.

1. The variables of the imported abstract machines cannot be used outside the local invariant since they will certainly disappear in the course of refinement.
2. Only Booleans, integers, enumerated sets and total functions (arrays) may be declared.
3. Only simple assignment, conditional and `case of` statements, sequentially composed substitutions, loops and operation calls may be used in operations.

The fundamental properties of the refinement relation are transitivity and monotonicity. Transitivity ensures that an implementation preserves and implements the properties of the initial abstract machine. Monotonicity ensures that it is equivalent to use an abstract machine or one of its refinements; therefore, an implementation is equivalent to the programming module to which it is translated.

10.4   Formal development lifecycle

The applications developed with B at GEC Alsthom follow the standard "V" lifecycle. The left descending branch is devoted to development and comprises several phases: specification, preliminary design, detailed design and coding. The development starts with a structured analysis specification of the system. The result of this phase is a top-down decomposition that defines the various functions of the system. This informal functional specification is accompanied by another document called the detailed specification which contains some implementation detail. One may wonder why structured analysis is used for specification instead of AMN in our formal development process. It is because our customers are used to reading them in order eventually to approve such functional descriptions. Furthermore, railway designers feel comfortable with the specification style used within the structured analysis, i.e. the functional description.

At the preliminary design stage the designers reformulate and package in AMN the functions described at the upper levels of the top-down functional decomposition. More precisely, an abstract machine that specifies the topmost function of the system is defined and implemented using the abstract machines that specify the functions of the first level of the top-down decomposition. The implemention of these abstract machines is also part of the preliminary design. In fact, it is fair to say that preliminary design work terminates when the layer where the main functions are implemented with the abstract machines that specify the main data of the system is reached. However, since the concept of "main" is quite subjective, it is not easy to fix a precise boundary to preliminary design.

Detailed design work consists of implementing the abstract machines that specify the main data of the system. During this phase, lower-level abstract machines are specified and developed. At the end of this phase all the implementations are available. The coding phase is the translation of all the implementations into programming language modules. The translation is done either automatically, if a code translator is available, or manually otherwise.

In the standard "V" lifecycle, three phases constitute the right ascending branch dedicated to verification:

1. unit tests, where each individual procedure is tested by simulating the calling environment;
2. integration tests, in which modules are assembled and the interfaces are tested;
3. functional tests, in which the compliance of the sofware with its requirements is checked using test scenarios or simulations.

In our formal development lifecycle, as illustrated in Figure 10.1, unit tests are no longer required as long as all operations have been fully specified and their proof obligations have been discharged. In fact, the proof process covers all the paths in the control flow graph of each operation and all the possible values of the variables.

The integration tests are reduced since only the interfaces between formally developed and non-formally developed modules have to be checked. The interfaces among formally developed modules are verified within the proof process. In fact, each time an operation

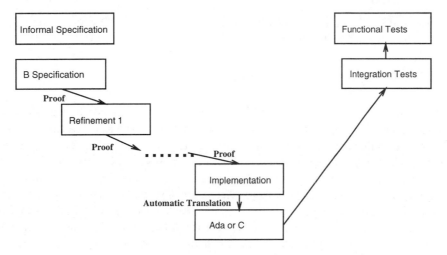

Figure 10.1 B development.

of an abstract machine is called, there is an associated proof obligation verifying that the operation is called from a state satisfying its precondition.

As far as the functional tests are concerned, the testing effort remains unchanged. One must check the compliance of the produced code with the user requirements.

10.4.1   Proofs

One of the most innovative aspects of formal development is that of proof obligation. Ideally, before an abstract machine is imported or implemented the designer must discharge all its proof obligations. To do this, the support environment provides an automatic proof obligation generator and an automatic prover. Unfortunately, this prover is not as effective as we would like it to be, and it may fail to discharge some proof obligations. Either this failure represents a design error or it is a consequence of shortcomings in the prover. In the latter case, the user may add some particular mathematical rules to help the prover in discharging the proof obligation.

In all the applications we have developed, a complete proof has been performed at the end of the preliminary design. However, our experience has shown that the detailed design often modifies the preliminary design and hence some of the proofs that have been carried out must be redone. So, since formal proof is a time-consuming activity, our intention for forthcoming projects is just to verify informally, at the end of preliminary design, that those proof obligations that could not be discharged automatically are not design errors. The complete formal proof will be performed at the end of the detailed design, when a stabilized situation has been reached.

As we pointed out earlier, the user may provide additional rules that help the prover in discharging proof obligations. Of course, these rules must be validated; therefore, in our lifecycle there is a formal validation phase which is performed by a separate validation team also responsible for the functional tests.

10.5   Safety envelope allocator

The most recent program developed with the B-Method is a subcomponent of a computerized interlocking (CI) system developed for the SNCF. The rôle of a safety CI system is to set up safe, protected routes for trains as they move within the geographic zone it administrates (the **domain**). The CI system comprises a master component called the **regional manager** that knows the planned routes and the positions of the trains within the domain and issues requests to two safety-critical systems, the **points controller** that, besides locking and unlocking points, guarantees that points considered as locked are and remain effectively locked, and the **envelope allocator** that administrates virtual track sections, called **envelopes**, while ensuring that they do not overlap and that each one is exclusively allocated to a single train.

Below we present the first development steps of the formal design of the envelope allocator. We start giving an informal specification of the system, next we present the implementation constraints that are imposed and finally we deal with the formal design.

10.5.1   Informal specification

An envelope covers an entire train and represents the portion of the network where the train can move without risking collision with other trains or terminal buffers. Its front border is the location where the train would stop if the emergency brake were to be activated. It is worth noting that this border varies with the position and the speed of the train and that it may be located at any position within an actual track section. A particular situation arises when the train crosses a set of points. In such a case, the envelope must be extended on a portion of the other emerging track in order to prevent trains on this track from getting excessively close to the crossing train, as shown in Figure 10.2.

The envelope allocator communicates with three systems: the regional manager, the train and the points controller. At the request of the regional manager, the envelope allocator creates an envelope for a train entering the domain, destroys the envelope of a train leaving the domain, moves the front border of the envelope of a train forwards in order to permit forward movement, joins the adjacent envelopes of two trains being coupled and splits the envelope of a train being divided into two independent trains. The envelope allocator sends acknowledgment messages back to the regional manager, including a status return code and the positions of the front and back borders of the envelopes.

When a train enters the domain, it sends to the envelope allocator its configuration (length, number and identity of carriages, etc.) and, as and when it moves forward, it sends the last safety position of its rear carriage. Then, the back border of its envelope is moved forward, freeing space for other trains, and consequently, allowing trains to occupy the freed portions of the line.

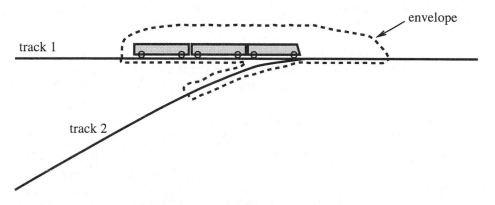

Figure 10.2 Envelope at a crossing (switch).

The envelope allocator communicates with the points controller in two circumstances: when it requests for the controlled state of a set of points before moving the front border of an envelope over them and, when it requests for the unlocking of a set of points after moving the back border of an envelope over them.

10.5.2 Implementation constraints

All our safety-critical applications follow the same architecture. A real-time operating system kernel periodically activates the basic input–output program and the application program. The frequency of activation of the basic input–output program is greater than that of the application program, therefore, it memorizes the input data and delivers it to the application program when this one is activated. It is the application program that is formally developed. This program is sequential, deterministic and non-distributed. It does not respond to interrupts and must terminate within a predefined cycle time.

Our applications must be protected against execution failures due to compilation errors or run-time environment errors (hardware failures, etc.). To prevent these situations, we make use of a program encoding technique that associates variables with signatures that record their history. These signatures are computed at compile time and loaded with the program. At execution time, they are computed once again and compared with the stored ones. In case of disparity, a hardware exception is raised and the emergency brake is activated. This technique traps almost all execution failures and it is as effective as, for example, the majority voting techniques also used in safety-critical applications. It is called **encoded preprocessor** (Chapront, 1992) and implies some restrictions on B implementations, e.g. limited use of arrays, of complex arithmetic expressions, etc.

There is another important implementation constraint. The detailed specification document describes the main functions of the envelope allocator in terms of finite-state automata. Consequently, the definition of the variables and of the operations of abstract machines will be strongly influenced by this implementation choice.

10.5.3 Formal design

The structure of the first layers of the envelope allocator is a tree of abstract machines that follows the functional top-down decomposition of the system. At the top there is the *global_treatment* machine that specifies the global safety invariant and the procedure called at every execution cycle of the system.

10.5.4 The *global_treatment* machine

State model

The underlying idea of our model is that envelopes are disjoint sets of elementary track segments of the railway network. However, since an envelope may cover a physical track section only partially, the segments we shall consider cannot be the track sections. A finer representation is required. So, we divide the tracks conceptually into units of measure that permit accurate location of the trains. Formally, we specify the railway network as a binary relation whose elements represent pairs of consecutive abscissae in the physical tracks or, dually, units of measure of the physical tracks. Let *ABSCISSA* be the set of all possible abscissae. The railway network is then represented by the binary relation

$$graph \in ABSCISSA \leftrightarrow ABSCISSA$$

which contains no cycles:

$$graph^+ \cap \text{id}(ABSCISSA) = \emptyset$$

where $graph^+$ is the (non-reflexive) transitive closure of *graph* and id is the identity function.

Notice that here we deal with abstract abscissae that will not be implemented. An implementation of an abscissa will be an ordered pair where the first projection is an identifier of a physical track section and the second projection is a natural number denoting a relative position in this track.

An auxiliary function is required for the determination of safety envelopes. As described in Figure 10.2, whenever a train approaches sufficiently close to a set of points its safety envelope must include these points and a portion of the emerging track in order to prevent trains on this track from getting too close. So, we introduce the function *protect* which associates each segment of *graph* with the set of segments that should be protected with it:

$$protect \in graph \rightarrow \mathcal{P}(graph)$$

(where $\mathcal{P}(S)$ denotes the power set of S) such that

$$\forall a_1, a_2.((a_1, a_2) \in graph \Rightarrow (a_1, a_2) \in protect(a_1, a_2))$$

Just as the network and the protected zones around points are physical constants of the system, *graph* and *protect* are constants of our specification.

Four variables are introduced in order to specify the safety envelopes associated with trains.

- *mb* is the set of protected **mobiles**, i.e. the set containing the identifiers of the trains inside the domain of the envelope allocator.
- *re* is the total function that associates the appropriate **route envelope** with each mobile in *mb*, i.e. the set of consecutive segments that constitute the intersection of its safety envelope and its route along the network.
- *rb* is the total function that associates a **right protected border** with each mobile in *mb*, i.e. the rightmost abscissa of its route envelope.
- *lb* is the total function that associates a **left protected border** with each mobile in *mb*, i.e. the leftmost abscissa of its route envelope.

Let *MOBILE* be the set of train identifiers; the following predicates formally characterize these variables:

$$mb \in \mathcal{F}(MOBILE) \tag{1}$$
$$re \in mb \to (ABSCISSA \rightarrowtail ABSCISSA) \tag{2}$$
$$\forall m .(m \in mb \Rightarrow re(m) \subseteq graph) \tag{3}$$
$$rb \in mb \to ABSCISSA \tag{4}$$
$$lb \in mb \to ABSCISSA \tag{5}$$
$$\forall m .(m \in mb \Rightarrow re(m)^{\mathsf{card}(re(m))} = \{ lb(m) \mapsto rb(m) \}) \tag{6}$$

The first predicate expresses that *mb* is a finite subset of *MOBILE*; predicates (2)–(6) express that, since there are no cycles in *graph*, the route envelope of a mobile is made of contiguous segments of *graph* starting at its left protected border and ending at its right protected border. The safety property of the envelope allocator is formalized by the predicate

$$\forall m_1, m_2.(m_1 \in mb \land m_2 \in mb \land m_1 \neq m_2 \Rightarrow$$
$$\mathsf{union}(protect[re(m_1)]) \cap \mathsf{union}(protect[re(m_2)]) = \emptyset)$$

which defines the safety envelope of a mobile as its route envelope together with the protected zone around it, and which expresses that the safety envelopes of two distinct mobiles do not intersect.

Notice that this definition allows contiguous route envelopes, which is required before two mobiles are to be coupled or which results from the dividing of a mobile in two distinct mobiles.

Initialization

The initialization of *global_treatment* expresses that the empty set is the initial value of each variable. It is easy to check that the initialization establishes the invariant since the initial values satisfy the invariant.

The perform_elementary_cycle operation

The abstract machine *global_treatment* specifies only the main operation *perform_elementary_cycle*, which is called every cycle of execution by the operating system kernel. Its specification is very simple; it just expresses that the variables may be modified and that their new values satisfy the machine invariant. This is a common and very abstract description of how the system must behave. All we say is that the system may move into a new state that preserves the invariant. Obviously this operation preserves the invariant of the machine. Consequently, the verification of this machine is very simple. In fact, one need only prove that the initialization establishes the invariant.

The *global_treatment* machine is the following:

MACHINE
  global_treatment
CONSTANTS
  graph,protect
PROPERTIES
  $graph \in ABSCISSA \leftrightarrow ABSCISSA$
  $\wedge\, graph^+ \cap id(ABSCISSA) = \emptyset$
  $\wedge protect \in (ABSCISSA \times ABSCISSA) \rightarrow \mathcal{P}(ABSCISSA \times ABSCISSA)$
  $\wedge\, \forall\, a_1, a_2.((a_1, a_2) \in graph \Rightarrow (a_1, a_2) \in protect(a_1, a_2))$
VARIABLES
  mb,re,rb,lb
DEFINITIONS
  invariant == (
  $mb \subseteq MOBILE$
  $\wedge\, re \in mb \rightarrow (ABSCISSA \rightarrowtail ABSCISSA)$
  $\wedge\, \forall\, m.(m \in mb \Rightarrow re(m) \subseteq graph)$
  $\wedge\, rb \in mb \rightarrow ABSCISSA$
  $\wedge\, lb \in mb \rightarrow ABSCISSA$
  $\wedge\, \forall\, m.(m \in mb \Rightarrow re(m)^{\mathrm{card}(re(m))} = \{lb(m) \mapsto rb(m)\})$
  $\wedge\, \forall\, m_1,m_2.(m_1 \in mb \wedge m_2 \in mb \wedge m_1 \neq m_2 \Rightarrow$
        $\mathrm{union}(protect[re(m_1)]) \cap \mathrm{union}(protect[\, re(m_2)]) = \emptyset)$
)
INVARIANT
  invariant
INITIALISATION
  $mb := \emptyset$
  $\|\ re\ := \emptyset$
  $\|\ rb\ := \emptyset$
  $\|\ lb\ := \emptyset$

```
OPERATIONS
  perform_elementary_cycle=
    BEGIN
      mb,re,rb,lb : (invariant)
    END
END
```

10.5.5   The *global_treatment* implementation

The implementation of *global_treatment* is just an algorithmic refinement of the *perform_elementary_cycle* operation. It imports the *local_treatments* machine which supplies the implementation with the constants and variables of *global_treatment* and also with the specification of the procedures that perform the main functions of the system. The actual implementation also imports the abstract machines which define the input and output operations and the time management operations that permit it to communicate and synchronize with the other components of the global CI system. For the sake of simplicity we group these in a single abstract machine *input_output* offering two operations *get_inputs* and *flush_outputs*.

The implementation of *global_treatment* is the following:

```
IMPLEMENTATION
  Imp_global_treatment
REFINES
  global_treatment
IMPORTS
  local_treatments, input_output
OPERATIONS
  perform_elementary_cycle=
    VAR ready IN
      get_inputs
    ; ready ← is_envelope_allocator_ready
    ; IF ready = TRUE THEN
        login_mobiles       /* may introduce or split mobiles */
      ; warn_mobiles        /* may send a warning message to mobiles */
      ; allocate_track      /* may extend the envelope of a mobile */
      ; free_track          /* may reduce or remove the envelope of a mobile */
      ; couple_mobiles      /* may couple two contiguous envelopes */
      ELSE
        initialize_envelope_allocator
      END
    ; flush_outputs
    END
END
```

Notice that no coupling invariant is necessary since *local_treatments* declares the same constants and variables as *global_treatment*: the constants and the variables of *global_treatment* are implemented with the constants and the variables of *local_treatments*.

10.5.6   Local treatments

The machine *local_treatments* contains the operations that specify the main functions of the safety envelope allocator. As seen above, the implementation of the machine *global_treatment* calls these operations. The machine *local_treatments* is not completely described here. We concentrate on the two major functions of the system namely track allocation and freeing.

State model

As as has been said before, *local_treatments* declares the same constants and variables as *global_treatment*. However, its invariant is weaker than the invariant of *global_treatment*. In the former, we are no longer concerned with safety properties expressed in the later.

Initialization

The initialization of *local_treatments* is identical to the initialization of *global_treatment*.

The allocate_track operation

The allocation of portions of track to a mobile is provided by the operation *allocate_track*. It is specified non-deterministically with a two-branch CHOICE substitution. The first branch expresses that *allocate_track* may have no effect. This is the case when the envelope allocator has not received an allocation request from the regional manager or when it executes statements without a visible effect on envelopes and borders. The second branch of the CHOICE substitution expresses that *allocate_track* may extend the route envelope of one the mobiles inside the domain of the envelope allocator. In the later case, there is a mobile, *mob*, a route envelope, *env*, a left border, *left*, and a right border, *right*, such that *mob* is a member of the mobiles inside the domain, *env* is a route envelope made of contiguous segments of *graph*, *left* is the leftmost abscissa of *env*, *right* is the rightmost abscissa of *env* and *env* includes the present route envelope of *mob* and satisfies the safety properties of the system. Neither the mobile nor the features of the extended envelope are precisely described. However, they must satisfy the safety properties related to envelopes. At the implementation level, the mobile and the allocation distance are extracted from a request transmitted by the master component of the system.

The free_track operation

The freeing of portions of track is provided by the operation *free_track*. Like *allocate_track* this operation is specified non-deterministically with a three-branch CHOICE substitution. The first branch expresses that *free_track* may have no effect. This is the case when the envelope allocator has not received the position of one of the mobiles inside the domain or when it executes statements without visible effect on envelopes and borders. The second branch of the CHOICE substitution expresses that *free_track* may shrink the route envelope of one of the mobiles inside the domain. In this case, there is a mobile, *mob*, a route envelope, *env*, a left border, *left*, and a right border, *right*, such that *mob* is a member of the mobiles inside the domain, *env* is a route envelope made of contiguous segments of *graph*, *left* is the leftmost abscissa of *env*, *right* is the rightmost abscissa of *env* and the present route envelope of *mob* includes *env* and satisfies the safety properties of the system. The third branch of the CHOICE substitution deals with mobiles leaving the domain of the envelope allocator. In that case *free_track* removes the mobile and all its attributes. As in the case of allocation, neither the concerned mobiles nor the features of envelopes are detailed. The unique constraint is that they must satisfy the safety invariant. At the implementation level, the mobile and the features of the new envelope are deduced from a message coming from a train.

The *local_treatments* machine is the following:

MACHINE
   local_treatments
CONSTANTS
   graph,protect
PROPERTIES
   $graph \in ABSCISSA \leftrightarrow ABSCISSA$
   $\wedge graph^+ \cap id(ABSCISSA) = \emptyset$
   $\wedge protect \in (ABSCISSA \times ABSCISSA) \rightarrow \mathbb{P}(ABSCISSA \times ABSCISSA)$
VARIABLES
   mb,re,rb,lb
INVARIANT
   $mb \subseteq MOBILE$
   $\wedge re \in mb \rightarrow (ABSCISSA \rightarrowtail ABSCISSA)$
   $\wedge rb \in mb \rightarrow ABSCISSA$
   $\wedge lb \in mb \rightarrow ABSCISSA$
   $\wedge \forall m.(m \in mb \Rightarrow re(m) \subseteq graph)$
   $\wedge \forall m.(m \in mb \Rightarrow re(m)^{\mathsf{card}(re(m))} = \{lb(m) \mapsto rb(m)\})$
INITIALISATION
   $mb := \emptyset$
  $\| re := \emptyset$
  $\| rb := \emptyset$
  $\| lb := \emptyset$
OPERATIONS
  allocate_track=
   BEGIN
    CHOICE
     skip
    OR
     ANY *mob, env, right, left* WHERE
      $mob \in mb$
     $\wedge env \in ABSCISSA \rightarrowtail ABSCISSA$
     $\wedge env \subset graph$
     $\wedge re(mob) \subseteq env$
     $\wedge right \in ABSCISSA$
     $\wedge left \in ABSCISSA$

$\wedge\ env(mob)^{\text{card}(env(mob))} = \{left \mapsto right\})$
$\wedge\ \forall\ mob'.\ mob' \in MOBILE \wedge mob' \neq mob \Rightarrow$
$\qquad\ \text{union}(protect[re(mob')]) \cap \text{union}(protect[env]) = \emptyset$

 THEN
  $re := re \Leftarrow \{\ mob \mapsto env\ \}$
  $\|\ rb := rb \Leftarrow \{\ mob \mapsto right\ \}$
  $\|\ lb := lb \Leftarrow \{\ mob \mapsto left\ \}$
 END
 END
END
;

free_track=
 BEGIN
  CHOICE
   skip
  OR
   ANY *mob, env, right, left* WHERE
    $mob \in mb$
   $\wedge\ env \in ABSCISSA \rightarrowtail\!\!\!\rightarrow ABSCISSA$
   $\wedge\ env \subset graph$
   $\wedge\ env \subseteq re(mob)$
   $\wedge\ right \in ABSCISSA$
   $\wedge\ left \in ABSCISSA$
   $\wedge\ env(mob)^{\text{card}(env(mob))} = \{left \mapsto right\})$
   $\wedge\ \forall\ mob'.\ mob' \in MOBILE \wedge mob' \neq mob \Rightarrow$
     $\text{union}(protect[re(mob')]) \cap \text{union}(protect[env]) = \emptyset$
   THEN
    $re := re \Leftarrow \{\ mob \mapsto env\ \}$
    $\|\ rb := rb \Leftarrow \{\ mob \mapsto right\ \}$
    $\|\ lb := lb \Leftarrow \{\ mob \mapsto left\ \}$
   END
  OR
   ANY *mob* WHERE
    $mob \in mb$
   THEN
    $mb := mb - \{\ mob\ \}$
    $\|\ re := \{\ mob\ \} \lhd\!\!\!- re$
    $\|\ rb := \{\ mob\ \} \lhd\!\!\!- rb$
    $\|\ lb := \{\ mob\ \} \lhd\!\!\!- lb$
   END
  END
 END
END

10.5.7 The *local_treatments* implementation

The implementation of *local_treatments* is also an algorithmic refinement. Recall that the detailed specification describes the main functions of the envelope allocator in terms of finite state automata. Their implementation is the direct consequence of this choice. Each operation of *local_treatments* has been decomposed into more basic operations that are triggered depending on the value of an automaton state variable. Therefore, the implementation of *local_treatments* imports an abstract machine called *automata* which declares the constants and variables of *local_treatments* and which offers the operations that decompose the operations of *local_treatments*.

The values of the state variable of the allocation automaton are WAIT_ALLOC_REQUEST, CHECK_ALLOC_REQUEST, ALLOCATE, CONTROL_SWITCH, and SEND_ALLOC_ACKNOWLEDGMENT. In the first state, the system looks for a request from the master component of the system. If a message has arrived, its validity is then checked. If the message is valid, the allocation operation is performed. If a set of points is reached while increasing the envelope of the mobile, the status of these points must be checked. Once an allocation has occurred, an acknowledgment message must be sent back to the regional manager.

The values of the state variable of the freeing automaton are WAIT_LOCALIZATION_MESSAGE, FREE, UNLOCK_SWITCHES. In the first state the system looks for a localization message coming from a mobile. Once a localization message is received from a mobile, a freeing operation is performed and a list of points to be unlocked is generated. A request is then sent to the points controller to unlock these points.

```
IMPLEMENTATION
  imp_local_treatments
REFINES
  local_treatments
IMPORTS
  allocation, freeing
OPERATIONS
  allocate_track=
    VAR automaton_state IN
      automaton_state ← current_allocation_state
    ; CASE automaton_state OF
        EITHER WAIT_ALLOC_REQUEST THEN
          look_for_alloc_request
        OR CHECK_ALLOC_REQUEST THEN
          check_alloc_request
        OR ALLOCATE THEN
          perform_allocation
        OR CONTROL_POINTS THEN
          control_points
        OR SEND_ALLOC_ACKNOWLEDGMENT THEN
          send_alloc_acknowledgment
```

```
            END
          END
        END
     ;
     free_track=
        VAR automaton_state IN
           automaton_state ← current_freeing_state
        ; CASE automaton_state OF
             EITHER WAIT_LOCALIZATION_MESSAGE THEN
                look_for_localization_message
             OR FREE THEN
                perform_freeing
             OR UNLOCK_POINTS THEN
                unlock_points
             END
           END
        END
     END
```

All the operations invoked in this implementation come from the machine *automata*. Apart from *current_allocation_state* and *current_freeing_state* which return the current state of the allocation and freeing automata, all the other operations are associated with the actions to be performed in a given state.

The *automata* abstract machine, which we do not present here, is implemented with the abstract machines that introduce and encapsulate the data required for the effective implementation of the system: network, messages, mobile attributes (length, number of vehicles,...), points, etc.

10.5.8   Tools

Although it was not the intention at the beginning of the technology transfer programme, the development of tools supporting the B-Method has been a major aspect of our experience in formal methods. In 1991, BP Innovation Center provided us with preliminary tools to analyze the B abstract machines and to produce the corresponding proof obligations. Very soon, it became clear that these tools had to be completed and improved in order to handle industrial applications. Consequently, we decided to develop a set of tools supporting the full B-Method.

The most recent version of B environment has been used for the development of the safety envelope allocator. The following tools are provided by this environment.

- *Type checker*. This tool detects type errors and errors related to intermodule visibility of variables or constants.
- *Proof obligation generator*. This generates the proof obligations associated with a module. A preliminary analysis is performed in order to discharge simple proof

obligations. Therefore, only the proof obligations requiring a non-trivial proof are generated.

- *Automatic prover*. This analyzes a proof obligation and consults a mathematical rule base to simplifying and discharge the proof obligation. A file containing user-defined rules may be consulted in case of failure of the proof.
- *Interactive prover*. This tool permits an investigation of the reason for which a proof fails. All the mathematical rules that have been applied during the proof are traced. The goal on which the proof has failed is displayed. The user can then determine whether the failure corresponds to an error in the source code or to a shortcoming in the mathematical rule base.
- *Ada and C translators*. Implementations are translated into C or Ada using these tools.
- *LaTeX document generator*. This produces a document that can be processed by LaTeX and hence viewed or printed.
- *Cross referencer*. This tool finds out where a variable is used, declared or modified.
- *Dependence graph generator*. This determines which other modules that a given module depends on.

Besides these tools, the environment includes a development manager tool that permits a group of users to work concurrently on a development. Very often, a development is a project composed of B modules. A Motif-based user interface facilitates tool usage.

The development of tools was quite a challenge. Indeed, in order to deal with large applications, we developed appropriate algorithms to be used in the proof obligations generator, the prover and the translators. For instance, in order to cope with large refinement operations, the proof obligations generator makes use of some aspects of the substitution theory that were not originally introduced for this purpose. None of the standard proof techniques (resolution, integer programming, etc.) has been used within our prover. Instead, based on some pragmatic heuristics, the prover kernel consults a large mathematical rule base and transforms formulae in order to simplify and discharge them. We are faced with two major issues: divergence (as a result of commutative and distributive laws) and efficiency. Our objective is to upgrade the prover to the point where 80% of proof obligations can be discharged automatically. In this respect, there is still much work to be done. The C translator makes use of a sophisticated algorithm in order to cope with the separation and the duplication of the data space associated with B machines.

A useful and interesting byproduct of this development was that we acquired a deep knowledge of all aspects of the B-Method, in particular the syntax and semantics of the abstract machine notation, substitution and refinement theories and set theoretic foundations. Consequently, we were able to provide efficient tool support to our users. This aspect of the experience is very important when a new technology is being introduced in an industrial setting.

This thorough investigation of techniques for supporting industrial applications has considerably improved the quality of our environment. The latest version of our environment is being commercialized by DIGILOG, a software house, and is being used by other companies.

All the tools, except the LaTeX document generator and the cross referencer, have been intensively used in the development of the safety envelope allocator.

10.6   Issues

The introduction of a new technology is not an easy task. Having developed four complete applications in B, we are now just about able to draw reasonable conclusions about our past experience and how B (or any other formal method) must be introduced. We have classified the problems into four different categories, each of which is detailed in the next four subsections.

10.6.1   Sociological issues

The software engineers' society, like any other human society, is regulated by its own beliefs and rituals. Introducing formal methods in such a society is like introducing new beliefs and rituals in a human society. The established order of things is shaken up and the new vision is preached. Therefore, it is natural to see reticence and resistance from both developers and project leaders.

Project leaders are usually faced with the situation where their background can no longer be directly useful in the technical aspects of the project. We are faced with people who are mostly concerned with respecting project planning and costs. It is therefore crucial to make project leaders sensitive to the advantages of a formal development. This is usually achieved by adequate training. Unfortunately, this type of training has never been set up and project leaders have had to follow internal training courses mainly aimed at developers. Even with such training, it is sometimes necessary for high-level managers to intervene in order to persuade project managers to continue using formal methods.

Developers usually take a different view. They are concerned with the resolution of issues such as how to develop a system that complies with its specification, how to write programs that do not produce run-time failures without being constrained by a development method. They expect a development method that comes with a complete set of tools, a development guide, user guide, training, examples, etc. It is clear that even now we cannot deliver these items completely, and thus some disillusionment and doubt have appeared and still remain in the developer's mind.

10.6.2   Development organization issues

Formal development does not naturally fit within the V life cycle. As mentioned before, our specification is written in terms of structured analysis "boxes and arrows". The translation into a formal description of the sytem is difficult because the two notations deal with two different philosophies. No translation guide is currently provided. There is another transition which is not natural either. The detailed specification document (written before the formal design) generally makes use of implementation algorithms and data structures. Writing B machines requires a reformulation of these data structures and algorithms into abstract mathematical objects and properties. Additional issues, such as the programming constraints due to the use of encoded processor techniques, make project planning difficult. The duration and the cost of some of the systems developed with B have been poorly estimated. Even the complexity of the B machines (number of proof obligations, etc.) cannot be accurately estimated by purely mechanical means.

10.6.3   Technical issues

Besides the psychological inhibitions concerning the utilization of a new development method, developers here were confronted with a very new problem: proof. In fact, the proof process is a major concern of B developers. Conventional programming practice is not suited to formal development and the most difficult task is to convince (experienced) programmers that another way of thinking must be adopted for formal development. We frequently cite the example of structured programming vs assembly languages, whereby an experienced assembly language programmer may find structured programming a very restrictive programming style because for instance the `goto` statement is prohibited. An analogous situation may exist between the use of B and the use of classical programming languages. For example, a programmer will normally write a classical `while` statement without thinking of its invariant and variant. Not only must the formal developer provide a loop invariant that states the properties of the variables modified or used once the loop is terminated, but also it must explicitly give the relationship between the implementation data structures constructed within the loop and the corresponding abstract data coming from the upper level of refinement.

Formal methods novices also tend to expect miracles such as proof obligations being discharged automatically. They must be informed from the outset that proof is difficult but necessary work.

Other factors influence the complexity of proof such as the software architecture, the choice of invariant, the complexity of operations and the refinement of conditionals. The following section investigates these issues.

Software architecture
We have noticed that B novices are tempted to specify large and complex applications using exclusively abstract machines that introduce many constants, variables and operations. This often results in a set of overcomplicated machines, having unecessary links. These are then difficult to fit together, to proof and to refine. In fact, our experience has shown that the complexity of the proof is directly proportional to the complexity of the specified application architecture.

We propose a less restrictive approach to specification. We think that refinements can be used not only for implementation purposes but also as a means to introduce specification details progressively. With this approach we can partition the specification constraints and introduce them gradually at the adequate levels of detail. Also, we can circumvent a number of restrictions imposed by the abstract machine notation, e.g. the absence of sequentiality in the operations of abstract machines and the restricted set of data structures at implementation level.

Of course with this approach it is harder to determine precisely the borders between the design phases of the software lifecycle since the preliminary design may include refinements and the detailed design may introduce specification constraints. So, we consider now the complete B development as a specification of the actual executable program.

Determination of the invariant

The complexity of the invariant plays a major rôle in the complexity of the proof. As said before, one of the factors that introduces complexity is the use of intricate architectures.

Another factor is the right choice of abstraction level. Since B permits both abstract and concrete descriptions, one may be tempted to use overly concrete descriptions within abstract machines (Bicarregui and Ritchie, 1993). As one can easily imagine, the implementable entities are much more complicated than abstract objects and may lead to considerably more proof obligations. Thus we encourage designers to use high-level data structures and non-deterministic substitutions (such as $:\in$, ANY, CHOICE) in abstract machines.

Another factor, which is closely related to the previous ones, is the choice of the characteristic properties of a system. Let us explain this notion with an example. As the reader can easily imagine, the non-overlapping of envelopes is not the only safety property of the envelope allocator. The system must also ensure that the mobiles are effectively covered by the envelopes, that the envelopes only include controlled and locked points, that the acknowledgment messages should convey the exact description of envelopes, etc. However, we thought that introducing all these properties at once would lead us to deal with too many concepts. Therefore, we decided to formalize at the top level of the specification what we considered to be the most characteristic safety property of the system and to introduce the other safety properties in lower-level machines or refinements.

Refinement of conditionals

Generally speaking, the introduction of complex control flow structures must be postponed as long as possible. From a proof point of view, it is easier to deal with predicates than with control flow structures. Another important topic is how a conditional must be refined. Suppose that in an operation, a conditional IF C1 THEN R1 ELSE S1 END is refined by another conditional IF C2 THEN R2 ELSE S2 END. For the sake of simplicity, we assume that R1, R2, S1 and S2 are deterministic. According to the definition of the conditional substitution (Abrial, 1995), we have four proof obligations to be proved for which the premises contain $C1 \wedge C2$, $C1 \wedge \neg C2$, $\neg C1 \wedge C2$ and $\neg C1 \wedge \neg C2$. Consequently, the number of proof obligations for nested conditionals grows exponentially. In order to avoid this, it is advisable to write conditionals in such a way that C1 and C2 have the same expression. Consequently, only two proof obligations are generated for each conditional.

Complexity of operations

In B implementations, one may use the statement sequencing operator represented by
; . There is sometimes a temptation to use B as a programming language without taking proof aspects into account. Deeply nested conditionals, nested loops and generally
speaking any complex control flow construct combined with the sequencing operator (;)
will produce a large number of proof obligations. It is advisable to avoid complex constructs. To this end, one may replace the branches of a conditional by calls to operations
that model these branches. These operations are then refined as necessary. By doing this
replacement, the proof deals no longer with branch refinements but with their abstract
definition.

Loops

Loops are useful in everyday programming. In B, they must be used with particular care,
however, because of the loop invariant property. Loop invariants form a barrier in the implementation, i.e. the global properties defined in the invariant of the implementation are
"lost". In other words, the loop invariant hides the global invariant of the implementation. The user must state the invariant properties appropriate to the loop.

10.6.4   External issues

An important issue is the relationship with customers. Except for SACEM, for which
the customer was prescribing formal methods, none of our customers has actually asked
for formal development. Hence, sometimes, we are faced with customers asking for unit
tests in addition to proofs.

  Most of these requests are a direct consequence of a lack of information, training and
validated tools. Extra effort is necessary in order to convince customers of the benefits
of formal development. Concerning information and training, we are confident that with
a wider appreciation of formal methods (via the introduction of formal methods in engineering curriculae, books with real-life examples, etc.), such methods will become more
easily accepted by customers. Concerning support tools, an important effort is being undertaken by RATP, SNCF, INRETS (the French Research Institute on Transport Security), DIGILOG and GEC ALSTHOM in order to develop and validate an industrial set
of tools. In particular, it is planned that the mathematical rule base used by the proof tools
will be formally validated using an independent theorem prover.

10.7   Evaluation

In this section we evaluate the use of the B-Method for the development of the envelope
allocator from several points of view.

The program

The safety envelope allocator is the largest application we have ever developed with the B-Method. The resulting program is about 35 000 lines of Ada contained in 108 packages. The large majority of the packages are relatively small and the biggest does not exceed 1000 lines of code. Also, the procedures are quite small, the biggest does not exceed 100 lines. The modularity and the relatively small size of the procedures are a direct consequence of the layer philosophy of the B-Method and of the strict data encapsulation principles of AMN. The former encourages the decomposition of implementations into separate machines and the later imposes procedure calls. Despite the number of procedure calls the execution time of the program fitted within the imposed cycle time. We cannot evaluate objectively the ratio of code expansion due to B since the encoded processor technique imposes writing rules that would not be used in a standard B development.

The costs and the planning

The preliminary design phase lasted 6 months and involved three full-time engineers. It produced the global architecture and the first layers of the application. An almost complete proof of the preliminary design has been carried out at the end of this phase. The detailed design phase lasted 7 months and involved two engineers. The complete proof could not be achieved before the delivery of the program. These figures are beyond our initial estimations. We must add that the envelope allocator is part of a new generation of computerized interlocking systems and that it was difficult to foresee its complexity and size. In fact, the initial cost and planning were estimated for a smaller program than the obtained one. However, we must admit that we underestimated the formal development of complex applications and, more particularly, its refinement and proof. Consequently our cost and planning estimations should be improved and take into account the specificities of formal development.

The B-Method

The first fact we want to point out is that we could use the B-Method to develop, from specification to code, a medium-sized non-trivial application. The B-Method permits us to understand the informal specification better, to detect some inconsistencies or deficiencies in it and to think more deeply about the architecture of the system. It also forces us to search for the simplest implementation solutions. We think this led us to produce a quite modular and maintainable code, and, since the basic machines were proved, to have a better confidence in the produced code.

However, we encountered some difficulties, mainly in defining a tractable architecture that was easy to prove and easy to split between the members of the project in order to have a balanced distribution of work. We had also some difficulties finding the simpler refinement relation between the abstract data and the concrete data. We think that we should had introduced intermediate levels of abstraction in order to facilitate the proof. We are still far from optimal usage of B in our projects mainly because of the lack of experience of developers. Continuous use of expert consultancy guided by user feedback is required in order to improve the quality of the usage of B.

The proof

About 13 500 proof obligations have been generated by the environment, of which 4000 are associated with preliminary design and 9500 with detailed design. 90% of the proof obligations associated with preliminary design had been discharged, whereas only 50% of those associated with detailed design could be discharged. One of the reasons is that, partly because of the non-trivial relation between abstract and concrete variables, and partly because of the encoding processor technique which uses biased arithmetic and Boolean calculus, the theorem prover could not automatically discharge more than 30% of the proof obligations associated with low-level implementations, whereas it usually discharges about 60%. Consequently, since we underestimated the proof task, we had to cut proof short in order to deliver the program without too long a delay.

Although the formal proof could not be carried out completely, it has helped us in finding significant errors and deficiencies at both the preliminary and detailed design stages. Furthermore, we noticed that some of the errors detected during tests could have been detected by proofs.

The tools

The formal developement of the envelope allocator produced 120 abstract machines and 110 refinements or implementations. It is clear that without automated tools, the management and the analysis of these components, as well as the generation and proof of the associated proof obligations are infeasible. Except for the machine which introduced the data representing the physical network and that had to be split, the type checker and the proof obligations generator could be used without any blocking anomalies. However, they will be improved in order to handle an incremental style of development. On some occasions the automatic theorem prover was flooded by the number of generated hypotheses. In these cases we had to change its tactics in order to reduce the number of generated hypotheses. Of course this reduces its effectiveness. Our interactive theorem prover is difficult to use, even for experienced proof practitioners; it will be completely redesigned and a user friendly interface will be provided.

10.8   Conclusions

We shall certainly use B in the development of our future safety-critical software systems. However, many aspects of formal development can be improved, especially the refinement process, the development and user guides and the tools. In the future, three other applications will make use of the B-Method and our development environment.

Successful usage of formal methods in industry depends on the following factors. Academic and research communities must pay more attention to industry's concerns. Powerful but practically unusable methods have no future in industry. On the other hand, industry managers must be more sensitive to the benefits of formal methods by evaluating industrial applications that have already been successfully developed.

Acknowledgement

We would like to thank Benjamin Clements for reviewing drafts of this paper and for his pertinent comments on its technical content.

Chapter 11

Z Applied to the A330/340 CIDS Cabin Communication System

Ute Hamer and Jan Peleska

11.1 Introduction

11.1.1 The CIDS system

The Cabin Intercommunication Data System (CIDS) is an airborne fault-tolerant dual computer system to control the cabin communication functions implemented in the Airbus A330/340 family. It comprises applications such as the public address system, cabin interphone system, sign operation (e.g. fasten seatbelts, no smoking), display of sensor information for the cabin crew (e.g. door and slide sensors), emergency evacuation signaling, testing of the emergency power supply unit and control of the cabin illumination. Amongst other reasons, the necessity to implement this heterogeneous set of functions on one computer system is given by the strict space limitations that have to be observed in the design of airborne computer systems. The CIDS system does not directly control safety-critical aircraft components, such as the engines, for example. However, since CIDS implements applications where a malfunction might indirectly impair human lives (e.g. emergency call function of the interphone system, emergency evacuation signalling), it has been classified according to DO178A criticality level 2b (this is the second-highest criticality level and corresponds to level B in the new revision, DO178B (RTCA, 1992)).

As a subcontractor to Deutsche Aerospace Airbus GmbH, DST have developed most of the application layer and some parts of the operating system software (both authors have been members of the project team, the second author in the position of the DST project manager). The Deutsche Aerospace Airbus GmbH have defined the CIDS system requirements and developed the operating system software and the computer hardware. The software development process was strictly controlled according to the requirements of DO178A. Throughout the software requirements specification phase and the software design phase, structured methods (structured analysis, real-time analysis, structured design) due to Hatley and Pirbhai (1987) and Ward and Mellor (1985) were applied with the support of a commercially available CASE tool. During the specification process, several of the application functions turned out to be surprisingly complex. The CASE methods applied completely failed to provide a sufficient means to overcome this complexity and to produce trustworthy specification results. Therefore DST decided to apply formal specification techniques using the Z notation (Spivey, 1992; Wordsworth, 1992) as an extension of the CASE specifications for the most critical and complex application functions.

11.1.2 CIDS cabin illumination

This chapter presents one of these formally specified functions, the CIDS cabin illumination function (CIL). It will be described in detail in the following sections. To introduce the basic concept of the CIL functionality, consider the aircraft cabin layout shown in Figure 11.1.

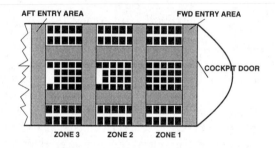

Figure 11.1 Aircraft cabin layout (simplified).

The CIL application allows for separate control of the illumination of cabin zones (e.g. first class, business class) and entry areas. To change the illumination status, the cabin crew uses panels as shown in Figure 11.2. The commands for cabin zones allow the illumination level for each zone to be chosen separately, with intensities *dim2, dim1, bright*. If the illumination level in zone 1 is off and the user presses button *dim1*, the illumination units will be switched to this intensity throughout the zone. This will be acknowledged to the user by activating a button indicator light in the *dim1* button of zone 1. Pressing the *bright* button of zone 1 will change the intensity from *dim1* to *bright*, switch off the *dim1* button indicator and turn on the *bright* button indicator. Pressing the *bright* button a second time will switch illumination and button indicators of zone 1 off. Commands to switch on/off night lights can be given, if the illumination of one zone has otherwise been switched off.

Similarly, the user can control the illumination status for entry areas. In addition to the user commands, certain sensors have an impact on the level of illumination. For example, if the cockpit door sensor signals "door open", the forward entry area lights must be dimmed to avoid distracting the cockpit crew.

To allow a flexible software-controlled adaption of the functions to different cabin layouts (e.g. different numbers of seat rows in each zone), the illumination units are connected to a bus used by the CIDS system to control various peripherals in the cabin. The CIL application function switches the intensity of an illumination unit by sending a com-

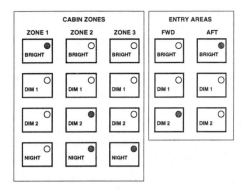

Figure 11.2 Forward attendant panel (FAP) — lights module.

mand to the unit's bus address. CIDS configuration data defines the mapping of bus addresses to cabin locations. Moreover, the functionality can be configured by means of "software switches" that enable or disable certain CIL features.

11.1.3   Overview

Section 11.2 presents the original system requirements specification for the cabin illumination functions. Section 11.3 justifies the suitability of Z for the application and presents the Z specification derived from system requirements. In Section 11.4, we will sketch the transformation process from specification to design, with a focus on the derivation of software architecture design. The heuristic approach presented in this section has been successfully applied at DST to several projects.

11.2   Airbus A330/340 CIDS cabin illumination – informal requirements specification

In this section the requirements (DA Airbus GmbH, 1993) for the CIDS cabin illumination function (CIL) are presented. Explanations of technical terms used in the requirements document and other information that might be helpful for the reader who is not acquainted with the CIDS system have been added as footnotes. Otherwise the text has been left in its original form[1].

---

[1]Because of the usual space limitations, the specification presented in this book has been slightly abridged. The complete document can be obtained from the authors. It contains the specification and design of additional functionality regarding the illumination of the crew rest compartments, lavatories and window, centre and aisle areas in the cabin zones.

11.2.1   General

This system function controls the dimmable illumination of different areas independently. Control information shall be received from the FAP, the MPB, AAPs[2] and some discrete inputs. The system software shall control the corresponding ballast units[3] in the cabin via the top lines and via DEU, type A[4].

The function of the cabin illumination shall be divided into at most four entry, two crew rest and five cabin zones[5], which are defined in number and configuration in the CAM[6] and which shall be controlled individually. Each of those zones is controlled by three commands from the FAP, AAPs, MPB and some discrete input commands. Their implication and effects are listed below. BRIGHT/off will denote the alteration between 100% and off, DIM I/off the alteration between 50% and off, DIM II/off the alteration between 10% and off.

Generally the first activation of a command switches on the illumination with corresponding indications on the control panels; the second activation switches them off. The illumination status shall be transmitted on the CIDS MPB[7].

All functions which are controlled from the FAP shall also be operable from the AAPs or via the MPB. The functions and the presence of these panels shall be defined in the CAM.

Signal–command sources and sinks

Sources   The different command sources are received from (1) units interfaced directly to the Director[8] (forward attendant panel (lights module[9]), multipurpose bus (MPB), cabin pressure controllers (CPC1 + CPC2)[10], cockpit door switch[11], landing gear control and

---

[2]Forward attendant panel (FAP), multipurpose bus (MPB) and additional attendant panels (AAP) provide user interfaces to input CIL commands and to observe system response via indicators. For the CIL application, these interfaces are identical. Figure 11.2 sketches the design of an FAP. The MPB is a computer interface that allows to control the functions normally available on panels from a remote computer.

[3]Illumination units.

[4]The **top line** is a bus connected to the CIDS system. This bus runs through the whole cabin. Its purpose is to provide interfaces to peripherals (e.g. illumination units) controlled by the CIDS. To allow control of different types of peripherals, a standard bus interface, the decoder/encoder unit (DEU) is used. Each illumination unit can be controlled by the CIDS computer by sending a command to the DEU address where the illumination unit is connected.

[5]Our Z specification will refer to three cabin zones and two entries, since the additional areas do not contribute anything to the specification concepts; cf. Figure 11.1.

[6]The Cabin Assignment Module (CAM) stores data for the configuration of the CIDS system. These data describe the cabin layout (e.g. a mapping of DEUA addresses to entry areas and cabin zones) and enables/disables CIDS functions by means of "software switches".

[7]The status information transmitted to the MPB is in one-to-one correspondence to the status of the button indicators on the panels.

[8]The CIDS computer is called Director.

[9]The FAP also carries other buttons to control additional CIDS functions apart from cabin illumination. These buttons have not been shown in Figure 11.2.

[10]CPC1 and CPC2 are sensor interfaces which indicate whether the cabin pressure is correct (i.e. high).

[11]Another sensor indicates whether the cockpit door is open.

interface unit (LGCIU)[12], oil pressure switch (EIUs)[13] and (2) units interfaced via DEU, type B, and the middle line data buses[14] to the Director (additional attendant panels).

Sinks   These are the illumination ballast units (interfaced to DEU A).

Functions

MAIN ON command   The MAIN ON function shall be active on ground only (landing gear compressed). When the MAIN ON command is given or when CIDS is switched on, the illumination of the cabin entries shall switch to bright with corresponding indications on all panels. The night lights shall switch off. When the MAIN OFF command is given the illumination of the cabin, entries, reading lights, attendant work lights and lavatories shall be switched off[15]. The night lights shall also switch off. A MAIN ON command shall then switch on the cabin illumination. If the system is in the MAIN OFF status and any illumination zone–area is switched on manually, the status shall change to MAIN ON without switching on other lights.

BRIGHT, DIM I or DIM II command   When BRIGHT, DIM I or DIM II command is given, all lights in the appropriate zone shall switch to the selected intensity with corresponding indications on the FAP and AAPs. When above-mentioned commands are given, the night lights shall switch off in the appropriate zone.

ENTRY AREA commands   When an ENTRY BRIGHT, DIM I or DIM II command is given, all lights in the appropriate areas shall switch to the selected intensity with corresponding indications on the FAP and AAPs.

Automatic dimming function of entry areas   This function shall be carried out only if in the given area the light was switched on to BRIGHT, DIM I or DIM II. The automatic dimming function of the FWD entry area shall be controlled by two discrete inputs COCKPIT DOOR OPEN and OIL PRESSURE LOW. If COCKPIT DOOR OPEN is active and OIL PRESSURE LOW is not active, the illumination in the assigned area shall switch to a CAM-related intensity. This shall only be performed for CAM-assigned ballast units.

Night light function   The basic CIDS shall provide two different night light functions named solutions I and II. With solution I, the CAM-related illumination ballast units will be used for this function. Solution II describes the use of additional 28 V lights connected to DEU, type A.

---

[12]This interface provides the actual state of the landing gears. This is evaluated to decide whether the aircraft is on ground (state *down AND compressed*) or in the air (state *up AND locked* or *down AND locked*).

[13]The state of the oil pressure switch is evaluated to determine whether the engine is running (oil pressure = *high*).

[14]The **middle line** is a bus installed in the cabin. It is similar to the top line described above, but interfaces to other types of peripherals (e.g. AAPs).

[15]Note that reading lights and attendant work lights are controlled by separate applications. Therefore they will not be mentioned in the Z specification shown in this chapter.

If a night light command is given a second time, the illumination will be switched off completely in the respective zone(s). This function is valid for solution I and II.

Solution I When the general illumination in a cabin zone is switched off completely, the CAM-assigned ports shall automatically switch to a CAM-assigned intensity in this zone (night light autofunction)[16]. When a NIGHT LIGHT command is given (e.g. from the FAP), the CAM-assigned night lights shall switch on, if the illumination in the corresponding zone is switched off completely[17]. It shall be possible to operate the night lights zonewise. The operation of the cabin zones with BRIGHT, DIM I or DIM II overrides the night light function in the corresponding cabin zone.

Solution II Functions of solution II are identical to solution I, but instead of the illumination ballast units, additional 28 V night lights, connected to DEU, type A, will be used.

Cabin decompression function   In the event of cabin decompression, the illumination in the cabin, entries, lavatories and crew rest areas shall switch to bright. For that, the input signals from the CPCs shall be monitored (CPC1 + CPC2). If input one or two is active the above-mentioned lights shall switch on. When both inputs signals are deactivated then the illumination must keep the described switch status. During all phases, the operation of the illumination system shall be possible (e.g. FAP). If assigned in the CAM, the operation shall be blocked as long as one of the input signals is active[18].

FAPinop reaction   If the FAP fails and this failure is detected by the system's internal BITE[19], the illumination which is controllable from the FAP shall switch to BRIGHT. The operation of the illumination shall then not be blocked for all other command sources.

11.3   Z software requirements specification

11.3.1   Implementation considerations influencing the specification

When selecting an appropriate specification language, it is necessary to take certain implementation considerations into account, to make sure that the intended system behaviour is properly reflected by the semantics of the specification. For the CIDS system, the following boundary conditions influenced our decision to choose the Z notation to model the behaviour of applications.

---

[16]The night light autofunction must be enabled in CAM.

[17]If the illumination in the corresponding zone is active and the night light autofunction is enabled, pressing the night light button will not have any effect. When the night light autofunction is disabled pressing the night light button will result in an activation of the corresponding button indicator. This serves as a night light pre-selection: switching off the illumination will now automatically activate the night lights, as long as the pre-selection is active.

[18]Note that the cabin decompression function is one of the safety-critical CIDS features that motivated the 2b classification according to DO178A.

[19]Built-in test equipment.

- The underlying operating system layer schedules each application sequentially by means of a function call inside a single task continuously "looping" on a processor. We refer to this sequence of application function calls as the **CIDS application cycle**.

- The number of functions and their corresponding resources (e.g. memory) are statically allocated on system start-up. No dynamic process or memory allocation is performed.

- The CIDS director is designed as a fault-tolerant redundant master–standby system consisting of two processors with local memory, bus system, interfaces, etc. However, this redundancy is "invisible" at the application level. Each application function can be designed as if it were running on a single-processor system.

- Interface drivers operate in parallel to the CIDS application cycle, but do not write concurrently into memory areas which are accessed by applications.

- At the beginning of each CIDS application cycle, the data which has been accumulated by the input drivers is made available by copying the information into memory areas being readable by applications. During that time, no application function is active.

These considerations justify the decision to consider the CIDS application layer as a sequential system. The system's static structure implies that it is not necessary to use a specification language allowing management of dynamic objects, as it would, for example, be necessary for specifying an X-windows user interface. Therefore the Z notation is a proper candidate for specifying CIDS applications.

The Z specification to be presented in the following sections was written with two main objectives in mind.

- *Easy traceability to system requirements.* It should be "sufficiently" obvious how to re-trace the system's behaviour[20], as pre-planned in the system requirements, in the Z software requirements specification. This is of particular importance, since the informal nature of the system requirements document does not allow for any sort of proof which shows the Z specification's completeness with respect to system requirements.

- *Easy transformation from software requirements to software design.* The Z specification should also be developed in a way that does not require more than one transformation or refinement step to reach an implementable level of abstraction.

With these objectives in mind, less emphasis was made on reaching other quality criteria of specifications, e.g. reusability or the elegance which can be achieved by trying to find the weakest predicates still completely describing the desired functionality.

---

[20]In this context behaviour means the interfaces of the application, the functions and the data structures influencing the functionality.

11.3.2   Basic data items – types and sets

This section formally introduces the basic data items of the cabin illumination (CIL) software requirements specification: these items are addresses of DEUs connecting the CIDS bus to illumination units, location identifiers denoting specific locations inside the cabin, and state values of peripherals connected to the CIDS director which are relevant to the CIL specification.

Let *ADDRESS* be the set of all DEU-A addresses combined with their ports to which any illumination unit is attached. At our level of abstraction, the distinction between DEU address and port number as well as the specific address range is irrelevant; we only need to know that any illumination unit can be activated by means of a unique address. We use $a \in ADDRESS$ as the (unique) identifier for an illumination unit:

$[ADDRESS]$

The following items introduce location identifiers. *LOCATION* is the free type containing all identifiers: $z1, z2, z3$ denote the cabin zones (such as "first class", "business class", etc.); fwd, aft are the names of cabin entries. Each of the sets *ZONES* and *EA* combines location identifiers of one type.

$$
\begin{aligned}
LOCATION &::= z1 \mid z2 \mid z3 \mid fwd \mid aft \\
ZONES \quad &== \{z1, z2, z3\} \\
EA \quad &== \{fwd, aft\}
\end{aligned}
$$

The following types are used to describe state information of peripherals. *DIM* denotes the state of an illumination unit with increasing intensity *off*, $dim1$, $dim2$, *bright*. $onNl2$ denotes the "ON state" of night lights solution II, which differs from the intensities $dim1$, $dim2$, *bright*, since these light units are of a different hardware type. *SWITCH* is used to describe whether an indicator for specific buttons on a panel is illuminated (*active*) or not (*passive*). *LGCIU* gives state information from the landing gear control unit: on ground, landing gears are in state *downCompressed*; in flight they are either *downLocked* or *upLocked*. *PRESSURE* denotes the state of the cabin pressure; *high* is the normal state, while *low* denotes the emergency state of insufficient cabin pressure. *DOOR* is the state of the cockpit door. The values of *FEATURE* are used as general flags to indicate whether a certain CIL feature is enabled owing to the CAM configuration.

$$
\begin{aligned}
DIM \quad\quad &::= dim1 \mid dim2 \mid bright \mid off \mid onNl2 \\
DIM_0 \quad\quad &== \{dim1, dim2, bright, off\} \\
DIM_1 \quad\quad &== \{dim1, dim2, bright\} \\
SWITCH \quad &::= passive \mid active \\
LGCIU \quad\quad &::= downCompressed \mid downLocked \mid upLocked \\
PRESSURE &::= low \mid high \\
DOOR \quad\quad &::= closed \mid open \\
FEATURE \quad &::= disabled \mid enabled
\end{aligned}
$$

The relation $<_{dim}$ introduces an ordering between the dim steps in the obvious sense:

$$\_<_{dim}\_ : DIM_0 \leftrightarrow DIM_0$$

$off <_{dim} dim2$
$dim2 <_{dim} dim1$
$dim1 <_{dim} bright$
$\forall\, a, b, c : DIM_0 \mid a <_{dim} b \wedge b <_{dim} c \bullet a <_{dim} c$

11.3.3   CIL application interface – inputs

The CIDS operating system provides a service layer to each application that allows it to handle inputs in the style of an event-driven system. To find the appropriate level of abstraction for the interfaces in our Z specification, this section provides a respecification of these system services using the Z notation.

Panel events
If any button is pressed on an AAP or FAP–MPB, a corresponding event will be visible to the application layer for one CIDS application cycle. Since the source of this panel event (i.e. an AAP or the FAP or the MPB) does not have any impact on the corresponding CIL operation, it is not necessary to include the source in the event model. Moreover, conflicting commands such as pressing the *ZONE 1 BRIGHT* command at AAP 1 and the *ZONE 1 DIM1* command at AAP 2 are simply resolved by discarding the second (and any additional) conflicting command. This leads to the event model described by schema *PanelEvents*, to be interpreted as follows.

1. $zoneEvent(z) = d$ means that the d button of zone z has been pressed at one of the panels. If no button for zone z has been pressed during the last CIDS application cycle, z will not be contained in the domain of *zoneEvent*.
2. $z \in nlEvent$ means that the night light button of zone z has been pressed.
3. $eaEvent(e) = d$ means that the d button of entry area e has been pressed.
4. $mainEvent = active$ means that the MAIN button has been pressed.

```
__PanelEvents_____
  zoneEvent : ZONES ⇸ DIM₁
  nlEvent : ℙ ZONES
  eaEvent : EA ⇸ DIM₁
  mainEvent : SWITCH
```

System states and system events   The CIL application also evaluates information provided by other subsystems of the Airbus A330/340. This information is stored in the operating system as state–event pairs. It is always possible to read the actual information value. As soon as a value changes, this will be indicated by the operating system by setting a corresponding event flag for the duration of one CIDS application cycle. The state–event pairs are specified by schemas *SystemStates* and *SystemEvents*. Components *CPC*1, ..., *oilPres* carry the actual state value of the cabin pressure controllers 1 and 2, the landing gears, the state of the FAP, the cockpit door and the oil pressure controller. *CPC*1*Event*, ..., *oilPresEvent* indicate that the corresponding state value has just changed.

```
┌─ SystemStates ──────────────────────────────────────────
│  CPC1 : PRESSURE
│  CPC2 : PRESSURE
│  LGEARst : LGCIU
│  FAP : SWITCH
│  cockDoor : DOOR
│  oilPres : PRESSURE
│
└──────────────────────────────────────────────────────────
```

```
┌─ SystemEvents ──────────────────────────────────────────
│  CPC1Event : SWITCH
│  CPC2Event : SWITCH
│  LGEARstEvent : SWITCH
│  FAPEvent : SWITCH
│  cockDoorEvent : SWITCH
│  oilPresEvent : SWITCH
│
└──────────────────────────────────────────────────────────
```

The above schemas are state schemas, because any update to their components is performed by the operating system layer, which is outside the scope of our specification. Moreover, during each CIL execution the event and state values remain unchanged.

Therefore the application layer can regard these values as state information. Moreover, these schemas are not initialized in the CIL initialization, because the operating system takes care of that.

11.3.4   CIL application interface – outputs

The effect of a CIL operation becomes visible in a change of state (i.e. brightness) of the illumination units connected to specific DEUA addresses and a state change for button indicators from *active* to *passive* and vice versa.

Interface to illumination units   Changing the brightness of an illumination unit is performed by the application by writing a value associated with the brightness to a memory location associated with the corresponding DEUA address. As a consequence, the memory area reserved for control of DEUA devices serves as the interface to the illumination units and at the same time reflects the actual state of all illumination units. Schema *ILLstate* defined in Section 11.3.6 below presents an abstraction of this memory area. Consistent with the implementation, each CIL function will operate on this state schema by changing the brightness values of DEUA addresses.

Interface to indicators To switch a button indicator, a function is provided taking the button identifier and the desired $SWITCH$ value as inputs. Again, we can abstract from explicitly setting the same indicator at every panel. We will explain in Section 11.3.6 that the actual state of the indicators can serve as a simple description of the actual state of cabin illumination in terms of locations and corresponding brightness values. Therefore schemas $ZONEINDstate$, $EAINDstate$, $MAININDstate$ are defined below to store the actual state of indicators for cabin zones, entry areas and the MAIN button. Since in the implementation any state change will be "synchronously" accompanied by a corresponding function call to set the indicator, each operation's impact on the button indicators will be modelled at the specification level simply as a state change for the above-mentioned schemas.

11.3.5 Definition of CAM tables – axiomatic definitions

In our context CAM tables can be viewed as global constants that can be accessed from anywhere in the specification. Therefore, in Z, they are modelled as axiomatic definitions.

The following axiomatic definition gives the Z definition of the CAM tables "assignment of DEU, type A, outputs" from the CIL system specification.

CAM_CAB The illumination units identified by a certain subset of $ADDRESS$ (namely, the domain of the partial function CAM_CAB) are associated with cabin zones: if illumination unit a is contained in the domain of CAM_CAB, then CAM_CAB(a) is the cabin zone where the illumination unit is installed. Note that since CAM_CAB is a partial function, we know that each illumination unit can be associated with at most one cabin zone.

CAM_EA Each illumination unit with address a in the domain of CAM_EA is contained in the entry area CAM_EA(a).

CAM_NL1 or CAM_NL2 Each illumination unit a with an address in the domain of either CAM_NL1 or CAM_NL2 is used as a night light solution I or II in the corresponding cabin zone, CAM_NL1(a) or CAM_NL2(a).

CAM_FAP To handle the FAP INOP reaction, this CAM table defines the cabin locations being controllable by the FAP.

The interpretation of the invariants specified in the axiomatic definition's predicate part is as follows.

1. If a is a night light solution I, then it is also used as a "normal" illumination unit of the associated cabin zone.
2. Each illumination unit associated with a cabin zone or an entry area cannot be associated with another area at the same time.
3. The night lights solution II are separate illumination units, they are not used for "normal" illumination of any cabin area.

$$
\begin{array}{|l}
\text{CAM\_CAB} : ADDRESS \twoheadrightarrow ZONES \\
\text{CAM\_EA} : ADDRESS \twoheadrightarrow EA \\
\text{CAM\_NL1} : ADDRESS \twoheadrightarrow ZONES \\
\text{CAM\_NL2} : ADDRESS \twoheadrightarrow ZONES \\
\text{CAM\_FAP} : \mathbb{P}\ LOCATION \\
\hline
\text{CAM\_NL1} \subseteq \text{CAM\_CAB} \\
\text{dom\,CAM\_CAB} \cap (\text{dom\,CAM\_EA} \cup \text{dom\,CAM\_NL2}) = \varnothing \\
\text{dom\,CAM\_EA} \cap \text{dom\,CAM\_NL2} = \varnothing
\end{array}
$$

CAM table CAM_EADIM defines a specific intensity for a certain illumination associated with the forward entry area. The illumination units with addresses in the domain of CAM_EADIM are used for the entry area dimming function described below.

$$
\begin{array}{|l}
\text{CAM\_EADIM} : ADDRESS \twoheadrightarrow \{ \mathit{off}, \mathit{dim}1, \mathit{dim}2 \} \\
\hline
\text{dom\,CAM\_EADIM} \subseteq \text{dom}(\text{CAM\_EA} \rhd \{\mathit{fwd}\})
\end{array}
$$

The following CAM tables are flags for the configuration of the CIL application. "Enabled" means the following in each case.

CAM_DECOMP CIL will automatically switch illumination to *bright* in case of cabin decompression. *CAM_BLOCK* During cabin decompression, all illumination commands will be blocked, so the illumination will stay in state *bright*.

CAM_NLAUTO If the illumination is switched off completely in a zone owing to a *dim1, dim2, bright* command the night lights associated with this zone are automatically switched on. (If lights are switched off by means of the *main* command, the night lights are switched off, too.)

$$
\begin{array}{|l}
\text{CAM\_DECOMP} : FEATURE \\
\text{CAM\_BLOCK} : FEATURE \\
\text{CAM\_NLAUTO} : FEATURE
\end{array}
$$

CAM_NL1_DIM denotes the intensity for night lights solution I in case of manual or automatic night light activation.

$$
\begin{array}{|l}
\text{CAM\_NL1\_DIM} : DIM_0
\end{array}
$$

11.3.6   Specification of system states – state schemas

In this section, we will provide the system's state description. It is always a good idea to try to find state variables that are directly observable or at least of "obvious significance" from the application's point of view. In our case, the idea for the description of the states was as follows.

- The indicators on the panels' illumination command buttons reflect the state of illumination in the location associated with each button, as it is intended by the user.
- The intensity of each illumination unit $a \in ADDRESS$ reflects the state of illumination as it has actually been switched by the CIL application.

State description for button indicators
For this specification's level of abstraction, the difference between the FAP, MPB and AAPs is irrelevant, since the effect of pressing a button only depends on the button's function, not on the panel where the button has been pressed. We define certain groups of buttons with similar functions and model each group as a mapping, as defined in schema *ZONEINDstate*.

- *zoneInd* models the state of $dim1$, $dim2$, $bright$ buttons defined for each cabin zone: $zoneInd(z) = dim1, dim2, bright$ means that the $dim1$, $dim2$, $bright$ indicator of zone z is active. Otherwise, we have $zoneInd(z) = off$. Note that this automatically models the requirement that in each zone at most one of the buttons may be active.
- *nlInd* models the night light buttons associated with each cabin zone: $nlInd(z) = active$ means that the night light indicator for zone z is active.

The meaning of the state invariants defined in the schema's predicate part is the following. If the illumination in zone z is not switched off, then the corresponding night light indicator must be *passive*, if the night light autofunction is enabled in CAM_NLAUTO.

ZONEINDstate
$zoneInd : ZONES \rightarrow DIM_0$
$nlInd : ZONES \rightarrow SWITCH$

$\forall z : ZONES \bullet$
$\quad nlInd(z) = active \Rightarrow (zoneInd(z) = off \vee \text{CAM\_NLAUTO} = disabled)$

Schema *EAINDstate* models the state of the entry area buttons. *eaInd* is defined in analogy to *zoneInd*.

EAINDstate
$eaInd : EA \rightarrow DIM_0$

Schema *MAININDstate* models the state of the MAIN button. The predicate part states, that the MAIN button will be passive if and only if the illumination has been switched off in every location, as far as this is under manual control.

MAININDstate
ZONEINDstate
EAINDstate
$mainInd : SWITCH$

$mainInd = passive \Leftrightarrow$
$\quad \text{ran } nlInd = \{passive\} \wedge \text{ran } zoneInd = \{off\} \wedge \text{ran } eaInd = \{off\}$

State description for illumination units

The collection of all illumination units is described as the mapping *ill* from *ADDRESS* to the set *DIM*. For example, $ill(a) = bright$ means that an illumination unit is associated with address a and this unit is switched to intensity *bright*.

ILLstate
$ill : ADDRESS \nrightarrow DIM$

$\text{dom } ill = \text{dom CAM\_CAB} \cup \text{dom CAM\_EA} \cup \text{dom CAM\_NL2}$
$\forall a : \text{dom } ill \bullet (ill(a) = onNl2 \Rightarrow a \in \text{dom CAM\_NL2})$

Correspondence between button indicators and illumination units

In this subsection we summarize the consistency conditions existing between the states of button indicators and the actual state of illumination. The schema *ZONEinvariant* states consistency conditions between buttons related to cabin zones and the corresponding state of illumination.

1. If the state of illumination in zone z is not *off*, the intensity is consistent with the active zone button indicator.

2. If the state of illumination in zone z is *off* and the night light indicator of zone z is *active*, then every night light solution I associated with zone z is active with intensity according to CAM_NL1_DIM. Moreover, every night light solution II is switched on. Every other illumination unit associated with zone z is switched *off*.

3. If the state of illumination in zone z is *off* and the night light indicator of zone z is *passive*, then every illumination unit associated with zone z (including night lights solution II) is switched *off*.

4. If the illumination of zone z is in state $d \neq off$, then every night light solution II associated with zone z is *off*.

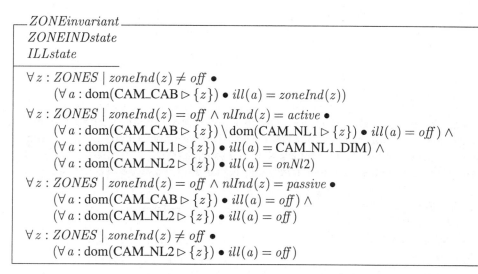

$\_$*ZONEinvariant*$_____$

ZONEINDstate
ILLstate

$\forall z : ZONES \mid zoneInd(z) \neq \textit{off} \bullet$
$\quad (\forall a : \mathrm{dom}(\mathrm{CAM\_CAB} \rhd \{z\}) \bullet \textit{ill}(a) = zoneInd(z))$

$\forall z : ZONES \mid zoneInd(z) = \textit{off} \wedge nlInd(z) = active \bullet$
$\quad (\forall a : \mathrm{dom}(\mathrm{CAM\_CAB} \rhd \{z\}) \setminus \mathrm{dom}(\mathrm{CAM\_NL1} \rhd \{z\}) \bullet \textit{ill}(a) = \textit{off}) \wedge$
$\quad (\forall a : \mathrm{dom}(\mathrm{CAM\_NL1} \rhd \{z\}) \bullet \textit{ill}(a) = \mathrm{CAM\_NL1\_DIM}) \wedge$
$\quad (\forall a : \mathrm{dom}(\mathrm{CAM\_NL2} \rhd \{z\}) \bullet \textit{ill}(a) = onNl2)$

$\forall z : ZONES \mid zoneInd(z) = \textit{off} \wedge nlInd(z) = passive \bullet$
$\quad (\forall a : \mathrm{dom}(\mathrm{CAM\_CAB} \rhd \{z\}) \bullet \textit{ill}(a) = \textit{off}) \wedge$
$\quad (\forall a : \mathrm{dom}(\mathrm{CAM\_NL2} \rhd \{z\}) \bullet \textit{ill}(a) = \textit{off})$

$\forall z : ZONES \mid zoneInd(z) \neq \textit{off} \bullet$
$\quad (\forall a : \mathrm{dom}(\mathrm{CAM\_NL2} \rhd \{z\}) \bullet \textit{ill}(a) = \textit{off})$

For the entry areas, the illumination units associated with their location are given by
CAM_EA. In the case of a running engine ($oilPres = high$) with open cockpit door, the
illumination units with address space dom CAM_EADIM must be dimmed to the CAM-
defined value, if this is less than the actual brightness value indicated by the corresponding entry area button.

$\_$*EAinvariant*$_____$

EAINDstate
ILLstate
SystemStates

$\forall e : EA \mid eaInd(e) \neq \textit{off} \bullet$
$\quad (\forall a : \mathrm{dom}(\mathrm{CAM\_EA} \rhd \{e\}) \setminus \mathrm{dom\,CAM\_EADIM} \bullet \textit{ill}(a) = eaInd(e)) \wedge$
$\quad (\forall a : \mathrm{dom}(\mathrm{CAM\_EA} \rhd \{e\}) \cap \mathrm{dom\,CAM\_EADIM} \bullet$
$\qquad (cockDoor = closed \vee oilPres = low \vee eaInd(e) <_{dim} \mathrm{CAM\_EADIM}(a)$
$\qquad\qquad \Rightarrow \textit{ill}(a) = eaInd(e)) \wedge$
$\qquad (cockDoor = open \wedge oilPres = high \wedge \mathrm{CAM\_EADIM}(a) <_{dim} eaInd(e)$
$\qquad\qquad \Rightarrow \textit{ill}(a) = \mathrm{CAM\_EADIM}(a)))$

$\forall e : EA \mid eaInd(e) = \textit{off} \bullet (\forall a : \mathrm{dom}(\mathrm{CAM\_EA} \rhd \{e\}) \bullet \textit{ill}(a) = \textit{off})$

11.3.7   Description of CIL operations – operational schemas

Auxiliary schemas
Schema *NOop* is used to indicate that the CIL state remains unchanged in situations where
an operation does not have any effect (e.g. because it is disabled in CAM).

```
┌─ NOop ──────────────────────────────────────────────────────────
│ ΞZONEINDstate
│ ΞEAINDstate
│ ΞMAININDstate
│ ΞILLstate
└──────────────────────────────────────────────────────────────────
```

The following schema describes the control of the MAIN button indicator which depends on the state of the other indicators. The schema is only used in sequential composition with other operational schemas: the other schemas provide the pre-state, *MAINadjust* describes how the main button indicator is then adjusted to the new CIL state.

```
┌─ MAINadjust ────────────────────────────────────────────────────
│ ΔMAININDstate
│ ΞZONEINDstate
│ ΞEAINDstate
├──────────────────────────────────────────────────────────────────
│ mainInd' =
│         if ( active ∈ ran nlInd ∨ ran zoneInd ≠ { off } ∨ ran eaInd ≠ { off })
│         then active else mainInd
└──────────────────────────────────────────────────────────────────
```

Initialization operation

On system initialization, the following state of illumination is adopted.

1. For cabin zones and entry areas, the associated illumination units are switched *bright*. Night lights solution II and all other indicators related to these locations are switched off.

2. The main button indicator is switched *active*.

```
┌─ ZONEINDINITop ─────────────────────────────────────────────────
│ ZONEINDstate'
├──────────────────────────────────────────────────────────────────
│ zoneInd' = { z : ZONES • z ↦ bright }
│ nlInd' = { z : ZONES • z ↦ passive }
└──────────────────────────────────────────────────────────────────
```

```
┌─ EAINDINITop ───────────────────────────────────────────────────
│ EAINDstate'
├──────────────────────────────────────────────────────────────────
│ eaInd' = { z : EA • z ↦ bright }
└──────────────────────────────────────────────────────────────────
```

```
┌─ MAININDINITop ─────────────────────────────────────────────
│ MAININDstate'
│ ───────────────────────────────────
│ mainInd' = active
└──────────────────────────────────────────────────────────────
```

```
┌─ ILLINITop ─────────────────────────────────────────────────
│ ILLstate'
│ ───────────────────────────────────
│ ill' = { a : (dom CAM_CAB ∪ dom CAM_EA) • a ↦ bright }
│        ∪ { a : dom CAM_NL2 • a ↦ off }
└──────────────────────────────────────────────────────────────
```

$INITop == ZONEINDINITop \land EAINDINITop \land MAININDINITop \land ILLINITop$

Operations related to the main button

The main ON or OFF operation only changes the system state if the landing gears are in state *downCompressed* as it is indicated by schema *MAINisBlocked*. In the non-blocked state, the main command will switch the illumination completely *off*, if the previous state of the main button was *active*. (As a consequence, all CIL indicators will also be switched off.) If the previous state was *passive*, the illumination will be switched on with exactly the same effect as on system initialization.

```
┌─ MAININDopPassive ──────────────────────────────────────────
│ ΔMAININDstate
│ ───────────────────────────────────
│ mainInd = active
│ mainInd' = passive
└──────────────────────────────────────────────────────────────
```

```
┌─ MAINILLopPassive ──────────────────────────────────────────
│ ΔILLstate
│ ───────────────────────────────────
│ ill' = { a : dom ill • a ↦ off }
└──────────────────────────────────────────────────────────────
```

```
┌─ MAINisBlocked ─────────────────────────────────────────────
│ SystemStates
│ ───────────────────────────────────
│ LGEARst ∈ { downLocked, upLocked }
└──────────────────────────────────────────────────────────────
```

$MAINop == (MAINisBlocked \land NOop)$
$\qquad \lor (\neg\, MAINisBlocked \land (MAINILLopPassive \land MAININDopPassive$
$\qquad\qquad \lor [MAININDstate \mid mainInd = passive] \land INITop))$

Switching operation for cabin zones

In this section the functions to control cabin illumination by means of the buttons $dim1$, $dim2$, $bright$ for each zone are specified.

The total operation is divided into the cases *switch passive* $\rightarrow$ *active* and *switch active* $\rightarrow$ *passive*. Moreover, the control of the button indicators is separated from the control of the illumination units.

Schema *ZONEINDopActive* specifies the control of the button indicators for case *switch passive* $\rightarrow$ *active*. Inputs $(z?, d?)$ specify that the button for brightness $d?$ has been pressed in zone $z?$.

The pre-condition to perform the transition into a new illumination state with brightness $d?$ is that the button $(z?, d?)$ is not already active. According to our definition of $zoneInd$, this is expressed by the condition $zoneInd(z?) \neq d?$.

In this case, the button indicator will be activated and any zone button previously active for zone $z?$ will be switched off.

Note that both switching operations are specified by the expression $\{z? \mapsto d?\}$, since only one zone button is allowed to be active at a time. Otherwise the zone buttons are left unchanged.

If the night light autofunction is enabled (CAM_NLAUTO $= enabled$), the night light button indicator of zone $z?$ must automatically be switched off, as soon as one of the illumination states $dim1$, $dim2$, $bright$ is taken. If the night light autofunction is disabled, the night light indicators will remain unchanged.

Note that we have taken care to specify that *ZONEINDopActive* does not alter any of the button indicators described in schema *EAINDstate*. This is necessary, because later on the schema will be used in $\wedge$ combination with schema *EAinvariant*. Therefore it operates in fact on the complete button indicator state space, although only changes of *ZONEINDstate* are visible in the schema. This situation will be clarified in all schemas by using the $\Xi \ldots INDstate$ expressions.

$\underline{\quad ZONEINDopActive \quad\rule{8cm}{0pt}}$
$\Delta ZONEINDstate$
$\Xi EAINDstate$
$z? : ZONES$
$d? : DIM_1$
$\rule{7cm}{0.4pt}$
$zoneInd(z?) \neq d?$
$zoneInd' = zoneInd \oplus \{z? \mapsto d?\}$
$nlInd' =$
$\qquad$ **if** CAM_NLAUTO $= enabled$ **then** $nlInd \oplus \{z? \mapsto passive\}$ **else** $nlInd$

Schema *ZONEINDopPassive* handles the case *switch active* $\rightarrow$ *passive*. The previously active zone indicator $d?$ of zone $z?$ is switched off. The night light indicators will automatically be activated, if the night light autofunction is enabled in CAM.

$$
\begin{array}{|l}
\hline
\_ZONEINDopPassive_____ \\
\Delta ZONEINDstate \\
\Xi EAINDstate \\
z? : ZONES \\
d? : DIM_1 \\
\hline
zoneInd(z?) = d? \\
zoneInd' = zoneInd \oplus \{z? \mapsto off\} \\
nlInd' = \\
\quad \textbf{if } \text{CAM\_NLAUTO} = enabled \textbf{ then } nlInd \oplus \{z? \mapsto active\} \textbf{ else } nlInd \\
\hline
\end{array}
$$

Schema *ZONEILLopActive* handles the case *switch passive → active* for the illumination units. Night lights solution II that might have been previously active are switched off. Since night lights solution I are illumination units inside the associated cabin zone, their previous state will be automatically overridden by setting the new intensity for the zone.

$$
\begin{array}{|l}
\hline
\_ZONEILLopActive_____ \\
\Delta ILLstate \\
ZONEINDstate \\
z? : ZONES \\
d? : DIM_1 \\
\hline
zoneInd(z?) \neq d? \\
ill' = ill \oplus \{x : \text{dom}(\text{CAM\_NL2} \rhd \{z?\}) \bullet x \mapsto off\} \\
\quad\quad \oplus \{x : \text{dom}(\text{CAM\_CAB} \rhd \{z?\}) \bullet x \mapsto d?\} \\
\hline
\end{array}
$$

Schema *ZONEILLopPassive* handles the case *switch active → passive* for the illumination units. If the night light autofunction is enabled or if the user has pre-selected the night light function by pressing the night light button of zone $z?$, night lights solution I and II will be turned on in zone $z?$. The solution I night lights are switched to their CAM-defined intensity. Otherwise the illumination units of zone $z?$ are switched off.

$$
\begin{array}{|l}
\hline
\_ZONEILLopPassive_____ \\
\Delta ILLstate \\
ZONEINDstate \\
z? : ZONES \\
d? : DIM_1 \\
\hline
zoneInd(z?) = d? \\
ill' = ill \oplus \{x : \text{dom}(\text{CAM\_CAB} \rhd \{z?\}) \bullet x \mapsto off\} \\
\quad \oplus \{x : \text{dom}(\text{CAM\_NL1} \rhd \{z?\}) \mid \\
\quad\quad (nlInd(z?) = active \vee \text{CAM\_NLAUTO} = enabled) \bullet x \mapsto \text{CAM\_NL1\_DIM}\} \\
\quad \oplus \{x : \text{dom}(\text{CAM\_NL2} \rhd \{z?\}) \mid \\
\quad\quad (nlInd(z?) = active \vee \text{CAM\_NLAUTO} = enabled) \bullet x \mapsto onNl2\} \\
\hline
\end{array}
$$

Schema equation *ZONEop* combines the above schemas controlling cabin illumination by means of zone buttons into a total function.

$$ZONEop == ZONEILLopActive \wedge ZONEINDopActive \vee$$
$$ZONEILLopPassive \wedge ZONEINDopPassive$$

Entry area commands

Schemas *EAINDop, EAILLopPassive, EAILLopActive* specify the behaviour of the entry area illumination commands. Here we have to take into account a special situation: if the cockpit door is open and the oil pressure is high (this reflects the fact that the aircraft has a running engine), certain illumination units in the *fwd* entry area must not be switched to a state that is brighter than the one indicated in table CAM_EADIM. This mechanism is implemented in order to avoid blinding the cockpit personnel. It is reflected by schema *EAILLopActive*.

$$
\begin{array}{|l}
\hline
\;EAINDop \underline{\hspace{8cm}} \\
\Delta EAINDstate \\
\Xi ZONEINDstate \\
\Xi EAINDstate \\
ea? : EA \\
dim? : DIM_1 \\
\hline
eaInd(ea?) = dim? \Rightarrow eaInd' = eaInd \oplus \{ea? \mapsto off\} \\
eaInd(ea?) \neq dim? \Rightarrow eaInd' = eaInd \oplus \{ea? \mapsto dim?\} \\
\hline
\end{array}
$$

$$
\begin{array}{|l}
\hline
\;EAILLopPassive \underline{\hspace{7cm}} \\
\Delta ILLstate \\
EAINDstate \\
ea? : EA \\
dim? : DIM_1 \\
\hline
eaInd(ea?) = dim? \\
ill' = ill \oplus \{x : \mathrm{dom}(\mathrm{CAM\_EA} \rhd \{ea?\}) \bullet x \mapsto off\} \\
\hline
\end{array}
$$

$$
\begin{array}{|l}
\hline
\;EAILLopActive \underline{\hspace{7cm}} \\
\Delta ILLstate \\
EAINDstate \\
\Xi SystemStates \\
ea? : EA \\
dim? : DIM_1 \\
\hline
eaInd(ea?) \neq dim? \\
ill' = \textbf{if } ea? = fwd \wedge cockDoor = open \wedge oilPres = high \\
\quad\quad \textbf{then } ill \oplus \{x : \mathrm{dom}(\mathrm{CAM\_EA} \rhd \{ea?\}) \bullet x \mapsto dim?\} \oplus \\
\quad\quad\quad\quad \{x : \mathrm{dom}\ \mathrm{CAM\_EADIM}\ | \\
\quad\quad\quad\quad\quad\quad \mathrm{CAM\_EADIM}(x) <_{dim} dim? \bullet x \mapsto \mathrm{CAM\_EADIM}(x)\} \\
\quad\quad \textbf{else } \{x : \mathrm{dom}(\mathrm{CAM\_EA} \rhd \{ea?\}) \bullet x \mapsto dim?\} \\
\hline
\end{array}
$$

The complete operation for entry areas is described by the equation

$$EAop == EAINDop \land (EAILLopActive \lor EAILLopPassive)$$

Automatic dimming operation for forward entry area

If the oil pressure controller signals "oil pressure high" (i.e. engine running) and the cockpit door sensor signals "door open", then the CAM-assigned illumination units located in the forward entry area will be switched to the CAM-defined intensity I if the actual intensity is not already lower than I. As soon as the door closes again or the oil pressure becomes low, these illumination units resume their previous state.

___*AUTODIMop*_____

$\Xi EAINDstate$

$\Xi SystemStates$

$\Delta ILLstate$

$cockDoor = open \land oilPres = high \Rightarrow$
$\quad ill' = ill \oplus \{a : \mathrm{dom\,CAM\_EADIM} \mid$
$\qquad\qquad \mathrm{CAM\_EADIM}(a) <_{dim} eaInd(fwd) \bullet a \mapsto \mathrm{CAM\_EADIM}(a)\}$
$cockDoor = closed \lor oilPres = low \Rightarrow$
$\quad ill' = ill \oplus \{a : \mathrm{dom\,CAM\_EADIM} \bullet a \mapsto eaInd(fwd)\}$

Night light operation

The following schemas describe the operation of the night light buttons. If the night light button indicator of zone $n?$ is passive, it will be turned on, if the night light autofunction is disabled or the zone illumination has previously been turned off. In the former case this will serve as a pre-selection, so that night lights will automatically be turned on, as soon as the zone illumination has been switched off. If the night light autofunction is enabled and the illumination is active, pressing a night light button will have no effect, because when switching off the zone illumination the night lights will automatically be turned on in any case.

___*NLINDop*_____

$\Delta ZONEINDstate$

$\Xi EAINDstate$

$n? : ZONES$

$nlInd(n?) = passive \Rightarrow nlInd' =$
$\qquad \textbf{if } \mathrm{CAM\_NLAUTO} = disabled \lor zoneInd(n?) = off$
$\qquad \textbf{then } nlInd \oplus \{n? \mapsto active\} \textbf{ else } nlInd$
$nlInd(n?) = active \Rightarrow nlInd' = nlInd \oplus \{n? \mapsto passive\}$
$zoneInd' = zoneInd$

Toggling the night light button will only affect the illumination units assigned as night lights solution I or II, if the cabin illumination of zone $n?$ has been turned off.

$$
\begin{array}{|l}
\_\_NLILLop _____ \\
ZONEINDstate \\
\Delta ILLstate \\
n? : ZONES \\
\hline
nlInd(n?) = passive \Rightarrow ill' = \\
\qquad \textbf{if } zoneInd(n?) = off \\
\qquad \textbf{then } ill \oplus \{x : \mathrm{dom}(\text{CAM\_NL2} \rhd \{n?\}) \bullet x \mapsto onNl2\} \\
\qquad\qquad \oplus \{x : \mathrm{dom}(\text{CAM\_NL1} \rhd \{n?\}) \bullet x \mapsto \text{CAM\_NL1\_DIM}\} \\
\qquad \textbf{else } ill \\
nlInd(n?) = active \Rightarrow ill' = \\
\qquad \textbf{if } zoneInd(n?) = off \\
\qquad \textbf{then } ill \oplus \{x : \mathrm{dom}(\text{CAM\_NL2} \rhd \{n?\}) \bullet x \mapsto off\} \\
\qquad\qquad \oplus \{x : \mathrm{dom}(\text{CAM\_NL1} \rhd \{n?\}) \bullet x \mapsto off\} \\
\qquad \textbf{else } ill
\end{array}
$$

$NLop == NLILLop \wedge NLINDop$

Operations related to cabin decompression

In case of cabin decompression, the indicators will be set so that they reflect the "all bright" state.

$$
\begin{array}{|l}
\_\_DECOMPINDopActive _____ \\
\Delta ZONEINDstate \\
\Delta EAINDstate \\
\Delta MAININDstate \\
\hline
mainInd' = active \\
zoneInd' = \{z : ZONES \bullet z \mapsto bright\} \\
nlInd' = nlInd \oplus \{z : ZONES \mid \text{CAM\_NLAUTO} = enabled \bullet z \mapsto passive\} \\
eaInd' = \{e : EA \bullet e \mapsto bright\}
\end{array}
$$

The cabin decompression function will only become active if it is enabled in CAM and at least one of the cabin pressure controllers CPC1, CPC2 indicates "pressure low". In this case the illumination units will be switched to bright. Only if the condition for *fwd* entry area dimming holds will the associated illumination units be dimmed (cf. Section 11.3.7).

$$
\begin{array}{|l}
\_\_DECOMPILLopActive _____ \\
\Delta ILLstate \\
\Xi SystemStates \\
\hline
ill' = \{a : \mathrm{dom}\,\text{CAM\_NL2} \bullet a \mapsto off\} \oplus \\
\qquad \{a : (\mathrm{dom}\,\text{CAM\_CAB} \cup \mathrm{dom}\,\text{CAM\_EA}) \bullet a \mapsto bright\} \oplus \\
\qquad \{a : \mathrm{dom}\ \text{CAM\_EADIM} \mid \\
\qquad\qquad cockDoor = open \wedge oilPres = high \bullet a \mapsto \text{CAM\_EADIM}(a)\}
\end{array}
$$

$DECOMPop ==$
   $[SystemStates \mid \textbf{CAM\_DECOMP} = enabled \wedge (CPC1 = low \vee CPC2 = low)]$
      $\wedge \ DECOMPINDopActive \wedge DECOMPILLopActive$
   $\vee \ [SystemStates \mid \textbf{CAM\_DECOMP} = disabled \vee CPC1 = high \wedge CPC2 = high]$
      $\wedge \ NOop$

FAPinop reaction

If an FAP failure occurs, the illumination in every cabin location controlled by the FAP must be switched to *bright*. These locations are given by CAM table CAM_FAP. Although schema equation *FAPinop* does not look very appealing, its structure is quite simple and reuses the existing CIL operations. For each location – cabin zones and entry areas – it is first checked whether the location is controlled by the FAP and whether its actual illumination state is not already *bright*. If both conditions are true, the corresponding operation will be activated, if necessary by piping the location and the desired intensity into the function.

$FAPinop ==$
$((([ZONEINDstate; \ z! : ZONES; \ d! : DIM_1 \mid$
      $zoneInd(z1) \neq bright \wedge z1 \in \textbf{CAM\_FAP} \wedge z! = z1 \wedge d! = bright] \gg ZONEop) \vee$
   $[ZONEINDstate; \ z : ZONES \mid zoneInd(z1) = bright \vee z1 \notin \textbf{CAM\_FAP}] \wedge NOop)_9^o$
$((([ZONEINDstate; \ z! : ZONES; \ d! : DIM_1 \mid$
      $zoneInd(z2) \neq bright \wedge z2 \in \textbf{CAM\_FAP} \wedge z! = z2 \wedge d! = bright] \gg ZONEop) \vee$
   $[ZONEINDstate; \ z : ZONES \mid zoneInd(z2) = bright \vee z2 \notin \textbf{CAM\_FAP}] \wedge NOop)_9^o$
$((([ZONEINDstate; \ z! : ZONES; \ d! : DIM_1 \mid$
      $zoneInd(z3) \neq bright \wedge z3 \in \textbf{CAM\_FAP} \wedge z! = z3 \wedge d! = bright] \gg ZONEop) \vee$
   $[ZONEINDstate; \ z : ZONES \mid zoneInd(z3) = bright \vee z3 \notin \textbf{CAM\_FAP}] \wedge NOop)_9^o$
$((([EAINDstate; \ ea! : EA; \ dim! : DIM_1 \mid$
      $eaInd(fwd) \neq bright \wedge fwd \in \textbf{CAM\_FAP} \wedge ea! = fwd \wedge dim! = bright] \gg EAop) \vee$
   $[EAINDstate; \ ea : EA \mid eaInd(fwd) = bright \vee fwd \notin \textbf{CAM\_FAP}] \wedge NOop)_9^o$
$((([EAINDstate; \ ea! : EA; \ dim! : DIM_1 \mid$
      $eaInd(aft) \neq bright \wedge aft \in \textbf{CAM\_FAP} \wedge ea! = aft \wedge dim! = bright] \gg EAop) \vee$
   $[EAINDstate; \ ea : EA \mid eaInd(aft) = bright \vee aft \notin \textbf{CAM\_FAP}] \wedge NOop)_9^o$
$MAINadjust)$

The FAP inop reaction is triggered, when the FAP system status is passive:

$FAPctrl == [SystemStates \mid FAP = passive] \wedge FAPinop$
      $\vee \ [SystemStates \mid FAP = active] \wedge NOop$

Top-level structure of the specification

The CIL application provides two top-level entries. The initialization – as specified by schema *INITop* in Section 11.3.7 – is activated only once on CIDS system startup. In this section the second top-level entry is described: this is the schema equation *CIL* below, representing the control structure which specifies how each of the CIL functions is activated during one CIDS application cycle.

Since each event only lives for one cycle, it is important to activate the associated functions at once. Moreover, we wish to separate the examination of a function's trigger conditions from the operation itself. Therefore *CIL* specifies the control structure of a sequential system checking for each function whether it should be activated. If the relevant activation conditions hold it will trigger the operation, at the same time providing the inputs required. With respect to trigger conditions, we make the following distinctions.

- Event expressions describing conditions for function activation are handled by the top-level control structure.
- Data conditions (e. g. values of input parameters and of CAM tables) preventing or otherwise influencing the function execution are processed within each function.

Schema equation *UserOp* below specifies the trigger conditions for the CIL operations accessible to the user, i.e. zone operations, entry area operations, night light operation and reaction to the MAIN button. The control structure has been designed such that first the existence of corresponding events is checked. Then the function is triggered. If the function has input parameters, they will be provided by the control structure as a result of the event evaluation. The reason for not letting the user functions themselves evaluate their associated events is that these operations may be reused in a context where the events are not active, e.g. for the FAP inop reaction described in Section 11.3.7. An operation (e.g. ZONEop) may be triggered more then once in this sequence, if several active events (e. g. dimming commands for several zones) require its execution. Schema equation *UserOpZones* defines the part of *UserOp* handling events for cabin zone commands.

$UserOpZones ==$
$\quad ((([PanelEvents;\ z!: ZONES;\ d!: DIM_1\ |$
$\qquad z1 \in \text{dom } zoneEvent \land z! = z1 \land d! = zoneEvent(z1)] \gg ZONEop) \lor$
$\qquad [PanelEvents\ |\ z1 \notin \text{dom } zoneEvent] \land NOop)_9^9$
$\quad (([PanelEvents;\ z!: ZONES;\ d!: DIM_1\ |$
$\qquad z2 \in \text{dom } zoneEvent \land z! = z2 \land d! = zoneEvent(z2)] \gg ZONEop) \lor$
$\qquad [PanelEvents\ |\ z2 \notin \text{dom } zoneEvent] \land NOop)_9^9$
$\quad (([PanelEvents;\ z!: ZONES;\ d!: DIM_1\ |$
$\qquad z3 \in \text{dom } zoneEvent \land z! = z3 \land d! = zoneEvent(z3)] \gg ZONEop) \lor$
$\qquad [PanelEvents\ |\ z3 \notin \text{dom } zoneEvent] \land NOop)$

Schema equation *UserOpEA* defines the part of *UserOp* which handles events for entry area commands.

$UserOpEA ==$
$\quad ((([PanelEvents;\ ea!: EA;\ dim!: DIM_1\ |$
$\qquad fwd \in \text{dom } eaEvent \land ea! = fwd \land dim! = eaEvent(fwd)] \gg EAop) \lor$
$\qquad [PanelEvents\ |\ fwd \notin \text{dom } eaEvent] \land NOop)_9^9$
$\quad (([PanelEvents;\ ea!: EA;\ dim!: DIM_1\ |$
$\qquad aft \in \text{dom } eaEvent \land ea! = aft \land dim! = eaEvent(aft)] \gg EAop) \lor$
$\qquad [PanelEvents\ |\ aft \notin \text{dom } eaEvent] \land NOop)$

Schema equation *UserOpNightLights* defines the part of *UserOp* handling the events for the night light function.

$UserOpNightLights ==$
$\quad(([PanelEvents;\ n!: ZONES \mid z1 \in nlEvent \wedge n! = z1]\gg NLop)$
$\qquad \vee [PanelEvents \mid z1 \notin nlEvent] \wedge NOop)\S$
$\quad(([PanelEvents;\ n!: ZONES \mid z2 \in nlEvent \wedge n! = z2]\gg NLop)$
$\qquad \vee [PanelEvents \mid z2 \notin nlEvent] \wedge NOop)\S$
$\quad(([PanelEvents;\ n!: ZONES \mid z3 \in nlEvent \wedge n! = z3]\gg NLop)$
$\qquad \vee [PanelEvents \mid z3 \notin nlEvent] \wedge NOop)$

Schema equation *UserOpMAIN* defines the part of *UserOp* which handles the MAIN button event.

$UserOpMAIN == ([PanelEvents \mid mainEvent = active] \wedge MAINop$
$\qquad\qquad\qquad \vee [PanelEvents \mid mainEvent = passive] \wedge NOop)$

The user operations are summarized by

$UserOp == UserOpZones \S\ UserOpEA \S\ UserOpNightLights \S\ UserOpMAIN$

We allow one exception to the two rules given above: the predicate schema *UserIsBlocked* is evaluated on the top-level control structure, although it evaluates state information and CAM data. The reason for this is that none of the operations summarized in *UserOp* will be triggered if the condition *UserIsBlocked* holds. Therefore the condition is evaluated only once to determine whether any *UserOp* function may be triggered at all.

_UserIsBlocked_____
$SystemStates$
_____
$CPC1 = low \vee CPC2 = low$
CAM_DECOMP $= enabled$
CAM_BLOCK $= enabled$
_____

Schema equation CIL now represents the top-level specification for the sequential composition of isolated CIL operations. If the corresponding events are active, the operations to react on cabin decompression, failure of the FAP or on events possibly requiring an execution of the automatic dimming function are triggered. Then condition *UserIsBlocked* is checked. If it does not hold, the user operations summarized in *UserOp* will be triggered, if corresponding events are active. The user operations may have an impact on the MAIN button indicator. This is covered by triggering *MAINadjust* after having executed the *UserOp* operations. Furthermore, the schema equation states that the global invariants defined in Section 11.3.6 must be respected by each operation. Since the functions have already been specified completely, introduction of the invariants results in an "overspecified" description of the CIL functionality. This was intended to produce two different "views" of the application system: the operational schemas provide the functional view, the invariants the data view with its associated safety conditions. If the pre-condition theorems (Wordsworth, 1992) for each operation prove to be correct, each operation is also consistent with the invariants. Therefore the two views, combined with the pre-condition calculation, provide a means to strengthen the specification's trustworthiness.

$$
\begin{aligned}
CIL &== \\
&(([SystemEvents \mid CPC1Event = active \lor CPC2Event = active] \land DECOMPop \lor \\
&\quad [SystemEvents \mid CPC1Event = passive \land CPC2Event = passive] \land NOop)\,_9^\circ \\
&([SystemEvents \mid FAPEvent = active] \land FAPctrl \lor \\
&\quad [SystemEvents \mid FAPEvent = passive] \land NOop)\,_9^\circ \\
&([SystemEvents \mid cockDoorEvent = active \lor oilPresEvent = active] \land AUTODIMop \lor \\
&\quad [SystemEvents \mid cockDoorEvent = passive \land oilPresEvent = passive] \land NOop)\,_9^\circ \\
&(\neg\ UserIsBlocked \land (UserOp\,_9^\circ MAINadjust) \lor UserIsBlocked \land NOop)) \land \\
&ZONEinvariant \land ZONEinvariant' \land EAinvariant \land EAinvariant'
\end{aligned}
$$

11.4   Transformation of software requirements into software design

In this section we will sketch how to transform the software requirements specification written in Z into a software design possessing the attributes of a "good" design according to design heuristics of software engineering. The transformation of isolated Z schemas into executable programs by means of data refinement and function refinement has been thoroughly investigated (Morgan, 1994; Morgan and Vickers, 1994). Therefore we will focus on another issue, namely the derivation of a suitable architectural design from the overall structure of the Z software specification. Recall that the CIL application will be developed as a sequential function, so we do not consider any aspects of concurrent process design. Therefore, in our context, architectural design means

- decomposition of the application into sequential modules,
- definition of module interfaces, and
- design of the sequential call structure ("function A first calls function B, then function C").

11.4.1   Quality criteria for software design

Observation of the following criteria usually helps to produce a clear and efficient software design. These criteria mostly apply to sequential systems implemented with conventional programming languages.

Module cohesion   The **Cohesion** of a module denotes the degree of functional homogeneity of the activities performed by the module. It is regarded as good software engineering practice if each module only implements (a part of) functionality being defined as a homogeneous application function in the software requirements specification. In general, this will result in easy traceability from design to specification and in better maintainability in case of specification changes and error localization. An important aspect of module cohesion is the module's interface design: it should always be the case that a module execution makes use of every input parameter. Otherwise the module will probably combine different types of functionality, with each "subfunction" requiring a different subset of inputs.

Data hiding packages   Complex data structures should not directly be accessed by application functions. Instead, the algorithms retrieving and manipulating the data should be encapsulated in **data hiding packages** implementing the data structure and exporting a set of access functions for the application[21]. This will avoid the repeated implementation of algorithms in several application functions and facilitate changes of the data structure and the algorithms.

Module reuse   Modules should be designed to be reusable whenever this is possible without affecting their cohesion.

Separation of control and data transformation   To conquer the complexity of software design, it is useful to separate complex decision making from algorithmic data processing. The following rules are helpful to distribute the application's overall complexity in a suitable way.

- System control signals (e.g. the components of schema *SystemEvents*) should be separately evaluated in transaction centres. These functions evaluate control structures and activate the corresponding data processing functions.
- Data conditions (i.e. control structures evaluated according to the actual state of application data) should be evaluated in separate transaction centres, if the conditions are complex. In time-critical applications, this concept can be applied to avoid unnecessary function calls if the corresponding pre-condition for the data processing is false[22].
- Functions performing data transformations should not implement decision structures which evaluate system control signals.
- The call structure should be designed such that the transaction centres performing system control are implemented in the top level of the call tree, the transaction centres evaluating data conditions in the tree's middle layer and the data transformation functions in its leaves.

---

[21]We prefer not to call the packages "abstract data types", since they do not necessarily provide a set of access functions that completely characterize the underlying data type.

[22]Note that this concept is often unsuitable for library functions which are called by many different applications and should therefore be sufficiently robust. In this case, pre-conditions and other data conditions should be evaluated by the data processing function itself.

11.4.2   Software design activities

For the development of software design, we recommend a mixed top-down and bottom-up approach: while the architecture is developed in top-down fashion, basic interface and data manipulation functions are designed in bottom-up manner. These basic functions represent the leaves of the function call tree. Therefore it is necessary to keep these "targets of decomposition" in mind, while the top-down design is developed. For this reason, the design activities described below are executed rather in a "recursive" manner than in the exact sequence as we have chosen to present them.

Collection of system interfaces   Schemas *PanelEvents*, *SystemStates*, *SystemEvents* of Section 11.3.3 indicate the system inputs required by the application. We can assume the following operating system services to be available. Service getZoneEvent will implement the function *zoneEvent* of schema *PanelEvents* by returning for each zone z? the value $dim2$, $dim1$, $bright$, if the corresponding button has been pressed during the previous CIDS application cycle. Otherwise getZoneEvent returns *off*. Similarly, functions are provided to retrieve the other events summarized in *PanelEvents*. To retrieve the actual value or event of system states, functions getSystemStates and getSystem-Events are defined. They input an identifier for $CPC1, \ldots, oilPres$ and return the corresponding state or event value. As an output interface to control the button indicators, the operating system provides a function putButtonIndicator, which takes a button identifier and the desired $SWITCH$ state as input. To control the illumination units, a predefined memory area is given, where the commands for illumination units can be stored. The operating system provides a function illumination to perform the mapping of DEUA addresses to corresponding memory locations and writes each command to the required location.

Designing the state space   Design of the state space is driven by the specification of state schemas in Section 11.3.6. Each of these schemas gives rise to a data hiding package. This is illustrated by Figures 11.3 and 11.4 for the subspace manipulated by zone operations.

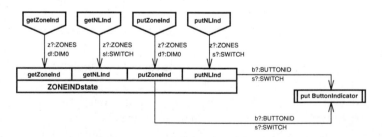

Figure 11.3   Data hiding module for the control of zone indicators and storage of indicator states.

The basic approach is to model the data structures together with a set of functions to access them. However, the access functions should be designed not only according to the data structure's characteristics, but rather according to the access operations performed in the specification's operational schemas. In case of *ZONEINDstate* this is rather straight-forward: the functions putZoneInd, putNLInd take a pair *argument* $\mapsto$ *image* as input and implement functional overriding $f' = f \oplus \{argument \mapsto image\}$. The state information is always changed together with the corresponding call to putButtonIndicator. It only has to be observed that function putZoneInd may require two calls to putButtonIndicator, namely switching off the indicator previously active and activating the new one.

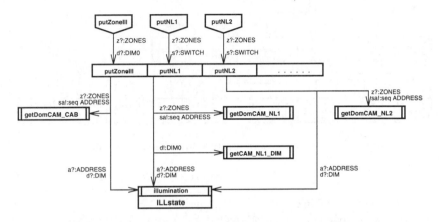

Figure 11.4 Data hiding module for the control of illumination units.

The package to access the *ILLstate* is more complex to design. The predefined operating system service illumination serves as a data hiding access function. Inspection of the operational schemas shows that *ILLstate* is never retrieved, because all relevant state information is included in *ZONEINDstate*, *EAINDstate*, ... As a consequence, we do not need any "getILLstate" functions. In case of the operations required for zone commands, the following functions are suggested. Schemas *ZONEILLopActive* and *ZONEILLopPassive* require manipulation of illumination units in cabin zones according to expression $\{x : \mathrm{dom}(\mathrm{CAM\_CAB} \rhd \{z?\}) \bullet x \mapsto d?\}$. Therefore we define a service putZoneIll that inputs zone $z?$ and required intensity $d?$ and switches the illumination units of the complete cabin zone accordingly. To support this operation function getDomCAM_CAB inputs a zone $z?$ and returns the domain of the corresponding range restriction. This could be effectively implemented by storing a second CAM representation which keeps addresses of one zone in a specific array. Similarly, functions putNL1, putNL2 are designed to implement expressions $\{x : \mathrm{dom}(M \rhd \{z?\}) \bullet x \mapsto d\}$ with $M = \mathrm{CAM\_NL1}, \mathrm{CAM\_NL2}$. Note that it is not suitable to control both night light solutions by a single function, because schema *ZONEILLopActive* shows that they are not always switched simultaneously.

Top-level architecture   Figure 11.5 shows the top-level architecture which has been derived from schema equation *CIL* in Section 11.3.7. Since the separation of system control events from application data processing has already been performed on specification level, the transformation into the call tree's root is straight forward. Function CIL checks system events to decide whether DECOMPop, FAPctrl, AUTODIMop should be activated. If condition *UserIsBlocked* does not hold according to the system status, UserOp will be called to process the user-controllable functions, followed by a call to MAINadjust in order to adapt the MAIN button indicator's actual state.

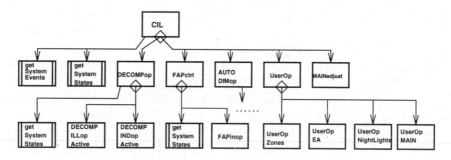

Figure 11.5 Top-level architecture for CIL software design.

Lower-level architecture   Figure 11.6 shows transaction centers processing data conditions in the case of zone commands. UserOpZones checks for zone button events and calls ZONEop for each event, providing the associated zone and required intensity as input parameters. The structure of ZONEop has been directly derived from schema equation *ZONEop* in Section 11.3.7. Functions ZONEILLopActive, ZONEINDopActive, ... represent the data transformation functions which implement the corresponding schemas, making use of the basic packages for data manipulation.

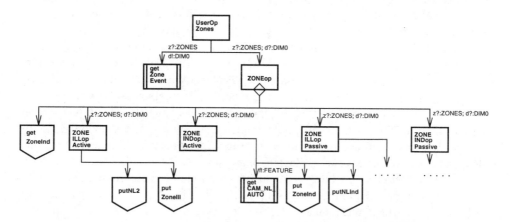

Figure 11.6 Zone operations and data manipulation functions.

Since all modules have been directly derived from schemas in the specification, the desired cohesion is automatically enforced by the design transformation.

11.5   Conclusion

In this chapter the Z specification of the Airbus A330/340 cabin illumination function, together with the associated transformation process system requirements → software requirements specification → software design has been presented. To summarize, the most important benefits derived from the application of Z were the following.

- The Z notation's powerful means to describe state spaces using mathematical data types provided the basis to develop a specification which reduced the overall complexity and could easily be verified.
- The understandability of the specification and its acceptable size were made possible by the Z constructs to produce modular and reusable specifications.
- While the checking facilities of the CASE tool provided little or no help at all in finding logical errors in the specification, the Z type checker applied (Deutsch System-Technik GmbH, 1993) uncovered a considerable number of logical errors in the early specification phases.
- The techniques applied to derive design from the Z specification considerably reduced the effort during the design and implementation phases. The development of a design architecture and of implementable data structures and algorithms from the specification turned out to be rather straight forward.
- The Z specification could be applied effectively to define trustworthy and significant test cases for integration testing. The concept to derive test cases from Z specifications in a systematic way has been described in Hörcher and Peleska (1994). It also allows for the automation of a considerable amount of the test evaluation effort. To this end DST have developed a prototype tool in cooperation with Christian Albrechts Universität Kiel, which is currently being evaluated (Hörcher and Peleska, 1994; Mikk, 1994).

Conventional CASE methods turned out to be insufficient to tackle the more complex functions of a safety-critical application system. This problem can be overcome by combining CASE methods with formal specification and verification methods. This approach was described in Peleska (1993a,b). At present it is being extended further as a joint effort between Christian Albrechts Universität Kiel, DST and the second author.

We regard the application of Z as an important factor for the successful completion of the CIDS applications developed by DST. It not only provided a technique to develop trustworthy specifications, but also helped to reduce the costs for implementation and integration, because the specification allowed the derivation a software design with minimum complexity.

Acknowledgements

We would like to thank Manfred Endreß of Deutsche Aerospace Airbus GmbH for his excellent cooperation during all development phases of the CIDS project. The final version of this article was produced while the second author was visiting lecturer at the University of Capetown. We wish to express our gratitude to Chris Brink and his group who provided both the opportunity and the stimulus to finish this work.

Chapter 12

Specifying the Kernel of a Secure Distributed Operating System

David Guaspari, Mike Seagar and Matt Stillerman

12.1 Introduction

THETA has been developed at Odyssey Research Associates (ORA) to provide a secure operating system for a heterogeneous distributed network. (For present purposes, a secure system is one that protects data from unauthorized access or modification.) Both the prototype version of THETA (Hartman, 1994) and the revision currently underway are based on the design of Cronus (Schantz *et al.*, 1986), which was developed at BBN. Following Cronus, THETA provides client programs with a persistent object database that is transparently distributed and replicated. Although the protection mechanisms of Cronus are more sophisticated than those of a typical operating system, they do not meet the standards required for protecting classified information.

The subject of this chapter is the redesign of the THETA **kernel**, a distributed program that runs on each computer belonging to a THETA network. The main tasks of the kernel are to route messages, to identify and authenticate users, and to provide access checking. A client program gains access to THETA objects only by interacting with its local THETA kernel fragment, and these kernel fragments interact with one another to effect non-local access. This mediation is a key part of the security mechanism.

The other main components of THETA are the **managers**, which manage the actual repositories of THETA objects. Clients generally send requests to the managers via the THETA kernel. The managers provide most of the object abstraction and the replication of objects. They implement a type hierarchy for objects and provide **access control lists**, a discretionary security mechanism analogous to the Unix notion of permissions. THETA is layered on top of more conventional secure operating systems and relies on them for local resource management and some local security enforcement. (We call the local operating system of each host its constituent operating system, or COS.) Actually, THETA is layered only partially, because a client program may still interact directly with its COS.

The new design has three aims: to make THETA more portable, to make THETA easier to maintain, and to simplify and clarify the **assurance argument** — the combination of formal and informal arguments offered as evidence that the information protection mechanisms succeed. We are using formal techniques, principally formal specifications, to help achieve both portability and a high assurance of correctness. A key requirement for portability is a precise definition of the interfaces between the kernel and its applications, its host operating system, and the network.

THETA is currently implemented in C. We are redesigning the kernel and reimplementing it in both Ada and C, allowing the kernel to run on a large number of hardware platforms. We expect the two versions to be very similar in design.

To judge this work the reader needs some context. First, THETA has been developed under government contract, and therefore the calculus of risks and benefits differs from that applicable to bringing a consumer product to market. Second, security work has its own peculiarities: end users are often obliged by certifying agencies to use products developed according to certain rigorous standards, and those standards may include or encourage the application of formal techniques. Finally, matters such as training and technology transfer are not a serious problem. ORA is full of mathematicians and experts in formal methods, and our technical staff is not rigidly divided between "formal methodists" and "others".

12.2   Background

We should begin by explaining a little about the peculiar nature of information security. The requirement that a secure system protect information from improper disclosure can be expressed as follows: users are associated with security levels, which are arranged in a partially ordered set; the information a user obtains from the system should be affected only by the activities of users with levels at or below his own.

This requirement, naturally formulated in terms of information theory, is complex and presents problems for both top-down and bottom-up ways of understanding (and verifying) a would-be secure system. The problem for top-down analysis is that security is not preserved by ordinary notions of refinement. For example, the chaotic system whose behaviours are entirely random is secure because it generates no meaningful information: observations of such a system will not allow us to infer anything about the activities of any other user. However, every system is a "procedural refinement" of the chaotic one — because the behaviours of any process are also (potential) behaviours of the chaotic system. So the procedural refinement of a secure system may be insecure. Data refinement is also problematic. For example, typical operating systems delete a file by changing a flag, but leaving intact the bit sequence representing the contents of that file. A security design must concern itself with the possibility of inadvertent or malicious operations that break the "directory" abstraction and access that bit sequence by some alternative means.

The problem for bottom-up analysis is that secure parts may not add up to a secure whole: whether the composition of two "secure" processes is "secure" depends in non-obvious ways on the precise way in which the intuitive information-theoretic notion of security is formalized. McCullough (1988, 1990) showed that a reasonable "minimal" definition of security is not composable and proposed a stronger definition that is. Since then a cottage industry has arisen devoted to defining other kinds of composable security properties.

THETA deals with these logical complexities in a conventional way—by implementing an approximation to the intuitive notion of security, an approximation expressible in the style of Bell and La Padula (1973). Essentially, we must show that THETA maintains a certain collection of invariants on the state of the system. These invariants arise from the requirements of security in the world of paper documents, by limiting the locations in which users may read or write. We must then make a separate, and somewhat *ad hoc*, argument that information flows through other channels (e.g. by modulating the use of some visible system resource) are not a serious threat.

The problems with refinement limit what we can conclude from presenting the description of a system in levels of accumulating concreteness and detail. In particular, we cannot conclude that a system is satisfactorily secure simply by showing that its most abstract description characterizes a secure system and that its implementation refines that abstract description. Nonetheless, a description by means of refinement is essential for organizing our understanding, and as a way of ensuring that the understanding remains consistent. Someone wanting to use our specification to understand the security properties of the system must choose some level of the specification and analyze its security properties with respect to the kinds of observations representable at that level.

12.3   Methods

We have many reasons for formally specifying the kernel. Some are generic:

- to clarify our own understanding of the design and implementation;
- as a guide to writing the documentation;
- as an aid to long-term maintainance (which includes the training of new implementors).

Some are specific to secure systems:

- to help define a "security policy" (describing how the system protects information);
- to provide the basis for an "assurance argument" (showing that it implements the policy).

End users rely on a certifying agency to declare a (would-be) secure system fit for their purposes, and certifying agencies base their judgments on the persuasiveness of the security policy and assurance arguments.

We were also eager to use some of the specification and verification tools developed at ORA and evaluate their performance on a complex real-world system.

This section briefly describes our attempts to choose methods that met our goals, and the compromises involved.

12.3.1   The problem

We quickly concluded that there exists no ready-made formalism that would easily accommodate all aspects of the kernel from its top-level view as a distributed system down to the Ada implementations of individual code modules. Thus, whatever method we chose, certain understandings about the functioning of the system would remain informal. We simply resigned ourselves to that fact.

Consider first a bottom-up view. At the bottom of the system are modules of Ada code. To represent their integration into the distributed THETA kernel, one must go outside the semantic model of Ada, which defines the meaning of a single program, not of a collection of programs that somehow cooperate. In our view the best ready-made techniques for specifying and reasoning about Ada code are embodied in the Larch/Ada specification language and the Penelope system for formally verifying Ada code (Guaspari *et al.*, 1990). These techniques apply to a subset of sequential Ada (though we have also developed some tentative ideas for specifying and reasoning about tasking). However, there remains a non-trivial gap between our best available view of the ultimate components and any view of the system as a whole.

Now consider the view from the top down. The end-user should see a unitary system. One step below that is the level that concerns us, a more concrete view in which the system is manifestly distributed (and therefore concurrent). That is the level at which the kernel appears.

The kernel's message routing involves elaborate protocols that, among other things, search through the system for migratory objects. The mechanics of the kernel-to-kernel protocols can be naturally described in a process algebra semantics such as LOTOS (Brinksma, 1985; Bolognesi and Brinksma, 1987), which was devised specifically for such purposes. We decided, however, that a process algebra specification would involve both too much detail and detail of the wrong kind. For example, the details of the "locator" protocols are largely irrelevant to understanding the system-wide properties we especially wished to consider. The strategy actually used to locate recipients — broadcast queries, consulting caches of previous replies, etc. — is largely *ad hoc*, arrived at by experimental tinkering to improve performance. For our purposes the important thing is not to describe or predict the precise route of a message or the precise way in which that route would be chosen, but rather to describe the invariants that any satisfactory route must maintain — invariants such as "the termini of each leg of the journey must have an appropriate security range". However, the notion of state is not directly or conveniently expressible in typical process algebras.

Our needs suggested a state machine model in which we could express invariants on states and on histories (sequences of state transitions). That still leaves open the question of how best to express the desired invariants. We could explicitly construct the domains of states, transitions, and histories, and use ordinary logic to define the predicates of interest. Alternatively, we could represent the model in a temporal logic, where states are defined explicitly and histories are present implicitly in the semantics of the temporal operators. Our previous experience suggested that temporal logic would not be appropriate, since it seemed better suited for describing the behaviour of reactive systems —

behaviour such as "Every time A happens, the system must do B before the next C" — than the kinds of invariants we wished to enforce.

These considerations, plus hindsight, justified the following plan. A simple formalism expressed in terms of state machines and ordinary logic would be suitable for the most abstract representation of the system. That model could be expressed straightforwardly in many of the formal notations — such as LSL, Z, or PVS — in which we have expertise. Larch/Ada, described below, seemed the obvious choice for describing the code modules themselves, though it could not fully describe modules whose behavior is essentially concurrent. The Penelope system could be used to develop both the abstract state machine description in LSL, also described below, and the specification of code modules in Larch/Ada. Penelope would also support formal verification of the code. Whatever hierarchy of refinements we provided between these two pictures would have to contain a gap, bridged by informal explanations gluing the distributed modules together outside the semantic model of Penelope and Ada.

We therefore concluded that our initial bias toward our own collection of Ada methods and tools should be indulged—particularly since we wanted to leave open the possibility of formally verifying modules of the code. There seemed to be no theoretical grounds for thinking that any other methods would be superior and the practical advantages would be considerable: experts would be on tap 24 hours a day and training would either be unnecessary or easily arranged. It would also be possible to ask for (small) modifications of the tools to meet our needs.

12.3.2 Our methods

In summary, we 'wrote specifications in Larch (Guttag *et al.*, 1985, 1990; Guttag and Horning, 1993) (a notation for first-order logic) and Larch/Ada (ORA, 1989a,b) (a formal specification language for sequential Ada). The code, specification, and English-language documentation are maintained in noweb (Ramsey and Marceau, 1991; Ramsey, 1994). We used the Penelope system (Guaspari *et al.*, 1990) to check the syntax and static semantics of the specifications—and, occasionally, to prove properties of the specifications and to prove the correctness of the corresponding Ada code.[1]

We applied other off-the-shelf formal techniques opportunistically, whenever it seemed convenient to do so. We built a simple model of THETA in Romulus (ORA, 1994), which can be used to check that components of the design satisfy a particular composable security property called restrictiveness (McCullough, 1988, 1990). We also checked the Ada code with AdaWise (Barbasch, 1993), which automates tests for certain common dynamic semantic errors.

These methods and tools are briefly described below.

---

[1] Formal machine-checked proofs have not been a major goal of our work. Such proofs as we have done have been mathematically trivial, though sometimes arduous, exercises that served as sanity checks.

Larch   Formally, the Larch Shared Language (LSL) is a notation for describing axiomatic theories in a well-organized, modular way. Its great virtue is simplicity: an LSL **trait** defines a theory of ordinary first-order logic, together with certain assertions about that theory, such as the assertion that it implies some other theory. The structuring constructs are few and almost self-explanatory. We have found it convenient to extend Larch somewhat, and in what follows "Larch" and "LSL" refer to our extended language. Our changes and the reasons for them are briefly described in Section 12.4.5.

Larch is a general methodological program that has two parts: developing a reusable library of mathematics (expressed in LSL) that is independent of any programming language; developing specification notations, called **interface languages**, that are tailored to particular programming languages. An interface language provides a way to specify a program by relating its behaviour to the behaviour of abstractions defined in LSL. For example, we can define the abstract notion of an unbounded stack in an LSL trait and use that notion to specify a bounded stack package in Ada along lines suggested by the following informal description of "push": if the stack is full, the executable push operation raises an exception; otherwise, pushing updates the stack as does the mathematical push operation defined in LSL. The same LSL trait could be used to specify a push operation in C, where an attempt to push an element onto a full stack is signalled not by raising an exception, but by returning an appropriate integer status code.

This style of specification is called "two-tiered" specification. The specification of a particular program module consists of a **mathematical tier** (a theory defined in LSL), and an **interface tier** (annotations defined in the appropriate shared language).

Two-tiered specifications pay an extra dividend on THETA: we have written very little Larch/Ada and a great deal of LSL, and we expect to reuse the LSL for specifying the kernel's implementation in C. (There is an interface language for C, called LCL (Guttag and Horning, 1993, Chapter 5).)

Larch/Ada   Larch/Ada (ORA, 1989a,b) is an interface language for Ada. Our specifications sometimes use features of Larch/Ada that are in draft form and not currently supported by Penelope.

Penelope   Penelope (Guaspari *et al.*, 1990) is an interactive tool that permits the incremental development of Larch/Ada specifications, Ada code implementing those specifications, and machine-checked proofs that the code is correct. The underlying formal model of Ada semantics covers virtually all of the machine-independent features of sequential Ada. Penelope currently implements a subset of that model, which includes generics, packages and private types, and exception raising and handling.

AdaWise   AdaWise (Barbasch, 1993) can be regarded as a kind of super-lint for Ada programs. It checks, for example, whether a program depends on the order in which its constituent modules are elaborated (roughly speaking, initialized) at program startup. That order is implementation dependent. Penelope does not make AdaWise redundant: AdaWise accepts arbitrary Ada programs and does its checks automatically, although the corresponding checks in Penelope, when applicable, are in principle more powerful.

noweb noweb (Ramsey and Marceau, 1991) is a simplified variant of Knuth's Web (Knuth, 1992), which supports "literate programming" — documentation that organizes the description of specification fragments and code fragments in the most informative expository order. We maintain a single marked-up set of source files containing specification, English-language commentary, and Ada. The noweb tools can "weave" these source files to produce LaTeX source for printing documentation organized for readability and can "tangle" these source files to produce code and specification in syntactically and semantically legal form.

We have successfully used a version of Web to maintain the code for the Penelope system through several years of implementation and many changes in the team of implementors (Ramsey and Marceau, 1989).

Romulus Romulus (ORA, 1994) allows a user to model a system as a collection of interconnected processes, to show that the components are secure, and then to apply a somewhat sophisticated theory of composable security properties to show that the overall system is secure.

12.4 The technical work

THETA applications invoke operations on objects. An invocation involves sending a message from the application to a manager of the object, and possibly receiving a reply from the manager.

The message passing is encapsulated in THETA libraries, and so is largely transparent to the application developer. Also transparent to the developer is the location of the target object, which may reside on any machine in the THETA network. The THETA kernel handles the tasks of locating the target object and routing messages between the application and the process managing the object.

All accesses to and responses from each object are governed by THETA's security policy. All THETA users and objects are associated with security clearances, and the relationship between a user's clearance and that of an object determines whether an invocation is allowed to take place. The THETA kernel is largely responsible for enforcing the security policy, although object managers also have some responsibilities in this regard.

In the next sections we describe the kernel's design and our formal model of the kernel and its role within THETA. At the most abstract level, our formal model of THETA tries to capture the distributed nature of the system, the message passing among applications (both manager and client programs are considered to be applications), and the THETA security policy. At that level there is no notion of a THETA kernel or any mechanism for transmitting messages or enforcing the security policy; we simply state the effect such mechanisms are intended to achieve. We will briefly describe this abstract model and then a refinement in which the specific kernel mechanisms begin to appear.

12.4.1   The design of the portable kernel

The THETA kernel is a distributed program. Client programs may register with the kernel. Thereafter, they may invoke operations on specific objects and receive replies. The objects may reside on any of the THETA host computers and may be replicated on a number of hosts—the location and replication of an object are typically transparent to the client. Managers may also register with the THETA kernel, asserting that they manage certain objects. Invocations of operations on those objects anywhere on the network may be routed to those managers. Clients and managers communicate only with the part of the THETA kernel running on the local host computer. Network communication occurs only between one THETA kernel fragment and another.

A fragment of the portable kernel consists of a security database containing security-related information about THETA users, such as their clearances, one or more message switches, which route messages among applications, a network minder, which handles all interactions between the kernel fragment and the network, and a login mechanism. There can be at most one instance of this software running on a host computer at any time. Registered clients and managers may communicate directly with (one of) the message switch(es) running on their local host computer. The security database is viewed as an approximately static set of THETA configuration data, to be used by other parts of THETA. The message switches transmit messages by communicating with one another and, whenever network communications are required, with the network minder. Roughly speaking, this data describes how THETA is installed on the local host computer and describes some aspects of the global THETA network. The login software handles one end of a protocol in which a user and the kernel establish an authenticated communications channel with one another.

The kernel can run in one of two modes: multilevel secure or multiple single level. In multilevel secure mode, a single trusted message switch on each host interacts with all local managers and clients. In multiple single level mode there is a set of message switches, each responsible for a single security level: all clients and managers must be running at a single security level and will interact only with the message switch for that level. The mode of a THETA kernel is chosen by the system administrator, and a single network can simultaneously support kernels in both configurations.

Because THETA is expected to run on a variety of trusted systems, whose natures vary widely, the new design must be highly portable. THETA depends on the constituent operating system of its host to provide a number of facilities, so some parts of the kernel are specific to each COS on which THETA runs. However, we are trying to minimize and to isolate the machine-dependent code.

12.4.2   Developing the formal specification

The specification is still under development, but its outline and structure are unlikely to change much. As noted above, we have mostly written a sequence of LSL theories representing successively more detailed levels of the specification. The sequence was chosen to highlight things of particular interest, for the sake either of the security argument or of our own understanding.

At each level we define

- a notion of state and an invariant indicating which states are "valid" (in particular, so far as security is concerned),
- a set of events visible at this level of abstraction and a corresponding set of transitions — a transition (s, e, s') represents the act of moving from state s to state s' after engaging in event e,
- invariants defining which transitions and sequences of transitions are "valid".

The top-level view of the world   Our most abstract model deals with the world as a whole, consisting of a collection of named hosts. A host is booted if its THETA kernel is booted. As far as THETA is concerned, an unbooted host has no actual properties, though it has potential properties, since there may be constraints on the configurations in which it may become booted. The state of each booted host consists of the following.

- *trange* is a range of security levels — all information accessed by the host must lie within this range.
- *applix* is a collection of (registered) application processes, each uniquely named by some systemwide ID.
- *sockets* is a collection of ports through which messages may be sent and received. Ultimately the sockets on a host will become part of its kernel.
- *connex* is a graph representing the port-to-port connections the host believes to exist. A host's beliefs about connections involving its own ports are authoritative, but its beliefs about other connections may be wrong.

Sockets, connections, and applications themselves have structure. For example, an application is associated with a security range, a collection of associated objects, and a collection of mailboxes (which are the kinds of message ports specific to applications).

The events are associated with the sending or receiving of messages, and there is also a special "null" event that marks all internal state changes. For example, one kind of non-null message event is associated with the forwarding of a particular kind of message — one that is stamped with a global ID denoting its recipient but containing no further routing information about how that recipient is to be found. Internal state changes, associated with null events, include such things as the creation of a new application or a change in the connection graph *connex*. In order to highlight security concerns, the top-level description need only insist that such null-event transitions proceed from one valid state to another.

The top-level view of the world is represented pictorially in Figure 12.1. The picture represents an application called β on host 3 sending a message to object o that happens to reside on host 2. The message goes from mailbox mm of β to socket ss of its kernel, is transmitted by the kernel to socket s on host 2, and is relayed by the kernel on host 2 to mailbox m of the application α that manages object o and finally delivers the message.

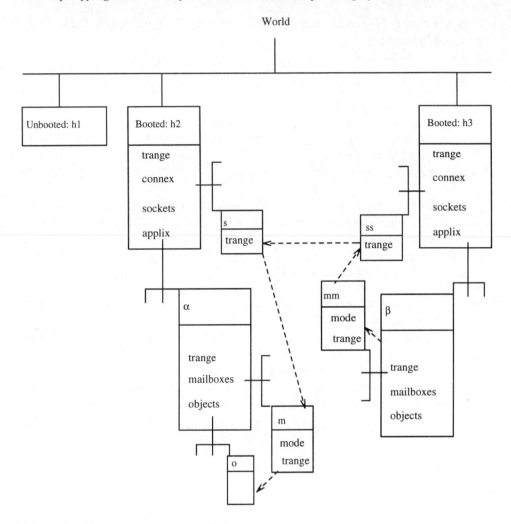

Figure 12.1 Top-level view of the world.

Figure 12.2 shows part of an LSL trait, HostsAndWorlds, defining this view of the world. The opening lines of the trait (up to the key word **introduces**) incorporate definitions previously stored in the library of traits. So, for example, these lines assume that certain constraints on the system parameters are satisfied, add the definitions of sockets, applications, etc., and define the state of the world as an association of a host name with its current state. Predicates defining a "valid" state of the world are declared in the **introduces** section and defined in the **asserts** section (which is abridged). For example, a valid booted host is one whose applications and connections are in valid states, and whose sockets and applications are operating within the ranges permitted for that host.

HostsAndWorlds : **trait**

assumes SystemParameters
includes Applications, Sockets, Connections, UnbootedHost
Booted_Host **tuple of** applix:Applications,
                       sox:Sockets,
                       trange:Theta_Range,
                       connex:Connection_Graph
Host_Descriptor **union of** unbooted:Unbooted_Host,
                           booted:Booted_Host
includes {World_}FiniteMapping(World, Host_Name, Host_Descriptor)

introduces

        valid : Host_Descriptor $\rightarrow$ Bool
        valid : World $\rightarrow$ Bool

asserts

      $\forall$ bh:Booted_Host, w:World

          valid_unbooted : valid(unbooted([]))

          valid_booted : valid(booted(bh)) $=$ valid(bh.applix) $\wedge$ valid(bh.connex)
                            $\wedge$ within(bh.sox, bh.trange) $\wedge$ within(bh.applix,
                           ·bh.trange)

          valid_world : valid(w) $= \ldots$

Figure 12.2 The top-level trait.

The next level   At the next level of abstraction appear more features that will ultimately belong to the THETA kernel. Here we will mention just one. At the top level, the existence of unregistered processes on the host is ignored, as they cannot make use of THETA communications. At the next lower level we wish to represent the act of registering a process with the kernel. Accordingly, the relevant notion of state at that lower level includes a collection of processes, some of which are registered and some not. The top-level notion of an application corresponds at the next level to that of a **registered** process. Every process has a local name assigned by its COS. By registering, a process acquires a globally unique THETA name, which is represented abstractly by maintaining a suitable map from local to global names.

Refinements   LSL does not provide a built-in mechanism for defining refinement between such levels or for generating the appropriate proof obligations. We did all that by hand, defining maps from lower-level states and events to higher-level states and events, and stating (as theorems to be proven) that these maps preserved the validity of states, transitions, and transition sequences. The theorems to be proven are, as pieces of mathematics, trivial, but the proof exercise did uncover some silly errors (discussed further in Section 12.4.2).

Getting started

The actual process, of course, was not nearly so rational as described. Three people contributed to the initial development of the specification: an expert on protocols, who saw everything as a protocol; an expert on Larch/Ada, who saw everything as an invariant; an expert on THETA, for whom every abstraction overlooked a potentially significant nugget of implementation subtlety. The new kernel was in the process of being designed, answers to many of our questions did not yet exist, and some of our questions raised design issues never before considered.

Only one member of the group had significant experience with writing formal specifications. The difficulties faced by an inexperienced specifier should not be underestimated: to begin with, where to begin? Also, when, at least initially, even the techniques to be used are open questions, the amount of freedom can be paralyzing.

We necessarily began "wastefully", pursuing scattered aspects of the design, often using different notations, using mutually inconsistent formulations, and with too much worry about detail. We took a step back and decided to begin with the kernel's fundamental job — mediating message passing between application processes — and began to develop the hierarchy of specifications described above. This is the stage at which we finally concluded, by a combination of reason and faith, that LSL and Larch/Ada would suit our purposes.

With the style of specification established and agreement on the basic formal vocabulary, developing subsequent levels of the specification became much simpler. There was still a great deal of discussion about where in the specification we should introduce certain details, but we were able to discuss such questions in the context of an existing framework, rather than debating style and terminology as we had in the early stages of the project.

The initial groping was a pencil and paper exercise, as some desired features of Larch had not yet been implemented in Penelope. However, the specification's complexity grew quickly and it became difficult to maintain the consistency of the specification by hand. Penelope proved a great help when, in response to our pleas, the necessary features were added. At that point we were not trying to prove any theorems or to verify any code, but the static semantic checking allowed us to concentrate on more interesting aspects of the work.

Enthusiasts for formal specification who wish (correctly) to emphasize that thinking is more important than the blind application of automated tools have sometimes seemed to denigrate the use of tools altogether. In fact, formal techniques cannot be applied to problems of practical size without automated support.

The gaps

The refinements discussed so far have been fairly clean, but there is a large gap in the level of abstraction between the lowest level of the LSL description and the implementation. The one member of the project who was immersed in both the specification and the implementation had a fairly good intuitive idea of how to relate the LSL specification to the code, but when a newcomer to the project found this gulf to be a source of some anguish. Thus the specification was serving its purpose in guiding the implementation and as an introduction to the kernel design, but was not fully adequate to bring a new person up to speed.

We plan to write at least a natural language description of this intuitive mapping, but a complete chain of formalism down to the level of the code is beyond the scope of our current effort.

The lowest-level modules

The last step, specifying individual code modules in Larch/Ada, is straightforward. Figure 12.3 contains some of the specification of a package for creating and manipulating intervals of security levels.[2] We will discuss this specification briefly, to illustrate the style of specification and its benefits. The most important benefit is that writing an interface specification requires you to answer a systematic set of intelligent questions. We also used Penelope to verify the (trivial) body of this package, principally as an exercise, with results described below.

The annotation `with trait SecurityLevels` says that the trait *SecurityLevels* defines the mathematical tier of the specification. *SecurityLevels*, not shown here, includes a mathematical description of the sort *Theta_Range*, whose values are all intervals of security levels. In particular, the trait defines $interval(l, h)$ to be the interval bounded below by l and above by h, and it defines operations *lo* and *hi* that return, respectively, the lower and upper bounds of an interval. Notice that a nuisance case arises if $l \not\leq h$, so that $interval(l, h)$ ought to be empty. Is there only one such empty interval? There will be more than one if we insist on the rule that $lo(interval(l, h)) = l$. If we decide there should only be one, what should be its lower and upper bounds?

The mathematical tier makes some conventional decisions about this nuisance, but they will not concern us, as can be seen by inspecting the annotations for the declaration of type `theta_range`. The `based on` annotation says that every value of the programming language *type* `theta_range` should be thought of as some abstract value in the LSL *sort Theta_Range*. The type and the sort are different things, even though we chose to overload an identifier and use the same name for both of them. The `invariant` annotation points to one of the differences: it says that every defined variable of type `theta_range` has some non-empty element of *Theta_Range* as its value. Thus the legitimate values of the type constitute a proper subset of the values in the sort. A client of package `security_levels` will be relying on the implementation of the package to maintain this invariant.

One way in which the invariant is maintained can be seen from the annotations of `make_range`: if this function returns normally, it returns as its abstract value the range bounded by its arguments; however, any attempt to create an empty security range does not terminate normally and does not return a value, but raises an exception instead.

---

[2]For expository purposes, the code in Figure 12.3 has been simplified.

```
with types;
with theta_levels; use theta_levels;
--| with trait SecurityLevels
package security_levels is

    empty_range : exception;

    type theta_range is private;
    --| BASED ON Theta_Range;
    --| INVARIANT: x:theta_range => not (is_empty(x))

    function make_range (low,high: in theta_level)
                        return theta_range
    --| WHERE
    --|    RETURN interval(low,high)
    --|    RAISE empty_range <=> not(low <= high)
    --| END WHERE

       ...

    function meets(r1,r2: in theta_range) return boolean
    --| WHERE
    --|    RETURN exists l: Theta_Level :: l \in r1
    --|                                 and l \in r2
    --| END WHERE;


       ...

private

    type theta_range is
      record
        lo: theta_level := system_low;
        hi: theta_level := system_low;
      end record;

end security_levels;
```

Figure 12.3 Implementing security ranges.

Two things prompted us to think that the type invariant for theta_range and the specification of make_range deserved some careful thought. First, the nuisance cases in the mathematical part suggested a potential source of implementation bugs. Second, Larch/Ada contains a "slot" waiting expectantly for the invariants of a private type and the exception-raising behaviour of a subprogram.

Larch/Ada also "asks" whether variables of type theta_range are to be regarded as defined upon declaration. The initialization annotation is omitted in this specification, so the answer defaults to "no": clients are thereby warned that variables of type theta_range should be explicitly initialized before they are read.

Concretely, a theta_range is implemented as a pair of security levels. The design decision to treat a newly declared theta_range variable as abstractly undefined does not determine what the concrete representation of a newly declared variable should be: we could leave its fields undefined, we could initialize them to values denoting an empty interval (so that you could always tell by inspection whether a variable has been left uninitialized), or we could initialize them to some values that would be least likely to cause harm if the user erred by failing to initialize them explicitly. The third alternative seemed the most prudent — and therefore, by design, the visible specification of this package is weaker than the specification it actually satisfies, since it is actually safe to use a theta_range variable without explicitly initializing it. This careful consideration of detail was all but forced on us by writing the formal specification.

The formal verification of this package showed that two wrongs had, in practice, been making a right. The utility meets determines whether two security ranges overlap. Two implementors agreed on the "obvious" algorithm for doing this: $interval(l_1, h_1)$ overlaps with $interval(l_2, h_2)$ just in case both $l_2 \leq h_1$ and $l_1 \leq h_2$. You might be able convince yourself of that, as we convinced ourselves, by drawing pictures of intervals on the number line — in which case you, like us, would be wrong: the "obvious" solution is not correct for an arbitrary partial order, though it is correct if the partial order is a lattice.

The actual THETA code took the form of a generic package to which the type of security levels and their ordering relation were parameters, and the original specifications of this package assumed only that the order of security levels was a partial order. Penelope did not permit us to prove the one-line implementation of that generic meets program because it did not in fact satisfy that specification. However, all the executable instances of this package that we created did behave correctly because the actual parameters to each instance had an extra property not assumed in the specification of the generic (namely, the property of being a lattice).

12.4.3 Products of the formal work

The most tangible product of the formal work is a manuscript, still incomplete at 400+ pages, containing the formal specifications for the kernel, the kernel's code, and extensive informal commentary. The principal intangible product has been the self-teaching that writing this manuscript entailed. We have used Penelope to check the static semantic consistency of the LSL and to check a few simple refinement proofs, which are briefly summarized in the associated informal commentary. We have not checked the static semantics of the Larch/Ada specifications, since they often use features that Penelope does not currently support. We have carried out some simple code proofs, but have not yet decided whether to make a systematic effort to identify and verify key code modules.

(Because Penelope does not yet support all of Larch/Ada or all of the Ada features we wish to use, the code proofs are "demonstrations" involving work-arounds.)

We have used the specification, with reasonable success, to introduce new workers to the specification project, although, as noted above, it is not completely self-sufficient. We are also using it to help produce the "formal top-level specification" — a design document, required by certifying agencies, that gives an overview of the system's security policy.

12.4.4 The formal work and the implementation

The design and the implementation of the new kernel are still in progress. We want the specification to help clarify the design and want the specification and design to evolve together. As noted above, the principal benefit of the specification exercise to date has been that it required us to figure out, in a clear way, what THETA and the THETA kernel are supposed to be doing.

The refinements of the LSL specifications were not neutral: if they did not compel certain implementation choices, they were nonetheless made with particular implementation ideas in mind. It soon enough became necesssary to try these ideas, and we began work on a preliminary version of the code. The wisdom of catching errors early works in both directions: we needed some coding experience that would validate those large-scale design commitments that were becoming embedded in the specification. There is some danger that we will never return to complete the specification and will lose the "lifecycle" benefits that a completed specification would provide. However, we are avoiding the converse danger of wasting time on marginal aesthetic improvements to the specification.

To date, the implementation consists of just over 5000 Ada statements[3] divided among about 40 packages and a dozen significant procedures. The specification guided development of the code, but we have not provided an argument showing that the code corresponds to the specification. We plan to review the code to ascertain that we can make, at the least, an informal correspondence argument.

12.4.5 Tools

Our principal automated tools have been Penelope and noweb, together with AdaWise, Romulus, standard Unix utilities (RCS, make, etc.), and an ad hoc collection of shell scripts. We discuss some of these tools below, and we also discuss LSL and Ada as "intellectual tools"—in particular, the extensions that we have made to LSL and the overall suitability of Ada for formal treatment and for the implementation of critical systems.

---

[3] We used a simple code counter called *countada* to arrive at this number. *countada* is basically a semicolon counter; it is available by anonymous ftp from the Public Ada Library at wuarchive.wustl.edu.

Larch

We have already described the strengths of Larch. We list here some limitations and inconveniences, first from the point of view of this particular exercise and then in general.

Particular criticisms LSL is algebraic, rather than state based. Since we decided to formulate our basic model as a state machine, we incurred the nuisance of carrying around explicit state parameters in all our operations.

LSL does not provide a notion of "subsort". So, for example, we are unable to introduce a sort of valid states and define operations on valid states; rather, we must define a "valid" predicate on the sort of all states and qualify our definitions of operations on states in terms of this predicate. The clutter increases when we construct further sorts (and subsorts) from these. We made errors in some definitions by forgetting to carry along the appropriate qualifying predicates. We discovered these errors either because we could not carry out the proofs (qualifiers omitted from the hypotheses) or because the proofs were so easy that we knew we must have been trying to prove the wrong thing (qualifiers omitted from the conclusions).

As already noted there is no built-in mechanism for constructing state machines and their histories, or defining refinements between such models. However, it would be straightforward to store generic constructions of these mechanisms in library traits.

General criticisms The Larch project centres on the exploration of specifications, using term rewriting as the underlying logical engine. Term rewriting is just substitution, so users easily understand it, and users can search automatically for certain logical errors by letting the rewriter roll and then eyeballing the output for unwanted consequences.

This approach limits the axioms in an "official" Larch trait to equations.[4] We prefer axioms written in a richer logic, because we find them easier to understand. For example, one can define "x is present in the array A at some index between lo and hi" equationally by using a recursive definition. The more obvious and natural definition, however, uses a logical quantifier: *"there exists* an index i in lo..hi such that A(i) = x". This more natural definition is easier to understand and is easier to get right in the first place.

So we made additions to the logical notation that include free use of logical quantifiers.[5] We added a schematic shorthand for declaring sorts whose values are mappings — declaring a sort of mappings makes the corresponding "lambda abstraction" available. We also extended the built-in "background theory" automatically included in every trait. Official LSL is parsimonious: the only built-in theory is the theory of Booleans. However, we have found little value in not having things such as the theory of integers automatically available.

Finally, in order to describe the basic types of Ada, we were obliged to add schematic shorthands for Ada array types, enumeration types, and record types. Without these schemas there would be no convenient way to define sorts on which to base these types.

---

[4]This is not strictly true, because LSL permits structural induction for arbitrary properties of inductively defined data types. Still, it is true enough to be useful.

[5]Revisions to "official" LSL that would permit free use of logical quantifiers are currently under way.

These changes mean that we cannot use the Larch prover as our proof checker. We have instead implemented a simple sequent calculus proof checker for first-order logic. In addition to the basic logical steps, the checker provides a few simple proof tactics, built-in decision procedures for Booleans, linear arithmetic, and equality, and a limited ability to do term rewriting.

Finally, we note that Larch is axiomatic and puts the responsibility for defining consistent theories on the user. Other systems enforce a discipline for introducing axioms that guarantees that only consistent theories may be created. (In such systems one cannot in general even formulate a theory without performing non-trivial theorem proving.)

Penelope

As noted, Penelope was invaluable for maintaining the static semantic consistency of the LSL specifications. We also used Penelope to carry out a handful of proofs that served as sanity checks of certain simple logical consistencies — for example, showing that the refinement map from the second level of the specification to the first preserved validity. These proofs uncovered several oversights but no conceptual errors. For example, one trait provided declarations of certain sorts and operations, but failed to include traits needed to define them. In another trait, the definition of a "valid" predicate on a composite sort omitted clauses asserting the validity of its components and of the relations between them. We also discovered that the pencil-and-paper proofs that we had memorialized in an earlier version of the documentation, though conceptually correct, were full of nonsense such as expressions that failed to sort check.

Certain other errors might be regarded as artifacts of the formalization itself. In several cases the author of a specification omitted the parentheses in an expression and instead used indentations to suggest the intended associations of operators visually. Penelope's parser inserted the missing parentheses "correctly", thereby changing the intended meaning of the expression. If the specification were being used only for communication with another person, the author's error would not have mattered, since the intention would have been correctly conveyed. (If the specification had been constructed interactively with the Penelope editor, these mistakes would have been avoided in the first place.)

The Penelope implementation under which we first carried out the proofs was overtaxed by the problem. This prompted some effort to improve Penelope's handling of memory, after which performance (as measured by the time to replay the original proofs and by the response time to changes in the proofs) improved dramatically.

AdaWise

In Ada, execution of a main program begins by elaborating all the compilation units on which the main program depends — doing so in an order partly, but not always fully, determined by the source text. AdaWise scanned the kernel code for sensitivity to the compiler's choice of this elaboration order and discovered some cases in which a subprogram could be called before its body was elaborated (which would result in "crash on takeoff" with an unhandled exception). This common error, a portability problem, is easily repaired by pragmas that constrain the compiler's choice of elaboration order.

noweb

The specification document generated from our noweb source has been a success. Our home-grown system for maintaining that source is far less satisfactory, principally because noweb is essentially batch oriented and Penelope is incremental and interactive. A noweb user proceeds by iterating the following cycle, as needed: tangle the noweb source, analyze the result (with Penelope, in our case), obtain error reports, modify the noweb source. However, we typically correct the tangled file interactively with Penelope, and then have no easy way to invert tangle so that this corrected file is appropriately deposited in the noweb source: tangling may have assembled the text that Penelope sees from many pieces scattered throughout the document. So the corrections developed with Penelope had to be added to the noweb source by hand. This step is error prone, but the result can of course be checked by retangling and reapplying Penelope.

Ada

Ada is complex, which raises questions about the practicality of applying formal techniques to Ada and about the prudence of using Ada in critical systems. These questions arise at two levels: understanding the semantics of the source code, and reliably translating the source into predictable object code.

The Penelope model is evidence of the strongest kind that a very large subset of sequential Ada has a clean semantics. Further, Ada's support for modularity, abstraction, and generics (parameterized modules) has enabled Larch/Ada specifications to follow the structure of Ada source code closely and idiomatically. (By contrast, the C interface language LCL must provide ways to impose a structure on C code.) We also expected that these features would permit portability and reuse that allowed the costs of careful development to be amortized over many applications. Here we had some disappointments. One of the commonest problems of Ada compilers is a weakness in handling generics. We have been unable to use a sophisticated set of list handling packages (Musser and Stepanov, 1989) because they relied on deeply nested generics, which neither of our validated Ada compilers could handle. Thus generics, a feature intended to promote code reuse, seems on this occasion to have hindered it. Finally, as noted earlier, Ada compilers are not always available on specialized hardware platforms, which places a rather effective limit on portability.

The question of reliable compilation is not a purely technical one. Even if the source code is restricted to a semantically "safe" subset for which straightforward (and presumably reliable) compilation techniques are adequate, there is no guarantee that a compiler will use such techniques. That has been left to the market place. For example, certain compilers aimed at the real-time market recognize some form of a "simple tasking" pragma — whose effect is to enforce the use of a language subset in the source and then to exploit that fact to generate more efficient code and/or to link in a simplified run-time environment with predictable performance characteristics. There does not seem to be — and certifying agencies have not thus far chosen to create — a similar market for Ada compilers for secure systems.

The Ada run-time environment needs special consideration. Certifying agencies typically require a design in which the essential guarantees are provided by the actions of a small "trusted computing base". Incorporating a large or complex run-time environment into each executable is therefore problematic. Further, implementing secure systems may require not a minimal runtime environment, but one permitting positive control of such things as the scheduling of tasks. For example, one natural implementation of the THETA kernel would isolate the processing at any single security level within its own task. In order to limit "covert" signalling between two tasks running at different security levels, we would need some control over task scheduling.

Romulus

As already noted, Romulus is a tool for modeling and reasoning about security properties. For technical reasons, Romulus can model and reason about only one THETA configuration at a time. Since there are an infinite number of possible configurations of THETA, there is no way to use Romulus to draw conclusions about all possible instances of THETA.

So we constructed a model of and analyzed a typical THETA configuration. The configuration we chose used multiple single-level message switches. These switches are secure for the trivial reason that the level of any possible output is always greater than or equal to the levels of any possible inputs. This reasoning does not apply to the netminder, whose inputs and outputs can be of any security level, so we had to consider the precise details of its behaviour. (We used a simplified model of the behaviour.) To carry out the proof, we had to ensure that the netminder independently certified the security labels on all messages passing through it — that is, the netminder cannot assume that the labels generated by the message switches are correct.

The model and proofs were quick to construct — taking a newcomer to Romulus about two days. Although these proofs were done for just one configuration, the conclusions obviously generalize to all instances of THETA, and provided useful insights into the design.

12.5   Evaluation

The kernel's redesign and reimplementation are still underway: the portable kernel does not yet implement all the kernel's functions. This partial kernel has been successfully tested on a network of two machines, one of them running the existing THETA kernel, and the other running the partial kernel and processes that simulate the actions of managers and clients.

Still, some interim conclusions are possible.

12.5.1 What we would do differently

What would we do differently next time? It is convenient to divide the anwer, artificially, into a discussion of the process and of the supporting tools.

Process

Writing the formal specification did not contribute as much to creating the design (as distinct from recording it) as had been hoped. This failing resulted, at least in part, from allotting too little time to the initial phases of design, and of becoming entangled in the ubiquitous snare, "get some code running". In part, this failing also resulted from being initially unclear about what the specification effort should provide. Our limited resources also meant that there was too little review of the design or of the correspondence between code and design: outside a few periods of intense design work and discussion only one person worked on this part of the project.

It is only fair to note one thing we would automatically do better the next time: we would get off to a better start. We suspect that formal methods experiments typically start from scratch, so that the intellectual capital developed—understanding the application domain, developing libraries of specification concepts, etc.—is subsequently lost and that development cost cannot be amortized over an entire "product line".

Tools

The tools that we used were adequate in their own right, but did not make up a coherent development environment. Since, in particular, some of them were predominantly batch processors and some (to varying degrees) incremental, it would have been difficult ever to make them work together well. We have already mentioned our difficulties integrating noweb with Penelope. Similar difficulties arise in integrating noweb with an Ada debugger or an Ada library system. (The problem for integrating with the Ada library is to avoid unnecessary recompilations of library units.) Cobbling together patches is time consuming and has predictably mediocre results. We were much too cavalier, at the outset of the project, about the burdens these problems would impose.

The problem with tools is both pragmatic and theoretical. The immediate pragmatic problem for a would-be user of formal methods is to choose some technique whose tools can be made to work reasonably well with the rest of a development environment that is already in place and cannot be radically changed. The more theoretical problem is that, as already noted, one often wishes to apply different specification techniques to different aspects of a problem or to different levels of abstraction, and there is little support, either conceptual or automated, for doing that.

12.6 Conclusion

A very crude estimate of the time spent on the formal specification and proofs (artificially separating it from coding) is a total of 15 person-months, split among five people, from the spring of 1993 through the end of 1994. We used these methods in hopes of improving the quality of our system, satisfying our customer about that quality, and helping with the long-term maintenance of the kernel. We also hope that the intellectual capital acquired by doing the formal work will be useful in future work on distributed systems.

The main benefit to date has been a well-organized understanding of the kernel and its role. In particular, we have a standardized and rationalized vocabulary for describing the kernel and the security properties we want to guarantee. We have good reason to attribute much of that success to the formal work: developing the formal specification made it plain that no one else had been forced to think about the system in quite the way we needed.

We cannot yet judge the longer-term usefulness of our work. One small piece of evidence is our using the formal specification to introduce one new worker to the project. As noted above, the unpolished formal specification was useful but not sufficient to stand by itself.

Acknowledgements

Funding for this material has been provided by the US Government under its Department of the Air Force (Rome Laboratory) contract number F30602-92-C-0145 to Odyssey Research Associates Inc., and is also discussed in Seager *et al.* (1995), where more emphasis is placed on security concerns.

Chapter 13

Formal Specification of an Aerospace System: the Attitude Monitor

**Andrew Coombes, Leonor Barroca, John S. Fitzgerald,
John A. McDermid, Lynn Spencer and Amer Saeed**

13.1 Introduction

This chapter describes the experience of a group of researchers in formally specifying an existing aerospace product, by means of a number of experimental techniques developed by the British Aerospace (BAe) Dependable Computing Systems Centre (DCSC). In performing this work, two organizations were involved: BAe Defence (Military Aircraft), and the DCSC, a BAe-funded research centre based in the Universities of York and Newcastle. The DCSC is an ongoing project aiming to develop solutions for intermediate term problems occurring in the software development of (primarily) avionic systems. Work within the DCSC includes research in the following: formal methods, requirements analysis, timing analysis of programs, and human computer interaction.

13.2 Project Background

The system discussed in this chapter resulted from work on the Experimental Aircraft Programme (EAP). A need was identified to stop or reduce cross-winds from adversely affecting the performance of the aircraft. In order to achieve this, a gust alleviation filter was proposed, which would activate gust-damping flaps on the aircraft whenever cross-winds were detected. Although this component is not inherently considered to be safety-critical, it was placed within the flight control system, which makes it safety critical "by association". It was an element of this filter, an attitude monitor, which was studied.

There are a number of reasons why this was seen as a particularly good opportunity to demonstrate the work of the DCSC against a real project.

- It provides the opportunity to compare experimental design techniques against ones used in practice.
- If developed further, it would involve meeting standards for level 1 (i.e. safety-critical) software (although the standards used for EAP are internal company standards, they closely reflect external standards).
- The system being developed has to fit within the constraints of an existing system.

- It includes "non-functional" issues in its requirements, such as the use of redundancy (diverse data sources) as a technique for achieving desired levels of integrity.

The approach taken by the work reported in this chapter resulted from research undertaken by the DCSC intended to achieve the following:

1. produce better justifications (of conformance to a standard) and traceability of design decisions;
2. develop methods which are capable of dealing with large systems;
3. provide assistance in analyzing design tradeoffs early in the development process (especially architectural concerns).

In addressing this case study, five philosophical questions were posed by BAe, representing their concerns in this area.

1. What subset of the information supplied is necessary and sufficient for a formal statement of requirements against which designs can be verified?
2. Why is this a minimum set?
3. How should the information be expressed?
4. What evidence can be provided to show design conformance?
5. How can the information be captured and expressed in the development context?

It was intended that the work should provide some answers to these questions.

13.3   Methods

The attitude monitor was specified using three techniques: safety specification graphs, architectural specification method and Zables. A fourth technique, a goal-based approach to structuring the specification and its associated design arguments, was used to provide a framework for justifying the design strategy adopted. These methods are described in slightly more detail in the following subsections.

The choice of these techniques was primarily based upon the objective of demonstrating their utility in "typical" aerospace projects. In the form presented here, the specification has paid little attention to standards, either external or company. However, it was recognized that the application would typically require certification, and therefore the techniques were chosen for their potential to produce or organize evidence which would support certification.

A range of techniques was applied to a common problem for two related reasons: first, to see their relative strengths and weaknesses; second, to see whether they could usefully be combined to provide a more "complete" method.

13.3.1 Safety specification graphs

A crucial concern in the development of high-integrity systems is to provide quality documentation that records the results of system development in a well-structured format. Poor, or incomplete, documentation is often a major obstacle to demonstrating that high-integrity demands imposed on a system have actually been met. Essential tasks for the provision of effective approaches to recording documentation are

- the judicious selection of information to be recorded,
- and the structuring of information in formats that are amenable to analysis.

The notion of a **safety specification graph** (SSG) (de Lemos *et al.*, 1994) has been introduced as a means to record the results of requirements analysis and safety analysis, and their interrelationships. An SSG (an example of which is shown in Figure 13.4) is a directed acyclic graph, in which the vertices represent the safety specifications and the edges encode the relationships between the specifications at adjacent layers of the graph. These relationships must be confirmed to ensure that the specifications maintain safe behaviour and that integrity levels have been appropriately allocated. When more than one specification is related to a specification of a previous layer, if the specifications are exclusive alternatives the edges are annotated with an "⊕", while if they are complementary the edges are annotated with a "⊙".

The SSG approach helps to establish levels of abstraction for the statement and analysis of safety properties. Relevant assumptions are formally recorded, and the specifications are traceable to the safety requirements they aim to satisfy (including non-functional requirements such as integrity levels). The SSG provides a mechanism for recording all the options which have been explored.

The basic principles of the SSG can be employed to provide traceability from top-level requirements to detailed specifications. This introduces the possibility of providing links from top-level requirements through to the allocation of integrity requirements on particular functions (such as the need to provide "data to an integrity of level 1 ...") and to the specifications stipulated at the architectural level. Imposing the discipline of identifying such links during development has the benefits of ensuring that high-integrity requirements are appropriately allocated and supports the demonstration for their satisfaction.

13.3.2 Zables — description of technique

The Zables notation has been developed to allow for abstract specifications of software moding requirements using both a tabular and the Z notation. It is based on the tabular style of specification developed to re-specify part of the A-7E aircraft (Parnas *et al.*, 1978).

The A-7E approach uses a number of tables to describe the modes the system can be in, the events that cause mode transitions and the conditions under which the system functions are to be carried out (in terms of modes and external events).

The Zables notation consists of a similar set of tables which are defined with specific format and contents. A mapping between these tables and a Z subset has been defined and implemented so that a tabular specification can be "translated" into a Z specification to form the basis of the moding behaviour of the system. This also has the added benefit of being amenable to systems engineers who are more familiar with tabular and graphical notations than formal mathematical ones.

Four tables in particular are used. The mode class table is used to list the system variables which determine the modes the system can be in. The contents of this table form the Z state schema. The mode table identifies the system modes and gives the definition of each mode in terms of values that the system variables can take. For example, a system variable might be *weight_on_wheels*; two modes might be *On_Ground* which is defined (in part) by *weight_on_wheels* = *True* and *In_flight* which is defined by *weight_on_wheels* = *False*. Each mode in the mode table becomes a schema in the Z specification. The mode names can be referred to in the rest of the specification.

The mode transition table identifies valid transitions between modes and the changes in value of the system variables and other external events which cause that transition. Each mode transition is translated into a Z operation schema which causes a change in the state. The pre-condition of the schema is the initial mode and the conditions and events which cause the transition; the post-condition is the final mode.

Finally action tables are used to identify when particular actions are to be performed. These might be dependent on being in a particular mode, entering a mode, certain events occurring or conditions holding, or a combination of these. Actions may be simple assignments to output variables or more complex calculations which are named in the action tables and defined elsewhere in the specification. Each action is translated into a Z operation schema which does not change the state. The pre-condition of the operation is the conjunction of modes, events and conditions which determine that the operation is to be carried out. The post-condition is either the assignment of output variables or a reference to the action definition.

13.3.3   Architectural specification method

The third set of techniques applied to the attitude monitor problem work at a lower level of abstraction than safety specification graphs and Zables. SSGs can be used to guide the process of assurance that design strategies will respect safety requirements, and Zables can be used to analyze overall moding behaviour. Once one begins to consider the architecture of an implementation, one to has to take into account constraints imposed by external factors, e.g. the need to distribute certain computations to specific items of equipment in an aircraft cockpit. Once an implementation structure has been decided, it is important to be able to ensure that the components of the structure (programs or hardware) will cooperate to perform the required computations in a timely manner: the allocation of realistic timing budgets to system components is a considerable headache for avionics engineers.

We will refer to system design at this level as **architectural specification**. An architectural specification of a system represents the system structure, functionality and temporal behaviour. We could extend this to include other important aspects of the system, such as resource consumption. However, we will concern ourselves with these three aspects because they represent the three most pressing concerns of avionics engineers at the present.

In the DCSC, we have been developing formal techniques for describing and analysing designs at this level, grouped under the title of the architectural specification method (ArchSM). In the rest of this section, we will introduce the notations used for describing system structure, functionality and timing properties.

We have allowed pragmatism to dictate the choice of notations. Rather than try to invent a new all-embracing formalism for architectural specification, we have tried to build on techniques which already have a formal or formalizable basis and some (even modest) history of successful application in the avionics industry.

Representing system structure At the architectural specification level, a system is viewed as a collection of independent agents which interact in a well-defined way by reacting to instantaneous events raised by agents in the structure or by external agents. Later in the design process, the communication initially defined in simple terms of signals between the components will be realized by more complex communication protocols involving areas of shared data.

One notation, developed within BAe, which can be used to represent system structure is a subset of the DORIS Real Time Networks notation (Simpson, 1993). DORIS's structural aspects can be used to define an initial system design in terms of the agents–activities of which it is composed and their interactions. At detailed design levels, the DORIS methodology allows communication between agents to be described via a rich repertoire of shared data structures. However, at the level of specification in the study described here, communication between agents is identified only in terms of the events that trigger and are raised by each agent.

Representing temporal behaviour We have chosen to represent the timing behaviour of systems with a graphical notation, based on the language of timed statecharts. This has the advantage of being accessible to people with a less mathematical background, while being sufficiently expressive and formal. A further consideration was that some BAe engineers are already familiar with the notation through experience of the Statemate tool (Harel *et al.*, 1990). Indeed, state-transition diagrams have been widely used as a design tool in avionics projects for some time.

Statecharts (Harel, 1987) are an extension of state machines and state diagrams for the specification of reactive systems. Timed statecharts (Henzinger *et al.*, 1992) extend the notation by adding time constraints. Figure 13.1 shows a very simple timed statechart.

Each box represents a system state, and each arrow a transition between states. The distinguished initial state is indicated by the arrow without a source state. Transitions

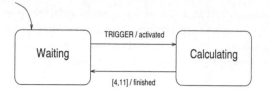

Figure 13.1 A very simple timed statechart.

are labelled with the name of an event which triggers the transition (e.g. "TRIGGER" above — names of events due to external agents are written in capital letters), the names of any events raised by the transition (e.g. "activated") or time bounds within which a transition is available for taking. The bounds are measured from the time the source state for the transition is entered, e.g. 4 and 11 time units on the lower transition. Transitions can also be labelled with conditions which must hold for a transition to be available. In the above example, the machine cycles between the two states, entering the calculating state when the even "TRIGGER" occurs and leaving it between 4 and 11 time units later. The examples in Section 13.4.5 will give a clearer idea of how the statecharts are used in practice.

Representing functionality   We have chosen Z (Brien and Nicholls, 1992) as a formalism for representing functionality, again because of its familiarity to groups of BAe engineers. Each agent in the system has a Z specification modelling its local state variables and the computations it performs. In relating the timed statechart model of a component of the system to the Z specification of functionality, we associate an operation (action) to a state in a state machine model. In this case the operation is invoked when the state is entered, and the invariant of the operation is related to the system being in that state. If there are time bounds on an outward transition out of that state, this time interval usually represents the minimal and maximal time allowed for the execution of the operation. Conditions on labels refer to the values of variables changed by the actions within the states.

Reasoning about timing and functionality   The production of rigorous arguments about designs is important for the assessment process. In ArchSM, real time logic (RTL) (Jahanian and Mok, 1986, 1987) can be used to construct such arguments about timing properties of systems whose timing behaviour is expressed using the timed statechart notation. RTL has been applied to reasoning about the allocation of timing budgets to cockpit equipment in the development of a pilot waypoint entry system, and this study is reported elsewhere (Barroca *et al.*, 1994). However, the construction of formal proofs about ArchSM specifications is a research issue beyond the scope of this paper.

13.3.4 Goal structuring

Goal structuring (Coombes *et al.*, 1994; Morris *et al.*, 1994) provides a framework for recording design rationale throughout the system development process. The starting point is to identify the top-level aims for the system (which may be inconsistent at the starting point). The framework is then applied at every level of abstraction of the system, recording decisions made and alternatives considered, in addition to the rationale for choosing a particular approach.

The approach is intended to engender several classes of traceability relation, support for safety argumentation, explicit assumptions about the system and its environment, and also to provide an opportunity to justify each decision made in the design process.

Goal specification is achieved by developing a hierarchy of goal structures (see Figure 13.2).

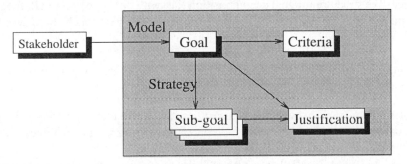

Figure 13.2 Goal structure.

The goal structure consists of six main elements.

- *Goal.* This represents a single "requirement" that the system is intended to achieve at a particular level of abstraction. The term "goal" is preferred to requirement, since a set of requirements are typically considered to be consistent (that is, no two requirements are mutually incompatible), whereas it is conceivable that any two goals are (particularly at the earlier levels of the analysis) inconsistent, and that tradeoffs need to be made between them.
- *Stakeholder.* This represents an enterprise (i.e. an individual or a group) who is concerned with the satisfaction of a particular goal. Every goal of the system should have one stakeholder.
- *Criteria.* The criteria describe an objective measurement of whether or not a particular goal has been satisfied. In many cases, the goal will serve as the criterion (e.g. the goal "to provide electronic communication between employees" is either satisfied or not). However, in some cases, the goal will be less deterministic (e.g. maximize productivity), in which case, a separate criterion needs to be established.
- *Strategy.* This denotes the set of subgoals used to satisfy a particular goal. In some cases, there may be a choice between possible strategies, in which case, a meta-strategy is used.

- *Justification.* Whenever a goal is decomposed into a set of subgoals, a justification is used to show why it is believed that these subgoals satisfy the goal.
- *Model.* Whenever one wishes to express goals, it is necessary to describe the environment in which these goals will be satisfied (to return briefly to the goal of providing electronic communications between employees, it is clear that this is expressed within the context of a company, however, the physical distribution of this company will have a direct impact upon how the goal is achieved). At the initial stages in the analysis, the model will describe the environment of the system under development; however, at later stages, the model will also encompass commitments made by previous strategies.

The above structure is repeated for each of the subgoals that arise from a goal (possibly with different stakeholders, and with a richer model). Although Figure 13.2 seems to imply a tree-like structure for goal decomposition (i.e. with only one root goal), the reality is that there will normally be more than one root goal, many of which share descendant nodes.

Traceability relationships   Traceability relationships which exist within the goals structure are as follows.

- *Between goals.* This will allow a specification user to identify why any particular goal has been suggested (i.e. which parent goals it has), and also to estimate the "knock-on" effects of changing one goal to another.
- *Stakeholder to goal.* When goals are found to conflict, tradeoffs need to be made. These tradeoffs can only meaningfully be made if the affected parties are aware of the decision. The traceability from stakeholder to goal allows the affected parties to be identified for any goals conflict situation.
- *Between models.* Tracing the relationship between models at different levels of detail permits assumptions (about the system's environment) to be identified.
- *Between justifications.* Within the context of a safety-critical system, the justifications of the goal structure provide an important function: as parts of the safety case. By tracing the justifications associated with different goals, it is possible to build the safety case. Justifications can also be used to provide the justification for particular choices of subgoals, something that is of extra value when the specification is revisited in maintaining the system.

13.4   Technical description of work undertaken

13.4.1   Background

In a retro-fit to an existing aircraft, one of the requirements was for a gust alleviation filter to be added to the flight control system (FCS). One of the inputs to this filter is the acceleration of the aircraft with the component due to gravity eliminated. The purpose of the attitude monitor system was therefore to provide as input to the filter the gravity vector components of the aircraft. Although the gust alleviation filter is not in itself safety critical its use in the FCS makes it safety critical and so the data provided has to be of sufficiently high integrity.

Two possible solutions were considered. The first solution was to use the aircraft attitude data (roll angle, pitch angle and yaw angle as shown in Figure 13.3) which was already provided by the AMSUs (air motion sensor units). However, this was not considered to be of sufficiently high integrity and it was not possible to upgrade the AMSUs to provide the data to a high integrity. The second solution was to use body rate data (rate of change of roll, pitch and yaw) which was generated to a high level of integrity by the AMSUs and from this derive the attitude data (by integrating it with respect to time[1]). The drawback to this solution was that attitude data derived in this way is liable to drift over the duration of the flight.

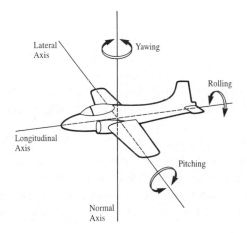

Figure 13.3 Axes and attitudes of an aircraft.

A solution was therefore proposed whereby attitude data from AMSU would be used for the gust alleviation filter, but it would be cross-monitored with another dissimilar, independent but low-integrity attitude source — the inertial navigation unit (IN). If the difference between these two sets of data exceeded a particular threshold for longer than a specified time then the high integrity body rates were to be used to derive the attitude data for a limited time period until the aircraft could be returned to straight and level flight and reversion laws could be selected (which was the condition under which the two sources were most likely to return to within the threshold).

An additional consideration in the design of the monitor was that the roll angle of the aircraft cannot be monitored at a pitch angle above 85° as AMSU data is frozen at these

---

[1]The gravity vector is determined from the aircraft bank, heading and inclination. Rates of change of bank, heading and inclination are not the same as the rates of roll, yaw and pitch. However, for the purposes of simplifying the description, the terms roll, yaw and pitch are used uniformly.

angles (bank angle is indeterminate at 90° pitch). However, at such levels of pitch the roll angle does not need to be taken into account in determining the gravity component of the aircraft acceleration anyway. The monitor was therefore designed such that monitoring of the roll angle is suspended and attitude data is generated (from the body rate data) once the pitch of the aircraft exceeds 83° even though at this pitch the roll angle is not required. This protects against a failure of the monitor occurring which would not be detected until pitch returned below 83° by which time there would not be a reliable value from which to start the attitude generator.

13.4.2   Overview of technique application

The techniques which are introduced in Section 13.3 are now used to develop the specification of the attitude monitor. The use of the techniques is as follows.

- *SSGs.* These start with a very high-level requirement (i.e. that of alleviation of gusts), and identify a composite strategy based on taking information directly from low-integrity sources when a comparison of data with another low integrity source matches; and integrating data from a high-integrity source otherwise.
- *Zables.* The Zables take an abstract view of the final level of requirements and determine moding behaviour which shows how we alternate between the two components of the SSG-identified strategy.
- *ArchSM.* ArchSM is used to represent the structure of a design. The architectural specification is based on information obtained from the SSG analysis (e.g. actual test comparison and calculation of integral) and from the Zables analysis (e.g. suggestion for main system state variables). The specification also includes timing properties.
- *Goals.* The goals provide an abstraction of the development process in terms of the goals that are established at each step, and through the justifications for decisions that are made throughout the process.

13.4.3   Safety specification graphs

In this section we conduct the requirements analysis of an aircraft function, from identification of the requirements imposed on the behaviour of the aircraft to the requirements that emerge for the avionics. The preliminary analysis is conducted informally, the formal analysis being deferred until the detailed requirements for the avionics emerge.

Aircraft analysis
The purpose of the aircraft analysis is to identify the requirements imposed on the aircraft that are of interest for this case study.

Aircraft requirement
- $R_{Aircraft}$. The flight of the aircraft must be robust to gusts of winds up to a specified strength.

Protection against gusts of wind is not safety critical. This would be reflected in the integrity level associated with $R_{Aircraft}$.

Avionics analysis
The avionics analysis aims to establish how $R_{Aircraft}$ can be realized by the avionics. Since any scheme for realizing $R_{Aircraft}$ must be accommodated within an existing avionics system, an important aspect of the analysis is to ensure that constraints imposed by the present avionics subsystems are adequately considered.

Avionics requirements
An analysis of the present avionics subsystems leads to the identification of the following two strategies.

- S_{FCS}. Provide a gust alleviation function within the FCS.
- S_{GA}. Provide an independent system with a gust alleviation function.

The first strategy, S_{FCS}, was adopted, leading to the following requirement.

- R_{GAF}. Develop a gust alleviation filter as a new component of the FCS.

The decision to provide a gust alleviation filter within the FCS associates an integrity level of 1 with R_{GAF}. In order to realize strategy R_{GAF}, the acceleration of the aircraft with the component due to gravity eliminated must be provided to the filter. When the pitch is high, the computed acceleration is sensitive to small changes in the pitch, and roll has an insignificant effect. When the pitch is low, the reverse holds (the acceleration is sensitive to roll but not pitch). Only one strategy for providing the gravity vector component was possible.

- S_{AMSU}. Compute gravity vector component using data provided by AMSU.

AMSU requirement
In order to satisfy S_{AMSU}, the following requirement emerges.

- R_{AMSU}. The AMSU must provide high integrity roll and pitch data, while the pitch value is below 83°.

Each layer of the SSG shown in Figure 13.4 records specifications as they emerge from the analysis. The root of the graph is the top-level specification ($R_{Aircraft}$); the next layer records the two alternative strategies for realizing $R_{Aircraft}$. The strategy S_{FCS} is further analyzed to identify its emergent requirements, such as R_{GAF}. The two strategies for achieving R_{GAF} are recorded, and the emergent requirement R_{AMSU} is identified (this requirement will be the primary focus for the subsequent analysis).

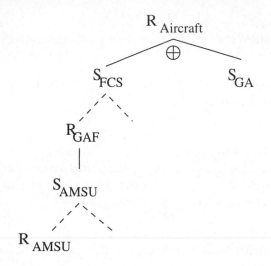

Figure 13.4 Specification graph for gust alleviation.

AMSU analysis

The subsequent analysis focuses on the role of the AMSU. Firstly, a model is provided to characterize precisely what is meant by high integrity attitude data; then the model is elaborated to analyze strategies for obtaining high-integrity data.

Definition: High-integrity data

The attitude data provided by the AMSU is of high integrity if it is within a predefined value of the actual attitude of the aircraft, at sample points.

The above can be formalized by introducing the following variables and constant:

Variables	Base	Comments
Pitch	$\mathbb{R}_+$	Aircraft's pitch.
OutputPitch	$\mathbb{R}_+$	Pitch from AMSU.
Roll	$\mathbb{R}_+$	Aircraft's roll.
OutputRoll	$\mathbb{R}_+$	Roll from AMSU.
Sample	$\mathbb{B}$	Indicates sample point.

Constant	Base	Comments
Tolerance	$\mathbb{R}_+$	Maximum tolerable error permitted for integrity level 1.

R_{AMSU}. At a sample point the output attitude data must be within the specified *Tolerance* of the actual value (unknown):

$$Sample \Rightarrow \mid OutputPitch - Pitch \mid < Tolerance \wedge$$
$$\mid OutputRoll - Roll \mid < Tolerance$$

Sources of attitude data

The AMSU has two sources of attitude data: raw attitude data and attitude data rates. This suggests two possible strategies for providing the attitude data.

- $S_{RawData}$. Use attitude data directly.
- $S_{GenerateData}$. Use attitude data rates to generate attitude data.

$S_{RawData}$ is not feasible owing to low integrity of attitude data. Although the attitude data rates are of sufficiently high integrity, $S_{GenerateData}$ is not feasible, over an entire flight, owing to drift in generated attitude data.

To overcome the deficiencies of the individual strategies, a scheme ($S_{Combine}$) that aims to exploit the strengths of both strategies is suggested. This involves cross-monitoring the AMSU data with IN data. If the difference does not exceed a predefined threshold, follow $S_{RawData}$. If the difference does exceed the threshold, follow $S_{GenerateData}$ until straight and level flight resumes.

The attitude data provided by the AMSU and the IN is described by the following state variables:

Variables	Base	Comments
AMSU_Pitch	$\mathbb{R}_+$	AMSU pitch data.
IN_Pitch	$\mathbb{R}_+$	IN pitch data.
AMSU_PitchRate	$\mathbb{R}_+$	AMSU pitch rate.
AMSU_Roll	$\mathbb{R}_+$	AMSU roll data.
IN_Roll	$\mathbb{R}_+$	IN roll data.
AMSU_RollRate	$\mathbb{R}_+$	AMSU roll rate.

To formalize $S_{Combine}$ the model must be elaborated to describe attitude data information at previous sample, and constants introduced for the monitor thresholds, errors and sample rates.

Variables	Base	Comments
PrevPitch	$\mathbb{R}_+$	Previous pitch data.
PrevRoll	$\mathbb{R}_+$	Previous roll data.
PrevOutPitch	$\mathbb{R}_+$	Previous pitch data output.
PrevOutRoll	$\mathbb{R}_+$	Previous roll data output
Roll_Thresh	$\mathbb{R}_+$	Maximum allowable difference between roll data of different sources.

Constants	Base	Comments
Pitch_Thresh	$\mathbb{R}$	Maximum allowable difference between pitch data of different sources.
RawError	$\mathbb{R}$	Error in AMSU raw data, if monitor check is passed.
ΔSample	**T**	Sampling interval.
ΔError	$\mathbb{R}$	Error growth when rate option is employed.

Assumptions

as1.   If the values for attitude data provided by the AMSU and the IN are within the specified threshold, the raw data of the AMSU is of sufficient integrity.

$$| \, AMSU\_Pitch - IN\_Pitch \, | < Pitch\_Thresh \Rightarrow | \, AMSU\_Pitch - Pitch \, | < RawError \, \wedge$$
$$| \, AMSU\_Roll - IN\_Roll \, | < Roll\_Thresh \Rightarrow | \, AMSU\_Roll - Roll \, | < RawError.$$

as2.   The growth in error (i.e. the drift in the attitude data values) by generating the data from the rates is bounded by $\Delta Error$.

$$\forall \, Error :$$
$$| \, PrevOutPitch - PrevPitch \, | < Error \Rightarrow$$
$$| \, PrevOutPitch + AMSU\_PitchRate \times \Delta Sample - Pitch \, | < Error + \Delta Error.$$

$$\forall \, Error :$$
$$| \, PrevOutRoll - PrevRoll \, | < Error \Rightarrow$$
$$| \, PrevOutRoll + AMSU\_RollRate \times \Delta Sample - Roll \, | < Error + \Delta Error.$$

The two approaches for providing attitude data can be formalized as follows:

$$RawData \equiv OutputPitch = AMSU\_Pitch \wedge OutputRoll = AMSU\_Roll.$$

$$GenerateData \equiv$$
$$OutputPitch = PrevOutPitch + AMSU\_PitchRate \times \Delta Sample \, \wedge$$
$$OutputRoll = PrevOutRoll + AMSU\_RollRate \times \Delta Sample.$$

The strategy can be characterized by modes of operation. The current mode of operation is encoded in the state variable *Mode*. This variable can take the following values: *Normal*, *Vertical*, *Latched*, *Tripped*. *Normal* corresponds to the situation where the differences in the roll and pitch values from the AMSU and IN are within the predefined thresholds and the *OutputPitch* value is below 83°. *Vertical* corresponds to the situation where the aircraft is considered to be in vertical flight (i.e. output pitch is at least 83°). *Latched* corresponds to the situation where the differences in the roll or pitch values from the AMSU and IN exceed the predefined thresholds. *Tripped* corresponds to the situation where the *Latched* mode has persisted for more that 0.5 seconds.

The relationship between the modes and the approaches for providing attitude data are stated in the following rules.

R_{Normal}. During *Normal* the raw data from the AMSU is output to the filter:

$$Mode = Normal \wedge Sample \Rightarrow RawData$$

$R_{Vertical}$. During *Vertical* either the raw data or the generated data from the AMSU is output to the filter:

$$Mode = Vertical \wedge Sample \Rightarrow RawData \vee GenerateData$$

$R_{Tripped}$. During *Tripped* the generated data from the AMSU is output to the filter:

$$Mode = Tripped \wedge Sample \Rightarrow GenerateData$$

$R_{Latched}$. During *Latched* the generated data from the AMSU is output to the filter:

$$Mode = Latched \wedge Sample \Rightarrow GenerateData$$

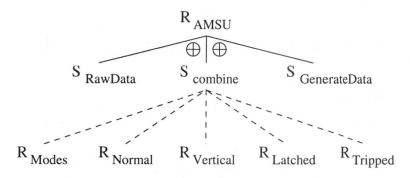

Figure 13.5 Specification graph for gust alleviation.

The root of the graph, for the AMSU (see Figure 13.5), is the specification R_{AMSU}; the next layer records the three alternative strategies for realising R_{AMSU}. The strategy $S_{Combine}$ is further analyzed to identify its emergent requirements, and the approach for obtaining attitude data within each mode (e.g. R_{Normal} specifies how the attitude data is obtained during *Normal*). The last layer of the graph is only a partial refinement of $S_{Combine}$; to complete the specification rules describing the transitional behaviour of the modes would have to be introduced.

The following section builds on the preliminary analysis of the moding behaviour, presented here by formally defining the transitional behaviour between the modes, and characterizing the actions that are to be performed within each mode. That is to say, the transitional behaviour between the modes (R_{Modes}) and the approach for obtaining the attitude data within each mode (e.g. R_{Normal} specifies how the attitude data is obtained during *Normal*).

13.4.4 Zables

This section illustrates how the Zables approach is used to identify the system modes and the activities performed in each mode.

1. Mode class table The mode class table identifies those system variables which determine the modes of the system. In this case study we are interested in the pitch angle of the aircraft, the status of the monitor threshold, the time since the monitor tripped and the status of the pilot reset button:

Condition	Type
pitch	*pitch_angle*
status	*monitor*
timesincetrip	*counter*
reset	*boolean*

This gives rise to the following Z state schema:

```
attmon
  pitch : pitch_angle
  status : monitor
  timesincetrip : counter
  reset : boolean
```

2. Mode table The mode table introduces each mode and gives its definition in terms of values of the various system conditions defined in the mode class table. In this example four modes have been identified:

Mode	System Condition	Value
normal	*pitch*	*lt_83*
	status	*within_threshold*
vertical	*pitch*	*ge_83*
tripped	*status*	*exceeds_threshold*
	timesincetrip	*< limit*
latched	*status*	*exceeds_threshold*
	timesincetrip	*≥ limit*

So for example the system is in *normal* if the pitch angle of the aircraft is less than 83° and the difference between the two sources of data is within the threshold. *normal* can now be used throughout the rest of the specification as an abbreviation for this conjunction of conditions.

Each mode is interpreted as a Z schema, for instance *normal*:

```
normal
  attmon
  
  pitch = lt_83 ∧
  status = within_threshold
```

These schemas can now be used in the rest of the Z specification.

3. Mode transition table   The mode transition table identifies the valid transitions that can occur and the events and conditions that cause them. The table is defined so that the different system variables are identified at the top of the table and each row in the table is a valid transition showing the initial and final modes. Where a system condition changes value it is represented as @*T* or @*F* in the relevant column. Where the value of a system condition is relevant (but does not change) it is represented as a *t* or *f* in the appropriate column.

Initial mode	pitch lt_83	pitch ge_83	status within	status exceeds	time < limit	time ≥ limit	reset	final mode
normal		@*T*						*vertical*
normal				@*T*				*tripped*
vertical	@*T*		*t*					*normal*
tripped	*t*		@*T*		*t*			*normal*
tripped						@*T*		*latched*
latched	*t*		*t*				@*T*	*normal*

So for example, a transition from *normal* to *tripped* occurs if the value of the system variable *status* changes to *exceeds*.

Each mode transition is translated into a Z operation schema which causes a change in the state. The change in the value of the system variable which causes the transition is treated as an input to the schema.

```
┌─ normal_to_tripped ─────────────────────────────
│ Δattmon
│ status? : monitor
├─────────────────────────────────────────────────
│ normal ∧
│ status? = exceeds_threshold ∧
│ tripped'
└─────────────────────────────────────────────────
```

4. Action table   The action tables identify the actions and the conditions under which those actions are to be carried out in terms of modes and events. Two special events, *in_mode* and *enter_mode*, are defined.

Mode/Action	Output _att	Generate _att	Store _values	Init _counter	Increment _counter
normal	*in_mode*		*in_mode*		
vertical		*in_mode*			
tripped		*in_mode*		*enter_mode*	*in_mode*
latched		*in_mode*			*in_mode*

These actions are all defined in terms of the system modes. For example, the action *Output_att* is performed continuously while in the *normal* mode but not in any other modes. The action *Init_counter* is performed once on entering the *tripped* mode. Each action (represented by one column in the table) is translated into a Z operation schema. This defines in what circumstances the action is to be performed but does not state what the action is. These operation schemas do not change the state unless the action occurs on entering a mode, for example

$$\begin{array}{l} \underline{\quad Output\_att \quad} \\ \Xi attmon \\ result! : Action \\ \hline normal \wedge \\ in\_mode = True \wedge \\ result! = act\_output\_att \end{array}$$

$$\begin{array}{l} \underline{\quad Init\_counter \quad} \\ \Delta attmon \\ result! : Action \\ \hline tripped \wedge \\ enter\_mode = True \wedge \\ result! = act\_Init\_counter \end{array}$$

13.4.5 Architectural specification method

Having analyzed the proposed attitude monitor system in terms of safety and moding behaviour, we can move closer to a final design. The architectural specification techniques introduced in Section 13.3.3 can be used to describe the functionality and timing behaviour of the chosen architecture using techniques with a formal basis, with further potential for proof.

In this section, we use the ArchSM to present the following solution to the attitude monitor problem, based on the composite strategy developed via the use of safety specification graphs in Section 13.4.3:

> Use attitude data (roll and pitch) provided directly by the AMSU for the calculation. Use roll and pitch data from an independent source (IN) to cross-monitor the first data. If the difference between these two sets of data exceeds defined thresholds, then use high-integrity body rates for a limited period of time.

Partitioning the system

The solution adopted for the attitude monitoring problem suggests a tripartite system structure. Defining this structure is a creative step between the requirements definition and a first high level design. The main system components (Figure 13.6) are

- the monitor which checks the AMSU attitude values,
- the attitude generator which is initialized when the monitor trips (roll or pitch thresholds exceeded) and generates the data from the high-integrity body rates,
- the normal generator which is the source of attitude data in the absence of a trip condition.

The monitor communicates with both the other agents. At the current level of abstraction, we assume that a signal is sent to initiate or to stop the attitude generator (as the normal generator is always running). Later in the development process, in a more detailed design, communication will be expressed in terms of the data shared by the agents. In the rest of this section, we will concentrate on recording the functionality and timing behaviour of the monitor.

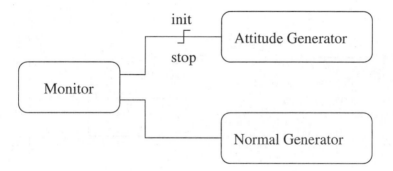

Figure 13.6 The partition of the system.

Since the monitor does most of the processing described above, it seems natural to decompose it further. It is the monitor that compares the values of the AMSU and the IN data, but it also evaluates the thresholds periodically. One possible decomposition of the monitor is therefore into

- the threshold evaluator which calculates the threshold difference between attitude data from the two sources at which the monitor will switch to high integrity body rates (this threshold varies with pitch),
- the comparator which compares values from the two sources and determines if a trip condition has occurred,
- the latch which determines whether a trip condition is transient (in which case it resets) or whether the condition lasts for a certain minimum amount of time (in which case it latches, permitting only external reset by the pilot).

The behaviour of the monitor

Figure 13.7 shows part of the simplified behaviour of the monitor. Drawing the corresponding statechart has helped us to identify which aspects of the system's behaviour are not clearly described in the documentation, and also to abstract some of the detail and to present the behaviour in a more clear way.

This problem is not particularly rich in timing constraints. However, there is one imposition that the trip condition has to be true for 0.5 seconds for the monitor to be latched. There is also a constraint that processes such as the threshold calculator agent execute periodically.

Monitor

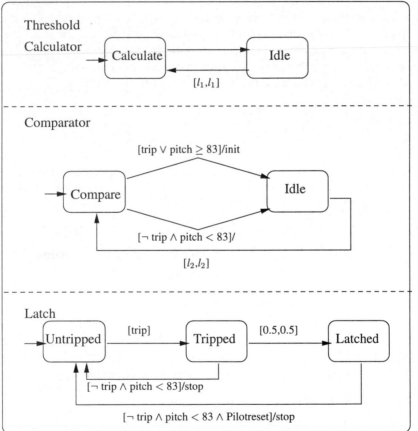

Figure 13.7 The state machine for the monitor.

The behaviour of the monitor can be defined as follows.

- The threshold calculator behaves in a periodic way calculating the two threshold values (the roll and pitch). The corresponding state machine is very simple; a transition occurs to state *Idle* when the calculation is terminated and it will restart the calculation (back to state *Calculate*) after a fixed time has elapsed.

- The comparator has a similar behaviour, establishing periodically whether a trip condition has occurred (data is invalid or the thresholds have been exceeded when comparing data from the two sources[2]) or whether the pitch angle has exceeded 83° (the plane is in vertical mode). In any of these cases an initialization signal (*init*) is sent to the attitude generator. A transition to state *Idle* occurs once the verification and comparison of values is terminated (in Figure 13.7 this transition is split into two to show the conditions under which the event is generated) . We do not show here the state machine for the attitude generator, but it will contain a transition triggered by the initialization signal (*init*).

- When a trip condition is set by the comparator (*trip*), the latch will start counting time; this is represented, in the corresponding state machine, by a transition from *Untripped* to *Tripped*. It will remain in this latter state until 0.5 seconds have elapsed with the trip condition set (in which case a transition to *Latched* will occur). If the trip condition ceases to exist (and the pitch angle does not exceed 83°) before 0.5 seconds a transition back to *Untripped* will be triggered. While in state *Latched* it can only return to *Untripped* if the trip condition disappears, the pitch angle does not exceed 83° and there is an external reset by the pilot. The interaction between the monitor and the attitude generator is not shown in Figure 13.7; once the generator has been initialized by the comparator, the latch will send a signal to stop it when it resets.

The functionality of the attitude monitor

The functionality of the threshold calculator is very simple. θ is the threshold value for the pitch (fixed at 3°), and ϕ is the threshold value for roll; its value is a function of the IN and AMSU pitch and of the roll rate. This is described in a Z schema associated with the *Calculate* state in the statechart. However, here we will show only the schema associated with the *Compare* state. Three values are output (*Init*, *Monresult*, θlim). The attitude generator is initialized (*Init* = true), as a result of this function, in the following cases:

1. either roll or pitch data are invalid;
2. pitch data from the AMSU and the IN sources differ for more than the threshold;
3. AMSU pitch exceeds 83° (*AMSU_pitch* $\geq$ 83), in which case the roll monitoring is suspended;
4. AMSU pitch does not exceed 83° (*AMSU_pitch* $<$ 83) and the roll data from the AMSU and the IN sources differ by more than the threshold.

A trip condition (*Monresult* = false) occurs if:

1. either roll or pitch data are invalid;
2. pitch data from the AMSU and the IN sources differ by more than the threshold;

---

[2]The difference between the roll values from the two sources is only checked if the pitch has not exceeded 83°.

3. the AMSU pitch does not exceed 83° and the roll data from the AMSU and the IN sources differ by more than the threshold.

The specification of the functionality does not include the definition of the validity of data (two input Boolean values *Valid_roll* and *Valid_pitch* are used); an ancillary Boolean function *threshold* (not specified here) determines whether the thresholds have been exceeded in which case it gives as result the value true.

[*Angles*]

$$
\begin{array}{l}
\hline
\text{\textit{Compare}} \\
\hline
IN\_pitch?, AMSU\_pitch? : \mathbb{R} \\
IN\_roll?, AMSU\_roll? : \mathbb{R} \\
Valid\_roll?, Valid\_pitch? : \mathbb{B} \\
\theta?, \phi? : Angles \\
Monresult!, Init!, \theta lim! : \mathbb{B} \\
\hline
\theta lim! = (AMSU\_pitch? \geq 83) \\
Init! = (\neg Valid\_roll? \vee \neg Valid\_pitch? \vee \\
\quad threshold(IN\_roll?, AMSU\_roll?, \phi?) \vee \\
\quad threshold(IN\_pitch?, AMSU\_pitch?, \theta?) \vee \\
\quad AMSU\_pitch? \geq 83) \\
Monresult! = (Valid\_roll? \wedge Valid\_pitch? \wedge \\
\quad \neg threshold(IN\_pitch?, AMSU\_pitch?, \theta?) \wedge \\
\quad (AMSU\_pitch? \geq 83 \vee \neg threshold(IN\_roll?, AMSU\_roll?, \phi?))) \\
\hline
\end{array}
$$

The previous schema represents the computation associated with the state *Compare* in the comparator state machines. Entering the state corresponds to initiating the corresponding action, and the termination of the action will coincide with the state being left. There are no timing constraints other than these computations are executed periodically.

13.4.6   Goals approach

In this section we will summarize the development of the system with respect to a goals hierarchy and relate it to decisions made in the previous sections. Note that for the sake of space we omit the details of models and stakeholders from this analysis. Figure 13.8 indicates the outline structure of the goals identified in the system. Top-level goals are denoted by rectangles, and derived goals by ellipses.

The development starts with the requirements that the aircraft is resistant to gusts of wind and that the aircraft can provide a "safe flight".

Three of the first goals of the analysis (G1, G2 and G3) are directly taken from the safety specification graph of Section 13.4.3 (these three are those corresponding to the

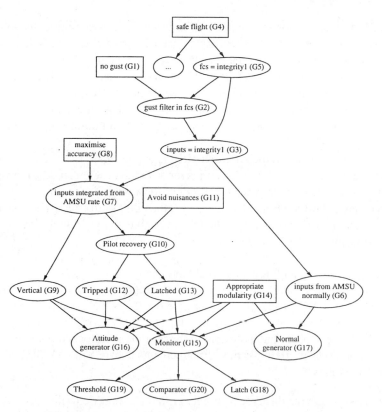

Figure 13.8 Goals structure for attitude monitor.

requirements in Figure 13.4). The two other top-level goals come from existing requirements on the aircraft.

Considering the goal of "safe slight" (G4), one criterion might be no more than one accident per 10^5 hours of operation (during normal, peacetime operations). The strategy adopted to achieve this includes the development of all flight control software to integrity level 1. The justification for this arises from commonly accepted practice in industry.

At the next level, the goal is for the flight control software to be of integrity level 1 (G5). The criterion for this is that the software (and its development processes) meets the standards established for integrity level 1. The strategy includes ensuring that the inputs to the FCS are also generated by integrity Level 1 software.

Ensuring integrity level 1 inputs can, initially, be divided into two cases:

- taking inputs from the AMSU when the value of the AMSU is close to that of the IN and when the pitch is less than 83° (G6), this corresponds with the mode *normal*;
- taking inputs from the integral of the pitch rate whenever the pitch is greater than or equal to 83° and after the AMSU has differed from the IN (even if the AMSU and IN subsequently agree) (G7).

Informally, the justification for the first case is based on the assumption that low integrity components which achieve the same purpose can be treated as being of a higher integrity whenever they agree, so long as they can be seen to be independent.

Taking inputs from the integral of the pitch rate is acceptable for a short duration[3] since the pitch rate input comes from an integrity level 1 source. However, after a long period, the drift of the pitch value becomes unacceptably high. Thus the justification must show that the generation of pitch data only takes place for a short duration.

- The period for which the aircraft's pitch is greater than or equal to 83° cannot be sustained for long periods (this corresponds to the goal G9 and the mode *vertical*), since this will eventually lead to a stall of the aircraft.
- Whenever the AMSU and IN "disagree", the pilot is informed, and can take recovery action. It is assumed that the pilot will take recovery action before the pitch drift becomes excessive (G10).

In the second case, an additional external goal comes into play, that of making the aircraft easy to operate through the avoidance of unnecessary alarms (G11). Under certain circumstances, the IN and AMSU can disagree briefly, before returning to approximate values. Under such circumstances, performing a recovery action (which involves bringing the aircraft to level flight and resetting the attitude monitor) constitutes a nuisance, which contradicts G11. To avoid this, disagreements between the AMSU and IN are divided into two classes.

- In those where the disagreement only lasts for a short time (in this case, the mode is returned to normal), generated data is only used as long as the disagreement lasts (this is termed "tripped" and relates to G12).
- In those where the disagreement lasts for greater than some fixed threshold, the pilot is warned as before, and the justification is as before (this is "latched" mode, G13).

Each of the goals which represents a mode (i.e. G6, G9, G12, and G13) need to be encapsulated within functional units which correspond to the aircraft's architecture. In this case, the justification must show that each of the mode goals can be satisfied by the composition of units. At this stage, a new top-level goal, G14 (related to a higher-level goal, namely ensuring that the system is designed using good engineering practice), is also introduced dealing with the need to ensure appropriate modularity. G6, G9, G12, G13 and G14 are satisfied by the introduction of three new subgoals corresponding to top-level architectural components:

- the monitor (G15), which detects which mode the system is in,
- the attitude generator (G16), which provides attitude data generated from body rate data,
- normal generator (G17), which provides data directly from the AMSU.

---

[3]We do not quantify "short" here. However, we do note that it is of the order of minutes.

In justifying these components against their parent goals, we note that the combination of monitor and attitude generator meet the requirements of G9, G12 and G13, and that the monitor and normal generator meet the requirements of G6. With respect to G14, we note that unnecessary duplication of functionality has been avoided, and that a high degree of functional cohesion has been achieved within units.

In decomposing the monitor into subcomponents (G18, G19 and G20), the justification which is used is similar (i.e. that the monitor is refined by the composition of G18, G19 and G20, and that these subcomponents provide an "appropriate" level of decomposition).

13.5   Evaluation

Ideally, we would like to be able to answer the five questions posed by BAe, and set out in Section 13.2. This is not entirely possible as it is difficult, for example, to determine what is the minimum information required. However, the case study has thrown some light on the questions. We address the last three first.

Starting with question 3, we have shown how the requirements and high level design could (not should) be expressed. The formalisms used are expressive, but not familiar to systems engineers. The use of statecharts and tabular specifications (Zables) indicates ways in which the specifications can be made more accessible.

The example shows the traceability needed as a basis for demonstrating design conformance. In principle, formal analysis of the specifications should be carried out (e.g. to conform to IDS 00-55 (Ministry of Defence, 1991a,b). We have not presented full formal analyses and it is a moot point whether or not they would be cost effective (see also Barroca and McDermid (1992)).

The examples show several ways of expressing the requirements and design information. However, as this was a retrospective analysis, we could shed no light on "capturing" requirements. (Note we would prefer to avoid the term "capture" as requirements are negotiated, dependent on what can be designed and realized, not found and brought into captivity.)

This brings us to the issue of necessity and sufficiency. This question can only be answered in context — where the context is defined by the set of stakeholders. Arguably the approaches are necessary and sufficient for safety — but they do not address usability, maintainability, etc. In general, there is an overlap between the needs of stakeholders, but never any guarantee that a new stakeholder will not introduce a new requirement category, e.g. numerical accuracy. Thus we can never say that an approach, or set thereof, is necessary and sufficient.

13.6   Conclusions

There is much more to be done, and space does not permit a full discussion, but there are a few important trends:

- the traceability afforded by the SSG/Goal structures is clearly valuable, and will form a basis of our approach;
- representational issues are crucial, and work needs to go into formalisms such as the Zables, statecharts etc. to produce usable specification languages;
- more work is needed on representing high-level designs, especially ensuring that they reflect the underlying computational model;
- work is needed on specification analysis, both in providing mechanisms, and in determining what is the right balance between inspection, mechanizable (decidable) checks and full formal proof.

We hope to develop an effective set of techniques for developing dependable computing systems building on the strengths of the above techniques and the experience gained in applying them.

Acknowledgement

The authors gratefully acknowledge the assistance of British Aerospace Defence (Military Aircraft), System Engineering Department, in providing the material given in this chapter.

Chapter 14

Developing a Security-critical System using Formal and Conventional Methods

John S. Fitzgerald, Peter Gorm Larsen,
Tom Brookes and Michael Green

14.1   Introduction

This chapter describes an experiment conducted by a UK company to investigate the costs and benefits to be derived from the modest application of formal methods in the development of a security-critical system component.

Although the present volume bears witness to the increasing number of commercial applications of formal methods, the evidence available to individual companies researching the application of this new technology is often felt to be weak. To receive serious consideration, studies should be of realistic scale and in areas relevant to a company's commercial domain. Many firms have invested heavily in the certification of their processes to standards such as the ISO9000 series, so studies should take account of how formal methods will fit into a real development process using prescribed procedures and tools. Perhaps above all, such studies ought to involve some measure of cost and effectiveness of applying the technology.

For British Aerospace (Systems and Equipment) Ltd. (BASE), the European Systems and Software Initiative (ESSI) has provided the opportunity to conduct an experiment on the development of a realistic system. Two teams of engineers, chosen for their similar levels of experience, are separately developing software prototypes of a **trusted gateway**, a communications device which ensures that messages having a high security classification are not routed to a low-security processing system. One team uses a standard development methodology; the other used the same methodology, supplemented by formal specification in VDM-SL (International Standards Organization, 1993). As the development proceeds, researchers monitor progress and cost, as well as examining the quality of the designs and programs built.

This chapter reports on the first, system design, phase of the experiment. We begin by discussing the background to the experiment, describing the main phases in the development process and the format of the experiment itself (Section 14.2). The techniques and tools used are introduced in Section 14.3. The specification developed by the engineer in the system design phase is then presented in some detail (Section 14.4), along with an account of how the tool support for formal specification was used. Section 14.5 reviews the technology transfer activities associated with the project. In Section 14.6, we present some of the more significant findings from the requirements analysis and system design activities. The practical consequences of these findings form the subject of the concluding section.

Readers interested primarily in the business and process implications of the study are directed to Sections 14.2, 14.6.8 and 14.7. Section 14.4 is the most technical, and may be omitted by readers unconcerned with the details of the specifications produced.

14.2 Background to the project

14.2.1 Motivating forces

The trusted gateway project came into being as a result of a combination of factors: the development of the system to a high assurance level was already part of a BASE process improvement plan; funding (in this case external) was available for comparative studies in the application of formal methods in the context of process improvement; a pilot study of the formal aspects of the trusted gateway showed that it formed a tractable but realistic case study in a commercial domain of relevance to the company.

BASE has a policy of continuous process improvement in both the system and software design areas, the primary aims of which are to reduce development times and costs, to improve the quality of the product and to reduce the risk involved in new development. To this end, a defined development methodology and CASE tools to support it are being introduced.

One important area of risk is external assessment. BASE is a supplier of secure message handling systems to the military market. Such systems have to be evaluated by an independent third party to ensure that they contain no security loopholes. Re-engineering and re-submission for assessment may be needed to meet the recommendations of an unsuccessful evaluation, so any step which can be taken to reduce that risk is beneficial to the development process.

BASE is currently developing a trusted gateway for use in a product. The possible application of formal specification techniques to the gateway's development was discussed with researchers in the University of Newcastle upon Tyne, and was thought to be suitable for a case study. In parallel with this, the European Systems and Software Initiative (ESSI) was set to fund investigations into techniques which could improve the systems and software development process. A successful proposal was made under ESSI, allowing the trusted gateway to be used as the basis of an experimental comparison between two developments, each following the same process but for the addition of formal specification in one development. The comparison of the two design methodologies should yield insights into the cost and benefits of applying formal techniques to the design of small security-critical systems.

14.2.2   Levels of assurance for security-critical systems

Security-critical systems are developed to meet levels of assurance described in the Information Technology Security Evaluation Criteria (European Community, 1991), which define the methodologies and development processes which must be employed to achieve each level. The rating for a given system is divided into two: a **functionality class** which describes the security features and functions used by the system and the **assurance level** which describes how well they have been implemented. It is the assurance level which is determined by the development process employed.

Assurance levels range from E1 to E6. Some of the information required at each level is shown in Table 14.1. As the assurance level increases, the demands on the developer become more stringent and the amount of information which has to be supplied increases.

Table 14.1 Requirements for assurance levels

Assurance level	E1	E2	E3	E4	E5	E6
Information security target	X	X	X	X	X	X
Formal security policy				X	X	X
Function description (informal)	X	X	X	X	X	X
Function description (semiformal)				X	X	
Function description (formal)						X
Architectural design (informal)	X	X	X			
Architectural design (semiformal)				X	X	
Architectural design (formal)						X
		State		Describe		Explain
			Level of rigour			

At lower assurance levels it is sufficient to provide a statement of the target, function description or design (e.g. "access control is provided"). At intermediate levels description is required (e.g. "access control is provided by a password mechanism"). At the highest levels of assurance an explanation is required (e.g. a detailed description of the password mechanism and a justification for the assertion that it controls access). As the level of assurance increases, so does the degree of formality expected in descriptions and explanations.

The development of certain safety-critical systems for military applications also requires the use of a methodology in which formal methods are mandated. In both areas, standards require that the tools used in the design process be certified to the highest levels of assurance. The lack of such tools greatly increases the difficulty of producing security-critical systems of any size or complexity.

The trusted gateway experiment aims to simulate the development of a security-critical system to level E5.

14.2.3   The development process

The development process used in this experiment is based on a modified version of the traditional "V" life cycle model (Royce, 1970), with requirements being defined, designed to and verified at each level of the design decomposition. A characteristic of the model is that each main development step (e.g. production of a software module design) is accompanied by the development of a test plan against which the relevant product (e.g. the software module) will be tested.

For this project, the process can be divided into three main phases: system design, software design, and implementation. The end of each phase is marked by a review of its products, including an inspection of designs and documentation conducted by senior engineers and quality assurance experts.

The system design phase.   The engineers performing this task are systems rather than software or hardware specialists, and the model constructed is essentially independent of the implementation medium. The phase commences upon receipt of a **requirements document** from the customer. This contains a variety of individual requirements in plain language which are often incomplete, ambiguous and contradictory. A major part of this phase is spent in negotiation with the customer to clarify the requirements and arrive at a specification for a system which is both implementable and satisfies the customer's requirement. Queries raised against requirements are logged and the clarification received from the customer is added to the requirement. In this manner the evolution of the requirement from its initial statement to the final version can be traced (see Section 14.3.1). The number of queries, their type and complexity can be used as an indication of the extent to which the systems engineer has been able to clarify the requirement (see Section 14.6.4).

This analysis yields a less ambiguous and more complete set of requirements clauses, which are grouped into functional categories. For each clause, a test is described which will later be used to demonstrate compliance against the customer requirement.

Following the Yourdon method of analysis and design, a logical system model defining the data and functions is then prepared using CASE tools (Section 14.3.1). Links are recorded between the functions defined in the model and the requirements they purport to satisfy, thereby establishing traceability from the original requirements to design.

The software design phase.   This task is performed by engineers skilled in the implementation medium (in this case, software). An implementation model is derived from the logical model by adding detail on how implementation is to be carried out and how the required functions are to be partitioned between the processors in the system. Tests for each of the identified subprocesses are prepared. The implementation model and test plan are then reviewed. Specifications for the software modules and the associated tests are prepared, reviewed and any required changes incorporated. The major outputs from this phase are the software design specification, the software module specifications, the software test specification and the software module test specifications.

Implementation phase. The modules are coded in the target language and tested on the intended processor. The system is then integrated, all modules being incorporated and tested together. Finally, the system tests defined in the design phase are run to determine whether the system satisfies the customer's original requirement. The outputs from this phase are the software code and test results documentation.

14.2.4 The trusted gateway experiment

In the experiment, two teams develop trusted gateways to the level of software prototype, following the same development process from the same initial customer specification. One team uses the standard design methodology (based on Yourdon with the Ward and Mellor (1985) notation) supported by the Teamwork and RTM CASE tools. The other team uses the same techniques and tools, but additionally uses the VDM-SL formal specification language to describe at least the security enforcing functions in the system. The use of VDM-SL is supported by the IFAD VDM-SL Toolbox. A central authority plays the role of customer and records, independently for each team, the questions and answers against the requirements.

The central authority also tracks problems and progress on the project. At the conclusion of each design stage, a comparative review takes place, but no information from the review is passed back to the corresponding teams. The differences identified between the paths are recorded in the experiment log.

At the end of the system design phase, a substantial change in the customer requirement, unanticipated by the design teams, is introduced. This serves as a way of comparing the ease of change of the designs with and without formal specifications.

The members of the teams have similar backgrounds and skill levels. However, it is recognized that differences in working approach may contribute to differences in the pattern of progress made by the two teams. The results presented here should therefore be treated with some caution, but it is believed that major trends will be identified by this procedure.

14.3 Techniques used

14.3.1 Requirements tracing and system description

The initial phase in the project involves capturing and analyzing customer requirements supported by the Requirements and Traceability Maintenance (RTM) toolkit. Starting from the customer requirements document, the requirements clauses are engineered, either by focusing two clauses into one when they have the same meaning, or by splitting one requirement into several where one customer requirement actually contains several parts. The aim of this process is to derive a set of requirements of uniform complexity which can form the basis of subsequent development.

The design itself is developed using the Teamwork CASE tool, which supports the Yourdon top-down functional decomposition approach with extensions to cover the timing and process control aspects of a system. System models are represented by data flow diagrams such as that given in Figure 14.2: the particular processes shown there (as circles) are discussed in Section 14.4.2.

The data flowing between processes (shown as arrows) are defined in a data dictionary associated with the Teamwork model. The data definitions are given as English text in the conventional development path, and as VDM-SL type specifications with explanatory English text in the formal development path. Teamwork supports hierarchical decomposition of processes into simpler processes. At the lowest level of decomposition, a process is defined by a process specification (or P-spec). In the conventional development path, P-specs were written in a mixture of English text, pseudocode and mathematical equations. In the path using VDM-SL, the P-specs hold VDM specifications for those processes which have been formally specified, again with supporting English text.

The evolution of customer requirements through the requirements engineering and design stages is recorded using RTM. Each modification of a requirement is recorded, as are any queries and customer responses related to the requirement. This traceability provides a basis for justification of the final, engineered, requirements. Each process and data definition in the Teamwork database is linked to requirements in the RTM database. Automated checking ensures that every customer requirement is related to some element of the design and that no unjustified processes are introduced.

In parallel with the development of the Teamwork model, the system test specification is produced, again using RTM to record the test requirement derived from each customer requirement. These are in turn linked to the test results as they become available. In later development stages, RTM continues to be used to maintain traceability down to individual code modules and final object code.

14.3.2   Formal specification

For the trusted gateway experiment, certain factors were felt to be important in the choice of specification language: the language should be reasonably accessible to computer-literate engineers; it should be well established with extensive support in the wider engineering community; and tool support must be available.

The Vienna Development Method (VDM) was chosen for the project. Its specification language (VDM-SL) is currently being standardized under the auspices of the International Standards Organization (ISO) and the British Standards Institution (International Standards Organization, 1993; Plat and Larsen, 1992). The specification language is model oriented: a specification consists of a collection of type definitions modelling the system state at the chosen level of abstraction. Computations are specified as operations on this model. Operations may modify the state as well as computing output values from inputs.

VDM enjoys a substantial measure of support and large user community. The VDM bibliography (Larsen, 1994) contains more than 500 references, including tutorial texts such as Jones (1990), Andrews and Ince (1991) and Latham *et al.* (1990), the language reference manual Dawes (1991) and the guide to proofs in VDM (Bicarregui *et al.*, 1994). In addition, users of VDM have their own electronic mailing list (Fitzgerald, 1994).

A number of tools have been developed to support VDM-SL, such as those discussed in Bloomfield *et al.* (1989), Jones *et al.* (1991) and Elmstrøm *et al.* (1994). For the trusted gateway project, the IFAD VDM-SL Toolbox was chosen, primarily because it enables interpretation of an executable subset of VDM-SL (Larsen and Lassen, 1991), making it possible to validate specifications by systematic testing using test suites. This kind of validation does not provide the degree of certainty about the correctness of the specification which a formal proof would supply; but it is an easy way to increase confidence in the correctness of a specification. The Toolbox runs with GNU Emacs on Sun Microsystems Unix hardware, all of which was already available at BASE.

14.4 Specifying the trusted gateway

At the time of writing, the results from the system design phase have been analyzed. This section presents the bulk of the system model produced as a result of this first phase. First the functionality of a trusted gateway is explained. We then present the first-level Teamwork model and the corresponding VDM-SL specification contained in the Teamwork P-specs. We conclude the section by illustrating how tool support was used in the production of the formal specification.

14.4.1 Trusted gateways

A major requirement of a secure system is the prevention of accidental disclosure of classified or sensitive information to third parties. When two systems are connected, the information flow between them must be controlled and information in certain categories prevented from being transferred. A trusted gateway is a device designed to perform this task, as illustrated in Figure 14.1.

The trusted gateway developed in this project works on streams of messages. The input is a stream of characters, from which valid messages must be extracted. It reads characters from the input port and determines whether they form a valid message. If they do not they are sent to an error output port. If they do form a message, they are read into memory and analyzed for the presence of character strings from two lists (called **categories**) stored in the gateway: one of strings indicating high security classification for the message, and one of strings indicating low security. If only low-classification strings are present, the message is output through one output port. Otherwise, the message is output to through another output port (connected to a highly trusted system).

The rough description given above is expanded upon in the customer requirements document. However, even there, a number of issues are unclear: restrictions on what strings can appear in the two categories, for example. Furthermore, exception conditions

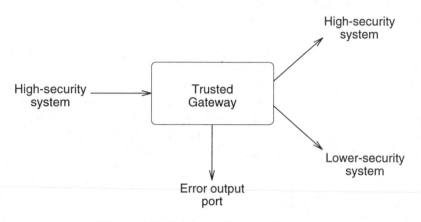

Figure 14.1 Function of a trusted gateway.

need to be defined for this device. For example, what is to be done if the message cannot be classified, or the message is longer than a predefined number of characters? These are typical of the issues raised in the the systems design phase. In our experimental development of the trusted gateway, it appears that the use of a formal specification language to represent such concepts as message validity allows more of these questions to be precisely answered at this early stage than is otherwise the case.

14.4.2   Teamwork diagrams and P-specs

Teamwork provides a diagrammatic notation for the functional decomposition of the system, which the engineer used as a basis for deciding what parts of the system to specify formally. A simplified form of the first level of decomposition of the system, as produced by the systems engineer in VDM-SL design path, is shown in Figure 14.2.

The system design in Figure 14.2, has two main functions, Segregate_Message and Classify_Message, shown as processes (circles) in the Teamwork model. These two processes communicate via an information store, called Message_Data, and read system configuration information from the System_Data store. The Segregate_Message process analyzes the input. If a valid message is found, it is placed in the Message_Data data store as ValidMessage. Input which does not form part of a valid message is sent to an output handler output_C via the data store. The Classify_Message operation reads the ValidMessage and determines its security classification. The message is written to out_A or out_B accordingly.

The additional processes Purge, Initialise_System_data, output_A, output_B and output_C enable the flow control to be modelled. For clarity, flow control is not shown

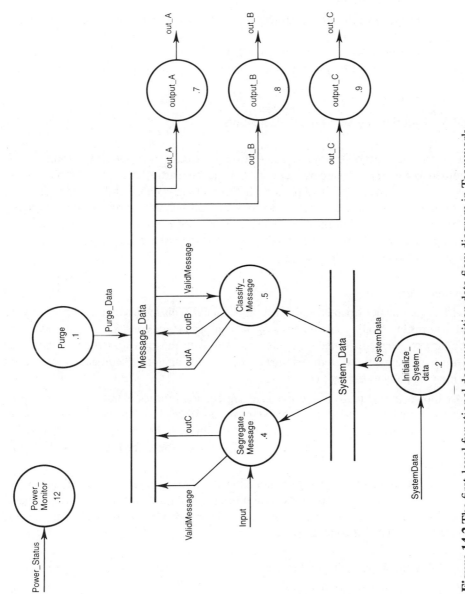

Figure 14.2 The first-level functional decomposition data flow diagram in Teamwork.

here, although this is to be found in the Teamwork diagrams produced by the engineer. By the end of the system design phase, all of the processes except Power_Monitor were given a formal specification.

The other type of information stored in the Teamwork model is the data dictionary, which contains the definitions of all of the data types used, such as Message_Data and its constituent parts. Because of restrictions in the tool, the VDM-SL data type definitions in the formal methods design path were supplied as comments in the Teamwork model.

14.4.3   Building the VDM-SL Specification

The VDM specification for the trusted gateway was built using the IFAD Toolbox, and recorded as part of the design by including the relevant parts of the specification in the P-spec for each formally specified process. In this section, we present the specifications of the two main processes: Segregate_Message and Classify_Message. We do not present the full specifications, but show enough to illustrate their main characteristics. Readers wishing for an introduction to the details of the VDM-SL notation, are referred to any of the texts listed in Section 14.3.2.

Message segregation

VDM-SL is a model-oriented specification language. This means that a system is specified in terms of a model constructed using data types and type constructors supplied in the specification language. Since the trusted gateway deals mostly with strings of characters forming messages, the systems engineer modelled the input as a sequence of characters (written formally as the type char*).

As shown in Figure 14.2, the message segregation process extracts valid messages from the input buffer, so that they can be passed on to the classification process. Characters from the input which do not form part of a valid message are output through port C. The valid message will be the subject of the classification described in the Classify_Message process.

Before fully specifying message segregation, the systems engineer realized that he had to define precisely what constitutes a valid message. After clarifying the requirements relating to this, he specified the Boolean function *IsAValidMessage0*, which returns true if a message satisfies the validity test:

$$IsAValidMessage0 : \text{char}^* \times \text{char}^* \times \text{char}^* \to \mathbb{B}$$

$$IsAValidMessage0\,(mes, somf, eomf) \triangleq$$
$$\exists s : \text{char}^* \cdot$$
$$mes = somf \frown s \frown eomf \land$$
$$\text{len}\,mes \leq max\text{-}msg\text{-}length \land$$
$$\neg\,occurrence\,(somf, s) \land$$
$$\neg\,occurrence\,(eomf, s)$$

This says that a message *mes* is valid if it starts with the start of message string (*somf*[1]) and ends with the end of message string (*eomf*); it must be smaller than the maximum message length (a constant for the present example set to 10 000 characters) and neither *somf* nor *eomf* must occur in the central part of the message.

The *IsAValidMessage*() function illustrates an interesting tension between tool support and specification style. It simply states that there exists some string *s* which is a valid body of the message. The existential quantification is made over the whole (infinite) type of character strings. Such general quantifications are not executable by the interpreter in the IFAD VDM-SL Toolbox. Therefore it has been necessary to write an additional, more direct, definition of this function to permit testing. However, this is not complicated because one just needs to split the message into its three components and then check the required properties separately:

$$IsAValidMessage : \mathsf{char}^* \times \mathsf{char}^* \times \mathsf{char}^* \to \mathbb{B}$$

$IsAValidMessage\,(mes, somf, eomf)\;\triangleq$
    $\mathsf{len}\ mes \leq max\text{-}msg\text{-}length \wedge$
    $\mathsf{len}\ mes \geq (\mathsf{len}\ somf + \mathsf{len}\ eomf) \wedge$
    $mes(1, \ldots, \mathsf{len}\ somf) = somf \wedge$
    $mes((\mathsf{len}\ mes - \mathsf{len}\ eomf + 1), \ldots, \mathsf{len}\ mes) = eomf \wedge$
    $\mathsf{let}\ s = mes(\mathsf{len}\ somf + 1, \ldots, (\mathsf{len}\ mes - \mathsf{len}\ eomf))\ \mathsf{in}$
    $\neg occurrence\,(somf, s) \wedge$
    $\neg occurrence\,(eomf, s)$

The auxiliary function *occurrence* is very easy to define:

$$occurrence : \mathsf{char}^* \times \mathsf{char}^* \to \mathbb{B}$$

$occurrence\,(substring, string)\;\triangleq$
    $\exists i, j \in \mathsf{inds}\ string \cdot string\,(i, \ldots, j) = substring$

This truth-valued function yields true if *substring* occurs anywhere in *string*. Note that the quantification is over a finite set (the indices of the string), so this function is easily interpreted in the Toolbox.

Now we return to the model of the trusted gateway's state, so far as the Segregate_Message process is concerned. The data flow diagram and requirements document suggested that the following elements are required in a model: the input buffer; the start and end of message functions; the valid message (if one is found); an output port for input characters not forming part of any valid message. Formally, the engineer wrote[2]

---

[1] *somf* stands for "start of message function", the technical term used to describe the distinguished string which indicates the beginning of a message. Likewise, *eomf* is the "end of message function".

[2] We only show that part of the model relevant to the following discussion.

```
state Gateway of
    buffer          : char*
    somf            : char*
    eomf            : char*
    ValidMessage : char*
    outC            : char*
                    . . .
```

inv $mk\text{-}Gateway(\text{-}, somf, eomf, ValidMessage, \ldots) \triangleq$
    $\text{len } somf \geq min\text{-}somf \wedge \text{len } somf \leq max\text{-}somf \wedge$
    $\text{len } eomf \geq min\text{-}eomf \wedge \text{len } eomf \leq max\text{-}eomf \wedge$
    $\text{len } ValidMessage \leq max\text{-}msg\text{-}length \wedge \ldots$

end

The invariant asserts that the length of the start and end of message strings must be in a certain range, and that the length of *ValidMessage* must not exceed the maximum length of messages as specified in the requirements specification (10 000 characters).

Using these state components and the auxiliary definitions above, the systems engineer specified an operation which produced a valid message stored in the state component *ValidMessage*. Although an implicit version of the operation could be given, the following definition was used because of its executability in the IFAD VDM-SL Toolbox interpreter:

$Segregate\text{-}Message : () \overset{o}{\to} \mathbb{B}$

$Segregate\text{-}Message () \triangleq$
    if $\exists i, j \in \text{inds } buffer \cdot IsAValidMessage(buffer(i, \ldots, j), somf, eomf)$
    then let $s\text{-}s = \{i \mid i \in \text{inds } buffer \cdot \exists j \in \text{inds } buffer \cdot$
                    $IsAValidMessage(buffer(i, \ldots, j), somf, eomf)\}$ in
        let $e\text{-}s = \{j \mid j \in \text{inds } buffer \cdot$
                    $IsAValidMessage(buffer(least(s\text{-}s), \ldots, j), somf, eomf)\}$ in
        $(outC := outC \frown buffer(1, \ldots, least(s\text{-}s) - 1);$
        $ValidMessage := buffer(least(s\text{-}s), \ldots, least(e\text{-}s));$
        $buffer := buffer(least(e\text{-}s) + 1, \ldots, \text{len } buffer);$
        return true)
    else $(outC := outC \frown buffer;$
        $buffer := \text{" "};$
        return false)

Superficially this looks complex, but it is actually straightforward and is, of course, accompanied by a commentary in the P-spec. If a valid message is present, the value *s-s* is the set of indices marking the start of a valid message in the input buffer; the value *e-s* is the set of indices marking the ends of valid messages. The first valid message is between the earliest start and end. This is put into *ValidMessage*, and everything before it discarded by appending to *outC*. The buffer is updated accordingly and the operation returns the value true. If no valid messages are present, the whole buffer is discarded and the operation returns false. The auxiliary function *least* simply yields the least value of a non-empty set of natural numbers.

Classification analysis

The Classify_Message process takes the valid message in state variable *ValidMessage* and analyzes it for the presence of strings indicating its level of security. It outputs the contents of *Valid_Message* to the relevant port. The parts of the state which are used for this classification process are as follows:

state *Gateway* of

$$\cdots$$

$\quad$ *ValidMessage* : char*
$\quad$ *catA* $\quad\quad$: char*-set
$\quad$ *catB* $\quad\quad$: char*-set
$\quad$ *outA* $\quad\quad$: char*
$\quad$ *outB* $\quad\quad$: char*

inv *mk-Gateway*(..., *ValidMessage*, *catA*, *catB*, ...) $\triangleq$
$\quad$ ... $\wedge$
$\quad$ card *catA* $\geq$ *min-no-catA* $\wedge$ card *catA* $\leq$ *max-no-catA* $\wedge$
$\quad$ card *catB* $\leq$ *max-no-catB* $\wedge$
$\quad$ *catA* $\cap$ *catB* = { } $\wedge$
$\quad$ *somf* $\notin$ *catA* $\cup$ *catB* $\wedge$ *eomf* $\notin$ *catA* $\cup$ *catB* $\wedge$
$\quad$ $\forall$ *string* $\in$ *catA* $\cup$ *catB* $\cdot$
$\quad\quad\quad$ len *string* $\geq$ *min-len-class* $\wedge$ len *string* $\leq$ *max-len-class*

$\quad$ end

The component *ValidMessage* holds a valid message extracted from the input buffer; *catA* is the set of low-security classification strings; *catB* is the set of high-security classification strings; *outA* is the low-security output; *outB* is the high-security output.

The invariant records requirements that the number of entries in the two categories of classification strings must not exceed certain limits, and that there there must be some minimal number of low-classification strings. In addition it is required that the two categories must not overlap and neither *somf* nor *eomf* may be used as classification strings. Finally, each string in the two categories must have some minimum and some maximum length.

With these state components, the message classification operation is defined as

$\quad$ *Classify-Message* : () $\overset{o}{\to}$ ()

$\quad$ *Classify-Message* () $\triangleq$
$\quad\quad$ if $\exists$ *classA* $\in$ *catA* $\cdot$ *occurrence* (*classA*, *ValidMessage*)
$\quad\quad$ then if *freeB* (*catA*, *catB*, *ValidMessage*)
$\quad\quad\quad\quad$ then *outB* := *outB* $\frown$ *ValidMessage*
$\quad\quad\quad\quad$ else *outA* := *outA* $\frown$ *ValidMessage*
$\quad\quad$ else *outB* := *outB* $\frown$ *ValidMessage*

If no low-classification string is found, the contents of *ValidMessage* are appended to the high-classification output port, even if no high-classification strings are present. If a low-classification string is found a further check is necessary to determine any "free" high-classification strings. A free high-classification string is one which does not occur in *ValidMessage* as a substring of a a low-classification string. This is checked by the *freeB* auxiliary function, whose simple definition is omitted here. The *freeB* check arose because the systems engineer queried the possibility that some strings in the classification categories may contain substrings drawn from the other category, e.g. "secret" and "not-secret-at-all". The query was raised by the systems engineer while considering the definition of the state invariant. Here, as in a number of other cases, the engineer using VDM-SL raised issues which have not been addressed at all in the system design produced in the conventional path.

14.4.4   Using the Toolbox to construct the VDM specification

The VDM-SL specifications used in the P-specs of the Teamwork model can be extracted, via an automatic script, and compiled into a single VDM specification. This specification can then be loaded into the IFAD VDM-SL Toolbox. The data dictionary entries were written so that the data type information could be assembled into a VDM-SL state definition enabling the process specifications to be written as a set of operations on this state.

The IFAD Toolbox supports specifications written within LaTeX documents, allowing syntax, type-checking and execution of specifications written in the (ASCII) interchange syntax defined in the language standard (International Standards Organization, 1993). This encourages the interleaving of specification and commentary. In the rest of this section, we present examples of P-specs as they are stored in the Teamwork model. First, the P-spec of **Classify_Message** is

```
\subsection{Classify Message}

Locate the classification string(s) within the message and
load the message into the relevant output area.

{\bf Note} The implementation MUST output a control signal to
notify the scheduler which output has data for outputting.

\begin{vdm_al}

        Classify_Message: () ==> ()

        Classify_Message()==
        if exists classA in set catA &
                occurrence(classA,ValidMessage)
        then
```

```
                if freeB(catA,catB,ValidMessage)
                then
                        (outB := outB^ValidMessage)
                else
                        (outA := outA^ValidMessage)
        else
                (outB := outB^ValidMessage);
```

\end{vdm_al}

In order to test the operations specifying the central functionality of the system, several auxiliary operators were built to load data into the state and to export data from the state. These additional operators corresponded to the other processes on the Teamwork diagram. A single operation called Test_All calls these in order, acting as a test rig. The Teamwork note covering the test operation is given below:

```
\subsection{The Test\_All operation}

This operation is used to test all of the operations of the
system in turn.  It follows a logical pattern where the system
is purged, initialised, then the message is read, the first
valid message (if any) is extracted, classified and output
and any non-message data is output.

{\bf Note} In the event of a message being detected, one of the
outputs $outA$ or $outB$ will contain a message, the other will
be empty.  If no message is found, both $outA$ and $outB$ will
be empty. $outC$ will contain all non-message data. $buffer$
should be empty at the end of all executions of $Test\_All$.

\begin{vdm_al}

        Test_All : seq of char * seq of char * seq of char
                * set of (seq of char) * set of (seq of char)
                ==> ( seq of char * seq of char * seq of char *
                    seq of char * seq of char )

        Test_All(message,Start,Stop,classA,classB)==
                (
                outA := "";
                outB := "";
                outC := "";
                Purge();
                Initialise_System_Data(Start,Stop,classA,classB);
                buffer := message;
                while Segregate_Message() do
                        (
```

```
                Classify_Message();
                Purge()
                );
        return(mk_(buffer,ValidMessage,outA,outB,outC))
        )
```

```
\end{vdm_al}
```

This operation can be used to build up an automatic test script using single calls such as

```
Test_All("fdgstrlowstpldjfg",
        "str","stp",
        {"low","nothigh","aab"},
        {"high","notlow","abb"})
```

which return values such as:

```
mk_( [   ],
     [   ],
     "strlowstp",
     [   ],
     "fdgldjfg" )
```

In this example, `Test_All` is given a message string containing a low classification message with junk data at the start and end of the buffer. The expected, and actual, result is that the input buffer is emptied, the internal data store is emptied (purged), the message appears on the low classification output, no message appears on the high classification output, and the junk data appears on the third output port.

Test scripts can be run in batch mode, along with the Toolbox's coverage monitoring software, which indicates what functions have been called, how many times they have been tested, and whether or not all paths through a function have been tested.

14.5 Technology transfer

14.5.1 Courses

A one-week week course on the use of formal methods, VDM-SL and the IFAD-VDM Toolbox was provided to the engineers, managers and quality assurance staff involved in the formal methods path. Other engineers within BASE were also trained so as to give the opportunity for the engineer to discuss problems on site. The course was felt to be of the correct length, but was very intensive. A reason cited by the engineers for the rapidity with which they came to understand the formalism was the availability of a tool which provided animation facilities, making it easier for them to gain a deeper understanding of the different constructs in VDM-SL. Additional examples of both how to use the tool and examples of performing specification testing would have been valuable.

Because of constraints on time and resources, the engineers were not given formal training in the use of RTM and Teamwork. However, an informal introduction and extensive support on tool use were provided in equal measure to both teams. As with consultant support in the use of VDM-SL, care was taken not to influence the content of the design, only to support the methods used.

14.5.2   Consulting support

None of the engineers involved had had previous exposure to the use of CASE tools on a project. The basic project model, an initial system context diagram and first level data flow diagram were supplied to form a common starting point. Neither of these diagrams was complete, data flows being missing, and not all processes being represented. During the project help was on hand to answer questions both on the methodology and the use of the tool set. In all but the simplest of cases, specific answers were not given, but a description and example of how to solve the problem was.

Consultation on the use VDM and the of the IFAD Toolbox was available by fax and phone from external experts. They were requested not to solve the specific problems identified, but to provide guidelines on how it could be solved, leaving the final decision to the engineer.

14.6   Evaluation

In this section, we discuss five significant aspects of the system design phase of the trusted gateway's development: costs, response to changing requirements, characteristics of the requirements analysis, the derived requirements and specifications, and the use made of consultants.

14.6.1   A note of caution

A small experiment such as this cannot claim to show the absolute worth (or otherwise) of formal methods. To address such an issue convincingly would require the costly engineering equivalent of the clinical trials used to test medical treatments. Rather, the experiment is intended to add something to the public body of evidence on the costs and benefits of applying these techniques, as well as teaching lessons for future experiments of this nature. As such, it is important that we identify the provisos which must be placed on our conclusions. Experiments involving human beings are subject to many outside influences, including the backgrounds and attitudes of those involved, which affect our ability to draw conclusions from them. For this reason, we have sought only to identify gross features in the data analyzed so far.

There are a number of sources of bias in the experiment. In particular, the engineers following the formal development path may have made a greater effort than would normally be the case, both because to the degree of assessment on their work and because of the desire to demonstrate competence in newly-acquired formal specification skills. In fairness, it should be noted that these factors may also be at work in the conventional development path, where the engineers are under the same microscope.

It has been suggested that developers using formal methods have enjoyed a greater degree of support than those using conventional methods. We would stress that this applies only to the use of VDM-SL and the Toolbox. Both groups of engineers had the same support for RTM and Teamwork.

Differences in individual working practices may lead to differences in the extent to which engineers avail themselves of assistance. One possible effect is that the extra workload imposed on the systems engineer through the use of VDM-SL reduces the amount of effort devoted to familiarization with the other techniques.

14.6.2   Costs

The number of hours used to perform the system design phase was logged for both design paths. No account was taken of additional work which the engineers may have performed but not recorded. Comparing the two showed that using formal methods required roughly 25% more effort than following the BASE design process. Some elements of this overhead are expected as additional work has to be performed to analyze the requirements in sufficient detail to allow for formal modelling, but the engineer performing this task commented that much of this additional effort would have been saved if he had had the experience and skill he had acquired at the end of the programme at the beginning.

The additional time can be compared to one of the results obtained in the DARTS programme (Adams, 1994) in which a design using VDM was compared to a Teamwork design. In the system design phase, the VDM path also required roughly 25% more effort. The agreement between these two figures is striking, although we note that the comparison in DARTS is not quite the same as that made here. The DARTS results compare VDM against a Teamwork design; we are comparing Teamwork designs, one of which additionally uses VDM.

14.6.3   Handling requirements changes

In Section 14.2.4, we noted that a change would be made to the customer requirements document in the later stages of the system design phase, to give some indication of the ease or difficulty with which the specifications could be modified. Initially, the customer requirement had stipulated that the gateway had only two output ports (those on the right of the gateway in Figure 14.1), with any spurious input being ignored. The change required that these spurious input characters be routed through a port on the input side of the device, i.e. these characters should be directed out without being placed in the gateway's memory, modelled by *ValidMessage*. Since the change is on the input side of the gateway, only the message segregation process was affected. First, the additional output port was added as an extra component of the state, *outC* : char*. Then the *Segregate-Message* operation was modified, only two lines being added to describe output at *outC*. The operation is repeated below with the lines which were added or modified shown bold:

$$\textit{Segregate-Message} : () \xrightarrow{o} \mathbb{B}$$

$\textit{Segregate-Message}\,() \;\triangleq$
    if $\exists i, j \in$ inds *buffer* · *IsAValidMessage* (*buffer* $(i, \dots, j)$, *somf*, *eomf*)
    then let $s\text{-}s = \{ i \mid i \in$ inds *buffer* · $\exists j \in$ inds *buffer* ·
                       IsAValidMessage (*buffer* $(i, \dots, j)$, *somf*, *eomf*)$\}$ in
        let $e\text{-}s = \{ j \mid j \in$ inds *buffer* ·
                 IsAValidMessage (*buffer* (*least* $(s\text{-}s), \dots, j$), *somf*, *eomf*)$\}$ in
        (**outC** $:=$ **outC** $\curvearrowright$ **buffer** $(1, \dots,$ **least** $(\textbf{s-s}) - 1)$;
        ValidMessage $:=$ *buffer* (*least* $(s\text{-}s), \dots,$ *least* $(e\text{-}s)$);
        buffer $:=$ *buffer* (*least* $(e\text{-}s) + 1, \dots,$ len *buffer*);
        return true)
    else (**outC** $:=$ **outC** $\curvearrowright$ **buffer**;
        buffer $:=$ " ";
        return false)

Incorporating the changes took only a short period of contemplation and a few minutes to implement. Retesting the specification took a longer period of time. The batch-mode test facility in the Toolbox was particularly valuable at this stage: the modified specification can be retested on the pre-modification test data as well as any new tests, increasing the engineer's confidence in the modification.

14.6.4 Query analysis

The customer requirements document dealt with the trusted gateway at a number of different levels of abstraction and governed the development process as well as the functionality of the system. Examples of typical clauses are as follows:

    3.1.3   The system shall be written in a high level language
    …
    3.1.11   The maximum number of characters in a block of text delineated by valid start and stop sequences shall be 10,000 characters
    …
    3.8.1   A facility to detect the removal of external power shall be provided

Approximately 40 questions on the requirements were submitted by the engineer using the conventional methodology during the system design, and about 60 from the engineer using VDM-SL. Two questions were raised against Requirement 3.1.11 by the engineer employing formal techniques. They were

3.1.11   Does the maximum size of the message, of 10,000 characters, include the start and end functions?

3.1.11   What do you as the customer want to happen if a message is received that has more than 10,000 characters?

It is worth noting that no questions were raised against this requirement by the engineer following the conventional path.

It is interesting to compare the areas of concern covered by the engineers' questions. All the questions were independently passed to several other experienced engineers from different departments (systems, software and quality), who were asked to allocate each question to the following categories:

- function, clarification of what the system has to do;
- data, to specify the data used by the system;
- exceptions, to determine what the system does in a particular situation;
- design constraints, to explore the envelope of system behaviours and implementation constraints.

The results were averaged: the normalized results are shown below and graphically in Figure 14.3.

	Formal Design	Conventional Path
Function	42	60
Data	31	10
Exception Conditions	14	8
Design Constraints	14	22

This suggests significant differences in the patterns of results. A much higher proportion of queries relate to data in the VDM-SL path compared with the non-VDM-SL path. A lower proportion of queries deal with identifying design constraints: this is seen as a positive attribute at an early stage of the development cycle. Although some of the differences may be accounted for by different working practices of the two engineers, the difference is felt to be sufficiently marked for the result to be treated seriously.

The formal path raised 50% more queries against the customer requirements during the system design phase than the conventional path. If the number of queries back to customers was increased by this amount in normal programmes, questions might be asked about the development team's competence. In fact, many queries raised can be answered locally, making use of experience in design methods and particular classes of product. Comparison of the system designs (Section 14.6.6) suggests that the conventional path in the system design phase leaves implicit a number of assumptions which the formal path

% Questions in category

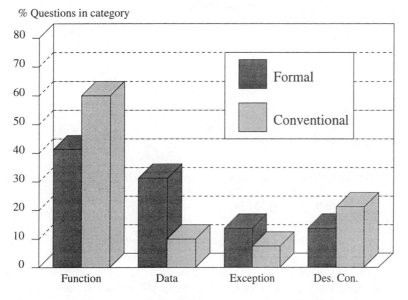

Figure 14.3 Distribution of questions across categories for each source.

has made explicit. The engineer using formal specification appears to have less opportunity simply to fail to record an assumption, or to leave ambiguity in the specification, so that even if assumptions are made without direct reference to the customer, they are nevertheless recorded explicitly.

14.6.5 Comparison of the derived requirements

The first part of the design effort is applied to engineering the requirements from the customer specification and security policy to obtain a coherent, unambiguous set of requirements which define the system to be built. Both approaches used the RTM tool to perform this task. At the conclusion, both had received answers which clarified requirements. The number of derived requirements was approximately 90 for the conventional approach and 105 for the formal methods. This difference is not considered significant.

14.6.6 Comparison of the specifications

The kernel of the trusted gateway is the most important function in the system. Consider the following descriptions, from the two design paths, extracted directly from the Teamwork model.

The security-enforcing function is encapsulated in the function *Classify-Message* first introduced in Section 14.4.3 above.

The definitions of auxiliary functions are omitted for clarity:

$Classify\text{-}Message : () \xrightarrow{o} ()$

$Classify\text{-}Message\,() \triangleq$
  if $\exists\, classA \in catA \cdot occurrence\,(classA, ValidMessage)$
  then if $freeB\,(catA, catB, ValidMessage)$
      then $(outB := outB \frown ValidMessage)$
      else $(outA := outA \frown ValidMessage)$
  else $(outB := outB \frown ValidMessage)$

The conventional process produced the following specification for the message classification process:

> *A switching statement shall be provided for all combinations of classifications which can be contained within a message. In the event that no classification can be established, the highest classification for the system shall be assumed and the message processed accordingly. All correct messages received by the system shall be passed unchanged to an output port. The TGS shall check the message for the presence of pre-defined character strings. A function shall provide the capability of assigning a message to an output port dependent upon the character string. The Trusted Gateway shall if a character string in category A is present output the message to port A. If a string in both security categories (A and B) is present, the block of text shall be written to output port B.*

The senior BASE engineers in the comparative review at the end of the system design phase felt that, once the VDM-SL notation was known, the formal description and commentary in the P-Spec provided a more detailed and unambiguous description of what occurs in the gateway than the conventional specification. It resolves a number of issues, such as occurrence of high-classification strings as substrings of low-classification strings, which have so far been ignored in the conventional development. It was felt that, when passed on to the next stage of the design process, there will be less room for error in designing a function to implement this process. It is expected that the formal description will be expanded to a more implementation-like description which defines in more detail the process leading to code which precisely satisfies the requirement.

Boswell's description (1993) of the formalization of a security policy model in Z shows similarities with our approach. In particular, we note the same "tension between abstraction and 'completeness' " in determining how much of the customer requirement is to be written in formal notation. It is also notable that our approach addresses integration of formal techniques into an existing development process in the way suggested in his conclusions: by using an informal technique for recording detailed requirements in conjunction with formal description of abstract requirements.

14.6.7   Use of consultants in the design process

Extensive use was made of consultants in the design path using VDM-SL. It is believed that engineers attempting to use formal methods for the first time must have access to experts who can either solve the problem or at least identify possible solution areas for the engineer to pursue. This expertise may be supplied by outside consultants as in this project, or (better) by a small group within the company who are familiar with the technique. Attempting to introduce formal methods without such cover will be doomed to failure.

14.6.8   Summary of the results

The formal development path required roughly 25% more effort to produce the system specification. The design produced was more abstract, but also more detailed in the description of the required security enforcing functions. More effort was expended on defining the data required by the system and in determining the behaviour of the system when exception conditions occur. It is believed that the overhead will be recovered in the subsequent software design and implementation processes. It is vital that expertise in the use of formal methods be accessible to the engineers using the technique.

14.7   Conclusions

In this paper we have described the first phase in the development of a security-critical system by two development teams, one using formal specification techniques, the other not. We have seen how VDM-SL specifications can be used in conjunction with CASE tools with the result that there is a substantial increase in the effort devoted to requirements analysis, particularly in the area of defining the data types used by the system.

At the end of this first development phase, it appears that using formal methods allows the system to be modelled at different levels of abstraction, helping to define the required functionality exactly and identifying unsuspected exceptions conditions and deciding, with the customer, on the policy to adopt when they are detected. Although formal methods are not mandated at the lower assurance levels for security-critical systems, their use is an aid to ensuring correctness and in demonstrating this to the evaluators. The limited application of these techniques on future projects is felt to be worthy of consideration.

Although it is unlikely that a formal method would be required in its entirety in all programmes, there is a niche where formality could be helpful. The stress on data modelling highlighted by this study suggests that using the type definition parts of VDM-SL, and being selective about where they are used, may yield benefits for "real" projects. It would be costly to train large numbers of engineers to use the totality of VDM, but the training needed to equip an engineer with the skills required to write data definitions is more affordable. This will bring the advantage of well-specified system data at an early stage in the design process. In addition, the data definitions can be checked to ensure that they are syntactically correct and are in an internationally recognized (ISO Standard) format. Tools could be developed to extract the information from the system data dictionary to allow automatic checking of the data definitions.

The advantages can be summarized as follows:

- an international standard to follow in defining data used in projects;
- the ability to reuse data definitions in future projects;
- formal and precise specification for vital functions;
- the ability to test specifications against requirements;
- an introduction route for formal methods with low startup costs.

This project displays several important characteristics worth bearing in mind when setting up future formal methods projects. We began by identifying a tractable problem in formal specification, and a pilot study was used to assess its suitability. Care was taken in the choice of notation, tool and consulting support. Our aims were limited: we have not concerned ourselves with formal proof or refinement. We have sought a measurable process improvement, with a clearly defined goal of assurance to high ITSEC levels. Formal methods were employed in the context of an existing development process, with VDM-SL specifications playing a role in design reviews. We feel that this use of formal system modelling with testable specifications in the context of an existing development method is a promising way forward for commercial developers of security-critical systems.

Acknowledgements

The authors gladly acknowledge the support for the Trusted Gateway programme given by British Aerospace (Systems and Equipment) Ltd. and the Commission of the European Union (ESSI Grant 10670). J.S. Fitzgerald is grateful for the support of the Engineering and Physical Sciences Research Council of the UK through a Research Fellowship.

Chapter 15

The Use of Z within a Safety-critical Software System

Vivien Hamilton

15.1 Introduction

Rolls-Royce and Associates Limited (RRA) have been contracted by the UK Ministry of Defence to conduct a pilot study into techniques for developing safety critical software. This study involves the development, in realistic project conditions, of a protection system for a crane handling hazardous materials. State-of-the-art commercial tools and techniques have been used. Part of the purpose of the project was to evaluate the application of two Interim Defence Standards, 00-55 and 00-56 (Minstry of Defence, 1991a,b), which are discussed in Section 15.2.4. The purpose of the project was also to provide an appraisal of the suitability, cost-effectiveness and practicalities of the tools and techniques employed.

This chapter discusses the background to the project, the standards and methods used, the technical work which was undertaken, and an evaluation of the success of the project.

15.2 Background

15.2.1 The company

Rolls-Royce and Associates Limited (RRA) is a major engineering company and is part of the Rolls-Royce Industrial Power Group.

A significant area of our business is the design, manufacture and through-life support of a range of power plants for the UK Ministry of Defence. This rôle also encompasses the preparation and maintenance of the complete plant safety case. From this and other applications, in other industries, we have over 30 years experience of specifying, developing, constructing, installing and commissioning high-integrity protection, control and instrumentation systems.

In designing such systems, we were among the first to develop a lifecycle suitable for developing safety-critical software which incorporated formal specification, static analysis and dynamic testing as part of the validation process.

We also provide consultancy and contract research and development in all parts of the high-integrity systems and software lifecycle. Services provided include third-party verification and validation, safety analyses incorporating hazards identification and risk classification, and third-party software quality assurance assessments.

RRA has been influential in the development of standards including the two Defence Standards evaluated by this project, and IEC 880 (International Electrotechnical Commission, 1995), and is represented on the British Computer Society Safety Critical Systems Technical Committee.

We have a broad range of skills in software engineering, including specification, analysis, design, coding, testing and maintenance. These skills cover a wide range of applications, project sizes and target hardware. We have experience of working to a range of national and international standards. Wide use is made of automation throughout the software development lifecycle, especially for testing.

Formal methods, including formal specification, program proving and static analysis have been used on a variety of civil and defence projects.

15.2.2   Preceding projects

The process selected for the development of the software for this project has been developed from previous projects requiring similar integrity levels. In particular, a project in the mid-1980s (Hill, 1991; Hamilton, 1992) to produce a safety-critical protection, control and instrumentation system, was used for comparison purposes. This project, which at the time was one of very few using formal methods, had been used in producing the original draft of Defence Standard 00-55 (Ministry of Defence, 1991a).

In this earlier project, a Ward–Mellor (Ward and Mellor, 1985) analysis was performed after the production of the formal specification and although conventional design and code reviews were held, proof of correctness of the design was performed as part of the static analysis of the final source code.

Subsequent projects had explored more up-to-date approaches piecemeal, but a complete application of the two defence standards had not been performed.

15.2.3   The application

The application selected for the pilot study was the control and protection system for a crane handling hazardous material within a large containment tank.

The crane consists of a trolley which moves on rails at the sides of the tank, a bridge which spans the tank, and a hoist which moves vertically within the tank. On the end of the hoist is a grab which grasps, holds and releases the hazardous material.

This project involved the requirements capture for the control and protection system, the system design, and the development of one subsystem, the safety-critical software-based protection system. For the software-based protection system, formal software specification and design was used. The hardware on which it resides was also designed using a modern semiformal method — specifically, VHDL (Institute of Electrical and Electronic Engineers, 1988) — and a powerful graphical toolset, Mentor Graphics.

As this was a research project and the project funds were limited, it was necessary to select a fairly simple application. The requirement for the project included monitoring the position and speed of the three moving elements of the crane, to ensure that the loaded grab could not collide with any the obstructions in the tank. The software also has to ensure that the grab places its loads gently and does not allow them to fall. Monitoring the rate of acceleration also protects the loads from sudden jolts.

In addition to these functional and safety requirements, the software requirements also included input/output handling, scheduling and self-testing.

15.2.4   Interim Defence Standard 00-55

At the time of the project, Interim Defence Standard 00-55 (Ministry of Defence, 1991a) was the current defence standard for development of safety-critical projects. The standard had, however, seen limited application and was due to be updated. Hence feedback on the practicalities of its implementation was important.

As with all good standards, IDS 00-55 endeavoured to specify what must be achieved and what must be done, without being prescriptive in how it should be done. It did, however, have stringent requirements about the methods and tools used, and the reviews conducted.

The most controversial aspect of IDS 00-55 was the requirement that formal methods should be used for this type of software. Critics, both within the UK Ministry of Defence and among industrial contractors, had claimed that formal methods were unduly expensive, immature and in many cases totally impractical. RRA's previous experience, however, suggested that this was not the case. It was expected at the start of the project that although it might not be practical (or in some cases possible) to comply with the whole of IDS 00-55, the majority of the standard could be successfully met. It was also felt that the methods it promoted were more likely to result in a dependable product and were therefore desirable for high-integrity applications.

It was also planned that the updated version of 00-55 would require contractors to apply a software quality assurance system compliant with ISO 9000-3 (International Standards Organization, 1991). Practical experience on how 00-55 related to this standard was also required.

Interim Defence Standard 00-56 (Ministry of Defence, 1991b), was less controversial than 00-55. It provides a standard for safety systems to identify hazards and to apply appropriate design techniques to minimize the consequence and probability of the hazards.

15.3   Developing the system specification

The process of requirements capture was performed using CORE (British Aerospace System Designers, 1985). CORE is a method for requirements engineering which involves considering all parties who will have an interest in the system (e.g. users, operators, systems that interface with it, etc.). The viewpoint of each such party is then modelled. This assists in ensuring that all requirements are captured.

Once the system requirements had been modelled using CORE, a preliminary hazards analysis was performed. This enabled the identification of those features which were safety related or safety critical. These "safety features" included both safety functions and safety properties. The safety functions are functions that the system must perform, such as "tripping" if certain constraints were exceeded. The safety properties are properties (or invariants) that must hold for the system to remain in a safe state. These included, for example, the permissible range for the various speeds. These safety features were expressed in Z (Spivey, 1992), so that they could be used in the later project stages, when it would be necessary to prove that the software implemented the safety features.

The CORE analysis was then converted into a structured analysis. The structured analysis method used was based on Ward and Mellor (1985), but modified to give a more object-based style. Conventionally, Ward–Mellor type structured analysis decomposes the system according to functional criteria. Object-oriented approaches are claimed to produce more maintainable software, because of the emphasis on encapsulation and abstraction. An object-based style avoids the extremes of multiple inheritance, while still achieving most of the advantages. The context diagram, state transition diagrams and entity–relationship diagrams are used to identify candidate objects. Analysis then proceeds with data flow diagrams. Non-primitive processes (i.e. those that decompose into other processes) are based on objects rather than functions. This approach can occasionally produce low-level data flow diagrams with unconnected processes, but it tends to reduce data flow at the higher levels.

The entity–relationship diagram was mapped directly from the CORE viewpoint diagram. State transition diagrams, data flow diagrams, and data structure diagrams were then created. During this exercise, a more detailed understanding of the requirements evolved. A high-level system design was then performed, and three subsystems were identified: a safety-related software-based control system, a hardware interlock system and a safety-critical software-based protection system.

The requirements, expressed in English, were then allocated to the three systems. For the purposes of exploring the application of IDS 00-55, the safety-critical software protection system was deemed to be a suitable size. It was small enough to be produced by a small team (two developers plus two part time verifiers) in the project timescales, but it provided sufficient functionality to test the methods and tools. This subsystem was therefore selected for further development.

15.3.1   Selection of a formal language

The decision was made to use Z as the specification language. The reasons for this included the fact that Z itself is mature, and has good tool support. It also supports modularity, and it was felt that this would help to ease the transition to the target implementation language, Ada. Ada was chosen as the implementation language for several reasons:

- it is the UK Ministry of Defence preferred language;

- it was designed as a solution to the software crisis of the 1970s and as such includes many desirable features such as support for abstraction;
- there is currently a great deal of interest in safe subsets of Ada, and their ability to provide verifiable software.

Good tool support is very important for industrial projects, where productivity is always of concern. Tools are not selected purely by the range of functionality provided. One of the most important considerations in many industrial projects is the maintainability of the software for the lifetime of the system for which it is being developed. In selecting a tool therefore, the pedigree of the tool vendor is critical. The vendor must provide good support, and some assurance that the tool will still be available for the lifetime of the product being developed. A tool which already has a reasonable number of users therefore has a considerable advantage over a brand new product, both from the point of view of having a greater likelihood of long-term support and because a large user base also makes it likely that any initial faults in the tool will have been corrected. The tool must be reliable, well supported, and reasonably easy to use and integrate with other tools, as well as providing the required functionality. CADiZ (York Software Engineering, 1993), which provides development support, syntax checking and type checking for Z, fulfilled these normal commercial criteria.

IDS 00-55 also places additional requirements on the integrity of the tools used to support the software development process. If the tool contains errors, there is a risk, which may be very small, that an error in the tool may mask an error in the software product. For example, the tool may fail to report a type or syntax error in the specification, which may lead to misunderstandings later in the software development. According to the vendors, CADiZ has itself been formally specified, and has been developed under an ISO 9000-3 compliant quality system, so the chances of residual faults in CADiZ leading to errors in the formal specification are minimized. Checking such claims was not performed under this project, although it would obviously have to be done under a production contract.

It is important to remember that when abstract specification is used, the naming of processes and data is very important. Unlike software variables in a program, which have a physical location in computer memory, an abstract data item has no physical representation. If its name is meaningful, however, the relation between the specification and the real-world item will be readily apparent. A specification is much clearer and easier to understand if the link between the data items and the real world items which they represent is intuitive. If, however, important information is omitted from the specification (such as that one item is in one set of units and another is in a different set), the operations being performed on these items will be confusing.

Z is an abstract specification language. Although methods have been proposed for using refinement as a constructive process from specification to final implementation, such as Morgan (1994), it was decided that these were not yet practical in an industrial context. A more practical solution is to specify the system formally, to use conventional methods to create a design, to express this formally and then to use refinement as a verification process to check that the design correctly implements the specification. There is industrial experience for applying refinement in this manner, for real systems which have accuracy, timing and efficiency constraints. For non-trivial systems, refinement as a constructive process relies entirely on the skill and expertise of the engineer; tool support is immature, and the number of people who are capable of using the methods but also retain a practical understanding of the application is limited.

It was decided that MALPAS Intermediate Language (IL) (Ward, 1989) would be used as the design description language. MALPAS is a set of tools for performing static analysis. To enable the tools to be used for a variety of languages, and to remove the ambiguities of many languages, the MALPAS tools operate on a functional language called IL. Using IL as the design description language therefore meant that the refinement proofs could be conducted with the aid of the MALPAS tools. Although MALPAS IL does not have a written formally defined semantics, it is designed to be unambiguous, is well understood, and has an excellent track record in industry. The availability of an Ada translator to assist with the process of turning the design implementation back into IL, and therefore to assist with the formal arguments about the correctness of the code with respect to the design made this option attractive.

15.3.2   Use of structured analysis

The success of structured analysis arises from its ability to enable software engineers to decompose the problem into pieces that are sufficiently small for it to be easily understood. The links between the elements are then represented graphically — a form which is much easier to absorb than text. The elements used in structured analysis include entity–relationship diagrams, data structure diagrams, data flow diagrams and state transition diagrams. These perform similar rôles to the various types of schemas used in Z. Thus structured analysis can be used to deduce the structure of the Z specification. Structured analysis also provides an easy-to-use "map" of the schemas in the Z specification.

Previous projects which used structured analysis and design tended to be free of a whole class of errors which are often seen in software. These errors are flow errors, and arise when an input or output is missing or is surplus to requirements. This may happen at the overall program level, or at the procedure or module level. These errors are readily identifiable when structured analysis and design is used however, and are generally removed during the initial development of the analysis or design.

Typically, when structured analysis and design are used, problems occur at the process specification level (i.e. where the specification is textual rather than diagrammatic). Problems also occur on the diagrams when iterative and sequential processes are used. These arise because the "syntax" of the diagrams is deliberately ambiguous to allow them to be as expressive as possible.

By using Z, the ambiguity is removed. Thus, a general idea of how the system works can be obtained from viewing the diagrams, and a precise understanding of the elements of the specification can be gathered from studying the Z schemas.

The actual production of Z schemas also tends to remove misunderstandings at this early stage, by forcing the specifier to think about the specification in a very precise, rather than a loose, sense. It is much easier to notice when a case has not been considered and to understand the scope of conditions in a Z specification, than in a structured English process specification.

Similarly, data schemas in Z can readily be made to include safety requirements, such as invariants on range or combinations, and these can be incorporated into formal proofs during the verification stages.

A well-designed state transition diagram can be treated formally by means of Petri-nets (a state transition diagram is a special case of a finite state machine). There is no direct conversion into Z notation although a simple, first attempt can be achieved by appending states. However, the requirements for the state transition diagram are usually easier to capture than the Z invariants which are needed to describe the system in a more formal and more abstract way. Once a state transition diagram has been developed, it can be used as an aid to reasoning to elicit the invariants for the Z specification. In the process, omissions and errors in the state transition diagram may also be noticed.

15.3.3   Structure of the specification

As with the system level structured analysis, the structured analysis for the software was performed with an object-based slant. The partitioning used in the data flow diagrams was centred around data structures rather than common functionality. This approach was particularly appropriate given that the implementation language was to be Ada.

The object-based approach also ensures that when the specification is converted into a formal notation, it is easier to generate high-level abstract functions, and the use of global definitions is much reduced.

Expressions written in a formal notation do not constitute a useful formal specification without additional supporting material. For a specification to be useful, it needs comment and explanation to make clear the intention of the formal expressions and show the link between notation and the real world system.

For each of the Z schemas in this project, an English description of what the schema was intended to achieve was first written. This was informally reviewed by another engineer within the team, before the formal version was developed. The English descriptions were retained as comments in the formal specifications, and in some cases extra detail was added to explain the formal treatment further. The net result was that the amount of English description far exceeded the amount of Z, although it is the Z that is definitive.

The layout of a specification can greatly enhance readability. For example, if the English description appears over the page from the related Z, the reader will be unable to see them both together. During the review process, the recommendation was made that in future documents, effort should be made to ensure that the description and the Z notation always appear on the same page, or on facing pages.

The specification was written for one frame or cycle (i.e. all inputs read once, all outputs generated once), and proofs were then performed over the closure of many cycles. The inputs represent the values of the analog sensors and the outputs represent the values used to drive actuators. The only state variables used were the values of the inputs from the previous frame. These are required both for error checking and for the calculation of certain values (such as acceleration) which are calculated over many cycles.

At the time of writing the specification, the actual values of most of the constants (such as the limits of travel and the maximum safe speeds) had not been defined. They were therefore included in the specification as named constants, with undefined values. This has an advantage in that the proofs are performed for all values of the constants, and any constraints on the relationships between the values of the constants have to be made explicit. Therefore, if at some future date, the system is changed such that some or all of the constants change value (e.g. because the tank is enlarged), the specification and proofs are still valid, provided that the constraints on the constants have been met.

Defining initialization requirements can be very difficult, particularly for fault-tolerant, real-time systems. In such systems, it is often possible for the software to undergo a reset while the system is operational. So, in the initial state of the software, it is possible for the state variables which represent the real-world system to have a range of values.

When the software re-initializes, it must first determine the state of the system and it must ensure that the system remains in a safe state while it does so. However, unless initialization is formally defined, it is not possible to complete the closure over all cycles, which is necessary if proofs are to be performed.

The amount of initialization required had been kept to a minimum by the use of data flow analysis. The vast majority of variables were always written before being read, and hence their initial values were irrelevant.

The non-functional system requirements included the requirement for a software and hardware self-test system. The exact requirements of self-test are implementation dependent, so their functionality cannot be specified as part of the software specification except in a very abstract way. A variable representing the state of self-test was therefore simply "parachuted" into the schema which monitored the health of the system; other methods which could have been used are a dummy input variable or an undefined "gremlin" function.

For a safety-related or safety-critical project it is important that there is traceability between the safety documentation and the software documentation. Each schema therefore referenced the safety requirements which it satisfied. In addition, two-way cross-reference tables were produced.

The specification consisted of sixteen Z schemas, occupying twelve A4 pages.

15.4   Verifying the specification

Validation is the process of ensuring that the system which is being developed is the system that is needed. Thus validation includes any process which lets the user examine whether he or she is getting what is needed.

Verification is the process of ensuring that the system is being built correctly. Some development and verification processes include an element of validation. For example the software designer may realize that the functionality specified does not seem sensible, and raise a query, which results in the correction of an error in the specification.

The primary reason for using formal methods is to ensure that there are as few errors as possible in the final product.

Software errors are ultimately caused by human error: typing errors, errors of understanding, or errors of thought. It is just as likely for the engineer writing the formal specification to make a mistake as it is for a programmer to do so. Thus it is as important for the formal specification to be verified as it is for the program to be tested.

Additionally, any errors which remain in the formal specification after verification are unlikely to be noticed during the software design process, since this uses the formal specification as a baseline. It may be that an engineer will fortuitously notice an error in the specification during the development process, but this can not be relied upon.

Errors in the specification, if found at all, are likely to remain until the system has been built and subsequently does not perform as desired. This means that correction of the errors will entail considerable rework, effort and delay to the project.

This situation is not unique to formally specified projects, but the use of a formal specification provides additional opportunities for verification at the early stages of the project. Thus the net effect of using formal methods is to "front load" the costs of the project. More time and money is spent in the specification stage, but this is repaid by making the latter project stages run more smoothly. In this project, several different methods of verification were performed on the specification, each having different strengths.

The most rigorous and time-consuming method of verification is discharge of proofs about the specification itself. This can be used to find conflicts between one part of the specification and another (the specification is then unsatisfiable or may deadlock), or differences between specified actions.

The Z notation has a defined syntax, and is supported by automated tools, and it is therefore possible to perform syntax and type checking. Since this is an automated process it is a very quick and reliable method of detecting errors in this category.

The specification can be translated into an executable form. Ideally this would be done by an automated tool, but in this pilot study the specification was manually translated. Once translated, the executable prototype, or animation, can be used by the person most familiar with the needs of the system to explore its behaviour under unusual as well as normal operating conditions. This approach therefore provides validation of the specification.

The final approach is peer review. In informally specified projects, this is commonly the only form of verification performed on the specification. Peer review on this project was performed after syntax and type checking (since removing errors with a tool is cheapest), but before construction and discharge of proofs and animation.

Peer reviews can detect errors in the way that the language is used, or in the understanding of the application, but their effectiveness depends on the people involved, and the particular conditions of the project. Peer reviews are the only method of ensuring that the specification is clear and meaningful and that the comments are correct.

15.4.1 Syntax and type checks

Syntax and type checking was performed by the engineers writing the specification, using CADiZ. CADiZ was found to be very easy to use, and the engineers soon gained confidence in its abilities to find mistakes. For the engineers who were new to Z, it was useful as a learning tool, since the error messages were easy to understand. CADiZ therefore proved useful as a training aid. The engineers also felt that a syntax checker that parses the specification after it has been written was easier to use than a syntax-directed editor.

It is important that syntax and type errors are removed before attempting any further verification, since the existence of such errors is likely to lead to misunderstandings in peer reviews, and renders any proofs performed potentially meaningless.

One of the strengths of CADiZ is that it can handle the whole specification at a time, rather than just checking individual schemas.

CADiZ includes hypertext and browsing facilities, so that when an error message appears for a type check, the name of the variable concerned can be selected from the error message, and its declaration and usage automatically tracked by the tool. This makes the process of debugging early drafts relatively easy.

Note that semantic checking, evaluations of schema operations, etc., are not performed by CADiZ, and the formal proofs and informal reviews are therefore used to check these.

15.4.2 Animation in Ada

Animation provides a means of validating the specification as it gives the user an opportunity to experiment with different inputs to see what outputs the system generates.

The Z specification was translated manually into Ada. In performing this translation, it had been expected that difficulties would be encountered as a result, for example, of the non-determinism inherent in abstract specification. This proved not to be a problem, and relatively few mappings between the Z constructs and the Ada constructs were required. This suggests that the process would be relatively easy to automate, and it is understood that the makers of CADiZ are in the process of developing such a tool.

DEC Ada, which is the native Ada on the host machine, was used for the animation. This is a full implementation of Ada, and has a comprehensive debugging environment. For the animation, the full scope of the language, as opposed to a subset, was used. Thus tasking was available to model concurrent processes and exceptions could be used to model error handling.

During the translation, each schema was mapped to an Ada procedure. The Z decorations (?, ! and ') were mapped to (_in, _out and _Tick) to satisfy internal naming conventions. The predicate of the schema was mapped to the body of the Ada procedure. The procedures were collected into packages consistent with the structured analysis hierarchy. Schema conjunction was achieved by invoking the Ada procedures as concurrent tasks.

In the absence of formal semantics for the Ada used, it was not possible to produce formal proofs of the correctness of the transformation from Z to Ada. However, the translation process was reviewed, and rigorous arguments created to demonstrate that the animation was a true representation of the specification.

Once the specification had been converted into Ada, harnesses to drive the code and to check the output values were created using IPL's AdaTEST. AdaTEST, as its name suggests, is a tool which provides assistance in many aspects of the testing process, including creating harnesses and stubs, checking results and checking coverage. The execution of the animation was file driven, rather than being fully interactive, but using AdaTEST immensely simplified the task of driving the animation and checking that the results were as expected. It also meant that the animation tests are fully repeatable and can be stored under configuration control.

To ensure that the tests which were run on the animation fully exercised the functionality, coverage analysis was performed on the animation tests. The coverage achieved was one hundred per cent statement coverage, decision coverage and Boolean operand coverage. AdaTEST also gives a metric for Boolean operator four-way coverage. This metric ensures that for conjunction and disjunction, all combinations of *true* and *false* are exercised (i.e. if the expression contains a single "AND", four tests are necessary; for two "AND"s, eight tests are needed). The variables may have some relationship to each other which means that not all combinations are semantically feasible, so for this metric, the target achieved was one hundred per cent of the feasible combinations.

The most important point about an animation is that it is easy to use, so that it encourages the users to explore whether or not it has the correct functionality. Although the animation for this project was not interactive, it was very easy to add new tests.

The test scripts and test results were actually included in the software specification record. For future projects, however, only the test data and a certificate that the animation actually passes the tests will be included. Publishing the full test scripts and results tends to swamp the useful information, and the files are stored under configuration management and subject to review procedures.

The test data used on the animation was initially produced by the specification writers. It was reviewed by an independent verification and validation team, and extra tests were requested. As a result of these extra tests, a subtle error in the specification was detected. It appears from this that animation is a worthwhile exercise, especially when the tests are designed by someone independent of the specification writers.

15.4.3   Discharge of proofs

It was felt that correctness had been demonstrated by the tests performed on the animation. The proof obligations remaining were therefore satisfiability and domain correctness.

As the specification was relatively short and simple, it was possible to discharge these proofs manually. The actual discharge of the proofs was not too onerous. A factor in this was probably the fact that the specification is for a pure safety system, i.e. the requirements for the functionality of the software and the requirements for the safety of the system are one and the same. This situation is not always the case for a safety-critical system which often has requirements for functionality over and above its requirements for safety. For example, when a control system is implemented in software there will probably be many possible control algorithms that are safe but are not the optimum control solution. The case of the system being permanently shut down is often among the safe, but unacceptable solutions.

The proofs were included in the specification record document, and subjected to rigorous peer review by other members of the design team and by members of an independent verification and validation team.

15.5   Tool support

The development environment for the project was a network consisting mainly of DEC workstations and fileservers running the DEC VAX/VMS operating system. The network also included UNIX machines and PCs. In this way, it was possible to provide the different platforms required by the various tools.

In general, transfer of files around the network was straightforward; however, transfer of files between the configuration management system running under VAX/VMS and the structured analysis tool, running under UNIX, did prove to be a significant overhead.

Project documentation was produced using a desktop publishing tool, Framemaker, running under UNIX. The majority of the tools (e.g. the structured analysis tools, Ada-TEST, etc.) produced output which could be directly imported into Framemaker.

In safety-critical projects, a very large amount of documentation must be produced, and an easy-to-use automated process for producing documentation has significant advantages in saving cost and time. The only part of the project where the documentation tool could not be integrated was in the production of the Z specifications and proofs. The output from CADiZ could not be integrated, and although of a very high quality, the necessity to transfer and convert files manually is time consuming and can lead to the introduction of errors or problems in configuration control.

15.6   Later project stages

15.6.1   Production and verification of the design

It was decided that Ada would be used for the design. When originally designed and specified, the intention of the US Department of Defense was that the Ada language would be used for the high-level design as well as the implementation detail. In this way, it was hoped that it would encourage good practice in software engineering.

Ada is object based; it supports some of the object-oriented paradigm (such as encapsulation and abstraction), although it does not support multiple inheritance. In order to ensure that the full benefits of using Ada as an implementation language for the target hardware were realized, it was necessary to use an object-based design method. With

Ada as a design language, syntax and strong type checking facilities were provided by the Ada compiler. The design could also be formally described and verified in the same manner as would eventually be used for the code (see Section 15.6.2).

Since the module designs would be represented in Ada, and powerful flow checking facilities would be available with the MALPAS tools, it was decided that the data dictionary facility in the structured design tool would not be used. It was felt that the necessity to duplicate entries in the data dictionary would have too high a likelihood of introducing errors. This meant that the structured design tool was used only as a documentation aid to produce structure charts. The structured design tool requires a completed data dictionary in order to be able to do any checking, so without the data dictionary, it was not possible to use the structured design tool to check the design.

Ada package specifications were produced to represent the top level design and English descriptions in the form of comments were used to describe the intended functionality of the procedures.

The design differed from the animation in several respects. The design and implementation were restricted to a "Safe" subset of Ada, whereas the animation had used the full scope of the language. The subset chosen was that supported by the Alsys CSMART compiler (Alsys, 1993). This subset was designed from a consideration of which language features can be compiled in a dependable manner. Two other subsets were considered: "Safe Ada" and "SPARK" (Program Validation, 1990). "Safe Ada" consists of only those features which are most likely to be correctly used by programmers without introducing errors. SPARK was mainly designed from a consideration of which features can be successfully analysed. All three subsets are similar, but not quite identical. CSMART has the advantage that it has a compiler developed specifically for the subset. This means that any language features which are outside the compiler cannot be compiled. The compiler itself is also much simpler and smaller than a full Ada compiler. CSMART can also contain features that are banned in SPARK, where the reason for the ban is that the way the compiler may implement them is potentially unsafe. Since the implementation of CSAMRT is fixed, such features have a defined implementation.

The animation also had abstract representations of implementation-dependent features (including input and output) and did not have to be coded in an efficient way, since modelling the time constraints was outside the scope of the animation.

The design is also written so that it will be easily maintainable, and, so far as practicable, it uses reusable modules. No such considerations are necessary for the animation.

A formal design description was then produced by using MALPAS to translate the Ada into MALPAS IL. During the translation process, the translator performs some validation of the Ada, and generates warnings for any Ada features which are liable to misuse. As a result of this process an error in the design was detected.

The translation is not fully automatic. Manual intervention was necessary to cope with certain features of Ada, where rules for translation of the general case of the syntax cannot be formulated, but where a model for a specific application of the syntax can be developed. Examples of these are described below.

Certain operations in the Ada were invoked as functions within a complex predicate. This leaves the choice of the order in which the functions are called to the compiler, and can cause problems if the functions have side effects, or if there is data flow from one function to another. The translator assumes a particular order and does not take into account a possibly large number of alternatives. In many cases, where the number of alternatives is very large, it would be infeasible to analyse all combinations. Thus a manual review of the potential effects of varying the order has to be used instead.

Certain features of the Ada Language Reference Manual are Implementation dependent. In this project, this included use of the package `System`, and the package `Calendar`.

The model of the source code was enhanced by a call to a check procedure to ensure that the flag representing constraint error had not been set, at every point where a constraint error could be raised.

Exceptions other than *Constraint Error* were handled by a combination of techniques: showing that various constraints could not be raised, and manually adding to the IL model to allow to the tool to demonstrate that exception conditions would not occur.

The compiler handles derived types in the same way as the parent type. This is valid provided that operators and functions previously defined for the parent type are not redefined for the derived type and the compiler flags any type compatibility problems. These checks were performed manually.

The translator models attributes of dynamic types as functions.Some amendments to simplify the model were made to change `'FIRST` and `'LAST` to constants where the types are in fact static.

Static analysis must be performed bottom up. It is, however, possible to have valid Ada code where the bodies of two packages are each dependent on the other's specification. In order to analyze the packages, it is necessary to split the pacakges into smaller parts, until all such mutual dependencies have been removed. Before splitting up the packages, it is necessary to ensure that there are no hidden dependences which would invalidate the split.

The translator models package elaboration sections as callable procedures. However, as package elaboration can cause problems owing to elaboration order, most of the package elaboration sections were empty and hence modelled as null procedures. The translator does not allow procedures with no outputs, so an abstract variable had to be defined to be used as the output of these procedures.

The translator does not fully support instantiations of generics, which need additional manual amendments to the model.

The purpose of the static path analysis on the design is to show that the design is free of flow errors and anomalies. MALPAS performs flow analysis on the IL model produced by the translator. The results of the flow analysis need to be interpreted, since MALPAS is incapable of distinguishing between genuine errors (such as a variable being overwritten before its value has been read) and anomalies deliberately introduced (such as those created by defensive programming).

Additionally, MALPAS does not use semantic information in its flow analyses. This can result in MALPAS flagging potential errors which are semantically infeasible. An example of this is where a path exists which cannot be executed because the conditions for executing it are contradictory. Such a path is said to be infeasible. The MALPAS semantic analyzer will endeavour to identify such paths and to remove them from the semantic analysis results, but is unable to do so if the contradictory conditions rely on anything other than simple logical or mathematical relationships. The semantic analysis results are not available to the flow analysis tool, and hence anomalies which only occur on semantically infeasible paths need to be identified manually. In addition to complicating the task of analyzing the software, proliferation of semantically infeasible constructs tends to confuse anyone reading the code. In safety-critical code, it is therefore desirable to minimize such constructs.

Since it had been shown by formal argument that the animation was a true representation of the specification, a MALPAS translation of the Ada animation was used as the specification to check that the design correctly implemented the functionality, and that the variables used were adequate. The comparison of the specification form and the design description was then performed using MALPAS. In addition a manual review between the Z specification and the MALPAS procspecs was performed.

For the design (concrete implementation) to be a valid refinement of the (abstract) specification, it must have the following properties.

- *Implementable*. The specification was shown to be implementable (i.e. a set of inputs, outputs and state variables can be found for which the specification does not evaluate to *false*). This property must be preserved in the implementation.
- *Adequacy*. The domain (the range of values that the inputs can take) of the implementation must represent the domain of the specification. The types of the variables may have changed from an abstract form to a concrete form (e.g. a set may be implemented as an array), but there must not be any values which are valid for the specification for which there is no equivalent value in the implementation.
- *Initial State*. The initial state in the implementation must map onto the initial state of the specification.
- *Domain Rule*. For all operations in the specification, and all data values in the implementation, if the conditions permit the abstract operation to return a result, the conditions must also permit the concrete operation to return a result.
- *Result Rule*. For all operations in the specification, there must be an operation in the implementation that will produce results that map to the results of the equivalent abstract operation, for all possible concrete data values.

For this project, since the design had been written in Ada, and had been compiled and run, it had been demonstrated that it was implementable. In strict terms the adequacy criterion was not met, because the specification used integers (having infinite range) and the implementation was limited to the range allowed by the compiler. However, the input space of the operations is limited by the range allowed by the hardware, and the concrete data ranges can easily accommodate this.

The other proof obligations were satisfied with the aid of MALPAS. Some minor faults were detected and corrected.

15.6.2   Production and verification of source code

The source code was produced in Ada from the detailed design with only the final implementation details needing to be added at this stage. With the hardware design fixed, and the storage requirements of the software determined, it was possible to design the memory map and to fix the locations of input and output variables which are memory mapped. In Ada, "representation clauses" are used to direct the compiler on such matters. During the hardware and software design phases, the requirements for self-testing had been finalized, and the self-test software was therefore added at this stage. This was again a manual process.

The code consisted of 45 Ada modules, each consisting of between five and thirty executable lines.

Static analysis was performed on the source code, using similar methods to those applied to the design. Since the refinement from the specification to the design had already been proved, it was only necessary to prove the refinement from the design to the final implementation. Further, because of the close mapping between the design and the source code, the approach used for the design could be adopted for the analysis of the source code, thus making the task quicker than would otherwise have been the case.

Unit testing of the source code was performed on the VAX host. This was carried out using IPL's AdaTEST to drive the units and to check that all the necessary coverage metrics were achieved. These included the same set of requirements as were imposed on the design. The same set of tests that were used at the specification stage were re-run on the code for additional confidence that no change to the functionality had taken place during source code generation.

Once unit testing had taken place all the modules were linked together and a previously designed set of integration tests were run. Once again this was performed on the VAX host using IPL's AdaTEST.

15.6.3   Validation of the final system

Once the system has been built, it is possible to validate it fully. The actual system can be tried out in realistic situations. For software developed using rigorous methods under a strong quality assurance system, this should be a confirmatory, rather than a debugging, exercise.

An independently written acceptance test schedule was generated from the software requirements. This document detailed a large number of tests that would test the systems functionality. These tests concentrated on ensuring that the various tolerances within the system met the requirements. This set of tests also tested the system over many software frames and ensured that the timing requirements were adequately met. The tests were reviewed by the safety engineers to ensure that they fully exercised and demonstrated the safety features of the system.

The acceptance testing was carried out by an independent engineer with the software running on the designated target system.

The project has been a success in achieving its main objectives of

- demonstrating that IDS 00-55 can be applied to a realistic safety application under real project conditions,
- highlighting omissions from IDS 00-55 and IDS 00-56,
- demonstrating the effectiveness of modern software engineering techniques,
- providing a prototype project for the development of procedures for applying IDS 00-55 and IDS 00-56, and
- providing a prototype project for the assessment of the software tools.

In addition, the project has advanced the understanding of the rôles of the independent verification team and the independent safety auditor. These rôles are specified by IDS 00-55, which is fairly prescriptive about what the verification team should do, but gives little guidance on the rôle of the independent safety auditor.

Compared with standard (low-integrity) commercial software, software productivity for safety-critical software is inevitably low. This is not necessarily because the methods slow the production rate, but rather because demonstrating that the software is error free is very time consuming; typically it can account for 70% of the development costs. Finding errors late in the process, and having to change the software as a result, tends to impact particularly badly on costs and timescales, so the "front-loaded" approach of formal methods is worthwhile.

As expected, error rates were very low. The conventional in-phase verification techniques such as peer reviews were conducted thoroughly and thus detected most of the latent faults. Thus the software products which were subject to the formal verification activities were already in a good state. Animation, static validation of the specification, formal verification of the design and static analysis of the source code were successful, in that each detected a significant error. Each error was then able to be corrected before continuing with the next phase. None of the testing phases (unit testing, integration testing, system testing and validation testing) detected any faults in the software, despite their thoroughness. Two of the faults detected by the formal verification activities should have been detected by system level testing had the verification activities not already ensured their removal. The other two may or may not have been detected by thorough testing; they could easily have remained in the system had formal verification not been performed. The absence of any errors discovered during testing strengthens the argument for using these activities as activities aimed at providing confidence in the software, and for use of these activities to estimate the software reliability.

Z proved to be fully capable of expressing the specification, and amenable for translation into Ada as part of the animation and the design. The translation into Ada was a relatively simple manual task, and a tool which automated this would be useful.

CADiZ proved to be a practical and easily used tool for assisting in writing and checking the Z specifications, and the team had a great deal of confidence in it. It does not, however, support proof generation and discharge, and an integrated tool of similar pedigree would be welcome.

MALPAS was extensively used as a development and verification aid. The Ada translator proved to be effective in its own right in identifying potential programming errors. The use of MALPAS during the design phase proved more effective at discovering errors than structured design tools.

One aspect investigated in this project was the learning curve needed to get engineers up to speed in the formal techniques. While very experienced formal methods practitioners were available to drive the planning stages of the project, to perform the rôle of the verification team, to provide guidance and to assess the project, the engineers performing the actual development were experienced software engineers with limited previous experience of formal methods. One of the criticisms levelled against formal methods has been that the learning curve is too great for industry to be able to use them widely. However, it was found that the learning curve involved in introducing experienced software engineers to formal methods was not unduly large. Engineers were productive in writing specifications under supervision after a one week training course. It should be borne in mind, however, that if the whole team were to be new to formal methods, or if inexperienced software engineers were to be used, serious difficulties may be encountered.

The use of broad spectrum languages and tools (Ada, MALPAS and AdaTEST) in several different project phases was felt to have eased the learning curves involved in introducing engineers to the project methods. For software which is required to have a very high level of integrity, the application of standards such as IDS 00-55 tends to result in a requirement for a large number of methods and tools. Such a situation can lead to problems in maintaining the software over the long lifetimes (e.g. 30 years) that are often required for real-time embedded software systems. A formal environment consisting of a broad spectrum notation, with browsing, syntax, semantic, and proof tools as well as code generation, which was capable of supporting the project from specification to verification of object code would have an advantage in this respect.

Acknowledgement

This work was carried out with the support of the UK Ministry of Defence Procurement Executive, Bath.

Chapter 16

Multiparadigm Specification of an AT&T Switching System

Peter Mataga and Pamela Zave

16.1   Introduction

This chapter describes the formal specification of a real AT&T switching system. While the specified system is vastly simpler than some major AT&T products (which offer hundreds of features), it includes all of the commonly used telecommunications features. It is also an order of magnitude more complex than the "plain old telephone service" (POTS) which is the subject of essentially all published specifications of telecommunications systems. Section 16.2 introduces some of the features and functions of the specified system.

The principal theme of this chapter is complexity. Section 16.3 discusses some deeper aspects of the specified system. It explores why each aspect is complex, and what specification techniques seem best in each case for representing and managing that complexity. Section 16.3 shows or describes partial specifications written as Jackson diagrams, as finite automata, as statecharts, and in Z.

The result of Section 16.3 is a clear mandate for the use of a multiparadigm approach. Each notation offers specialized features and semantics that make the specification of some aspect of the switching system concise and readable. If we give up these special advantages, then the size of the specification will explode beyond practical limits.

Sections 16.4 through 16.7 explain how partial specifications written in multiple languages (six in all) are composed in the specification of this switching system. The foundations of the multiparadigm method were laid down by Zave and Jackson (1993). In this study we emphasize how the partial specifications constrain each other. We also focus on overcoming typical obstacles, namely the need to compose languages with incompatible semantics, and the need to check consistency across language boundaries.

Non-trivial examples of multiparadigm specification are difficult to find, so we have tried to make this a useful one. We have tried to convey the flavour of the problem, the advantages of using multiple languages on it, the style of the decomposition and composition employed, and the motivation behind the reasoning processes applied to it.

Some details have been suppressed for clarity. For those who are interested, the full specification (Zave and Mataga, 1993a,b; Mataga and Zave, 1993) is available from the authors. The major specification techniques have also been given a more rigorous, more problem-independent treatment elsewhere (Zave and Jackson, 1994).

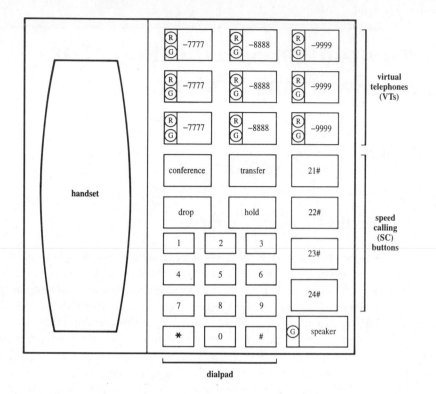

Figure 16.1   Telephones connected to the switching system have at least the hardware features shown here.

16.2   Some features of the switching system

The system supports modern telephones with at least the hardware shown in Figure 16.1.

A virtual telephone (VT) is a hardware resource, belonging to a telephone and support-ing time multiplexing of calls at that telephone. A telephone can participate in as many calls simultaneously as it has VTs. The green light of a VT helps to indicate the status of the call assigned to that VT, if any.

The VT that is selected controls the shared resources of the telephone, such as the voice channel, handset, built-in speakerphone, dialpad, and function buttons. At most one VT is selected at a time, and a selected VT's red indicator light is always lit. The VT se-lected at a telephone can be changed by pressing VT selection buttons. Selecting a new VT usually has the effect of disconnecting any call at the previously selected VT, but a selected VT can be deselected without disconnecting the call assigned to it by pressing the hold button first.

Each VT has a directory number (DN), as shown by the four-digit labels in Figure 16.1. One telephone can have multiple DNs, and one DN can be shared by the VTs of multiple telephones. Shared DNs have profound consequences on call processing, as a few scenarios will illustrate.

A call to a shared DN usually rings at every telephone sharing the DN. If the call is answered, then the answering VT becomes connected and every other VT (that was previously ringing) remains as a participant in the call with a **reserved** status. A reserved VT can be connected to the talking VTs of the call very easily — all a user needs to do is select it. A set of VTs that ring simultaneously and remain part of a call after it is answered constitute one example of a **cluster**.

A cluster is also formed at the caller's end of the call. Every telephone sharing the calling DN usually contributes a reserved VT to a calling cluster; these reserved VTs can join the talking VTs just as easily as the reserved VTs on the called end.

The VTs of a cluster form a sort of committee representing the cluster DN to the call. The switching system considers them interchangeable, so a cluster lasts as long as it contains at least one connected VT. In other words, a cluster cannot be the source of a call disconnection operation until its last VT disconnects.

Use of the conference button joins two calls at this telephone so that people at three telephones can confer. Use of the drop button disassembles a conference or, if the currently selected call is not a conference, acts as a disconnect or as a cancel. Use of the transfer button joins two calls from this telephone and removes this telephone, so that the resulting configuration connects the far parties of the original two calls.

Speed calling enables a user to enter frequently used DNs quickly. The speed-calling (SC) codes at each telephone can be assigned separately to DNs. An SC code can be entered by pressing an SC button or dialing two digits followed by "#".

Three types of call forwarding are offered by the switching system. Calls to a DN can be forwarded when the DN is busy, when the DN rings but there is no answer, or under all circumstances. For each DN and each type of forwarding, the forwarding destination can be set separately and the capability can be turned on or off separately.

16.3   Some complex aspects of the switching system

16.3.1   Connections

The major function of a switching system is to create and destroy voice connections. One might imagine that voice connections could be represented by an equivalence relation on telephones, with each equivalence class being a connected set of telephones, but the features of the system specified here require a much more complex representation.

First, the participants in a call are VTs rather than telephones. This might seem like a mere change of nomenclature, but it introduces the possibility that the same telephone could have several VTs participating (playing different roles) in the same call.

Second, two distinct connection relationships (inter- and intracluster) must be represented. Two connected VTs in the same cluster are related in such a way that if one is disconnected, the other is unaffected. If a call consists solely of two VTs in different clusters, however, the disconnection of one of them will destroy the entire call.

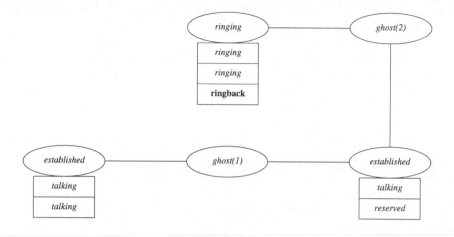

Figure 16.2   A sample call graph. Clusters are depicted as ovals and labelled with cluster states. VTs in clusters are depicted as rectangles and labelled with VT states. Billable connections are depicted as lines between clusters.

Third, even at the cluster level a call cannot be represented as a simple equivalence class (of clusters). It is a graph whose nodes are clusters and whose edges are billable connections. Some of the clusters are **ghosts** having no VT members. This graph is shaped by the history of the call, particularly by the use of forwarding and conferencing features. It includes all the historical information necessary to ensure correct call processing and billing in the future.

Figure 16.2 shows some aspects of the graph of a complex call. The two established clusters and the first ghost cluster were previously an isolated call. The ghost is present because the isolated call was set up with the help of call forwarding. The ghost is necessary because there must be two billable connections: one billed to the caller and one billed to the forwarder.

The second ghost cluster was originally a normal cluster from which a call to the ringing cluster was dialled. This normal cluster had one VT which was at the same telephone as a VT in the rightmost established cluster. A conference operation at that telephone merged the roles of the two VTs into the one talking VT in the established cluster. The ringing cluster contains a special VT which is a generator of the ringback tone; all of the talking VTs in the call can currently hear ringback.

So what is the nature of the complexity in this aspect of the specified system? A call is representable by a graph, but the graph is hierarchical—its nodes are clusters of VTs. Both clusters and VTs have states. There are many structural constraints relating the call, cluster, and VT levels. The inevitable consequence of these constraints is that a typical call operation changes the representation at all three levels.

Furthermore, there is an inherent difference between operations that create call structures and operations that destroy them. Creation operations tend to be requested very explicitly by telephone users. Destruction operations do not; they are usually the system's attempt to clean up after the users have disconnected and disappeared.

Z (Spivey, 1992) has two great representational strengths. One is the richness and flexibility of its notation. The other is the fact that any state invariant is implicitly asserted to hold before and after any state change (Hayes *et al.*, 1994).

These strengths can be put to good use in specifying connections. The flexibility of the notation makes it straightforward to represent connection graphs, with all their miscellaneous levels, states, and other attributes. We extended the usual notation (using extensibility features built into Z) to make infix operators capable of updating the call representation at all three levels simultaneously. These operators are similar in purpose to the well-known specification technique of promotion, but they push the notation much further, and make the idea practical in a situation where normal promotion would be too clumsy.

Many representational details are covered by invariants, so that the specifications of operations are much briefer than they would be if they had to specify the outcome of each operation completely. The effect is particularly dramatic for destruction operations. When a cluster is deleted, for instance, invariants ensure that the affected call is pruned back automatically to the largest useful graph; this pruning can remove a chain of ghost clusters and connections without any explicit instructions to do so.

More details about the Z specification of connections can be found elsewhere (Mataga and Zave, 1994).

16.3.2 Digit analysis

Users of the switching system dial digits to indicate call destinations; they can do this by dialling full DNs or shorter SC codes. Users also dial digits to enter other feature commands, including ten different set-up commands for call forwarding and speed calling. Dialling episodes are further complicated by the need for iteration and error recovery. Users may dial a sequence of feature commands in one dialling episode. Users may also dial erroneous entries, may cancel incomplete entries using the drop button, or may quit dialling without completing the latest entry.

Obviously the strings of symbols entered by users during dialling episodes must be parsed so that the switching system can interpret them properly as call-processing commands. The best way to specify a parse is to supply a corresponding formal grammar. A grammar is a completely declarative specification of a parsing algorithm.

The digit grammar turns out to be regular. Ordinary regular grammars and regular expressions are inadequate, however, because they have no built-in features for simplifying the exceedingly complex subexpressions that result from separating correct and error cases.

A better choice is the diagrams originally introduced as part of the Jackson structured programming method (Jackson, 1975) and later extended for telecommunications applications (Zave and Jackson, 1989). These are regular expressions represented graphically as non-recursive trees, with labelled non-terminals and built-in features for error handling.

Figures 16.3 through 16.5 show three fragments of a simplified version of the dialling grammar. If a set of sibling nodes is unannotated, then the parent non-terminal node is defined as the concatenation of the siblings. If a set of siblings is annotated with small circles, then the parent is defined as exactly one of the siblings. If a parent has only one child annotated with an asterisk, then the parent is defined as zero or more repetitions of the child. Leaf nodes labelled *dial-...*, *SC*, *drop*, or — (empty sequence) are terminals of the grammar, while all other leaf nodes are non-terminals of the grammar, and must be defined (have the same labels as parents) in other diagrams. The large circles will be explained in Section 16.7.

Figure 16.3 is the top of the tree. The labels "POSIT" and "ADMIT AS SOON AS POSSIBLE" indicate that each *complete dialing entry* is to be parsed as a *correct entry* if that is possible. If it is not possible, then the first input that makes it impossible completes the *complete dialing entry* and ensures that it will be parsed as an *erroneous entry*.

Figure 16.4 illustrates a few other notational conveniences. Each *DN* is a string of exactly seven digits. The pattern *dial-(2..4)* matches any of three dialled digits. The non-terminal *correct multievent entry* is defined as any one of *setup command, DN entry,* or *pickup code*. The non-terminal *incomplete entry*, because of the ! annotation in its child, is defined as any proper, non-empty prefix of a *correct multievent entry*.

16.3.3   Telephone states

The state of the specification must include the states of individual telephones. There are two reasons for this. The switching system controls some aspects of the states of telephones, such as the status of the audio channel. The switching system must also keep track of some aspects that it does not control, such as whether or not the telephone is offhook, because it needs this information to interpret input signals from the telephone correctly.

The telephone states themselves are not complex. The state transitions, on the other hand, are surprisingly many and varied. This is illustrated by Figure 16.6, which is a finite automaton specifying the relationship between some Boolean components of the state of a telephone and the events that can change their truth values.

The states of the automaton in Figure 16.6 encode whether the telephone is *onhook* or *offhook* (two mutually exclusive and exhaustive alternatives), and whether the audio channel is inactive, is being directed through the handset, or is being directed through the built-in speakerphone (another set of alternatives). The transition labels denote disjoint classes of event that the telephone can generate as inputs to the switching system. These classes do not include all the events that the telephone can generate, but they do include all the events that can affect these particular state components.

The compound transition labels have been made as mnemonic as possible. For example, members of *speaker-with-target* and *speaker-without-target* are both generated by pressing the speaker button. The difference is that a *speaker-with-target* occurs when some VT at the telephone (the "target") is selected, and a *speaker-without-target* occurs when no VT at the telephone is selected. These event classes are discussed further in Section 16.7.

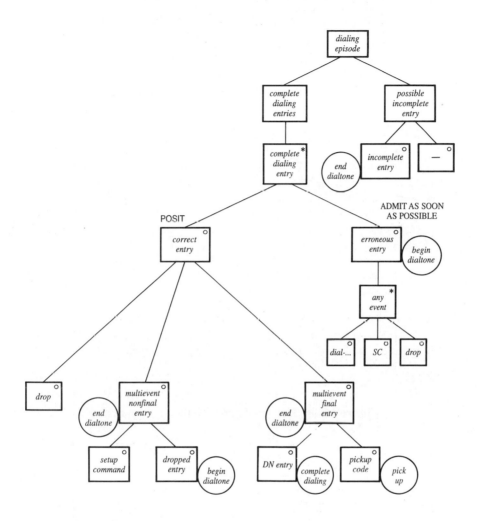

Figure 16.3 A Jackson diagram in the digit grammar.

Note how understanding of the complex relationships in Figure 16.6 is enhanced by the graphical notation. It is difficult to imagine a textual representation that would be as successful.

Figure 16.7 is a specification of the telephone states involved when a user is attempting to perform conference or transfer operations. These operations require at least two button pushes, so there must be some memory of the first when the second arrives. Statecharts are finite automata augmented with many features, in particular hierarchical states (Harel, 1987). Figure 16.7 is a statechart, chosen because the state information involved in the conference–transfer protocol is inherently hierarchical.

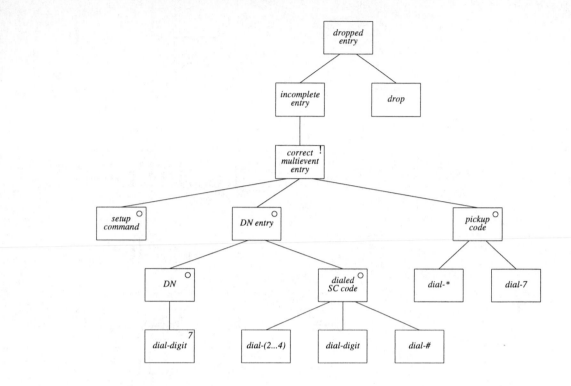

Figure 16.4 A Jackson diagram in the digit grammar.

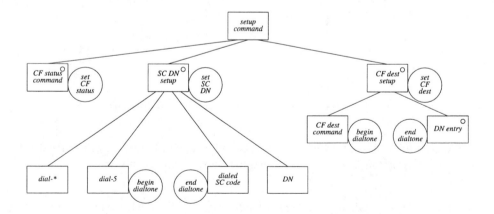

Figure 16.5 A Jackson diagram in the digit grammar.

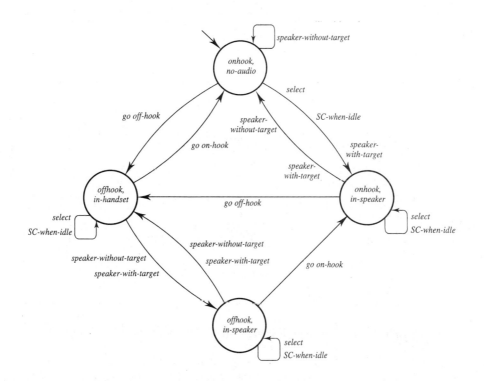

Figure 16.6 A finite automaton constraining some components of the telephone state.

16.4 Foundations of language composition

The subject matter of a formal specification is the observable phenomena of the real world. These phenomena can all be formalized in terms of a set of unique individuals and a finite set of relations on individuals. In other words, the set of possible specificands (Wing, 1990) can be restricted to the models of one-sorted first-order predicate logic with equality (Jackson and Zave, 1992).

The basic idea supporting composition of partial specifications written in different languages is that every partial specification is equivalent to an assertion in first-order logic. The vocabulary of a partial specification is the set of atomic relations found in its assertion. The meaning of a composition of a set of partial specifications is the conjunction of their equivalent assertions.

It has been shown that many useful languages and notations can be given complete semantics in first-order logic, using the particular first-order encoding of temporal phenomena presented in Section 16.5. These semantics provide precise, flexible, and intuitive explanations of how partial specifications in different languages work together (Zave and Jackson, 1993).

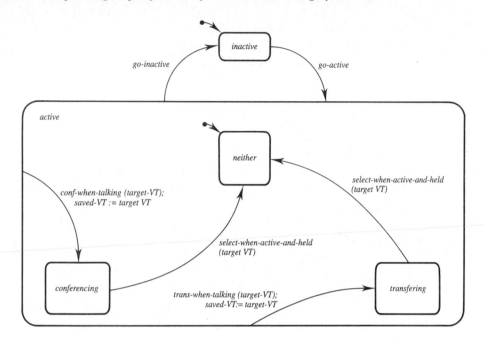

Figure 16.7 A statechart constraining some components of the telephone state.

Although the basic idea is sound and offers many advantages, two kinds of difficulty are almost inevitable in using this multiparadigm approach on a large scale. The particular value of a realistic case study is that we can confront these difficulties realistically. Our experience shows that the obstacles are surmountable — that serious problems can be avoided, and that the insights gained in avoiding them improve the general organization and coherence of the specification.

One of the difficulties is that for some popular specification languages it is not feasible to give a complete semantics in first-order logic, either because their assumptions about representation of the real world are too different from ours, or because they are too feature rich to contemplate such a project. Both objections apply to Z. As the reader will see, this obstacle can be overcome by relying on a partial semantics of Z in our style — covering only those aspects of the Z specification that interact directly with other languages. If the translatable subset of Z is small enough and carefully chosen, it can be translated both conveniently and accurately.

The other difficulty is that the specification must be internally consistent, and some of the reasoning needed to show consistency crosses language boundaries. In principle it would be possible to translate all the specifications into logic, and to manipulate them within that formal system. In practice this form of reasoning seems absurdly indirect and inefficient.

This obstacle can be overcome because, as the reader will see, the organization of the specification is far from arbitrary. Partial specifications constrain each other in very restricted ways. Analysis and exploitation of the organization of the specification can replace global, low-level reasoning with proof obligations on individual partial specifications. These local proof obligations can be discharged using higher-level, language-dependent technology.

16.5 Temporal properties of the specification

Our specification regards the switching system and its telephones as a big state machine. The inputs are events occurring at telephones (they are caused by user actions). These events cause state changes. The "output" of the system is its current state, which includes the current connections and the states of all indicator lights and sounds on telephones.

Input events are assumed to be atomic and sequential. A state change in response to an event is assumed to occur before any subsequent event.

This model of a switching system and its telephones is rather unrealistic, as it ignores communication delays, the distributed nature of the domain, and the possibility of slow system responses. Nevertheless, we believe it is the right model for feature specification, for the following reasons.

Telecommunications features are always specified in terms of sequential input events and instantaneous responses, because that is the only way that users (and engineers, for that matter) can understand them. The complexity of telephone features and their interactions is very great. It is a very different kind of complexity from that presented by distributed, concurrent systems. The two must be kept separate, because addressing them both simultaneously is a foolish and doomed endeavour.

The two kinds of complexity can be kept separate, simply because the simplified feature model is a viable approximation of reality. It may not be clear to the switching implementation which of two events at two different telephones occurred first, but if the implementation chooses an order arbitrarily and then behaves consistently according to that choice, observers at the two telephones will not be able to detect an anomaly. When input events are occurring too fast for the switching implementation to keep up with them, the implementation can queue them without loss and respond to them in queued order. Users can tolerate and adjust to this situation, as long as the implementation ensures that it is not severe or frequent.

Other circumstances also help to make the specification simple from a temporal point of view. There are no preconditions on events, as any event can occur at any time. There are no liveness properties, as nothing in this model happens "eventually". All we have are safety properties: state invariants and event post-conditions. Event post-conditions assert that if an event with certain characteristics occurs during a state with certain characteristics, then the state after the event has certain characteristics.[1] Needless to say, state invariants and event post-conditions must be consistent with one another.

---

[1] There are a few exceptions to the specification properties described in this section, but they are minor and do not affect the overall organization of the specification. The only ones noticeable to a reader of this chapter concern telephone switchhooks: *onhook* and *offhook* components of the state are physical, and therefore not under the control of the switching software. A *go-offhook* event cannot occur when a telephone is *offhook*, and a *go-onhook* event cannot occur when a telephone is *onhook*.

Returning to the common semantics in first-order logic, an essential feature of this common semantics is a representation of temporal phenomena. It assumes that events are unique and atomic. They are formalized as individuals, and differentiated from other individuals by the unary relation *event(e)*.

We also assume that events are totally ordered in time. This is formalized by a first-order theory asserting that the binary relation *earlier(e_1, e_2)* is a non-dense total order over the events.

Because events are non-dense and totally ordered, we can postulate a unique pause between each adjacent pair of events during which the relevant state of the world cannot change and can be observed. These pauses can be formalized as individuals satisfying the unary relation *pause(p)*. The relation *earlier(e_1, e_2)* is extended to pauses, so that the set of all temporal phenomena (events and pauses) becomes a total order in which events and pauses alternate strictly, beginning with a pause and ending (if there is an end) with a pause.

The significance of pauses is that every state component is formalized as a relation with a pause argument. For example, *offhook(t, p)* is true if and only if telephone *t* is offhook during pause *p*.

A few sample assertions will illustrate how these relations are used. This one states that for any telephone, during any pause, *offhook* and *onhook* are exclusive and exhaustive alternatives:

$$\forall t \forall p ((\text{offhook}(t,p) \lor \text{onhook}(t,p)) \land \neg(\text{offhook}(t,p) \land \text{onhook}(t,p)))$$

The next assertion means that a *go-onhook* event cannot occur at a telephone that is *onhook*. The relation *source-telephone(e,t)* is true if and only if telephone *t* is the source of event *e*. The relation *ends(e, p)*, true if and only if *e* is the event that ends pause *p*, is defined in terms of *earlier(e_1, e_2)*.

$$\forall t \forall p \forall e (\text{onhook}(t,p) \land \text{source-telephone}(e,t) \land \text{ends}(e,p) \Rightarrow \neg\text{go-onhook}(e))$$

The final assertion means that after a *go-offhook* event, a telephone is *offhook*. The relation *begins(e, p)*, true if and only if *e* is the event that begins pause *p*, is defined in terms of *earlier(e_1, e_2)*.

$$\forall t \forall p \forall e (\text{begins}(e,p) \land \text{source-telephone}(e,t) \land \text{go-offhook}(e) \Rightarrow \text{offhook}(t,p))$$

16.6   State components

16.6.1   State-oriented decomposition

From Section 16.5 we can infer that the specifier's primary job is to state completely the post-conditions on state components.

As the examples in Section 16.3 suggest, many of the factors that influence which specification language is appropriate for which partial specification have to do with its state

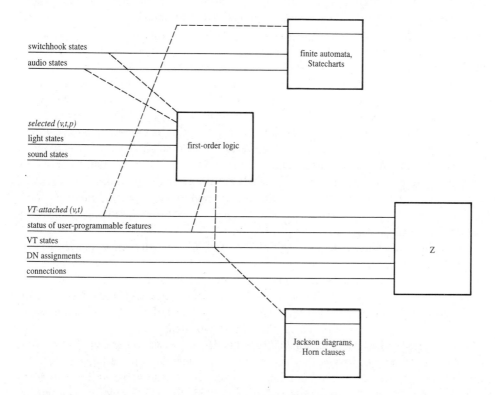

switchhook states

audio states

selected (v,t,p)

light states

sound states

VT attached (v,t)

status of user-programmable features

VT states

DN assignments

connections

finite automata,
Statecharts

first-order logic

Z

Jackson diagrams,
Horn clauses

Figure 16.8   Modules (collections of partial specifications) in the switching specification constraining each other by means of shared state components. Regarding lines as directed from left to right, the lines entering a module on its left represent part of its vocabulary. Solid lines represent relations that the module constrains, and dashed lines represent relations that it only examines.

components. For instance, Z is used to specify connections because of the features it offers for representing complex call states. The use of Jackson diagrams for digit analysis makes it unnecessary to specify parsing states—they are implicit in the grammar. Various forms of automata are chosen by matching their state representations to the properties of the relevant state components.

As a result of these factors, the decomposition into partial specifications is based primarily on grouping similar or closely related state components, and the choice of language for each partial specification is based on the nature of the state components in it.

Figure 16.8 shows the decomposition of the specification into four major pieces (each one containing one or two partial specifications) based on state components. Each module is labelled with the languages used in it.

To make the specification more orderly and to limit the complexity of global reasoning, there is a further rule: each state component is constrained by at most one partial specification. A state component may belong to the vocabularies of any number of partial specifications, all of which may examine it, but only one partial specification may constrain it (assert invariants and post-conditions governing it) as well.

The idea of partitioning a specification into modules on the basis of state components is a familiar one—it is the basis of data abstraction and object-oriented design. One of the differences between partial specifications and objects is that objects access the states of other objects by means of operational procedure calls, while partial specifications simply make assertions about the relations in their vocabularies, both shared and unshared.

In Figure 16.8, the solid lines at the left of each module indicate the state components constrained by the module. Most of the labels are informal designations for groups of relations. For example, "VT states" stands for the relations $idle(v, p)$, $held(v, p)$, $dialing(v, p)$, $ringing(v, p)$, $reserved(v, p)$ and $talking(v, p)$, each true if and only if the VT v is in the indicated state during pause p.

The relation $VT\text{-}attached(v, t)$ is true if and only if VT v is attached to telephone t (it is a total function from VTs onto telephones). The relation $selected(v, t, p)$ is true if and only if VT v is the selected VT at telephone t during pause p.

The light states, sound states, and $selected(v, t, p)$ state components are relatively simple and have relatively little structure exploitable by the use of a higher-level language. That is why they are constrained using plain first-order logic.

The module specified with Jackson diagrams and Horn clauses constrains no state components. (As mentioned above, the Jackson diagrams encode implicit parse states, but these are local to the partial specification and not directly observable in the real world of the switching system.) The function of this module in the whole specification will be explained in Section 16.7.

16.6.2   Intermodule constraint through shared state components

Whenever partial specification S_2 examines a state component that is constrained by partial specification S_1, a channel of influence is available from S_1 to S_2. In Figure 16.8, dashed lines from state components to modules show the state components examined but not constrained by those modules.

You will note that there is relatively little intermodule constraint through shared state components. The preferred mechanism (explained in Section 16.7) is better structured, and bears most of the burden of propagating influence among partial specifications.

So why is intermodule constraint through shared state components used at all? As will be shown, the mechanism presented in Section 16.7 relies on a partial order on partial specifications (the order within the switching specification is indicated by left-to-right position in Figure 16.8). This mechanism can only propagate information from lesser to greater in the partial order. So the less-structured mechanism of shared state components must be used whenever information must be propagated from greater to lesser in the partial order. Note that, in Figure 16.8, all uses of shared state components propagate information from right to left—the partial specification constraining the state component always lies to the right of the partial specification examining it.

"Propagation of information" has an operational flavour to it, but we are just trying to describe how partial specifications constrain each other. Recall that composed partial specifications are really just conjoined assertions. They do not execute, they are not members of a hierarchy, and they do not communicate with each other in any operational sense.

Also note that intermodule constraint is minimized as much as possible. For example, the specification is written so that the simple VT states are all that the other partial specifications need to know about the state of connections. As a result, the much more complex call-graph components need not be shared.

A partial specification is most readily reusable if its scope is kept as small as possible. For example, it is better to write a partial specification describing one telephone than to have it describe all telephones simultaneously. A partial specification describing one telephone, however, must be applied to all telephones. That is the function of the small extra boxes on top of two of the modules in Figure 16.8.

These extra boxes represent "wrappers", a specification construct that (among other things) wraps a specification inside a universal quantifier. Although wrappers have been formalized in higher-order logic (Gunter *et al.*, 1994), a wrapped module is still equivalent to a first-order assertion. The top wrapper applies the automata module to every telephone. The bottom wrapper applies the Jackson–Horn module to every dialling episode, i.e. every distinct situation in which a VT is continuously in the *dialing* state.

Most of the specification languages used have been given complete first-order semantics, so the relationship between the higher-level languages and the atomic relations in their vocabularies is straightforward. The only semantic problem is presented by Z, because it does not have a complete first-order semantics. This problem is solved by focusing on the shared relations, as follows.

Recall that in the common semantics, all state components take the form of atomic relations with a pause argument. Obviously this includes state components that are shared by the Z specification and other partial specifications, for example $ringing(v, p)$ and $CF\text{-}feature\text{-}status(f, n, u, p)$ (during pause p, call-forwarding feature f has activation status u for DN n).

Now consider these two features of Z: basic types such as [*VT,feature,DN,status*] and global variables whose types are either power sets of a basic type or power sets of Cartesian products of basic types:

$ringing : \mathbf{P}\mathit{VT}$

$CF\_feature\_status : \mathbf{P}(feature \times DN \times status)$

These two features are very easily translated into first-order logic. A basic type such as *VT* corresponds to a unary relation $VT(v)$ true if and only if v is a *VT*. A variable such as *ringing* corresponds to a binary relation $ringing(v, p)$ true if and only if v is a member of the set *ringing* during pause p. A variable such as *CF_feature_status* corresponds to a quaternary relation $CF\text{-}feature\text{-}status(f, n, u, p)$ true if and only if (f, n, u) is a member of the set *CF_feature_status* during pause p. These relations are the shared state components, exactly.[2]

So far we have shown that there exists a translatable representation in Z for all shared state components, but the translatable representation may bear no resemblance to the way state information is actually specified in Z. For example, it has nothing to do with the call-graph structures discussed in Section 16.3.1.

This is not a problem because of the particular role of invariants in Z (Jackson, 1995). We can write the Z specification exactly as we please, and then we can declare translatable variables for all shared state components as a redundant representation. The translatable variables do not affect the existing specification in any way; they are not mentioned in it and their values are never manipulated directly. All we need are invariants that relate the values of the translatable variables to the values of the more complex state representations in the "real" specification. (These invariants are typically easy to write.) The invariants guarantee that the translatable variables always have the correct values.

16.6.3   Consistency of state components

Obviously partial specifications that constrain state components must do so in a consistent manner. This is a matter of the consistency of individual partial specifications, which is outside the scope of this chapter. Our concern here is to reduce all issues of consistency between partial specifications to proof obligations on individual partial specifications.

The only consistency obligation raised by state components is that only one partial specification can constrain each state component. The others that share it must use it in a "read-only" manner.

The situation is a little tricky because there is no formal notion of constraint in first-order logic; it must be added as a metaconcept. Fortunately all we need to do is to tag the relations in the vocabulary of a partial specification as "constrained" or "not constrained." Consider the partial specification consisting entirely of $\forall x (P(x) \Leftrightarrow Q(x))$, with $Q(x)$ tagged as constrained and $P(x)$ tagged as not constrained. This specification means that Q must always agree with P.

The resulting local proof obligations are as follows. For each partial specification that examines some state-component relations $E_1, \ldots, E_n$ and constrains some state-component relations $C_1, \ldots, C_n$, and for each possible set of relations $E_1, \ldots, E_n$, there must exist relations $C_1, \ldots, C_n$ satisfying the specification.

16.7   Event classes

16.7.1   Event classification

In addition to making assertions about phenomena (relations), a partial specification can also define new relations in terms of the relations of its vocabulary. These defined relations can appear in the vocabularies of other partial specifications as if they were directly observable phenomena, providing a second means of influence and constraint among par-

---

[2]Our convention in handling formal names is that capitalization is irrelevant, and all separators (space, hyphen, underscore) are equivalent. This enables us to satisfy the naming conventions of many languages without explicit name translation.

tial specifications (Zave and Jackson, 1993). This means of influence, applied particularly to the classification of events, is used heavily within our switching specification.

In the terminology of this chapter, an **event type** is a set of events whose members are directly observable in the real world, such as the set of all *offhook* events. Each event type is formalized as a unary relation on events, and the event types partition the set of all events.

Event classes are also sets of events characterized by unary relations on events, but they are defined within the specification. Event classes may overlap freely—in addition to its single type, an event may belong to any number of event classes.

The definition of an event class within a partial specification typically makes use of state components constrained by that partial specification. Thus the event classification carries with it some information about the state at the time that the event occurred, which is how it propagates information among partial specifications. An example will illustrate this.

Figure 16.9 is an augmented version of Figure 16.6. It differs from Figure 16.6 mainly in having definitions of new event classes. Any transition label containing a slash contributes to these definitions. A transition labelled *select/select-when-active* means that the transition applies in the usual way to any *select* event occurring in its source state, and that any *select* event occurring in its source state is also defined to belong to the class *select-when-active*. The event class *select-when-active* is the set of all events causing transitions whose labels contain *select-when-active* after the slash. Any other partial specification with *select-when-active(e)* in its vocabulary can rely on the fact that any such event occurred when its telephone was active, i.e. had an active audio channel.

Figure 16.9 shows how any automaton-based notation (including statecharts) can be augmented for definition of event classes based on the states in which events occur. We have also augmented Jackson diagrams for event classification, as shown in Figures 16.3 and 16.5. If a large circle is attached to the right side of a box representing a non-terminal of the grammar, then the last event parsed as belonging to each instance of that non-terminal is given the classification in the circle. If a large circle is attached to the left side of a box, then the first event parsed as belonging to each instance of the non-terminal is given the classification in the circle. Algorithmic checks are necessary to ensure that event classification is unambiguous despite backtracking in the parse. We have found this notation to be extremely powerful and convenient.

How do partial specifications use or absorb nonlocal state information by means of event classification? This is easy, because every specification language employed in this project allows event classes as vocabulary relations. From the perspective of a partial specification with event classes in its vocabulary, it makes no difference whether those event classes are directly recognizable in the real world or are defined with the help of directly and indirectly observable information.

Figure 16.10 shows how the modules of the switching specification constrain each other through defined relations. Event types and classes have been introduced in this section; event attributes will be discussed in Section 16.7.3. Note that the event classes defined by a module are always based on the state components constrained by that module. Note also that the "automata" module uses some defined event classes; this is why

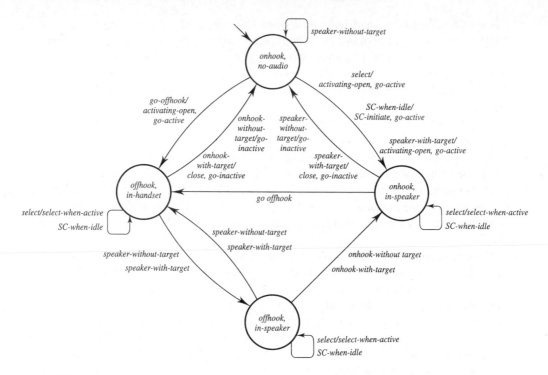

Figure 16.9 A finite automaton augmented with definitions of event classes.

the transition-causing labels in Figures 16.6 and 16.9 are sometimes more elaborate than *go-offhook, go-onhook,* etc.[3]

To prevent circular definitions, the graph of definitions and uses (as in Figure 16.10) must be acyclic. This is the origin of the partial order on partial specifications alluded to in Section 16.6.

Figures 16.8 and 16.10 combined show essentially all the vocabulary of all the major pieces of the specification.

Like sharing of state components, definition of new relations is a purely declarative specification mechanism, with no operational aspect whatsoever. Like sharing of state components, partial specifications are influencing one another through mutual assertions on a shared vocabulary of relations.

16.7.2   Z operations

Strictly speaking Z has no temporal semantics, but there is a widely used convention that a Z operation corresponds to an event class, and that the unprimed and primed variables in

---

[3]The reader may also notice that the transition-causing labels are more elaborate in Figure 16.9 than in Figure 16.6. This is because additional discriminations are needed to define the new event classes properly.

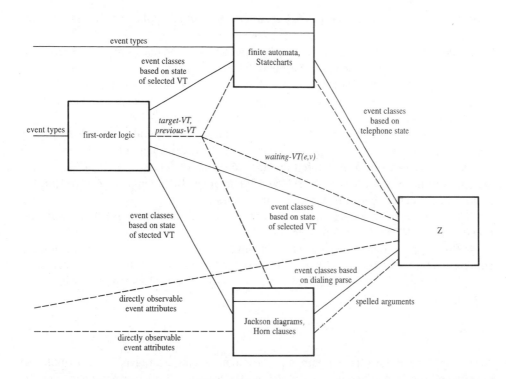

Figure 16.10   Modules (collections of partial specifications) in the switching specification constraining each other by means of defined relations. Regarding lines as directed from left to right, the lines entering a module on its left represent part of its vocabulary. Solid lines represent event types or classes, and dashed lines represent event attributes (binary relations on events and their attributes).

the operation schema describe the state before and after events in that class, respectively. Our partial translation of Z into the common first-order logic semantics is based on that convention.

The operations of the Z specification are chosen to be natural and convenient within its context of representation choices and style. They are interesting from a complexity standpoint because there is a large conceptual gap between them and the event types observable in the real world. The non-Z modules perform a many-to-many mapping from event types to Z operations. Without the assistance of this mapping, the Z operations would have to correspond to raw event types, and the Z specification would be much more complex and much less readable.

What follows are examples of the nature of the conceptual gap between event types and Z operations. The examples mention these Z operations: *open* is to a VT what going offhook is to an old-fashioned telephone—it initiates activity; *close* is to a VT what going onhook is to an old-fashioned telephone—it terminates activity; *complete-conf* merges two calls as described in Section 16.3.1; *complete-dialing* supplies a DN and attempts call set-up.

(1) Events of one type, occurring in different contexts, can correspond to several different operations. When a telephone is onhook and the selected VT is talking through the speakerphone, the event *press-speaker* is classified as a *close*. When a telephone is onhook and completely idle, the event *press-speaker* is classified as an *open* of the currently selected VT (which is now active through the speakerphone).

(2) Events of several different types can turn out to be different ways of performing the same operation. An *open* operation can be performed through three raw events. It can be a *press-speaker*, as explained in the first example. It can be a *go-offhook* when the speakerphone is not in use (the selected VT is opened). It can be a *select* of the VT to be opened, under several different circumstances.

(3) Events can be ignored if they occur at the wrong time. *Dial* events are always ignored unless a VT in the *dialing* state is selected.

(4) Some operations are requested by means of a sequence of events. Requesting a conference takes two button pushes, only the second of which is classified as a *complete-conf*. Dialing a DN takes several button pushes, only the last of which is classified as a *complete-dialing* operation.

16.7.3   Arguments

All of the Z operations have arguments. Argument values are regarded as attributes of events, and are formalized as binary relations on events and other individuals. For example, most of the Z operations have a VT-valued argument named *target_VT?*. In the common semantics this translates to a relation *target-VT*(e, v) true if and only if VT v is the argument of event e.

Some arguments are directly observable in the real world. For instance, each event of type *dial* has an observable attribute relation *dialed-symbol*(e, s). However, most of the attribute relations are defined.

Three VT-valued attributes show up often as arguments to Z operations: *target-VT*, *previous-VT*, and *waiting-VT*. The target of an operation is the VT directly affected or referred to by it. The *previous-VT* is the VT that was selected immediately before the operation. Some operations affect both their targets and their *previous-VT*s. For example, an operation that opens a VT must also close any previously opened VT, since at most one VT can be opened at a time. These attribute relations are defined in the "logic" module, mostly on the basis of what VT is selected at the time an event occurs.

The *waiting-VT* is one of the two VT-valued arguments of a conference or transfer operation. It is defined by an augmented version of the statechart shown in Figure 16.7.

The most interesting arguments are those determined by dialling sequences. Although inherently complex, they are extremely easy to specify, because we have given the specification languages we are using some powerful semantics tailored to problems of this nature. The language semantics does all the work, and the specifier needs to write little.

Rather than give a complete presentation of the specification techniques being used, we shall confine ourselves to an example.

As specified in Figure 16.5, a *Set_SC_DN* operation of the Z specification is requested by first entering the command code "*5" (after which the user hears a new dialtone), then by entering an SC code, then by entering a DN. After the operation, the SC code will stand for the DN.

As explained in Section 16.7.1, the semantics of the Jackson diagram ensures that the last event of an event sequence parsed as an instance of the non-terminal *SC DN setup* is classified as a *Set_SC_DN* operation, i.e. it satisfies the relation *set-SC-DN(e)*. Since the Z operation *Set_SC_DN* has an argument *entered_SC_code?*, our task now is to define the relation *entered-SC-code(e, c)*.

In Section 16.5 we introduced a temporal theory on the relations *event(e)*, *pause(p)*, and *earlier(e_1, e_2)*. The temporal theory also includes some other relations and assertions. *episode(s)* is true if and only if *s* is the unique identifier of a set of events. *episode-member(e, s)* is true if and only if event *e* belongs to episode *s*. *subepisode(s_2, s_1)* is true if and only if its arguments are both episodes, and all the events of s_2 are also events of s_1.

Let s_1 identify the set of dialling events entered by a user in requesting a *Set_SC_DN* operation, and let s_2 identify the subset of those events used to determine the SC code. Then, by virtue of the semantics outlined above, we know that *episode(s_1)*, *episode(s_2)*, and *subepisode(s_2, s_1)* are true.

Just as the Jackson diagrams have built-in semantics for defining event classes, they also have built-in semantics for defining episode classes and an episode-valued event attribute. Each non-terminal of the grammar corresponds to an episode class (unary relation on episodes), so the Jackson diagram asserts automatically that *SC-DN-setup(s_1)* and *dialed-SC-code(s_2)*. Each event classified has an attribute which is the episode whose parse caused it to be classified, so the Jackson diagram asserts automatically that *operation-episode(e, s_1)* is true, where *e* is the *Set_SC_DN* operation.

The definition of *entered-SC-code(e, c)* is conveniently written as a Horn clause in Prolog syntax:

entered_sc_code(E, C) :– *set_sc_dn(E)*, *operation_episode(E, S1)*,
        subepisode(S2, S1), *dialed_sc_code(S2)*, *match_as_sc_codes(S2, C)*.

It can be paraphrased operationally as, "to find the argument of event *e*, find the episode s_1 that goes with *e*, then find a subepisode s_2 of s_1 with type *dialed-SC-code*, then find an SC code *c* that matches the episode s_2".

We now have all the necessary pieces except a relation *match-as-SC-codes(s, c)*, true if and only if *c* is an individual, unique SC code with a digit spelling that matches the dialing events in episode *s*.

Fortunately this relation is easy to come by, for reasons shown graphically in Figure 16.11. The spellings of SC codes are immutable state of the specification (not mentioned previously, because immutable state components present few challenges). Episodes and SC codes are both sequences (totally ordered sets) with isomorphic formalizations in terms of individuals and relations. This makes specifying the *match* predicate trivial— we reused a relation from a standard library concerning sequences.

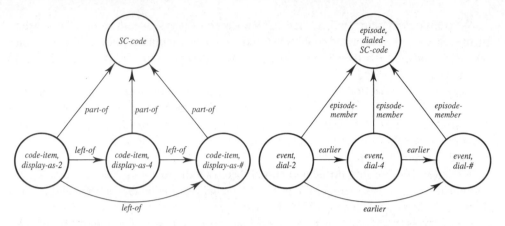

Figure 16.11   Formal representation of an SC code and a *dialed-SC-code* episode. A circle is an individual. A label inside a circle is a unary relation satisfied by the individual. Each arrow is labelled by a binary relation, and indicates that the relation is true with the origin individual as the first argument and the destination individual as the second argument.

The language semantics called upon in this technique are unfamiliar and perhaps subtle; they rely on isomorphisms of temporal and spatial "data structures." At the same time, the specification work is easy—the argument relation was defined by writing a single Horn clause. This combination of concise specification and powerful semantics is exactly what we are seeking in multiparadigm specification.

16.7.4   Consistency of event classes

There are two ways in which event classes could cause inconsistencies among partial specifications in a specification.

First, all of the languages with event classes in their vocabularies (finite automata, statecharts, Jackson diagrams, Z) assume that the event classes in the vocabulary of a particular partial specification are disjoint. Showing that they are, in fact, disjoint is an important proof obligation.

The obligation can be satisfied with a straightforward inductive proof. The induction step requires showing that for each partial specification, assuming that the event classes in its vocabulary are disjoint, the event classes it defines are disjoint, and each event class it defines belongs to the vocabulary of only one partial specification (Zave and Jackson, 1994). Even when a partial specification does not satisfy the induction hypothesis, it can usually be made to satisfy it by means of a minor rearrangement of the specification.

Second, a partial specification can assert that events of a particular class, or with particular attributes, cannot occur in a particular state. Since the event classes and most of the event attributes are defined within the specification, there could be an inconsistency between the definitions of an event class and its attributes, and assertions about the event class. This issue casts suspicion on all pre-conditions, including type and uniqueness constraints on arguments.

Fortunately, in the switching specification, only the Z specification places pre-conditions on event classes. These pre-conditions are sometimes explicit, and sometimes implicit in state invariants and post-conditions on event classes.

Determining that the definitions of event classes and event attributes guarantee the satisfaction of all event pre-conditions requires some reasoning in first-order logic and some higher-level, language-dependent analysis.

The higher-level analysis determines, for each Z operation event class, all of the ways in which an event could be a member of that class. These "ways" correspond to paths through the definition graph (Figure 16.10). Each path has the form $< T, (S_1, C_1), \ldots, (S_n, C_n) >$ where T is an event type, S_i is a partial specification, and C_i is an event class. Events in T are in the vocabulary of S_1 and could be classified by it as belonging to C_1. Events in C_i are in the vocabulary of S_{i+1} and could be classified by it as belonging to C_{i+1}. C_n is the Z operation event class being analyzed.

Language-dependent reasoning also determines, for each pair (S_i, C_i), the pre-condition G_i guaranteed by S_i in its definition of C_i. G_i is expressable in first-order logic, because it is a fragment of the semantics of S_i.

The pre-condition R required and relied on by Z is also expressable in first order logic, because it is always a condition on the shared, translatable relations discussed in Section 16.6.2. This is to be expected — the shared, translatable relations are exactly those through which the Z specification and the other partial specifications interact.

The final step is now obvious. For each path leading to a Z operation event class, it is necessary to prove the first-order theorem

$$G_1 \wedge \ldots \wedge G_n \Rightarrow R$$

This may seem like an intimidating process, but it should be remembered that the Z specification is designed to interact relatively little with the others, and so its operation pre-conditions tend to be few and simple. For example, all of the event classes based on the dialling parse (see Figure 16.10) have as their sole pre-condition

$$\exists!v(target\_VT(e,v) \wedge dialing(v,p))$$

where e is the event and p is the pause preceding it. This condition is guaranteed by the first-order logic specification for all events in all classes in the vocabulary of the Jackson diagrams. Since all event classes based on the dialling parse are are contained in the union of these vocabulary classes, the pre-condition is established.

16.8   Conclusion

The complete specification of the switching system described here consists of about 25 pages of Z text, and about 15 pages of text and diagrams in other languages.

For purposes of comparison, the industrial specifications from which real switching systems are implemented are typically written in English, and have hundreds of pages per feature. To be fair, much of the bulk is caused by the inclusion of design detail (which we have carefully avoided). Even though this design detail is ultimately necessary, its inclusion in the specifications — along with a general lack of organization and abstraction — makes it impossible to obtain precise answers to subtle questions about functional behaviour. Other published specifications of switching systems typically confine themselves to one feature (POTS). This switching system has 12 substantive features, and it is well known that the complexity of feature interactions grows exponentially with the number of features.

It is really important to be able to specify systems of realistic complexity concisely, and not just to win specification "beauty contests". Multiparadigm techniques result in specifications small enough to think about clearly, to analyze and improve.

For telecommunications software the need for tractable specifications is particularly great, because there is so much need for this software to be extensible, and so many mysteries about how aggregated features interact (Zave, 1993). Conceptual models embodied in tractable formal specifications seem to be the only hope for unravelling these mysteries.

Chapter 17

Formal Methods Technology Transfer: Impediments and Innovation

Dan Craigen, Susan Gerhart and Ted Ralston

17.1 Introduction

A significant concern currently facing formal methods advocates is the transfer of a formal methods capability from the research and prototype application realm, to the broader software engineering community. Even though there have been successful applications of formal methods technology, in which improvements in quality and reductions of cost and time to market have been reported, there has been limited diffusion to, and adoption by, software engineers — even in niche markets such as critical systems. Technology transfer is not solely an issue of developing an eminent technology; there are also political, sociological and economic forces at play. Formal methods are not alone in having to overcome significant impediments to diffusion and adoption. As reported by Fichman and Kemerer (1993), structured methodologies and object orientation also suffer from low adoption trajectories.

In this chapter, we analyze the state of formal methods with regards to technology transfer (diffusion and adoption) to industry. Our general view is that formal methods advocates are facing significant, though not unique, impediments in diffusing their technology to industry. We will use an "innovation diffusion" model (Rogers, 1983; Fichman and Kemerer, 1993) to analyze data from a survey of industrial applications of formal methods (Craigen *et al.*, 1993). The innovation diffusion model provides a framework with which to understand the forces advancing and/or retarding the diffusion of formal methods. With this understanding, we will be better placed to enhance the diffusion of formal methods to industry.

This paper differs from three previously published papers on the survey (Craigen *et al.*, 1995; Gerhart *et al.*, 1993, 1994). The first paper focuses on formal methods research and development issues arising from the survey. The second paper presents survey results in software engineering terms. The third paper focuses on the safety- and security-critical applications.

17.2 International survey case studies

The international survey of industrial applications of formal methods had three primary objectives:

- to better inform deliberations within industry and government on standards and regulations;
- to provide an authoritative record on the practical experience of formal methods to date;
- to suggest areas where future research and technology development are needed.

The "methodology" of our survey was based on "common sense" and not based on a rigorous social scientific approach. On a case-by-case basis, we proceeded along the following lines.

1. An initial questionnaire was sent to prospective interview subjects.
2. The survey team reviewed relevant project literature.
3. Two members of the survey team interviewed project participants. A second questionnaire formed the basis of the interviews.
4. Raw notes on the interview, along with other information, formed the case study report. Reports were sent to participants for comment.
5. The survey team analyzed the results.

The questionnaires were structured so that we could determine what formal methods were being used, what results were being reported, what the rôle of the project team was within the organization, what was the evolution of the project, and what was the application. In order to ameliorate potential bias of the survey team, a review committee was established. The review committee commented on interim and draft reports. We leave it to our other papers and the final report for a discussion and application of our "common sense" analysis.

Twelve projects were the object of our survey. We divided the projects into three clusters: regulatory, commercial, and exploratory. Regulatory cases were either safety or security critical and generally attracted the attention of government regulatory authorities. Commercial cases were driven by entrepreneurial profit imperatives. Exploratory cases were driven by organizations investigating the potential utility of formal methods. For expository purposes, in this paper we collapse the exploratory cases into the regulatory and commercial clusters.

Tables 17.1 to 17.6 summarize the survey cases and also provide a summary of the specific formal methods used. The first two tables summarize the regulatory cluster; the subsequent four tables summarize the commercial cluster.

17.3   Adoption of innovations

The analytic framework used in our analysis of the survey cases is borrowed from the study of innovation carried out in the 1970s and 1980s by several scholars and industry associations (E.M. Rogers, Nathan Rosenberg, Richard Collins, The Sloan School of Management, the American Electronics Association, and the US National Academy of Sciences, to name but a few). The framework has come to be accepted by both academia

Table 17.1 Case descriptions: part I (regulatory)

Case	Who	What	Why	How
DNGS: Darlington Nuclear Generator Trip Computer	Ontario Hydro, AECL, Atomic Energy Control Board of Canada (AECB), consultants	Decision-making logic for the shutdown systems implemented in software	Safety critical; AECB would not license DNGS without convincing demonstration of correctness of code	Three separate teams developed formal spec, program function tables, and proof of equivalence
MGS: Multinet Gateway System	Ford Aerospace, US National Computer Security Center, MITRE Corp.	Secure Internet device for transmitting datagrams	Security critical; aimed at high rating by US Trusted Computer System Criteria	Followed prescribed computer security methodology
TBACS: Token Based Access Control System	NIST SW Engineering and Security Technology groups	Security properties of a smartcard (for network access)	Gain experience using FMs and underlying tools	Specifier located with developer and worked in parallel
TCAS: Air Traffic Alert and Collision Avoidance	UC Irvine, US FAA, aviation working group	Intended to reduce the risk of mid-air and near mid-air collisions	Clarify complex components to increase assurance in TCAS II functionality	Groups worked together to develop method, redo specification from pseudocode
SACEM	GEC Alsthom, Paris regional train network and Paris Rapid Transit Authority	Automatic train protection system	Increase volume by 25% to obviate building new line, maintaining safety	Applied various FMs and other techniques to assure regulators

Table 17.2 Formal methods usage: part I (regulatory)

Case	Requirements	Design/Scale	Assurance	Other
DNGS	A-7/SCR style (tabular descriptions of requirements)	Pre- and post-conditions (1362 LOC Fortran, 1185 LOC Assembler.)	Hand proofs of consistency	No FM tools, but extensive testing and SW hazard analysis
MGS	Gypsy and graphical notation for security model–system structure	Gypsy implementation methodology (10 pages math, 80 pages Gypsy, 6 KLOC OS)	Proof of security properties	Non-FM security analyses
TBACS	Defined security policy and smartcard system model	Reverse engineered model from emulation code (300 LOC FDM from 2500 LOC C)	Security proofs and indentification of flaws	Estimations of effort–payoff, input to new standards
TCAS	Reverse engineered two subsystems using Statecharts variant	None (7 KLOC pseudocode, specifications comparable size)	Review by domain experts of formal requirements	Aimed for reviewable notation and basis for safety analysis
SACEM	Hoare logic and B to express requirements	Hoare logic and B to relate requirements to C code (9 KLOC verified code)	B tool for verification	FM one of many safety techniques

and industry as a useful way to analyze strategies for innovation adoption and identifying impediments. Other models of technology transfer exist (e.g. Tornatsky and Fleisher (1990) and Przybylinski *et al.* (1991)), but are not discussed here.

In our version of the framework, our analysis uses the following criteria.

- *Relative advantage*: an analysis of the technical and business superiority of the innovation over technology it might replace.

Table 17.3 Formal methods usage: part II (commercial)

Case	Who	What	Why	How
HP	Bristol (UK) Applied Methods Group, Waltham (US) Medical Instruments division	System component; real-time database of patient monitoring data	Evaluate general utility of FM and an HP specific FM (HP-SL) in product environment	Waltham developer interested in FM
CICS (Customer Information Control System)	IBM Hursley and Oxford PRG	Large transaction processing system	Re-engineering, adding features, improving quality and reducing development costs	Formally specified using Z at module interfaces
Cleanroom	IBM Federal Systems Division	COBOL restructuring facility (COBOL/SF)	Full-scale FM development process; COBOL/SF a technical challenge	Combined FM, review, statistical testing
Inmos	Inmos Ltd. (Bristol, UK) and Oxford PRG	Components of 3 generations of transputers	Tractable research and development example led to reduced testing and increased assurance	Specify and transform into implementation language

- *Compatibility*: an analysis of how well the innovation meshes with existing practice.
- *Complexity*: an analysis of how easy the innovation is to use and understand.
- *Trialability*: an analysis of the type, scope and duration of feasibility experiments and pilot projects.
- *Observability*: an analysis of how easily and widely the results and benefits of the innovation are communicated.
- *Transferability*: an analysis of the economic, psychological and sociological factors influencing adoption and achieving critical mass (Fichman and Kemerer, 1993).

Table 17.4 Formal methods usage: part II (commercial)

Case	Requirements	Design/Scale	Assurance	Other
HP	HP-SL to produce top-level specification	HP-SL (55 pages) carried through levels of specification to code	Rigorous reviews via Bristol methods, test generation from specifications	FM taught along with more general SE methodology
CICS	Reflect changes in market	Z specifications used to implement new code (50 KLOC)	Z specifications augmented English descriptions, replaced pseudocode	Technology transfer from Oxford PRG, resulting in industrial feedback into Z
Clean-room	Specification using grammars, transformations, etc.	Refinement with design verification through reviews (80 KLOC with 20 KLOC reused)	Reliability testing, stepwise refinement and reviews of correctness questions	Case-based Cleanroom courses, ongoing support from Cleanroom developers
Inmos	FPU to be consistent with IEEE floating point standard	Transformation tool generated Occam then VHDL (100 page Z specification of FPU)	Reduced testing, discovered error in rounding algorithm	Positive interaction between FM group and developers

Principal factors are

- *Prior technology drag*, the presence of large and mature installed bases for prior technologies,

- *Irreversible investments*, the cost of investing in the new technology,

- *Sponsorship*, the presence of an individual or organization that promotes the new technology (promotion includes subsidization of early adopters and the setting of standards),

- *Expectations*, the benefits accruing from expectations that the technology will be extensively adopted.

Table 17.5 Case descriptions: part III (commercial)

Case	Who	What	Why	How
LaCoS: Large Correct Systems	ESPRIT: CRI, Lloyds Register, Matra Transport and others	RAISE Trials (Rigorous Approach to Software Engineering)	Evaluate industrial utility of RAISE and technology transfer	Wide variation of applications
SSADM	Praxis (Bath, UK)	Toolset for SSADM	Feasibility analysis of requirements and to improve understanding	High-level Z specification, object-oriented design
Tektronix Oscillo-scope	Research and development laboratory and engineers in business unit	Family of oscilloscope products	Shorten time to market with a reusable platform	Z specifications of oscilloscope system and user interfaces

Adoption of a superior innovation may still be negated by concerns, on the part of early adopters, arising from two early adoption risks: "transient incompatibility" and "risks of stranding" (Fichman and Kemerer, 1993). Transient incompatibility refers to risks accruing from delays in achieving a sufficiently large community interested in the new innovation. Stranding refers to the risks arising due to the failure to achieve critical mass. A well-known example is the ongoing use of the QWERTY keyboard, even though better keyboard layouts have been designed.

17.4 Adoption analysis

In this section, we present an analysis of the survey data using the adoption framework.

17.4.1 Relative advantage

In general, the survey shows that the use of formal methods had a positive impact on most key evaluation criteria relevant to relative advantage across the three clusters. The use of formal methods clearly enhanced the ability to demonstrate increased assurance in safety-critical systems over existing methods, thereby aiding certification by the regulatory bodies. In the case of the commercial cluster, in terms of key commercially oriented criteria (e.g. cost, quality, time to market), formal methods were marginally positive. The observed marginally positive benefit may understate the relative advantage of for-

Table 17.6 Formal methods usage: part III (commercial)

Case	Requirements	Design/Scale	Assurance	Other
LaCoS	Use of RAISE for modelling	Follow RAISE method to derive specificationss and code	RAISE proof editor and reviews	Develop pedagogical material and specification library
SSADM	Z specification used to test requirements, understanding and complexity	Z specification (340 pages) informally translated to Objective C (37 KLOC)	Specification used to improve communication	Met BS 5750 quality requirements, used only primitive tools
Tek-tronix	Capture vocabulary and architecture	200 000 KLOC abstracted as two 15 page Z specifications	None, specifically reported	Z specification has been replaced by object library

mal methods because of the learning curve associated with the first application. In terms of lifecycle stages, formal methods showed a net positive impact.

Relative advantage, as used in the innovation adoption model, typically is measured in terms of economic profitability (the aforementioned criteria primarily involve economic performance issues). However, relative advantage may also be observed in terms of the success (or failure) of an innovation used during a crisis or other decisive event. Rogers (1983) notes "a crisis emphasizes the relative advantage of an innovation and affects its rate of adoption". (The rôle of crisis as an instigator of change is similar to that observed by Kuhn (1970) in the emergence of new scientific theories.) Relative advantage may also be emphasized by a strong promotional effort, which underscores the influence of perception over reality.

With respect to crisis, it is arguable that the data collected in the survey points to some sort of crisis. The-long lamented and misnamed "software crisis" is an obvious candidate. A crisis is, according to *The Concise English Dictionary*, "a momentous juncture in war, politics, commerce, domestic affairs, etc.". While, with regards to software development, we have not reached that "momentous juncture" where revolutionary, not evolutionary, change is necessary, we are on the cusp of a transition from a "chronic software condition" to a true crisis. The evidence of gradual adoption, as shown in both the regulatory and commercial clusters, seems to imply that the real software crisis — the inability of traditional design and programming practices to handle complexity in an intellectually controllable and reliable manner — is emerging (Gibbs, 1994).

Evidence of a strong promotional effort on formal methods is abundant with respect to many years of government funding and early adopter subsidies on both sides of the Atlantic (e.g. the Multinet Gateway and LaCoS cases). The evidence, however, that this promotional effort has led to adoption is limited at best. It is arguable that the effect of government efforts has resulted in a negative perception, most manifest in the essentially inaccurate but (more importantly) widely believed anecdotes regarding high costs, Feynman-like workforce skills, and horrendous failures of formal methods. Part of the motivation for the survey was to redress this imbalance. In addition, the government subsidies (particularly in North America) can be argued to have retarded the exposure of the early formal methods adopters to the demands and survival skills of the commercial software marketplace.

One difficulty we encountered in determining the relative advantage of formal methods is the lack of strong scientific evidence that the technology is, in fact, effective. Various surveys have provided reasonably systematic anecdotal evidence of effective industrial use of formal methods. However, none of the formal methods application projects has used strict, scientifically based, measurement criteria. One indicator of a lack of scientific rigour is that we found that conventional industry metrics were not used in almost all the cases surveyed. The explanation given was that formal methods were not compatible with commonly used industry metric systems. Only two of the cases, CICS and SSADM, attempted to produce and record statistics pertaining to productivity, quality, or reliability. Project management tools used for estimating costs, resource utilization, and time — which often produce this kind of data — were uniformly not applied. Hence, it is possible that the putative benefits accrued to formal methods may, in fact, arise for other reasons, such as, excellent staff or an improvement in process.

It would appear the claims of formal methods advocates are primarily based on bias, belief and anecdote. Mind you, formal methods advocates are not alone in making such claims; most software engineering claims are based on dubious scientific grounds. This is not to say that the claims are necessarily false, only that they are scientifically unproven.

17.4.2   Compatibility

There is limited evidence in the case studies of formal methods integrating successfully with existing development methods or the installed toolbase. In several of the case studies, a choice was made to separate formal methods analysis from conventional practice.

Cleanroom may demonstrate the highest degree of compatibility through its meshing of inspection, reliability analysis, formal design refinement, and testing. SSADM successfully integrated formal methods with object orientation. In the CICS case, the existing IBM software development process was modified by adding an additional step into the then current IBM process architecture. In the remainder of the cases, the formal methods activity was either carried out separate from, or in parallel with, the conventional development processes.

Compatibility, as described by Rogers (1983), is divided into three aspects: values, requisite knowledge and skills, and complexes.

Values

Values play a major rôle in formal method adoption, both pro and con. The long history of controversy in the field (e.g. De Millo *et al.* (1979) and Fetzer (1988)) shows a range of extremist views, moderate positions, and blissful ignorance. There are also strong camps within the field. For example, a major debate that occurred during the FM'89 workshop (Craigen and Summerskill, 1990) was between the adherents of using formal methods for high-level specifications and minimal use of proof, and adherents of an approach in which hardware, code and operating systems were verified to the fullest extent possible. Both approaches are valid and have significant benefit. Our study concluded that the high-level specification approach, as generally followed by users of Z, was of general industrial benefit. There was also, in relative terms, success in technology transfer to industry. On the other hand, the verification adherents were arguing that "mathematically predictable systems" could be achieved only if one is developing an entire system on solid scientific foundations. While hardware verification has penetrated into the hardware industry, it is our impression that adoption is not as extensive in comparison to the adoption of high-level specifications. (However, the public relations disaster associated with the Intel Pentium chip flaw, and the accrued \$400+ million in costs, may accelerate adoption of formal methods and other technologies (Glanz, 1995).)

In our case studies, we found several different groups directly involved in the cases. We classify the case studies by their dominant characteristic, although most cases had additional characteristics.

Firstly, there are the cases consisting of long-time advocates of formal methods with vested academic or industrial careers: SSADM (Praxis' use of formal methods as "house methods"), CICS (Oxford Programming Research Group's use of Z), COBOL/SF (IBM's use of the Cleanroom methodology), Tektronix (researchers demonstrating and promoting Z), LaCoS (European Union sponsorship of RAISE), and TBACS (researcher experimented with a formal method on a smartcard application). Next, there are the cases consisting of individuals or groups looking for improvements in products and/or processes: Inmos (where improvements were sought that led to the employment of formal methods experts), TCAS (where the method evolved from a need to improve the specification of an important US Federal Aviation Administration system), and SACEM (where insecurity about the effects of changing from hardware to software led to the exploration of new techniques). Finally, there are the cases consisting of individuals or groups coerced to apply the technology: Darlington (where formal methods were used in support of achieving accreditation), MGS (where formal methods were necessitated by security obligations), and HP (where a transfer receptor group was available during a brief exploration period).

In all cases, values were significant in that some groups committed themselves, for whatever reasons, to major experiments. For example,

- in CICS, academic researchers at Oxford PRG committed themselves to work directly with developers at IBM Hursley, an atypical academic process,
- in SACEM, a manager committed to a long-term exploration of various techniques and the regulators committed to understanding the approach, and

- in HP, technology receptors committed themselves, to a point, requiring definite improvements in process before further adopting the HP formal method, in competition with object-oriented approaches.

We should ask where values come from. The individual trained in an engineering school has, and should have, different values from an individual trained in computer science. Engineering is but one professional discipline with a certifying body. (Individuals calling themselves "software engineers" are illegally representing themselves in many jurisdictions. The term "engineer" is limited only to those so certified by a recognizable professional body.) Computer science is a subject, or collection of subjects, basic to many professions. Inherent to both computer science and engineering is mathematics, with computer science directly involved in pursuing new approaches to abstraction, a core concept of mathematics. However, computer science has not fully developed its themes of "applied mathematics", which is the rôle formal methods plays in software development. In the above cases, there were many individuals who valued the rôle mathematics could play in their projects.

Knowledge

While it is reasonable to claim that the required knowledge for employing formal methods is not widely disseminated, it is hardly scarce. Many universities teach formal methods concepts and have done so for a decade. Many books, tutorials, and other materials are available. These observations suggest that felicitous conditions must exist for a successful application of formal methods, including either (i) a sufficient number of knowledgeable researchers or developers, or (ii) sufficient time and resources to develop the capability. Unfortunately, increasing market competition, and the consequent organizational re-engineering or restructuring, has reduced the opportunities for investigating and investing in new technologies.

It is of interest to compare and contrast the differing adoption trajectories of automated deduction and computer algebra tools. We contend that the latter tools are on a more rapid adoption trajectory since the supported mathematics is consistent with the knowledge and practice of the user community (generally scientists and engineers); mathematical logic, the core mathematics of automated deduction tools, is not as widely disseminated, or understood in the pure application (in contrast to research) sense.

Complexes

By "complexes" we ask whether the innovation is self-contained, or whether it requires additional linkages to other technologies and capabilities. Clearly, there is a "complex", i.e. an interwoven set of ideas, as displayed in our method synopses (Craigen *et al.*, 1993, Volume 1, pp. 79–110).

- Representations involve recently evolved and, sometimes, arcane notations.
- The steps performed and the artifacts produced are described in various levels of detail.
- The tools available range from total dependence, as with the GVE, to none, as in Cleanroom.

- The rôles involved and the definition of skills involved are included. Only RAISE aspired to define itself as an industrial process.

Many concepts are involved in formal methods with methods differing not only in how the concepts are applied but also whether they are required, recommended, or ignored. This complex of concepts may be a barrier to adoption forcing the selection of a single, relatively self-contained method, rather than enabling selection among different methods. Cleland and MacKenzie (1995) recommend a taxonomy of methods and applications to address this difficulty.

17.4.3   Complexity

Rogers defines complexity as "the degree to which an innovation is relatively difficult to understand and use". Complexity and adoption are inversely related. In general terms, formal methods are perceived as being of high complexity, accessible only to highly trained individuals, and unsuitable for practicing software engineers. In our view, we believe this perception of formal methods to be ill founded. Many formal methods concepts are rather basic and accessible — requiring simple mathematical concepts. As noted in our report: "Given the elementary nature of the mathematics of most formal methods, the greater problem may be in the ability of formal methods users to properly model their systems and carry through their designs."

Notations

An area of superficial complexity — yet, potentially, a significant inhibitor to adoption — is the notations used by the formal methods community. In some regards, the problems of notation are similar to those of user interfaces. Norman (1988) cites a number of cases in which user interfaces (or notations) were changed to facilitate adoption. The phone system is a particularly pertinent example. In the early days, many subscribers shared the same telephone line. A subscriber would recognize when a call was for him or her by the number and tone of the rings (much like Morse code). Since most subscribers were not knowledgeable of Morse code, the ringing pattern was not intuitive and easily confused. Improvements were also required in making a phone call. At one time, all phone calls had to be processed by an operator and the caller gained the operator's attention by using a hand crank to transmit an electronic signal. The operator would then make the appropriate connections. An early problem was to replace the hand crank with the now omnipresent digital scheme, so that the caller could, in essence, program their own calls by dialling a set of digits. Digits are a form of notation that a massive portion of the population understand, so adoption was eased. Instead of coming face to face with the complexities of telephony, telephone users were removed some levels from the complexity through the use of a rotor (now usually a digital pad) and dedicated lines.[1]

---

[1]However, the increasing complexity of available functionality is making it more difficult for telephone users to form a model of what actually is being achieved by dialling certain digits and symbols.

It appears that the notations used with many formal methods are viewed as being complex and poorly compatible with existing industrial capabilities. In general, the notations are arcane and baroque; consequently, they are difficult to read and write. The notations tend to be driven by mathematical and computing imperatives. Sometimes, the notations faithfully reflect or add to the complexity of the underlying conceptual framework and there are many mathematical and computing ideas which are not yet common currency (e.g. fixed-point theorems, variable capture).

Notational complexity (and incompatibility) appeared most forcefully in the TCAS, MGS, and HP cases. In the first two instances, improvements occurred so that relevant non-formal-methods experts actively engaged in system development or accreditation. In the latter case, the medical instruments domain experts did not come to terms with the notation and so relevant reviews did not occur. The TCAS experience is particularly instructive. Early versions of their formalism held true to predicate calculus style of notation. The notation was, however, incomprehensible to the engineering audience and even Leveson's group came to recognize that they were making errors because of the notation (e.g. unintended variable capture); hence, for the description of state transitions, the notation was recast into tabular representations (of disjunctive normal form formulae) that were similar to decision diagrams. This form of notation was readily adopted by project stakeholders.

Hiding complexity

In Roger's discussion of complexity, he reports on the work of another researcher who analyzed the different rates of adoption of canasta and television in the, so-called, upper and lower classes. Canasta was viewed as being of high complexity. To learn the game, detailed personal explanation was required and its procedures were difficult to master. Television, in contrast, required only a simple twist of a knob.[2] However, it is clear that the technology underlying television is much more complex than the rules of canasta. The big difference is that the technological complexity of television is hidden from its users; only the technically or professionally interested need understand the inner workings. In a similar manner, aspects of formal methods can be adopted relatively easily. For example, the use of so-called "push-button" tools in which formally based analyses are performed automatically and only the results of the analyses are reported are similar to turning a TV dial. Examples of such tools include (i) checking that array indices are within bounds, (ii) the semidecision procedures of Nelson and Oppen (Nelson, 1981), (iii) the binary decision diagram (BDD) based analyses of propositional formulas of Clarke *et al.* (1992), and (iv) the "Prover Technology" of Logikkonsult (Ståalmarck, 1990). The BDD technology has been successfully used, for example, in a variety of computer-aided design applications. Logikkonsult's Prover Technology (based on results from complexity theory) has been successfully used by a number of large Swedish firms. The predominant tools of our survey are language well-formedness checkers (especially for Z). Language well-

---

[2]Whether a similar analysis carried out today would result in the same conclusions is debatable. The simple twisting of the knob has been replaced by remote controls and televisions have been generalized into "entertainment centres".

formedness checkers are, in some regards, examples of push-button tools; they check for syntactic and semantic linguistic ambiguities or errors. In comparison, there is general agreement that it can take up to six months for an individual, with a reasonably sophisticated mathematical and computing background, to become proficient in the use of state-of-the-art automated deduction tools.

While not particularly evidenced by the results of our survey, recent observations have shown that push-button tools that complement engineering procedures are being adopted much more rapidly than automated deduction systems that require highly skilled individuals in the relevant technology. Here, in addition to complexity, issues of relative advantage accrue.

Allied to the concept of push-button tools and, in essence, the hiding of technology, is the approach followed by Tektronix. In the Tektronix project, highly skilled formal methods consultants were used to construct the reusable software architecture. The consultants used their specification language of choice (Z) and performed the modelling and analyses that they deemed appropriate. However, the ideas were not presented to the implementors in terms of Z, but couched in the object-oriented framework with which the implementors were expert. Hence, a transition occurred, where the relevant design artifacts were communicated, but the complex formal methods analysis and technology hidden. Tektronix obtained the benefits from formal methods that they required and they did not need to train substantial portions of their staff to achieve their goals. On-site or nearby expertise in the technology can ameliorate adoption difficulties arising from complexity. The Tektronix and CICS case studies particularly exemplify our observation.

Education

One means of mitigating complexity issues is an aggressive educational program. It has been our observation that moderate (on the order of a few weeks to a few months) levels of education and training, when coupled with follow-on work on real projects, considerably helped understanding of such formal artifacts as notation, specification language structure, and rudimentary proof checking. IBM Hursley (CICS case study) followed this educational theme and have built a coterie of staff that are well versed in formal methods techniques.

Nascent technology

Computing science is a nascent technology. Many unifying principles, coherent descriptions, professional practices, etc. still need to be developed. We are still in a transitional state from being an industry partially dependent upon craft, to one primarily based on scientific and engineering principles. The resulting inchoate state has a complex web of knowledge which is difficult to learn. The current state of formal methods reflects industrial and academic reality. As noted earlier, a taxonomy of methods and applications may help to ease these concerns.

17.4.4   Trialability

Rogers refers to this adoption criterion as "divisibility", the notion that an innovation is not totally "take it or leave it". We generalize the adoption characteristic to focus on how well formal methods may be applied in trial.

Addressing the former issue, there are points of view expressed in the literature that define formal methods as very much a "total experience", required to verify code as well as to ensure the validity of specifications. However, practice, as shown in our case studies and in many more examples, suggests there are many opportunities for selective use of formal methods. For example, an early interesting formal methods approach focused on loop invariants and is still a worthy practice even when specifications are absent or informal because the reasoning process reduces to questions about proper uses of language operations ("is this pointer always in bounds") or to well-defined functions ("computes the total over a vector" or "searches a list for an element"). At the other end of the process, formal methods are often advocated as modelling techniques, capturing, for example, the state structure and state transitions of a system. Other techniques include developing specifications for the purpose of test planning and the well-defined approaches of design by reification.

From another perspective, trialability addresses whether it is possible to define experiments that will provide meaningful, timely information about the value of formal methods for specific applications or in specific organizations. Example experiments include the following.

- Given method X, does it apply to application A?
- Knowing methods U, V, and X, does one of these methods provide added value for application A?
- Can practice P (e.g. testing) be reduced by use of specification approach U?

All such questions have the additional parameter of the organization performing the work, whether academic, industrial research laboratories, development organizations, government regulators, etc. We lack a systematic guidebook to formal methods to help an organization define its choices for a trial. However, general technology transfer experience provides guidance as to how to design experiments by, for example, identifying stakeholders, suggesting measures of improvement, and identifying processes for "thawing" organizational fears (Przybylinski *et al.*, 1991).

Several case studies showed instances of selective applications of formal methods. CICS used Z primarily for specification of system interfaces and relied primarily on inspection (as opposed to verification) to reveal specification errors. TCAS showed a large-scale and evolutionary application of a state-based notation to express system requirements, with later development of verification tools. MGS, on the other hand, was a top-to-bottom application, as required by security contracts. Similarly, SACEM evolved a full-scale formal methods approach, embedded in a larger regime of other forms of reliability analysis.

From the perspective of designing trials of formal methods, it would be hard to say that any trials were ever exactly designed. Rather, interested groups started using formal methods, for whatever reason, and the experiments evolved. Assuming this is the normal adoption process, the interesting questions are when and why the experiments are terminated. One often-overlooked explanation is that modern organizations rarely remain stable in their personnel structure or business orientation long enough for experiments to evolve. Government agencies have acted to stabilize their relevant environments (e.g. with the MGS and LaCoS cases). However, cases such as HP and Tektronix are more typical, in that a brief window of opportunity exists within which the experiment occurs. The SACEM and CICS cases differ from the previous cases in that the product under evolution was sufficiently long term so as to allow the methods, uses and users to mature.

In summary, our survey provides considerable evidence of how formal methods are tried, how the trials proceed, and how the outcomes are portrayed. We urge further documentation of past cases within organizations to extract more experience and recommend our interview forms for data capture and our feature analysis for experience evaluation. Indeed, versions of our methodology might well be adapted for the design of trials (e.g. understanding the organization and the application), identifying the reasons for wanting formal methods, documenting existing practices, identifying those features (e.g. cost of product or reuse) where formal methods could contribute, and identifying those features of primary concern to the organization.

17.4.5   Observability

Rogers defines "observability" as "the degree to which the results of an innovation may be diffused to others". Rogers provides the example of pre-emergent weed killers, that is, weed killers that are applied prior to the emergence of weeds. Adoption was retarded in the US Midwest because farmers using the weed killer had no dead weeds to show to the neighbours. Fortunately, in some instances, formal methods have been shown to be an effective bug killer (e.g. the reported improvements in quality with CICS).

For various reasons, some unfathomable, formal methods appear to be more observable in the negative than the positive. For example, the magazine *American Programmer*, which primarily focuses on the practicing software engineer, carried a special issue on formal methods in May, 1991. The general feeling was that the articles were well crafted and reasonably explained the technology. Yet, that issue was badly received by the subscribers and many did not want to see such a special issue again. "Formal methods" has acquired a pejorative connotation to such an extent that many players are looking for ways to reposition the field. The negative tone has resulted from ill-argued, but widely disseminated, critiques (De Millo *et al.*, 1979; Fetzer, 1988), ill-considered claims as to the felicity and appropriateness of the technology, and from attempts to use immature toolsets in industrial settings. When attempting to transfer a sophisticated technology, one must carefully pave the way for adoption and carefully explain the potential benefits, detriments, caveats and constraints.

In general, our survey suggests that there was little organizational observability of formal methods technology outside of the specific project groups and, certainly, very little adoption outside of the original project group. A specific instance of lack of observability was with the Tektronix project. The software architecture project was, in fact, the object of two surveys: one on formal methods, the second on object-oriented programming. The individual involved with the second survey did not know that formal methods had been an important component of the project. Industrial proprietary issues and government secrecy have also impeded observability. For example, little is known about the US government's use of formal methods in developing security-critical applications, and IBM has been slow to publish results on CICS and other projects. Both industry and government have substantive reasons for their positions (preservation of integrity and secrecy; maintenance of a competitive advantage), but there are harmful consequences on observability.

Our survey was originally published in 1993 and a sequence of papers have resulted. In general terms, there has been substantial interest in the survey and the results. We believe that the survey report has helped to increase the observability of formal methods and has helped to suggest potential applications for formal methods, transition paths, strengths and weaknesses. Interest in the survey is suggestive that there is a hunger for balanced reporting on actual use and results of formal-methods-related developments. Given the somewhat negative tone of our discussion on the observability criteria, it is heartening to note that there is still a degree of open-mindedness in the software engineering fraternity.

17.4.6 Transferability

The survey data indicate that formal methods suffered from prior technology drag and the perception of irreversible investment. It is clear that sustained government sponsorship has both benefitted and retarded formal methods. Formal methods have largely lost the expectations game.

Prior technology drag
With respect to competing methods, ideas and techniques (but not necessarily the complete methodology) from both structured methods (e.g. DeMarco, Yourdon, Jackson) and object orientation have been adopted and regularized. The presence of these methods has impeded adoption of formal methods. Compared with the situation a decade earlier, the use of the structured methods and object orientation has resulted in demonstrable improvements. The introduction of formal methods has not yet led to demonstrations of significant improvements over the gains achieved by these other methods.

Irreversible Investment
The perception on the part of potential new adopters of irreversible investment is definitely a major impediment to the adoption of formal methods. This situation is an example of where perception and reality diverge. The survey data shows the up-front costs in tools and education for all twelve cases were relatively minor and roughly comparable with the costs of introducing any new method or technique. While not trivial, the evidence generally shows the costs are not onerous. Tool support is a relatively minor cost,

with basic tools to assist in writing and reading formal specifications available for a few hundred dollars to up to as much as a few thousand dollars for automated deduction systems. It should be noted that these tools are far from industrially rugged when compared with CASE products. Education and training costs for system designers and programmers were deemed acceptable in most of the cases, lasting from a few weeks to a few months.

Sponsorship

Government sponsorship has figured strongly in the development of formal methods. Government has played two distinct rôles: first, as a prospective (and eventually actual) user of the technology; second, as a subsidizer of early adopters. The first rôle has largely been successful in bringing about necessary developments in mathematical theories, logics, automated tool support, and education and training. The effectiveness of the government in the second rôle is somewhat more problematic. The goal of providing the means of developing better software as a result of applying more scientific rigour to what is otherwise a largely *ad hoc* activity has had an impact in the fields of security and safety-critical systems, fields in which the responsibilities of governments as evaluators and certifiers are undisputed. However, this government perspective has, for the most part, ignored outside market and industrialization trends that have been evolving over the past decade in terms of sophisticated environments of tools, changing demands for accessibility by users, lower cost structures, and different programming and development process paradigms. The effect has been to retard the ability of early adopters to integrate with the larger software engineering community.

Expectations

Evidence in the survey shows formal methods have not benefitted from positive expectations that it would become a dominant and widely used technology. Further, formal methods has suffered from negative expectations as an *a priori* impediment (Hall, 1990). Given that expectations involve psychological and sociological attitudes of the potential adopter community (in this case, programmers and software engineers), there is a notable faddishness to the number and attributes of entrants into the "better software" business, which, accompanied with marketing publicity, creates a "honeymoon" period during which an innovation enjoys immediate popularity. Additionally, grapevine reviews, aided in recent years by the explosion of networked user groups, have spread a variety of largely negative messages.

Formal methods have not experienced a honeymoon period enjoyed by other software engineering methods. Almost from its inception, formal methods have been viewed by the mainstream software development industry in largely negative terms. At best, formal methods are perceived as an evil that is either to be avoided (because of cost, education and overselling) or, if mandated (as per government requirements), then performed in damage limitation mode. This perception stems from multiple interrelated causes.

First, as discussed earlier, formal methods have a tendency to produce arcane notations which are hard to understand and tend to create an impression of impenetrability (e.g. the reaction of HP production engineers).

Second, the claims of greater precision or "correctness" have been difficult to justify in rapidly growing markets (such as the shrink-wrap software marketplace) which solve such quality and reliability problems through patches and updates in a relatively timely and sufficiently adequate manner.

Third, formal methods practitioners have cultivated an attitude of aloofness and superiority with respect to the rest of the software industry. This aloofness and superiority is manifest in the general absence of formal methods practitioners at major industry gatherings (e.g. Comdex and Software World), a lack of involvement in significant standardization bodies ("significant" in terms of major industry trends such as open distributed computing, networking, quality, multimedia, object technology), and, perhaps most significantly, the lack of any general-purpose, and widely used commercial products developed using formal methods.

17.5   Summary of analysis

In this section, we provide a summary of our analyses. We focus on whether formal methods are aided or impeded by the traits of the specific criterion. Our conclusion is that formal methods have a low adoption trajectory.

17.5.1   Relative advantage

Overall, formal methods, as shown in our survey, enjoy a moderately high degree of relative advantage over other methods. This conclusion is supported by the evidence of clear technical superiority of formal methods in use on high assurance and safety-critical systems, coupled with a demonstrated ability to achieve intellectual control of legacy systems or technologies which are new and unfamiliar. This positive finding is attenuated by the lack of a clear demonstrable business superiority over other methods (e.g. object-oriented design) in terms of cost, quality, and time to market. Hence, formal methods do not compellingly pass the economic profitability test. In addition, as noted above, the strong promotional effort by government has not resulted in a positive perception of formal methods in the broader software development community.

17.5.2   Compatibility

For most formal methods, advocates have failed to demonstrate how the technology could contribute to, and benefit from, other approaches to the grand goal of higher software quality. An exception is Cleanroom, which meshes inspection, reliability analysis, formal design refinement, and testing, while other cases attempt some degree of pairwise composition. Failure on the part of formal methods advocates to consider compatibility issues thoroughly may present an impediment. The impediment could be addressed by using a wider knowledge base, more open minds, and better communication channels.

17.5.3   Complexity

In general terms, formal methods suffer from a perception of high complexity, thereby impeding adoption. The perception of complexity has arisen from diverse sources, including poor notations, inability to package the technology so as to present only the appropriate concepts, and the problems arising from a nascent technology. Complexity can be mitigated by aggressive educational programs, push-button tools, and a formal methods taxonomy.

17.5.4   Trialability

Numerous uses and ways of using formal methods have been presented in the literature. In our survey, we have gleaned some data about how well they worked, how much they cost, and what motivated them. The main impediment to undertaking any such trial in today's economic climate is the pressure for rapid time to market, compounded by the decreasing number of research laboratories to undertake more leisurely experiments. We urge that current and future trials of formal methods be systematically documented, and recommend our interviews and analytic framework for consideration.

17.5.5   Observability

Formal methods have suffered from poor observability and, more generally, for what observability does exist, formal methods have been perceived negatively. Our case studies showed very little observability in the participating organizations. Negativism has generally been due to philosophical diatribes, misunderstandings of the potential rôles of formal methods, and the use of immature and unreliable tools (and concepts) on production developments. Arguably, the costs of the SACEM and Darlington cases generally indicate negative results of full-blown code verification. The lack of scientific criteria for measuring relative advantage reduces formal methods observability.

17.5.6   Transferability

Formal methods has shown a low rate of transferability. The gains from using formal methods have not significantly improved the coding or design process sufficiently so as to warrant a complete substitution for existing techniques. This prior technology drag was by no means completely black and white, in that formal methods approach was, in some cases, merged with existing practice (SSADM, SACEM, Inmos), while in others it was performed in isolation (CICS, Tektronix). The perception (as opposed to the reality) of substantial up-front investment costs persists, even in companies that have had first-hand experience and a basis to compare. Government sponsorship has, on balance, had a neutral impact, with the positive effects of subsidization of research and early adoption, counterbalanced by the retarding effect of isolating early adopters from market and industry forces. Lastly, the weight of negative anecdotes, coupled with an absence of systematic study and assessment, has resulted in formal methods losing the expectations game.

17.6   Conclusion

In this paper, we have used an innovation diffusion model to analyze the likely adoption trajectory of formal methods. Using the diffusion model, we have improved on our "common sense" analysis by being significantly less *ad hoc*. Our findings for formal methods are similar to those of Fichman and Kemerer (1993) regarding the low adoption trajectories of both structured methods and object orientation. The innovation diffusion model suggests where there are impediments and accelerators to the diffusion of formal methods. By recording these impediments and accelerators and providing a case-based analysis, we have tried to disseminate to formal methods advocates the kinds of concerns that they must address if formal methods are to be more than an academic and technical curiosity.

References

Abowd, G., Allen, R. and Garlan, D. (1993) Using Style to Give Meaning to Software Architecture. In *Proceedings of SIGSOFT'93: Foundations of Software Engineering, Software Engineering Notes*, **118**(3):9–20, December.

Abrial, J.-R. (1995) *The B Book: Assigning Programs to Meanings*, Cambridge University Press, to appear.

Adams, G. (1994) *Analysis of the Reliability of the DARTS Channels*, Document DARTS-277-WTC-231193-C, DARTS Consortium (Esprit ESP/2354), February.

Allen, R. and Garlan, D. (1992) A Formal Approach to Software Architectures. In J. van Leeuwen, editor, *Proceedings of IFIP'92*, Elsevier Science, September.

Allen, R. and Garlan, D. (1994a) Formalizing Architectural Connection. *Proceedings of the Sixteenth International Conference on Software Engineering*, IEEE Computer Society Press, Los Alamitos, May.

Allen, R. and Garlan, D. (1994b) Beyond Definition/Use: Architectural Interconnection. *Proceedings of the ACM Interface Definition Language Workshop, SIGPLAN Notices*, **29**(8), August.

Alsys (1993) *CSMART and the Certification of Safety-Critical Systems*, Report AL/RRA/CSCS-/SR1, Version 1.0, 13 December. Available from Alsys Ltd., Partridge House, Newtown Road, Henley-on-Thames, Oxon., RG9 1EN, UK.

Andrews, D. and Ince, D. (1991) *Practical Formal Methods with VDM*, McGraw-Hill International Series in Software Engineering, London.

Archinoff, G.H., Hohendorf, R.J., Wassyng, A., Quigley, B. and Borsch, M.R. (1990) Verification of the Shutdown System Software at Darlington Nuclear Generating Station. In *Proceedings of the International Conference on Control & Instrumentation in Nuclear Installations*, The Institution of Nuclear Engineers, Glasgow, No. 4.3, May.

Atomic Energy Control Board (1991) *Proposed Standard for Software for Computers in the Safety Systems of Nuclear Power Stations*. Final Report for contract 2.117.1 for the AECB, Canada, by Professor David L. Parnas, McMaster University, Communications Research Laboratory, Hamilton, Ontario L8S 4K1, Canada.

Barbasch, C.A. (1993) *AdaWise User's Manual*, Report TM-93-0036, Odyssey Research Associates, Ithaca, NY, USA, July.

Barroca, L. and McDermid, J.A. (1992) Formal Methods: Use and Relevance for the Development of Safety-critical Systems. *The Computer Journal*, **35**(6):579–599, June.

Barroca, L.M., Fitzgerald, J.S. and L. Spencer (1994) *The Architectural Specification of an Avionic Subsystem*, Technical Report DCSC/TN/94/24, BAe DCSC, Department of Computer Science, University of York, UK.

Barwise, J. (1989) Mathematical Proofs of Computer System Correctness. *Notices of the American Mathematical Society*, **36**(7):844–851, September.

B-Core (UK) Ltd. (1993) *B-Toolkit User Manual.* Available on request from B-Core (UK) Ltd., The Magdalen Centre, The Oxford Science Park, Oxford OX4 4GA, UK.

Beatty, D.L. and Bryant, R.E. (1994) Formally verifying a microprocessor using a simulation methodology. In *Proceedings of the 31st Design Automation Conference*, ACM Press, New York, pp. 596–602, June.

Bell, D.E. and La Padula, L.J. (1973) *Secure Computer Systems: Mathematical Foundations and Models*, Report M74-244, The MITRE Corporation, USA, May.

Best, D., Kress, C., Mykris, N., Russel, J. and Smith, W. (1982) An Advanced-Architecture CMOS/SOS Microprocessor. *IEEE Micro*, pp. 11–26, August.

Bevier, W.R. and Young, W.D. (1992) Machine Checked Proofs of the Design of a Fault-Tolerant Circuit. *Formal Aspects of Computing*, **4**(6A):755–775.

Bevier, W.R., Hunt, Jr., W.A., Moore, J.S. and Young, W.D. (1989) An Approach to Systems Verification. *Journal of Automated Reasoning*, **5**(4):411–428, December.

Bicarregui, J.C. and Ritchie, B. (1993) Invariants, Frames and Postconditions: A Comparison of the VDM and B Notations. In Woodcock and Larsen (1993), pp. 162–182.

Bicarregui, J.C., Fitzgerald, J.S., Lindsay, P.A., Moore, R. and Ritchie, B. (1994) *Proof in VDM: A Practitioner's Guide*, Springer-Verlag FACIT Series, London.

Bloomfield, R., Froome, P. and Monahan, B. (1989) SpecBox: A toolkit for BSI-VDM. *SafetyNet*, **5**:4–7.

Boehm, B.W. (1981) *Software Engineering Economics*, Prentice Hall, Englewood Cliffs.

Boehm, B.W. (1988) A Spiral Model of Software Development and Maintenance. *IEEE Computer*, **21**(5):61–72, May.

Bolognesi, T. and Brinksma, H. (1987) Introduction to the ISO Specification Language LOTOS. *Computer Networks and ISDN Systems*, **14**:25–59.

Boswell, T. (1993) Specification and Validation of a Security Policy Model. In Woodcock and Larsen (1993), pp. 42–51.

Bowen, J.P. (1993) Formal Methods in Safety-Critical Standards. *Proceedings 1993 Software Engineering Standards Symposium*, IEEE Computer Society Press, pp. 168–177.

Bowen, J.P., editor (1994) *Towards Verified Systems*, Real-Time Safety Critical Systems Series, Volume 2, Elsevier Science, Amsterdam.

Bowen, J.P. and Gordon, M.J.C. (1994) Z and HOL. In Bowen and Hall (1994), pp. 141–167.

Bowen, J.P. and Hall, J.A., editors (1994) *Z User Workshop, Cambridge 1994*, Proc. of the 8th Z User Meeting, University of Cambridge, 29–30 June 1994, Workshops in Computing, Springer-Verlag, London.

Bowen, J.P., He, J. and Page, I. (1994) Hardware Compilation. In Bowen (1994), Chapter 10, pp. 193–207.

Bowen, J.P. and Hinchey, M.G. (1994a) Formal Methods and Safety-Critical Standards. *IEEE Computer*, **27**(8):68–71, August.

Bowen, J.P. and Hinchey, M.G. (1994b) Seven More Myths of Formal Methods: Dispelling Industrial Prejudice. In Denvir *et al.* (1994), pp. 105–117.

Bowen, J.P. and Hinchey, M.G. (1995a) Ten Commandments of Formal Methods. *IEEE Computer*, **28**(4):56–63, April.

Bowen, J.P. and Hinchey, M.G. (1995b) Seven More Myths of Formal Methods. *IEEE Software*, **12**(4), July.

Bowen, J.P. and Hinchey, M.G., editors (1995c) *ZUM'95—9th International Conference of Z Users*, Lecture Notes in Computer Science, Springer-Verlag, Heidelberg.

Bowen, J.P. and Stavridou, V. (1993a) Safety-Critical Systems, Formal Methods, and Standards. *IEE/BCS Software Engineering Journal*, **8**(4):189–209, July. Also appears in revised form in Bowen (1994), Chapter 1, pp. 3–33.

Bowen, J.P. and Stavridou, V. (1993b) The Industrial Take-up of Formal Methods in Safety-Critical and Other Areas: A perspective. In Woodcock and Larsen (1993), pp. 183–195.

Bowman, W.C., Archinoff, G.H., Raina, V.M., Tremaine, D.R. and Leveson, N.G. (1991) An Application of Fault Tree Analysis to Safety Critical Software at Ontario Hydro. *Probabilistic Safety and Management Conference*, February.

Boyer, R.S. and Moore, J.S. (1979) *A Computational Logic*, Academic Press, ACM Monograph Series, Boston.

Boyer, R.S. and Moore, J.S. (1988) *A Computational Logic Handbook*, Academic Press, Boston.

Boyer, R.S., Goldschlag, D., Kaufmann, M. and Moore, J.S. (1991) Functional Instantiation in First Order Logic. In *Artificial Intelligence and Mathematical Theory of Computation: Papers in Honor of John McCarthy*, pp. 7–26, Academic Press.

Breuer, P.T. and Bowen, J.P. (1994) Towards Correct Executable Semantics for Z. In Bowen and Hall (1994), pp. 185–209.

Brien, S.M. and Nicholls, J.E. (1992) *Z Base Standard, Version 1.0*, Technical Monograph PRG-107, Oxford University, Programming Research Group, November.

Brilliant, S.S., Knight, J.C. and Leveson, N.G. (1989) The Consistent Comparison Problem in N-Version Software. *IEEE Transactions on Software Engineering*, **15**(11):1481–1484, November.

Brinksma, H. (1985) The Specification Language LOTOS. In *Proceedings NGI-SION Symposium 3*, Amsterdam, NGI.

British Aerospace System Designers (1985) *CORE—The Method*, Report BAe-WSD-R-CORE-SWE-512, British Aerospace, Pembroke House, Pembroke Broadway, Camberley, Surrey GU15, 3XD, UK.

Brock, B.C., Hunt, Jr., W.A. and Young, W.D. (1992) Introduction to a Formally Defined Hardware Description Language. In V. Stavridou, editor, *Theorem Provers in Circuit Design: Theory, Practice and Experience*, Proceedings of the IFIP TC10/WG 10.2 International Conference, IFIP Transactions A-10, North-Holland, pp. 3–36.

Brock, S. and George, C. (1990) *The RAISE Method Manual*, Computer Resources International A/S.

Bruns, G. and Anderson, S. (1994) The formalization and analysis of a communication protocol. *Formal Aspects of Computing*, **6**(1):92–112.

Bryant, R.E. (1986) Graph-based Algorithms for Boolean Function Manipulation. *IEEE Transactions on Computers*, **C-35**(8):677–691, August.

Burch, J.R. and Dill, D.L. (1994) Automatic Verification of Pipelined Microprocessor Control. In D.L. Dill, editor, *Computer-Aided Verification, CAV'94*, Springer-Verlag LNCS 818, pp. 68–80.

Burns, A., McDermid, J.A. and Dobson, J. (1992) On the Meaning of Safety and Security. *The Computer Journal*, **35**(1):3–15, February.

Butler, R.W. (1991) NASA Langley's Research Program in Formal Methods. In *COMPASS'91 (Proceedings of the Sixth Annual Conference on Computer Assurance)*, Gaithersburg, MD, June, IEEE Computer Society Press, Los Alamitos, pp. 157–162.

Butler, R.W. and Finelli, G.B. (1993) The Infeasibility of Quantifying the Reliability of Life-Critical Real-Time Software. *IEEE Transactions on Software Engineering*, **16**(5):66–76, January.

Carranza, M. and Young, W.D. (1992) Verifying a Fuzzy Controller. *Proceedings of the Second IFIP International Workshop on Industrial Fuzzy Control and Intelligent Systems*, pp. 194–203, December.

Carrington, D. and Stocks, P. (1994) A Tale of Two Paradigms: Formal Methods and Software Testing. In Bowen and Hall (1994), pp. 51–68.

Carter, W.C., Joyner, W.H. and Brand, D. (1978) Microprogram Verification Considered Necessary. In *National Computer Conference*, AFIPS Conference Proceedings, Volume 48, pp. 657–664.

Cellary, W., Gelenbe, E. and Morzy, T. (1988) *Concurrency Control in Distributed Database Systems*, Studies in Computer Science and AI, North-Holland.

Chapront, P. (1992) Vital Coded Processor and Safety Related Software Design. In H.H. Frey, editor, *Safety of Computer Control Systems 1992 (SAFECOMP'92)*, IFAC Symposium, Pergamon Press, Oxford, pp. 141–145.

Clarke, E., Grumberg, O. and Long, D. (1992) Model Checking and Abstraction. *Transactions on Programming Languages and Systems*, **16**(5):1512–1542.

Cleaveland, R., Parrow, J. and Steffen, B. (1993) The Concurrency Workbench: A Semantics Based Tool for the Verification of Concurrent Systems. *ACM Transactions on Programming Languages and Systems*, **15**(1):36–72, January.

Cleland, G. and MacKenzie, D. (1995) Inhibitors to Formal Methods Exploitation – Cause or Symptom? In *Proceedings of the Workshop on Industrial-Strength Formal Specification Techniques (WIFT'95)*, Boca Raton, Florida, IEEE Computer Society Press, Los Alamitos, April.

Cohn, A.J. (1988) A Proof of Correctness of the Viper Microprocessor: The First Level. In G. Birtwistle and P.A. Subramanyam, editors, *VLSI Specification, Verification and Synthesis*, Kluwer Academic Publishers.

Collins, B.P., Nicholls, J.E. and Sørensen, I.H. (1989) *Introducing Formal Methods: The CICS Experience with Z*, IBM Technical Report TR12.260, IBM UK Laboratories Ltd., Hursley Park, UK.

Cook, J.V. (1986) *Final Report for the C/30 Microcode Verification Project.* Technical Report ART-86(6771)-3, Computer Science Laboratory, The Aerospace Corporation, El Segundo, CA, September. Export Controlled.

Coombes, A., Morris, P. and McDermid, J.A. (1994) Causality as a means for the expression of requirements for safety-critical systems. In *Proceedings of COMPASS'94, 9th Annual Conference of Computer Assurance*, 27 June – 1 July, Gaithersburg, MD, USA, IEEE Computer Society Press, pp. 223–231.

Craigen, D. and Summerskill, K., editors (1990) *Formal Methods for Trustworthy Computer Systems (FM89)*, Workshops in Computing, Springer-Verlag.

Craigen, D., Gerhart, S. and Ralston, T. (1993) *An International Survey of Industrial Applications of Formal Methods.* Atomic Energy Control Board of Canada, U.S. National Institute of Standards and Technology, and U.S. Naval Research Laboratories, NIST GCR 93/626. National Technical Information Service, 5285 Port Royal Road, Springfield, VA 22161, USA, March. Also published by the U.S. Naval Research Laboratory (Formal Report 5546-93-9582, September 1993) and the Canadian Atomic Energy Control Board reports INFO-0474-1 (Volume 1) and INFO-0474-2 (Volume 2), January 1995.

Craigen, D., Gerhart, S. and Ralston, T. (1995) Formal Methods Reality Check: Industrial Usage. *IEEE Transactions on Software Engineering*, **21**(2):90–98, February.

Craigen, D. and Summerskill, K., editors (1990) *Formal Methods for Trustworthy Computer Systems (FM89)*, Workshops in Computing, Springer-Verlag.

Cyrluk, D. (1993) *Microprocessor Verification in PVS: A Methodology and Simple Example*, Technical Report SRI-CSL-93-12, Computer Science Laboratory, SRI International, Menlo Park, CA, December.

Cyrluk, D., Rajan, S., Shankar, N. and Srivas, M.K. (1994) Effective Theorem Proving for Hardware Verification. In Kumar and Kropf (1994), pp. 287–305.

DA Airbus GmbH (1993) *Cabin Intercommunication Data System System Specification, A330-/340, CIDS*, Deutsche Aerospace Airbus Industrie No. 2370M1F000101, Volume I, Issue 5.

Dawes, J. (1991) *The VDM-SL Reference Guide*, UCL Press/Pitman Publishing, London.

Dean, C.N. and Hinchey, M.G. (1995) Introducing Formal Methods through Rôle-Playing. *ACM SIGCSE Bulletin*, **27**(1):302–306, March.

Delisle, N. and Garlan, D. (1989) Formally Specifying Electronic Instruments. In *Proceedings of the Fifth International Workshop on Software Specification and Design, Software Engineering Notes*, **14**(3):242–248, May.

Delisle, N. and Garlan, D. (1990) Applying Formal Specification to Industrial Problems: A Specification of an Oscilloscope. *IEEE Software*, **7**(5):29–37, September.

De Millo, R.A., Lipton, R.J. and Perlis, A.J. (1979) Social Processes and Proofs of Theorems and Programs. *Communications of the ACM*, **22**(5):271–280, May.

Denvir, T. Naftalin, M. and Bertran, M., editors (1994) *FME'94: Industrial Benefit of Formal Methods*, Springer-Verlag LNCS 873.

Dijkstra, E.W. (1976) *A Discipline of Programming*, Prentice Hall, Englewood Cliffs.

Dijkstra, E.W. (1981) Why Correctness must be a Mathematical Concern. In R.S. Boyer and J.S. Moore, editors, *The Correctness Problem in Computer Science*, Academic Press, London, pp. 1–6.

Di Vito, B.L., Butler, R.W. and Caldwell, J.L. (1990) *Formal Design and Verification of a Reliable Computing Platform for Real-Time Control*, NASA Technical Memorandum 102716, NASA Langley Research Center, Hampton, VA, October.

Dix, A. (1991) *Formal Methods for Interactive Systems*, Academic Press, London.

DST Deutsche System-Technik GmbH. (1993) *Using Z and DST-fuzz: An Introduction*, DST Deutsche System, Kiel, Germany.

Dürr, E.H. (1992) VDM^{++} – A Formal Specification Language for Object-oriented Designs. In *Technology of Object-oriented Languages and Systems*, Proceedings of TOOLS Europe 1992, Prentice Hall International, pp. 63–78.

Dürr, E.H. (1994) *The Use of Object-oriented Specifications in Physics*. Ph.D. thesis, Utrecht University, The Netherlands, October.

Dürr, E.H. and Plat, N. (1995) *VDM^{++} Language Reference Manual*. Document number AFRO-/CG/ED/LRM/V10, Afrodite (ESPRIT-III project number 6500), February.

Dyer, M. (1992) *The Cleanroom Approach to Quality Software Development*, John Wiley & Sons, Series in Software Engineering Practice.

Elmstrøm, R., Larsen, P.G. and Lassen, P.B. (1994) The IFAD VDM-SL Toolbox: A Practical Approach to Formal Specifications. *ACM SIGPLAN Notices*, September.

European Community (1991) *Information Technology Security Evaluation Criteria*, European Community Office for Official Publications, June.

European Space Agency (1991) *ESA Software Engineering Standards*, ESA, 8–10 rue Mario-Nikis, 75738 Paris Cedex, France, ESA PSS-05-0 Issue 2, February.

Fagan, M. (1986) Advances in Software Inspection, *IEEE Transactions on Software Engineering*, **12**(7):744–751, July.

Fetzer, J.H. (1988) Program Verification: The Very Idea. *Communications of the ACM*, **31**(9):-1048–1063, September.

Fichman, R.G. and Kemerer, C.F. (1993) Adoption of Software Engineering Process Innovations: The case for object orientation. *Sloan Management Review*, Winter.

Fitzgerald, J.S. (1994) The VDM Forum: A New e-mail List for Researchers, Practitioners and Teachers. *FACS Europe*, **1**(2):17, Spring.

Flinn, B. and Sørensen, I.H. (1992) CAVIAR: A Case Study in Specification. In I. Hayes, editor, *Specification Case Studies*, 2nd edition, Prentice Hall International Series in Computer Science, Hemel Hempstead.

Floyd, R.W. (1967) Assigning Meanings to Programs. In J.T. Schwartz, editor, *Proceedings of the Symposium of Applied Mathematics*, Mathematical Aspects of Computer Science, American Mathematical Society, **19**:19–32.

Formal Systems (Europe) Ltd. (1992) *Failure Divergence Refinement, User Manual and Tutorial*, Formal Systems (Europe) Ltd., Oxford, UK.

Froome, P.K.D. (1990) *SpecBox*, Adelard Software, UK.

Fuchs, N.E. (1992) Specifications are (Preferably) Executable. *Software Engineering Journal*, **7**(5):323–334, September.

Garlan, D. (1995) Making Formal Methods Education Effective for Professional Software Engineers. *Information and Software Technology*, **35**(5), May.

Garlan, D. and Delisle, N. (1990) Formal Specifications as Reusable Frameworks. In D. Bjørner, C.A.R. Hoare and H. Langmaack, editors, *VDM'90: VDM and Z – Formal Methods in Software Development*, Springer-Verlag LNCS 428, pp. 150–163.

Garlan, D. and Shaw, M. (1993) An Introduction to Software Architecture. In V. Ambriola and G. Tortora, editors, *Advances in Software Engineering and Knowledge Engineering*, World Scientific Publishing Company, Singapore.

Garlan, D. and Shaw, M. (1994) Software Development Assignments for a Software Architecture Course. In *Software Engineering Resources: Proceedings of the ACM/IEEE International Workshop on Software Engineering Education*, Technical Report 94/6, Department of Computing, Imperial College, London, May.

Gerhart, S., Bouler, M., Greene, K., Jamsek, D., Ralston, T. and Russinoff, D. (1991) *Formal Methods Transition Study Final Report*, Technical Report STP-FT-322-91, Microelectronics and Computer Technology Corporation, Austin, TX, August.

Gerhart, S., Craigen, D. and Ralston, T. (1993) Observations on Industrial Practice Using Formal Methods. In *Proceedings of the 15th International Conference on Software Engineering*, Baltimore, MD, May.

Gerhart, S., Craigen, D. and Ralston, T. (1994) Experience with Formal Methods in Critical Systems. *IEEE Software*, **11**(1):21–28, January.

Gibbs, W.W. (1994) Software's Chronic Crisis. *Scientific American*, **271**(3):86–95, September.

Gladden, G.R. (1982) Stop the Life Cycle – I Want to Get Off. *ACM Software Engineering Notes*, **7**(2):35–39.
Glanz, J. (1995) Mathematical Logic Flushes Out Bugs in Chip Designs. *Science*, **267**, 20 January.

Goldberg, A. (1984) *Smalltalk-80: The Interactive Programming Environment*, Addison-Wesley.

Goldschlag, D.M. (1991) *Mechanically Verifying Concurrent Programs*. Ph.D. thesis, University of Texas at Austin, USA.

Gordon, M.J.C. (1985) *Why Higher-Order Logic is a Good Formalism for Specifying and Verifying Hardware*, Technical Report 77, University of Cambridge Computer Laboratory, UK, September.

Gordon, M.J.C. and Melham, T.F., editors (1993) *Introduction to HOL: A Theorem Proving Environment for Higher Order Logic*, Cambridge University Press, Cambridge.

Guaspari, D., Marceau, C. and Polak, W. (1990) Formal Verification of Ada Programs. *IEEE Transactions on Software Engineering*, **16**(9):1058–1075, September.

Gunter, C., Gunter, E. and Zave, P. (1994) *Formalizing Specification Modules in Higher-Order Logic*, AT&T Bell Laboratories, Technical Report, in preparation.

Gupta, A. (1992) Formal Hardware Verification Methods: A Survey. *Formal Methods in System Design*, **1**(2/3):151–238, October.

Guttag, J.V. and Horning, J.J. (1993) *Larch: Languages and Tools for Formal Specification*, Springer-Verlag Texts and Monographs in Computer Science, New York.

Guttag, J.V., Horning, J.J. and Wing, J.M. (1985) *Larch in Five Easy Pieces*, Technical Report 5, Digital Equipment Corporation, Systems Research Center, 130 Lytton Avenue, Palo Alto, CA 94301, July.

Guttag, J.V., Horning, J.J. and Modet, A. (1990) *Report on the Larch Shared Language*, Technical Report 58, Digitial Equipment Corporation, Systems Research Center, 130 Lytton Avenue, Palo Alto, CA 94301, April.

Hall, J.A. (1990) Seven Myths of Formal Methods. *IEEE Software*, **7**(5):11–19, September.

Hall, J.A. (1994) Formal Methods in the Development of an Information System for Air Traffic Control. Draft manuscript, October.

Hamilton, V. (1992) Formal and Conventional Development Methods, *International Atomic Energy Authority Specialists Meeting*, Chalk River. Available from Rolls-Royce & Associates Ltd., PO Box 31, Raynesway, Derby DE24 8BJ, UK.

Harel, D. (1987) Statecharts: A Visual Formalism for Complex Systems. *Science of Computer Programming*, **8**:231–274, August.

Harel, D., Lachover, H., Naamad, A. and Pnueli, A. (1990) Statemate: A Working Environment for the Development of Complex Reactive Systems. *IEEE Transactions on Software Engineering*, **16**(4):403–414, April.

Hartman, B.A. (1994) *An Introduction to THETA*, Report TM-94-0012, Odyssey Research Associates, Ithaca, NY, USA, February.

Hatley, D.J. and Pirbhai, I.A. (1987) *Strategies for Real-Time System Specification*, Dorset House Publishers, New York.

Hayes, I.J. (1985) Applying Formal Specification to Software Development in Industry. *IEEE Transactions on Software Engineering*, **11**(2):169–178, February.

Hayes, I.J. (1990) *Specifying Physical Limitations: A Case Study of an Oscilloscope*, Technical Report 167, Department of Computer Science, University of Queensland.

Hayes, I.J. and Jones, C.B. (1989) Specifications are not (Necessarily) Executable. *Software Engineering Journal*, **4**(6):330–338, June.

Hayes, I.J., Jones, C.B. and Nicholls, J.E. (1994) Understanding the Differences Between VDM and Z. *ACM Software Engineering Notes*, **19**(3):75–81, July.

He, J., Page, I. and Bowen, J.P. (1993) Towards a Provably Correct Hardware Implementation of Occam. In G.J. Milne and L. Pierre, editors, *Correct Hardware Design and Verification Methods*, Springer-Verlag LNCS 683, pp. 214–225.

Heitmeyer, C.L. and Jeffords, R. (1995) *Formal Specification and Verification of Real-Time Systems: A Comparison Study*, Technical Report, Naval Research Laboratory, Washington DC, USA.

Heitmeyer, C.L. and Lynch, N. (1994a) *The Generalized Railroad Crossing: A Case Study in Formal Verification of Real-Time Systems*, NRL Memorandum Report NRL/MR/5540–94–7619, Naval Research Laboratory, Washington DC, USA, December.

Heitmeyer, C.L. and Lynch, N. (1994b) The Generalized Railroad Crossing: A Case Study in Formal Verification of Real-Time Systems. In *Proceedings of RTSS'94, Real-Time Systems Symposium*, San Juan, Puerto Rico, December 1994, pp. 120–131, IEEE Computer Society Press, Los Alamitos.

Heitmeyer, C.L., Jeffords, R.D. and Labaw, B.G. (1993a) *Comparing Different Approaches for Specifying and Verifying Real-Time Systems*, Technical Report, Naval Research Laboratory, Washington DC, USA.

Heitmeyer, C.L., Jeffords, R.D. and Labaw, B.G. (1993b) A Benchmark for Comparing Different Approaches for Specifying and Verifying Real-Time Systems. In *Proceedings 10th International Workshop on Real-Time Operating Systems and Software*, New York City, 10–11 May 1993, IEEE Computer Society Press, Los Alamitos.

Heninger, K.L. (1980) Specifying Software Requirements for Complex Systems: New Techniques and their Application. *IEEE Transactions on Software Engineering*, **6**(1):2–13, January.

Heninger, K.L., Kallander, J., Parnas, D.L. and Shore, J.E. (1978) Software Requirements for the A-7E Aircraft, *NRL Memorandum Report 3876*, United States Naval Research Laboratory, Washington D.C., November.

Henzinger, T., Manna, Z. and Pneuli, A. (1992) Timed Transition Systems. In J.W. de Bakker, C. Huizing, W.-P. de Roever and G. Rozenberg, editors, *Real-Time: Theory and Practice*, Springer-Verlag LNCS 600.

Hester, S.D., Parnas, D.L. and Utter, D.F. (1981) Using Documentation as a Software Design Medium. *Bell System Technical Journal*, **60**(8):1941-1977, October.

Hill, I.D. (1972) Wouldn't it be Nice if We Could Write Computer Programs in Ordinary English – or Would it? *The Computer Bulletin*, **16**.

Hill, J.V. (1991) *Software Development Methods in Practice*. In C. Churchley, editor, *Microprocessor Based Protection Systems*, Elsevier.

Hinchey, M.G., and Jarvis, S.A. (1995) *Concurrent Systems: Formal Development in CSP*, McGraw-Hill International Series in Software Engineering, London.

Hoare, C.Λ.R. (1969) An Axiomatic Basis for Computer Programming. *Communications of the ACM*, **21**(8):666–677.

Hoare, C.A.R. (1985) *Communicating Sequential Processes*, Prentice Hall International Series in Computer Science, Hemel Hempstead.

Hoare, C.A.R. (1987) An Overview of Some Formal Methods for Program Design. *IEEE Computer*, **20**(9):85–91, September.

Hoare, C.A.R. and Gordon, M.J.C. (1992) *Mechanized Reasoning and Hardware Design*, Prentice Hall International Series in Computer Science, Hemel Hempstead.

Hoare, C.A.R. and Page, I. (1994) Hardware and Software: Closing the Gap. *Transputer Communications*, **2**(2):69–90, June.

Hörcher, H.-M. and Peleska, J. (1994) The Role of Formal Specifications in Software Test. Tutorial presentation at the *Formal Methods Europe '94 Symposium*, Barcelona, Spain.

Hunt, Jr., W.A. (1994) *FM8501: A Verified Microprocessor*, Springer-Verlag Lecture Notes in Artificial Intelligence 795, Berlin.

Hunt, Jr., W.A. and Brock, B.C. (1992) A Formal HDL and FM9001 Verification. In Hoare and Gordon (1992), pp. 35–47.

Iglewski, M., Madey, J., Parnas, D.L. and Kelly, P. (1993) *Documentation Paradigms (A Progress Report)*, CRL Report 270, McMaster University, CRL (Communications Research Laboratory), TRIO (Telecommunications Research Institute of Ontario), July.

Institute of Electrical and Electronic Engineers (1988) *IEEE Standard VHDL Language Reference Manual*, IEEE STD 1076-1987, New York.

Intel Corporation (1993) *Pentium Processor User's Manual, Volume I: Pentium Processor Data Book*, Intel Corporation, Santa Clara, CA.

International Electrotechnical Commission (1986) *Software for Computers in the Safety Systems of Nuclear Power Stations.*

International Electrotechnical Commission (1995) *Software for Computers in the Safety Systems of Nuclear Power Stations*, First Supplement to IEC 880. In preparation.

International Standards Organization (1991) *ISO 9000-3: Quality Management and Quality Assurance Standard Part 3*, Guidelines for the application of ISO 9001 to the development, supply and maintenance of software, June.

International Standatds Organization (1993) *Information Technology Programming Languages – VDM-SL First Committee Draft Standard CD 13817-1*, Document Number ISO/IEC JT-C1/SC22/WG19/N-20, November.

Inverardi, P. and Wolf, A.L. (1995) Formal Specification and Analysis of Software Architectures Using the Chemical, Abstract Machine Model. *IEEE Transactions on Software Engineering*, to appear.

Jackson, D. (1995) Structuring Z Specifications with Views. *ACM Transactions on Software Engineering and Methodology*, to appear.

Jackson, M.A. (1975) *Principles of Program Design*, Academic Press, London.

Jackson, M.A. and Zave, P. (1992) Domain Descriptions. In *Proceedings of the IEEE International Symposium on Requirements Engineering*, IEEE Computer Society Press, Los Alamitos, pp. 56–64.

Jahanian, F. and Mok, A.K. (1986) Safety Analysis of Timing Properties in Real-Time Systems. *IEEE Transactions on Software Engineering*, 12(9):890–903, September.

Jahanian, F. and Mok, A.K. (1987) A Graph-Theoretic Approach for Timing Analysis and its Implementation. *IEEE Transactions on Computers*, 36(8):961–975, August.

Jahanian, F. and Stuart, D.A. (1988) A Method for Verifying Properties of Modechart Specifications. In *Proceedings of RTSS'88, Real-Time Systems Symposium*, December, IEEE Computer Society Press, Los Alamitos.

Janicki, R. (1993) *Towards a Formal Semantics of Tables*, CRL Report 264, McMaster University, CRL (Communications Research Laboratory), TRIO (Telecommunications Research Institute of Ontario), September.

Jeffay, K. (1993) The Real-Time Producer/Consumer Paradigm: A Paradigm for the Construction of Efficient, Predictable Real-time Systems. In *Proceedings of the 1993 ACM/SIGAPP Symposium on Applied Computing*, Indianapolois, IN, pp. 796–804, February.

Jones, C.B. (1990) *Systematic Software Development using VDM*, 2nd edition, Prentice Hall International Series in Computer Science, Hemel Hempstead.

Jones, C.B., Jones, K., Linsay, P. and Moore, R. (1991) *Mural: A Formal Development Support System*, Springer-Verlag, London.

Joyce, J. (1988) Verification and Implementation of a Microprocessor. In G. Birtwistle and P.A. Subrahmanyam, editors, *VLSI Specification, Verification and Synthesis*, Kluwer Academic Publishers, Boston, MA.

Kaufmann, K. (1991) A Mechanically-Checked Correctness Proof for Generalization in the Presence of Free Variables. *Journal of Automated Reasoning*.

Kaufmann, K. (1992) An Extension of the Boyer–Moore Theorem Prover to Support First-Order Quantification. *Journal of Automated Reasoning*, **9**(3):355–372, December.

Knuth, D.F. (1992) *Literate Programming*, CLSI Lecture Notes, No. 27, Stanford University.

Kozen, D. (1983) Results on the propositional mu-calculus. *Theoretical Computer Science*, **27**:-333–354.

Kronlöf, K., editor (1993) *Method Integration: Concept and Case Studies*, John Wiley and Sons, Series in Software Based Systems, London.

Kuhn, T.S. (1970) *The Structure of Scientific Revolutions*, University of Chicago Press.

Kumar, R. and Kropf, T., editors (1994) *Preliminary Proceedings of the Second Conference on Theorem Provers in Circuit Design*, Bad Herrenalb, Germany, September, Forschungszentrum Informatik an der Universität Karlsruhe, Germany, FZI Publication 4/94.

Lamport, L. (1991) *Temporal Logic of Actions*, Technical Report 79, Digital Equipment Corporation Systems Research Center, 130 Lytton Avenue, Palo Alto, CA 94301, December.

Larsen, P.G. (1994) *The VDM Bibliography*, IFAD, Odense, Denmark, January.

Larsen, P.G. and Lassen, P.B. (1991) An Executable Subset of Meta-IV with Loose Specification. In Prehn and Toetenel (1991).

Latham, J., Bush, V.J. and Cottam, I.D. (1990) *The Programming Process: An Introduction Using VDM and Pascal*, Addison-Wesley, London.

Leeman, G.B., Carter, W.C. and Birman, A. (1974) Some Techniques for Microprogram Validation. In *Information Processing '74 (Proceedings of the IFIP Congress 1974)*, North-Holland, pp. 76–80.

de Lemos, R., Saeed, A. and Anderson, T. (1994) On the Safety Analysis of Requirements Specifications. In *Proceedings of SAFECOMP'94*, 23–26 October, Anaheim, CA, USA, pp. 217–228.

Leveson, N.G. (1986) Software Safety: What, Why and How. *ACM Computing Surveys*, **18**(2):-125–164, June.

Leveson, N.G. and Stolzy, J.L. (1987) Safety Analysis Using Petri Nets. *IEEE Transactions on Software Engineering*, **13**(3):386–397, March.

Lincoln, P. and Rushby, J. (1993) The Formal Verification of an Algorithm for Interactive Consistency under a Hybrid Fault Model. In C. Courcoubetis, editor, *Computer Aided Verification*, Springer-Verlag LNCS 697, pp. 292–304.

Littlewood, B. and Strigini, L. (1993) Validation of Ultrahigh Dependability for Software-based Systems. *Communications of the ACM*, **36**(11): 69–80, November.

Luckham, D.C., Augustin, L.M., Kenney, J.J., Vera, J., Bryan, D. and Mann, W. (1995) Specification and Analysis of System Architecture Using Rapide. *IEEE Transactions on Software Engineering*, **21**(4):336–355, April.

MacQueen, D., Harper, R. and Milner, R. (1986) *Standard ML*, Technical Report ECS-LFCS-86-2, University of Edinburgh, Department of Computer Science, UK.

Mahony, B.P. and Hayes, I.J. (1991) Using Continuous Real Functions to Model Timed Histories. In P.A. Bailes, editor, *Proceedings of the 6th Australian Software Engineering Conference (ASWEC91)*, pp. 257–270, Australian Computer Society, July.

Mander, K.C. and Polack, F.A.C. (1995) Rigorous Specification using Structured Systems Analysis and Z. *Information and Software Technology*, **37**(5), May.

Mataga, P. and Zave, P. (1993) *A Formal Specification of Some Important 5ESS Features, Part III: Connections and Provisioning*, Technical Report BL0112650-931001-24, AT&T Bell Laboratories, USA.

Mataga, P. and Zave, P. (1994) Formal Specification of Telephone Features. In Bowen and Hall (1994), pp. 29–50.

May, D. (1990) Use of Formal Methods by a Silicon Manufacturer. In C.A.R. Hoare, editor, *Developments in Concurrency and Communication*, University of Texas at Austin Year of Programming Series, Addison-Wesley, Chapter 4, pp. 107–129.

May, D., Barrett, G. and Shepherd, D. (1992) Designing Chips that Work. In Hoare and Gordon (1992).

McCracken, D.D. and Jackson, M.A. (1982) Life Cycle Concept Considered Harmful. *ACM Software Engineering Notes*, **7**(2):28–32.

McCullough, D. (1988) Noninterference and the Composability of Security Properties. In *Proceedings of the Symposium on Security and Privacy*, Oakland, CA, April 1988, pp. 177–186, IEEE Computer Society Press.

McCullough, D. (1990) A Hookup Theorem for Multilevel Security. *IEEE Transactions on Software Engineering*, **16**(6):563–568, June.

McMillan, K.L. (1993) *Symbolic Model Checking*, Kluwer Academic Publishers, Boston.

Melton, R. and Dill, D.L. (1993) *Murφ Annotated Reference Manual*, Computer Science Department, Stanford University, Stanford, CA, March.

Mikk, E. (1994) *Translation of Z Specifications into Executable Code for Automatic Evaluation of Test Results*, Technical Report, Christian Albrechts Universität zu Kiel, Germany.

Mills, H.D. (1975) The New Math of Computer Programming. *Communications of the ACM*, **18**(1):43–48, January.

Milner, R. (1989) *Communication and Concurrency*, Prentice Hall International Series in Computer Science, Hemel Hempstead.

Ministry of Defence (1991a) *The Procurement of Safety Critical Software in Defence Equipment* (Part 1: Requirements, Part 2: Guidance), Interim Defence Standard 00-55, Issue 1, MoD, Directorate of Standardization, Kentigern House, 65 Brown Street, Glasgow G2 8EX, UK, 5 April.

Ministry of Defence (1991b) *Hazard Analysis and Safety Classification of the Computer and Programmable Electronic System Elements of Defence Equipment*, Interim Defence Standard 00-56, Issue 1, MoD, Directorate of Standardization, Kentigern House, 65 Brown Street, Glasgow G2 8EX, UK, 5 April.

Morgan, C.C. (1994) *Programming from Specifications*, 2nd edition, Prentice Hall International Series in Computer Science, Hemel Hempstead.

Morgan, C.C. and Vickers, T., editors (1994) *On the Refinement Calculus*, Formal Approaches to Computing and Information Technology Series (FACIT), Springer, London.

Morris, P., Coombes, A. and McDermid, J.A. (1994) Requirements and Traceability. In *Requirements Engineering: Foundation of Software Quality (REFSQ'94)*.

Mukherjee, P. (1995) *Computer-Aided Validation of Formal Specifications*, Technical Report TR-CSD 95-01, Royal Holloway College, University of London, UK, January.

Mukherjee, P. and Stavridou, V. (1993) The Formal Specification of Safety Requirements for Storing Explosives. *Formal Aspects of Computing*, **5**(4):299–336.

Mukherjee, P. and Wichmann, B.A. (1993) *STV: A Case Study in VDM*, Technical Report DITC 219/93, National Physical Laboratory, Teddington, UK, May.

Musser, D.R. and Stepanov, A.A. (1989) *The Ada Generic Library: Linear List Processing Packages*, Springer-Verlag, New York.

Neilson, D.S. and Sørensen, I.H. (1994) The B-Technologies: A System for Computer Aided Programming. In U.H. Engberg, K.G. Larsen and P.D. Mosses, editors, *Proceedings of the 6th Nordic Workshop on Programming Theory*, B-Core (UK) Ltd., BRICS Notes Series, University of Aarhus, Denmark, 17–19 October 1994, pp. 18–35.

Nelson, G. (1981) *Techniques for Program Verification*, Technical Report CSL-81-10, Xerox Palo Alto Research Center, USA, June.

Neumann, P.G. (1995) *Computer Related Risks*, ACM Press, Addison-Wesley, New York.

Nix, C.J. and Collins, B.P. (1988) The Use of Software Engineering, Including the Z Notation, in the Development of CICS. *Quality Assurance*, **14**(3):103–110, September.

Norman, D.A. (1988) *The Psychology of Everyday Things*, Basic Books, New York.

Normington, G. (1993) Cleanroom and Z. In J.P. Bowen and J.E. Nicholls, editors, *Z User Workshop, London 1992*, Proceedings of the 7th Z User Meeting, Springer-Verlag Workshops in Computing, pp. 281–293.

ORA (1989a) *Larch/Ada Reference Manual*, Report 89-37, Odyssey Research Associates, Ithaca, NY, September.

ORA (1989b) *Larch/Ada Rationale*, Report 89-38, Odyssey Research Associates, Ithaca, NY, September.

ORA (1992) *Introduction to EVES: Exercises and Notes*, Odyssey Research Associates, Ottawa, Ontario, Canada.

ORA (1994) *Romulus Overview*, Report TM-94-0019, Odyssey Research Associates, Ithaca, NY, March.

Owre, S., Rushby, J.M. and Shankar, N. (1992) PVS: A Prototype Verification System. In D. Kapur, editor, *11th International Conference on Automated Deduction (CADE)*, Saratoga, NY, June, Springer-Verlag Lecture Notes in Artificial Intelligence 607, pp.748–752.

Owre, S., Shankar, N. and Rushby, J.M. (1993) *The PVS Specification Language*, Computer Science Laboratory, SRI International, Menlo Park, CA, February.

Parnas, D.L. (1992) *Tabular Representation of Tables*, CRL Report 260, Communications Research Laboratory, McMaster University, Ontario, Canada, October.

Parnas, D.L. (1994) Mathematical Descriptions and Specificaton of Software. In *Proceedings of the IFIP World Congress 1994*, August.

Parnas, D.L. and Madey, J. (1992) Functional Documentation for Computer Systems Engineering (Version 2), CRL Report 237, Communications Research Laboratory, McMaster University, Ontario, Canada. To appear in *Science of Computer Programming*.

Parnas, D., Heninger, K., Kallander, J. and Shore, J. (1978) *Software Requirements for the A-7E Aircraft*, Naval Research Laboratory Memorandum Report 3876.

Parnas, D.L., Asmis, G.J.K. and Kendall, J.D. (1990) Reviewable Development of Safety Critical Software. In *Proceedings of the International Conference on Control & Instrumentation in Nuclear Installations*, The Institution of Nuclear Engineers, Glasgow, No. 4.2, May.

Parnas, D.L., Asmis, G.J.K. and Madey, J. (1991) Assessment of Safety-Critical Software in Nuclear Power Plants. *Nuclear Safety*, **32**(2):189–198, April-June.

Peleska, J. (1993a) Formales Software-Engineering mit Strukturierten Methoden und Z: Nachweisbare Korrektheit fuer sicherheitsrelevante Anwendungen. In H.-J. Scheibl, ed., *Software-Entwicklung – Methoden, Werkzeuge, Erfahrungen '93*, Technischen Akademie Esslingen. English version available as *Formal Software Engineering, Z and Structured Methods – Provable Correctness for Safety-critical Systems*, Technical Report, DST Deutsche System-Technik GmbH, Kiel, Germany.

Peleska, J. (1993b) CSP, Formal Software Engineering and the Development of Fault-Tolerant Systems. In J. Vytopil, editor, *Formal Techniques in Real-Time and Fault-Tolerant Systems*, Kluwer Academic Publishers.

Perry, D.E. and Wolf, A.L. (1992) Foundations for the Study of Software Architecture. *Software Engineering Notes*, **17**(4):40–52, October.

Phillips, M. (1990) CICS/ESA 3.1 Experiences. In J.E. Nicholls, editor, *Z User Workshop, Oxford 1989*, Proceedings of the 4th Annual Z User Meeting, Oxford, 14–15 December 1989, Springer-Verlag Workshops in Computing, pp. 179–185.

Plat, N. and Larsen, P.G. (1992) An Overview of the ISO/VDM-SL Standard. *SIGPLAN Notices*, **7**(8):76–82, August.

Prehn, S. and Toetenel, W.J., editors (1991) *VDM'91: Formal Software Development Methods*, Volume 1, Springer-Verlag LNCS 551.

Program Validation (1990) *SPARK — The Spade Ada Kernel*, 3rd edition, April. Available from Program Validation Limited, 26 Queens Terrace, Southampton SO1 1BQ, UK.

Przybylinski, S.M., Fowler, P. and Maher, J.H. (1991) *Software Technology Transfer*. Course notes for a tutorial at the 13th International Conference on Software Engineering, Austin, Texas, May.

RAISE Language Group (1992) *The RAISE Specification Language*, Prentice Hall/BCS Practitioner Series, Hemel Hempstead.

Ramsey, N. (1994) Literate Programming Simplified. *IEEE Software*, **11**(5):97–105, September.

Ramsey, N. and Marceau, C. (1989) *Using Literate Programming in Production*, Report 89-28, Odyssey Research Associates, Ithaca, NY, USA, July.

Ramsey, N. and Marceau, C. (1991) Literate Programming on a Team Project. *Software–Practice and Experience*, **21**(7):677–683, July.

Rockwell International (1990) *AAMP2 Advanced Architecture Microprocessor II Reference Manual*, Collins Commercial Avionics, Cedar Rapids, Iowa, February.

Rockwell International (1993) *AAMP5 Microarchitecture*. Collins Commercial Avionics, Cedar Rapids, Iowa, February.

Rogers, E. (1983) *Diffusion of Innovations*, Free Press, New York.

Royce, W.W. (1970) Managing the Development of Large Software Systems. In *Proceedings of WESTCON'70*, August. (Reprinted in *Proceedings of the 9th International Conference on Software Engineering*, IEEE Press, 1987.)

RTCA (1992) *DO-178B: Software Considerations in Airborne Systems and Equipment Certification*, Requirements and Technical Concepts for Aviation, RTCA Inc., Suite 1020, 1140 Connecticut Avenue NW, Washington DC 20036, USA, 1 December. (Also available as document ED-12B from EUROCAE, 17 Rue Hamelin, Paris Cedex 75783, France.)

Rushby, J. (1993) *Formal Methods and the Certification of Critical Systems*, Technical Report SRI-CSL-93-07, SRI International, Menlo Park, CA, USA, November.

Rushby, J. (1995) *Formal Methods and the Certification of Formal Methods and their Role in the Certification of Critical Systems*, Technical Report CSL-95-1, SRI International, Menlo Park, CA, USA, March. (Shorter version of Rushby (1993).)

Santoline, L.L., Bowers, M.D., Crew, A.W., Roslund, C.J. and Ghrist III, W.D. (1989) Multiprocessor Shared-Memory Information Exchange. *IEEE Transactions on Nuclear Science*, **36**(1):626–633.

Saxe, J.B., Garland, S.J., Guttag, J.V. and Horning, J.J. (1994) Using Transformations and Verification in Circuit Design. *Formal Methods in System Design*, **4**(1):181–210, January.

Schantz, R., Thomas, R. and Bono, G. (1986) The Architecture of the Cronus Distributed Operating System. In *Proceedings of the 6th International Conference on Distributed Computing Systems*, May 1986, pp. 259–259, IEEE Computer Society Press, Los Alamitos.

van Schouwen, A.J. (1990) *The A-7 Requirements Model: Re-examination for Real-Time Systems and an Application to Monitoring Systems*, Technical Report 90-276, Department of Computer and Information Science, Queen's University, Kingston, Ontario, Canada, May.

van Schouwen, A.J., Parnas, D.L. and Madey, J. (1993) Documentation of Requirements for Computer Systems. Presented at *RE'93, 1st IEEE International Symposium on Requirements Engineering*, San Diego, CA, 4–6 January, IEEE Computer Society Press, Los Alamitos.

Seager, M., Guaspari, D., Stillerman, M. and Marceau, C. (1995) Formal Methods in the THETA Kernel. In *Proceedings of the 2nd IEEE Symposium on Security and Privacy*, Oakland, CA, 8–10 May, pp. 88-100, IEEE Computer Society Press, Los Alamitos.

Shankar, N. (1992) *Mechanized Verification of Real-Time Systems Using PVS*, Technical Report SRI-CSL-92-12, SRI International, Menlo Park, CA, USA, November.

Shankar, N., Owre, S. and Rushby, J.M. (1993) *The PVS Proof Checker: A Reference Manual*, Computer Science Laboratory, SRI International, Menlo Park, CA, February.

Shaw, M. and Garlan, D. (1995) *Software Architecture: Perspectives on an Emerging Discipline*, Prentice Hall.

Simpson, H. (1993) *Methodological and Notational Conventions in DORIS Real-Time Networks*, Technical Report, Dynamics Division, British Aerospace.

Smith, M.K. (1993) *Track-Segment Safety in Nqthm*, Internal Note, Computational Logic, Inc., Austin, TX, September.

van de Snepscheut, J.L.A. (1983) *Trace Theory and VSLI Design*. Ph.D. thesis, Technische Hogeschool Eindhoven, The Netherlands, October.

Spivey, J.M. (1992) *The Z Notation: A Reference Manual*, 2nd edition, Prentice Hall International Series in Computer Science, Hemel Hempstead.

Srivas, M.K. and Bickford, M. (1990) Formal Verification of a Pipelined Microprocessor. *IEEE Software*, **7**(5):52–64, September.

Srivas, M.K. and Miller, S.P. (1995) *Formal Verification of a Commercial Microprocessor*, Technical Report, Computer Science Laboratory, SRI International, Menlo Park, CA. In preparation.

Srivas, M.K., Shankar, N. and Rajan, S. (1995) *Hardware Verification using PVS: A Tutorial*, Technical Report, Computer Science Laboratory, SRI International, Menlo Park, CA. In preparation.

Stålmarck, S.G. (1990) Modelling and Verifying Systems and Software in Propositional Logic. In B.K. Daniels, editor, *Safety of Computer Control Systems 1990 (SAFECOMP'90)*, IFAC Symposium, Pergamon Press, Oxford, pp. 31–36.

Stirling, C. (1989) An Introduction to Modal and Temporal Logics for CCS. In A. Yonezawa and T. Ito, editors, *Concurrency: Theory, Language, and Architecture*, Springer-Verlag Lecture Notes in Computer Science 491, pp. 2–20.

Stirling, C. (1991) Modal and Temporal Logics. In *Handbook of Logic in Computer Science*, Oxford University Press, pp. 477–563.

Tahar, S. and Kumar, R. (1993) Implementing a Methodology for Formally Verifying RISC Processors in HOL. In J. Joyce and C.-J.H. Seger, editors, *Higher Order Logic Theorem Proving and its Applications (6th International Workshop, HUG'93)*, Vancouver, Canada, Springer-Verlag LNCS 780, pp. 281–294.

Tornatsky, L.G. and Fleisher, M. (1990) *The Processes of Technological Innovation*, Lexington Books, New York.

Ward, N.J. (1989) The Static Analysis of Safety-Critical Software using MALPAS. In R. Genser, E. Schoitsch and P. Kopacek, editors, *Safety of Computer Control Systems 1989 (SAFECOMP'89)*, IFAC/IFIP Workshop, Pergamon Press, Oxford.

Ward, N.J. (1993) The Rigorous Retrospective Static Analysis of the Sizewell 'B' Primary Protection System Software. In *Proceedings of SAFECOMP'93*, pp. 171–181.

Ward, P.T. and Mellor, S.J. (1985) *Structured Development for Real-Time Systems*, 3 volumes, Yourdon Press Computing Series, Prentice Hall, Englewood Cliffs.

Windley, P.J. (1990) *The Formal Verification of Generic Interpreters*. Ph.D. thesis, University of California at Davis, June.

Windley, P.J. and Coe, M.L. (1994) A Correctness Model for Pipelined Microprocessors. In Kumar and Kropf (1994), pp. 35–54.

Wing, J.M. (1990) A Specifier's Introduction to Formal Methods. *IEEE Computer*, **23**(9):8–24, September.

Wood, W.G. (1992) *Specification of Operation and Controller Design Constraints for a Real-Time System*, Report, Software Engineering Institute, Carnegie Mellon University, USA, September.

Woodcock, J.C.P. and Larsen, P.G., editors (1993) *FME'93: Industrial-Strength Formal Methods*, Springer-Verlag LNCS 670.

Wordsworth, J.B. (1992) *Software Development with Z*, Addison-Wesley, Wokingham.

York Software Engineering (1993) *The CADiZ User Guide*, YSE Report, 9 July.

Zave, P. (1993) Feature Interactions and Formal Specifications in Telecommunications. *IEEE Computer*, **26**(8):20–30, August.

Zave, P. and Jackson, D. (1989) Practical Specification Techniques for Control-Oriented Systems. In G.X. Ritter, editor, *Proceedings of the 11th IFIP World Computer Congress*, North-Holland, pp. 83–88.

Zave, P. and Jackson, M.A. (1993) Conjunction as Composition. *ACM Transactions on Software Engineering and Methodology*, **2**(4):379–411, October.

Zave, P. and Jackson, M.A. (1994) Where Do Operations Come From? A Multiparadigm Specification Technique. Submitted for publication.

Zave, P. and Mataga, P. (1993a) *A Formal Specification of Some Important 5ESS Features, Part I: Overview*, Technical Report BL0112610-931001-33, AT&T Bell Laboratories, USA.

Zave, P. and Mataga, P. (1993b) *A Formal Specification of Some Important 5ESS Features, Part II: Telephone States and Digit Analysis*, Technical Report BL0112610-931001-34, AT&T Bell Laboratories, USA.

Zucker, J.I. (1993) *Normal and Inverted Function Tables*, CRL Report 265, Communications Research Laboratory, McMaster University, Ontario, Canada, December.

Zucker, J.I. (1994) *Transformations of Normal and Inverted Function Tables*, CRL Report 291, Communications Research Laboratory, McMaster University, Ontario, Canada, August.

Index

C.A.R. Hoare, Series Editor

POMBERGER, G., *Software Engineering and Modula-2*
POTTER, B., SINCLAIR, J. and TILL, D., *An Introduction to Formal Specification and Z*
REYNOLDS, J.C., *The Craft of Programming*
ROSCOE, A.W. (ed.), *A Classical Mind: Essays in honour of C.A.R. Hoare*
RYDEHEARD, D.E. and BURSTALL, R.M., *Computational Category Theory*
SHARP, R., *Principles of Protocol Design*
SLOMAN, M. and KRAMER, J., *Distributed Systems and Computer Networks*
SPIVEY, J.M., *The Z. Notation: A reference manual (2nd edn)*
TENNENT, R.D., *Principles of Programming Languages*
TENNENT, R.D., *Semantics of Programming Languages*
WATT, D.A., *Programming Language Concepts and Paradigms*
WATT, D.A., *Programming Language Processors*
WATT, D.A., WICHMANN, B.A. and FINDLAY, W., *ADA: Language and methodology*
WELSH, J. and ELDER, J., *Introduction to Modula 2*
WELSH, J. and ELDER, J., *Introduction to Pascal (3rd edn)*
WELSH, J., ELDER, J. and BUSTARD, D., *Sequential Program Structures*
WELSH, J. and HAY, A., *A Model Implementation of Standard Pascal*
WELSH, J. and McKEAG, M., *Structured System Programming*
WIKSTRÖM, Å., *Functional Programming Using Standard ML*